THE VIKING AGE IN
CAITHNESS, ORKNEY AND
THE NORTH ATLANTIC

THE VIKING AGE IN CAITHNESS, ORKNEY AND THE NORTH ATLANTIC

SELECT PAPERS FROM THE PROCEEDINGS
OF THE ELEVENTH VIKING CONGRESS,
THURSO AND KIRKWALL,
22 AUGUST – I SEPTEMBER 1989

EDITED BY

COLLEEN E. BATEY

JUDITH JESCH

CHRISTOPHER D. MORRIS

EDINBURGH UNIVERSITY PRESS
FOR
CENTRE FOR CONTINUING EDUCATION,
UNIVERSITY OF ABERDEEN
AND
DEPARTMENT OF ARCHAEOLOGY,
UNIVERSITY OF GLASGOW

Reprinted in paperback 1995

Edinburgh University Press Ltd
22 George Square, Edinburgh

Typeset in Lasercomp Ehrhardt
by Alden Multimedia Ltd, Northampton, and
printed and bound in Great Britain by
The Alden Press, Oxford

A CIP record for this book is available from the British Library
ISBN 0 7486 0632 7

The printing of this book is made possible by grants and
subventions from Caithness District Council;
Orkney Islands Council; Highland Regional Council;
the Centre for Continuing Education, University of Aberdeen; and
the Department of Archaeology, University of Glasgow.

The *held* (on the half-title page) is the symbol of the Viking Congress.
It was designed by Janus Kamban and first used at the
Tórshavn Congress in 1965.

CONTENTS

HER MAJESTY QUEEN ELIZABETH THE QUEEN MOTHER
PATRON OF THE ELEVENTH VIKING CONGRESS, 1989
(Photograph by Anthony Crickmay, Camera Press, London.)

THE ELEVENTH VIKING CONGRESS, CAITHNESS AND ORKNEY, 1989

PATRON
HER MAJESTY QUEEN ELIZABETH THE QUEEN MOTHER

Organising Committee

MICHAEL P. BARNES

COLLEEN E. BATEY (joint Organising Secretary)

CHRISTINE E. FELL

JAMES A. GRAHAM-CAMPBELL

CHRISTOPHER D. MORRIS (joint Organising Secretary)

DONALD OMAND (Local Secretary)

RAYMOND I. PAGE

ALAN SMALL

DAVID M. WILSON (Chairman)

Congress Secretary

JANET MOWAT

THE ELEVENTH VIKING CONGRESS.

Camster Cairns, Caithness. - 1989

MEMBERS AND ASSOCIATES

DENMARK
Hans Bekker-Nielsen, Odense
Ole Bruhn, Århus
Gillian Fellows-Jensen, Copenhagen
Ole Fenger, Århus
Jørgen Højgaard Jørgensen, Odense
†Torben Kisbye, Århus
Laurits Rendboe, Odense
Else Roesdahl, Århus
Preben Meulengracht Sørensen, Århus
Marie Stoklund, Copenhagen

ENGLAND
Michael P. Barnes and Kirsten Barnes, London
Paul C. Buckland, Sheffield
Christine E. Fell, Nottingham
Peter G. Foote, London
James A. Graham-Campbell, London
David W. Griffiths, Durham (Postgraduate)
Richard A. Hall, York
Judith Jesch, Nottingham
Susan E. Kruse and Gordon Gallacher, London
James T. Lang, London
Susan A. Margeson, Norwich
Raymond I. Page, Cambridge
David Parsons, Nottingham (Postgraduate)
Caroline E. Richardson, Newcastle Upon Tyne (Postgraduate)
Andrew Wawn, Leeds
David M. Wilson, London

FAROES
Símun V. Arge, Tórshavn
Hans Jacob Debes, Tórshavn
Steffen Stummann Hansen and Ann-Christine Larsen, Hørsholm
Ditlev L. D. Mahler, Tórshavn
Eivind Weyhe, Tórshavn

GREENLAND
Jette Arneborg, Copenhagen

ICELAND
Finnbogi Guðmundsson, Reykjavík
Þór Magnússon and María Heiðdal, Reykjavík
Guðmundur Ólafsson, Reykjavík
Mjöll Snæsdóttir, Reykjavík

IRELAND
†Thomas Fanning, Galway
Uaininn O'Meadhra, Dublin
Patrick F. Wallace, Dublin

NORWAY
Per Sveaas Andersen, Oslo
Olav Bø and Inger Hyllerås Bø, Oslo
Jan Ragnar Hagland, Trondheim
Eyvind Fjeld Halvorsen and Anne Marie Halvorsen, Oslo
Sigrid H. H. Kaland, Bergen
Irmelin Martens, Oslo
Gerd Stamsø Munch, Tromsø
Else Mundal, Oslo
Heid Gjøstein Resi, Oslo
Kolbjørn Skaare, Oslo
Birthe Weber, Oslo

SCOTLAND
Colleen E. Batey, London
Barbara Crawford and Robert Crawford, St Andrews
Alexander Fenton, Edinburgh
Ian Fisher, Edinburgh
Robert Gourlay, Inverness
John R. Hunter, Bradford
Anne Johnston, St Andrews (Postgraduate)
Raymond G. Lamb, Kirkwall

Christopher D. Morris, Durham
Donald Omand, Halkirk
Olwyn A. Owen, Edinburgh
Gillian Quine, Durham (Postgraduate)
Alan Small, Dundee
Brian Smith, Lerwick
†Robert B. K. Stevenson, Edinburgh
William P. L. Thomson, Kirkwall
Doreen Waugh, Edinburgh

LOCAL MEMBERS
Anne Leith Brundle, Kirkwall
Jess Campbell, Wick
Edwin Eunson, Kirkwall
Julie Gibson, Rousay
Peter Leith, Stenness
Ron MacDonald, Inverness
Robert A. S. Macrae, Orphir
Ingrid Mainland, Rousay
Jacqueline A. Marwick, Rousay
Janet Mowat, Halkirk
Leslie Myatt, Halkirk
Ross Noble, Kingussie
John Robertson, Kirkwall
Beverley Smith, Stromness
J. William Spence, Kirkwall
David M. Tinch, Kirkwall
James A. Watson, Stromness
Bryce Wilson, Kirkwall
John Young, Wick

SWEDEN
Marit Åhlén, Stockholm
Björn Ambrosiani, Stockholm
Lennart Elmevik, Uppsala
Anne-Sofie Gräslund, Uppsala
Helmer Gustavson, Stockholm
Ingmar Jansson, Stockholm
Kenneth Jonsson, Stockholm
Brita Malmer and Mats P. Malmer, Stockholm
Lena Peterson, Uppsala
Karl Inge Sandred, Uppsala
Inger Zachrisson, Stockholm

FOREWORD

Members and Associates of The Eleventh Viking Congress generally arrived in Thurso, Caithness on Tuesday, 22 August 1989, although some appeared to travel more in hope than expectation of arrival at this destination. Some indeed took longer than expected to arrive, in part due to British Airways' newly-introduced policy of flying only nine-seater planes between Aberdeen and Wick, and in part due to other, more complex reasons. At least one arrived earlier than expected. For those who did arrive on time there was the opportunity of partaking in a Thurso Town Walkabout, the first of a number of tours and excursions undertaken during the Congress which appear below in the Congress Diary.

The arrangements for this Congress were rather more complex than usual, as it was a two-centre affair, with a crossing of the Pentland Firth (mercifully calm!) to Orkney on 25 August. The full Congress continued until 28 August, concluding with a Congress Dinner at the Kirkwall Hotel. Members then either returned home on 29 August, or joined a three-day post-Congress Tour, departing on 1 September.

There was a very full programme of lectures and excursions, and many of the former have been included in revised forms in this volume. The title reflects the major themes examined throughout the Congress, but there were other papers delivered on English, Irish and Scandinavian themes. These have not been included in this volume, partly on grounds of size and practicability, and partly on grounds of overall coherence for the published Proceedings. We also miss a few papers prepared for, or delivered at, the Congress, but not delivered to the Editors. We hope these are published elsewhere. We give our thanks for their contributions at the Congress to: Per Sveaas Andersen, Raymond Page, †Thomas Fanning, †Torben Kisbye, Karl Inge Sandred, Brian Smith, Mjöll Snæsdóttir, Anne-Sofie Gräslund, Inger Zachrisson, Irmelin Martens, Gerd Stamsø Munch, Else Roesdahl, Björn Ambrosiani, Brita Malmer, Kolbjørn Skaare, Gro Steinsland, Helmer Gustavson and Lennart Elmevik.

An innovation at this Congress was the invitation to a number of British postgraduates working in the field of Viking Studies to take part at a subsidised rate: they contributed to the life of the Congress in several ways, some time-honoured, but also some by means of poster-sessions on their own researches. These were well-received and the Committee hopes that future Congresses may continue to highlight the work of the younger generations of Viking scholars by turning the innovation into a tradition.

A long tradition of Viking Congress parties was upheld, and we are grateful to the Caithness District Council, Highland Regional Council, Orkney Islands Council, Durham University, and the Danish, Norwegian and Swedish Consulates for their generous hospitality. In particular, we acknowledge with thanks the formal welcomes by Councillors John Young and Edwin Eunson, Convenors of the Caithness District and Orkney Islands Councils respectively, and by the Highland Regional Council, through Messrs Ron MacDonald and Ross Noble. The highlight was without doubt the Official Reception by our Royal Patron at The Castle of Mey. The personal interest in the Congress of Her Majesty Queen Elizabeth The Queen Mother is, we hope, reciprocated in our choice of frontispiece, and we acknowledge the gracious permission granted for the reproduction of Her Majesty's photograph.

Special thanks are due to the various guides on the excursions, including members of the Committee, but most particularly Robert Gourlay and Raymond Lamb, Regional Archaeologists for Highland Region and Orkney Heritage Society respectively. Raymond, in particular, in the planning of the memorable Sunday excursion on board *Orcadia* to Rousay, Egilsay and Wyre, and of the post-Congress Tours, gave unstintingly of his time and expertise to assist the Organising Secretaries. Donald Omand and Janet Mowat of Aberdeen University's Centre for Continuing Education at Braal in Halkirk acted as the lynchpins of the local organisation before, during and after the Congress; the rest of the Organising Committee owe them a deep debt of gratitude. We also wish to acknowledge the practical assistance of the Secretaries of the Departments of Archaeology at Durham University and Glasgow University and of Medieval Archaeology at University College London: Sheila Brown, Norma Wakeling and Angela Morrell.

We acknowledge with much appreciation here the following bodies for their grants for the organisation of the Congress: The Binks Trust; The British Academy; The Dame Bertha Philpotts Fund, Cambridge University and The Highlands and Islands Development Board's Social Fund. Generous grants and subventions towards the publication of this volume are acknowledged above.

Finally, the energy and inspiration of our Chairman, Sir David Wilson, must be acknowledged; his organisation of the business of Committee meetings is legendary and his choice of venues always apt. He has been a member of many Viking Congresses, the leading British scholar in Viking studies of his generation and internationally acclaimed. As he has now left the leadership of the British Museum to take well-earned retirement, we salute his achievement and hope that he will regard the publication of these papers as a suitable leaving present from his friends and fellow-members of the Viking Congress.

CHRISTOPHER D. MORRIS
On behalf of the Organising Committee

I

CONGRESS DIARY

NOTES ON FIELD EXCURSIONS

EDITED BY CHRISTOPHER D. MORRIS

As is traditional at Viking Congresses, in addition to the formal sessions when papers were presented (a selection of which are printed in this volume), a number of excursions to sites, monuments and museums were made. As a significant number of these places were unknown to many visitors, and as details of them are often difficult to track down, it was decided to include brief accounts of them (usually based on handouts prepared for the Congress) as a more permanent record for members of the Congress, and as a point of reference for purchasers of the volume. In some cases, the texts were prepared specifically for the Congress, and in some cases they were reproduced by the authors from other publications of their own. If the latter is the case, then the source has been given, and grateful thanks given for their reproduction here. Two general maps (Figs 1.1 and 1.21) have been provided, one for each area, supplemented by other illustrative material as appropriate. These also serve as location maps for subsequent chapters.

CAITHNESS (Fig. 1.1)

GENERAL REFERENCES

Baldwin, John R. (ed.) 1982. *Caithness. A Cultural Crossroads*, Scottish Society for Northern Studies, Edinburgh.

Batey, Colleen E. 1987. 'Viking and Late Norse Caithness: The Archaeological Evidence', in *Proceedings of the Tenth Viking Congress, Larkollen, Norway, 1985*, ed. Knirk, James, Oslo, pp. 131–48.

Bramman, John, Butler, Ken, Hughes, Brian, Miller, David, Myatt, Leslie, Saxon, Jack & Watson, George 1976. *Visits to Ancient Caithness*, Caithness Field Club, Wick.

Close-Brooks, Joanna 1986. *Exploring Scotland's Heritage: The Highlands*, RCAHMS, Edinburgh.

Omand, Donald (ed.) 1989. *The New Caithness Book*, Wick.

I

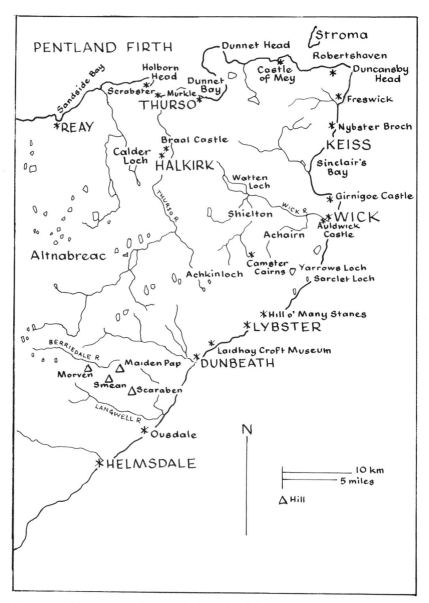

Figure 1.1: Caithness: map of sites visited and mentioned (A. L. Brundle).

Tuesday, 22 August

Old Thurso (Fig. 1.2)

Leslie J. Myatt

Thurso, the most northerly town on the mainland of Britain, is pleasantly situated and of considerable interest. With a present population of 9,000, it is an important centre in the north but was apparently also a settlement and seafaring centre in the Viking period. It was here, in *c.* 1040, that Thorfinn defeated the army of Moddan, Karl Hundason's nephew (Cowan 1982, 33).

There is uncertainty about the origin of the placename. A popular derivation is from the Old Norse *Thors-á*, meaning Thor's river, but placename scholars point out that it would be unusual in Old Norse for a river to be named after a god. A preferred origin is from *thjors-á*, 'bull river', and this is further supported by *Tarvendunum*, bull fort, shown on Ptolemy's map and identified as Holborn Head where the remains of a promontory fort are still to be seen. More recently Professor Thorson has suggested (Thorson 1968) that it may derive from *Thorshaugr*, 'Thor's mound'. This is based upon three 13th-century spellings (Thurseha, Turishau, Thorsau) and may be identified with a conical mound close to Thurso Castle.

There are three main stages in the development of Thurso as a town. The old part, which has now been carefully rebuilt, was centred mainly around the harbour area. At the beginning of the 19th century Sir John Sinclair of Ulbster (1754–1835), a great benefactor to the town, planned his 'new town' of Thurso which extends westwards across the present settlement from the road bridge across the river. Although not fully carried out, his plans included a reconstruction of the harbour by Telford. Nevertheless his design can be seen in Janet Street and in the areas around Rose Street. The third stage took place with the coming of the Atomic Energy Authority to Dounreay when further housing estates were built on both sides of the river at Mount Vernon and Ormlie. Here one may notice many of the Vikings such as Sweyn, Sigurd, Thorfinn and Haakon remembered in the street names!

1. Toll House

On entering the town by the A 882 road, the old toll house on the corner of the road junction to John o' Groats can be seen. Now used as an art gallery, this is one of three tolls which were in use until they were abolished in 1878. The other two were situated at entrances to the town by the Station Hotel and at the junction of Durness Street and Olrig Street.

2. Thurso Bridge

The first road bridge was not built over the river until 1800. It was financed by public subscription and built by Robert Tulloch, master mason. By 1881 this bridge was in need of repair, and widening was also necessary. It was decided to build a new bridge at a cost of £4,000. This is the present bridge which was opened in 1887 by the Earl of Caithness.

3. Janet Street

Overlooking the river are the elegant town houses of Janet Street. This is part of the 'new town' as planned by Sir John Sinclair and named after his mother Lady Janet Sinclair.

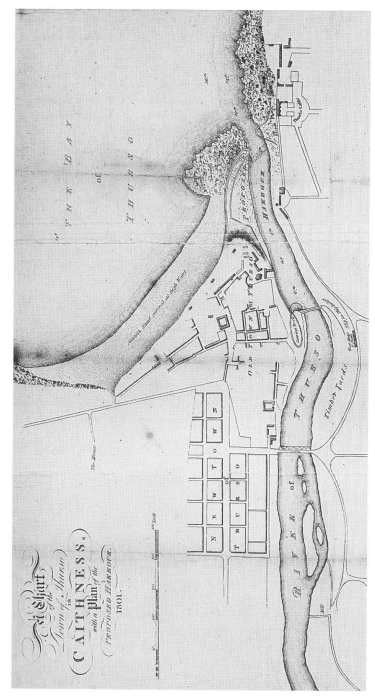

Figure 1.2: Thurso: plan 1801 (J. P. Campbell).

4. Sir John Square

Standing in the centre of Sir John Square, which was donated to the town by Sir Tollemache Sinclair in 1879, is the statue by Chantry of Sir John Sinclair. Dressed in trews and sporran, Sir John is seen wearing the uniform of the Rothesay and Caithness Fencibles of which he was the founder in 1794. Sir John, who was Member of Parliament for Caithness from 1780–1835, was responsible for the introduction of Cheviot sheep into the county in place of the Blackface. He was also editor of the *[Old] Statistical Account of Scotland*.

5. Railway Station

Although a more elaborate network of railways was at one time proposed in the county, including a branch line to Castletown, the existing single track connection from Thurso to Wick and Inverness via Georgemas Junction was opened in 1874.

6. Meadow Well

At one time situated in the meadow of Ormlie, this was for centuries the main town source of water. It was in use up to 1876 by which time its supply of water had become inadequate. Water was then piped, as today, from Loch Calder some 8 km away from the town. In recent years the fabric of the small circular building surrounding the well has been restored by the Thurso Rotary Club.

7. Rotterdam Street

The name of Rotterdam Street is an indication of the trade which was at one time carried out between Thurso and the Continent. Its original name was 'Black Gutter' but it was renamed in 1856 when it was widened and other improvements were carried out. Further rebuilding and restoration has been carried out in more recent years and it is interesting to note how modern buildings can be designed to blend in with the older buildings where they have been restored.

8. Robert Dick's House

Robert Dick (1811–66), born in Tullibody, Clackmannanshire, came to set up his business here as a baker in 1830. He was also a very keen and able naturalist and geologist, fields in which he was self-taught. He built up an extensive collection of plants, insects, shells and fossils. In 1834 he rediscovered the Northern Holy-grass (*Hierochloe odorata*) growing beside the Thurso river. This plant had been thought by botanists to be extinct in Britain. So devoted to his study of plant life was Dick, that it was not unusual to find him walking very long distances after his day's work to collect more specimens. Dick's death came rather prematurely at the age of 55, and he is buried in Thurso cemetery where to his memory was erected, by public subscription, a large obelisk.

9. Town Hall

Opened in 1871, this Gothic building was erected at a cost of £2,500. It houses the Court Room and Council Chamber together with a museum. Of particular interest in the museum are two Early Christian stones (see Gourlay, pp. 116–17 below). One, the Ulbster Stone, depicts on each side a cross together with a large number of Pictish symbols. The other, the Skinnet Stone, is sculptured partly in relief and partly with incised lines and depicts elaborately ornamented crosses on both sides. Also on view is a cross roughly hewn out of Caithness flagstone and bearing an inscription in Scandinavian runes. Professor Liestøl read this as '. . . made this overlay after Ingolf his/her father' (Liestøl 1984, 228). This cross was unearthed on top of a burial in 1896 when some old buildings were demolished at the east end of Old St Peter's church (see Batey, pp. 156–7 below).

10. Shore Street

Shore Street and the adjoining area comprises the oldest part of the town. Of particular interest is the 17th-century tower house dated 1686 and bearing the initials D. W. K. R. This circular turret contains a stair leading to the houses on the upper floor. A similar tower house may be seen in High Street.

11. Old St Peter's Church (Fig. 1.3)

Although most of what is now to be seen of this church probably dates from about the 16th or 17th century, it is generally supposed to have been founded by Gilbert of Moray who was Bishop of Caithness from 1222–45. Probably the

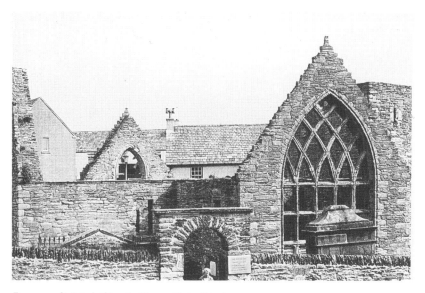

Figure 1.3: St Peter's Church, Thurso (C. E. Batey).

earliest part of the structure, and possibly dating from the 12th century, is the apsidal cell at the E end. This part of the structure, square on the outside and circular inside, is similar to that of St Margaret's chapel in Edinburgh Castle dating from this period. Worthy of note is the well preserved tracery in the window of the S transept. On the W wall is a stone dated 1357 with the letters TW and GG, but the style of lettering suggests that it is of much later date, probably 16th century.

It is recorded that, when the church was in use, there were painted panels above the pews. One of them depicted Abraham dressed in kilt and hose with a flowing surtout. At one time in the 18th century the vestry was used as a courthouse and a vault as a prison. The church was in use until 1832 when the new church of St Peter opposite Sir John Square was built at a cost of about £6,000. A number of interesting grave stones may be seen in the adjoining burial ground, and a cross with a runic inscription is now to be seen in the Town Hall Museum (see above, p. 6). A second runic inscription has recently been found (see Postscript below, pp. 9–10).

12. The Harbour

At the time when Sir John Sinclair was planning the new town of Thurso, an Act of Parliament was passed in 1802 granting the building of a new harbour. It was to be designed by Telford and to cost £7,000. Unfortunately insufficient money was forthcoming and the scheme had to be abandoned. Despite the inadequacy of good harbour facilities and the low depth of channel at the harbour mouth, it was used early in the 19th century at the beginning of the flagstone industry when polishing yards covered both banks of the river. Vessels entered at high water and at low water were beached. It was not until 1891 that the Duke of Portland laid the foundation stone of the present harbour to be constructed at a cost of £16,000. The work was never fully completed owing to severe storm damage and other technical difficulties.

The area around the W bank of the harbour mouth is known as Fisherbiggins. It has been rebuilt in recent years but retains the original character of this part of the town. Across the bay is Scrabster, adjacent to which the lighthouse was constructed in 1862. It is now the main harbour on this coast. From it operate a number of fishing boats, the Orkney ferry and a summer ferry service to Faroe.

13. Thurso Castle

The original castle of Thurso, which has long since disappeared, stood on a site at the S part of the town. Built by the Norse Earls, it was destroyed in the 12th century by King William the Lion when he was forced to enter the county with an army to suppress Earl Harald Maddadsson for his atrocities against John, the Bishop of Caithness.

The present castle stands near the entrance to the harbour. The first castle was built on this site in 1660 by George, the 6th Earl of Caithness of the Sinclair family. After Sinclair's death it fell into the possession of Glenorchy and was destroyed by the rightful heir, Sinclair of Keiss. It passed to the Sinclairs of Ulbster in 1719 when a new castle was built. Considerable changes were made in 1872 by Sir Tollemache Sinclair when it was remodelled in the style of the French Chateaux. Unfortunately by 1952 serious defects appeared in the structure and the upper parts had to be dismantled.

14. Harald's Tower

Standing on a small hill to the NE of Thurso castle is Harald's Tower. Nearby, in 1196, took place the battle of Clairdon Hill, between Earl Harald the Elder, son of the Countess of Athlone, and Harald the Younger, grandson of Earl Rognvald. Harald the Elder had dispossessed Harald the Younger of a large part of the county which he had inherited from his grandfather. The purpose of the battle was for Harald the Younger to attempt to recover his share of the earldom and his hereditary rights. Unfortunately Harald the Younger was killed; he was buried close to where he fell. A chapel was built over his grave but eventually it fell into decay. The present tower was built on the spot by Sir John Sinclair to commemorate the events which took place.

15. Pennyland Farm

Pennyland farm stands on the left hand side of the road leading westwards out of the town. It is the birth place of Sir William Smith (1854–1914), founder of the Boys' Brigade. Coming from a military family, he is reputed to have been seen drilling a group of 20 boys on Thurso beach when he was only 11 years old. He left Thurso at the age of 14 to live with an uncle in Glasgow where he became a Sunday School teacher at the Woodside Mission. He founded the Boys' Brigade in 1883 which predates the Boy Scout movement of Lord Baden Powell by some 25 years.

16. Pennyland Chapel

Overlooking the bay, and standing on the site of an early chapel, is the mausoleum of the Murray family.

17. The Bishop's Castle

Standing on the cliff edge at Burnside, overlooking the bay, are the remains of the Bishop's castle, the one-time residence of the Bishops of Caithness. Although little now remains to be seen, a partial excavation of the site was carried out in 1970 when part of the building plan was revealed (Talbot 1973). The castle was protected on the landward side by means of a drawbridge and a terrace extending along the bank was known as the 'Bishop's walk'. It was in this castle that Bishop Gilbert of Moray died in 1245. His remains were subsequently removed to Dornoch Cathedral. The castle fell into disuse some time during the 16th century, after it was seized from the Bishop by the Earl of Caithness. A triangular window, removed from the castle, is now built into Scrabster House.

REFERENCES

Bramman *et al.* 1976, nos 13 & 18: 22–3 & 30–1.

Close-Brooks, 1986, no. 8: 19 & 33–5.

Cowan, Edward J. 1982. 'Caithness in the Sagas', in *Caithness. A Cultural Crossroads*, ed. Baldwin, John, Edinburgh, pp. 25–44.

Liestøl, Aslak 1984. 'Runes', in *The Northern and Western Isles in the Viking World. Survival, Continuity and Change*, eds Fenton, Alexander & Pálsson, Hermann, Edinburgh, pp. 224–38.

Talbot, Eric 1973. 'A Report on Excavations at Bishop's Castle, Scrabster', *Northern Studies*, 2, 37–9.

Thorson, Per 1968. 'Ancient Thurso, a Religious and Judicial Centre', in *The Fifth Viking Congress. Tórshavn, July 1965*, ed. Niclasen, Bjarni, pp. 71–7.

Postcript: Runic Find at St Peter's Church
(Extract from *Caithness Courier*, 30 August 1989)

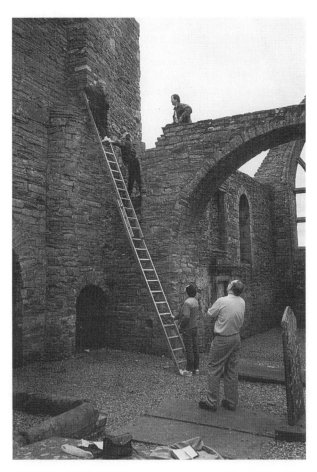

Figure 1.4: St Peter's Church, Thurso: inspection of runic stone, Viking Congress, 1989 (M. Åhlén).

Viking scholars are acclaiming a major find of an ancient runic stone in a Thurso church. The discovery of what is believed to be a memorial inscription dating back to the 10th century AD was made 25 feet up a wall of the town's old St Peter's Church. [Fig. 1.4]

The unusual markings were first noticed by Dounreay worker George Watson while he was helping carry out survey work on the historic roofless church. Mr Watson, of St Andrew's Drive, Thurso, alerted the organisers of the 11th Viking Congress which got underway in Thurso last week.

Five expert runologists from Britain and Scandinavia visited the church last Thursday armed with a step-ladder and a high intensity lamp. Professor Raymond Page, of Corpus Christi College, Cambridge, disclosed the 'major find' at the final session of the congress in Thurso. Professor Page had gone to inspect the rune along with Swedes Helmer Gustavson, Lena Peterson and Marit Åhlén, Norwegian Jan Ragnar Hagland and Highland Regional Council Archaeologist Bob Gourlay.

He said Dr Gustavson, from Stockholm, had been able to identify a runic inscription, 70 centimetres long by 21 cm broad, and 13 cm high, on the W face of the church's tower wall. Dr Gustavson and his colleagues believe the memorial was provided by a grieving Viking husband for his late wife who bore the name Gunnhildr. Said Prof Page: 'This is one of the very few memorials of this kind found in the far North of Scotland. It's very rare indeed.'

It is planned to have casts made of the rune and, if possible, to remove the piece of stone from the wall.

Wednesday, 23 August

Castle of Mey (Fig. 1.5)
Robert B. Gourlay

The Royal residence of the Castle of Mey lies on sloping ground overlooking the Pentland Firth and with views across to the Orkneys. Once known as Barrogill Castle, it has now reverted to its original name.

The castle consists of an original Z-plan tower of 16th century date with numerous additions and alterations. It was built by the Sinclairs about 1567 and remained in their possession more or less until the late 19th century. After a period of neglect it was acquired and restored by Her Majesty Queen Elizabeth the Queen Mother about 1960.

The main block runs E-W, and stands three storeys and an attic in height. The thick walls are pierced with numerous gunloops. To the SE projects a square wing, while to the NW is a smaller square stair-tower. Both wings rise a floor higher than the main building. At the E end of the main block is a massive chimney block, almost as thick as a small tower, and containing a double set of flues.

The original entrance was in the NW tower and opened onto the main stair.

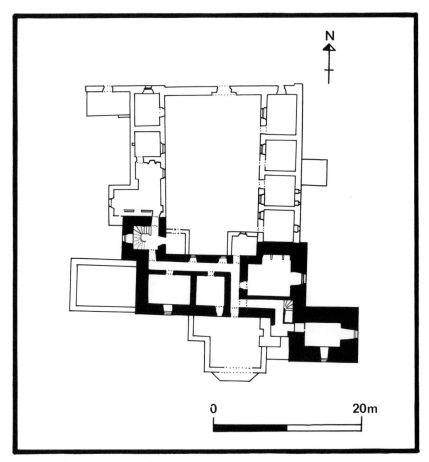

Figure 1.5: Castle of Mey: plan (D. Low, Highland Regional Council, after RCAHMS).

From there a vaulted passage gave access to the three vaulted chambers of the main block basement, including the wine-cellar and the original kitchen with its massive fireplace and ingle-neuk. The hall, later the dining room, was on the first floor with two other apartments, and the sleeping quarters above. The heightening and crenellation of the angle-turrets is a 19th-century addition. To the N is a curtain walled courtyard entered by a round-arched gateway.

Wick
Donald Omand

Like many another town, the history of Wick is obscure, but it is highly possible that the oldest nucleus of a settlement lay close to the mouth of the river where the small haven provided shelter. There are early references to Wick in the *Orkneyinga saga* when Earl Rognvald came to Caithness and was entertained at

Vik, perhaps at Auldwick (Old Wick) Castle, an early stronghold to the S of Wick (see below, pp. 14–15). In the Bodleian Library, Oxford, an old map dated to *c.* 1250 has Wick as the only settlement noted in Caithness.

In the year 1503 Wick was made the seat of the sheriff court; in 1589 it was raised to the status of royal burgh by King James VI. The town must have looked a sorry sight when the accolade of royal burgh (giving it important trading rights) was bestowed upon it, as it had been burned and looted the previous year by the Earl of Sutherland as part of a feud with the Earl of Caithness, who virtually owned the town and the lands around it. Wick in the late 16th and 17th centuries was apparently still a very small town, as – judging from a map of 1608 by Timothy Pont – it was divided into four straggling groups of buildings scarcely 1·6 km (1 mile) in length.

A clearer picture of the royal burgh emerges in 1660 when documentation indicates a settlement of 500 people, with ten merchants, six tailors, five weavers, four smiths, five shoemakers, four coopers and four glovers. Although Wick itself had no vessels (Thurso had two sloops) trade was taking place including such items as: timber, tallow, hides, wool, millstones, beef, mutton, port, butter, cheese and whisky. In the early 18th century Wick was still a 'small town of little trade'; in 1760 it was described as 'pleasantly situated in a little bay which has no harbour'. Relative to Thurso the town's population growth was slow, as a writer of 1735 observed that the population of Thurso was approaching 3,000 people, about three times the figure for Wick. In the 1790s, the population was at a similar level when the contributor to the *Statistical Account* was bemoaning the fact that the town had no harbour.

The great spur to the town's development was the phenomenal growth of the herring fishery, primed by the construction of Telford's harbour (begun in 1803 and completed in 1810) on the south side of Wick River. By the year 1816, the new planned settlement of Telford's 'Pulteneytown' was well established. It took its name from a one-time director, who eventually became Governor, of the British Fisheries Society, Sir William Pulteney. Other streets in the new town have the names of directors and officials of the Society, such as: Argyle Square, Vansittart Street, Kinnaird Street, Huddart Street, Breadalbane Terrace and Smith Terrace.

With the accelerating success of the fishing (particularly the summer herring catch), an increasing number of families left the land to try their luck at sea. The new harbour with all its attendant facilities meant that fishing could now become a full-time occupation, a radical change from the traditional role of crofter-fisherman. The neatly laid out new town of Pulteney, with its focus on Argyle Square and its central green, was soon teeming with people from all parts of Caithness. Eye witnesses have also recorded the crowds of incoming High-landers who filled the harbour quays eagerly seeking work.

By 1835 there were 830 boats fishing from Wick and by 1862 the figure had exceeded 1,100, crews coming from all over Britain to fish for the 'silver darlings'. In those hectic days of the zenith of the herring fishing, the population of Wick could swell from 7,000 to 18,000 people. Such a thronging populace was good for business – as the thriving markets on the North Head (in July) and the High Street (in November) could testify. At the latter, the curers settled with the fishermen for past fishing and engaged them for the coming season at a fixed price. A feel for the days when Wick was the herring capital of the world can still be gained from a visit to its excellent Heritage Centre in Bank Row (see also Fig. 1.6).

Wick and herring may no longer be linked synonymously in the public mind, but a new product has substituted the herring in that respect: Caithness Glass, which opened its factory in Wick in the early 1960s and has had considerable commercial success, with subsidiary units in Oban and Perth.

To the rapidly expanding new town was added a distillery, in 1826. Most of its product is used for blending but some is bottled as a distinctive malt whisky known as 'Old Pulteney'. Perhaps over-indulgence of the product prompted the comment in the *New Statistical Account* that, 'at all seasons of the year whisky is drunk in considerable quantities, but during the fishing season enormous potations are indulged in'. The writer was inspired to comment further about the inhabitants of Wick parish: 'Maniacs are very rare. Idiots . . . are remarkably common'!

In the early 19th century 'greater Wick' consisted of four settlements:

Figure 1.6: Wick Harbour and the herring fishery (J. P. Campbell).

Broadhaven and Louisburgh (both of which were established by Sir Benjamin Dunbar of Hempriggs), Wick and Pulteney. For many years Wick and Pulteney had their separate town councils until the two settlements amalgamated into one burgh in 1902. The considerable expansion of Wick in the late 18th and early 19th centuries largely destroyed traces of the older burgh, with the 16th century church of St Fergus and part of Parliament Square being among the few survivors.

The long sinuous High Street, a continuation of the main road from John o'Groats is the spine of old Wick, with a number of lanes and closes off-shooting from both sides. One of these, Tolbooth Lane, commemorates the former Tolbooth, long since gone, whose successor was the town hall, with fine cupola, built in Bridge Street in 1828. The focal point of the old town would have been the market place and the site of the former market cross is indicated by stones set into the road.

There is a tradition that the original parish church of Wick stood near the eastern extremity of the High Street at Mount Hooly, a name that suggests early ecclesiastical associations. The church was then transferred to the western end of the High Street. Perhaps a number of buildings stood on the western site before Wick Old Parish Church was dedicated in 1830. It is reputed to be one of the widest kirks in Scotland, its rafters resting on the side walls without any other interior support. In 1843, the minister (the Rev. Charles Tomson) 'came out' in the Disruption and took most of the congregation with him to form the Free Church (now Bridge Street Church). Close by the Old Parish church is the interesting fragment of a much older church, dedicated to St Fergus but usually called Sinclair's aisle as it was supposedly built by George Sinclair, 4th Earl of Caithness, in the 16th century.

From: Omand, Donald. (ed.) 1989. *The New Caithness Book*, Wick, 124–6.

REFERENCE

Close-Brooks 1986, no. 7: 31–3.

Castle of Old Wick (Figs 1.7 & 1.8)
Robert B. Gourlay

Known locally as the Old Man of Wick, this plain, ruined tower house stands on a dramatic cliff promontory cut off from the landward approach by a ditch. It consists of a simple keep tower with no diagnostic dating features, but was probably constructed during the late 12th or 13th century AD. As the Norse Earls of Orkney held Caithness during this period it may reasonably be described as a Norse fortification.

The fragmentary remains of a rampart and gatehouse survive on the landward side of the ditch, once crossed by means of a drawbridge. Four floors, marked by scarcement ledges, each held a single room beneath a simple pitched roof. A door at first floor level on the seaward side gave access to the tower, but this has now

Figure 1.7: Castle of Old Wick (J. P. Campbell).

collapsed. Access to other floors must have been by wooden ladders, as there is no staircase within the wall. There are also no chimneys or fireplaces, and a small chamber on the first floor – probably a latrine – is the only feature which disturbs the monotony of the walls. Two tiny windows on each floor provided the only internal light.

On the seaward side of the promontory are two rows of grassy mounds, indicating the presence of a range of buildings either side of a central passage which seems to end in a small courtyard. These presumably represent domestic buildings for servants and horses, and probably the kitchen and bakehouse are also in this area. Old Wick is similar in design to another undated castle at Forse (ND 224 338). Both are recorded as the property of the Cheyne family during the 14th century.

REFERENCES

Bramman *et al.* 1976, no. 15: 25.
Close-Brooks 1986, no. 46: 103.

Thursday, 24 August

Halkirk (Fig. 1.9)
Donald Omand

The derivation of the place name Halkirk appears to be from the Old Norse *Há-kirkja*, meaning High church. There is a large number of chapels in the parish

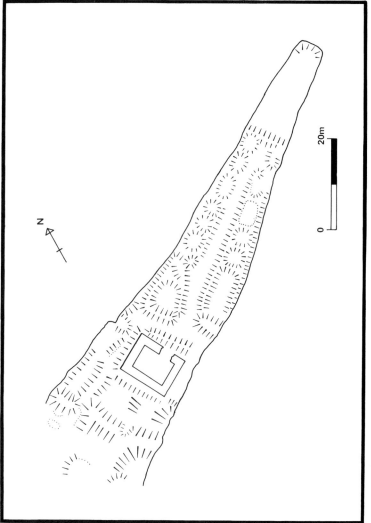

Figure 1.8: Castle of Old Wick: plan (D. Low, Highland Regional Council, after R. G. Lamb).

dedicated to saints, e.g. to Columba at Dirlot and to St Trostan, who has two dedications in Halkirk parish, at Westfield and Westerdale, and five dedications in all in Caithness. The old parish kirk on the outskirts of the village stands on or close to a site known as *Tor Harlogan*, signifying an early dedication to this missionary who crossed the Moray Firth from Buchan.

At the nearby chapel of St Thomas, Skinnet, stood a beautifully carved Class I Pictish symbol stone, one of the two outstanding examples (the other being the Ulbster stone) found in Caithness. Both stones are now housed in Thurso Museum (see above, p. 6). Unfortunately, the Skinnet Stone, probably dating to

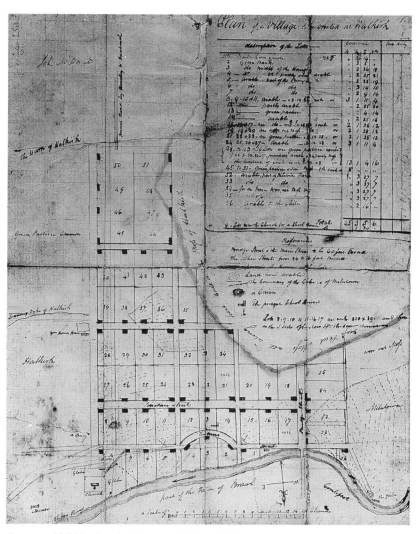

Figure 1.9: Halkirk: plan of settlement (J. P. Campbell).

the 7th–9th century AD, has been broken into a number of pieces, a sorry fate for this beautiful piece of relief monumental sculpture.

Perhaps the original focus of settlement in the area where Halkirk village now stands was the old castle at Braal, now a roofless rectangular keep pleasantly situated among woodlands on the west bank of Thurso River (see below, pp. 19–21). [The adjacent new castle of Braal, of late 19th-century date, has been converted into flats.] An 18th-century traveller, Cordiner, commented on the 'aged trees spreading near the castle' and the river which 'yields plenty of salmon'. He wrote favourably of the large garden by the castle with its 'rows of fruit trees, bearing plenty of apples, pears and cherries'.

Braal Castle was at one time the principal seat of the Earls of Caithness. As far back as 1375 King Robert II granted Brathwell (Braal) Castle to his son. In 1222, there occurred a dark deed that put the name of Braal on the pages of Scottish history. The incident was caused through the insistence of Bishop Adam to double the butter tax that he received as tithes from his flock. Greatly resisting this imposition, an angry crowd made for Braal Castle, residence of the Earl of Caithness, who was asked to protect the people from the prelate's exactions. One legend had it that the Earl refused to intervene in the dispute; another, that he advised the mob to burn the bishop in his butter. Whatever the advice, the unfortunate prelate was seized and put to death. So incensed was the Scottish King Alexander II by the crime that he came north with soldiers and avenged the bishop's death by causing much bloodshed in the area. Adam was succeeded by the distinguished Bishop Gilbert Moray. Following the barbarous crime at Braal, Gilbert decided to move the bishopric to Dornoch, where the cathedral church of the see now stands.

Halkirk parish continued to be the stage where many bloody skirmishes and clan feuds were enacted (such as the desperate battle at Harpsdale between the Keiths and Gunns) but more settled times had arrived before John Sinclair of Ulbster, grandfather of Agricultural Sir John, died leaving a sum of money for the construction of a stone bridge over the Thurso River, opposite the lands of Comlifoot. However, as twelve years elapsed before the work was begun, the story soon gained credence that the delay was due to the influence of the devil. When the structure was finally completed, it was believed that the devil made a rendezvous there every night. Little wonder few folk would cross the bridge after sunset!

It was almost another 60 years before the indefatigable Sir John Sinclair reputedly mustered his tenants and pushed a road through from Latheron to Georgemas, and ultimately to the bridging point of the river at Comlifoot, Halkirk. The 19th century had turned before Sir John Sinclair drew up his plans for a settlement at his grandfather's bridge, using land that was not suitable for the plough: the moss of Halkirk. The plan for a new village was drawn up in 1803 and, in the fashion of the time, was laid out on a grid-iron basis with each of the 22·3 × 0·4 ha (55 × 1 acre) holdings delineated and numbered.

The principal thoroughfare at Bridge Street was to be 18·3 m (60 ft) broad and the lesser streets to measure 7·3–7·9 m (24–26 ft) in width. Dotted along the streets were communal wells, two of which survive on Bridge Street. Family names are commemorated in Sinclair Street, Lane and Square as well as in George and Camilla Street. An inn site was allocated on Bridge Street (opposite the end of Sinclair Street) with space for shops to the south of it. It was envisaged that Halkirk would grow into a thriving market centre, but the nearness of Thurso ensured that this would not be so. Only now is the original grid plan being filled in.

The handsome village hall known as the Ross Institute is so named after John Ross, who was born at Gerston in 1834 and emigrated to Otago, New Zealand, in 1861. The business which he developed soon expanded until it had branches in all the main towns of New Zealand. In 1911 the Ross Institute was opened, the electric clock (the first in a public building in Scotland) in its tower being a donation of another son of Halkirk, David Murray.

Many people in the area were saved from destitution by receiving contributions from the fund of the Halkirk Village Society, whose accounts in the early part of the last century showed a figure of £300, an enormous sum for those times. Further provision was made for the needy with the construction of the Poor House (now converted into flats) at Halkirk in 1856. It served the W end of the county, the E having a poorhouse, now virtually ruinous, at Ben-a-chielt, by the Causewaymire road.

Distillation of the 'barley bree' has had a long association with Halkirk. For nigh on 100 years the spirit was distilled at Gerston. The earliest distillery foundation, which goes as far back as 1825, survived some 50 years producing whisky of considerable merit, which was a favourite of Prime Minister Sir Robert Peel. There is now little trace of the original distillery, but not long after its demise another distillery, the Ben Morven, was established close by in 1886. The Still House is all that remains of this once large complex. Ben Morven never acquired the distinction of its predecessor and after a period of financial difficulty, it closed in 1911.

From Omand, Donald. (ed.) 1989. *The New Caithness Book*, Wick, 137–9.

Braal Castle, Halkirk (Fig. 1.10)
Robert B. Gourlay

The ruins of Braal Castle sit on the west bank of the Thurso River near the village of Halkirk. The tower is a rectangular, rubble-built structure, measuring internally about 10 m square, and survives to the level of the top of the second storey. The roof features have all disappeared, to some extent due to the reduction of the wall top in recent years because of dangerous masonry.

The castle probably dates from the 14th century. In 1375 or 1376, King Robert II granted to his son David Stewart 'the Castle of Brathwell and all the

Figure 1.10: Halkirk: Braal Castle (J. P. Campbell).

lands thereof'. In 1452, King James II granted the lands of Brathwele to Admiral Sir George Crechtoun of Carnis. In 1457 the castle was in the possession of George, Earl of Caithness, who along with several others, had a remission from Queen Mary for taking the Castle of Ackergill (N of Wick) for forcibly confining Sir Alexander Keith, the Captain, and John Skarlet, his servitor, in the place of Girnigo, Brawl, and other places.

The entrance is at first floor level, with the staircase within the wall thickness at the right hand side. The unvaulted basement had no external door and was lit by two narrow vertical loop-holes. On the first floor are deep, broad window recesses in the N and W walls. These are arched and furnished with stone seats. In the E wall are a fireplace and latrine, with a closet in the SW angle. There are no surviving floors and, due to the dangerous condition of the building and disturbance to the fabric through vandalism, the opening was closed off and access to the interior discontinued.

Lybster
Donald Omand

The place name Lybster, like so many in the settled parts of lowland Caithness, is of Norse origin (including *bólstaðr* = farm). But, clearly, people were living in the area long before: witness the diverse monuments of ancient times, including the spectacular stone age burial tombs at Camster.

It seems likely that the mouth of the Reisgill Burn (Old Norse *hrís* = brushwood, and *gil* = ravine) was an attractive area for early settlement as, on the N brae above the harbour, a cross and a shallow depression were found carved on a stone. This stone was removed to the old church of St Mary's (built in 1836) and subsequently located beside the central parish kirk at the north end of the village. Further evidence of an early ecclesiastical interest in the area is provided by the old name of Lybster Bay, *Haligoe*, 'the holy geo', and the Brethren Well to the W of the burn mouth. Moreover, during the early 19th century, excavation of the land by the river, to provide a harbour, led to the discovery of a substantial burial ground. Such place name evidence, along with the carved cross and cemetery, might suggest an early monastic settlement at the head of the bay.

We could speculate, then, that on their arrival in this area, possibly in the late 8th or 9th century AD, the Norse came upon a peasant society of Picts already christianised through the zealous missionary activity of the Celtic Church. The bay was named *Haligoe* by the Norse and their early settlement to the E of the inlet perhaps focussed on their hall, the *skáli*, now commemorated in the name of Skaill at the S end of the village.

There was, of course, no 'village' in those times. Indeed, there was no village in the whole of Latheron parish even as recently as the 1790s! The 19th century had dawned before the first planned settlement in the parish became a reality; its originator was the local laird, Patrick Sinclair, a character of considerable energy, who had a capacity for losing money.

Patrick Sinclair was a cousin of Sir John Sinclair of Ulbster, that distinguished son of the county better known as 'Agricultural Sir John'. Patrick joined the Black Watch and while in Canada served under General Amherst. After a varied career he returned to Lybster in 1784 to his home at the Hall or Ha', now usually referred to as Lybster Mains. In his fifties he married and decided to extend his house, whose oldest parts may date back to the 17th century. A library and a reception room were built, with fine plaster ceilings and decorative cornices. Around the turn of the century Patrick Sinclair planted

40 ha (100 acres) of his estate with birch, alder, elm and ash. The old trees are now dying off but have been replaced with young conifers.

Agricultural Sir John's land innovations no doubt influenced his cousin at the Ha' as reclamation and drainage schemes were initiated, and he even experimented with growing wheat in various parts of his estate, which stretched from Swiney in the S to Clyth burn in the N. In the year 1810 Patrick Sinclair decided that he could best encourage the growth of the fishing industry by constructing a wooden pier at the mouth of the Reisgill Burn. There were already a few boats engaged in lobster fishing, which was rapidly expanding along the Moray Firth. Having built the new pier, he decided to rename the sea inlet Amherst Bay, in memory of his commanding officer in Canada. In 1820 Lt General Sinclair died at the age of 83, the oldest general in the British army. His grave lies in what was once his own land at the Ha'.

As an increasing number turned to the summer herring fishing, many people (including those dispossessed of land in parts of Sutherland) were attracted to the vicinity of Lybster village, which Patrick Sinclair first planned in 1802. Soon, the small village had an influx of people who had a variety of trades such as coopers, fishcurers, boatbuilders, ships' chandlers and shopkeepers. So rapid was the growth of activity at the harbour that in 1817 the Fishery Board for Scotland officially recognised Lybster as a fishing station. To mark the success of Lybster as a fishing port, the General fixed a miniature herring barrel to the south-east gable of the Ha', where it can still be seen.

The early development of the village coincided with the important new lines of communication in Caithness being laid out under the supervision of the eminent Scottish civil engineer, Thomas Telford. In fact, the line of Telford's new road (now the A9) ran across the north end of the main street of the village which was named Quatre Bras, commemorating the battle in which General Sinclair's two sons had taken part. Here, too, the Free Church was built in 1848.

In 1820 Temple Frederick Sinclair, Patrick's son, succeeded to the estate and he continued the development of the linear village by laying out a square off the lengthy main street. Temple, like his father, was a staunch Whig and so he named the four sides of the square after politicians of the Reform Ministry of the 1830s: Grey's Place, Russell Street, Jeffrey Street and Althorpe Street. The junction of the old coast road and the southern end of the planned square became known as The Cross. Two houses in the village with dates of 1802 and 1833 above their porches are reminders of the foundation of the settlement and its first phase of expansion.

A feu disposition, dated 1833, from Temple Sinclair to James Sutherland, Fishcurer, 5 Grey's Place, Lybster, gives an interesting insight into how carefully the village layout was planned. Sutherland was obliged to 'build and erect a substantial stone house and to cover the same with blue slates'. The street in front was 'to be 50 feet in width, whereof 24 feet are to be laid with the common materials of the high road and six feet reserved on each side for a foot pathway . . . to be flagged with stone'. The road and pathway were to be made 'at the sole expense of the feuars', proportional costing depending on the length of the house frontage. To ensure that the paths and streets were kept in good repair, the sum of 3/- (15p) had to be paid annually by each feuar to the proprietor, who had decreed that no outstairs, outshots, dunghills or other nuisances were to encroach on the street!

By the late 1830s the parish had developed the classic coastal Highland economic way of life of dual dependence on land and sea. In 1838 the *New Statistical Account* reported that 2,592 people in the parish were employed in fishing for herring with 325 boats in Latheron parish: 71 at Clyth, 101 at Lybster, 10 at Swiney, 32 at Forse, 32 at Latheron and 76 at Dunbeath. By this time Lybster, with a population of around 400, had become the third greatest herring station in Scotland after Wick and Fraserburgh.

Some harbour improvements were made in 1832 when a stone pier was erected along the west bank of Reisgill Burn where it entered the sea. In the 1850s much of the main quay was built. The west wall of the harbour basin was constructed to a length of 91 m (300 ft) and a weir was made near the outlet of the Burn spanned by a fine 18·6 m (61 ft) high bridge. The substantially improved developing harbour led to an import trade of coal, timber and salt. The peak of the herring fishery was reached in the 1870s, but within a decade the dark clouds of recession had gathered. Despite the gloom, harbour improvements continued and the lighthouse was built in 1884.

By the beginning of the First World War, the industry had all but collapsed and local folk would never again witness dozens of tiny boats sailing heavily to port with the 'silver darlings'. Nor would they wonder at the throng of fishery workers from the W filling the night air with the haunting music of the Gael. By the 1930s the harbour was a desolate area, but an energetic harbour committee soon restored its picturesque appeal as well as increasing its safety as a haven.

From: Omand, Donald (ed.) 1989. *The New Caithness Book*, Wick, 120–4.

Dunbeath
Donald Omand

The establishment and growth of many villages and towns in the N of Scotland was intimately linked with the mass movement of people, often involuntarily, from the countryside. This dislocation, in Caithness, was in the main due to landlords finding it more profitable to lease their land in some other way. This 18th and 19th century monetarism often had drastic social consequences, with entire valleys being cleared of people. For example, in the SE of Caithness, the straths of Ousdale, Berriedale and Langwell were virtually emptied. Many of the evicted people from Langwell, some 28 families in all, formed a crofting village on a barren, grudging shoulder of peaty land perched above the perilous cliffs at Badbea, just after the turn of the 19th century. The sad little settlement has long since died; a monument, erected in 1912 to the memory of those who had lived there, is an added pathos to the scene.

Like the Langwell valley, the lovely Dunbeath Strath was emptied of its people in the 1840s, when 80 families were forced to move elsewhere to make a living. Many of them became involved in the herring fishery which had begun at the rivermouth about the year 1790. So prolific were the catches that, by 1838, 76 boats were fishing from the tiny harbour. Small settlements arose to the north (Portormin) and south (Balcladich) of the rivermouth. Others developed near the Telford bridge and at Inver, which had the market hill nearby.

The Dunbeath Strath has come to be associated with writer Neil Gunn who was born in the house adjacent to the village shop. As a boy, Neil explored the river in detail getting acquainted with the antiquities, particularly the broch not far from his home. On the opposite bank of the river to the broch was Milton Inn, athwart the pre-Telford road, where Glenorchy's troops sheltered prior to the battle of Altimarlach near Wick in 1680.

A visit to Laidhay Croft Museum (see below, pp. 29–30) gives an insight into the basic but cosy dwellings and outhouses the crofters lived in during the 19th and early 20th centuries. Laidhay provides a stark contrast to the castle of Dunbeath which may date as far back as the 13th and 14th centuries. The castle looks N towards the harbour to some of the restored buildings of the Dunbeath Preservation Trust, whose unique heritage project work can be seen in the strath and at its headquarters in the old village school (see below, pp. 24–8).

From: Omand, Donald (ed.) 1989. *The New Caithness Book*, Wick, 118–19.

The Dunbeath Archaeological Survey (Fig. 1.11)
Alex. Morrison

The Dunbeath lands were possessed by one or other branch of the Caithness Sinclairs for more than three centuries until 1945, when they passed finally out of Sinclair hands. The estate was purchased by Mr R. Stanton Avery, of Pasadena, California, in 1977. Mr Avery, who had already contributed funds to educational and cultural organisations and to medical and environmental research in the United States through the Durfee Foundation, a private grant-awarding body, set up the Dunbeath Preservation Trust. Part of the Deed of Declaration of the Trust states that funds shall be directed to 'the preservation, enhancement and development for educational and other charitable purposes in every respect of all or any part of the general locality of Dunbeath, Caithness (including Dunbeath Estate) with particular reference to its resources in respect of prehistoric sites, ancient monuments, historic buildings, social history and general environment including its flora, fauna and geology'.

A major project in which the Dunbeath Preservation Trust is involved, together with students and staff of the Archaeology Department of the University of Glasgow, is the systematic field survey and recording of archaeological and historical remains in the region. This has involved walking over the estate from the coast to its farthest inland boundaries. The survey has been supervised since 1985 by Dr Alex. Morrison. Known sites have been checked and planned and many new sites have been discovered, particularly in areas which have not been regarded as suitable for agriculture or settlement in recent times. It has also been important to note the deterioration in the condition of some of the remains in the relatively short time since they were first systematically recorded and described by the Royal Commission on the Ancient and Historical Monuments of Scotland in 1910–11. Some of this deterioration is undoubtedly due to natural processes of weathering and subsidence, but grazing animals and the hand of man seeking materials for making roads, dykes and other structures are responsible to an even greater extent. It is hoped that, as survey gives way to excavation of selected remains over the years, close examination of the surrounding areas of deserted sites will uncover even more detailed evidence of human activities and start to fill in some of the framework provided by the field survey.

Working simultaneously on various fronts, the Dunbeath Preservation Trust hopes to gather detailed information in all relevant fields of study. Ornithological and botanical studies have begun, and a start has been made in the collection of local and oral history, with some involvement of local schoolchildren. Part of the work of the Preservation Trust has been and will be to support the restoration and preservation of more recent buildings of historical value. The first steps in this direction can be seen at the site of the salmon-fishing station set up at Portormin in the early 19th century. The ice house and salmon-fishers' bothy were recently repaired and expertly restored to their original internal and external appearance. In 1990 the broch of Dun Beath at the junction of the Houstry Burn and Dunbeath Water was stabilised and partly restored under the supervision of Mr Iain Banks of the then Archaeological Projects Glasgow group in the Department of Archaeology of the University of Glasgow. A further project will be to restore the old coaching inn at Milton. Work is going ahead on the repair and enhancement of public walkways from which many of the historical and archaeological sites and buildings can be seen.

The culmination of this first stage of the Trust's work has been the planning of a Dunbeath Heritage Centre as a repository for the data being collected and to present, audio-visually and in the form of museum exhibits, the results of the continuing research into the history, archaeology and natural sciences of the Dunbeath area. This research extends from the environments and settlements of the first hunters and farmers to the continuing problems of modern economic exploitation of the landscape. This initiative has been supported and partly funded by the Countryside Commission, Nature Conservancy Council, Highlands and Islands Development Board and the Dunbeath Preservation Trust. The old schoolhouse in Dunbeath village was acquired by the Trust and work on the Centre commenced in 1988. Apart from the audio-visual theatre, the exhibits

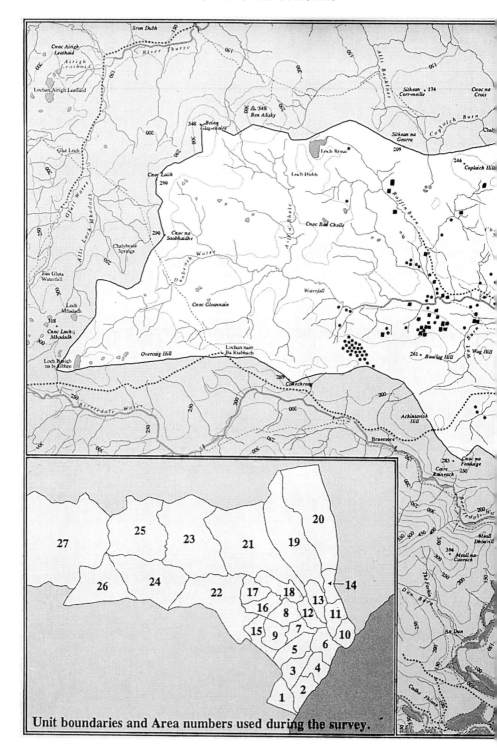

Figure 1.11: Dunbeath Estate: map of archaeological sites (A. Morrison & L. McEwan).

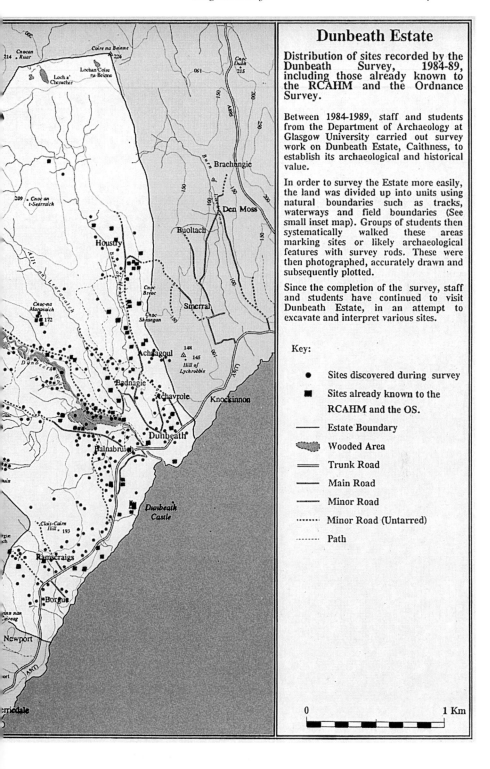

Dunbeath Estate

Distribution of sites recorded by the Dunbeath Survey, 1984-89, including those already known to the RCAHM and the Ordnance Survey.

Between 1984-1989, staff and students from the Department of Archaeology at Glasgow University carried out survey work on Dunbeath Estate, Caithness, to establish its archaeological and historical value.

In order to survey the Estate more easily, the land was divided up into units using natural boundaries such as tracks, waterways and field boundaries (See small inset map). Groups of students then systematically walked these areas marking sites or likely archaeological features with survey rods. These were then photographed, accurately drawn and subsequently plotted.

Since the completion of the survey, staff and students have continued to visit Dunbeath Estate, in an attempt to excavate and interpret various sites.

Key:

●   Sites discovered during survey

■   Sites already known to the RCAHM and the OS.

——   Estate Boundary

   Wooded Area

   Trunk Road

——   Main Road

——   Minor Road

·······   Minor Road (Untarred)

·······   Path

0   1 Km

cover eight major themes: 'Shadows of my past', a central tableau of figures from the Stone Age to the 20th Century; Archaeology and Research; Natural History; Geology and Topography, with a view up the Strath of Dunbeath; Oil, with a binocular view of the Beatrice oil platform; The Modern Estate and Trust; The Life and Work of local writer Neil Gunn; A Local Photo Gallery. The Heritage Centre was officially opened by Her Majesty, Queen Elizabeth, the Queen Mother, on 28 August 1989.

Laidhay Croft Museum (Fig. 1.12)
Donald Omand   Geoffrey P. Stell

Laidhay exhibits most of the features common to the older croft-buildings of eastern Caithness. The croft, which comprised 16 acres of arable together with rights over 15 acres of rough grazing, came into the possession of the Bethune family in 1842 with whom it remained until 1968. The thatched croft-buildings comprise a modified long-house nucleus, measuring 105 feet 5 inches in length and incorporating the dwelling, byre and stable. A fine detached barn stands to the NE and the remains of a cart-shed to the S. At the beginning of this century the living quarters were subdivided into two (latterly three) rooms and a kitchen and dairy, the end room and the kitchen being equipped with a fireplace and the 'middle room' containing a range of four box-beds. The large kitchen fireplace was at that time of a hob-hearth type, incorporating iron fire-bars and an ash-pit or 'lazy-hole'. The floor is of flagstones bedded in sand, and the flags were washed with buttermilk to give them an attractive blue shine. The roof over the kitchen still includes one surviving cruck truss or 'Highland couple'. From the

Figure 1.12: Laidhay Croft Museum (J. P. Campbell).

kitchen the scullery or dairy and the byre are entered by a doorway in the centre of a stone partition, but this wall does not appear to have been part of the original arrangement when there was probably no permanent division between kitchen and byre. A long table for various dairy utensils was placed against the rear wall of the scullery, and the byre with its cobbled floor and drain had flagstone partitions for the beasts tethered against the same wall.

The barn is an excellent specimen of its type. It is neatly built of mortared rubble with a thatched roof carried on three 'Highland couples' or crucks, each roof-truss being made up of several members lapped and pegged together and set into the lower third of the side-walls. The timbers are mainly of birch, but the roof structure includes many re-used boat timbers especially among the purlins (the longitudinal members) and the cabbers or common rafters. The remains of the winnowing door can be seen in the side-wall opposite the main entrance, and when opened was intended to create a through draught from the prevailing wind for winnowing purposes.

The layout and construction of the older type of Caithness croft-building such as Laidhay is ultimately derived from a type of long-house or byre-dwelling that was once a common feature of the Scottish rural landscape prior to the age of agrarian improvements in the 18th and 19th centuries. During this later period, however, modified long-houses continued to be built in parts of the country such as Caithness where they became clearly associated with individual small-holdings or crofts, as opposed to the old communal run-rig system of agriculture based on group-farms.

From: Stell, Geoffrey P. & Omand, Donald 1976. *The Caithness Croft*, Laidhay Croft Museum.

REFERENCE

Close-Brooks 1986, no. 23: 60 & 64–5.

Grey Cairns of Camster (Figs 1.13 & 1.14)
Robert B. Gourlay

The Grey Cairns of Camster comprise two magnificent and well-preserved examples of Neolithic chambered tombs. While they are presently visible in their open moorland setting, the next few years will see the setting of the cairns change as recently planted trees begin to grow up around the site. Both the round and long cairns have been carefully restored and provided with roof lights, and a somewhat uncomfortable scramble on hands and knees along the entrance passages allows three virtually intact chambers to be viewed at first-hand.

The Round Cairn is almost in its original state, although its primary drystone kerb has been concealed by partial collapse of the overlying cairn material. The low, narrow passage, leads into an ante-chamber and then the burial chamber itself – each element separated from the other by a pair of massive slabs set on end. Within the inner chamber can be seen most of the original corbelled roof,

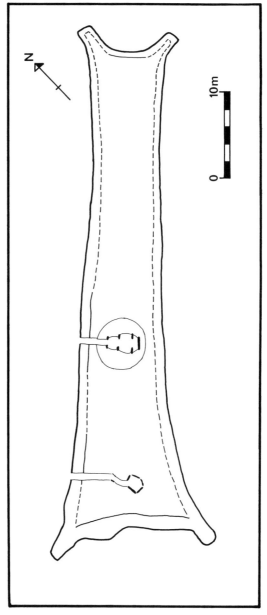

Figure 1.13 (and opposite): Camster Cairns: plans (D. Low, Highland Regional Council, after A. Henshall).

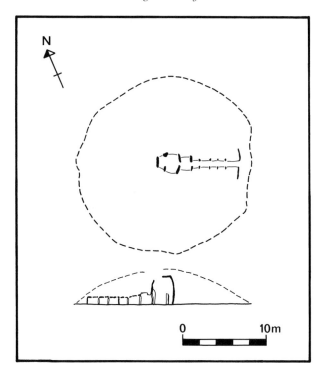

Figure 1.14: Camster Long Cairn (J. P. Campbell).

and the characteristic 'back-slab'. Excavated in the last century, burnt bone, pottery and flint tools were found in the chamber along with the remains of several skeletons in the chamber and passage.

Camster Long Cairn was excavated over many years, showing it to be a complex structure of several phases. It has since been restored to its present condition. It consists of a huge, elongated cairn covering and adapting two earlier, circular cairns of different style and construction. The right-hand passage on the E side of the cairn leads into a simple polygonal chamber. The original size of the circular cairn which originally covered this tomb can be estimated from the position of the bend in the passage where it was extended to the edge of the later long cairn. The left hand entrance leads through a short passage into a tomb of similar arrangement to the Round Cairn. This, too, was at first covered by a circular cairn, but both were later incorporated into the 69 m long monument with its horned facades at both ends – both of which are 'blind' and have no entrance leading from them.

The cairns were constructed during the 4th and 3rd millenia BC, and may have remained in continual use for 1,000 years or more.

REFERENCES

Bramman *et al.* 1976, no. 1: 6–7.
Close-Brooks 1986, no. 93: 164–5.

Hill o' Many Stanes, Mid Clyth (Fig. 1.15)
Robert B. Gourlay

Unique to Caithness and the adjacent fringes of Sutherland is a group of monuments known as 'stone rows'. The 'Hill o' Many Stanes' at Mid Clyth is much the best preserved of these curious fan-shaped settings, and lies on the southern slope of a low hill. From the viewpoint at the top of the site some 22 rows run southwards, fanning out slightly as they go, and now containing about 200 visible stones. These are small slabs of local stone all less than 1 m in height, and lie with their long axes along the rows.

The plan suggests that the 'fan' is in two parts: in the centre, and less obviously on the E side is what appears to be the main fan pattern, while a smaller, separate fan on the W has a bend at its northern end. As recently as 1871 about 250 stones were visible, and if the pattern is filled in, it is likely that originally there may have been as many as 600 stones.

None of these sites has yet been excavated, and so dating must be guesswork, but it is generally assumed that they are Bronze Age in date. Many such sites have a mound or cairn at or near the narrower end – also not understood in the absence of excavation. These sites have been investigated in some detail in recent years through the survey work of local amateur archaeologist Mr Leslie Myatt, as a result of which their link with archaeoastronomical sightings is well attested.

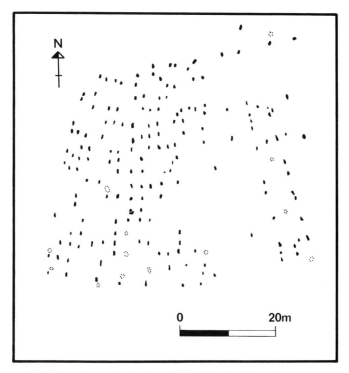

Figure 1.15: Hill O'Many Stanes: plan (D. Low, Highland Regional Council, after J. Close-Brooks).

REFERENCES

Bramman *et al.* 1976, no. 9: 12–13.
Close-Brooks 1986, no. 90: 161.

Friday, 25 August

Sinclair and Girnigoe Castles (Figs 1.16 & 1.17)
Robert B. Gourlay

Set on a precipitous, cliff-girt promontory N of Wick are the dramatic ruins of a former stronghold of the Sinclair Earls of Caithness. The ruins represent what is left of the original Castle Girnigoe, built in the late 15th century by Earl William of Caithness, and a later and more ambitious addition built in the early 17th century and known as Castle Sinclair.

Despite its earlier date, the ruins of the first castle remain in the better condition. Defended by the cliffs and a rock-cut ditch, they comprise a tall, five-level tower and a series of lower buildings which occupy all available space on the steep promontory. At the seaward end, two of the ruined buildings have steep stairs giving access to the sea.

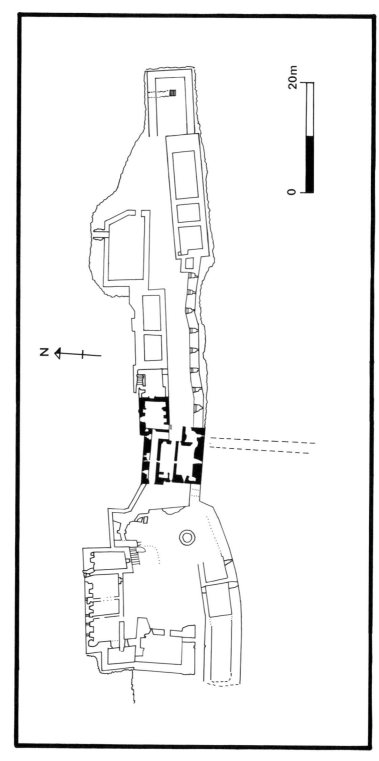

20m

0

N

Figure 1.16: Castle of Sinclair/Girnigoe: plan (D. Low, Highland Regional Council, after RCAHMS).

Figure 1.17: Castle of Sinclair/Girnigoe (J. P. Campbell).

The addition, or Castle Sinclair, is much more ruinous, but signs of elaborately carved mouldings and corbels attest to its architectural pretensions. It may be built over, or perhaps incorporate, an earlier gatehouse. It lies within an outer rock-cut ditch which would have defended the original bailey. The castle was abandoned after a siege in 1690 during one of the family's numerous inheritance disputes, and never occupied afterwards.

A further feature of the complex may be represented by the promontory to the E of the site, which is cut off by a low, grassy bank. As there are no visible internal features, this may belong to a much earlier period.

The nature of the site and subsequent erosion make this a most hazardous site to visit, and great care should be taken by any visitor who attempts the interior areas.

REFERENCES
Bramman *et al.* 1976, no. 17: 28–9.
Close-Brooks 1986, no. 40: 94–5.

Nybster Broch, Auckengill (Fig. 1.18)
Robert B. Gourlay

The broch at Nybster was excavated about 1900 by Sir Francis Tress Barry, who was also responsible for excavations at a large number of other such sites. His collaborator on many of the excavations was the artist and sculptor John Nicolson. Many of his drawings and volumes of record photographs from the

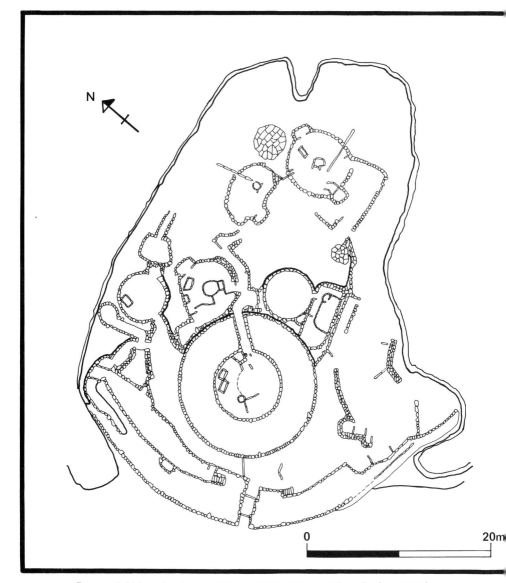

Figure 1.18: Nybster broch: plan (D. Low, Highland Regional Council, after RCAHMS).

excavations, along with objects and other memorabilia, have been gathered together and presented to the public in the John Nicolson Museum at Auckengill, soon to be incorporated into the 'Northlands Viking Centre'.

The broch is unusual in many ways. The inner court of the broch itself is extremely small (6·2 m), although this compares with two other such sites at

Skirza Head and Ness. While the entrance passage has the usual door check, there are no intra-mural cells or guard chambers. The wall is circular, between 4·2 and 5·0 m in thickness. Excavation has revealed considerable evidence of additional buildings on the promontory within the protection of a massive cross-promontory wall – curiously without an external ditch. The buildings are circular or cellular in shape, and while there are none of the galleried structures attached to other brochs in Caithness, many of these structures are likely to date from the Pictish period.

Adjacent to the broch is the newly moved and reconstructed monument known as 'Mervyn's Tower'. Built by John Nicolson to commemorate Sir Francis Tress Barry, it was moved both to take it clear of the broch itself (it was based on one of Tress Barry's spoil heaps) and to save it from collapse.

On the elegant and beautifully-drawn plan from the excavation, many of the details of structures revealed by excavation but now overgrown or invisible are clearly shown. Finds from the site included a long-handled bone comb; a bronze pin with annular head; several fragments both of rotary and saddle querns; and the decorated upper stone of a rotary quern with radial grooves and flutings.

Freswick Links: A Multi-period Site (Fig. 1.19)
Colleen E. Batey

The earliest documented excavation on the site was undertaken by Sir Francis Tress Barry in the 1890s, when the Iron Age broch, Freswick Sands, in the northern part of the Links was excavated. This excavation was only one of a series of eight he undertook along the East Caithness coast – including Nybster (with John Nicolson: see above, pp. 34–7) at Auckengill, and Ness and Skirza to the north. He characterised the broch tower and noted various structures outside, but paid little attention to the Norse material, which artefactual analysis indicates overlay the ruins.

In 1924 and 1926, A. J. H. Edwards, then of the National Museum of Antiquities in Edinburgh, excavated a series of three crude stone structures, which he interpreted as earth-houses. They were pre-Norse in date and sealed by Norse middens. Local informants still recall this work and have been most instructive in suggesting the precise location of these sites, inland and S of the broch.

Work on the Viking and Late Norse deposits was initially undertaken by A. O. Curle and V. G. Childe in 1937–8 and 1941. These results have been published and re-examined in great detail subsequently. A series of structures, some remaining intact and others less complete, were excavated, but there are severe limitations in the results as published by the original excavators. Very little consideration was applied to the associated midden and occupation deposits of these structures, which originally resulted in a less than complete understanding of the site.

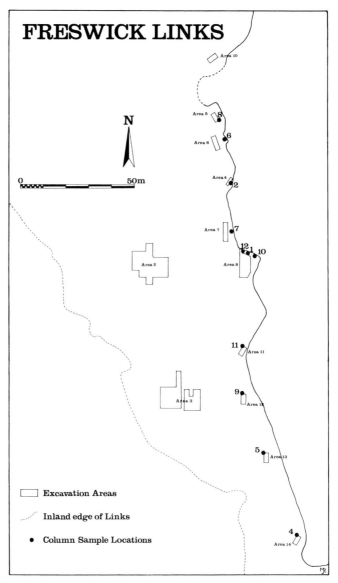

Figure 1.19: Freswick Links: overall plan (M. J. Rains: Crown copyright).

The work of A. O. Curle in 1937 and 1938, followed to a lesser extent by that of V. G. Childe in 1941, provided indications of the extent and nature of the Norse site at Freswick. However, the recent reappraisal of that work indicates a rather later date for the site occupation than initially published. Curle considered the site to be Viking, as did Childe, and although the relative lateness in date of some of the finds from the earlier excavations – the number of which was very limited – was fully recognised, the site remained classified as a Viking site. Detailed artefactual study, and indeed reinterpretation of this earlier excavation material, confirms a date bracket of the 11th to 13th centuries and is to be termed Late Norse, following Bigelow's definition in Shetland. Earlier Viking material, although very limited in quantity, is known from the site – but without clear structural associations.

Less formal work has been undertaken at the site since these excavations and before the work undertaken by Durham University. Collection by A. D. Lacaille in the 1940s and 1950s has suggested Mesolithic and Bronze Age activity on the site, represented by extensive flint scatters. Locally-held material, in part exhibited for the Congress in Wick, is predominantly dated to the Viking and Late Norse periods; such collections are largely made up of complete items, possibly suggesting a certain selectivity in the material retained.

Work by Durham University on the Links commenced in 1978 and that phase of work was completed in 1984. Excavation beneath Freswick House or Castle was undertaken in 1979. The publications of significant parts of this work are now available, and the remaining sections are with editors. This work was undertaken as a response to severe erosion of rich midden deposits at the site. The earlier excavations concentrated on the structural remains, whereas the modern thrust concerned the ecofactual aspects of the site, through a detailed study of the middens. A programme of work was established particularly to examine the middens at the cliff edge, and structural remains were not especially sought.

Extensive sampling and sieving on site took place, down to 1 mm in most cases and, in the case of cultivation traces examined, down to 500 microns. The data-base thus achieved remains unparalleled even to date in the period represented – the prohibitive cost of such an exercise would militate against its precise repetition! In an attempt to gain a quicker understanding of the midden material in the areas examined, a series of columns 30 cm square were taken through the deposits (in addition to the four 1 m × 50 cm columns taken from the cliff-edge trenches). The time required to process the many tonnes sampled, and then to analyse the material, has resulted in a considerable delay in the publication of the rest of the archaeological data, and so the columns were processed in advance of the rest.

The excavations via small trenches (4 m × 2 m) at the cliff edge and extensive sieving of the deposits has revealed in great detail aspects of the economic basis of the site. There are excellent conditions for bone preservation on the site and this, combined with the large-scale sieving of deposits, has resulted in the recovery of many small fish bones which do not commonly survive – head and fin bones, for example. The preservation conditions enable these small bones to be studied in relation to modern samples, and this has obvious uses in the study of the history of fishing and fish movements.

Analysis of the fish bone material, which forms the bulk of the assemblage, suggests large-scale fishing activity was taking place at Freswick in the Late Norse period (this had not even been suspected prior to this work), and that fish

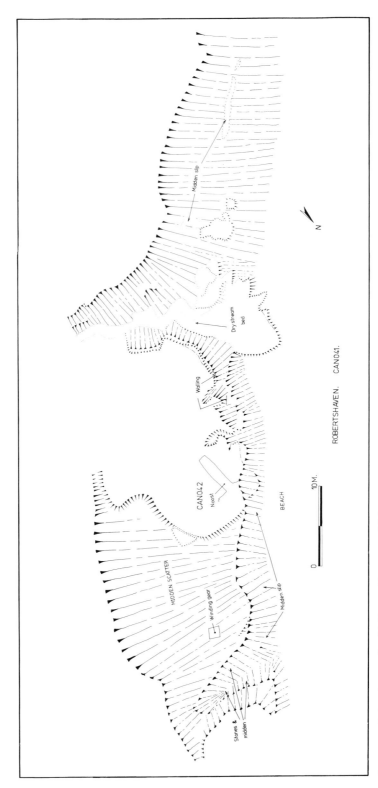

Figure 1.20: **Robertshaven: plan (N. Emery: Crown copyright).**

in excess of 1 m in length, sometimes rather larger, were being brought to the site. It seems likely that the Freswick settlement was acting as a processing centre, possibly for the area, although at present this cannot be proven. Aspects of seasonality in the catch, preferred species and indeed the influence of post-depositional factors have been studied by Andrew Jones, formerly of the Environmental Archaeology Unit at York.

Other elements examined include mammal bones, bird bones and sea mammal bones, although they are all less significant than the fish material. However, there is evidence for cattle and sheep exploitation at the site. Pollen analysis by Jacqueline P. Huntley of Durham University shows clearly that, although cereals were being cultivated in the pre-Viking period in the area around Freswick, there is a *lacuna* in the Viking and Late Norse periods. This has been difficult to understand since cultivation marks have been identified at several parts of the site. Such cereal traces as survive on the vegetal tempered pottery must be from imported grain – could this have been in exchange for the processed fish? There are clearly implications from this work for our understanding of Late Norse economic networks in Mainland Scotland.

However, ^{14}C analysis now identifies some of these cultivation traces as Pictish, which is supported in the pollen record. We now have to compare carefully the faunal remains in the Late Norse contexts with those from the Pictish – superficially, they do seem remarkably similar in several respects.

On the site today, buildings of particular note are Freswick House or Castle, which is predominantly 16th century and later, but which directly overlies a southerly extension of the Late Norse site on the Links. Nearby, a Mausoleum, Doocot and Bridge (with prisoner's chamber and the coat of arms of the Sinclairs), are thought to be of roughly contemporary build with the Castle.

REFERENCES

Batey, Colleen E. 1987. *Freswick Links, Caithness. A Re-appraisal of the Late Norse Site in its Context*, British Archaeological Reports, British Series 179, 2 Vols. Oxford (and references therein).

Batey, Colleen E. 1989. 'Recent work at Freswick Links, Caithness, Northern Scotland', *Hikuin*, 15, 223–30.

Robertshaven, John o' Groats (Fig. 1.20)

Colleen E. Batey

The eroding middens and structures which are visible to the E of John o' Groats were first identified and recorded during the Caithness Coastal Survey in 1980–82. A seasonal stream cuts through the heart of the visible site and has revealed extensive traces of midden. Preliminary examination suggests the same fish-rich middens and vegetal tempered pottery as distinguished at Freswick. Survey suggests that the site extends over some hundreds of square metres: inland to the standing later structure, some 50 m and to the W of the visible wall, some 50 m and roughly twice that to the E of that wall. It is suggested that this site is of similar date to Freswick, although preliminary thermoluminescence dates suggest a rather later period for those deposits sampled. It is perhaps circumstantial that Clouston noted only two *bu*s in Caithness: one at Freswick and the other at Duncansby, the area where Robertshaven lies!

REFERENCES

Batey, Colleen E. 1984. *Caithness Coastal Survey 1980–82; Dunnet Head to Ousdale*, Department of Archaeology, Durham, Occasional Paper no. 3, 24–6, 59 & 100.
Batey, Colleen E. 1991. 'Archaeological Aspects of Norse Settlement in Caithness, North Scotland', in *The Norse of the North Atlantic* ed. Bigelow, Gerald F.,=*Acta Archaeologica* 61 (1990), 29–32.

ORKNEY (Fig. 1.21)

GENERAL REFERENCES

Orkney is well-served in terms of general accounts of the islands, their people, history and environment. The following are all recommended for their own distinctive contributions:

Berry, R. J. 1985. *The Natural History of Orkney*, The New Naturalist, London.
Berry, R. J. & Firth, H. N. (eds) 1986. *The People of Orkney*, Aspects of Orkney 4, Kirkwall.
Schei, Liv K. & Moberg, Gunnie 1985. *The Orkney Story*, London.
Shearer, John, Groundwater, William & Mackay, John D. (eds) 1966. *The New Orkney Book* ('prepared for use in the schools of Orkney'), London & Edinburgh.
Thomson, William P. L. 1987. *History of Orkney*, Edinburgh.

For the aspects particularly considered during the Congress (i.e. the Pictish, Viking and Late Norse periods), the following general accounts should be consulted:

Wainwright, Frederick T. (ed.) 1962. *The Northern Isles*, Edinburgh & London. Chapters VII–X by Wainwright and Radford, C. A. Ralegh.
Renfrew, A. Colin (ed.) 1985. *The Prehistory of Orkney BC 4,000–1,000 AD*, Edinburgh. Chapters 9 & 10 by Ritchie, Anna and Morris, Christopher D.
Brundle, Anne L. 1989. *A Haven for Vikings. Life, death & treasure hoards in Norse Orkney*, exhibition booklet, Orkney Museums Service, Kirkwall.

Many of the sites visited during the Congress are well-known, and members received copies of the standard guide:

Ritchie, Anna & Graham. 1988. *The Ancient Monuments of Orkney*, Historic Scotland guidebook, Edinburgh, 3rd edn.

In the following section, references will be made to this and to other more detailed archaeological guides:

Lamb, R. G. 1982. *The Archaeological Sites and Monuments of Scotland, 16. Rousay, Egilsay and Wyre (with adjacent small islands), Orkney Islands Area. An Archae-ological Survey*, RCAHMS, Edinburgh.

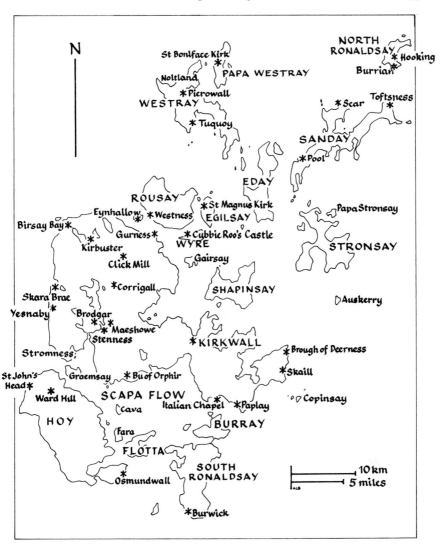

Figure 1.21: Orkney: map of sites visited and mentioned (A. L. Brundle).

Lamb, R. G. 1987. *The Archaeological Sites and Monuments of Scotland, 27. Shapinsay, St Andrews and Deerness (with adjacent small islands), Orkney Islands Area. An Archaeological Survey*, RCAHMS, Edinburgh.

Ritchie, Anna. 1985. *Exploring Scotland's Heritage: Orkney and Shetland.* RCAHMS, Edinburgh.

Friday, 25 August

Scapa Flow and South Isles

Churchill Barriers

See Ritchie 1985, no. 1, 21.

Scapa Flow

See Hewison, William S. 1985. *This Great Harbour Scapa Flow*, Aspects of Orkney, 3, Stromness.

The Italian Chapel

See Ritchie 1985, no. 2, 22.

Saturday, 26 August

Kirkwall

Origins and Development (Figs 1.22–1.25)

Raymond G. Lamb

The usurper *jarl* Rognvald Brusason – Thorfinn's rival – established himself and a large household, well provisioned, in Kirkwall for the winter of 1046 (*Orkneyinga saga*, xxix). When the relics of St Magnus were transferred here from Birsay, apparently *c.* 1136 (*Magnúss saga skemmri*, xviii) Kirkwall is explicitly named as a market-centre which still had few buildings (*O.S.*, lvii). The Cathedral of St Magnus was begun by Rognvald Kali Kolsson in 1137 as the new seat of the Orkney bishopric: the Bishop's Palace was probably begun soon after. We infer that Kirkwall by 1046 was an appropriate place for a *jarl*'s

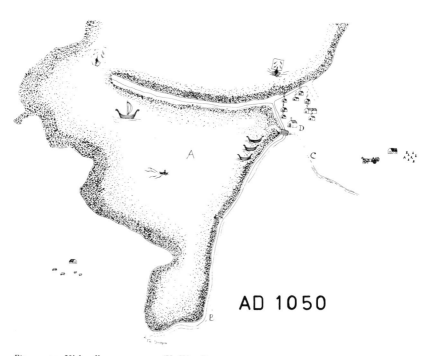

Figure 1.22: Kirkwall: map AD 1050 (K. Wood).

household to overwinter and had buildings suitable for the purpose; that by that time it was developing as a mercantile centre; taking these inferences together we can deduce that the merchants who used Kirkwall did so under the patronage and protection of the *jarl*. By the 1130s it was sufficiently dominant to attract the rapidly emerging main *cultus* – that of St Magnus – away from the older, rural power-centre at Birsay, and the transfer of the bishopric inevitably followed. The foundation of the Cathedral under the most determined kind of royal patronage, ensured the development of the market centre into a mediaeval city with ecclesiastical and administrative functions.

To understand the town-plan it is important to know that the long main street – represented by Bridge Street, Albert Street, Broad Street, Victoria Street, Main Street – originally ran along the waterfront, as it still does at Stromness and Lerwick (although those towns are no older than the 17th century). Most of the original harbour, the Oyce or Peerie Sea (A on Fig. 1.22), has been filled in, and most of that infilling has taken place since 1865. Shallow-draught ships of Viking type could have come as far south as the spot where the Catholic Church now stands (B), 800 m from the present harbour. From here it is only 2 km across a flat, sea-level isthmus to Scapa Bay, and ships trapped by adverse winds may well have been hauled across the isthmus to be launched from the other bay. From a maritime viewpoint, therefore, this is an attractive situation, and the narrow isthmus between the eastern and western parts of the Mainland ensures that land traffic also must pass Kirkwall.

There has been little archaeological research in the town. The late Neil McGavin excavated several small trenches in 1978, but all of these were well to the west of the main street, in areas which throughout the Middle Ages were in the Peerie Sea, with the exception of a trench inside Tankerness House, which picked up an old shoreline. More about the original water-front was learned during major roadworks in 1986, when new drains were installed under Broad Street. Observation of these roadworks enabled the mediaeval water-front to be defined in the vicinity of the Cathedral.

The four pictorial maps (Figs 1.22–1.25) were drawn by Karen Wood for use in local history teaching in Orkney schools; much of the detail is doubtful, but they show in outline, four stages in the development of the town.

AD 1050 (Fig. 1.22): The original mercantile settlement, a group of merchants' booths loosely grouped in the area later known as 'The Burgh'. There are waterfronts facing north – the present Shore Street, still a waterfront, and facing west, where the shoreline is represented by Bridge Street. Both waterfronts are beaches on which ships are drawn up for loading. To the south the settlement is bounded by the Papdale Burn (C), flowing into the Peerie Sea. We have shown a chapel (D) near the burn (stream), where St Olaf's Chapel later stood, although St Olaf's Chapel as we know it probably was built around 1100 and we do not know for certain that there had been an older church on the site. There must

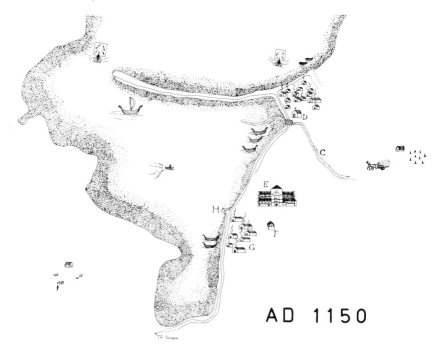

Figure 1.23: Kirkwall: map AD 1150 (K. Wood).

have been a *jarl*'s residence with at least one large feasting-hall, but the location of this is unknown.

AD 1150 (Fig. 1.23): Kirkwall at the height of its glory, when Rognvald Kolsson had his court here. By the Papdale Burn, St Olaf's Chapel (D) (of which one re-positioned Romanesque door-way survives in St Olaf's Wynd off Bridge Street) has briefly held the relics of St Magnus, but these are now in the new Cathedral (E) which is well under way. The Bishop's Palace (F) is shown, although we do not know for certain that it had been begun by this time, or what it looked like in its first phase. The Cathedral is placed on a virgin site well to the south of the Burgh with its merchants' booths and probably still the location of the *jarl*'s residence. The main access to the Cathedral is by boat, from the Peerie Sea. South-west of the Cathedral, a new settlement (G) grows up, to accommodate the various ecclesiastical personages who serve the Cathedral and its liturgies. The bishops control this new settlement, which becomes known as the Laverock, and encourage merchants to do business there. Thus there develop two rival mercantile centres – the Laverock under the bishops and the Burgh under the *jarls*. The rivalry continues today in the Christmas and New Year street-football games between the 'Uppies', the bishops' men, and the 'Doonies', who inhabit the Burgh.

An unknown factor is an older settlement in Laverock, found during the roadworks of 1986. It is a settlement site of the late Iron Age to Pictish period, probably of broch type, built on the shore where the Royal Bank of Scotland now stands. On the map (H) it is shown as a small promontory with ruins on it. In all likelihood it had been abandoned by the time the Cathedral was founded, but we cannot rule out the possibility that it had continued for long enough to have influenced some early Norse settlement in this area, in which case the town might have originated around two distinct early centres.

AD 1500 (Fig. 1.24): The use of deeper-draught ships has influenced the development of the harbour. The cog type of ship came in during the 13th century, and instead of being beached for loading, it needed wharfage, which is created on the Burgh waterfronts (J). The 1986 excavations also revealed a wharf (K) immediately west of the Cathedral – this had been created by cutting back the bedrock to a vertical face; the position of this waterfront is about the middle of Broad Street. The Cathedral has, of course, now reached its full development. A flight of steps leads up from the wharf to the west door – there is a Kirkwall tradition that ships were sailed 'up to the steps of the Cathedral'. Very soon after 1500 however, if not a little before, this wharf was deliberately filled in to create new land, and from about 1520, houses were built on this reclaimed land on the west side of Broad Street. Meanwhile, the Burgh has expanded south of the Papdale Burn, forming the 'Midtown' – Albert Street (L). The street, however,

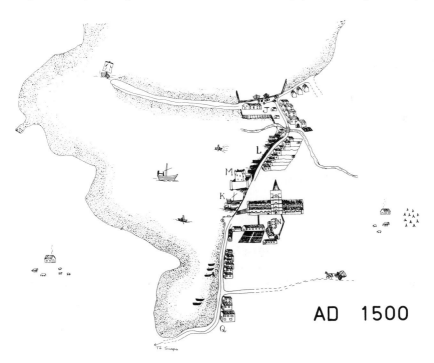

AD 1500

Figure 1.24: Kirkwall: map AD 1500 (K. Wood).

is still a waterfront – there are no buildings on the Peerie Sea side. But at the south end of the Midtown, *c.* 1380, Earl Henry St Clair built a new castle (M); this would have been seen by the bishops as an aggressive move.

Two towers (N), both square in plan, are shown on the Cathedral side of the Bishop's Palace. The larger was known as the Manse Tower and may have dated from the thirteenth century. Both were demolished around 1800. The round tower now at the north end of the Bishop's Palace did not yet exist in 1500; it was added by Bishop Reid (1541–58). Soon after, when the bishopric estates were broken up, the earls took over the bishop's palace and then built themselves a new Earl's Palace (P on Fig. 1.25) to the east. Built in the first decade of the 17th century, it was already in ruins by 1700. West of the Bishop's Palace were other ecclesiastical buildings, possibly including a college of canons. The Laverock has extended southwards to the inner end of the Peerie Sea (Victoria Street and Main Street), along the road to Scapa and the west Mainland (Q).

AD 1865 (Fig. 1.25): A strip of land on the west side of the street has, since the seventeenth century, been reclaimed from the Peerie Sea. In the Burgh, in Midtown and in Laverock, there are now houses on both sides of the street. Those on the west side had access to the shore, where boats can land, and barges were used to carry goods, offloaded from ships in Kirkwall Bay, into the Peerie Sea where merchants had sheds and warehouses (R) along the shore. In 1838 a

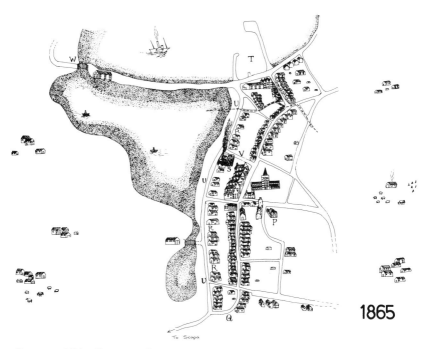

Figure 1.25: Kirkwall: map AD 1865 (K. Wood).

gasworks (S) was built; originally it stood on the shore and the coal arrived in barges. After 1830 steamships revolutionised the Orkney economy. It became possible to ship live cattle to markets in the south, so Orkney rapidly changed over from subsistence farming to the raising of cattle for export. The new prosperity brought about a great increase in bulk goods being shipped into Kirkwall. The only access to the harbour was still along the main street. Carts often got stuck at the narrow bridge over the Papdale Burn, which is set on a sharp corner (Leonard's the Newsagent's Corner). In 1865 the town council started an enormous engineering scheme. A new harbour (T) was built so that steamships could come alongside a pier. The Kirkwall Hotel subsequently was opened to serve the comfort of commercial travellers. The Papdale Burn was covered over. Land was reclaimed from the Peerie Sea on which a new road (U) was built behind the houses on the main street. This new road is called Junction Road because it joins Kirkwall and Scapa harbours. The last remnant of the St Clair castle was demolished to make way for Castle Street (V), which connects Junction Road to Broad Street. Finally, the channel into the Peerie Sea was bridged (W) to allow a new road route to Stromness – the present main road – to be created. There was talk of a railway, but it was never built. In the 20th century, reclamation of the Peerie Sea has continued to the west of Junction Road. The Peerie Sea is now reduced to a small ornamental pond.

Also see Ritchie 1985, no. 10, 36–38.

St Magnus' Cathedral, Kirkwall

Raymond G. Lamb

The Cathedral was begun in 1137, immediately after Rognvald Kali Kolsson's success in seizing Orkney from Pall Hakonarson. *Orkneyinga saga* stresses the vow that Rognvald had made to found an unprecedentedly magnificent church in Kirkwall in the name of his uncle, St Magnus. The Cathedral was the *jarl*'s own personal project, and from the circumstances of its foundation and from the stress laid on the miracles attributed to the intercession of St Magnus in *Orkneyinga saga* and the Magnus sagas, we can deduce that its prime purpose was to house the relics and to be the centre of the *cultus* of St Magnus, which now received vigorous official promotion. The relics themselves, shortly before, had been transferred to Kirkwall from the older ecclesiastical centre in Birsay, and the transfer of the bishopric to the new church inevitably followed. A parallel for the transfer of an officially-promoted *cultus* along with a bishopric, from an old rural power-centre to a new urban one, is the move of St Sunniva's relics from Selje to Bergen in 1170, followed by the establishment of the episcopal seat in that town.

The oldest part of the building is the western section of the quire, which originally terminated in an eastern apse, in the position where the organ screen is now. The foundations of the apse were discovered during repairs to the floors in the 1920s. The emphasis being on the relics of the saint, it is likely that the apse housed the shrine, with the high altar being in the quire a little to the west. The layout would have been designed to provide a ceremonial route for pilgrims approaching the shrine. In the 13th century the emphasis shifted from the relic-cult to the increasingly elaborate liturgies of a functioning Cathedral, with need to provide in the quire seating for more and more ecclesiastical dignitaries, canons, and a larger choir. In common with most Romanesque cathedrals, Kirkwall then lost its apse as the quire was extended eastwards; the change to the newer pointed arches is obvious. The relics of St Magnus were reinterred within the greatest pier on the south side of the quire; those of St Rognvald are in the corresponding pier on the north. A wooden casket in which the bones of St Magnus were housed within the pier, until their discovery and re-interment in 1923, is in Tankerness House Museum.

Before the enlargement of the east end, the nave and transepts had been built in the 12th-century Romanesque style. The central crossing however has pointed arches, and so either an original Romanesque central tower had collapsed not long after its erection (as happened not uncommonly with Norman towers) and was rebuilt in the newer style, or the start on the tower had been delayed. The church as originally designed would have been meant to have twin western towers. The most important reason why these were never built was revealed by the roadworks in Broad Street in 1986. The surface of the flagstone bedrock slopes down from east to west, at much the same angle as the slope of Palace Road (the road to the south of the Cathedral); above the bedrock is a thick layer of clay. The west front of the Cathedral is virtually at the top of the old beach. It would have been a most unstable foundation for towers, as the clay tends to slide down the surface of the bedrock. As it is, the early 13th-century west front is tending to pull away from the rest of the building, as revealed by the slant of the westernmost of the nave piers.

Also see Crawford, Barbara E. (ed.) 1988. *St. Magnus Cathedral and Orkney's Twelfth Century Renaissance*, Aberdeen; Ritchie 1985, no. 49, 97–9.

The Bishop's Palace, Kirkwall

Raymond G. Lamb

It is likely that Bishop William began a stone palace for himself in parallel with the earliest work on the Cathedral. The building is a hall, with the main accommodation on the first floor above an undercroft. Such a first-floor hall was a Romanesque idea, new to the North, and in contrast to the ancient Scandinavian timber-building tradition. Another grand building of the type is to be seen in Rousay at The Wirk (see below, pp. 53–4).

W. Douglas Simpson analysed the Bishop's Palace and drew comparison with King Haakon's Hall in Bergen. He suggested that the undercroft is the original work of Bishop William. Everything above (including the vaulted ceiling of the undercroft) has been rebuilt in the 16th century, along with the building of Bishop Reid's round tower. Two square towers, one of them probably quite large and likely to have been of 13th-century date, stood somewhere to the east of the hall; they were demolished *c.* 1800 and their exact location and relationship to the main building are not known, but a thick layer of demolition rubble which probably came from them was seen in 1986 under the road north-east of Bishop Reid's tower.

King Haakon before his attack on Scotland mustered his fleet in Elwick Bay, on the south side of Shapinsay, and after the battle of Largs, he returned via Kirkwall, where he fell ill. In his saga it is told how he died in a room adjoining the hall of the Bishop's Palace on the night of 15–16 December 1263. A Bishop's Chapel is also mentioned in the account. The body was laid out in the main hall, and then temporarily interred in the Cathedral in front of the shrine of St Magnus, before being removed to Bergen in the following spring. The choice of the Bishop's Palace as the suitable place to which to take the King, suggests that it then offered the most befitting accommodation available in Kirkwall. The Earl, perhaps, was still making do with a traditional timber hall.

Also see Simpson, W. Douglas, 1961. *The Castle of Bergen and the Bishop's Palace at Kirkwall*, Aberdeen University Studies 142, Edinburgh & London; Ritchie & Ritchie 1988, no. 28, 64–5; Ritchie 1985, no. 41, 85–7.

Highland Park Distillery, Kirkwall

The following notes are quoted from: Lamond, John & Tuček, Robin. 1989. *The Malt File. The independent guide to single malt whiskies and their distilleries*, Malt Whisky Association, London, 87.

Established	1798
Age/Strength	12 years, 40% abv
Distillery	Highland Park
Address	Kirkwall, Orkney
Map reference	HY 452095
Colour	Pale straw with pale-yellow depths
Nose	Pleasantly peaty with a hint of smokiness
Finish	Long and distinguished
Flavour	Dry and well balanced
Water	From springs below the level of the distillery. The water has to be pumped uphill.
History	Founded by David Robertson. Enlarged from two to four stills in 1898 when owned by James Grant. Owned by Highland Distilleries since 1935.
Geography	Sited on a hillside, overlooking Scapa Flow to the south and Kirkwall to the north.
Notes	The distillery is built on the spot where the legendary 18th-century smuggler Magnus Eunson's bothy stood.

A local churchman as well as distiller, he apparently kept a stock of whisky under his pulpit. Hearing that his church was about to be searched by the excisemen, he had the kegs removed to his house where they were shrouded in white cloth. A coffin lid was placed next to the cloth and Eunson and his family knelt in prayer. The whispered word 'smallpox' quickly ended any idea of a search by the excisemen. A visitors' centre was opened in 1987, a special feature of which is a 15-minute audio-visual presentation on the history and notable features of Orkney.

The Earl's Palace, Kirkwall

Raymond G. Lamb

The tyrannical Earl Robert Stewart took over the bishop's palace and his son Patrick (from 1593) incorporated it in a new layout which involved the building of a new palace on previously unoccupied ground to the east. This was one of the finest Renaissance buildings in Scotland. The luxurious taste and extravagant living of Earl Patrick are attested by the great kitchen and row of vaulted storerooms which make up the ground floor, below the magnificent first-floor hall with its oriel window and its fireplace with the notable 'straight arch' of joggled voussoirs.

Also see Ritchie & Ritchie 1988, no. 29, 66; Ritchie 1985, no. 36, 77.

Tankerness House Museum, Kirkwall

See Ritchie 1985, no. 23, 55.

Sunday, 27 August

Rousay (Fig. 1.26)

Taversoe Tuick Chambered Tomb, Rousay

See Ritchie & Ritchie 1988, no. 5, 25; Ritchie 1985, no. 98, 165.

Blackhammer Chambered Tomb, Rousay

See Ritchie & Ritchie 1988, no. 2, 22–3.

Midhowe Chambered Tomb, Rousay

See Ritchie & Ritchie 1988, no. 4, 24; Ritchie 1985, no. 96, 163.

Midhowe Broch, Rousay

See Ritchie & Ritchie 1988, no. 17, 46–9; Ritchie 1985 no. 60, 123–4.

St Mary's Church, Skaill, Rousay

Raymond G. Lamb

Also referred to as 'Swandro Church', 'Westside Church', 'Westness Church',

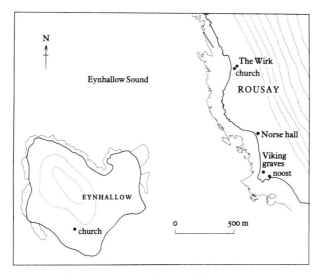

Figure 1.26: Map of Westside, Rousay and Eynhallow (N. Emery).

'Skaill Church', this is the shell of the former parish church of Rousay, abandoned in 1815, probably comprising post-Reformation fabric on medieval foundations. Architectural fragments are built into the walls. In spite of buttresses provided by General Burroughs late in the last century, the building is moving down the slope and is structurally threatened.

From: Lamb 1982, no. 111, 26.

The Wirk, Rousay

Raymond G. Lamb

At the NE corner of St Mary's churchyard is the debris-choked shell of a well-constructed stone tower with footings of a large hall-like building ajoining it to the E. The tower is referred to as a 'fortalice' in a document of 1556 and has been compared to Cubbie Row's Castle. It was crudely excavated in the 1920s and a report published by J. Storer Clouston in his *Early Norse Castles* (Kirkwall, 1931). From the quantities of ecclesiastical-looking carved stone which was lying around, Clouston deduced that the hall-like building was a church and that this was its W tower, which had been built first, and made defensible; the church itself was not completed although carved stones for incorporation in it had been collected. Previously, Dietrichson in *Monumenta Orcadica* (1906) had decided that The Wirk was a church tower, but a detached one associated with St Mary's, for which he adduced a Norwegian parallel.

During a visit in 1982 Mr J. G. Dunbar produced an interpretation which I am sure is the right one. The latrine shoots within the thickness of the tower wall suggest that it is a garderobe tower attached to the end of a massive first-floor hall, of the same type as the Bishop's Palace in Kirkwall. The walls partly exposed by Clouston, and interpreted by him as the foundation courses of his supposed church, are actually at first-floor level, the entire undercroft being still buried by the soil-creep which also conceals the true westward length of the hall. The broad scarcement still visible on the walls supported the timbers of the main hall. The steps within the tower led down to a doorway into the buried undercroft. If fully excavated, therefore, this would be a spectacular building, a statement of the enormous prestige of the magnate responsible for it.

In the 16th century the house of Brough was the seat of the Craigie family, the most important family in the island. The name Brough now applies to a ruined house immediately inland from the broch of South Howe, a house probably of 18th-century date. I suspect that the 16th-century reference to the 'house and fortalice of Brough' actually is to the festal hall and its tower, the house now bearing the name of Brough being a subsequent re-location. The hall and tower are probably of 13th- or early 14th-century date. They are possibly the work of one of Sigurd of Westness' successors. The location of this hall and St Mary's Church indicate a probable westward shift of the power-centre from Sigurd's time; it later reverted eastwards to Westness House which remained the laird's house until General Burroughs built Trumland.

Architectural Fragments from Westside and Eynhallow

Raymond G. Lamb

Linking the monastic church on Eynhallow with the old Rousay parish church of St Mary, Westside, and with the adjacent tower and hall of The Wirk, is a group of elaborately-carved architectural fragments, the origins and history of which is something of an enigma. The greatest number of these stones is built up as an ornamental gateway over the path to the kitchen-garden at Trumland House, and so obvious is the resemblance of these pieces – all carved in a red sandstone freestone alien to the island – to details of St Magnus Cathedral, that some islanders believe that these stones must have been brought quite recently from Kirkwall. From known recent history however, together with the incorporation of stones into the fabric of St Mary's, it is clear that this is not so.

Stones have been found in the vicinity of The Wirk on at least two occasions. The first was prior to 1870, when Sir Henry Dryden made his investigations, which are drawn upon by MacGibbon and Ross and by Dietrichson. Both these sources mention pieces, then at Westness House, which made up an arch. The other occasion was Storer Clouston's excavation, when stones were found at the foot of The Wirk and in the attached hall. An ornate finial with crocketed gables and sixteen human heads was found by an outside corner of the tower, as if fallen from its top, and a 16th-century armorial panel of Bishop Adam Bothwell was found in a similar situation. RCAHMS reported that the stones, which by the 1930s were at Trumland, had been collected from the neighbourhood of The Wirk and Westside Church.

More stones are built into the lichened walls of St Mary's Church (I am indebted to Sigrid Kaland who first noticed these). They are placed no higher than half-way up the walls at the E end; the church was disused after 1815 so it is unlikely they were inserted after that date. Some of them resemble pieces which before the 1983 fire were piled loosely on the west terrace of Trumland House (they have now disappeared, possibly shovelled away and disposed of with the fire debris). Another group of fragments was found when Eynhallow church was cleared out; these are still on the island, piled in a nettle-grown heap in a corner of the monastic buildings. Once again, the pieces are of non-local sandstone freestone, and they contrast with the crude stonework of the church, which is built of unmortared Rousay flag shaped only by splitting. In their fine quality the pieces find no obvious place on the buildings as they now stand.

The mixed date of the stones is especially puzzling. Storer Clouston's excavation found both a 16th-century armorial, and a finial; the description of that finial fits the unlabelled and unprovenanced finial now in Tankerness House Museum, which I would assign to the last quarter of the 13th century. It is in a fussy, 'Decorated' style for which parallels anywhere in Orkney are lacking. The archway stones now at the Trumland kitchen-garden – at least two different arched doorways are represented – include one with two orders of dogtooth ornament. Although there is no doorway on St Magnus Cathedral with this ornament, there is affinity of style with the early 13th-century work there.

J. G. Dunbar has examined the Trumland stones and the Tankerness House finial, and considers that the fineness of some of the work would be more appropriate to interior than to exterior stonework. The medieval precursor of St Mary's Church may have incorporated a family chantry with, perhaps, an elaborate canopied tomb in it, to which the finial could have belonged. Access to mason work of this high quality would not be implausible for the family responsible for The Wirk and its festal hall. Smashed up at the Reformation, fragments from the chantry were used in repairs or enhancements to the tower and hall (at which time the armorial also was installed); other fragments were casually used in the walls of the replacement church.

The fragments on Eynhallow, however, remain an enigma.

From: Lamb 1982, 10–12, with additions.

Westness Norse Settlement and Cemetery

See article by Sigrid H. H. Kaland below, pp. 308–17.
Also see Kaland, Sigrid H. H. 1973. 'Westnessutgravningene på Rousay, Orknøyene', *Viking* 37, 77–102.

Egilsay
St Magnus Church, Egilsay (Figs 1.27 & 1.28)

Raymond G. Lamb
Although a church in Egilsay is featured in saga and hagiographical accounts of the martyrdom of St Magnus in 1116 or 1117, the existing building,

Figure 1.27: Egilsay, St Magnus Church from the air (W. Vaughan).

conspicuously sited on nearly the highest ground on the island, probably dates from the second quarter of the 12th century. It is the only survivor of a distinctive group of great round-towered churches in Orkney and Shetland. The barrel-vaulted, square-ended chancel had an upper storey above the vault, entered from the nave by a doorway over the chancel arch; the nave has opposed N and S doorways near its W end and the curiously-tapering tower, which survives to a height of 14·9 m, is attached to its W wall. In use until the early 19th century, it is shown in Hibbert's drawing of 1822 to have had flagstone roofs, but these had been removed before Dryden's first visit in 1846; now in guardianship, and in good order.

Egilsay's church today is unique, but the curiously bottle-shaped round tower seems to have been a feature of a distinctive group of major Orkney and Shetland churches. The demolished parish church of Stenness (RCAHMS 1946, ii, no. 870, p. 297) had a half-round W tower, while Low, writing in 1774, described St Ninian's, Deerness, as having two round towers flanking the chancel (see below,

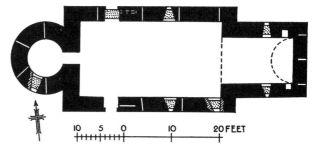

Figure 1.28: Egilsay, St Magnus Church: ground-plan (RCAHMS).

pp. 61–2, and Low 1879, 53–4). Information about Shetland is scanty, but from scattered sources it seems likely that the churches at Tingwall (inland from Scalloway), Ireland (on the W coast of Dunrossness, immediately N of St Ninian's Isle) and Papil (Burra) conformed to this general type.

From: Lamb 1982, 9 & 32.
Also see Fernie, Eric 1988. 'The Church of St Magnus, Egilsay', in *St Magnus Cathedral and Orkney's Twelfth Century Renaissance*, ed. Crawford, Barbara, Aberdeen, pp. 140–62; Ritchie & Ritchie 1988, no. 23, 57–9; Ritchie 1985, no. 50, 100.

Wyre

Cubbie Row's Castle (Fig. 1.29)

Raymond G. Lamb

Kolbeinn Hruga was a powerful magnate of the mid-12th century who has passed into folk-memory as the giant 'Cubbie Row'. This structure on a rounded hilltop is evidently the 'good stone-castle' which, according to *Orkneyinga saga*, he built in Wyre shortly before 1150 and in which, in *Hákonar saga*, the slayers of Earl Paul stood siege in 1231. The latter source differentiates between the 'castle' proper, represented by a nearly-square mortar-built tower surviving to a height of 2·4 m, and an 'outer castle' which must refer to the substantial outer wall with its outer ditch and counterscarp bank, and to the buildings between it and the tower. Excavated by HM Office of Works in the 1920s, it is in guardianship and in good order.

Figure 1.29: Cubbie Row's Castle, Wyre from the air (C. D. Morris. Copyright University of Durham).

There have been divergent opinions over the square-tower castles of which Rousay and Wyre have two out of three examples at present known in Orkney. The *Inventory* description of Cubbie Row's Castle is excellent, and the discussion of its date, which shows awareness of the Norwegian aspects is extremely scholarly. But it is interesting to observe how RCAHMS could not accept that this is a Scandinavian type of building, to which the late date of Scottish tower-houses is not relevant. St Magnus Cathedral is evidence enough that 12th-century Orkney had both the money and the awareness to get for itself the best that was fashionable in Northern Europe. W. D. Simpson, who uniquely was able to bring to bear an equally detailed and critical knowledge of English, Scottish and Scandinavian architecture, was strong in his condemnation of the doctrine of 'retarded work', and he regarded as unassailable the historical evidence for the 12th-century date of the castle in Wyre. He knew, of course, that *Hákonar saga* – in which the castle is described in sufficient detail to make clear that it existed in 1231 essentially as we see it today – is a reliable source, written within a half-century of the events it relates, and highly respected by Norwegian historians.

From: Lamb 1982, 10 & 33.
Also see Ritchie & Ritchie 1988, no. 21, 54–6; Ritchie 1985, no. 42, 87.

St. Mary's Chapel, Wyre (Fig. 1.30)

Raymond G. Lamb

This chapel, which stands at the foot of the hill occupied by Cubbie Row's Castle, has also been called Peter's Kirk; but the Marian dedication was accepted

Figure 1.30: St Mary's Chapel, Wyre, from the air (C. D. Morris. Copyright University of Durham).

by Archdeacon Craven and subsequently recorded by RCAHMS in 1929 from a good local source. It is a neat building, close in style and design to the chapel at Lybster, Caithness, and dating from the middle or second half of the 12th century; the nave has a round-arched W door and a round arch into the square-ended chancel. Ruinous by 1791, it was cleared and partly rebuilt in the late 19th century at the instigation of General Burroughs; now in guardianship, and in good order.

From: Lamb 1982, 33.
Also see Ritchie & Ritchie 1988, no. 27, 64; Ritchie 1985, no. 51, 101.

Monday, 28 August

Deerness (Fig. 1.31)

Skaill, Deerness (Fig. 1.32)

Raymond G. Lamb
The farmstead of Skaill, associated with the site of one of Orkney's most remarkable medieval churches, occupies the site of *Hlaupandanes*, the seat of

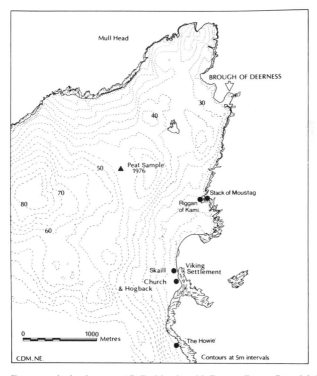

Figure 1.31: Deerness: the local context (C. D. Morris & N. Emery. Crown Copyright).

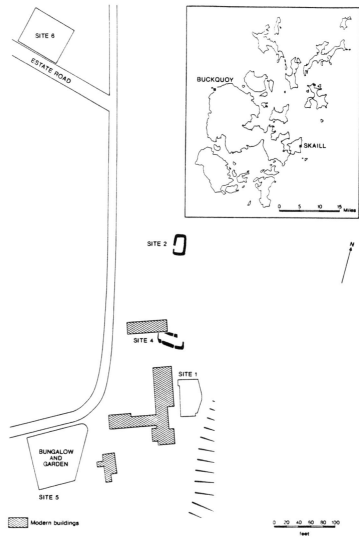

Figure 1.32: Skaill, Deerness: overall plan (P. S. Gelling).

Thorkel Fostri, a leading supporter of Earl Thorfinn the Mighty (ruled 1020–65). In the early 1960s, Mr J. R. Foubister reported that, in extracting lime-sand from the links immediately north of the wooden hen-house that forms the N boundary of the farmyard, he had encountered buildings. Mr Foubister suspended his sand-removal to allow excavation by the late Mr P. S. Gelling of Birmingham University. This grew into a long-term project which ran through the 1970s, in the course of which further Norse and later buildings were investigated in the farmyard itself, and substantial remains of prehistoric settlements were located and excavated both near to the church and, in the opposite direction, in two of the home fields 200 m NW of the farmstead. Mr Gelling's account of the Viking-period buildings recently appeared (Gelling 1984), while the prehistoric material, left unfinished at his death, is currently being prepared for publication by Mr S. Buteaux.

The area of the initial discovery (HY 5882 0650) contained late Pictish buildings which were replaced, apparently without any gradual transition, by some not very well-built early Norse houses. The Pictish phases produced a fragment of an incised cross-slab re-used as a paving stone. A more substantial Norse building, probably a steam-bath, was excavated in the farmyard at the SE corner of the hen-house (HY 5883 0647) and a glimpse of what may have been the main 11th-century house was obtained E of the byre (HY 5886 0645), below a very substantial rectilinear hall-type building possibly of 13th-century date. Viking-period structures also underlay a group of 16th-century buildings E of the hen-house (HY 5884 0648).

To the NW of the church and close beside the bungalow (HY 5881 0638), there was a considerable open-area excavation of a substantial late Bronze Age settlement which lay immediately below the ploughsoil. At the same time a trial trench was dug into the prominent mound known as the Howan (HY 5890 0633) SE of the church, which in 1930 was suggested as the site of a broch, and a dark deposit observed in the eroding shoreline. The Howan proved to be a sand-dune and the deeply-buried dark deposit is an ancient ploughsoil, in which ard-marks, probably of Bronze Age date, were found. In 1982 Mr Foubister encountered fragmentary prehistoric buildings between the Howan and the SE corner of the churchyard dyke (HY 5886 0635).

The latter years of the project were devoted to examining a multi-period settlement complex which began in the late Bronze Age and continued through the Iron Age into a 7th-century AD Pictish context; it was situated about 200 m NW of the farmstead (HY 5865 0657), an area spanning the fence between two fields (Gelling 1985).

From: Lamb 1987, 26.
Also see Gelling, Peter S. 1984. 'The Norse buildings at Skaill, Deerness, Orkney and their immediate predecessor', in *The Northern and Western Isles in the Viking World*, eds Fenton, Alexander & Pálsson, Hermann, Edinburgh, pp. 12–13; Gelling, Peter S. 1985. 'Excavations at Skaill, Deerness', in Renfrew, A. C. (ed.) 1985, pp. 176–82.

Deerness Parish Church (Fig. 1.33)

Raymond G. Lamb

The modern church at Skaill stands somewhat to the NW of the medieval one, which was dedicated either to St Mary or to St Ninian. There is today no trace of it, but Low's sketches of 1774 show a most remarkable Romanesque church,

Figure 1.33: Drawing of Deerness Church, Skaill (Rev. George Low, 1774).

which had a vaulted chancel provided with an upper floor set between twin eastern round towers. His description is as follows:

> The Church of Deerness is very remarkable, and part of it looks to be pretty ancient: the east end consists of a vault which crosses the breadth of the inside, and at each side of this is erected a small steeple. Thro' the vault or quire one enters the steeple on his right hand, and by a turnpike stair goes to a small apartment or vestry built between the steeples. From this last apartment he enters the second tower, which, or both probably, have had bells; these are now gone, said to have been carried away by Cromwell's soldiers. Tradition is not clear (and there are no records) who was the builder of this Church. The steeples are said to be monumental, and placed over a Lady's two sons buried there, but whether this is so or not is hard to determine. As this is the most remarkable country Kirk in these isles, I have added a sketch of it as follows.

From: Lamb 1987, 32; Low, G. 1879. *A Tour through the islands of Orkney and Schetland in 1774*, J. Anderson (ed.), Kirkwall, pp. 53–4.

Hogback, Skaill (Fig. 1.34)

James T. Lang
Hogback; red sandstone; Type B3, late 11th- early 12th-century.
Length: 172·7 cm; width at ends: 49·5 cm and 35·6 cm; height at ends: 22·9 cm and 19·7 cm.

Figure 1.34: Hogback stone at Deerness Church, Skaill (RCAHMS).

The ridge, worn at the head end, is plain and slightly arched, the highest point being 35·6 cm from the head end. Below it are four rows of tegulae, chiefly rectangular with clipped corners though some are trapezoid. The top row is 5·1 cm deep, the second and third rows 6·3 cm and the bottom row 7·0 cm. The width of a tegula from the lowest row is 6·3 cm tapering to 3·2 cm. The roof pitch tapers with the stone, the depth of the pitch being 30·5 cm at the head and 24·1 cm at the foot. Below the eaves one plinth is perpendicular whilst the other inclines inwards slightly; they are 7·6 cm deep at the head and taper to 5·1 cm. The ends are vertical and undecorated.

In the Session House of the church. It was found in the NE corner of the churchyard 9 ft from the E boundary wall at Skaill in Deerness parish. It lay on an ENE-WSW axis.

From: Lang, James T. 1974. 'Hogback monuments in Scotland', *Proceedings of the Society of Antiquaries of Scotland*, 105 (1972–4), 232.

Low's description (*op. cit.* 54–5) is as follows:

In the Churchyard observed a coffin-shaped stone without any inscription, the shape a triangular prism, one side plain, the other cut into such figures as the Heralds call Vairy. Tradition is silent to whom it belonged, but there is another of the very same dimensions, and carved with the same figures; the latter goes by the name of the Queen of Morrocco's grave stone, anent whose arrival and death they here tell us a long apocryphal story not worth repeating.

Also see Ritchie 1985, no. 53, 103.

Figure 1.35: Brough of Deerness from the air (C. D. Morris. Copyright University of Durham).

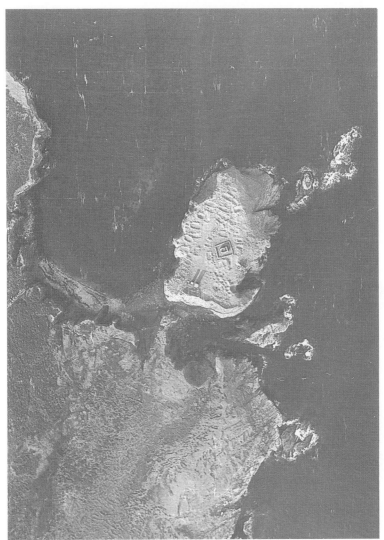

Figure 1.36: Brough of Deerness from the air (J. D. H. Radford).

Figure 1.37: Brough of Birsay, Birsay Bay and Birsay village from the air (Gunnie Moberg).

The Brough of Deerness (Figs 1.35 & 1.36)

See article by Christopher D. Morris in *Proceedings of the Tenth Viking Congress, Larkollen, Norway 1985*, ed. James Knirk, Oslo 1987, 113–29. Also see Morris, Christopher D., with Emery, Norman. 1986. 'The Setting for the Brough of Deerness, Orkney', *Northern Studies* 23, 1–30; Morris, Christopher D., with Emery, Norman. 1987. 'The chapel and enclosure on the Brough of Deerness, Orkney: survey and excavations, 1975–1977', *Proceedings of the Society of Antiquaries of Scotland* 116 (1986), 301–74.

Stenness

Maeshowe

For chambered tomb: see Ritchie & Ritchie 1988, no. 6, 26–8; Ritchie 1985, no. 95, 160–2.

For runes: see article by Michael P. Barnes below, pp. 349–69.

Tormiston Mill

See Ritchie 1985, no. 30, 70.

Ring of Brodgar

See Ritchie & Ritchie 1988, no. 15, 41–3; Ritchie 1985, no. 83, 149–51.

Stones of Stenness

See Ritchie & Ritchie 1988, no. 14, 39–40; Ritchie 1985, no. 84, 152.

Birsay (Figs 1.37 & 1.38)

The Brough of Birsay

Christopher D. Morris

Birsay has rarely been off the agenda of the Viking Congresses, and three articles have been published in the Proceedings over the years. Stewart Cruden's interim accounts of excavations on the Brough of Birsay in the 1950s and 1960s appeared in the 3rd and 4th Congress Proceedings (Cruden 1958; 1965), and have been followed by that of some of the work in the 1970s in the 8th Congress Proceedings (Hunter and Morris 1981). John Hunter also presented a review of later work at the 9th Congress.

The Brough of Birsay, projecting out into the Atlantic, is at the NW corner of Birsay Bay. This tidal island is separated by the 238 m wide Brough Sound from the Point of Buckquoy, although it is connected at low tide by a modern concrete track across the natural causeway of exposed rocks. The surface slopes from around 40 m above sea-level at the W to about 5 m at the E end. The cliff-edge level at the Point of Buckquoy is also around 5 m which suggests that the area now occupied by the Brough Sound was low-lying. Changes in sea-level, and also the effect of sea erosion allied with geological factors (discussed in Morris 1989, ch. 1.1) were, no doubt, the main factors in causing the breach between the Brough and the Point of Buckquoy.

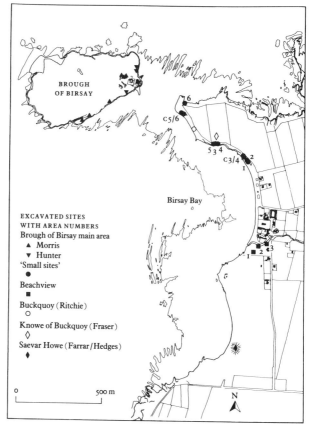

Figure 1.38: Birsay Bay: excavations (C. D. Morris & N. Emery. Crown Copyright).

The name for the Brough of Birsay derives from ON *borg*, fortress or stronghold, which can refer both to a broch, or, more likely in this case, the natural defensive qualities of an island difficult of access (Marwick 1952, 130). In its i-umlaut form, *byrgi*, as in *Byrgisheraƍ* or *Byrgisey*, appears to be used of narrow necks, peninsulas and enclosed places and would be entirely appropriate as a description. Such a neck of land is perhaps represented on the 17th century drawing of the Earl's Palace, Birsay (RCAHMS 1946, II, Fig. 68 opp. 12).

There has been much discussion of the significance of the entries in the *Orkneyinga saga* (chs 31 & 32) concerning the 'minster dedicated to Christ' at Birsay established by Thorfinn. Both Dr Ralegh Radford (1959; 1962; 1983) and Mr Stewart Cruden (1958; 1965) take the view that the buildings mentioned in the *Saga* can be identified with structures excavated on the Brough. Others (e.g. RCAHMS 1946, II, nos 1 & 6: 1–5, & 7; Lamb 1974; Lamb 1983) see these structures as 12th Century (rather than 11th), monastic in character, and favour a location for the 'minster' in the village area. However, it can now be argued that earlier structural elements *below* the chapel on the Brough no longer need to be associated with the so-called 'Celtic' church, and may themselves date from the Norse period by analogy with Brattahlid in Greenland (Radford 1983) and the Brough of Deerness (Morris 1990).

The earliest archaeological work on this site appears to have been by Sir Henry Dryden (1870, 13–17), who cleared out the chapel and whose description of the structure was utilised, and elaborated upon, by later writers (MacGibbon & Ross 1896, 135–41; Dietrichson & Meyer 1906, 19–20 & 80–3). The site came into the care of the Secretary of State for Scotland in 1934, and under the supervision of Dr J. S. Richardson considerable clearance took place, along with excavation, to lay the site out for the general public. This work was curtailed with the outbreak of war, and the only published account remains the short account in the RCAHMS Inventory (RCAHMS 1946, II, 1–5, & 7; Curle 1982, 13). As the accounts of some of the excavations have been preserved in the archives of SDD (Ancient Monuments Branch), now Historic Scotland, these will be summarised in a future volume (Morris, forthcoming). The finds from the excavations have, however, been published by one of Richardson's assistants, Mrs Cecil L. Curle (Cecil Mowbray), along with the finds from the later campaigns of Radford and Cruden (Curle 1982). Interim accounts of aspects of that work have been published (Cruden 1958; 1965; Radford 1959), but the Final Report is awaited.

Work was resumed on a small-scale in 1973 on the Brough. The area to the E of the chapel was known from previous work to be one with considerable depth of stratigraphy, and 'Room 5' had not been excavated. In order to assist with the analysis of the finds from the earlier excavations, an excavation in this area was undertaken by Dr John Hunter and the writer in 1973–4, and has been published as an appendix to her monograph (Hunter & Morris 1982). Essentially, four major periods were distinguished stratigraphically, and from analysis of the associated finds, together with some C-14 dating, the first may be assigned to the pre-Norse, Pictish, phase, and the later three to the Norse. Only the last relates to the laid out, standing building.

Following this work, a renewed large-scale series of excavations on the Brough were begun in 1974, which continued until 1982. These excavations were concerned both with the area in the care of the Secretary of State, and areas to the SW and towards the Peerie Brough; some of these were in areas subject to erosion on the coastal margins of the site. Interim accounts have been published (Hunter & Morris 1981; Hunter 1983), and the first Final Report volume is now available (Hunter 1986), to be followed by a second (Morris, forthcoming). The not-inconsiderable literature directly concerned with the archaeology of this site is appended.

REFERENCES

Cruden, Stewart H. 1958. Earl Thorfinn the Mighty and the Brough of Birsay, in *Third Viking Congress, Reykjavík 1956*, ed. Eldjárn, Kristján, Reykjavík, pp. 156–62.

Cruden, Stewart H. 1965. 'Excavations at Birsay, Orkney', in *The Fourth Viking Congress, York 1961*, ed. Small, Alan. Aberdeen University Studies 149, Edinburgh & London, pp. 22–31.

Curle, Cecil L. 1982. *The Pictish and Norse Finds from the Brough of Birsay 1934–74*, Society of Antiquaries of Scotland Monograph Series 1, Edinburgh.

Dietrichson, L. and Meyer, J. 1906. *Monumenta Orcadica. The Norsemen in the Orkneys, and the Monuments they have left . . .* Kristiania.

Dryden, Sir Henry E. L. 1870. *Ruined Churches in Orkney and Shetland*, Kirkwall.

Hunter, John R. 1983. 'Recent Excavations on the Brough of Birsay', *Orkney Heritage* 2, 152–170.

Hunter, John R. 1986. *Rescue Excavations on the Brough of Birsay 1974–82*, Society of Antiquaries of Scotland Monograh Series 4, Edinburgh.

Hunter, John R. and Morris, Christopher D. 1981. 'Recent Excavations at the Brough of Birsay, Orkney', in *Proceedings of the Eighth Viking Congress, Aarhus 1977*, eds Bekker-Nielsen, Hans, Foote, Peter G. and Olsen, Olaf, Odense, pp. 245–58.

Hunter, John R. and Morris, Christopher D. 1982. 'Appendix: Excavation of Room 5, Brough of Birsay, Clifftop Settlement, 1973–4', in Curle 1982, pp. 124–38.

MacGibbon, D. and Ross, T. 1896. *Ecclesiastical Architecture of Scotland from the Earliest Christian Times to the Seventeenth Century. Volume 1*, Edinburgh.

Lamb, Raymond G. 1974. 'The Cathedral of Christchurch and the Monastery of Birsay', *Proceedings of the Society of Antiquaries of Scotland* 105, 206–35.

Lamb, Raymond G. 1983. 'The Cathedral and the Monastery', *Orkney Heritage* 2, 36–45.

Marwick, Hugh. 1952. *Orkney Farm Names*, Kirkwall.

Morris, Christopher D. 1989. *The Birsay Bay Project Volume 1*, University of Durham, Department of Archaeology, Monograph Series 1, Durham.

Morris, Christopher D. 1990. *Church and Monastery in the Far North. An Archaeological Evaluation*, Jarrow Lecture 1989, Jarrow.

Morris, Christopher D. Forthcoming. *Brough of Birsay, Orkney. Excavations 1974–1981*, Society of Antiquaries of Scotland Monograph Series, Edinburgh.

Radford, C. A. Ralegh. 1959. *The Early Christian and Norse Settlements at Birsay*, Official guide, Edinburgh.

Radford, C. A. Ralegh. 1962. 'The Celtic Monastery in Britain', *Archaeologia Cambrensis* CXI, 1–24.

Radford, C. A. Ralegh. 1983. 'Birsay and the Spread of Christianity to the North', *Orkney Heritage* 2, 13–35.

Ritchie, Anna. 1986. *Brough of Birsay*, Historic Scotland Official Guide, Edinburgh.

Ritchie 1985, no. 57, 112–115.

Ritchie & Ritchie 1988, no. 20:52–3.

RCAHMS. 1946. *Twelfth Report with an Inventory of the Ancient Monuments of Orkney and Shetland*. 3 vols, Edinburgh, nos 1, & 6; 1–5 & 7.

Birsay Bay

See article by Christopher D. Morris below, pp. 285–307. Also, *Orkney Heritage* 2, 1983 ('Birsay: A Centre of Political and Ecclesiastical Power'); Morris, Christopher D. 1989. *The Birsay Bay Project Volume 1*, University of Durham,

Department of Archaeology, Monograph Series 1, Durham; Marwick, Hugh 1970. *The Place-Names of Birsay*, ed. Nicolaisen, William F. H., Aberdeen.

Birsay village, The Earl's Palace and St Magnus' Church (Figs 1.39 & 1.40)

Christopher D. Morris

As noted above, one school of thought would interpret the entries in the *Orkneyinga saga* regarding Thorfinn's 'minster dedicated to Christ' as referring to the Village area. In 1982, excavations took place in advance of restoration of the Parish Church of St Magnus, under the direction of Mr John W. Barber. The structural elements uncovered below the present Church have been accorded a probable 12th-century date, and attention drawn to the presence of carved stones and architectural detail. This indicates that the present building was preceded by a pre-Reformation church of some sophistication. However, the dating accorded to the remains does not enable associations with the historical data to be firmly stated, and so it cannot yet be claimed that the 'minster' was originally located in the village, rather than on the Brough.

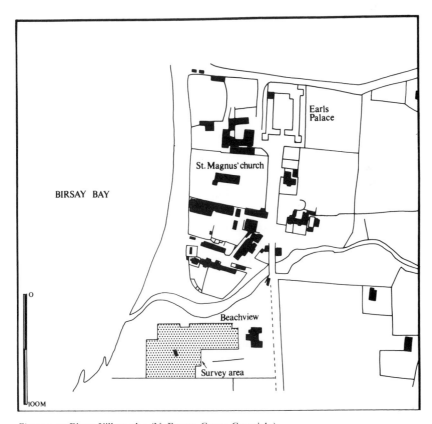

Figure 1.39: Birsay Village plan (N. Emery. Crown Copyright).

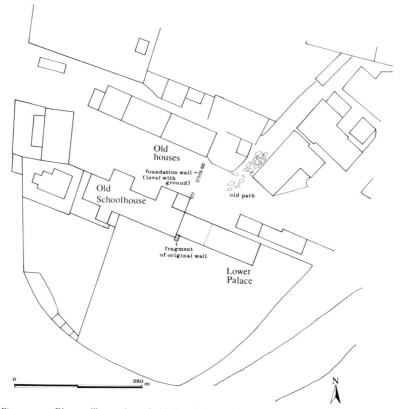

Figure 1.40: Birsay village: plan of old foundations and standing buildings (N. Emery, after R. Rendall. Crown Copyright).

Norse Christianity clearly focussed upon Birsay, but once Magnus's bones were transferred to Kirkwall, and the Cathedral was built there, naturally the focus of secular and ecclesiastical power was shifted away from Birsay. Little is known of events here between the 12th and the 16th centuries. However, by the 16th century much of Birsay had been transferred from the hands of the Earl to the Bishops, and in that century it is clear that the Bishops used a palace hereabouts.

A stone carved with 'Monsbellus' in 16th century handwriting survives here in two fragments (in the sill of a window in the S wall of the church and as a window-jamb in the S wall of 'Palace Cottage') and ties in with the evidence of a letter from Adam Bothwell, Bishop of Orkney 1558–88, signed at 'Monsbellus in Orkney' – presumably, therefore, Birsay. In 1529 'Jo Ben' described Birsay as having 'an excellent palace', although in the present state of knowledge we cannot be sure whether this might be a survival from the later Mediaeval period or a new foundation – perhaps from after 1498 by Bishop Edward Stewart, whose arms are on a stone here. Local tradition is certainly strong on the presence of walls and other features in the area to the S of the Parish Church which might tie up with this.

The significance of Birsay in the 16th century is reinforced by the building of an imposing Earl's Palace to the N of the Burn of Boardhouse. This was constructed with ranges of buildings around a courtyard with projecting rectangular towers at three corners; the northern range may well be a later addition. Although a fortified residence, complete with gun-loops, 17th- and 18th-century drawings show an elegant S facade with the initials of Robert, Earl of Orkney above the lintel over a central doorway and a date of 1574. Decorated ceilings to rooms were part of what was described as a 'sumptuous and stately building' in 1633, but 'sombre' and 'austere' are certainly the adjectives that now seem most appropriate.

It is probable that, in the construction of the Earl's Palace, stones from the older Bishop's Palace were re-used, and there has been a suggestion that it was incorporated into the Earl's Palace. Similarly, it has been suggested that the bridge over the Burn may be in part mediaeval below the 1872 reconstruction. What is certain is that, after the Reformation, the old Bishopric estate had been acquired by the Stewart Earls, and that by 1595 the whole of the Parish was included within a rental.

However, the regained significance of Birsay was short-lived, and Anderson has suggested that deterioration of the Earl's Palace is recorded from as early as 1653. The gaunt ruins of the Palace now are perhaps visible reminders of what has been described as the 'dark period' of Orkney's history under the Stewart Earls, but nevertheless the descriptions of 'Palace' for the village area and 'Barony' for the wider area to N and S are surviving memorials of those periods of greatness when Birsay had an importance out of all proportion to its situation and size.

Earl's Palace, Birsay

See Anderson, Peter D. 1983. 'Birsay in the Sixteenth Century', *Orkney Heritage 2*, 82–96. Also, see Rendall, Robert 1959: 'Birsay's Forgotten Palace', *Orkney Herald 21 April 1959*; Ritchie & Ritchie 1988, no. 30, 66–8; Ritchie 1985, no. 39, 81–3; Tyrrell, Edward 1911: 'Birsay Palace, Orkney', *The Antiquary*, 136–40, & 183–7.

St Magnus Church, Birsay

See Lamb, Raymond G. 1975. 'The Cathedral of Christchurch and the Monastery', *Proceedings of the Society of Antiquaries of Scotland*, 105 (1972–4), 200–5; Lamb, Raymond G. 1983. 'The Cathedral and the Monastery', *Orkney Heritage 2*, 36–45.

Figure 1.41: Beachview, Birsay: buildings under excavation (C. D. Morris. Crown Copyright).

Beachview, Birsay (Fig. 1.41)

Christopher D. Morris

There are now clear indications that buildings from the Viking and Late Norse periods remain to be discovered in the area to the S of the village. The placename 'Tuftaback', bank or slope of house-sites, might well be equated with the area to the S of the Burn of Boardhouse. Here, buildings and middens of some complexity have been uncovered on top of a mound-site [the 'Studio' site] composed of archaeological deposits presumably going back into Prehistory. A second such mound-site almost certainly exists below the modern building of 'Beachview' and extending down to the river-bank to the W of the bridge.

See Morris, Christopher D., pp. 303–4 below; also, see Morris, Christopher D. 1983. 'Excavations Around the Bay of Birsay', *Orkney Heritage 2*, 142–7.

Saevar Howe, Birsay

Christopher D. Morris

Beyond the village to the S are the Links, prominent at the S end of which is Saevar Howe, another multi-period mound-site, examined in the 19th century and more recently by John W. Hedges. Pictish buildings here were presumably built on top of a Prehistoric site, and were themselves superceded by Viking-Age dwellings. On top of these, explored by James Farrer, were the remains of a Christian Norse cemetery – although not recognised as such by him last century.

See Hedges, John W. 1983. 'Trial excavations on Pictish and Viking settlements at Saevar Howe, Birsay, Orkney', *Glasgow Archaeological Journal* 10, 73–124 & M40–102.

Harray

Corrigall Farm Museum, Harray

See Ritchie 1985, no. 27, 66–7.

Orphir (Fig. 1.42)

St Nicholas Church, Orphir

See article by Ian Fisher below, pp. 375–80. Also, see Ritchie & Ritchie 1988, no. 22, 56–7; Ritchie 1985, no. 48, 96.

Earl's Bu, Orphir

Colleen E. Batey.

The first excavations at the Earl's Bu, Orphir were recorded by Torfaeus in 1758 'on digging earth for the Bow or farm of Orphir, and near the round house called

Figure 1.42: Orphir: the Round Church and building remains from the air (C. D. Morris. Copyright University of Durham).

the Gerth – House of Orphir, they found large foundations, and laid very deep, which must have supported some great buildings'. Despite several references in *Orkneyinga saga* to activity at the site (e.g. ch. 66), reputedly the drinking-hall of Earls Paul and Harald, it seems that there was no local tradition concerning the hall at Orphir and that the earliest work at the site did not use the *saga* as a guide. Excavations at the site by Petrie in 1859 produced further structural remains in the immediate vicinity. 1899–1901 saw activity at the site by Johnston, following the discovery by a gravedigger of walling in the NW corner of the churchyard; Johnston went on to record the presence of a wall some 104 feet long by 4 feet wide, possibly of two phases. The wall foundations now visible are in part the result of work when the site was taken into Guardianship in the 1930s. It is quite obvious, even from surface indications, that many phases of activity are represented, and despite the good preservation of some of the walls – possibly rebuilt for display – the site is not easy to understand. It is presumed that the foundations date from sometime in the Late Norse period (i.e. 11th–15th centuries). It is clear that this site is in need of further work, and that geophysical work undertaken suggests a complex structural sequence underlying the apparently innocuous grassed area to the W of the standing remains.

See Johnston, A. W. 1903. 'Notes on the Earl's Bu at Orphir, Orkney, called Orfjara in the sagas, and on the remains of the round church there', *Proceedings of the Society of Antiquaries of Scotland*, 37 (1902–3), 16–31.

Excavation of a Horizontal ('Norse') Mill at Orphir (Fig. 1.43)

Colleen E. Batey   Christopher D. Morris

During the Congress, members visited the site currently under excavation to the N of the Earl's Bu. At that stage, an apparent 'passage', some 10 m long, expanded into a 'chamber' to the W some 2 m wide with walling upstanding to about 1 m in height. A curiosity was the apparent continuation of the passage to the W of the chamber. Both 'passage' and 'chamber' were covered and infilled with rich Late Norse middens with abundant artefactual and ecofactual material. At the time of the Congress field visit, the site was considered to be best interpreted as a souterrain from the pre-Norse period, possibly dating from the Roman Iron Age–Pictish period.

A tentative possibility, raised just before the visit, was that these remains might perhaps represent the remains of a horizontal mill, of the so-called 'Norse mill' type. Colleagues from Scotland, Ireland, Faroe and Denmark all concurred with this hypothesis; subsequently, renewed excavation in September 1989 and

Figure 1.43: Orphir: excavation of 'Norse mill' in progress (C. D. Morris).

the summer of 1990 confirmed the identification, and refined the dating – to within the Viking period. Further elements of the complex can now be identified, together with an earlier Bronze Age 'burnt mound' on top of which, and into which, the mill was built. Of interest is a small runic inscription incised on a bone (see Hagland, pp. 370–4 below).

See Batey, Colleen E. with Morris, Christopher D. 1992. 'Earl's Bu, Orphir, Orkney: Excavation of a Norse horizontal mill' in *Norse and Later Subsistence and Settlement in the North Atlantic*, eds Morris, Christopher D. and Rackham, D. James, Archetype (Denbigh) for Glasgow University Dept of Archaeology, Occasional Paper no. 1.

Lavacroon, Orphir

Colleen E. Batey

To the W of the Earl's Bu can be seen an apparently insignificant mound, which is named 'Lavacroon'. After deep ploughing, detailed fieldwalking of the area over and around the mound indicated a disturbed structure and deposits comprising industrial debris and sherds of pottery dated to the 11th–12th centuries. Other finds included a steatite bar mould and part of a decorated glass bead dated to the 6th century. It is suggested that this site is a continuation of the Earl's Bu complex. Extensive geophysical examination indicates the presence at this site of substantial structural remains, including at least one roughly circular element some 30 m across, as well as more rectangular forms. Without excavation, it is not possible to ascribe a date bracket to these features, but the artefactual remains would strongly suggest a date within the Late Norse period.

See Batey, Colleen E., with Freeman, Claudine. 1987. 'Lavacroon, Orphir, Orkney', *Proceedings of the Society of Antiquaries of Scotland*, 116 (1986), 285–300; Johnson, Paul G. 1992. 'The Investigation of the Environs of the Earl's Bu, Orphir, Orkney by Remote Sensing', in *Proceedings of the Archaeological Sciences Conference. York 1991*, ed. Szymanski, J., forthcoming.

POST-CONGRESS TOUR

Tuesday, 29 August

Westray
Raymond G. Lamb

General

Westray today is the most economically successful of the North Isles and the only one with a consistently stable level of population. The farms give an impression of quiet prosperity, and there is a successful fish-processing factory served by Westray's own fishing fleet, which includes several large vessels recently built to the highest technical specifications for Westray owners.

The theme of this visit was the Norse settlement pattern, which offers strong contrasts to what is to be seen in Sanday. Westray's rental value, probably thirteen urislands, is about what we would expect for the island's size, whereas Sanday's thirty-six urislands is extraordinarily high. Sanday's settlement pattern is a complex patchwork of small tunships, with a correspondingly high number of mediaeval churches and chapels – over two dozen are reliably known. Westray, however, has only six known church or chapel sites, plus two dubious ones (Rousay, at exactly half Westray's urisland value, has seven known churches or chapels). In Sanday there is a hint of strong continuity of much of the settlement pattern from Pictish into Norse times, while in Westray, the paucity of chapels may reflect a smaller number of very large Norse estates which possibly had been established without much reference to what had gone before. The exploration of these aspects will, it is to be hoped, be furthered by a renewal of the excavations at the key site of Tuquoy (see Owen, pp. 318–39 below).

Westray features prominently in *Orkneyinga saga* at only one point in the story, the events of 1135 when Rognvald Kali Kolsson was trying to invade Orkney from his base in Shetland. Three prominent households figure in the story, and two of these are associated with important places in the island, the Bu of Rapness, and the village of Pierowall. The seat of the third and the most prominent of these households is not named, but circumstantially, Tuquoy is the likeliest place with which to associate it.

The Story of Helgi, Kugi and Haflidi

Páll Hákonarson could call upon the support of three leading men in Westray – Kugi of Rapness, Helgi, who lived at Pierowall, and an obnoxious fellow called Thorkell Flettir who had two unpopular sons named Thorsteinn and Haflidi. In 1135 Rognvald arrived in Shetland and the Shetlanders went over to his side. The North Isles of Orkney, and particularly Westray which is the Orkney end of what then was the most dependable sea route from Shetland, therefore became critical to Páll's defence plans. He called-up his forces, and overall charge of Westray was given to Kugi, with Thorkell getting the command of one of Páll's ships. The figure of Sveinn Asleifarson then enters the scene, and the machinations become complicated. Those wishing to study them are referred to *Orkneyinga saga*, from chapter lxv.

At one point Páll was hunting for Sveinn, and Páll knew that Thorkell knew where Sveinn was. As inducement to reveal information which, as it turned out, was of no practical help, Páll gave Thorkell a rich Stronsay estate confiscated from Sveinn's brother Valthjof. Soon after, we are told that Páll was storm-stayed in Papay while on his way to become a guest of Kugi's, indicating that his was then the leading household. In April 1136 Rognvald invaded Orkney, landing first in Westray. Páll was in Mainland and Thorkell was esconced in his Stronsay farm; Kugi and Helgi decided to accept the fact that Rognvald was now their overlord.

It seems that Kugi was unhappy about reneging on his allegiance to Páll; there was rumour of a conspiracy, and Kugi was suspected of leading it. Rognvald diplomatically pardoned Kugi but made one of his famous wry verses about him, and Kugi evidently was obliged to retire from public life and live quietly on his farm. And so he goes out of the story.

Meanwhile Thorkell was not left in peace; Sveinn attacked the Stronsay farm and burnt him in the house. In fear of Páll's vengeance the burners naturally threw in their lot with Rognvald, while Haflidi went to Páll and was well received by him. Then came the kidnapping of Páll by Sveinn, Rognvald became *jarl*, and he gave back to Sveinn all his family's former possessions. Haflidi however must have been mollified in some way, for he accepted the command of one of Rognvald's ships, and later was in the expedition which Rognvald mounted against Sveinn in Caithness. It seems, then, that Haflidi, not too scrupulous about his allegiances, came out on the winning side, while Kugi of Rapness, originally the head of the most important household in Westray, lost status. The Norse settlement at Tuquoy, the centre of what must have been among the largest of Norse estates in Orkney, is the likeliest place for Thorkell's and Haflidi's residence in Westray, and the refined elegance of the twelfth-century church, which (not, as otherwise would have been expected, the church associated with the Bu of Rapness) became a parish church, would fit nicely with Haflidi's return to Westray with his status and wealth enhanced.

Rapness

The Bu of Rapness, Kugi's seat, is on the opposite side of the ness from the road, and is not visible. Near it on the coast is one of the Peterkirk churches, on the site of a broch. It is likely that the admistrative importance of the Pictish church here was influential in determining the location and status of the early Bu. Peterkirk was not adopted as a parish church in the High Middle Ages, presumably because its position became more and more peripheral to the island's economic centre further north, and also on account of Kugi's loss of status.

Tuquoy: The Estate

The modern farmstead of Tuquoy (run by Tom Pottinger, one of Westray's most successful farmers) is 800 m inland from the coast where the mediaeval church is sited. It is anomalous in the rentals as a tunship named after a *kví* – just about the lowest status of Norse farm-designation in Orkney – with the high value of one urisland. This anomaly is readily explicable once it is understood that the original centre of the estate was adjacent to the church. For some reason, possibly the threat of the erosion which now is destroying the site, the original house and steading were abandoned and an originally peripheral settlement became the main residence. Both the documentary evidence and the recent excavations imply that the move was made before the 15th century was out.

Tuquoy evidently is the name of this originally peripheral house; the original name of the primary main settlement is not preserved.

The great wealth of this estate is even more remarkable when it is appreciated that it once extended beyond the present tunship of Tuquoy. The adjacent tunship to the west is Midbea, and to the west of Midbea is Noltland-be-west (i.e., western cattle land). The middle tunship, Midbea, signifies the middle of the baer, and *baer* is among the most dignified of ancient farm-designations. Furthermore, neither Midbea nor Noltland contains a chapel – there is only the expensive-looking church in Tuquoy tunship. This adds up to the original existence of an estate with the colossal value (adding up the values of the subsequent tunships) of four-and-a-half urislands, such as could only represent the holding of one of the greatest men in Orkney.

This was worked out by Hugh Marwick in his *Orkney Farm-Names* (1952). He did not, however, know that the remains of the original magnate farm itself are spectacularly eroding out of the low cliff adjoining the church. The place was known as an unidentified archaeological site in the 1960s, but was recognized as a Norse settlement less than ten years ago.

Cross Kirk, Tuquoy (Fig. 1.44)

This is one of the most refined of all the mediaeval churches of Orkney. It consists of an original twelfth-century chancel and short nave, which was later lengthened. The chancel is barrel-vaulted; the E window does not survive but MacGibbon and Ross record a tradition that it had resembled the surviving window in the S wall of the original nave. The chancel arch has inclined jambs. The original length of the nave has been indicated on the ground by the paving. The walls of the earlier work survive to a height exceeding 2 m, but the nave-extension is reduced nearly to ground level. MacGibbon and Ross record a tradition, presumably collected by Dryden, 'that the church was enlarged, and when certain people within memory were pulling it down, an old inhabitant begged them not to "pull down the Danes' work", alluding to the chancel and eastern part of the nave'. Marwick has suggested that the extension of the nave represents the elevation of the building to parish-church status, probably in the thirteenth century.

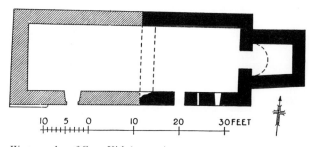

Figure 1.44: Westray: plan of Cross Kirk (RCAHMS).

Tuquoy: The Norse Magnate Farmstead

The remains are exposed in the shoreline to the west of the church. When first observed, the most prominent features were massive stone walls, leaning at crazy angles because their foundations (in sand) had been undermined, bearing traces of the same shelly lime render as occurs on high-status mediaeval buildings such as Cubbie Roo's Castle and The Wirk. Other buildings seen in section showed paved floors with drains running under them, and suggested the byres of a Norse farmstead.

Preliminary investigations by Olwyn Owen for the Scottish Development Department (Ancient Monuments) started in 1982 and have continued, on a small scale, in two subsequent years. These have confirmed the substantial nature of the buildings, the depth of surviving deposits, and the richness of the associated small-finds. The most recent work was on a pit, which had been exposed in the shoreline, which contained burnt stones and a rich assortment of organic matter. The buildings visible in the section and so far examined by excavation belong to the High Middle Ages. It is inherently probable that the lower levels go back to the start of the Viking Age, but only further excavation can reveal these. Ms Owen recounts the results so far in the paper below, pp. 318–339).

Pierowall (Fig. 1.45)

Pierowall Bay is the best harbour in the north of Orkney, and the base of the successful Westray fishing fleet. It offers ready access to the true sea to the north, unobstructed by shoals or reefs, in contrast to the rock-beset coasts of Sanday and North Ronaldsay with their dangerous tide-races. From Pierowall would have been, in terms of mediaeval navigation, the most dependable passage to Shetland, and it would have been for this reason that Rognvald made Westray the first objective in his invasion of Orkney.

The *Saga* (ch. lvi) states that Helgi lived on Westray in a *þorp*. Pierowall is the only location in Orkney to which the *Saga* elsewhere applies the designation 'thorp'. Evidently Helgi lived not in an isolated magnate farm as Kugi did, but in something more akin to a village.

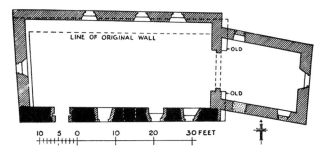

Figure 1.45: Westray: plan of Pierowall church (RCAHMS).

Archaeologically, Pierowall is famous as the location of the largest group of Viking graves to have been found in Britain. The discoveries were made last century, and unfortunately there is no record which enables the site to be pinpointed exactly. All that was preserved was the considerable collection of weapons and brooches in the National Museum (now the Royal Museum of Scotland) in Edinburgh, from which Arne Thorsteinsson has reconstructed the grave-groups (published among the papers from the *Proceedings of the Fifth Viking Congress, Tórshavn*). He has deduced a minimum of seventeen burials from the surviving collection.

This cemetery, which lay somewhere under the sand-dunes behind the village, would be consistent with a small mercantile settlement, and the 'thorp' is likely to have originated as a small *kaupstaðr* in the same way as Kirkwall. The parallel with Kirkwall is quite close. As was originally the case at Kirkwall, the long main street runs around the bay, the buildings favouring the inland side of the street, and with various private jetties and slipways running into the sea (the steamer pier, now enlarged and augmented to form a substantial harbour, was provided at the north-east end, where there is deeper water). The main mediaeval church is located by the shore about half-way along the street. The extensive dunes inland from the village were mostly formed during a period of extensive sandblow in the late 17th and 18th centuries. Before then, it would have been an easy haul across the isthmus to Noltland Bay, and as at Kirkwall, the skippers of small cargo vessels may once have welcomed this chance of getting out at the expense of a portage, when trapped in the main harbour by persistent adverse winds.

In the account of Kirkwall (pp. 44-9 above) I suggested that the mercantile settlement originally grew up under the patronage and protection of the *jarl*. Pierowall is likely to have developed in the same way. It may even have its origin in one of the periods when Orkney was divided up into portions for rule by several *jarls*, as was the case for a few years following the death of Sigurd (1014) when Einar, Brusi and Thorfinn each had a third. Each *jarl* may have tried to develop a *kaupstaðr* in his own third. In subsequent history, of course, Kirkwall acquired urban institutions and developed into a mediaeval city, while Pierowall has always remained essentially as it began – a loose string of merchants' houses and warehouses. But unlike the other North Isles harbour villages – Kettletoft in Sanday and Whitehall in Stronsay, which were created by 19th-century commercial fishing – Pierowall's origins go back into the Viking Age.

The ruined parish church, Lady Kirk, was very heavily remodelled in the 17th century; there is a date-slab of 1674. Only the south wall of the nave, which is the earliest part of the standing fabric, may be of mediaeval date.

Noltland Castle (Figs 1.46 & 1.47)

Inland from the village is Noltland Castle, a fine example of a Scottish Z-plan tower-house begun *c.* 1560, and probably never quite finished. It is the work of

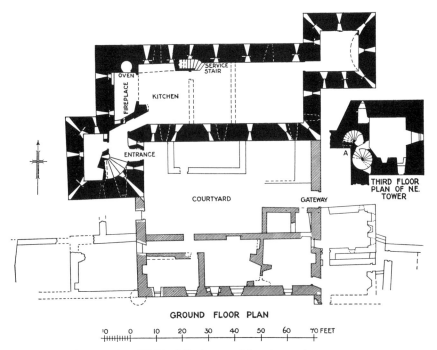

Figure 1.46: Westray: plan of Noltland Castle, ground-floor (RCAHMS).

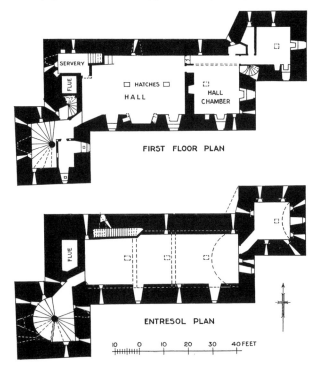

Figure 1.47: Westray: plan of Noltland Castle, first- and second-floors (RCAHMS).

Gilbert Balfour, a political adventurer who did very well for himself out of the displenishing of the Bishopric estates. It is over-generously provided with loopholes designed for defence with light hand-guns. A courtyard range, probably of 17th-century date, and ruinous, adjoins it.

Also see article by Olwyn Owen below, pp. 318–39; Ritchie & Ritchie 1988, nos 25, 26 & 31; 61–3 & 68–9; Ritchie 1985, nos 40 & 45; 84–5 & 94; Lamb, R. G. 1983. *The Archaeological Sites and Monuments of Scotland, 19. Papa Westray and Westray, Orkney Islands Area*, RCAHMS, Edinburgh.

Wednesday, 30 August

Sanday (Fig. 1.48)
Raymond G. Lamb

The Sea-route to Sanday

From Kirkwall, ships steam almost due north across Kirkwall Bay and then along the west coast of Shapinsay; the channel lies close inshore and at Ayre of Vasa the ship passes between the Vasa Skerry and the beach. On clearing the Galt peninsula at the north-western end of Shapinsay the route turns north-eastwards and the Green Holms appear to port. The larger of these islands, Muckle Green Holm, is the island named in *Orkneyinga saga* as *Hellisey*, where Sveinn Asleifarson hid in a sea-cave to evade his pursuers; there are many such caves on the east side of the island. As the Green Holms are passed, ships enter the tidal races known as the Fall of Warness and round the south-eastern corner of Eday to put in at the island's pier.

Eday is a sparsely-populated island, as most of the land is of poor agricultural quality; unlike most of Orkney, the Eday rock is sandstone, which produces rather acid soils, and furthermore, there is no local supply of shell-sand for liming the ground. In prehistoric times, however, Eday was densely settled, so that today it is archaeologically notable for the field systems and settlement remains preserved under the hill peat. In Viking and later times it was comparatively poor, as attested by a rental value of a mere two urislands. After leaving the pier, the view of Eday makes it clear that this island – *eiðs-ey*, 'isthmus-isle' – has been named from the viewpoint of a man at sea. The same is true of Westray and Sanday – Westray's position, and Sanday's white beaches, are the features most notable to sea-travellers.

General

Ships enter Sanday Sound (passing the low-lying Holms of Spurness, with ruined kelper's bothy), with Sanday to port and Stronsay to starboard. After passing the Holms, there is a view into the deep Bay of Stove, recognisable by the farm with a tall chimney at its head (the chimney once served a steam-driven threshing-mill, necessary in Sanday because of the lack of water power there). This farm is Stove, one of a small number of *stofa* names in Orkney, and

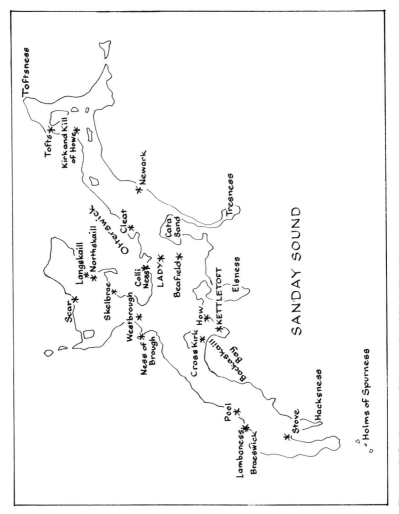

Figure 1.48: Sanday: map of sites mentioned (A. L. Brundle).

probably to be identified with *Volunes*, the place for which Sveinn was making when he hid in the cave in Hellisey, and the only Sanday place to be named in *Orkneyinga saga*.

After Bay of Stove is the low point of Hacksness, and then ships pass alongside the long hogback hill which forms the south-western peninsula of Sanday. Like Eday, this part of Sanday is sandstone, and it is the only part of the island to rise significantly above sea-level. It shows however the most distinctive quality about Sanday – the huge amount of wind-deposited sand. The side of the hill visible from the ship is entirely covered by deep, frequently shifting dunes which extend right to the top of the hill.

The hogback abruptly gives way to the flat, sea-level landscape which comprises all the rest of the island. Backaskail Bay has a wide sandy beach at its head, and then comes Bea Ness with the village of Kettletoft on its eastern side. As the ship turns towards the pier, the dangerous quality of the Sanday coast, extending away to the north-east, will be appreciated. The shoreline rises hardly above sea-level, and reefs extend far offshore; in thick weather it was easy for a ship to find herself on the rocks before the coast had been sighted. Sanday and North Ronaldsay (which continues the same landscape) were notorious for shipwrecks. Opposite Kettletoft is the headland of Elsness; the hillock with the square water-tank on it is a farm mound, the former site of the house and steading of Elsness which after destruction in the Jacobite troubles of 1746 was rebuilt on a new site. Another farm mound, Howe, still the centre of a successful farm, is visible on the skyline where the road from Kettletoft disappears from view.

Although it does not figure in the sagas, Sanday was the richest region in Orkney in mediaeval times, with a rental value of 36 urislands – about three times as much as we would expect if we were guided by size alone. Prehistoric settlement, too, is dense, and the underlying reason is clear enough: the soils formed on the shell-sand are light, easily-cultivated, well-drained, and rich in lime, therefore ideal for bere (barley), the staple crop until the 18th century. The settlement pattern is extremely complex; the high number of urislands is reflected in a patchwork of small tunships and a correspondingly high number of known chapel or church sites. In the High Middle Ages three parishes were formed, Lady, Cross and Burness, the last taking in North Ronaldsay. I suspect that the pattern in Sanday reflects an especially high degree of influence of the Pictish settlement pattern on the Norse. It certainly forms a contrast to Westray with its suggestion of dominance by large estates and its paucity of chapels.

The shell-sand attracted settlement and enabled farms to be prosperous; it also happens to create near-ideal conditions for archaeological preservation. The shape of the island seems to have changed drastically during the 5,000 to 6,000 years of human settlement here, with occasions when a great deal of sand has been on the move. Long-occupied settlements result in deep stratigraphies – the richest in Orkney – sealed by blown sand. The island's most distinctive settlement features however, the farm mounds, which are huge piles of deposits reaching heights exceeding five metres and areas of up to a hectare, do not seem to be related to sandblow, but have been formed by the same processes which have produced similar features in Arctic Norway.

Bea Ness and Cross Kirk

The fishing village of Kettletoft occupies the eastern side of Bea Ness. To the north-west, inland from Backaskaill Bay, is Bea Loch. These names greatly puzzled Hugh Marwick, who recognized that somewhere must have been a settlement of *baer* status, although as Howe is a high-value rental farm, he had difficulty in placing it. The situation is, in fact, quite parallel to Tuquoy. There was a substantial magnate farm adjoining the mediaeval parish church, which stands at the eastern side of Backaskaill Bay and as at Tuquoy, was dedicated to Holy Cross. The remains of the Norse settlement are deeply buried under a metre and more of blown sand, mostly to the east of the church. Accelerating erosion in recent years has exposed more and more of the deposits in section; included are some heavy stone walls with the same shelly lime render which is distinctive at Tuquoy. It will be noted that Backaskaill Bay thus has a *skáli* at one side and a *baer* at the other.

The South End

By 'the south end' is meant the hogback peninsula, the only hilly part of the island. On the western side, where the habitation is, is the bay of Pool sheltered by the promontory of Lambaness. Several Viking graves were found in this area last century.

The multi-period settlement at Pool is one of many sites in Sanday suffering from the ever-accelerating sea erosion. It manifested itself as a raw cliff showing in section some three metres of deposits including kitchen-middens, walls and flagstone floors. The upper part of the section contained fragments of steatite vessels, while lower down, a distinctive fine-quality Pictish pottery was found. It seemed therefore that the settlement spanned the critical Pictish-Viking transition period. By chance, it happened to coincide with the location postulated by Steinnes for one of his six 'huseby' centres – Steinnes was unaware of the archaeological site when he pinpointed this location. For these reasons the site was selected as a priority for rescue excavation by the Scottish Development Department; the campaign by Dr John Hunter ran for six seasons, finishing in 1987, and is described below, pp. 272–84.

Not apparent from the section in the cliff, and discovered with a shock in the course of excavation, was the Neolithic date of the lowest levels of the stratigraphy. This has, in fact, turned out to be one of the best Neolithic settlement sites in Europe. This unexpected discovery shows both the difficulty of estimating the dates of erosion-sectioned sites when no diagnostic artefacts happen to appear in the section, and the alarmingly high importance that Orkney sites can turn out to have, once they are properly examined. Another Neolithic settlement, possibly a 'village' akin to Skara Brae, is currently being eroded out of the shoreline at Bay of Stove.

The North End

As the South End is left, there.is (if the weather is clear) a good view over the flat landscape of the rest of Sanday, with North Ronaldsay in the distance. The long peninsula known locally as 'The North End' is a landscape of flat tracts of sandy plain, vast white beaches, and wastes of sand-dunes.

The first really obvious farm mound is Beafield, which is passed just before Lady Village. Beyond Lady, which is built on rising ground, the road descends gradually to the flat Plain of Fidge, with the tidal Cata Sand and the ridge of dunes extending out to the rocky point of Tresness. The Plain of Fidge, continuing north-east into the golf course, is probably of recent origin. It is devoid of antiquities but several old storm-beach lines exist among the dunes. No serious geomorphological study has ever been done of this fascinating region – such a study would be an interesting exercise in the relationship of natural and man-made influences in shaping the landscape. In the famous hurricane of February 1953 (in which the *Orcadia's* predecessor, the little coal-burning steamer *Earl Thorfinn*, was caught while on passage between Stronsay and Sanday, and had to run before the storm to Aberdeen), the sea flowed across the Plain of Fidge from Otterswick to Cata Sand. Away to the north, the farm mound of Cleat stands out prominently.

After the golf clubhouse is passed, the land rises slightly to a rock-based hillock with the farm of Newark, then runs for most of the rest of the route behind a ridge of dunes forming the shore. Several farm mounds can be seen on the flat plain to the left. Eventually the single road divides to form a loop around the extremity of the island. The most prominent of all farm mounds, Tofts, with its steep sides and flat top occupied by the farm buildings, cannot be mistaken. The flat Tofts Ness north-east of it apparently was occupied by dunes until *c.* 1810, when within the space of a few years, these shifted, revealing an extraordinary landscape of prehistoric mounds, burial cists, and settlement remains, which have been planned by the Royal Commission and investigated by Steve Dockrill of Bradford University for Historic Scotland. The highest point within the loop of road, west of the loch, bears the name of Kirk and Kill of Howe, adjoining the lands of a vanished farm called Eggleton. The latter appears to contain the element *eccles-*, from Latin *ecclesia*, while *Kill* can hardly be other than the *cill* element, from *cella*. These elements in both Brittonic and Gaelic forms occur in the south and west of Scotland but this is the only probable occurrence of *cill* and *eccles* in Orkney (unless the more dubious case of Egilsay and Kili Holm is accepted); what it signifies here is uncertain. Midden deposits attest to former settlement on the hilltop.

Burness

The remaining arm of the island is the former parish of Burness. Leaving Lady, the road skirts Otterswick, and the hill of Colli Ness, topped by remains of a Victorian volunteer battery, is seen. The chapel beneath the battery was the site of some bizarre and imperfectly-understood finds early last century. There is an enclosure around the hilltop, but this is too confused by the military use for its age to be certain. The upper part of the hill may be artificial, and contains remains of a substantial broch or similar Iron Age structure, on which the chapel, the foundations of which survived into the present century but now cannot readily be made out, had been built. Close to the west end of the chapel, flagstone-lined graves were discovered, close together in rows, lying with heads to the W on their right sides with knees bent. A gold ring reportedly was found but soon afterwards broken. A slab with a rude Cross of Calvary formed one of the grave-sides. An iron spear-head also is reported to have been found.

Farm mounds occur in Burness too, specially notable being Westbrough, where the house and steading have, within the last two centuries, come down off the mound, and now stand beside it. This is one of the mounds to have been sampled and radiocarbon-dated by Dr Donald Davidson; another is Skeabrae, a less prominent mound now topped by a water tank. The peninsula west of Westbrough, Ness of Brough, is the site of important but little-known Viking graves.

At the extreme north of Burness is Northskaill, a working farm on a mound which is more obvious when seen from the N side, and close by is Langskaill, where all surface trace of the farm buildings has vanished. Langskaill farm mound is overblown with sand on the land side, but towards the shore it is dramatically exposed as a spectacular section. This is the most rapidly eroding site in Orkney – some 15 m has been lost from its width in ten years – and we are worried that most of it will have gone before suitable investigations can be organised.

See Lamb, R. G. 1980. *The Archaeological Sites and Monuments of Sanday and North Ronaldsay, Orkney*, RCAHMS, Edinburgh.

Thursday, 31 August

Eynhallow (Figs 1.26 (p. 53), 1.49 & 1.50)

Raymond G. Lamb

General: The 'Holy Isle'

The first modern writer to refer to Eynhallow was 'Jo Ben', whose *Description of the Orkney Islands* was probably composed in the 1590s. He is aware that the name means 'the holy isle' – 'enhallow, quasi dicas Sancta Insula' – and he retails some quaint legends (blood flows from stalks of corn cut after sundown; horses will not remain tethered), which, he is careful to add, he does not believe. Writers in the 17th and 18th centuries state that no cats, rats or mice can live

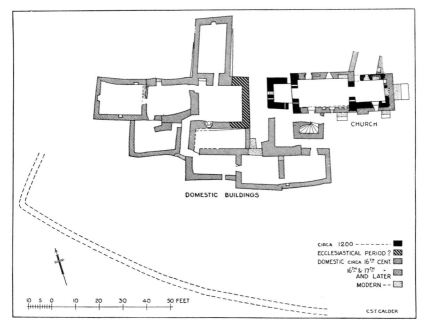

Figure 1.49: Eynhallow: overall plan of buildings (RCAHMS).

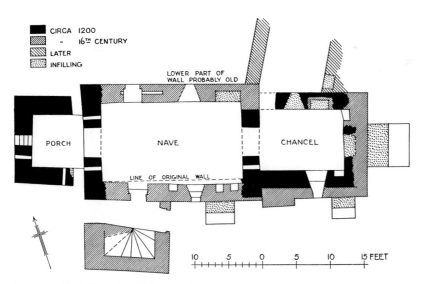

Figure 1.50: Eynhallow: plan of church and putative monastery (RCAHMS).

there, and there are traditional stories that Eynhallow originally belonged to the fairy-folk, appearing at times out of the mist and as readily disappearing, until a man succeeded in winning it into the mortal world by landing on it while clutching a piece of iron. Parallel legends, particularly the belief that certain creatures cannot thrive on the island, attach to Damsay, in the Bay of Firth, and to Burra Isle in Shetland – both of which appear to have supported ecclesiastical communities in the Middle Ages.

Jo Ben is not aware of the existence of a church and monastery on Eynhallow – in view of his interest in the place, this is significant, and suggests that the monastic community had not lasted until the Reformation, but had come to an end at a time sufficiently long before, for any memory to have faded (a church on Eynhallow is however mentioned in *The Booke of the Universal Kirk of Scotland*, 1588). Possibly it had succumbed to the general economic depression of the 15th century, which hit Orkney particularly hard, but had serious effects on Benedictine houses throughout Europe. The existence of this monastery (I use this term for convenience; *kloster* is to be understood, a religious house which might have been a nunnery for all that we know about it) has to be inferred from the place-name, the tradition of some special, otherworldly quality, and from the archaeological remains, for there is no medieval document which refers directly or indirectly to it (or, indeed, to any monastic establishment anywhere in Orkney).

'The holy isle', *eyin-helga*, is mentioned in passing just once in *Orkneyinga saga*. This is in chapter xcvii: '. . . he sailed immediately to Eynhallow and there captured Olaf, son of Sweyn Asleif's son . . .'. It is conjectured that Svein's enemy Jon Vængr had sought Svein's son on Eynhallow because the boy was at school there with the monks.

It is necessary to clear away a persistent confusion surrounding another island named in the *Saga*. In chapter xcv Svein escapes from Damsay to 'Hellisey', eludes his pursuers by hiding in a sea-cave, and then makes for Sanday in a boat which belonged to the monks. There is today no island named Hellisey in Orkney, and 19th-century scholars identified it with Ellyar Holm (or Helliar Holm), south of Shapinsay. Hugh Marwick, writing in John Mooney's *Eynhallow* (1949), correctly pointed out that the similarity of the names was superficial, Ellyar Holm must be named in the same way as Elwick Bay, *Ellidarvik* in *Hakonar Saga*. Marwick then assumes that Hellisey must be Eynhallow, Hellisey had monks on it and Eynhallow has an archaeologically identifiable monastery. This argument is faulty, for Eynhallow was certainly not the only monastic foundation in medieval Orkney. For Hellisey we need to look for a sea-cave-ridden island somewhere between Gairsay and Sanday, with a modern name; this is Muckle Green Holm, south of Eday, as noted by Finnbogi Guðmundsson (p. 264 of *Íslenzk Fornrit* edition of *Orkneyinga saga*). I have noted on Muckle Green Holm settlement remains and a field system possibly representing a monastic grange (Lamb 1984, 7 & 21).

Historiography

Until 1851 the church on Eynhallow went unrecognised, being concealed within a complex of thatched-roof cottages that had developed around it. In 1851 because of disease among the four families who lived there, the proprietor, D. Balfour, cleared the island and unroofed the buildings. This revealed the church, which was subsequently examined by Thos. Muir and Sir Henry Dryden while still more or less obscured by debris. In 1894 the island was bought by Thos. Middlemore of Melsetter, who had the buildings further cleared out and examined in 1897 by William Lethaby. In 1911 it was placed in Office of Works guardianship and further consolidation was carried out.

Eynhallow was visited in July 1865 by T. S. Muir, who hints that the place had already provoked discussion in ecclesiological circles. He provides a schematised-looking plan which is not to scale; among its more interesting features are the chancel arch, shown partly blocked by a domestic doorway, and the 'belfry stair' forming part of a south-western extension which Muir suggests formed the priest's accommodation. (The recognition of the establishment's monastic character came later.) He dates it to the 13th–14th centuries.

Sir Henry Dryden visited Eynhallow in 1866 and made a series of careful and detailed plans and sketches. These plans, much reduced, were used to illustrate MacGibbon and Ross' account, much of the text also probably relying heavily on Dryden. Dryden shows the chancel arch as if unblocked but notes that blocking is still in position, and also shows the history as follows: In the 11th–12th centuries a chapel was built of nave and chancel, with entrance at the W end of nave. In the 14th century a new chancel arch was inserted, N and S doorways made to the nave, a sacristy built at the W end, and a porch and parvise made outside the S doorway.

Archdeacon Craven, in 1901, reported that Mr Middlemore had recently cleared and enclosed the buildings. Dietrichson and Meyer, in *Monumenta Orcadica*, 1906, were first to suggest that the domestic buildings beside the church were monastic and that the complex represented a Cistercian house postulated from the *Melrose Chronicle* to exist somewhere in Orkney. The complex is compared with the Norwegian houses of Lyse (1146) and Hovedöen (1147). After Dietrichson's death, and in the light of further historical scholarship, Meyer revised his conclusion, suggesting that Eynhallow was most likely a Benedictine foundation *c.* 1100.

The Royal Commission on the Ancient and Historical Monuments of Scotland *Orkney Inventory*, 1946, gives a detailed description of the church and buildings, and plans made by C. S. T. Calder. RCAHMS is more cautious than Dryden in its dating of various parts of the church; it makes the W end and the lower inside parts of the chancel *c.* 1200 and the rest, including the greater part of the nave walls, 16th century or later. The complex of domestic structures it mostly dismisses as post-mediaeval.

John Mooney's *Eynhallow*, 1949, follows Dietrichson's original identification of the house as Cistercian. Behind this are enigmatic entries in the *Melrose Chronicle* and *Origines Cistercienses*. The *Chronicle* under the year 1175 has:

> Laurencius monachus noster, quondam abbas in Orcadia, ij idus Maii, electus est, et in crastina die ascensionis Domini a Jocelino episcopo Glasguensi, in ecclesia nostra honorifice in abbatem benedictus.

Interpreting 'monachus noster' as meaning that Laurence was of the Cistercian order, this is taken as implying that there was a Cistercian house in Orkney. But (i) it was possible for a monk to change orders, e.g. Benedictine to Cistercian; and (ii) there is nothing to indicate that Laurence had been abbot of Eynhallow rather than of any other Orkney house. The reference in *Origines Cistercienses* to a house 'Apemma' or 'Apenna', stated inconsistently to be in Orkney within the diocese of Sodor, is now generally thought not to refer to a house in Orkney. These historical problems are usefully summarised by RCAHMS.

The Buildings

There has been no really detailed architectural survey of the complex. The dating of the church is difficult. The W wall of the nave with its round arch is certainly Romanesque and probably nearer 1100 than 1200, and with it probably goes the western 'porch' (variously also described as tower or sacristy). The chancel arch, which is pointed, does seem to be an alteration of something already there, and although it could be 14th century, it could equally well be 13th century. The W 'porch' on the other hand could be later – the curious triangular W doorway and round-lintelled N doorway could be Romanesque or a good deal later. The basic fabric of the nave could be mediaeval; the windows and doors also happily parallel the unquestionably mediaeval church at Hvalsey in Greenland which, in its E window arch, provides an interesting parallel for the construction method used in the Eynhallow chancel arch.

The complex of domestic buildings displays many features, e.g. fireplace, quern alcove, that may be relatively modern, but their building history is evidently complex and their basic plan – an agglomeration of chambers – is very unusual in a purely domestic context. The plan recalls the complex of the so-called 'canons' houses' between the church and the cliff edge on the Brough of Birsay and also the complex building-ranges at Strandibrough, Fetlar, Shetland. Possibly, therefore, the Eynhallow complex is ultimately monastic in origin.

A very puzzling feature of Eynhallow is a collection of architectural fragments in red sandstone freestone, allegedly found in the clearance work last century and still lying around. The masonry of Eynhallow is of local grey stone split to shape and unmortared; these fragments are difficult to place on the buildings as they at present stand. They are discussed in relation to Westside, pp. 54–5 above.

The general impression given by Eynhallow church is of a building which is attempting to follow current architectural fashion, but is being built without adequate resources of money and expertise. The chancel arch, a pointed arch contrived, exactly as at Hvalsey, out of undressed and unmortared stones, is particularly revealing in this respect. It is likely that the church was originally begun somewhat before the middle of the 12th century, at first followed the Romanesque style set by St Magnus Cathedral, and then tried to convert to the pointed style in the 13th centry when that change reached Kirkwall. No firm conclusion can be reached as to the Order to which the house belonged, but a foundation-date in the first half of the 12th century makes it more likely to be Benedictine than anything else.

Other Antiquities on Eynhallow

There are considerable traces of prehistoric settlement. Most of the sites are strung along the low clifftop of the north-eastern corner of the island; they include houses of Bronze-Age and Iron-Age types. One of the latter was excavated in the 1920s by John Mooney, who was looking for traces of earlier monastic occupation. Although the island's name may well indicate some pre-12th-century ecclesiastical associations, the roughly circular foundation dug by Mooney is not, as he supposed, a Celtic hermit's beehive cell, but an ordinary Iron Age roundhouse.

REFERENCES

Barry, G. 1805. *History of the Orkney Islands*, Edinburgh. This prints the text of
    Jo Ben's 16th-century account.
Craven, J. B. 1901. *History of the Church in Orkney prior to 1558*, Kirkwall, 16.
Dietrichson, L. & Meyer, G. 1906. *Monumenta Orcadica*, Kristiania. Norwegian text
    126–33 with plan, English text 36–43.
Lamb, R. G. 1973. 'Coastal Settlements of the North', *Scottish Archaeological Forum*
    5, 76–98.
Lamb, R. G. 1984. *The Archaeological Sites and Monuments of Scotland 23. Eday and
    Stronsay (with adjacent small islands)*, Orkney Islands Area, RCAHMS,
    Edinburgh.
MacGibbon, D. & Ross, T. 1896. *Ecclesiastical Architecture of Scotland*, vol. 1,
    Edinburgh, 116–22.
Mooney, J. 1933. 'Laurence Abbot', *Proceedings of the Orkney Antiquarian Society* 11,
    1932–3, 27–30.
Mooney, J. 1949. *Eynhallow: the Holy Island of the Orkneys*, 2nd edn, Kirkwall.
Muir, T. S. 1885. *Ecclesiological Notes on some of the Islands of Scotland*, Edinburgh,
    68–9 & 252–4.
Ritchie 1985, no. 52, 101–3.
Ritchie & Ritchie 1988, no. 24, 59–61.
RCAHMS, 1946. *Twelfth Report with Inventory of Monuments in Orkney and Shetland*,
    3 vols, Edinburgh, II, no. 613, 230–4.
Sir Henry Dryden's drawings are in the National Monuments Record of Scotland,
    catalogue numbers ORD/94/7–11 for the plans, ORD/94/12 for the sepia view.

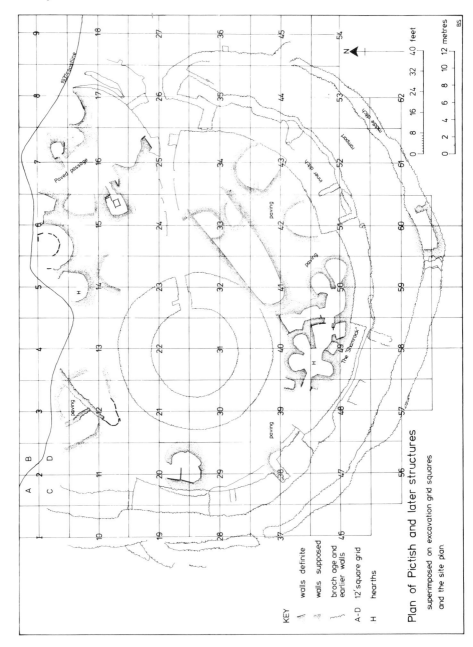

Plan of Pictish and later structures

superimposed on excavation grid squares
and the site plan

KEY

walls definite

walls supposed

broch age and
earlier walls

A-D   12' square grid

H   hearths

West Mainland

The Broch of Gurness (Figs 1.51 & 1.52)

Beverley Smith

One of the largest monuments in the care of Historic Scotland in Orkney is that of the Iron Age settlement at Aikerness in Evie – the broch of Gurness. Displayed to the public is part of Orkney's past from approximately two thousand years ago. A ruined broch tower with its surrounding buildings, ramparts and ditches still dominates the coastline which overlooks Eynhallow Sound, the waterway separating mainland Orkney from the island of Rousay. Constructed entirely of drystone masonry, this monument still serves to demonstrate the social conditions and the power which epitomize the Iron Age in Orkney. The status and wealth of the petty chieftains who lived at Gurness can be judged by the large internal area of the broch tower, the number of adjacent contemporary buildings (up to 14), the imposing entranceway between the deep ditches and the inaccessibility of the broch itself guarded by four doors or gateways. The settlement belonged to high status overlords for approximately three centuries.

By analogy with the more recent excavations of a broch settlement at Howe, Stromness (Ballin Smith (ed.), forthcoming), it is assumed that during the second to fourth centuries AD the Gurness broch went into decline. The collapse and reorganisation of buildings led to a diminution of the status of the settlement

Figure 1.52: Broch of Gurness from the air (C. D. Morris. Copyright University of Durham).

and that of its chieftain. The highly planned and organised broch settlement gradually became masked by rubble from its own buildings and was replaced by structures of less impressive styles and of poorer construction. These post-broch buildings were extremely difficult to excavate in the 1930s and many of them were missed or were removed as rubble. From the site records it has been possible to trace the location of some of these buildings (see Fig. 1.52) to produce a composite plan. Fieldwork and detailed analysis of the monument produced further evidence of post-broch structures and these too are reproduced on the plan (see also Smith in Hedges, 1987, ch. 2.2). Unfortunately it is not possible, on the evidence available, to redefine these post-broch buildings further. These structures could span several centuries and encompass both late Iron Age (Pictish) and Viking buildings.

In marked contrast to the broch buildings, the later structures were mainly cellular and of single-faced wall construction. They were dug into the broch rubble and reused the older walls as foundations. A group of these late buildings, now known as 'the shamrock', were reconstructed away from the site in front of the site museum. Adjoining these, and also partly reconstructed was a linear building over 18 m long, with a recognisably curved end. These structures seem to have been relatively short-lived and eventually the settlement declined to such an extent that the buildings became part of the rubble which made up the large mound on the site. Again, the problem exists of the dating of these late buildings and their contemporaneity.

If the buildings are problematic, the artefacts are less so. In 1939, at the end of the causeway to the settlement mound was found the indisputable grave of a Viking woman. The grave was stone-lined, and apart from the poorly preserved skeleton, contained two bronze oval brooches, an iron necklet, knife and sickle as well as a bone pin (*ibid.*, 73–4). Hedges also mentions the possibility that six other Viking-Age graves may have been found on the settlement mound during excavation. The finds include a folded bronze balance, two shield bosses, a glass linen smoother, two amber beads and one of jet, and a bronze ring headed pin SF 234 (*ibid.*, Fig. 2.39). Included in Hedges' list is also a skeleton of two hands with five bronze finger rings in place. He considers the majority of these finds as belonging to a period between the late 9th to the latter half of the 10th century.

The available evidence supports the suggestion that Viking settlers did not use the mound for habitation but moved to a new green-field site. The old settlement mound was, however, of sufficient prominence and importance for six graves to be dug within it and one Viking burial to be sited close to it.

See Hedges, John W. 1987. *Bu, Gurness and the Brochs of Orkney. Part II: Gurness*, BAR British Series 164, Oxford; Ritchie & Ritchie 1988, no. 16, 44–6; Ritchie 1985, no. 59, 121–2; Ballin Smith, Beverley (ed.), forthcoming. *Howe - occupation over 4 millennia, Stromness*, Orkney Society of Antiquaries of Scotland Monograph Series 9, Edinburgh.

Click Mill (Fig. 1.53)

Anne Brundle

The Click Mill in Birsay (HY 325 228) is a horizontal water-mill, built in the early 1820s by John Spence of Millbrig, as a replacement for one which had become ruinous (Fenton 1978, p. 400). The mill was used by the farm for the processing of oats and bere (a kind of barley, pronounced 'bear'). It is said it was last worked in the mid-1880s when John Kirkness, herd-boy at Millbrig, took oats there for grinding into 'grap' (P. K. I. Leith, personal communication).

Grap was the 'metteen' (whole grain) ground without removing any of the husks. It was fed to cattle and horses. If the millstones were set wider apart, the 'scrubs' (outer husks) were removed without crushing the kernels. This process was called 'shilling'. If the grain was then winnowed and ground, it could be used as 'shilled grap' (hens' feed) or it could be put through a calf-skin riddle to separate the 'suids' (inner husks) from the meal. Oatmeal was made into oatbread (oatcakes), porridge or brose. The suids might be fed to animals or they

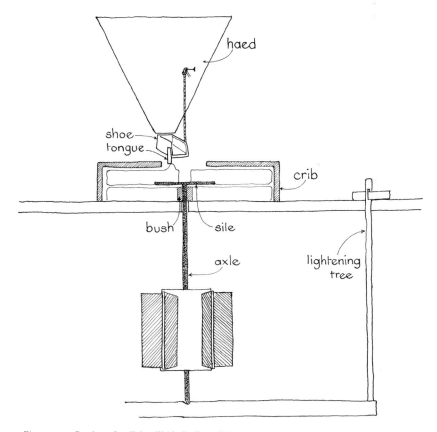

Figure 1.53: Section of a click mill (A. L. Brundle).

could be soaked and strained to produce a floury liquid called 'sooans' (P. K. I. Leith, personal communication). This was used to make scones (pancakes) and other dishes, including boiled sooans which was held to be 'very good for invalids, as it was supposed to be light on the stomach' (J. J. Leith, personal communication).

The horizontal water-mill is one of the simplest machines for turning grain into meal, since the wheel rotates on the same axle as the grinding stone, without any intermediate gears. There were such mills in the Mediterranean area about two thousand years ago and perhaps in Ireland about the 3rd century AD (Fenton 1978, 396). They are known in other parts of Britain, mainland Europe and Asia (Hume, 1981).

Though grain has been grown in Orkney for thousands of years, the oldest horizontal water-mill so far discovered here is a Norse example, currently under excavation at the Bu in Orphir (see Batey, pp. 77–8 above). Perhaps there are others to be found, but it is hard to say how many. Some places had no suitable stream; some farmers were obliged by their tenancies to grind their grain at the lairds' mills.

There were at least three horizontal mills on a single burn in Harray in the 15th century (Fenton 1978, 397), but the 18th-century observer George Low claimed he first saw a horizontal water-mill in Shetland in 1774, though he had been well-acquainted with Orkney since 1768 (John Hunter, 'Introduction', xiii, in Low 1978):

> Here I saw the first Schetland mill for grinding Oats and Bear, but this it does in a clumsey manner, little better than a hand-mill or quern, only it saves hand labour.
>   (Low 1978, 74)

Some hundred years later, John R. Tudor described 'Shetland mills' in much the same terms (Tudor 1883, 151), although by then the Click Mill in Birsay had been in use for almost sixty years.

The Click Mill is a small rectangular building of stone, roofed with flagstones covered with turf. The wheel, in the under-house at the south end, is unusual in having two rows of blades set one above the other (Fenton 1978, 400), presumably to get maximum force from the waterflow. Only part of the stone lade remains; the rest was destroyed in the 1920s when a contractor used the side of the burn as an easy source of road materials (Fenton 1978, 400). Since then, land improvements and new drainage have further changed the watercourses. The Burn of Kirkgeo now flows east and south of the mill (OS maps 1903 and modern) and only the Burn of Swartageo still lies close to the building.

The iron axle of the wheel rises through the floor and through a wooden plug (bush) in the lower millstone to an iron cross-piece (sile) which supports the upper stone (Hume 1981). Beside the stones is a lever (the lightning tree), linked to the end of the beam on which the mechanism pivots. Axle, wheel and upper stone are raised and lowered as one, to vary the settings for shilling and grinding, for barley and for oats and to allow for the stones wearing. Very fine adjustments could be made by putting wedges under the lever. For more details of the mechanism, see Fenton (1978) and Hume (1981).

The millstones are in a wooden casing (the crib). Above them hangs a 'haed' (hopper) in a wooden frame. From the 'haed' the grain pours into a wooden 'shoe', which has a wooden 'tongue' attached to it. A projection in the upper stone strikes the 'tongue' and shakes the grain into the mill, making the distinctive 'clicking' noise. The flow of grain is controlled by altering the slope of the 'shoe'. The grap or meal is channelled out of the stones over a rectangular pit in which a wooden 'meal box' stands. If necessary, grain could be winnowed at the mill, for there is a 'wind door' opposite the entrance.

The Click Mill was renovated by the Orkney Antiquarian Society, and passed into the care of the Office of Works in 1932. Since then further work has been undertaken. It is now a Guardianship monument in the care of Historic Scotland.

REFERENCES

Cruden, Stewart. 1947. 'The horizontal watermill at Dounby, on the mainland of Orkney', *Proceedings of the Society of Antiquities of Scotland*, 81 (1946–7), 43–7.
Fenton, Alexander. 1978. *The Northern Isles: Orkney and Shetland*, Edinburgh.
Hume, John R. 1981. *Click Mill*, Historic Scotland leaflet, HMSO, Edinburgh.
Low, George. 1978. *A Tour through the Islands of Orkney and Schetland* (1774, reprinted), Inverness.
Ritchie 1985, no. 34, 73.
Ritchie & Ritchie 1988, no. 32, 70.
Tudor, John R. 1883, *The Orkneys and Shetland: their Past and Present State*, Kirkwall and Lerwick.

Kirbister Farm Museum, Birsay

See Ritchie 1985, no. 29, 69.

Skara Brae

See Ritchie & Ritchie 1988, no. 13, 37–8; Ritchie 1985, no. 72, 138–40.

2

THE LANDSCAPE OF CAITHNESS AND ORKNEY

DONALD OMAND

INTRODUCTION

The Orkney Islands (389 square miles) contrast markedly in rock type, scenery and land utilisation with their northern neighbour, Shetland, but have a closer affinity in many respects with Caithness (685 square miles), from which they are separated (one is tempted to write *linked*) by the Pentland Firth, a mere 10 km in width at its narrowest part.

In the Pentland Firth is the island of Stroma, a part of Caithness. Stroma would have provided a convenient stepping stone for early mariners between Orkney and Caithness, the land of the Catti, which had Sutherland, the Southland of the Norse, for its neighbour.

GEOLOGY

A considerable area of Caithness and almost the entire Orkney Islands are composed of fairly gently inclined sedimentary strata sandstones and flagstones of Lower and Middle Old Red Sandstone (ORS) age. These strata were originally laid as a cyclothem, a rhythmic series of alternating sandstones, mudstones and limestones, in a large water-filled basin dated to well over 350 million years ago and known to geologists as Lake Orcadie. The highly fissile flagstones have proved an excellent source of building material since prehistoric times. With the population explosion of the 19th century came substantial quarrying operations, particularly in Caithness, where at its peak the industry employed nearly 1,000 people and Caithness flag was exported to many countries throughout the world. It is mainly in these flagstone beds, particularly the calcareous ones, that the high quality assemblages of fossil fishes have been found (Crampton & Carruthers 1914).

In Orkney a basement complex of much older Moinian rocks and granites forms a number of inliers in the ORS, such as on the island of Graemsay and in the West Mainland near Stromness and Yesnaby. Those Moinian rocks also appear in Caithness, mostly under the interior peatlands and are identified with a low-lying terrain. Rising beyond them are resistant quartzites which form the

Figure 2.1: The Caithness landscape looking towards Dunnet Head (J. P. Campbell).

dominant ridge of Scaraben (625 m). Pink granites are found in the south-east and west of Caithness and dark diorite in the vicinity of Reay village. However, in the lowlands of the north-east triangle of Caithness the flagstones of the ORS age predominate. What a contrast this landscape (Fig. 2.1) provides with the conglomerates (also of ORS age) in south-east Caithness, which have been chiselled into the tor-capped conical hills of Maiden Pap and Morven (705 m), the highest hill in the county.

At Dunnet Head, the most northerly promontory on the British mainland, lie rocks of Upper ORS age, which are continued on the other side of the Pentland Firth in the thick sandstones of the island of Hoy. Since the deposition of these sandstones there has been some volcanic activity, mostly as intrusive dykes, on both sides of the Pentland Firth.

Structure and Landscape

The general structure of Caithness is relatively simple in that it forms part of a basin of sedimentary rocks which extends from south of the Moray Firth up to Mainland Shetland. Geologically, then, Caithness and Orkney have a common heritage; structurally, the Orkney Islands form a dissected undulating platform that is tilted to the north and east. Folding and faulting appear to have played a more significant role in the structural evolution of Orkney than Caithness. A classic case of this control is provided in the superb natural anchorage of Scapa Flow which is bounded by fault lines. Its sheltered waters have a low energy wave environment which contrasts markedly to, say, West Mainland, the west coast of Hoy and most of the Caithness littoral (Crampton & Carruthers 1914; Phemister 1960).

The folding, faulting and submergence of the Orkney islands have given a distinctive drowned appearance to the landscape, with its whale-backed islands separated by firths and sounds that have proved such excellent shipping thoroughfares down through the ages. The Orkney archipelago, consisting of some 90 islands and skerries, 14 of them inhabited, appears to have been formed by the drowning of a plateau area that was subsequently folded and faulted. A series of natural depressions, probably the remnants of preglacial river systems modified during the Ice Age, divide the archipelago into three distinct groupings of the North Isles, Mainland and South Isles. Actually, a fall of only 37 m would unite all of these islands into one landmass (Mykura 1976).

Landscape

Since the ORS sediments of Caithness and Orkney were deposited over 350 million years ago, the land has been uplifted and erosion has taken place on a massive scale, removing great thicknesses of material to reveal ancient reliefs long buried under the deposits of the ORS sea. Examples of such exhumed landscapes in Orkney occur at Yesnaby, Brinkie's Brae (Stromness) and on the island of Graemsay. In Caithness, an outstanding example is the reappearance of the quartzite Scaraben range. It is likely that the excavation of the tor-capped conglomerate hills of Morven, Smean and Maiden Pap were sculpted at the same time. Current thinking is that much of the shaping of the landscape of Orkney and Caithness would have taken place during the Tertiary period, which was initiated some 70 million years ago, leaving a subdued lowland over much of Caithness and the low hills and shallow valleys that typify much of Orkney. A feature of the prolonged reduction of the landscape by various processes of weathering has been the remnants of erosion surfaces that survive, e.g. the dissected plateau of North Hoy (*c.* 300 m), the low-lying and subdued relief of the West Mainland of Orkney and the gently-rolling plain to the south-west of Halkirk in Caithness.

Because its landmass has been segmented into a number of islands, no river network has developed in Orkney, whereas well-established systems are found in Caithness, most of them reflecting an initial regional slope towards the south-east. The geological evidence suggests that in south Caithness the Langwell and Berriedale Rivers have been superimposed on to the present landscape from a surface long since vanished, as they traverse the outcropping rocks with a total disregard for structure (Crampton & Carruthers 1914; Mykura 1976).

Glaciation

The cooling of the climate towards the end of the Tertiary period led to a number of glacial episodes in Scotland, the first of these occurring *c.* 2 million years ago. Repeated glaciations left their mark on the landscape and, indeed, offshore, where thicknesses of sediments of around 1,000 m have been reported from the North Sea basin (Cameron, Stoker & Long 1987).

The most widespread of the Ice Age deposits in Caithness and Orkney is till, which covers most of the former and extensive areas of the latter. Excellent sections occur along river banks in Caithness and along the coast in Orkney. The so-called shelly till, which is typically blue-grey in Caithness and red or yellow in Orkney, received its calcareous content and a host of erratics as ice moved in a north to north-west direction across a landmass now covered by the North Sea. The turning of mainland Scottish ice towards the north-west may have been due to pressure from Scandinavian ice lying to the east. On both sides of the Pentland Firth there is evidence to suggest an older till underlying the shelly one. It has been suggested that the last major push of ice in Scotland may have failed to cover a number of peripheral areas including lowland Caithness and Orkney (e.g. Sutherland 1984). More recent work (Hall & Whittington 1989) using a variety of relative age criteria, has indicated that almost all the Quaternary deposits of south-east Caithness are of late Devensian age. Assuming that the shelly till of Caithness and the Orkney islands is a single till, then the evidence points to the Orcadian deposit as being of late Devensian age too. This in turn implies that the maximum limit of the last ice sheet must lie at least as far north as the Orkney-Shetland channel (Hall & Whittington 1989).

Glacial conditions on a very limited scale seem to have returned again, at least to Orkney, and more specifically to the island of Hoy, during what is termed the Loch Lomond Readvance dated to close on 11,000 BP. Evidence for this readvance on north-west Hoy is indicated by corries and associated terminal moraines.

Having such a high percentage of lowland, glacial erosion did not produce the dramatic scenic effects that are found over much of the Northern Highlands, yet

Figure 2.2: Ward Hill, Hoy (E. J. Brundle).

one cannot fail to notice the large number of rocky ridges that frequently run parallel to each other in Caithness. These features generally run with geological strike but have been emphasised by the passage of ice. Even the major through valley running from Wick to Thurso is likely to have been a preglacial feature whose form was accentuated as ice moved from the south-east towards the north-west.

In Orkney the passage of ice led to a smoothing of the pre-existing landscape, although on the higher North Isles of Rousay and Westray advancing ice emphasised the terraced appearance of the well-stratified sedimentary rocks. On the island of Hoy the two glacially deepened glens on either side of Ward Hill (Fig. 2.2), the highest in Orkney (477 m), coalesce to form the wide valley of Rackwick. The main axes of lochs like Harray, Stenness, Boardhouse and Swannay would seem to lie along preglacial depressions subsequently modified by ice (Mykura 1976). The evidence from Caithness suggests many of the lochs lie in rock basins (e.g. Sarclet, Yarrows and Achkinloch) while glacial deposits are so thin near the biggest lochs of Calder and Watten as to suggest that they too might lie in rock basins where ice has gouged the floor of existing depressions (Omand 1973).

Fluvioglacial deposits to the north of Rackwick on Hoy are too limited to be of economic importance; the major Caithness deposit is an esker system by the Thurso River to the south of Halkirk. Although largely worked out, it has been an important source of sand and gravel to the construction industry.

PEAT

Since the last of the glaciers vanished over 10,000 years ago the major impact on the appearance of the landscapes of Northern Scotland has been the accumu-lation of peat, mostly deposited since the Neolithic period. Peat results from the accumulation of partly decomposed plant remains whose normal decay has been inhibited by an excess of moisture, which severely curtails normal decomposi-tion by excluding oxygen and preventing bacteria from breaking down vegetable matter.

In Orkney the most extensive areas of peat are found in Hoy and the eastern sector of the West Mainland. In Caithness, like Orkney, most peat deposits are of the blanket bog variety and cover some 60 per cent of the landmass. The three principal accumulations are at Shielton, Achairn and Altnabreac, whose area exceeds 8,500 hectares, making it the largest peat bog in Britain. The area of peat cover in Orkney and Caithness was formerly much more extensive, but where the deposit was thin enough to be skinned it was removed so that the underlying till deposits could be prepared for agricultural purposes (Crampton & Carruthers 1914).

THE COAST

With a combined coast line of almost 1,000 km, both Orkney and Caithness are lands of superb seascapes. In Orkney the high cliffs tend to be restricted to the

Figure 2.3: St John's Head, Hoy (E. J. Brundle).

Figure 2.4: Duncansby Stacks (J. P. Campbell).

extremities of the archipelago; in Caithness they are also peripheral, occurring in the granites of the south-east coast near the Sutherland boundary. Orkney's awesome buttress of St John's Head in Hoy (347 m) (Fig. 2.3) makes the tallest Caithness cliffs of 120 m seem rather modest. In both areas cliff erosion is still active, as is the continuing abrasion of the skirting rock platforms.

The variety of forms in plan and in section of the hard rock coastline is quite astonishing and is attributable to a number of factors: variations in rock type, bedding, jointing, dip-strike relationships and exposure to marine erosion which is greatly assisted by long fetches and strong persistent winds.

The most characteristic feature of the rocky coasts is the geo, a long, narrow, structurally-controlled inlet found in the sandstone and flagstone beds. Geos can occur as extremely narrow slots, especially where they have been excavated along deeply weathered dykes. They can be quite spectacular in the well-jointed flagstones and have almost parallel sides when cut between two fractures. Where their form is joint controlled, geos trend at high angles to the strike of the rocks; where fault-controlled, they follow the line of least resistance.

The well-jointed flagstone and sandstone rocks are particularly susceptible to cave formation. The roof of a cave may eventually communicate with the surface by means of a chimney, sometimes of considerable proportions, such as the Gloups of Deerness in Orkney and Stroma in Caithness. When two caves on opposite sides of a small promontory unite, a natural arch will form, such as at Yesnaby (Orkney Mainland) and the Vat of Kirbister in Stronsay, Orkney, or the Brig o' Trams to the south of Wick. Should the roof of the arch collapse, isolated stacks like the Old Man of Hoy (137 m) and the flat-topped 'Clett' at Holborn Head near Thurso will form. The pyramidal stacks of Duncansby in north-east Caithness are the remnant pinnacles surviving rapid marine erosion of the relatively unresistant John o' Groats sandstone (Fig. 2.4).

Raised shorelines are a common feature of the Northern Highlands and can be located at a number of localities around the Caithness coast. The highest firmly identified sites lie near Dunbeath and have been levelled at 6 m above the high water mark. It appears that in Caithness the various rock notches and raised shorelines decline northwards from Dunbeath and eastwards from Reay.

Such raised shorelines have not been identified in Orkney but it is possible that they now lie under the sea. If so, this evidence along with the truncation of hill slopes by active marine encroachment, the presence of peat beds below the high water mark and a number of fresh water oyces (impounded waterbodies) close to sea level, point to the gradual submergence of Orkney since the last Ice Age.

The corrugated coastline of Caithness offers some extensive beach areas, but obviously not on a comparable scale to the much longer coastline of Orkney. Beach materials can, of course, be supplied by marine erosion of the substantial cliff areas, but undoubtedly the glacial deposits both on and offshore are a much greater source of nourishment for the creation of the low soft coastlines that, in

Figure 2.5: Carness Ayre, Orkney (D. Mackie, after T. Kent. Copyright The Orkney Library).

Orkney, constitute a variety of forms from shingle bars (ayres: Fig. 2.5) sometimes with oyces to fine sandy beaches. In both Caithness and Orkney the principal component of many sandy beaches is comminuted shells, so that lime content can reach as high as 90 per cent in some samples. In Caithness, at Sinclair's Bay and Dunnet Bay, there are two fine examples of a long dune range

Figure 2.6: Freswick Links from the air (C. D. Morris. Crown copyright).

running parallel to the coast and backed by a machair type zone with subsidiary dunes. At Freswick (Fig. 2.6) and at Sandside Bay the dunes are more irregularly distributed. In Orkney, blown sand covers extensive areas of the North Isles, particularly in Sanday, Westray, North Ronaldsay and to a lesser extent, Stronsay (Ritchie & Mather 1970; Mather, Smith & Ritchie 1974). On the Mainland the largest accumulations are at the Bay of Skaill (near Skara Brae) and Sandside Bay, Deerness. These lime sources have been extremely useful as an additional soil sweetener to generations of crofters and farmers who have utilised and improved the glacial soils, quarried the local stones for their houses and steadings, and used slabs of flagstones set on edge to compartment their fields, creating green and pleasant lands whose sheep and cattle have gained an international reputation for Orkney and Caithness.

REFERENCES

Baxter, A. N. & Mitchell, J. G. 1984. 'Camptonite-Monchiquite dyke swarms of Northern Scotland: Age relationships and their implications', *Scot. J. Geol.* 20 (3), 297–308.

Black, George P. 1978. *Orkney: Localities of Geological and Geomorphological Importance*, Nature Conservancy Council, Newbury.

Cameron, T. D. J., Stoker, M. S. and Long, D. 1987. 'The History of Quaternary Sedimentation in the UK section of the North Sea Basin', *J. Geol. Soc.* 144, 43–58.

Crampton, C. B. & Carruthers, R. G. *The Geology of Caithness*, Edinburgh.

Flinn, Derek 1981. 'A Note on the Glacial and Late Glacial History of Caithness', *Geol. Journ.* 16, 175–9.

Hall, Adrian M. & Whittington, Graham 1989. 'Late Devensian glaciation of southern Caithness', *Scott. J. Geol.* 25 (3), 307–24.

Jardine, W. G. & Peacock, J. D. 1973. 'Scotland', in, *A Correlation of Quaternary Deposits in the British Isles*, Mitchell, F. G., Penny, L. F., Shotton, F. W. & West, R. D., Geol. Soc. Lond. Spec. Rep. 4.

Mather, Alexander Smith, John S. & Ritchie, William 1974. *Beaches of Orkney*, Aberdeen.

Miller, Ronald 1976. *Orkney*, London.

Mykura, W. 1976. *Orkney and Shetland (British Regional Geology)*, Edinburgh.

Omand, Donald 1973. *The Glaciation of Caithness*, Unpub. M.Sc. Thesis, University of Strathclyde.

Omand, Donald (ed.) 1989. *The New Caithness Book*, Wick.

Phemister, J. 1960. *Scotland: The Northern Highlands (British Regional Geology)*, Edinburgh.

Price, Robert J. 1976. *Highland Landforms*, Inverness.

Ritchie, William & Mather, Alexander 1970. *The Beaches of Caithness*, Aberdeen.

Rock, N. M. 1983. *The Permo-Carboniferous camptonite-monchiquite dyke suite of the Scottish Highlands and Islands*, Rep. Inst. Geol. Sci. no. 82/14.

Sissons, John B. 1976. *The Geomorphology of the British Isles: Scotland*, London.

Sutherland, Donald G. 1984. 'The Quaternary Deposits and Landforms of Scotland and the Neighbouring Shelves: A review', *Quat. Sci. Review*, 3, 157–254.

Whittow, John B. 1977. *Geology and Scenery in Scotland*, Hardmondsworth.

3

BEFORE THE VIKINGS

THE PRE-NORSE BACKGROUND IN CAITHNESS

ROBERT B. GOURLAY

The people known to us as the 'Picts' are justly regarded as something of a mystery, prompting F. T. Wainwright, in 1955, to entitle his collection of essays on the latest ideas on these people *The Problem of the Picts* (Wainwright 1955). In the ensuing thirty-odd years the 'problem' has not gone away.

The brochs totter into disuse at an uncertain point in the first century AD, and with few exceptions, nothing is distinguishable in the archaeological record in Caithness until the late Viking remains at Freswick Bay a thousand years later. The Picts themselves first appear as a name mentioned by the Roman poet Eumenius in AD 297, where they are linked with the Irish *Hiberni* as enemies of the *Britanni* of eastern England. In AD 360, the Roman historian Ammianus Marcellinus again refers to them in the same terms, and adds that they were split into two groups known as the *Verturiones* and *Dicalydones*. Later still, other writers including Gildas and Adomnan refer to their presence and their power, until their credentials are finally established by the Venerable Bede, who, in his *Ecclesiastical History of the English People*, describes them as being with the Scots, Angles and Britons, one of the four peoples of Britain, again emphasising their division into a northern and a southern group. While it is therefore clear that we are dealing with a real and powerful people, their origins are misty in the extreme, and the identifiable remains of their passing – with the notable exception of their art – almost non-existent.

The recognition of the Picts as a 'people' probably serves more to confuse than illuminate. Scholars find it difficult to agree because of the lack of corroborative evidence, but they are probably the descendants of native Bronze Age incomers – suggested by their apparently non-Indo-European language – and thus of the broch-dwellers themselves. At any rate, we do not have to see them as newcomers to Scotland, but rather as a development of what has gone before. They seem not to have been a single people, but probably a confederation of tribal units whose political motivations derive from a need to ally against common enemies. Their centre of power, accordingly, seems to have shifted from S to N – probably dependent on the strengths of individual leaders. Thus, under King Brude or Bridei, for example, during the 6th century, the principal court and exercise of power was based near Inverness. Earlier, and particularly during the great raid of AD 367 on the Roman frontier, it lay in southern Pictland, maybe in Fife. Perhaps, because they were not a single people, their cultural artefacts may have been insufficiently alike for us now to identify them readily.

Perhaps most obviously missed are their homes. Houses of a period which can confidently be described as Pictish are now known from Orkney, at sites such as Buckquoy and Birsay, where they precede those of early Viking date. On the mainland, however, we are presented with a virtual blank, although Caithness has its own unique contender in the form of the structures known as 'wags'. On older maps of the area, large numbers of antiquities are labelled 'Pict's Houses', but these generally apply (erroneously) to broch sites. However, in a number of instances, later settlements surround the brochs themselves, and amongst them are structures of a particular form which might, through modern excavation techniques, be proven to be 'Pictish'. Other sites of similar type are found on their own. These are the 'wags', a type of monument found only in Sutherland and Caithness, and confined almost wholly to Latheron parish in the SE of the county. They are identified by a curious internal arrangement of pillars – either drystone or single flags – which stand around the interior, close to, but separate from the walls – thus dividing the perimeter into sections while creating an 'aisle' along the inside wall-face. Their shapes are very varied. Some are circular, others oval or kidney-shaped, while others are almost rectangular but with rounded ends. A few have secondary rooms, and could be descibed as 'cellular'.

One of the best examples can be seen at the Wag of Forse (Fig. 3.1; *1*) near Latheron, where a long, sub-rectangular building with small cells attached lies outside the ruins of what is surely a broch. Some of the stone pillars which supported the 'aisle' can be clearly seen here. Another example may be seen amongst the structures surrounding the broch at South Yarrows (Fig. 3.1; *2*), where the shape of the building has been determined by the external curvature of the broch wall (Fig. 3.2). A third is to be seen at Langwell (Fig. 3.1; *19*), where an 'aisled' structure adjoins one side of a circular building not unlike a hut circle. Elsewhere, their ruinous condition makes their plan difficult to unravel. Excavation will be needed to prove their Pictish date, but they are at present the chief contenders for the honour in Caithness. Their curious name, incidentally, appears to derive from the Gaelic *uaimhach* or 'little cave'.

It can be assumed that unless 'Pictish' is a term which really only applies to the politically-recognised element represented by the higher social strata of tribal society during the first millenium AD – a position which is far from impossible, and might explain the absence of ordinary, domestic structures – they would have been farmers much as the inhabitants of Caithness had been since the Neolithic. If so, we have yet to find traces of their agricultural landscapes – their fields, kilns, mills and so on. It is of course possible that these were the same as, or almost indistinguishable from, those of the Iron Age. Indeed, the lack of identifiably Pictish remains probably means that this was indeed the case.

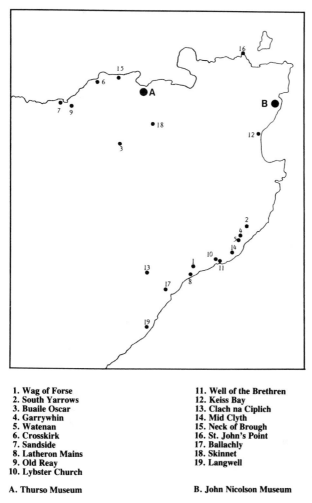

1. Wag of Forse
2. South Yarrows
3. Buaile Oscar
4. Garrywhin
5. Watenan
6. Crosskirk
7. Sandside
8. Latheron Mains
9. Old Reay
10. Lybster Church

11. Well of the Brethren
12. Keiss Bay
13. Clach na Ciplich
14. Mid Clyth
15. Neck of Brough
16. St. John's Point
17. Ballachly
18. Skinnet
19. Langwell

A. Thurso Museum

B. John Nicolson Museum

Figure 3.1: Pre-Norse background in Caithness: sites (R. B. Gourlay).

Elsewhere in Scotland, there are signs of the Pictish military presence in the form of fortified sites – on hillforts and duns – many apparently the re-use or refurbishment of sites first built during the Iron Age. Sites such as Craig Phadrig in Inverness and Dundurn, near St Fillans in Perthshire, have been demonstrated to have had Pictish period occupation. In Caithness, regrettably, such sites have yet to be identified. The main contenders must have been broch sites, but they are built to a different scale from the more southerly forts, and, as well as being perhaps unsuitable as Pictish fortifications, were probably too ruinous without undergoing considerable reconstruction. Hillforts, in the classic Iron Age tradition, do not exist in Caithness, and the author feels that those sites described as 'forts', such as Buaile Oscar (Fig. 3.1; *3*) on Beinn Freiceadain, and

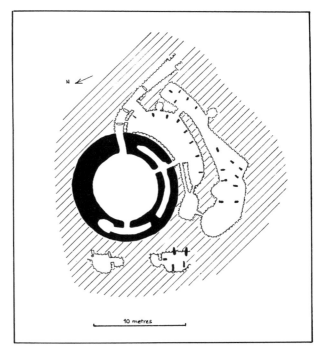

Figure 3.2: Broch and aisled buildings or 'wags', South Yarrow, Caithness (R. B. Gourlay, after RCAHMS).

Garrywhin (Fig. 3.1; *4*) are likely to be enclosures of a different kind and of much earlier date. Perhaps as the county lies well away from the main Pictish areas of conflict, such fortifications were unnecessary. In any event, these high status sites are as elusive as the domestic ones.

Not infrequently, the religious and burial practices of past societies leave substantial remains – even when, as in the Neolithic, little else survives. In recent years, a number of burial sites have produced fragments of the characteristically Pictish sculptures known as Class 1 *symbol stones* (see below), and are perhaps beginning to indicate a style of burial which may be Pictish (Friell & Watson (eds) 1984). Again, the best-investigated of these have been in Orkney and elsewhere outside the county. They consist of small mounds, or stone cairns, which may be both square or circular, and are often grouped together in small cemeteries. Often, the individual cairns are linked together, and may have shallow ditches surrounding them. The best examples of these can be seen at Garbeg, Drumnadrochit, and by Whitebridge, both near Inverness. Other groups show up over a wide area as cropmarks in arable fields. At Garbeg, one of the graves appears to have contained a broken fragment of a symbol stone as also did a stone cairn of similar size near Watenan (Fig. 3.1; *5*) in Caithness. This combination of graves and broken stones is clearly significant, and may eventually shed much light on the functions of the stones themselves. Beyond this, Pictish remains in Caithness consist wholly of their artwork in the form of these symbol stones and later cross-slabs. Let us now turn our attention to these.

It is misleading, really, to say that the stones are 'all that we have', as they are part of a rich and magnificent legacy of sculptural art which more than anything else identifies the Picts to us today. They fall into two main groups – those which carry Christian designs, and those which do not. Anthony Jackson dislikes the use of the term 'symbol' in describing the individual design elements, and prefers to use this term for groups of designs which he suggests have symbolic meaning (Jackson, A. 1984). Here, however, to avoid the creation of a new and confusing term, *each element* will be referred to as a symbol, as, unless Jackson's theory can be proven, that is patently what they are. The first category, therefore, consists of stones, usually undressed, which carry groups of symbols that are characteristically Pictish and non-Christian. These range from purely geometric designs such as the 'V-rod and Crescent' and the 'Double-disc and Z-rod' through elegant representations of native birds and animals and the more mundane 'Mirror and Comb' to abstract creatures of perhaps mythical origin such as the so-called 'Elephant'. Incised into the surface of the stones, they are for the most part graceful and elegant designs executed with a high degree of skill.

The meaning of the designs, however, remains a mystery, and although many theories have been put forward, none is satisfactory. It is not unlikely that they represent tribal, family, or individual totems, but the reason they were carved with such care onto stone remains unclear. It has been variously suggested that they represent tribal boundary markers, tribal or marriage alliances, or memorials describing the origins and status of the individual they commemorate. However, without more direct evidence, none of these theories is provable. The instances of *broken* stones in association with graves may yet prove crucial in understanding this problem.

There are seven Class 1 stones noted in Caithness, of which one, from Crosskirk (Fig. 3.1; *6*), is now missing, three are in the Royal Museum of Scotland, Edinburgh, and three remain in the county. The first of these latter is at Sandside House, Reay (Fig. 3.1; *7*) where it is built into a garden wall near the house; the second is built into a wall of the farmhouse at Latheron Mains (Fig. 3.1; *8*); the third, which came from the stone cairn at Watenan (Fig. 3.1; *5*), consists of two conjoining pieces, and is currently on display in the John Nicolson Museum, Auckengill (Fig. 3.1; *B*).

The second group also carry pre-Christian symbols, but in conjunction with the Christian cross. These are carved in relief, and are usually on carefully shaped and dressed stones. The conjunction of the cross and the earlier symbols might suggest that the latter were in some way connected with Pictish religion before their conversion to Christianity by Columba *c*. AD 560, when the saint undertook a mission from his base in Iona to the court of King Brude – taking

Figure 3.3: Pictish symbol stone from Ulbster, Caithness (J. P. Campbell).

time out along the way to cast the Loch Ness monster back into the depths! This conversion seems only to apply to the northern Picts, as those in the S were converted by St Ninian in the 5th century, according to Bede.

Two examples can be seen in Caithness today, each with its own particular interest. The slab known as the *Ulbster Stone* – not least from the disgraceful addition of that name to the stone itself in horrendous Gothic lettering – has the distinction of carrying more symbols than any other Pictish stone (Fig. 3.3). It can be seen in all its glory in Thurso Museum (Fig. 3.1; *A*), along with the *Skinnet Stone*, recovered from the chapel at Skinnet between Thurso and Halkirk (Fig. 3.1; *18*) in the mid-19th century. Both are fine examples of their type, and are better visited and seen than described here.

A third stone, originally from Latheron (Fig. 3.1; *8*) and now in the Royal Museum of Scotland, has the added distinction of carrying an inscription in Ogam. This script was probably developed in Ireland specifically for carving on stone, as it consists of short lines in groups on either side of a median line, and without difficult curves (Jackson, K. 1955). The groups of lines represent letters of the Latin alphabet, but transcription of the letters on the Latheron Stone produce a meaningless jumble of letters. If this is indeed Pictish, the language bears no relation to any other contemporary European tongue and is singularly unhelpful in unravelling the mystery of the stones. A second Ogam-inscribed stone, now in Edinburgh, came from Keiss Bay links (Fig. 3.1; *12*). It also bears the lower part of a fish, and the 'rectangle' symbol (Fig. 3.4).

Besides the stones described above there are a small number of other

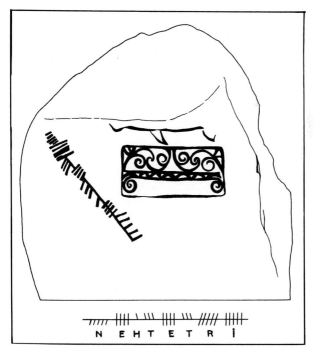

Figure 3.4: Class 1 symbol stone with ogam inscription, from Keiss Links, Caithness (R. B. Gourlay).

sculptured crosses which are probably contemporary, but lack the Pictish symbols. These fall into two categories – those which are on dressed slabs, and the simpler crosses carved on boulders. Built into the wall of a mausoleum in the graveyard at Old Reay (Fig. 3.1; *9*) is a fine example of a cross-slab bearing a wheel cross whose arms and base are covered in close panels of interlace and key patterns. A much-eroded spiral boss decorates the hub, while the upper arm of the cross shows the tool marks where a vandal of the 1980s recently obliterated the work of an earlier vandal when the stone was embellished with an unfinished memorial to one 'Robert McKay 17——' (Fig 3.5).

Half-hidden under a shelter on the S side of the church at Lybster (Fig. 3.1; *10*) is a large boulder bearing an unusual incised triple cross. It is thought originally to have come from near the Well of the Brethren (Fig. 3.1; *11*) during the construction of Lybster Harbour in the 1830s. At Clach na Ciplich (Fig 3.1; *13*), a simple, long-shafted cross is incised on a flat slab set upright on a peaty knoll. A third cross stands on the edge of the ruins of the chapel at Skinnet (Fig.

Figure 3.5: Cross-slab, Old Reay Churchyard, Caithness (R. B. Gourlay).

3.1; *18*), whence comes the cross-slab mentioned above, with a fourth and fifth known from the graveyard at Mid Clyth (Fig. 3.1; *14*). Of the last two, one still stands in the graveyard, while the second is now built into the wall of a barn at Roadside Farm.

Although all of these are likely to be contemporary with the Picts, they may perhaps owe their origin to the presence in the county of Irish priests, or *papar*. These eremitic monks spread out from Ireland during the early centuries of Christianity and established small cells in out-of-the-way places. Several such monastic sites are suspected in Caithness, although none has produced direct evidence of their use. One such site stands on a small promontory at Neck of Brough (Fig. 3.1; *15*), and another on St John's Point (Fig. 3.1; *16*), also known as Dunmey. A third example sits above the Dunbeath Water at Ballachly (Fig. 3.1; *17*), where a small rectangular building, thought to have been a chapel, sits atop a natural mound with a massive and most odd wall running from its foot towards the river. Much of the information about these sites relies on tradition and may not always be accurate. Only excavation will reveal the truth.

All in all, not much of the remains of the first millenium AD can be distinguished on the ground, but the county was clearly occupied, and probably thriving, during those ten centuries. Archaeologists, historians and art historians will doubtless continue to debate the issue on the basis of the available evidence, but what is most needed is *new* information in the form of identified and excavated sites, before the 'problem' can be resolved much further.

REFERENCES

Friell, J. Gerry P. & Watson, W. Graham (eds) 1984. 'Pictish Studies. Settlement, Burial and Art in Dark Age Northern Britain', *Brit. Archaeol. Reps*, British Series 125, Oxford.
Jackson, Kenneth 1955. 'The Pictish Language', in *The Problem of the Picts*, ed. Frederick T. Wainwright, Edinburgh, pp. 129–66.
Jackson, Anthony 1984. *The Symbol Stones of Scotland*, Kirkwall.
Wainwright, Frederick T. (ed.) 1955. *The Problem of the Picts*, Edinburgh.

Reprinted, with permission, from 'Chapter 5. The Picts', in *The New Caithness Book*, ed. Omand, Donald, 1989, Wick, 56–66.

4

CAITHNESS

AN ONOMASTIC FRONTIER ZONE

DOREEN WAUGH

The purpose of this chapter is to present an overall picture of Caithness placenames and to make some comments on what can be deduced from placename evidence about the history of settlement in this north-eastern corner of Scotland. Comments will be weighted towards the Norse onomastic input at the risk of giving a slightly inaccurate impression of the relative significance of the Scandinavians as name-givers, by comparison with the Gaels and Scots. There were, of course, inhabitants in Caithness prior to the arrival of the Scandinavians but it is not possible to be satisfactorily precise in dating names which are of early Celtic origin. One can never be sure whether a name is pre-Scandinavian (i.e. pre-9th century), or contemporary with the earliest Scandinavian settlers, or very slightly later, because reliable documentary evidence is non-existent. The most one can say is that there is a scattering of names of Celtic origin which substantially predate the main movement of Gaelic-speaking people into Caithness and which, because of their survival through the intervening centuries, must have been known to and used by the early Scandinavians. Examples of early Celtic placenames are Dunnet, Mey and Latheron.

Dunnet
Donotf   1223–4   OPS (Origines Parochiales Scotiae)
Dunost   1276   OPS
Dunneth   1455   RMS (Register of the Great Seal)
Donet   1539   RMS
Dunate   1549   RSS (Register of the Privy Seal)
Dunnat   1575   RMS
Celtic: *dūnos*, 'a fortress' (Watson 1926, 36)

Mey
Mai   1250   Matthew Paris (Moir 1973, 159)
May   1549   Sinclair Estate Papers
Maii   1578   RMS

Mei   1592   RMS
Celtic: *magos*, 'a plain' (Watson 1926, 500)

Latheron
Latherin   1476   Sinclair Estate Papers
Latheroun   1522   RMS
Ladrone   1546   Sinclair Estate Papers
Lathrone   1625   Sinclair Estate Papers
Celtic: *lath*, 'a mire, puddle' (Watson 1926, 122)

People often ask why there are so few of these apparently pre-Scandinavian names and a possible explanation will be offered later in the paper.

I have adopted the dating of *c.* AD 800 which is generally proposed for the initial appearance of Scandinavians in Caithness, although as Nicolaisen has said (1982, 75) 'the toponymic evidence is neutral' in respect of dating the earliest Scandinavian settlement. There is no reason to assume that settlement in Caithness was significantly later than settlement in Orkney and Shetland, but placename evidence does suggest that settlement in Caithness may have been less intensive than in the isles to the north because although all the commonly occurring habitative generics, such as *staðir*, *setr* and *bólstaðr*, all of which refer to farming units, can be found in Caithness names, examples are less numerous than in comparable territory in either Orkney or Shetland. This may be partially explained by greater Norse name loss in Caithness, given competition from both Gaelic and Scots in subsequent centuries, but it is also possible that the Scandinavian settlers favoured the security of an island home to the uncertainty of a frontier zone, which Caithness undoubtedly must have been.

Among the earliest Norse placenames in Caithness are those which refer to prominent topographical features, particularly those scattered around the coastline of Caithness. The name Caithness itself, although not wholly topographical in character, contains a topographical reference to the Old Norse (ON) *nes*, or headland, most probably Duncansby Head and the land behind it, which the Scandinavians must have seen as they approached by sea from the lee side of the Orkney Islands. The specific in the name is thought to refer to the local tribe inhabiting the areas, the Cats – an appellation which is still preserved in the modern Gaelic name for the neighbouring county of Sutherland, *Cataibh*, 'among the Cats' (Watson 1926, 30). One can certainly deduce awareness of an indigenous population from the coining of a name such as *Katanes*. Another early topographical name with which most people will be familiar is Wick, from ON *vík*, 'a bay', a term which is not very common in Caithness due to lack of appropriate situations. There are only two further examples – Dwarwick and Freswick – and the latter was certainly a Scandinavian settlement site. In fact, most of the early topographical names were adopted for use as habitative names at an early stage in their existence or, more likely than not, started life as descriptions of human habitation.

It has always seemed slightly odd to me that two of the most eye-catching topographical features in the Caithness landscape should not be described in Norse topographical terms. The Celtic name borrowed for Dunnet Head has already been mentioned and one might argue that a Celtic presence in the area led to an onomastic 'hands off' as far as the headland was concerned because the indigenous name was familiar from regular contact with the people who used it; but what about Duncansby Head? The name Duncansby, albeit Scandinavian, is certainly not topographical in origin and it, along with its neighbour Canisbay, is an onomastic misfit. Not only are Norse *bý*-names unlikely denizens of the north, being more at home in Yorkshire, but, to add further confusion, they are in these instances apparently compounded with the Celtic personal names, *Dungal* and *Cano* (Waugh 1987, 101). Were these also early Celtic inhabitants whose influence was sufficiently strong to minimise the Scandinavian presence in the area behind Duncansby Head, thus accounting for the missing topographical name? One can only speculate before moving on to the more common Norse habitative generics which occur in Caithness and which indicate a substantial settlement of Scandinavians, predominantly coastal in orientation.

The generics *staðir*, *setr* and *bólstaðr*, all of which refer to farms, occur regularly in the Northern Isles and, although in comparatively small numbers, they also occur in Caithness, which is what one would expect given the closeness of Caithness to Orkney, both in terms of distance and of physical similarity. There are very few examples of *staðir* in Caithness and I have had to deduce their existence by a process of analogy with Orkney names for which there is clear documentary evidence of derivation from *staðir* (Marwick 1952, 234–7). The *staðir*-names seem to be situated at the edges of what I would regard as firmly established Scandinavian communities, where clusters of Norse names suggest concentrated farming activity. For instance, Drumhollistan and Borrowston are in the vicinity of Reay (ON *rá*, 'a farm on the boundary, a farm on a long stretched out elevation'), Gerston is close to Halkirk (ON *Há-kirkja*, 'high church') and Calder (ON *Kálfadalr*, 'valley where calves were reared/penned'), and another example of Borrowston lies to the south of Wick, sandwiched between two *bólstaðr* farms, Thrumster and Ulbster. As in Orkney and Shetland, the emphasis in the *staðir* names seems to be on personal ownership, in that the specifics could be interpreted as Scandinavian personal names, although over-enthusiastic attribution of specifics to personal-name origin should be avoided. Tentatively, therefore, the specifics in the Caithness names could be *Holfr*, *Hólmr* or *Holi* in Drumhollistan (*druim* being a later Gaelic addition), *Geirr* in Gerston, and *Borgarr* in Borrowston. It seems, therefore, that *staðir* was appropriate for use at a time of apportionment of land to individuals within a community of farms.

Bólstaðr is probably the most widely occurring of the Norse habitative generics in Caithness, although it can be very difficult to identify because it is, more often than not, compressed into forms such as -mster, -pster, -bster, or even -ster, a modern reflex which, as the reader can imagine, creates its own set of problems when one is attempting to track down *setr* names. For example, one encounters names such as Stemster (ON *steinn*+*bólstaðr*), Achalipster (in which -lipster appears to derive from ON *hlíð*+*bólstaðr*), Brabster (possibly ON *breið(r)*+*bólstaðr*), and Wester (early forms of which prove that it derives from ON *vatn*+*bólstaðr*). In Shetland and Orkney the work of identification is easier because the modern reflex is most frequently -bister, or sometimes -bist in Orkney. The pronunciation of Caithness *bólstaðr*-names has obviously been affected by the presence of Gaelic speakers and, no doubt, by the earlier presence of speakers of Scots because the modern -bost form which occurs in the entirely Gaelic-speaking areas of Lewis and Skye is not common in Caithness. The use of *bólstaðr* in Caithness is particularly interesting because it shares a great deal of common ground with the Gaelic term *achadh* which seems to have started life as a reference to a field and only subsequently was it used as a name for a small farm (Nicolaisen 1976, 125). In fact, Norse *bólstaðr*-names sometimes form the specifics in subsequent Gaelic compounds in which the generic is *achadh*, as in Achalipster which has already been mentioned; Achlibster, which is a variant of the same name occurring in another part of Caithness; Achkeepster, Achscrab-ster and Achunabust. It seems reasonable to assume that, in Caithness at least, Norse *bólstaðr* and Gaelic *achadh* were used to describe farms which were initially similar in type and function. One has the impression that *bólstaðr* was a very elastic term and could vary according to the complexion of the surrounding landscape and possibly could vary according to Norse observation of the farming activities of an indigenous population.

Names containing *setr*, or possibly in some instances the form should be *sætr*, 'a shieling' (Fellows-Jensen 1984, 161), are very common indeed in Orkney and Shetland but much less so in Caithness, for a very interesting reason. At first I was puzzled but inclined to accept that, just as there is a small number of *staðir*-names in Caithness there is also a small number of *setr/sætr*-names; but I felt uneasy about making such an assumption because *setr/sætr* is so common in Orkney and Shetland that its relative infrequency in Caithness seemed to point to some major difference in degree or kind of land use and, as has been said with reference to *staðir*, to assume any such major difference seemed illogical given the proximity and similarity of the areas concerned, even if one accepts that Caithness was probably less densely populated by Scandinavians than the neighbouring islands of Orkney. However, I subsequently noted that where one might expect to find *setr/sætr* in Caithness names, one finds *ærgi*, a Norse borrowing from Gaelic *airigh*, 'a shieling' – and I would suggest that, in Caithness, contact with Gaelic-speaking people led to a preference for the word of Gaelic origin, which is similar in reference to the ON terms *setr/sætr* which occur in the islands where there was no regular contact with Gaelic speakers. The Caithness *ærgi*-names are very frequently combined with ON personal names, although one must remember the word of caution already expressed regarding the addictive quality of personal name spotting. It does, however, seem likely that personal name specifics would be appropriate for use in the apportionment of grazing land to individuals within the Scandinavian community. Examples of names containing *ærgi* are Skirza, Blingery, Halsary, Munsary, Badrinsary, Assery, Shurrery.

It has been suggested that names such as Sandside, in the Gaelic-speaking west of the county, may contain ON *sætr* (Nicolaisen 1976, 92), but the dating of early references to the Caithness examples at least (I cannot speak for Sutherland) does not clearly support such a contention. In many instances, the generic could simply be English *side*, a term which is very common in Caithness placenames from the time of the arrival of Scottish English in the county, probably *c.* AD 1400.

Gaelic (G) *airigh* is itself quite common in Caithness names, identifiable by Celtic word order in the compound and by the Gaelic specifics with which it is combined, e.g. Airigh nam Bruach Dubha, 'shieling of the dark bank', situated beside the stream (G: *abhainn*) of the same name. Furthermore, the eastern Gaelic form *ruighe* (common in areas such as Perthshire) also appears to occur in Caithness names, as in Rhianacoil, 'shieling beside the wood'. When one adds to this the Scots (Sc) form Sheilton (Sc: *shiel/sheil*) which appears in Canisbay Parish, one can see how much of a linguistic melting pot Caithness really is. It is not wholly surprising, given the nature of the land, that generics which now refer to small hill farms should most clearly demonstrate the range of languages which have been used by inhabitants of Caithness throughout the centuries.

One Norse generic which is certainly very scantily represented in Caithness placenames, and for which there is no obvious Gaelic substitute, is *garðr*, 'a yard or enclosed space'. It is ubiquitous in Shetland, as is its derivative *gerði* (Stewart 1987, 91–115), and quite common in Orkney, although Hugh Marwick (1952, 232) does suggest that it is unevenly distributed. In Caithness, there is one example of Garth on the north coast and one or two more names of uncertain etymology, such as Achsinegar, which may incorporate *garðr*, and this situation is markedly different from that obtaining in the isles to the north. Why were there so few farms of this type in Caithness? Was it because there were fewer Scandinavians in Caithness and, therefore, the urge towards expansion and diversification of the community was less pressing, or was it because the marginal land which might have become a *garðr* farm was already occupied, in some instances, by a group of Gaelic-speakers and, in others, was regarded as undesirable because the political situation in Caithness seemed insecure? One would like to be clairvoyant.

Certainly, at the peak of Scandinavian occupation, the north-east corner of the county must have been a relatively secure place in which to live because, with the exception of Canisbay, Duncansby and Mey, which were mentioned earlier, there is a blanket covering of Norse placenames, with a subsequent superstratum of Scots, and no further names which are indisputably of Gaelic origin have survived, if indeed they ever existed. There are some examples of *quoys* in this region, derived from ON *kví*, originally 'a cattlefold or a place where animals gathered for milking', and often subsequently enclosed as a small marginal farm because of the fertility of the soil, but the element is not a reliable indicator of extensive expansion and subdivision since there are relatively few *quoy*-names and several are later compounds with Scots specifics because ON *kví* in the form *quoy* was taken into the Caithness dialect of Scots and was in use for many centuries after the Scandinavian period. Many onomastic terms were borrowed from Norse into both Gaelic and Scots, not necessarily in a Caithness context, but the terms were used in Caithness as they were used in other parts of Scotland where Scandinavian influence had been felt and many, such as Sc: *geo*/G: *geòdha*, from ON *gjá*, 'a deep inlet of the sea', are still in everyday use.

In this impressionistic scamper through Norse generics in Caithness placenames, I have carefully avoided such etymological quagmires as the name Thurso, which has been the subject of much discussion in the past. I have given it and the numerous other problem names a great deal of thought but I would not be so rash as to claim that I have reached a conclusion, although in the case of Thurso I do marginally favour the suggestion (Thorson 1968, 75) that the final element is ON *haugr*, 'a how, mound'.

I should like now to move on briefly to Gaelic placenames which have already been mentioned frequently in the course of comments on Norse name elements. No dates have, so far, been attached to remarks about the presence of Gaelic speakers in Caithness, except that it has been implied that they were there from a very early stage in the Scandinavian colonisation of Caithness, probably in small numbers at first, but gradually increasing in numerical significance from the 12th century onwards. Their presence would have been most evident in Reay, Latheron and the southern part of Halkirk Parish, i.e. in the west and south of the county, in which areas Gaelic was still spoken in the early years of this century. When I first started investigating placenames in Caithness, I did a great deal of field work, particularly in Reay Parish. I was keen to ascertain the present extent of knowledge of the Gaelic placenames which had been recorded on the 6″ Ordnance Survey maps in the 1890s. The results of my survey were depressing but not altogether unexpected. Roughly 60 per cent of the names recorded at the end of the last century have now been completely forgotten, partly because the Gaelic language has been replaced by Scots but also because the names are no longer in regular use because the rural lifestyle which they reflected has been replaced by the 20th-century tendency to concentrate habitation in towns or larger villages, linked by fast motorable roads. I said earlier that I would return to the question of non-survival of names from the pre-Scandinavian period and I would suggest that the reasons are probably the same as those I have proposed for the disappearance of Gaelic placenames. The language changed and, simultaneously, the way of life changed in some way and I do not, therefore, find it particularly surprising that so few names have survived. They may, of course, have survived in a form which we cannot now recognise, just as some of the Gaelic names have survived in a different English guise. For example, the Gaelic name An t'Eas, 'the waterfall', has been ingeniously adapted into quasi-English as The Esses and is now said to refer to a winding or S-shaped section of the burn in the course of which the waterfall occurs.

The Gaelic generic which is most common in habitative names in Caithness is undoubtedly *achadh* which has already been mentioned because of the common ground it shares with Norse *bólstaðr*. As I have said, *achadh* often occurs as the generic in hybrid Gaelic/Norse compounds, particularly with Norse names containing *bólstaðr*. There is no evidence to suggest borrowing in the opposite direction, i.e. Gaelic placename as specific with Norse generic. The majority of *achadh*-names are of purely Gaelic origin which is what one would expect given that the element was productive throughout the period when Gaelic was spoken in Caithness and it even occurs as a quasi-borrowing into Scots in the form The Achins. Examples of purely Gaelic names containing *achadh* are Achnacraig, Achnagoul, Achorn and Achadh Chairnleith.

Gaelic *baile*, 'a farm, homestead, village', also occurs but it is not so common as *achadh* and it is most frequently combined with a Gaelic specific, giving the appearance of being more recent in form. Perhaps there was no Norse generic which was close enough to Gaelic *baile* in conception and physical realisation to merit the regular retention of the placenames in which it occurred as specifics in subsequent Gaelic place-nomenclature. The name Balruddery in Latheron Parish does, however, suggest that, on occasion, *baile* could be combined with a Norse name in *ærgi*, 'a shieling', which does not quite fit into the range of reference normally associated with *baile*. The explanation may be that in some instances, the generic is not *baile* but another Gaelic term *buaile* 'a sheepfold' – a term which, like ON *kví*, has come into use as a habitative generic after initially referring specifically to an area of land which had been used for the penning of animals and which, having been fertilised, then became desirable ground for cultivation. Some attested examples of *baile* and *buaile* are as follows: Ballone, Ballachly; Buaile nan Gobhar and Buaile Oscar.

A further Gaelic generic which gives a practical demonstration of what may have happened in the case of *achadh* as it developed in meaning from 'field' to 'farm' is *bàrd*, 'a park or fenced area'. Sometimes, in Caithness placenames, *bàrd* means exactly that, but sometimes it now refers to the small croft which has been established on and around the original field. For example, in Reay Parish, Bàrd na Cailliche refers to the park which was used by an old woman and Bàrdnaheigh is a croft name which probably originates from the Caithness Gaelic version of the field where the horse(s) were penned. Once again one can see how significant the presence of animals must have been in determining the subsequent use of the land.

The bulk of Gaelic placenames describe topographical features and, because many of these are on the now deserted moorland, they have been particularly subject to loss, which is very regrettable. At least they are preserved on maps and the Gaelic-speaking hillwalker, rare though he or she is, can enjoy thinking about the life lived by people in previous centuries as it is encapsulated in the recorded placenames.

Finally, I shall turn briefly to Scots or Scottish English in Caithness. It is just as difficult to date the arrival of speakers of Scottish English as permanent inhabitants of Caithness as it is to date that of Gaelic-speakers, even though their arrival postdates the arrival of Gaelic-speakers by a couple of centuries. I have suggested a date *c.* AD 1400 but it could well have been a little earlier. Place-names containing Scots terms become common in written records from the latter part of the 16th century. It is often difficult to tell Scots and Norse placenames apart, given names such as Greenland or Langland in which both specifics and generic could happily derive from either source. Written records are, more often than not, inadequate and one simply has to admit that either is possible. In other instances, however, a recognisably Scots specific can determine that a name is most probably recent in origin, as in the case of Heathery Quoy – one of the *quoy*-names derived from the Caithness dialect version of ON *kví* which was mentioned earlier. The ease with which Scots and Norse placenames intermingle is, of course, due to the similarity of the languages both in terms of sound system and in terms of lexical content, but a similar intermingling of Scots and Gaelic can be observed in the placenames. The already cited example of The Achins is a case in point, and there are further similar constructions such as The Craggans (from G: *creag*, 'a rock'), The Tullach (G: *tulach*, 'a mound'), The Sian (G: *sìthean*, 'a fairy hillock'). In fact, one of the most interesting aspects of name study in Caithness is being able to observe at first-hand what happens to local placenames when one language is gradually fading from use and is being replaced by another.

Scots specifics and generics, both habitative and topographical, are scattered throughout Caithness and I often think that the generics, in particular, have a unifying effect on the placenames of the county as they attach to either Norse, Gaelic or Scots specific. For instance, the Scots terms *mains*, 'the chief farm on an estate', *croft*, 'a small agricultural landholding', *brig*, 'a bridge', *burn*, 'a stream' and *moss*, 'moorland', occur in the following compounds among many others: Borrowston Mains, Mains of Brims, Philip's Mains, Croft of Northfield, Crofts of Achimore, Brigs o'Auckingill, Achiegullan Burn, Burn o'Winless, The Blind Burn, Drumhollistan Moss, Drags Moss, Moss o'Quintfall. It is also, however, true to say that the bulk of the *mains*-farms have either Norse or Scots specifics, i.e. the Scots took over the better agricultural land in Caithness from the Scandinavians not from the Gaels, and it is likely that the Scots initially made their presence felt in territory held by Scandinavians along the east and north coasts.

Scots may now be in the ascendancy but it too is subject to the same type of name loss that we encountered in Gaelic placenames. I suppose the fact that names are dying is paradoxical proof that they are very much alive and are constantly changing to fit the needs of users. Older Scots names, particularly those referring to topographical features which are no longer significant in modern usage, have been forgotten but, on the positive side, new names are being created in response to the same impulse which spurred the Scandinavians, the Gaels and the Scots in previous centuries to put their own distinctive onomastic imprint on the landscape.

REFERENCES

Fellows-Jensen, Gillian. 1984. 'Viking Settlement in the Northern and Western Isles', in *The Northern and Western Isles in the Viking World*, eds Fenton, Alexander and Pálsson, Hermann, Edinburgh, pp. 148–68.
Marwick, Hugh. 1952. *Orkney Farm-Names*, Kirkwall.
Nicolaisen, W. F. H. 1976. *Scottish Place-Names*, London.
Nicolaisen, W. F. H. 1982. 'Scandinavians and Celts in Caithness: the Place-Name Evidence', in *Caithness. A Cultural Crossroads*, ed. Baldwin, John, Edinburgh, pp. 75–85.
Origines Parochiales Scotiae (OPS) 1855. The Antiquities Ecclesiastical and Territorial of the Parishes of Scotland. The Bannatyne Club, 2 vols, Edinburgh.
Paris, Matthew (*c.* 1250), in *The Early Maps of Scotland 1973*, ed. Moir, Donald G., 3rd edn, Edinburgh.
Register of the Great Seal (RMS) 1882–1914. Registrum Magni Sigilli Regum Scotorum, eds Thomson, J. M. *et al.*, Edinburgh.
Register of the Privy Seal (RSS) 1908–83. Registrum Secreti Sigilli Regum Scotorum, eds Livingstone, M. *et al.*, Edinburgh.
Sinclair Estate Papers, Catalogue no. GD96. Unpublished Mey Estate Papers, in Scottish Record Office, Edinburgh.
Stewart, John 1987. *Shetland Place-Names*, Lerwick.
Thorson, Per 1968. 'Ancient Thurso, A Religious and Judicial Centre', in *The Fifth Viking Congress: Tórshavn 1965*, ed. Niclasen, Bjarni, pp. 71–7.
Watson, William J. 1926. *The History of the Celtic Place-Names of Scotland*, Edinburgh.
Waugh, Doreen J. 1987. 'The Place-Names of Canisbay, Caithness', *Northern Scotland* vol. 7, no. 2, 99–111.

5

NORSE EARLS AND SCOTTISH BISHOPS IN CAITHNESS

A CLASH OF CULTURES

BARBARA E. CRAWFORD

The relationship of the early bishops and the earls of Caithness is of outstanding interest in European history. It is an important example of the tension between Church and State which underlies the whole development of medieval society. Despite the remoteness of the location from the centres of political power in Scotland and Norway, the impact of the Church and increasing episcopal authority were felt here as much as anywhere else – and with more dramatic results. The story is of particular interest for several reasons: it shows that the Norse communities of Scotland which had developed out of the viking raids and settlements of the 9th and 10th centuries were just as subject to ecclesiastical authority as anywhere else. But the violence of the process may reflect the unusual nature of the circumstances, in which Scottish bishops and Scottish kings moved into a political community where Norse ecclesiastical and secular customs were already established. The weaning of Caithness away from the Norse world and the incorporation of this territory into the Scottish kingdom was not easily or peacefully achieved (Crawford 1985, 25–6).

Caithness was and is both a maritime and a territorial unit. In the centuries of viking domination of the maritime waterways Caithness was drawn into the viking world – as were the western coasts of Scotland. But more so than in the west, Caithness became part of an offshore political unit and was tied to the Norse earldom of Orkney by easy maritime contact across the Pentland Firth. The Orkney earls' domination of both sides of this waterway gave them great power in the trading and raiding world of viking overlordship. This domination extended south to the Moray Firth and sometimes included areas of the western seaboard of Scotland as well. But Caithness was also a territorial unit: you do not actually need ships to organise society or the land in Caithness as you do in Orkney. Nor did the kings of Scots need ships in order to extend their authority in Scotland north of the Moray Firth. They could march their armies north, despite the distance, and from the end of the 12th century they did so. In 1200 the camp of the Scottish army of King William the Lion was said to stretch 'from one end of the valley to the other' at Ousedale on the Caithness-Sutherland border and that, added the saga-writer, is 'quite a distance' (*OS*, Pálsson & Edwards, 197–8).

From the late 11th century it was apparently recognised by the kings of Norway that Caithness was part of the Kingdom of Scotland although the earls of Orkney are certainly said to have done homage to the kings of Scots for their Caithness earldom before then (*ES*, i, 483, 542; ii, 112–13). Despite the difficulties involved in thus being the vassals of two overlords it never happened that the two parts of the joint earldom were separated and became the preserve of different branches of the earldom family, as one might imagine would have been the obvious development. Even though the kings of Scots tried to grant the earldom of Caithness to other members of the earldom family, this was strenuously resisted by the earls of Orkney. After periods of difficulty it is notable how the earls voluntarily emerged out of their secure base in the islands and travelled south to submit to the Scottish king – at Inverness or Perth – to do homage and pay large sums of money to win back their Scottish overlord's goodwill (Crawford 1985, 32). They evidently valued their Caithness earldom too much not to want to keep it and enjoy it in peace with the Scottish king's sanction, while the kings themselves were able to command larger resources and use these resources to tie their remote Norse vassals down with oaths of homage and financial dues.

This is, of course, a process which went on all over Europe in the formation of monarchies and the medieval state. The taming of semi-independent magnates by feudal methods of political control was never a peaceful business, but in Caithness it was particularly violent and unusually so in that one bishop was attacked and physically maimed and another was stoned and burned to death in his own manor house. Bishops who met violent ends in the 12th and 13th centuries are rather few and far between. Thomas à Becket was the most famous, but the stand he took against Henry II was unusually provocative. Were the men and earls of Caithness similarly provoked by Bishops John and Adam? What was the provocation which resulted in these violent attacks? It seems to have been the process of implementing Scottish policies and Scottish ecclesiastical usage in an area where church structures had already been developed according to Norse patterns of Christian society (Crawford 1985, 28–30).

The land of the Picts in the province of Cat was conquered by the earls of Orkney entirely by their own efforts and without any assistance from the kings of Scotland. They could claim that they owed no obligation to anyone for their Scottish possessions. They would like to have claimed the same for their island earldom, but the tradition that they owed their position to a grant by Harald Finehair kept being repeated (whether correctly or not is still a matter of debate). In the case of Caithness, however, the earls moved across the Firth from their island base in the 9th century and by force of arms dominated as much territory as their manpower permitted. The kings of Scots at this point were far away in the south consolidating their own power across the Lowlands from their base in

Argyll. The earls' struggle was primarily with native Celtic chieftains and particularly with the rulers of the province of Moray (*mormaers* in Scottish terminology and *rí*, or King, in Irish). The two famous Viking warriors Thorstein the Red and Earl Sigurd Eysteinsson *hinn ríki* (the Mighty) conquered 'half Scotland' and Sigurd was buried in a howe on the banks of the River Oykell in the late 9th century (*ES*, i, 370–2; Crawford 1987, 57–8). But the process of conquest was not completed until the reign of Earl Thorfinn Sigurdsson who, we are told in *Orkneyinga saga*, 'turned his mind to the government of his land and people, and to the making of laws' (*OS*, Anderson, 189). This suggests that in the latter part of his rule Earl Thorfinn started to establish regular governmental administrative structures in Orkney (Crawford 1987, 83). If he did, then we can assume that these would have been imposed similarly by him in Caithness also. These administrative structures would eventually lead to the levying of tribute or tax (*skattr*), and the appointment of officials to collect such renders and deliver them to the earls' treasury. The question as to how such policies were refined into the creation of tax districts and a fiscal assessment system is one which is currently under discussion (Lindquist 1991, Andersen 1991). Basic to this development was the ruler's ability to defend his territory and dominate any subject peoples by maintaining an armed force (or in the earls' case a naval levy).

A particularly important aspect of Thorfinn's reign was the creation of a bishopric, that is, the erection of ecclesiastical structures for establishing the Christian religion on an organised footing, and particularly the appointment of bishops by the earl. As we know from *Orkneyinga saga* the first bishop's seat was established by Thorfinn at Birsay in close assocation with the earldom (*OS*, ch. 31). This marks a development from the previous situation where bishops had travelled round with the earls as court chaplains and remained very dependent on the secular power with no possessions of their own (Crawford 1983, 100–1). The bishop's Christ-Church in Birsay was still closely linked to the earl's seat of power but at least it was a fixed centre from which episcopal government could begin to function. Some measure of financial independence would probably be accorded at the same time with endowments of land by the earls.

Although the sparse information that we have about this process concerns Orkney, it is certain that similar developments would have taken place in Caithness (Crawford 1985, 27). As part of the earl's domain, Caithness would have come under the bishop of Orkney's authority, which also probably extended as far south as the River Oykell and the Dornoch Firth. The later evidence, of estates which the bishops of *Orkney* continued to hold in Caithness and of taxes which they continued to levy there, points to the conclusion that these were original endowments retained by the island bishops after the Scottish kings began to appoint their own bishops in Caithness in the mid-12th century. The lands in question are in the central part of Caithness in the parishes of Reay, Halkirk, and Bower; with the right to 'skatts' from Dunnet and Canisbay. There seems no other valid explanation as to why 16th-century bishops of Orkney should possess estates and have financial rights in another bishopric – a highly unusual situation.[1]

If this is the reason why these estates are in the possession of the bishops of Orkney then we can use this information as evidence for the extent of their endowment in Caithness at the time when Scottish bishops are first appointed to Caithness (mid-12th century). These lands and rights must have been given to the bishops of Orkney by the earl, and probably in the century prior to 1150 when the original endowment of the bishopric was established. Furthermore, a 16th century rental of the bishop of Orkney's lands in Caithness itemises the amount of 'skat malt' and 'skat silver' paid to the bishops by the parishes of Dunnet and Canisbay (NLS, Adv. MS49.7.19 [iv]). These may have been originally earldom 'skatts' which had *also* been granted to the bishops of Orkney by the earl at a date prior to 1150. If so, then the deduction one appears able to make is that the system of payments of 'skatt' by the farmers to the earls was already in place before the mid-12th century. This conclusion is entirely in accordance with current thinking about the taxation structure of the Orkney earldom and the establishment of the ounceland system, although the earliest direct evidence for the 'skatt' system is the late 15th-century Orkney Rentals. The fact that the Orkney bishops had lands and 'skatts' in Caithness appears to offer some proof that the system was in existence by 1150.

THE POSITION OF HALKIRK[2]

As well as being endowed with lands in Caithness the 11th-century bishops would also have a church built for them to be their 'seat' *(biskups-stóll)* in the earldom. If this was situated near one of the earl's own residences – as in Orkney – then it could have been at either Thurso, where the earls later had a castle; or Murkle, where they resided in the 13th century; or Duncansby, Thorfinn's favourite place of residence; or Brawl in upper Thursodale, an important earldom centre later. Is there any evidence for early churches at these earldom residences? Certainly Thurso became a very important centre and St Peter's (the parish Kirk) in the heart of the old town has recently been re-assessed as having an early 12th-century core (Gordon-Slade 1989, 307–9). Rune stones have been found here too which are rare finds anywhere else in Caithness. Moreover the bishops had a fortified residence at Scrabster, some two miles west of Thurso, first recorded in 1201 when Bishop John was attacked there by Earl Harald Maddadson. There is also a parish church at Halkirk, near to the earl's castle at Brawl although on the opposite bank of the Thurso River. Its name is first recorded as the place where Bishop Adam was murdered in 1222 while residing at his episcopal manor (*OS*, Anderson, 200–1). The original Old Norse form of the name (*Há-kirkja*) is always translated as 'high' church, meaning specially elevated (in a political sense) (Crawford 1991, 30). It is assumed that this name must stem from its association with the bishops. The fact that the name is Old Norse strongly suggests that it dates from the period prior to the Scottish bishops, i.e. before the mid-12th century. If so, its name points to it being the main church of the bishops of Orkney in Caithness, presumably having been built for them by the earl near to his estate at Brawl.

The impression that the church at Halkirk was exceptional is strengthened by the evidence that it was *not* originally a parish church, although it became one after Bishop Gilbert moved the chief diocesan seat to Sutherland in the years following Bishop Adam's murder. When Bishop Gilbert founded the constitution for his new Cathedral at Dornoch twenty parishes are listed in the diocese, and Halkirk was *not* among them.[3] However it *is* named as a parish – with a vicar – in Bagimont's Roll of Crusading tithes uplifted in 1275 *(CSR, no. 16)*. Thus we can tell that it became a parish in the period after the move of the Cathedral to Dornoch and must have been carved out of the existing parish of Skinnet. The fact that the two churches – Skinnet and Halkirk – are only $1\frac{1}{2}$ miles apart points to an unusual situation, and indeed by 1500 they had become a joint vicarage called the 'common churches of Caithness diocese' *(RSS*, i, no. 607). Skinnet is certainly an ancient church site for a 9th-century cross slab has been found there (Beaton 1909, 31–3; Romilly Allen & Anderson 1903, 31). When the Melrose Chronicle tells us that Bishop Adam was first interred before the altar in the baptismal church (prior to his translation to the Cathedral in 1239) it would have been Skinnet Church that was used (*ES*, ii, 450, 516).[4] At that time whatever church or chapel existed at Halkirk must have been extra-parochial and built for the bishop's own use on his estate. But, as said, the name strongly indicates a church of high status, and this may point to its use as a proto-Cathedral in the embryonic days of the new bishopric. The situation would therefore not be dissimilar to that at Birsay where the possible bishop's church (on the Brough) and parish church (in the village) are about the same distance apart. In the Foundation Charter for his new Cathedral Constitution Bishop Gilbert refers to the cathedral church prior to his time as having been served by only one priest, and explains his decision to build a new cathedral because of the poverty of the location and the frequent hostilities (*tum propter loci paupertatem tam propter frequentem hostilitatem*: *CSR*, 14). There has been some doubt as to which church was being referred to by him but the latter description must surely indicate either Skinnet or Halkirk rather than any previous church in Dornoch itself. The balance of probability is that it was Halkirk that was meant.

The name of Halkirk is therefore a relic of a pre-Scottish phase in the Christian Church in the north. It is a stranded name which gives us a hint of the Norse past in Caithness, a relic of a system which did not survive. We know little of this Norse system of church organisation but it may have been pre-parochial. The first historical evidence we have is all of a Scottish system and of the organisational abilities of a Scottish bishop who drew up a constitution for his new Cathedral in Dornoch in which the parishes are closely tied in to the

Cathedral financial and administrative arrangements. As I have pointed out elsewhere (Crawford 1985, 30) this was all very much part and parcel of the Scottish crown's establishment of feudal methods of government in the north and their use of loyal vassals – the de Moravias – to carry out their work for them. As archdeacon of Moray, Gilbert had been given a grant of frontier territory in Sutherland by his relative Hugh de Moravia. As Bishop he undoubtedly received more land for the endowment of his new Cathedral from the newly created earl of Sutherland, William de Moravia. Sutherland was the new growth point of secular and ecclesiastical power structures; and the earl of Caithness lost out badly in this process. However this was the end result of a very turbulent period which we have not yet considered. The disputes between earls and bishops in the later 12th century and first half of the 13th century were a result of the clash of cultures and the attempts by Bishops John and Adam to enforce their authority in the face of existing ecclesiastical custom in Caithness – a process which probably also threatened the authority of the earls in their Scottish dominions (Crawford 1974, 21; 1985, 28). This situation developed out of the growing power of the Scottish monarchy and the development of the Church as an independent institution in the 12th century.

PAPAL ANATHEMA AND ROYAL RETRIBUTION

Throughout Europe the Christian Church became institutionalised and developed a complex hierarchy culminating in the headship of the Pope at Rome. In the different countries its organisation became standardised and the resources of the church were developed, so that it was able to distance itself from kings and princes instead of needing their constant support and protection. There were notable clashes between Church and State in many parts of Europe. The anathema of the Church could be a source of weakness to rulers whose position was threatened. But it could also be a useful tool to rivals and a source of strength to kings dealing with recalcitrant nobles, and in the expansion of royal power. We see these factors coming into play in the story of the earls and bishops in Caithness.

The first of the two attacks on the Caithness bishops was that led by Earl Harald Maddadson against John in the bishop's castle at Scrabster in the year 1201 (*OS*, ch. 111). This was the culmination of a very tense relationship between bishop and earl which had clearly developed earlier; one of the flashpoints between them had been the dispute over the payment of one penny from every inhabited house in Caithness which the earl had made to the benefit of the church in Rome in the time of the first Scottish bishop of Caithness, Andrew (a payment modelled on the due normally known as Peter's Pence in England and recently instituted in Norway) (Crawford 1974, 17–18). Perhaps because of the Scandinavian nature of this due, perhaps because he himself had no income from his bishopric, Bishop John had forbidden the payment of this due 'by those who were appointed by him in his diocese', as a result of which the earl had complained to the papacy. One of Innocent III's very first letters was that written to the bishops of Orkney and Ross ordering them to compel John to allow this payment to continue (*CSR*, no. 3; *CPL*, i, p. 1; *DN*, vii, no. 2; *Inn. III*, no. 218). The clash between earl and bishop had therefore reached the ears of the head of the church a few years prior to the culmination of the quarrel in a physical attack on the bishop in his castle of Scrabster. This resulted in another letter being sent by Innocent III to the Bishop of Orkney detailing the penance to be laid on one of the Earl's followers, Lumberd, for having been involved in the outrage, and the individual responsible for cutting out the bishop's tongue (*CSR*, no. 4; *CPL*, i, 24; *DN*, vii, no. 3). Poor Lumberd seems to have become a useful scapegoat for he had already gone to Rome and was given the papal letter to take back to Bishop Bjarne of Orkney. On his return he had to walk naked and barefoot – except for breeches and a short and sleeveless woollen vest – throughout the countryside where the Bishop had been mutilated and in the surrounding region, for 15 days 'with his tongue tied with a thin cord and pulled out beyond his lips and the cord tied round his neck' (*lingua subtili funiculo religata, et paulisper extracta, ut promineat extra labia summitatibus eiusdem funiculi nexis in collo*). He had to carry rods in his hand and when he came to a church to be disciplined (whipped?), he had to lie on the ground, remain in silence, and fast until the evening, when he could partake of bread and water.

Nor was that all. Within a month of the above ordeal Lumberd had to leave for Jerusalem and spend three years there 'sweating in the service of the Cross' (despite the fact that Jerusalem had fallen again to the infidel in 1190): for 11 years he had to fast every sixth day on bread and water unless a priest gave him indulgence because of bodily infirmity or summer heat. Quite apart from the fascinating details which the Church thought up for a punishment to suit the crime, this letter is remarkable evidence for the concern of the head of the Church for events which had occurred on the northernmost fringes of Europe. It takes some effort of historical perspective to realise that a minor expedition of the earl of Orkney on the coast of Caithness in 1201 resulted in a letter being written by Pope Innocent III in August-September 1202 ordering the Bishop of Orkney to see that the above penance was carried out. Innocent III was of course a remarkable pope and one determined to govern the whole church in Europe as a world empire. This letter gives evidence of his energy and organisational ability. Both these letters concerning the situation in Caithness are among the first letters in the register of papal archives which begins about this date. Nor can we doubt that the directive would to some extent have been fulfilled, although the Church's methods of compulsion were purely spiritual unless it was able to employ the secular powers. In this instance it probably had a willing accomplice in Earl Harald, who apparently escaped any direct retribution by diverting blame to his follower Lumberd. Nonetheless Harald had already gone south to Perth in the spring of 1202 under safe-conduct of Bishop Roger of St Andrews through whose intercession he came to terms with King William, 'swearing that in all things he would stand by the judgment of the Church' (*ES*, ii, 356, quoting Fordun; Crawford 1985, 32). Apart from the fine of £2,000 which he paid to the Scottish king, Earl Harald would undoubtedly have had to make compensation to the Church also.

On this occasion, as on others, the Scottish king benefited from the Church's determination to punish violence against its members. William the Lion had been the first Scottish king to send an army as far north as Caithness in the 1190s after Earl Harald had been involved in attacking the king's vassals near Inverness in an attempt to protect his southern frontier against Scottish encroachment (Crawford 1985, 31). William had been preparing another expedition when Earl Harald submitted in 1202. The opportunity arose again after the men of Caithness attacked the next bishop (Adam) because of their antagonism to the increased tithes which this bishop attempted to collect. Here again we seem to have changes being made to traditional church payments which were no doubt seen as being the result of the imposition of Scottish custom by Scottish personnel (Crawford 1985, 28). This led to the second attack on a Caithness bishop – by the local farmers primarily, although the earl (son of Earl Harald) was closely implicated in the crime and blamed for not having done more to prevent it (*Scotichron*, 5, 115). After the burning of Bishop Adam in his manor-house at Halkirk in 1222 King Alexander mounted an expedition north and Earl John Haraldson submitted, resigning half his earldom to the king and bestowing lands and money on the Church. Another papal letter, of Honorius III, addressed to the Bishops of St Andrews, Glasgow, Dunkeld and Dunblane spills much ink on praising the king for his prompt action in preparing a retaliatory expedition to punish the perpetrators. It makes no mention of the horrible retribution imposed by Alexander on the Caithness farmers, but orders their lands to be placed under strict ecclesiastical interdict, to last until suitable satisfaction had been given (Theiner 1864, no. 49; *CSR*, no. 10). Details of the retribution were however widely known. The Icelandic Annals record that 80 men who had been present had a hand and a foot cut off, and many of them died (Storm 1888, 126). The fragmentary Annals of Duisk (a Cistercian Abbey in Ireland) record the burning of their bishop by the Caithness men, who were killed by the king of Scots and their sons castrated while their wives were thrown out – perhaps a conclusion drawn from the known confiscation of the perpetrators' lands (Nicholls 1983, 96). 'The punishments inflicted by him [King Alexander] for the burning of the Bishop, by mutilation and death, confiscation and outlawry from the land, are still in fresh memory' wrote the Icelandic saga writer some decades later (*OS*, Anderson, 201).

The violence of these clashes certainly gives the impression that the earls of Orkney-Caithness were anti-clerical and resentful of ecclesiastical authority and particularly of increased church taxes. Yet we have the remarkable evidence of the piety of the earlier 12th-century earls who built and endowed St Magnus Cathedral to the honour of a murdered member of the earldom family. Harald

Maddadson was not descended from that side of the earldom house, but we have evidence of his piety also and of his generosity to other ecclesiastical foundations – his grant of an annual mark of silver to the canons of Scone (*DN*, ii, no. 2), his protection of the convent of 'Bencoryn' (?Bangor, Co. Down) (*APS*, i, 116), as well as his organisation of the payment of Peter's Pence from Caithness to the Papacy (Crawford 1974, 18). The earl's relationship with Bjarne Kolbeinsson (bishop of Orkney, 1188–1223) was entirely amicable as far as is known, and Harald benefited from Bjarne's intercession with King Sverre on his behalf after the 'Eyskjeggar' rising in 1193. Bjarne was however his second cousin and undoubtedly put in office by the earl who considered it his privilege to choose his local bishop. It was when this control was threatened by the appointment of Scottish clerics over whom the earl would be able to exercise little influence in his Caithness earldom that the piety turned to resentment and devout Christians became vengeful anti-clerics. The first and third Caithness bishops, Andrew and Adam, were monks (Benedictine and Cistercian) and undoubtedly dedicated to maintaining their episcopal authority free of secular interference. Bishop Andrew was also a constant attender at the court of Malcolm II and William I and a close royal adviser (Crawford 1991, 31–2). There is no evidence of his presence in Caithness and much evidence that he was actively involved elsewhere; he was, however, in contact with Earl Harald over the grant of Peter's Pence from Caithness which he is said to have sanctioned.

PETER'S PENCE AND PENNYLANDS: AN EXCURSUS

When Earl Harald procured the agreement of Bishop Andrew and the leading landowners in Caithness to the anual payment of *denarium de qualibet domo in comitatu catenensi habitata* to the church of Rome, he was instituting a tax which had to be collected and transmitted overseas in an annual administrative process – just as Peter's Pence had also from England and the Scandinavian countries. It is well-known that the ancient tax of one penny paid to the papacy from every household in England annually was extended to Scandinavia in the 11th and 12th centuries (*KHLNM* sub 'Peterspenge'; Crawford 1974, 17–18). In the case of Norway it was imposed by the English Cardinal, Nicholas Breakspear, when he erected the diocese of Trondheim into an archbishopric in 1152–3 (Helle 1964, 30–1). Included in this were the bishoprics of the Norwegian settlements overseas, and in the first papal taxation record of *c.* 1192 it is said that one penny was paid *by every house* yearly in the Norwegian dioceses and in Orkney and Sodor (*Reg. Norv.* I, 223). What constituted a household? Considering the early date for this papal imposition it is of some interest to know how such a wide-ranging demand was put into effect, and how each 'house' was assessed.

As Peter's Pence was never paid in Scotland (Crawford 1974, 15), we have to look to England where the tax was long established and there was evidently a property qualification, at least by the late 11th century. The *Leis Willelmi* say that a man had to have livestock to the value of thirty pence before being obliged to pay Peter's Pence, and a lord's payment exempted his workmen (Jensen 1901, 17). A burgess had to possess property worth $\frac{1}{2}$ mark and a free man in the Danelaw had to have livestock worth $\frac{1}{2}$ mark. Similarly in Norwegian laws there is mention of a property qualification of possessions worth 3 marks above a man or woman's usual weapons and clothes (*KHLNM* sub 'Peterspenge'), and it would appear that such a man or woman must also have been head of a household, as the payment is clearly said to be paid on a household basis in the papal taxation record (Steinnes 1942, 145). In Sweden it was paid by every independent household and ownership of land constituted tax liability (*KHLNM* sub 'Peterspenge'). Evidently this payment was only levied on the wealthier sections of society and possession of land must have been the usual qualification. This seems to make it a property tax rather than primarily a personal tax.

When this due was imposed in the Northern and Western Isles it is likely that the church would have made use of existing administrative structures – as Earl Harald would also for the collection of his penny in Caithness. Such structures at this date were probably based on divisions which had been imposed over the islands and the northern and western parts of the Scottish Mainland during the period of rule of Earl Thorfinn (as discussed earlier, see p. 131) and refined since then. The ounceland/*tirunga* unit was rather large and must have been sub-divided for convenience in the process of developing assessment units for the collection of dues. *When* the ounceland was sub-divided into pennylands (which signified that the penny had come into use as a monetary unit in contrast to the ounce as a unit of weight) is a very difficult question to answer. In the west, earlier household divisions of 20 may have been utilised by the Norse earls, or local kings, for the Hebridean ounceland was divided into 20 units, and this may represent a continuation of a pre-Norse Dalriadic administrative structure. What the division into 18 which prevailed in the Northern Isles was derived from has not been established, but it seems likely that it would have related to a 'household' structure as well. It has been said of the situation in the Orkneys that 'it would probably not be very wide of the mark to think of the pennyland as corresponding to a typical agricultural holding or household unit' (Thomson 1987a, 25); the number of pennylands in the Orkneys (3,670) corresponded nearly enough with the number of farms and agricultural holdings at the height of the 19th century population growth (3,376), so that one can regard the Orkney pennyland as 'more or less equivalent to a small household unit' (Thomson 1987b, 116).

In enquiring into the origin of such units we are coming close to the basic matter of medieval exploitation of agricultural resources. We should not assume that the imposition of land assessments in the Scandinavian parts of Scotland was so very different from elsewhere. The division of agricultural resources into units large enough to sustain the extended family or 'household' are basic to western European society. We have only to refer to Bede's *terra unius familiae* (or the 'hide' as it was called in Anglo-Saxon) to find a common denominator, but the term varied in the different parts of northern Europe. The single-family farm in the Carolingian world was called the *mansus* (Herlihy 1960, 83) and indeed the latin word for the hide was *mansus*. The equivalent to the hide in the north of England was the 'carucate' which is generally assumed to be Anglo-Danish in origin (Harvey 1985, 92). This term translates OE *plogesland*, 'ploughland', which is an anglicisation of ON *plógsland* (Charles-Edwards 1972, 14). (Another term in Doomsday Book, the 'ploughland', has recently been interpreted as an assessment term for the whole agricultural potential of an estate (Harvey 1985, 92) and applied throughout Doomsday England in 1086.) Then there is the famous problem of the Doomsday 'manor' (*manerium*) long ago described as 'a house against which geld is charged' – a technical meaning which has recently been reinforced with a slight shift of emphasis to 'a house at which geld is collected' (Palmer 1987, 153). According to the political history of a region or a kingdom there was frequent need to re-assess the potential of estates for fiscal purposes, but the basis of that assessment was usually (?always) the social unit of the family holding whether called the 'household', *domus*, *mansus* or *manerium*. Once established this unit had a permanency in the landscape which governments constantly found useful for the assessment and collection of taxes and renders.[5]

If we can see the pennyland in this light, as the equivalent in Scandinavian Scotland of the hide in England, with a household/manorial centre against which the 'penny' or other levies could be collected in, the question then arises as to *when* the use of the penny coin is likely to have been so customary in the Northern and Western Isles and the neighbouring Mainland territories that it gave its name to the unit concerned. The first recorded incidence of the term 'pennyland' is in Shetland in 1299 (*DN*, I, no. 89).[6] Significantly, the *Orkneyinga saga* tells us that the term ploughland (*plógsland*) was apparently used in Orkney (as well as in northern England.) This is the name given to the unit of land on which a mark was laid by Earl Rognvald when he was seeking funds for the building of St Magnus' Cathedral in the mid-12th century (*OS*, ch. 76; *KHLNM* sub 'Plogland'). It is the only time that the term is ever used in the sources for a land division in Orkney, and as a result there has been an attempt to explain it as a misreading by a scribe for the name 'pennyland' (Andersen 1988, 65). However, we should not brush the ploughland on one side but face the fact that it may indeed have been the name of an Orkney assessment unit, at the time of the building of the cathedral in the 1140s which was later superseded by the term 'pennyland'. The building of St Magnus' has been shown to have close links with northern England (Crawford 1988, *passim*) so that influence in terminology from the same direction would not be too surprising.

Perhaps a change of name then took place as a result of the imposition of Peter's pence on the Norwegian dioceses by Cardinal Nicholas in 1153. Did the local clergy in Orkney use the already existing ploughland units for their new assessment purposes and did this give rise to the term 'pennyland'? It has been suggested before that the penny levy was connected with grants to the Church.[7] This is not unlikely given the growth in church taxation in the 12th century, and the imposition of Peter's Pence *could* provide an explanation for the use of the term 'pennyland'. This theory could, moreover, also help to provide an explanation for the occurrence of the pennyland unit in most of the Scandinavian offshore settlements around the Scottish coasts – all of which came under the authority of the archdiocese of Trondheim. As noted already the annual penny was theoretically paid to the papal see by every house in the diocese of Sodor (Man and the Hebrides). Should we in fact look to a church imposition rather than an earldom tax for the origin of the term 'pennyland' in both Northern and Western Scotland?

In the west the 'household' unit which is recorded as being in existence in Argyll in the pre-Viking age and which may have persisted through the Norse settlement period, was likely to be the basis for the collection of the new papal tax. In general it looks as if the Hebridean pennyland is much larger than the Orkney pennyland which may relate to the fertility of the land and the size of the population, although the situation regarding pennylands in the west is not at all straightforward.[8] In the first place the known incidence of pennylands does not correspond exactly to the boundaries of the archdiocese of Trondheim (Crawford 1987, Fig. 24). They are very notably absent from the Isle of Man where the 'treen' ($=tirunga$ or ounceland) was divided into four quarters and the quarterland farm 'varying in size from about thirty acres to about 100 acres, has been the normal farm unit of the island since the Middle Ages' (Megaw 1956, 153). They also appear to be absent from Islay, Colonsay, Jura and Gigha and here again the term 'quarterland' is used (as well as 'ploughland' in Islay) (Lamont 1966, 6). They *do* occur, moreover, in mainland Argyll, in SW Scotland – particularly in Galloway – as well as in Caithness. This distribution picture presents us with a problem in our efforts to understand the origins of this assessment unit.[9]

When considering the existence of pennylands along the western Mainland of Scotland and in the north Mainland we have to appreciate the reality of the political situation, which was that the Lords of the Isles and the earls of Orkney both held territory on the Scottish Mainland as vassals of the Scottish kings. In the 12th century the latter were trying to bring the north Mainland under their own direct authority, and we have seen the problems that ensued when they installed bishops in Caithness. This was happening at just the time when Peter's Pence was being imposed over the Norwegian dioceses. We can imagine that the bishop of Orkney might have attempted to impose Peter's pence in the Caithness half of the diocese, but that the attempt was thwarted by the new Scottish bishop, for Peter's pence was not paid from Scotland. We know of course that Earl Harald organised the payment of a very similar due from his

Caithness earldom, and can guess that this may have been as a direct result of the refusal of Bishop Andrew to allow the Norwegian tax payment. But the bishop could not refuse to allow the earl to organise a very similar alms payment to Rome himself and he is specifically said to have given his permission – although his successor Bishop John attempted to prevent it being paid by some of his own appointees. If in general the annual levy went ahead (which seems likely given the papal letter ordering the two bishops to see that it did) this could explain the usage of the term 'pennyland' in the diocese of Caithness, just as in Orkney.

In the Hebrides the imposition of Peter's pence coincided with the upheaval in the kingdom of Man when Somerled forced a partition of the kingdom and set up his own independent lordship in the southern Hebrides and the mainland territory of Argyll (Duncan & Brown 1957, 195). The secular lords concerned with this papal due were therefore the kings of Man who still dominated the northern Outer Hebrides, and Somerled's dynasty in the Inner Hebrides. As with Earl Harald in the north, these lords also ruled part of the adjacent Scottish Mainland, where the authority of the archbishop of Trondheim could not be exercised and Peter's pence would never have been levied. Yet we find pennylands in these coastal areas. For those areas coming under Somerled's lordship an explanation exists; there has survived the record of Reginald, son of Somerled, making an annual grant of one penny from every house 'from which smoke emitted' *totius terre sue* to the monastic foundation at Paisley (*c.* 1200) (*Paisley Reg.* 125). If this was to apply throughout his lands then it could have given rise to the name pennyland (or *peighinn* as it is in Gaelic) for the household unit on his Mainland estates. The phrasing of the grant certainly indicates knowledge of Peter's Pence and an imitation of that papal tax as he may have known it in the Isles. It is in general not at all clear exactly how extensive Reginald's 'terra' was, although in the charter mentioned above he calls himself King of the Isles, lord of Argyll and Kintyre. Certainly the sons of Somerled ruled from Glenelg to the Mull of Kintyre (Duncan & Brown 1957, 198; Barrow 1981, 109) – which corresponds closely to the west coast distribution of pennylands. They occur also in Cowal, which came within the traditional bounds of Argyll and belonged to the diocese of Argyll which was created about this same date as a territorial bishopric based on Somerled's lordship. As a Scottish bishopric it would not be likely to endorse payments of Peter's Pence, although probably supportive of Reginald's grant to the monks of Paisley.

North of Somerled's lordship pennylands are absent (although Ouncelands do occur). This most probably relates to the change of lordship and the fact that the Argyll of Moray (Wester Ross) was by the mid-12th century under the control of the McHeth family, and probably part of the bishopric of Ross (which it certainly was at a slightly later date). These were both powerful administrative units established with the support of the Scottish kings and this may help to explain the absence of pennylands, or any penny grant to the church. In the eastern part of Ross, similarly, pennylands do not occur and the southern-most limit of the unit here is the Dornoch Firth and the River Oykell, the ancient southern frontier of the Norse earls' area of influence.

If we turn to the kingdom of Man, which from the mid-12th century had been much reduced in extent by the growth of the house of Somerled, it appears that the kings found themselves left with control only of the Isle of Man and Lewis and Skye in the northern Hebrides. As already noted there is a total absence of pennylands from Man itself and an apparent near absence from Lewis, with a limited distribution in Skye (Easson 1987, Fig. 1). Historical evidence about the payment of Peter's pence from the Hebrides is entirely non-conclusive. Details of payment of Peter's pence from the whole of Norway, presumably including the *skattland*s (i.e. the dioceses in the islands off Scotland and in the north Atlantic) exist in a letter of 1321 but never for *skattland*s alone (Steinnes 1942, 159). It was certainly paid from Orkney as there are complaints about its non-payment in the 14th century. But was it *ever* paid from the Kingdom of Man and the Isles? The nearest we can get to any indication on that point is a letter of Innocent III's written to Reginald of Man (son of Godred) in 1200-1 'concerning the payment of Peter's Pence' (*Reg. Norv.* I, A24). This comes from a volume containing a list of rubrics of letters only, and the letters themselves do not survive so we will never know what Innocent III had to say on the matter of the payment of Peter's Pence from Reginald's kingdom. However, it was rather unusual for letters to be written to secular rulers about this papal tax and a strong presumption might be that a letter was required because of its non-payment. A few years later Innocent III also wrote to the Archbishop of Trondheim concerning its non-payment in his province, referring to *eos qui tibi super hoc presumpserit contraire* and giving weight to the ecclesiastical censure which the archbishop *in detentores census illius rationabiliter promulgaverit* (*DN*, vii, no. 6). But there is no evidence to link this non-payment with any particular part of the church province. It could of course be postulated that the private grant of one penny from every house in his lands made by Reginald, son of Somerled *c.* 1200, was made *because* of the failure to collect Peter's pence in the Hebrides by the archbishop of Trondheim; that in fact the papal tax was replaced by the secular lord's own grant – much as we have seen it was in Caithness. This would resolve the difficulty of an apparent double annual imposition of the penny tax being borne by the household units in the islands. They surely only paid one penny – the one that went to the monastic foundation at Paisley.

A church exaction assessed in the same way as Peter's pence was apparently collected in the Isle of Man in the 14th century. The evidence for this comes from the Bishops' List at the end of the *Chronicle of the Kings of Man* where it is recorded that after a papal interdict had been imposed on the islanders they had to pay one penny from every house from which smoke emitted (*dederunt ei de qualibet domo fumigante unum denarium*) in order for the interdict to be removed. This continued to be paid on the occasion when each successive bishop came to them from the islands (*Chron. Man.* f. 51r). It is very interesting that the same phrase was used for this ecclesiastical fine as was used for Reginald's grant of a century earlier, and that a household assessment was the basis for it. However, it was not an annual payment, but must have been a very occasional one, and so would be unlikely to have the effect of imprinting the name of 'pennyland' on the household unit used (probably the quarterland). One suspects that Peter's pence was never instituted in the Isle of Man, and that the above fine was the nearest thing that the church managed to get to such an imposition. This leaves the question of the northern Hebrides very much an open one, requiring further analysis of land assessment units in the islands before any firm conclusions can be drawn.

In conclusion it can be said that the payment of Peter's pence did make its mark in the Norwegian settlements around the Scottish Coasts in the 12th Century, although only in Orkney is there evidence that it was established as a regular due paid to the archiepiscopal see. In both Caithness and Argyll similar payments were instituted by the Earl of Orkney and the Lord of the Isles, using the same household assessment. In Man the household unit was also used for an occasional church due imposed by the papacy itself a century later. The use made in all these areas of a house unit points to a similar household assessment system and it is suggested that in Orkney and Caithness and some parts of the West this may have formed the circumstances in which the name pennyland was adopted for the taxable unit. The most positive indicator to come out of this preliminary investigation is that questions of landlordship and the control exercised by the earls and kings and Lords of the Isles over their dominions is undoubtedly a very significant factor in the distribution of pennylands and the most likely explanation for them. Whether the suggestion that the name can be linked with the imposition of Peter's pence – or imitations of it – will be upheld by further lines of enquiry into the problem remains to be seen. It is hoped that this preliminary discussion of the origin of the name 'pennyland' will serve to stimulate further study into its distribution and help to provide a definitive explanation for it.

Notes

1. The explanation given for these holdings by Bishop Graham in 1624 was that they were 'serving for the bishop's sojourning there when stayed at the Pentland Firth' (Peterkin 1820, 22) and those in the parish of Halkirk 'for service in convoyeing thame throw ye cuntrie of Caithnes' (*Ibid.* 24). But the scattered nature of the lands does not support such an explanation for the original possession. Nor does the grant of earldom skatts from the parishes of Dunnet and Canisbay suggest that these rights were given originally to enable the bishop of one diocese to travel through a neighbouring diocese.

2. It has not been possible to trace another 'Halkirk' in either Norway or the British Isles. The nearest I have found is Harkirk in Lancashire (Crosby parish) although the

specific first element there seems likely to derive from OE *hār*=grey, possibly meaning a boundary marker. (Harkirk nonetheless does lie in a parish which is full of Norse names.) The problem of the origin of this Lancashire name is compounded by the uncertainty of the nature of the 'kirk' site, for there is no actual evidence that it was a medieval church site even though a chapel and graveyard was constructed there in the 17th century by the local recusant family, the Blundells. This very fact does however suggest to me that the site would have been chosen because of earlier ecclesiastical associations – which are also indicated by the find of an early 10th-century Norse coin hoard, a frequent component of graveyards (Blackburn & Pagan 1989, 295). If Harkirk *was* an early church site it was pre- or extra-parochial but our lack of evidence for the status of the church or chapel does not allow us to postulate any parallel with the Caithness Halkirk. (I would like to acknowledge the help given by Doreen Waugh and Margaret Gelling in my attempts to establish the significance of the names Halkirk and Harkirk.)

3. In the foundation charter as it has survived 14 parishes assigned to the Cathedral prebends are listed by name: Clyne, Creich, Rogart, Lairg, Farr, Bower, Watten, Kildonan, Olrig, Dunnet, Canisbay, Skinnet, Durness and Dornoch. The six parishes reserved by the bishop for his own use are not listed (*CSR*, no. 9). However, in the papal bull of confirmation issued by Gregory IX in 1238 these are given as Kilmalie, Loth, Latheron, Wick, Thurso and Reay (*Registres de Gregoire IX*, 1069). This bull also makes clear, as Professor D. E. R. Watt has pointed out to me, that the bishop was patron of all the parish churches in his diocese, which is most unusual. One can only speculate that this may have been a result of Bishop Gilbert's reorganisation. It seems unlikely that the earls would have exercised no powers of patronage over churches in Caithness prior to this reorganisation. Would such a change have taken place with or without the earl's concurrence?

4. Calder (1887, 82) asserts that Adam's 'remains were disinterred from the common burying ground in Halkirk and removed to a more honourable sepulture in the cathedral church'. The Melrose Chronicle says, however, that the bishop had been 'committed to honourable burial, as was fitting, beside the holy altar in the baptismal church'. As Halkirk was not a parish church at this date it would never be described as 'the baptismal church'.

5. Bannerman, in discussing the house groupings of Dal Riata in his study of the 8th-century *Senchus Fer nAlban* (1974, 140–6) draws comparisons with 'houses' and 'assessment districts' in Wales, Ireland and Anglo-Saxon England. Charles-Edwards, in discussing the use of the term 'ploughland' in Northern England states the universal problem: 'what we must decide is whether a new method of land measurement was introduced by the Scandinavians, or, on the contrary, only a new word for the old standard holding' (1972, 14).

6. As Brian Smith has pointed out to me the 1299 document recording land prices and rents on Papa Stour says that there 'will never be found higher prices from all Papay than there have always been from of old (*en sua sem iafnan hefir gengt at fyrnd*), a mark of burnt gold for arable land from every pennyland'. It is difficult to know how to treat a statement of this kind – used in a legal deposition which is deliberately stressing that some crooked financial dealings have taken place contrary to established custom. But I do not think it can be used as positive evidence that the name 'pennyland' dated back prior to the mid-12th century (nearly 150 years before that statement was made).

7. Lamont (1981, 74). More recently a link has been postulated between pennylands and

the establishment of a parochial system along with the introduction of annual tithes in the later 12th-century (Andersen, 1988, 65).

8. William Thomson has recently applied his knowledge of the Orkney pennyland divisions to the Arran pennylands and many more studies of this kind are needed.

9. This is particularly the case as regards Galloway which never came under the control of either the earls of Orkney or of the Lords of the Isles and kings of Man. But Galloway was closely linked to the kingdom of Man and the Isles and we have to assume – *whatever* the explanation for the pennyland unit – that the lords of Galloway simply adopted this unit for their own purposes from their knowledge of it in the Isles (Oram 1987 50).

REFERENCES

Andersen, Per Sveaas 1988. 'The Orkney Church of the Twelfth & Thirteenth Centuries: A stepdaughter of the Norwegian Church?', in *St Magnus Cathedral*, ed. Crawford, Barbara E. Aberdeen, pp. 56–68.
—— 1991. 'When was Regular, Annual Taxation Introduced in the Norse Islands of Britain? A Comparative Study of Assessment Systems in North-Western Europe', *Scandinavian Journal of History*, 16, 73–83.
APS: *The Acts of the Parliaments of Scotland*, ed. Thomson, T. & Innes, C. Edinburgh, 1814–75.
Bannerman, J. 1974. *Studies in the History of Dalriada*.
Barrow, G. W. S. 1981. *Kingship and Unity*, London.
Beaton, D. 1909. *Ecclesiastical History of Caithness*.
Blackburn, Mark & Pagan, Hugh 1986. 'A revised Check-List of coin hoards', in *Anglo-Saxon Monetary History*, ed. Blackburn, M. A. S. Leicester.
Calder, James T. 1887. *Civil and Traditional History of Caithness*, Wick.
Charles-Edwards, T. M. 1972. 'Kinship, Status and the Origins of the Hide', *Past and Present*, 56, 3–33.
Chron. Man.: Chronica Regum Manniae & Insularum, trans. Broderick, G. 1979, Manx Museum & National Trust.
Crawford, Barbara E. 1974. 'Peter's Pence in Scotland', in *The Scottish Tradition*, ed. Barrow, G. W. S. Edinburgh, pp. 14–23.
—— 1983. 'Birsay and the Early Earls and Bishops of Orkney', in *Birsay; A Centre of Political and Ecclesiastical Power*, Orkney Heritage 2, 97–118.
—— 1985. 'The Earldom of Caithness and the Kingdom of Scotland, 1150–1266', in *Essays on the Nobility of Medieval Scotland*, ed. Stringer, K. J. Edinburgh, pp. 25–43.
—— 1987. *Scandinavian Scotland*, Leicester.
—— (ed.) 1988. *St Magnus Cathedral and Orkney's Twelfth-century Renaissance*, Aberdeen.
—— 1991 'Catanensis eccl. (Caithness)', in *Series Episcoporum Ecclesiae Catholicae Occidentalis Ab Initio Usque ad Annum 1198*, series vi tomus I, Ecclesia Scoticana, ed. Watt, D. E. R. (adiciente Crawford, B. E.), Stuttgart, pp. 29–33.
CPL: *Calendar of Entries in the Papal Registers relating to Great Britain and Ireland: Papal Letters*, ed. Bliss, W. H. & others, London 1893–.
CSR: *Caithness and Sutherland Records*, ed. Johnston, A. W. & others, London 1909–28.

Duncan, A. A. M. & Brown, A. L. 1957. 'Argyll and the Isles in the Earlier Middle Ages', *Proceedings of the Society of Antiquaries of Scotland*, xc, 1956–7, 192–220.

DN: Diplomatarium Norvegicum, Kristiania/Oslo, 1849–.

Easson, Alexis 1987. 'Ouncelands and Pennylands in the West Highlands and Islands of Scotland', in *Ouncelands and Pennylands*, ed. Macgregor, L. J. & Crawford, B. E., St Andrews, pp. 1–12.

ES: Early Sources of Scottish History 500–1286, ed. Anderson, A. O., Edinburgh, 1922.

Gordon-Slade, H. & Watson, George 1989. 'St Peter's Kirk, Thurso, Caithness c1150–1832', *Proceedings of the Society of Antiquaries of Scotland*, cix, 1989, 297–325.

Harvey, Sally, P. J. 1985. 'Taxation & The Ploughland in Domesday Book', in *Domesday Book: A Reassessment*, ed. Sawyer, P., pp. 86–103.

Helle, Knut 1964. *Norge Blir en Stat*, Universitetsforlaget.

Herlihy, D. 1960. 'The Carolingian *Mansus*', *Economic History Review*, 2nd ser. 13, 79–89.

Inn.iii: Die Register Innocenz III, ed. Hageneder, O. & Haidacher, A., Cologne, 1964.

Jensen, O. 1901. 'Peter's Pence', *Transactions of the Royal Historical Society*, xv, 171–247.

KHLNM: Kulturhistorisk Leksikon for Nordisk Middelalder, Copenhagen, 1956–78.

Lamont, W. D. 1966. *The Early History of Islay*.

Lamont, W. D. 1981 '"House" and "Pennyland" in the Highlands and Isles', *Scottish Studies*, 25, 65–76.

Lindkvist, Thomas 1991. 'Social & Political Power in Sweden, 1000–1300: Predatory Incursions, Royal Taxation & the Formation of a Feudal State', in *Social Approaches to Viking Studies*, ed. Samson, R., Glasgow, pp. 137–45.

Megaw, Basil R. S. & Eleanor, M. 1956. 'The Norse Heritage in the Isle of Man', in *The Early Christian Cultures of North-West Europe*, ed. Dickens, B. & Fox, C. pp. 143–70.

Nicholls, K. W. 1983. 'Late Medieval Irish Annals: Two Fragments', in *Peritia*, 2, 87–102.

Oram, Richard D. 1987. 'Davachs and Pennylands in South-West Scotland: A Review of the Evidence', in *Ouncelands and Pennylands*, ed. Macgregor L. J. & Crawford, B. E., pp. 46–59.

OS: Orkneyinga saga Anderson, trans. by Hjaltalin, J. A. & Goudie, G., Edinburgh 1873, reprinted 1973.

—— Guðmundsson, Íslensk Fornrit, XXXIV, Reykjavík, 1965.

—— Pálsson and Edwards, London, 1978.

—— Taylor, Edinburgh, 1938.

Paisley Reg.: Registrum Monasterii de Passelet, Maitland Club, 1832; New Club, 1877.

Palmer, J. J. N. 1987. 'The Domesday Manor', in *Domesday Studies* ed. Holt, J. C., pp. 139–53.

Peterkin, Alexander 1820. *Rentals of the Ancient Earldom & Bishopric of Orkney*, Edinburgh.

Registres de Grégoire IX: Les registres de Grègoire IX, ed. Auvray, L. & others, Paris 1896–.

Reg. Norv.: Regesta Norvegica, ed. Gunnes, E. I., Oslo, 1989.

Romilly Allen & Anderson J. 1903. *The Early Christian Monuments of Scotland*, III, Edinburgh.

RSS: *Registrum Secreti Sigilli Regum Scottorum*, ed. Livingstone, M. & others, Edinburgh 1908–.

Scotichron: *Scotichronicon*, Bower, Walter, ed. Taylor, S. & Watt, D. E. R. 5, 1990.

Steinnes, Asgaut 1942. 'Romaskatt og Folketal', *(Norsk) Historisk Tidsskrift*, 32, 1940–2, 137–82.

Storm, Gustav 1888. *Islandske Annaler indtil 1578*, Christiania.

Theiner, A. 1864. *Vetera Monumenta Hibernorum et Scotorum Historiam Illustrantia*, Rome.

Thomson, William P. L. 1987a. 'Ouncelands and Pennylands in Orkney and Shetland', in *Ouncelands and Pennylands*, ed. Macgregor, L. J. & Crawford, B. E., pp. 24–45.

—— 1987b. *History of Orkney*, Edinburgh.

6

THE VIKING AND LATE NORSE GRAVES
OF CAITHNESS AND SUTHERLAND

COLLEEN E. BATEY

In *The Proceedings of the Tenth Viking Congress*, I published a review paper of the current state of knowledge of the Viking and Late Norse settlement in Caithness from the archaeological evidence (Batey 1987a). The purpose of this chapter is to provide updated information on one element of that paper, that concerned with the graves, and to encompass the area today termed Caithness and Sutherland (Fig. 6.1). A brief outline of information on both the Pictish (pre-Viking) and Viking elements in this area has been presented elsewhere (Batey 1991). A summary of the published record will be presented here, followed by details of new finds notified after the preparation of the paper published in 1987. The evidence from modern-day Sutherland is not extensive, but there has been a notable new addition to the corpus of graves, and this will be outlined briefly here. The fuller publication will appear elsewhere (Gourlay, Low & Batey forthcoming).

THE PUBLISHED EVIDENCE: A SUMMARY

One of the major problems in examining the evidence from old 'excavations' is that often the precise find circumstances are not recorded and the details of immediate context are overlooked. This situation is, of course, not peculiar to Northern Scotland, but, as elsewhere, it does place clear limitations on the available evidence. The recovery in 1786 at Castletown on the north coast, for example, of a female skeleton accompanied by a pair of similar oval brooches, a jet armring and a roughly made bone bodkin (Fig. 6.2) (Wilson 1863, 265–6; Anderson 1874, 549–51) is relatively well-recorded. This was 'dug out of the top of the ruins of a Pictish house. . .' (Anderson 1874, 550), a traditional term for a broch, in this case at Castlehill (RCAHMS 1911, 87 no. 320). The additional information is given that it was found underlying a flat slab. One of the brooches was donated to J. J. A. Worsaae on a visit to Scotland (presumed to be shortly after the recovery of the grave) as part of an exchange for Danish antiquities (Anderson 1874, 550), and now presumably resides in the National Museum in Copenhagen. The rest of the assemblage remains in the National Museums of

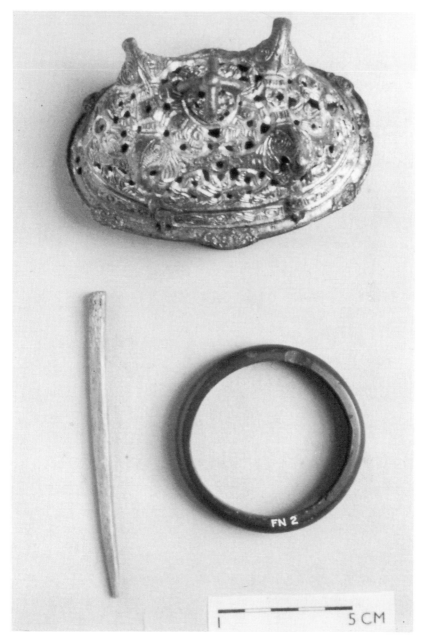

Figure 6.1: Castletown, Caithness. Grave group excluding oval brooch donated to J. J. A. Worsaae (Copyright NMS).

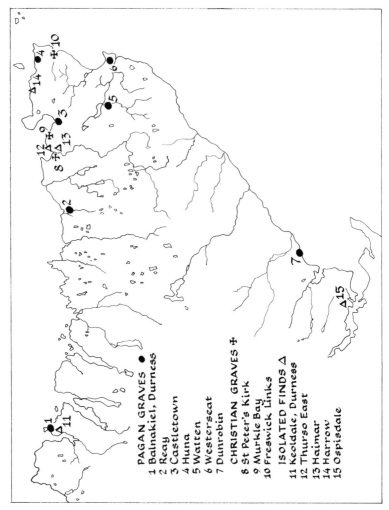

Figure 6.2: Location of Viking and Late Norse Graves in Caithness and Sutherland (A. L. Brundle).

Scotland, Edinburgh (NMS) where it was donated in 1787 by James Traill and is accessioned as IL221 (brooch), FN2 (jet ring) and FN3 (bodkin) (SAS 1892, 217 and 278).

The brooch type is interesting, differing in its degree of ornamentation from others in Northern Scotland. Jansson illustrates a similar type from sites in Sweden (Jansson 1985, 83–91) as Type P52, with examples cited from Birka (nos Bj 978 and Bj 965) being very close parallels to those from Castletown. This type is rather similar to Rygh Type 655 (Rygh 1885), whereas the others recorded from Caithness (discussed below) are Rygh Type 652 (Rygh 1885), a somewhat less flamboyant form of oval brooch and corresponding to Jansson's Type P51 (1985, 67–83 after Petersen 1928). These are of differing forms, although not necessarily indicating vastly differing dates of use in this Viking colony, but Jansson's work clearly suggests an earlier chronological position for the more common Type Rygh 652 (P51)in the 10th century than the more elaborate Rygh Type 655 (P52).

The relatively poor quality of the record for the dissimilar oval brooches recorded from the Westerseat area near Wick on the east coast, is more in keeping with the period. Even the year of discovery is open to dispute: Anderson in 1874 noted it as 1840 (Anderson 1874, 551–2), but in the Society of Antiquaries, Notices of Donations, a year later, they were recorded as recovered in 1841 (SAS 1875, 152–3) and the Society of Antiquaries' records themselves give a recovery date of 1837 (SAS 1892, 278). Located in a gravel hillock near the broch of Kettleburn at Westerseat, a pair of brooches (of Rygh Type 652) were recovered from a stone cist. The dimensions of the cist are variously recorded; Anderson supplied the information that it was a short cist (Anderson 1874, 551–2), but Brøgger noted that no dimensions were available (Brøgger 1930, 195). Recovery during gravel quarrying at the site was hardly likely to have produced a good record, and no further remains were noted, not even a skeleton. Apparently other cists were removed from the site without record before 1875 (OS Record ND 35 SE 20). The brooches were donated to the NMS in 1875 (accessioned as IL217 and IL218) by James Henderson, the landowner, and exhibited in both Edinburgh (1856) and Aberdeen (1859).

Further isolated groups of material which could suggest Viking burial are scattered throughout Caithness. In 1867, an iron spearhead of Viking type was found in a cist at the Mill of Watten (in central Caithness) with the remains of a skeleton (SAS 1872, 183; SAS 1892, 276). The spearhead was donated by R. MacAdam in 1871 and accessioned as IL210. Brøgger dates the spear to the late Viking period (Brøgger 1930, 195; Fig. 105, 196), although due to severe corrosion, the particular form is far from clear. Subsequent digging at the site in 1869 revealed two other graves. No further details are available, but it is interesting to note that Shetelig records a possible female grave at this site, although no detail is provided (Shetelig 1945, 8). There is a reference from Pope to a find of Scandinavian weapons at Haimar near Thurso on the north coast which included amongst it a number of swords (cited in Anderson 1874, 563). It is not clear whether this might have been a group of remains representing a number of graves with no recorded relationships.

In 1936, A. O. Curle surveyed the scattered remains of rivets, timber fragments, chain and skull fragments at Huna on the north coast (NMRS ms 28 (SAS 461), 20–21). Unfortunately the finds do not survive, and there remains only a sketch plan in the notebook. Although a settlement concentration nearby has been recorded more recently (Batey 1984, 34), unfortunately this was largely destroyed before either full recording or protective legislation could be brought into force. It is therefore difficult to find an immediate Viking context for this potential boat burial. However, the significance of the find cannot be overstated, since it is the only one to be even suggested for mainland Scotland to date. This is in contrast to the position in nearby Orkney, where several boat burials have been identified at Westness, Rousay (Kaland, this volume) for example, and more recently in late 1991 a fine example was recorded with triple burial and extensive artefact collection at Scar, Sanday (Dalland & Owen forthcoming).

To date, the largest group of graves from a single site which have been recorded (and in variable detail) are from Reay, on the north coast to the west of Thurso. This seems to be the only pagan cemetery recorded in the northern mainland of Scotland, although it is not impossible that some apparently isolated finds (such as Balnakeil, see below) might be part of larger burial groups. The sand dunes at Reay have been prone to severe wind erosion over several decades, and it is sometimes unclear from the record available how potential isolated finds may be correlated with graves which were previously examined by excavation. It does, however, seem likely that at least three definitely defined burials might be represented at the site – as well as the suggestion of a further unknown quantity. There have also been suggestions of a nearby settlement (NSA 1845, 13) exposed by extreme weather in 1751.

The earliest recorded grave from Reay was recovered in 1912, when the skeleton was accompanied by a buckle and a horse-bridle (Notes, 1912). The National Monuments Record for Scotland (NMRS) reports that 'a skeleton with the buckle of a horse bridle was found by James Forbes' (NC96NE13). The following year, a female grave was uncovered containing two oval brooches (Fig. 6.3), a buckle, a steatite whorl, a bridle-bit and probably the ringed pin recovered shortly after the main discovery (Brøgger 1930, 190). The brooch IL334 was clearly old when deposited, since it has an applied patch at one edge. The deposit was greatly disturbed and the finds scattered (Grieg 1940, 21–2), which has not assisted subsequent analysis. J. Curle adds to this group a possible iron buckle and a pair of cruciform tweezers, and the comment that the brooches were found face-to-face (Curle 1914, 295) (actually with the rear faces opposing). This latter feature is interesting since it is matched in the finds from the Viking grave at Claughton Hall, Lancashire (Kendrick 1935; illus. in Richards 1991, colour plate 10). The finds noted by Curle were in fact recovered after the excavation had

Figure 6.3: Reay. Oval brooches found in 1913 (from Curle 1914).

taken place and found in the vicinity of this grave. In view of the fact that there seems to be a cemetery group at this site, such an ascription of the finds may not actually have been correct. In 1926, the site was re-identified by many horse bones in the sand and associated with a circular structure (NC96NE13). Finds from the first stage of recovery were purchased from David J. Stephen of Reay in 1913 by NMS and accessioned as IL334–9 and IL341–2.

In August 1926, a male skeleton, complete from the knees upwards was found in the sand dunes at Reay. It was fully extended and laid on a paved surface and accompanied by several grave goods (Fig. 6.4) including an axe, shield boss, knife, sickle and buckle of iron, also a ringed pin and whetstone (Edwards 1927,

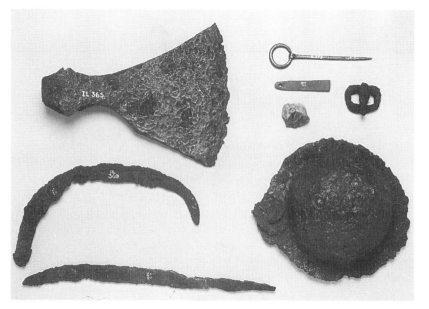

Figure 6.4: Reay. Male grave group found in 1926 (from Edwards 1927).

202; Brøgger 1930, 194, figs 102, 103). These were presented to NMS by Alan D. Pilkington of Sandside in 1926 (accessioned as IL365-375). It is not clear whether the 'several graves' noted subsequently by Edwards from the same hollow (Edwards 1927, 203), but not detailed, are in fact new find spots or a reference back to those already outlined above from earlier years. Other graves in the vicinity in long cists and lacking grave goods may date to the Christian Norse period (see below) (Edwards 1929, 139).

The significance of the material from Reay lies obviously in its quantity in relation to other sites on the mainland of Scotland. As the assemblage stands today, the group represented is rather small, but it is clear that the minimum number of individuals is under-represented due to the fact that the graves have been examined over a number of decades and in varying conditions. It is interesting to note that parts of a potential settlement may have been identified (see above) although this cannot be proved to be Norse in any way. However, the significance of the site in pre-Viking times is obvious (see, for example, the sculptural assemblage in Allen & Anderson 1903, 29 and 36) and it clearly continues into the pagan Viking period. In Sutherland, this situation could be matched in the area around Dunrobin and Golspie, which also seems to have a concentration of pre-Viking and Viking material (Allen & Anderson 1903, 42, 45–50; Batey 1991) although possibly spread over a larger geographical area. These are the only sites on the mainland to indicate this chronological bridging in any way at all, since at Freswick Links on the east coast there appears to be a gap in the site chronology at this crucial juncture (Morris & Batey, forthcoming).

A small number of Viking graves have been recorded from Sutherland, particularly in the area of Dunrobin Castle, Golspie, in the south of the region on the east coast. Early records indicate the recovery of a pair of oval brooches found in a grave near Dunrobin (Anderson 1874, 554; Grieg 1940, 17). These were transferred to Dunrobin Castle shortly after recovery sometime before 1855, and are now accessioned as DUOCM ARC 388a and 388b in the collections there. Also from the Dunrobin area, an iron axe and small iron ring were noted from the shore area (Grieg 1940, 17) and a hollow iron object, possibly a spearhead socket, came from a grave near to Dunrobin and is now in NMS as IL209 (Grieg 1940, 17; SAS 1892, 276). A single oval brooch has been recorded from Ospisdale (Anderson 1874, 554) and possibly associated with a steatite bowl, now lost (Grieg 1940, 18). Additional stray finds are noted by Small (1982, 183), but it cannot be judged whether they are grave finds.

The remaining potential grave group came from the area of Durness on the north coast, in what is now part of Sutherland, but which had a separate identity in the period of Norse influence in the North (Barbara Crawford, personal communication). The only references to potential graves in this area are supplied by Lethbridge and concern the site of Keoldale.

'. . . One of these was at Keoldale in Sutherland, within a short distance of a rifled barrow, which appears to have been that of a woman provided with tortoise brooches and padlocked chests'

(Lethbridge 1950, 96)

Three items illustrated by Lethbridge from Keoldale (Fig. 6.5), including a small bell, 'enamelled bronze brooch and two bronze and silver ear-rings'

Figure 6.5: Possible grave finds from Keoldale, Durness, Sutherland (from Lethbridge 1948; Scale approx. 1 : 1).

(Lethbridge 1948, Fig. 11, 87) may be from the grave group described in 1950, but this is not confirmed. The dating of the objects would conventionally probably be pre-Viking, but the inclusion of the small bell is of more than passing interest. The significance of such bells has been discussed elsewhere (Batey 1988; 1989). The find illustrated here is certainly of a very similar form to those recorded from Iceland, and rather simpler in form than that published from Freswick Links, Caithness (Batey 1988; 1989). Unfortunately the finds now appear to be lost. It is conceivable that this group of finds could represent a Viking grave as suggested by Lethbridge, and this now seems a more viable proposition in the light of the discovery in May 1991 of a pagan male Viking buried at Balnakeil, Durness (see below), only a short distance away from Keoldale.

All the graves discussed so far are pagan, being ascribed to a Viking context by

Figure 6.6: Runestone from St Peter's Church, Thurso (J. Campbell).

the nature of the accompanying grave goods. There is, however, a category of Norse graves which lack grave goods, and these are ascribed to the period of acceptance of the Christian religion. It is notoriously difficult to confirm that inhumations lacking distinctive artefacts belong to a specific cultural milieu, but in Caithness we have a lucky exception. In 1896, two graves were located near the ruins of St Peter's Church, Thurso on the north coast. The grave settings were of rough stones set on edge and orientated east-west (Allen & Anderson 1903, pt III, 36–7). The graves were of a child and an adult in a flexed position, and on top of the adult lay the fine runic inscribed cross illustrated in Figure 6.6. It is evident that the stone was intended as a grave cover and the inscription has been read as '. . . made this overlay after Ingolf his/her father' (Anderson 1897, 293–6; Allen & Anderson 1903, pt III, 37; Liestøl 1984, 228). The inscription has been dated to the 12th century, clearly in the Late Norse period, and it is likely that a contemporary church lay in the vicinity (discussed in Batey 1987b, 40). Without the cross-slab, these burials would have been chronologically indistinct, as was the case, for example, with a number of cist graves examined in earlier work at Freswick Links, on the east coast (Batey 1987b, 38–9 and 48). The same situation has also been noted at Reay (see above). This category of evidence is likely to be expanded as further detailed research is undertaken on these simple burials. However, the potential for classifying such burials is greatly enhanced by the use of modern dating methods (c.f. Hedges 1978, at Sandside, Graemsay in Orkney).

THE RECENT DISCOVERIES

In May 1991, human remains were identified in an area of exposure at Balnakeil Bay, Durness on the north coast of Sutherland. The find was reported to the Regional archaeologist and excavation followed. The remains were exposed and subsequent analysis of the skeletal material indicated that a boy of 8–13 years old had been buried at the site. The accompanying grave goods were varied and form a significant contribution to the corpus of mainland Scottish Viking material. The boy had been buried with a sword (of full size) which retained traces of its fragmentary scabbard, a spear and a shield, remaining only as an iron boss which might have been placed over the head of the deceased. In addition to the weaponry, a penannular brooch of simple form and possibly of Irish origin (see Fig. 6. 7) and a possible strap end were identified; also recovered were an antler comb and 14 antler gaming pieces, a bone needle case with needles surviving and three beads (R. Gourlay, Highland Regional Council, and T. Skinner, NMS, personal communications). Other fragments await positive identification, but could include a gaming board of wood, and there are several patches of textiles which have been preserved in the iron corrosion products. The discovery of this material poses several problems from the conservation and technological point of view and there will be an inevitable delay while this work is carried out (Gourlay, Low & Batey forthcoming).

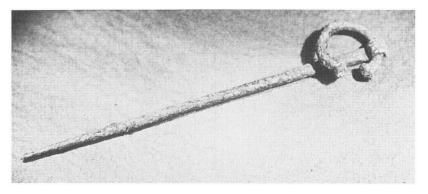

Figure 6.7: Balnakeil penannular brooch, front and rear (C. E. Batey).

At this stage it is too early to speculate on the immediate context for this burial, but its beach location, mirroring that at Reay, could suggest that other burials may await discovery and indeed that others may well have been lost to the sea. There is a history in the area of the collection of stray finds which could support this suggestion (R. Gourlay, personal communication). It is interesting to point out, however, that this young boy had been buried with an apparently full-sized set of weapons and also that other youngsters with grave goods have been excavated at Kneep, Lewis in the Western Isles (see Appendix below) and Scar in Orkney (Dalland & Owen, forthcoming).

During the winter of 1973–4 a single oval brooch was recovered from disturbed ground along the shoreline of Thurso East, on the eastern side of Thurso Bay. It was brought to the attention of NMS in 1984 and entered the collections in 1985, having been claimed as Treasure Trove (number TT338). The ground had been badly disturbed during the passage of heavy machinery which was involved in the salvage of two grounded trawlers in the bay. The embankment suffered severe damage from this activity and the brooch was recovered amongst the mud which had been churned up. Although it is most likely that this represents the site of a female Viking grave, since such finds are rarely found in other circumstances in areas outside the Viking homelands, further examination of the site by Robert Gourlay, the Regional Archaeologist,

Figure 6.8: Thurso East oval brooch (Copyright NMS).

failed to reveal anything further (Robert Gourlay and NMS, personal communications). As can be seen from Figure 6.8 the brooch is damaged in both the upper
and lower parts, but there remain traces of gilding on the underside and on the
upper part of the lower shell. Staining in the area of attachment, which lacks
traces of the iron pin, could suggest the textile traces so common on similar finds.
In this respect, and also in type, it is closely similar to those from the grave at
Kneep, Valtos (Welander, Batey & Cowie 1987, illus 3 and 4, 154–5) and, more
locally, at Reay (Grieg 1940, Fig. 4b, 21), i.e. Rygh Type 652.

The most recent find from Caithness which could indicate another grave spot
is a penannular brooch of Baltic type which was discovered near Harrow on the
north coast (Fig. 6.9). Although the piece is an isolated find, it could have been
associated with a grave deposit (Robert Gourlay, personal communication) and
is of a form not normally expected in this part of the Viking world. Its closest
parallels lie in the Baltic region, dated to the 9th century, and examples have
been recovered from the major trading centre at Birka in Sweden (Arbman 1940,
taf. 52–56). The pin itself seems likely to have been a replacement. Although the
brooch type is unexpected, it is interesting to note that the oval brooches from
the nearby site of Castletown (see above) are also of a Swedish form (Jansson
1985, 83–91). It is certainly worth pondering the fact that Eastern Viking
elements could be represented in the Western Viking world, rather than simply
those of Norwegian origin, which is our customary view. Jansson has already
drawn attention to an Oriental find in Iceland (Jansson 1978), a link which
demands a much greater feat of the imagination!

As with the pagan graves discussed, there is also new evidence available in the

Figure 6.9: Harrow brooch – mid-conservation (Copyright NMS.)

study of the Christian Late Norse settlers in Caithness. In the area around Murkle Bay on the north coast, a series of human skeletons have been recovered over the last 150 years. In the northern part of the bay in 1840 '[workmen] came upon a tremendous lot of human bones which appeared to have been deposited in a ditch', and nearby in the same year, human bones, iron spearheads and a 'brass' horseshoe were recorded (ONB 7, 1873, 13). In 1860 and 1872 the site once more produced human remains and an urn, when 'Mr Hobson . . . found pieces of an urn sticking out of the bank' (ONB 7 1873, 21). More recently, in 1981, approximately in the middle of the Bay, ploughing once more disturbed human remains and this occurred again in 1986. Examination of the site revealed that several crude stone cists had been disturbed, and one of a series of burials revealed in a relatively complete cist was sampled for a C14 determination. A date of 640 ± 60bp has been reported from the skeletal remains examined (GU 2135). This calibrates to AD 1260–1420 (at 2 sigma level, i.e. 95 per cent confidence), based on the use of the University of Washington Calibration Programme version 2.0. Identification of the human remains was undertaken by Margaret Bruce, School of Biomedical Sciences, University of Aberdeen, and the full report is lodged with the NMRS, Edinburgh. In summary, at least two individuals were represented from this one cist, an adult female and an adult male, but no age range is provided. (I am most grateful to Dr Noel Fojut of Historic Scotland for this information.)

   This burial would seem likely, therefore, to fall within the Late Norse period of activity in the general area and *a priori*, it is assumed the other human remains are broadly contemporary. However, what is the context for such a potentially large inhumation cemetery with long cists? Traditionally the site is recorded as a nunnery:

> A nunnery or monastery existed at a very early period at Murkle. Torfeus mentions that a queen of Norway died in it and that an Earl of Caithness was buried there in 960.
>
> (Auld 1868, 5)

However, the Ordnance Survey states that 'The supposed nunnery at Murkle, at a place locally known as Glosters, cannot be authenticated from Scottish records' (OS card no. ND16NE27). Despite this negative opinion, ploughing in the area has also revealed foundations of buildings. It is, therefore, probable that at least part of this long cist cemetery dates to the Late Norse period, although at this remove, it cannot be confirmed that the whole area was a single cemetery or indeed that it was related to any particular ecclesiastical activity in the immediate area.

CONCLUSION

Although the available evidence for the area is not extensive, it is clear that there is a range of material which enables comparison with the richer grave assemblages from Orkney and the Western Isles. The significance lies in the fact that, as in Orkney, new material is constantly being brought to light, and, even since 1978, when work began in earnest on examining the Caithness material, the picture has become much fuller. It is clear that the same detailed approach is still required for modern-day Sutherland.

1991 has seen an unprecedented wave of grave material being revealed and excavated – Balnakeil, Scar in Orkney and Kneep, Lewis (see Appendix to this paper), unfortunately all revealed through accident. The real significance lies in the fact that these have been subject to modern excavation techniques, for until relatively recently the only major group of finds to be so examined was at the cemetery of Westness, Rousay in Orkney (see Kaland, this volume). The single grave at Kneep, Lewis, excavated in 1979 (Welander, Batey & Cowie 1987) was significant because it integrated scientific analysis of the micro remains on the artefacts and technological information with a more conventional study of the grave group. In the early 1990s, we can be sure that this kind of activity will be undertaken as a matter of course.

Modern excavation conditions ought also to ensure that grave groups do not become mixed before detailed work can be undertaken. This is a problem which has dogged the study of old grave finds, in particular at sites such as Reay discussed here, and also at Pierowall, where Thorsteinsson has attempted to disentangle the confused records of finds recovered over decades (Thorsteinsson 1968). With this in mind, it is certainly worth considering the fact that the Reay oval brooches (IL334 and IL335) are dissimilar, although one of the brooches is similar to one of those recorded from Westerseat (IL217). It is not inconceivable that there has been confusion in the past.

Through careful scrutiny of the individual grave groups it will be possible to distinguish between those objects which were solely related to clothing and dress and those which were actually grave goods, deposited with significance for the after life. By examination of the elements which have often eluded the archaeologist in the past – the textiles and other organic remains, such as food – a much fuller picture can be presented. These aspects come together through the fruitful union of science and archaeology, the next stage on from isolated analysis of the artefacts, which are often all that remain of the earlier finds. A move towards a more predictive approach in the recovery of Viking graves – finding them before they are irrevocably damaged by either natural erosion or man-made damage, would enhance the quality of the record further. Consideration of the contemporary ground surface, surface treatment or marking of the grave location, and associated features such as stone settings, are all aspects of this record which can be lost without adequate safeguards. The single brooch from Thurso could have provided much greater information had it been *in situ*, with the rest of the assemblage; isolated as it is, we can only *suggest* that it was a grave find, just as with the brooch from Harrow.

The range of grave goods need not be extensive, however, as seen in the report which follows, of a recent find from Kneep Headland, Lewis, but it does have to be sufficient to enable us to distinguish the occupant as a person in the Norse milieu. Whether the occupant was a Scandinavian or not is another matter; again, in the future the interdisciplinary approach could well assist here through the examination of DNA in the skeletal remains. Through such developments, great strides are being made in our understanding of the archaeological record. When a database becomes available for such elements, the material from Caithness and Sutherland can then be incorporated and assist in comparisons throughout the rest of the North Atlantic cultural area.

REFERENCES

Allen, Joseph R. & Anderson, J. Romilly 1903. *The Early Christian Monuments of Scotland. A classified, illustrated, descriptive list of the monuments, with an analysis of their symbolism and ornamentation*, Edinburgh.
Anderson, Joseph R. 1874. 'Notes on the relics of the Viking Period of the Northmen in Scotland, illustrated by specimens in the Museum', *Proc. Soc. Antiq. Scot.*, X, 1872–4, 536–94.
Anderson, Joseph 1897. 'Notices of some recently discovered inscribed and sculptured stones', *Proc. Soc. Antiq. Scot.*, XXXI, 1896–7, 293–308.
Arbman, Holger 1940. *Birka I. Die Gräber*, 2 vols, Stockholm.
Auld, Alexander 1868. *Ministers and Men in the Far North*, 1st edn, Wick.
Auld, Alexander 1891. *Ministers and Men in the Far North*, 2nd edn, Edinburgh and Glasgow.
Batey, Colleen E. 1984. *Caithness Coastal Survey 1980–82: Dunnet Head to Ousdale*, Occasional Paper no. 3, Department of Archaeology, University of Durham.
Batey, Colleen E. 1987a. 'Viking and Late Norse Caithness: The Archaeological Evidence', in Knirk, James (ed.) 1987, 137–48.

Batey, Colleen E. 1987b. *Freswick Links, Caithness. A re-appraisal of the Late Norse site in its context.* BAR Brit Ser 179, 2 vols, Oxford.

Batey, Colleen E. 1988. 'A Viking-Age Bell from Freswick Links, Caithness', *Medieval Archaeology*, XXXII, 213–16.

Batey, Colleen E. 1989. 'Bjalla frá söguöld fundin á Skotlandi', *Árbok hins Íslenzka Fornleifafélags 1989*, 101–10.

Batey, Colleen E. 1991. 'Picts and Vikings in Caithness and Sutherland: A resumé', in Karkov, Catherine & Farrell, Robert (eds) 1991, pp. 49–60.

Brøgger, Anton W. 1930. *Den Norske Bosetningen på Shetland – Orknøyene. Studier og Resultater*, Oslo.

Curle, James 1914. 'On recent Scandinavian grave finds from the island of Oronsay and from Reay, Caithness', *Proc. Soc. Antiq. Scot.*, XLVIII, 1913–14, 292–315.

Dalland, Magnar & Owen, Olwyn (*Forthcoming.*) 'Excavation of the Viking Boat Burial at Scar, Sanday, Orkney'.

Edwards, Arthur J. H. 1927. 'Excavations of Graves at Ackergill and of an Earth House at Freswick Links, and a discovery of a Viking Grave at Reay, Caithness', *Proc. Soc. Antiq. Scot.*, LXII, 1926–7, 196–209.

Edwards, Arthur J. H. 1929. 'Excavations at Reay Links and at a Horned Cairn at Lower Dounreay, Caithness', *Proc. Soc. Antiq. Scot.*, LXIII, 1928–9, 138–50.

Fenton, Alexander & Pálsson, Hermann (eds) 1984. *The Northern and Western Isles in the Viking World. Survival, Continuity and Change*, Edinburgh.

Gourlay, Robert, Low, Dorothy & Batey, Colleen E. (*Forthcoming.*) 'The Viking Grave at Balnakeil, Durness, Sutherland', *Proc. Soc. Antiq. Scot.*

Grieg, Sigurd 1940. *Viking Antiquities in Scotland* (=*Viking Antiquities in Great Britain and Ireland*, vol. II, Shetelig, Håkon (ed.)), Oslo.

Hedges, John W. 1978. 'A long cist at Sandside, Graemsay, Orkney', *Proc. Soc. Antiq. Scot.*, 109, 1977–8, 374–8.

Jansson, Ingmar 1978. 'Ett rembeslag av orientalisk typ funnet på Island. Vikingatidens orientaliska bälten och deras eurasiska sammanhang', *TOR*, vol. XVII, 1975–7, 383–420.

Jansson, Ingmar 1985. *Ovala spännbucklor. En studie av vikingatida standardsmycken med utgångspunkt från Björkö – fynden*, Uppsala.

Karkov, Catherine & Farrell, Robert T. (eds) 1991. *Studies in Insular Art and Archaeology*. International Medieval Conference, Kalamazoo, 1988 (=American Early Medieval Studies, 1), Miami, Ohio.

Kendrick, Thomas D. 1935. 'The Claughton Hall Brooches', *Saga-Book of the Viking Society*, vol. XI, pt II, 117–24.

Knirk, James E. (ed.) 1987. *Proceedings of the Tenth Viking Congress, Larkollen, Norway 1985*. Universitetets Oldsaksamlings Skrifter Ny Rekke Nr 9. Oslo.

Lethbridge, Thomas C. 1948. *Merlin's Island. Essays on Britain in the Dark Ages*, London.

Lethbridge, Thomas C. 1950. *Herdsmen and Hermits*, Cambridge.

Liestøl, Aslak 1984. 'Runes', in Fenton, Alexander & Pálsson, Hermann (eds), pp. 224–38.

Morris, Christopher D. & Batey, Colleen E. (*Forthcoming.*) *Excavations at Freswick Links, Caithness, 1979–84*, Highland Region Monograph no. 1.

Niclasen, Bjarni (ed.) 1968. *The Fifth Viking Congress Tórshavn 1965*, Tórshavn .

NMRS ms 28 (SAS 461). Notebook of A. O. Curle. Manuscript held in National Monuments Record for Scotland, Edinburgh.

Notes, 1912. *Year Book of the Viking Society for Northern Research*, IV, 1911–12, 20.

NSA 1845. The *New Statistical Account of Scotland*, by the Ministers of the respective Parishes, 15 vols, Edinburgh and London.

Omand, Donald (ed.) 1982. *The Sutherland Book*, Golspie.

ONB 1873 & 1914. Ordnance (Survey) Notebooks held in the National Monuments Record for Scotland, Edinburgh.

Petersen, Jan. 1928. *Vikingetidens Smykker*, Stavanger Mus. Skrifter 2, Stavanger.

RCAHMS 1911. *Third Report. The Inventory of Monuments and Constructions in the County of Caithness*, Edinburgh.

Richards, Julian D. 1991. *Viking Age England*. English Heritage/Batsford, London.

Rygh, Oluf 1885. *Norske Oldsager. Ordnede og Forklarede*, Christiania.

SAS 1871. 'Donations to the Museum, 10th April 1871', *Proc. Soc. Antiq. Scot.*, 183 (Robert Macadam).

SAS 1875. 'Donations to the Museum, 8th March 1875', *Proc. Soc. Antiq. Scot.*, 152–3 (James Henderson).

SAS 1892. *Catalogue of the National Museum of Antiquities of Scotland*, Society of Antiquaries of Scotland, Edinburgh.

Shetelig, Håkon 1945. 'The Viking Graves of Great Britain and Ireland', *Acta Archaeologica*, XVI, 1–55.

Small, Alan 1982. 'Viking Sutherland', in Omand, Donald (ed.), pp. 180–4.

Thorsteinsson, Arne 1968. 'The Viking Burial Place at Pierowall, Westray, Orkney', in Niclasen, Bjarni (ed.), pp. 150–73.

Welander, Richard, Batey, Colleen E. & Cowie, Trevor 1987. 'A Viking burial from Kneep, Uig, Isle of Lewis', *Proc. Soc. Antiq. Scot.*, 117, 149–74.

Wilson, Daniel 1863. *Prehistoric Annals of Scotland*, vol. 2, London and Cambridge.

Appendix

THE DISCOVERY OF A CHILD BURIAL OF PROBABLE VIKING-AGE DATE ON KNEEP HEADLAND, UIG, LEWIS, 1991: INTERIM REPORT

TREVOR COWIE   MARGARET BRUCE   NEILL KERR

CIRCUMSTANCES OF DISCOVERY

The bleached remains of a human skull were spotted by two teenagers, Marie MacLean and Ross James, in an eroded hollow, or blow-out, high on the machair-covered slopes of Kneep headland during a family outing in May 1991.[1] Marie was already aware of the archaeological potential of the Kneep area, having previously been shown sites in the vicinity by Mrs Margaret Curtis, a local amateur archaeologist, in the course of a school excursion. She recognised the bone as human – in fact, part of the orbit of the skull – and showed it to her father, and together they returned to the site to see if further remains were exposed. In the course of scraping away the sand they recovered further skull fragments, the mandible and items which were subsequently identified as an amber bead and a stone pendant. At this point they realised the archaeological significance of the find and, replacing the pieces they had recovered, took steps to report the find to Mrs Curtis, who in turn notified the National Museums of Scotland. Although initial details were vague, the find-spot appeared to be in the vicinity of a richly furnished Viking female grave, found on the same headland in 1979 (Welander, Batey & Cowie 1987), and in view of the recovery of the two objects, it seemed possible that this grave might also be of Viking-Age date. On behalf of the National Museums of Scotland, the author (TC) immediately travelled to Lewis to investigate the site.

THE EXCAVATION

The site lies on Kneep headland (NGR c NB 100 365) overlooking Traigh na Berie, one of the largest and most scenic beach, dune and machair systems in Lewis (Fig. 6A.1). The headland itself is covered by blown sand supporting a thin turf cover (machair), broken in many places by large blow-outs, or sand bunkers, scooped out of the slopes by the wind. The find-spot lay within a large deflation hollow near the summit ridge of the headland, uphill and approximately 40 m NE of the site of the grave found in 1979.

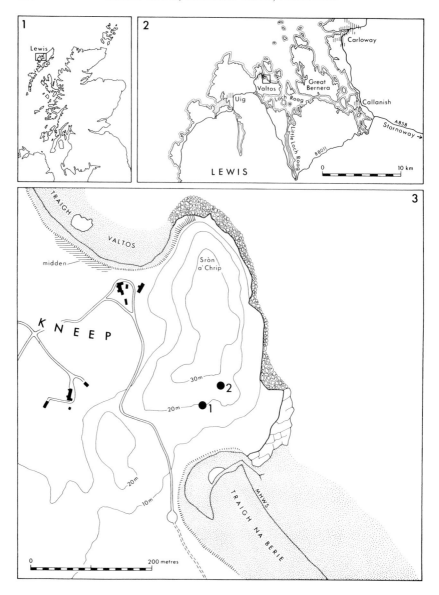

Figure 6A.1: Kneep Headland: location map showing the relative positions of the graves found in 1979 (*1*) and 1991 (*2*).

Figure 6A.2: Kneep Headland: the remains of the skeleton as revealed by excavation (Copyright NMS).

The bones had been found at a point where a bench of old ground surface had been exposed along the northern margin of the blow-out. In order to facilitate excavation, slumped turf and wind-blown sand deposits were cut back to expose the old land surface over an area of *c.* 4.5 × 2.5 m. Investigation of the find-spot subsequently revealed the crouched burial of a child, which appears to have been deposited immediately behind a large rock in a shallow grave-pit scooped in a layer of wind-blown sand, representing the fossil subsoil of the old ground surface (Figs 6A.2 & 6A.3); apart from greater root penetration, the fill of the grave was virtually indistinguishable from the surrounding sand, which tends to suggest that the pit was dug from a land surface actually composed of blown sand or, perhaps more likely, thinly vegetated with a light machair-type sward. It is unlikely that the rock itself was visible when the grave was excavated, for in preparing the pit, several flakes of stone appear to have been detached; some of these clearly lay underneath the skeleton, while others lay against the side or within the fill of the grave. Had the rock been visible on the surface, it might be expected that the gravedigger(s) would have taken steps to avoid it.

Whatever its condition at the time of burial, at some stage the land surface stabilised fully, allowing the formation of a recognisable soil profile. This was eventually tilled and enriched by manuring, for which there is evidence in the

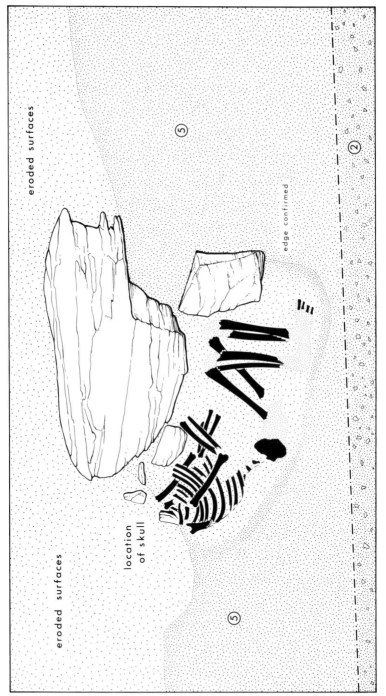

Figure 6.A.3: Kneep Headland: plan of the burial. Layer 2 = surface of buried soil; layer 5 = underlying wind-blown sand, into which grave-pit was scooped (M. O'Neil).

form of plough-marks, spade-marks and profuse charcoal flecks and fragments of shell, bone and pottery incorporated in the soil profile. It was probably the presence of the large rock and nearby outcropping bedrock which resulted in the fortuitous survival of the grave during this activity, for the ploughing may as a result have been shallower or intermittent in this area. At some unknown date, this old ground surface was inundated by extensive deposits of wind-blown sand, probably with intermittent phases of stability, until the formation of the present-day machair surface (and in due course the initiation of the current cycle of erosion). It is clear that the grave would not have survived present-day erosion for much longer for it was the exposure, drying out and undercutting of the buried old ground surface that had revealed the bones of the skull.

THE BURIAL

The results of examination of the human remains by Dr Margaret Bruce and the dental features by Neill Kerr (both of the University of Aberdeen) may be summarised briefly. The remains are those of a single individual, a child of about six years of age, of indeterminate sex owing to the immaturity of the skeleton. The estimate of age was corroborated by study of the dentition. The degree of attrition of the deciduous teeth and absence of caries suggests the diet was of an abrasive nature, with few carbohydrates. In summary, the 'good quality' bone and well-formed tooth enamel suggest the youngster was well-nourished, enjoyed a relatively healthy childhood and did not suffer from any severe infections or debilitating illnesses. The human remains shed no light on the cause of death.

The only artefacts likely to have been deliberately deposited with the burial are an amber bead and stone pendant found at the time of the original discovery (Figs 6A.4 & 6A.5). The bead is in good condition and measures 19 mm in diameter; the pendant is made from light grey and pink stone, and is 41 mm long. While superficially resembling a whetstone, the pendant shows no obvious sign of such use. In view of their apparent recovery near the jawbone, it is perhaps possible that the bead and pendant had been worn around the neck. Three iron nails were found in the fill of the grave but their significance is uncertain.

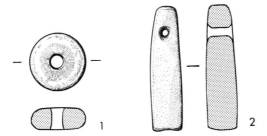

Figure 6A.4: Kneep Headland: the amber bead and stone pendant (M. O'Neil).

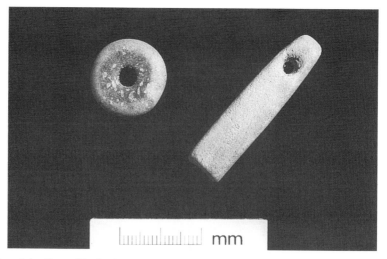

Figure 6A.5: Kneep Headland: the amber bead and stone pendant (Copyright NMS).

DISCUSSION

While neither the presumed grave goods nor the burial rite are particularly diagnostic, this burial must be seen against a background of vague local accounts of discoveries of human bones on the headland[2] and poorly provenanced stray finds including several pins of Norse date (Lacaille 1937; Close-Brooks, forthcoming) and, more tellingly, the rich female grave found in 1979. While the possibility of native burial traditions must continue to be borne in mind, the circumstantial evidence at least tends to suggest that we are dealing with another Viking-Age burial, probably of 9th–10th century AD date. If so, it forms a significant addition to the accumulating body of evidence for Norse settlement in the Uig area of Lewis (summarised in Welander, Batey & Cowie 1987, 168) – whatever form that took *vis-à-vis* the indigenous population.

A brief postscript demonstrates just how quickly that body of evidence is accumulating. In November 1991, a single bone was observed, eroding from a sand-bank on the slopes of the Kneep headland, near to the grave-site of 1979. The site was inspected by the author, but for several reasons it was felt that, rather than salvage the skeletal remains, which were only just beginning to emerge, the archaeological interests of the site would be best served by a planned season of excavation. The sand-bank from which the bones were emerging was therefore protected as an interim measure, subsequently complemented by regular monitoring of the site over the winter.[3] It was felt that investigation of the intact areas of buried soil available for excavation would almost certainly throw more light on the context of the rich Viking grave found in 1979, and in particular, would provide an opportunity – all too rare in the Western Isles – to assess whether or not these random discoveries might genuinely reflect the presence of a cemetery on the headland.

In the event, this strategy was vindicated: excavations were undertaken in Spring 1992 on behalf of Historic Scotland by the Centre for Field Archaeology (University of Edinburgh) and even the very limited area investigated revealed a further three extended inhumations in shallow graves, demarcated on the contemporary ground surface by oval settings of small boulders (I. Armit, personal communication; *Discovery and Excavation in Scotland, 1992*, 83).[4] This is clearly a headland which still holds very considerable scope for further investigation.

ACKNOWLEDGEMENTS

Full credit for the discovery of the burial in May 1991 goes to Marie MacLean (aged 15) and Ross James (aged 13), who spotted the bleached bones of the skull eroding from the sand, and who then, with their parents Pat and Don MacLean, and Bobbie James, took steps to ensure that their discovery was reported without disturbing the site further. I am grateful to Mr Kenneth MacLennan, Clerk of the local Grazings Committee, for permission to investigate the site. Thanks are due to Carol Cunningham, Mike Spearman and Richard Langhorne for their assistance in various ways while on Lewis, and to Dr Margaret Bruce and Neill Kerr for examining the skeletal remains; finally, I am especially indebted to Margaret and Ron Curtis for immediately informing the National Museums of Scotland of the discovery and for all their subsequent help.

NOTES

1. This is an extended version of a preliminary account of the discovery published in the *Hebridean Naturalist* (Cowie 1991).

2. In this context, mention may be made of an *adult* human molar tooth found in the eroded sand in the immediate vicinity of the child burial (Dr Margaret Bruce, personal communication).

3. Mr and Mrs G. R. Curtis, Callanish, Lewis, deserve recognition for undertaking the thankless task of monitoring the site over the winter – often in appalling weather conditions.

4. In the light of these new discoveries, the complete report on the child burial will be incorporated into the final report on the work carried out in 1992.

REFERENCES

Close-Brooks, Joanna (*Forthcoming.*) 'Excavation of a cairn at Kneep, Uig, Lewis', *Proc. Soc. Antiq. Scot.*

Cowie, Trevor G. 1991. 'The discovery of a child burial of probable Viking-age date on Kneep Headland, Lewis, 1991: preliminary report', *Hebridean Naturalist*, 11, 31–4.

Lacaille, Armand, D. 1937. 'A stone industry, potsherds and a bronze pin from Valtos, Uig, Lewis', *Proc. Soc. Antiq. Scot.*, 71 (1936–7), 279–96.

Welander, Richard D. E., Batey, Colleen E. & Cowie, Trevor G. 1987. 'A Viking burial from Kneep, Uig, Isle of Lewis', *Proc. Soc. Antiq. Scot.*, 117, 149–74.

7

THE NORTHERN HOARDS OF
VIKING-AGE SCOTLAND

JAMES GRAHAM-CAMPBELL

INTRODUCTION

In the 15 years since the publication of my survey 'The Viking-age silver and gold hoards of Scandinavian character from Scotland' (Graham-Campbell 1976),[1] no new hoards have been discovered in the Northern Isles or the North-East Mainland of Scotland, although the evidence has been reviewed by others (Morris 1985, 233–4; Batey 1987, 306–9; Crawford 1987, 128–36). However, new information on old finds has come to light and there are newly excavated single-finds of coins and hacksilver (see Appendix).

One more recent Scottish hoard survey has appeared (Smart 1985), but this is confined to coin and mixed hoards[2] and does not take account of a number of relevant papers published in the late 1970s and early 1980s. On the other hand, a new starting point for the study of this material is provided by Blackburn and Pagan's (1986) new listing of all hoards containing coins from Britain and Ireland, c. 500–1100, with revised deposition dates. Their results for Scotland are plotted and listed here (Fig. 7.1 and Table 7.1), with the addition of an old (pre-1852), unprovenanced coin hoard of the 940s, with a distinctive black patina (Stevenson 1966, xxi). However, the hoard tentatively suggested by Smart (1985, 69), on the basis of a run of Edward the Confessor pennies in Perth Museum, has not been included, for it needs to be demonstrated that they do not derive from one of the several large English hoards associated with the Conquest, perhaps given or sold to the museum by a private collector.[3] The 1988–90 mixed hoard from Lews Castle, Stornoway, on the Isle of Lewis,[4] and a recent find of Hiberno-Norse coins from, Perthshire,[5] are both also omitted as they are still undergoing conservation and study, but their discovery means that the number of hoards containing coins from c. 850–1100, known to have been found in Scotland, stands at 22 (recte 23[+]: see Graham-Campbell, forthcoming)[1].

CHRONOLOGY AND DISTRIBUTION

The adjustments made by Blackburn and Pagan to Dolley's (1966) deposition dates reveal two hoarding peaks or clusters (Fig. 7.1): one beginning in the 970s

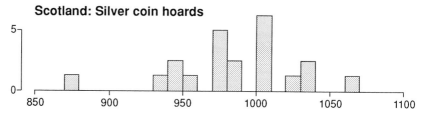

Figure 7.1: Deposition of silver coin and mixed hoards in Scotland, *c.* 850–1100, by decade.

Table 7.1. Deposition dates for silver coin and mixed hoards from Scotland, *c.* 800–1100 (after Blackburn & Pagan 1986).

51	Croy, Inverness	*c.* 845?
46	Talnotrie, Kirkcudbright	*c.* 875?
116	Skye (Storr Rock), Inverness	*c.* 935
123	Cockburnspath, Berwick	*c.* 940?
—	Unprovenanced	*c.* 940?
129	Skaill, Orkney	*c.* 950
162	Skye (no. 2), Inverness	*c.* 970?
168	Islay (Machrie), Argyll	*c.* 970
169	Port Glasgow, Renfrew	*c.* 970
171	Tiree, Argyll	*c.* 970
177	North Uist, Inverness	*c.* 985?

180	Iona Abbey, Argyll	*c.* 986
190	Tarbat, Ross	*c.* 1000
191	Kilmartin, Argyll	*c.* 1000?
192	Quendale, Shetland	*c.* 1000
193	Burray, Orkney	*c.* 1000
194	Inchkenneth, Argyll	*c.* 1000
209	Jedburgh, Roxburgh	*c.* 1025?
216	Parkhill, Lindores, Fife	*c.* 1030?
221	Caldale, Orkney	*c.* 1035
245	Dunrossness, Shetland	*c.* 1065?

which reflects the upsurge in hoard deposition and non-recovery in Ireland at this period, attributed by Dolley (1966, 33) to the unsettled conditions in the Irish Sea area in the years leading up to the 980 battle of Tara; and the other around the millennium. However, a more meaningful interpretation of these statistics may be arrived at by breaking down the overall Scottish pattern by region.

For this purpose, Viking-age Scotland can be divided into four (Fig. 7.2):

(i) the *South-East Mainland*, which will not be considered here as it is without primary Scandinavian settlement;

(ii) the *South-West Mainland*, which will also be passed over, since its only hoard is of doubtful Scandinavian character (Graham-Campbell 1976, 118);

(iii) the *West*, comprising the West Highlands and Islands;

(iv) the *North*, comprising the Northern Isles and the North-East Mainland area of Scandinavian settlement.

On this basis the twin peaks in hoard deposition may be re-examined, separating the coin and mixed hoards of the West from the North (Fig. 7.3). This analytical refinement reveals that the peaking and clustering in the 970s and 980s consists

Figure 7.2: Map of Viking-age coin and mixed hoards, and coinless hoards of Scandinavian character, from Scotland (after Graham-Campbell 1976, Fig. 1).

WEST

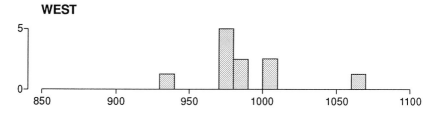

NORTH

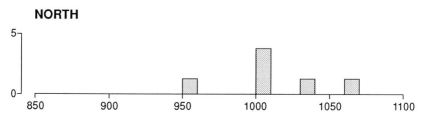

Figure 7.3: Deposition of silver coin and mixed hoards in the West and North of Scotland, by decade (*c.* 850–1100).

solely of hoards deposited in the West. On the other hand, the millennium is marked by hoard deposition and non-recovery in both regions.

The Garthbanks/Quendale/Dunrossness Hoard(s)

Doubt has been cast on the existence of one of the Shetland millennial hoards (Smart 1985, 68), on the grounds that that found in November 1830 'in some Cornland called the Tofts near Garthsbanks, a little way south of the House of Quendale in the Parish of Dunrossness', might be one and the same as the hoard recorded (in 1844) in the *Gave-Protocol* of the Coin Cabinet in Copenhagen as having been found 'i Dunrosness Præstegaard' (Dolley & Skaare 1973). This has been translated as 'from the policies of Dunrossness manse' (Dolley & Skaare 1973, 227), and as 'in the glebe of Dunrossness parish' (Stevenson 1986, 341). The manse and glebe of Dunrossness was at Skelberry, several miles to the north-east of Quendale House, near which the 1830 hoard was discovered. The latter consisted of 'some small and very thin old coins much wasted with some bits of uncoined silver' found in a horn, around which were six or seven silver 'hoops', which can be identified as specimens of 'ring-money' (Graham-Campbell 1976, 128–9, note (iv), plate 13), whereas the Dunrossness manse coin is stated to have been accompanied by others 'similar' and by 'adskillige ituhugne Sølvarmbaand' (several cut-up silver arm-rings).

The King's and Lord Treasurer's Remembrancer wrote from the Exchequer Chambers in Edinburgh, on 7 April 1831, to the Procurator Fiscal in Shetland,[6] requesting his assistance in the recovery of this 1830 hoard so that it might be 'transmitted to this office for the disposal of the Barons'. He had been 'informed that a Horn mounted with Silver was lately discovered in Shetland and found to contain a large quantity of old Coins – and they are said to have been soon after in the possession of the Minister of Dunrossness'. That this was the case by the end of 1830 is confirmed in the deposition taken by Andrew Duncan, the Sheriff Substitute of Zetland, on 7 December, a copy of which he sent to Lord Meadowbank. In this it is stated that 'the Coins appear to be chiefly of the reigns of "Ethered", "Athelstan", "Edwg", "Eadgar", and "Ethelred". One or two are said to belong to the period of the Heptarchy – vide the accompanying impressions taken in Sealing wax by permission of the present possessor of the originals, the minister of this parish'.

Immediately afterwards, on 18 January 1831, Lord Meadowbank (Alexander Maconochie) wrote to Sir Walter Scott that 'the drawings of the rings have been sent me – impressions of many of the coins have accompanied them as well as some pieces of the originals . . . the coins I mean to give the Antiquaries',[7] who indeed received 'two or three fragments' later that same year (Stevenson 1966, ix and xix). The source of six coins from this hoard in the Hunterian Collection, of Eadwig, Edgar (4 coins), and Æthelred II, has been assumed to be the Lord Treasurer's Remembrancer (Robertson 1961, xii). However, it has not been possible to establish whether he succeeded in laying his hands on the minister's coins,[9] but this must be their most probable source, given that none had been retained by either the finders or the landowner. According to the deposition already quoted, the finders' landlord at Quendale had told them to 'make their best of' the hoard and they had 'sold the Hoops and the other uncoined Silver in Lerwick, for three pounds Sterling, and the few Coins were given away or disposed of for mere trifles'.

The question remains whether the coin in Copenhagen could have been left over from the 1830 find. It is a triquetra penny of Harald Hardrada and so could not have been deposited before *c*. 1060, whereas the Anglo-Saxon coins mentioned above as being from Garthbanks/Quendale form a considerably earlier group, suggesting a deposition date of *c*. 1000. It is to be hoped that further information concerning this matter may yet come to light, but in the meantime, following Dolley and Skaare's original suggestion as endorsed by Blackburn and Pagan (1986, nos 192 and 245), it is proposed to continue to accept the existence of two 19th century finds from the same parish, rather than of one hoard with a chronological spread in its coins of over eighty years.

Historical Contexts

Consideration of the limited historical evidence may help to further the interpretation of the hoard peaks or clusters. In the words of Crawford (1987, 66), 'the evidence that we have suggests that there was a struggle for power in Hebridean waters in the 980s, and saga tradition remembered that [Earl] Sigurd [of Orkney] was the victor'. Hoards deposited on North Uist and Iona date to this period, but it is the millennial hoards which may serve to reinforce her claim that 'Earl Sigurd was indeed the most powerful figure in Scandinavian Scotland in the early eleventh century, and a great warrior with large resources of men, supplies and ships at his disposal' (Crawford 1987, 67), before he met his death at Clontarf in 1014 – a battle that is unmarked in the hoard record of both Ireland and Scotland.

On the other hand, with Blackburn and Pagan's (1986, no. 221) redating of the deposition of the Caldale hoard, near Kirkwall on Orkney, to *c*. 1035, it has been moved well out of the period of tyrannical rule by Sigurd's successor, Einar, which Crawford suggested as the explanation for its concealment (1987, 133).

Northern Hoards: The Picts

The Vikings who raided the Northern Isles and North-East Mainland of Scotland, from the late 8th century onwards, encountered a population rich in portable wealth. The Pictish treasure buried within a decade or two of 800 on St Ninian's Isle, Shetland, consisted of 28 pieces of ornamented silver, most notably eight vessels and 12 brooches, which would have weighed altogether about 2 kg on deposition (Small, Thomas & Wilson 1973). A similar hoard was found in the ruins of the Broch of Burgar, Orkney, in 1840, but is now lost; it also contained eight silver vessels, as well as silver combs, pins, brooches and chains, with amber beads (Graham-Campbell 1985). On the Scottish mainland, the hoard found in 1868 at Rogart in Sutherland was certainly larger and more important than is generally remembered from the few surviving objects (Small, Thomas & Wilson 1973, 81–2). Thus, each of the three areas comprising the Northern hoards region has on record its own major hoard of Pictish silver, all of which were deposited in the late 8th or early 9th century. They consist of the sort of material which would mostly have been melted down by Viking raiders for conversion into Scandinavian-style ornaments, such as arm-rings which seem to have fallen out of use amongst the Picts by this period, although their prestige penannular brooches were carried back to Norway where they were then copied (Graham-Campbell 1987).

Northern Hoards: Scandinavian Introduction

The Northern hoard record is blank for the first century and more of Scandinavian settlement, although there is amongst the Northern single-finds a perforated coin of Burgred (dating to 866–8) found in Norse occupation levels during the 1977 Saevar Howe excavations in Orkney. This presumably represents the casual loss of a personal ornament – in contrast to the deliberately cut halfpenny of Eadmund (939–46) which was placed in a pagan male burial at Buckquoy, further round the Bay of Birsay. The Buckquoy coin and the remaining eight single-finds of Anglo-Saxon and Norwegian coins, from both Orkney and Shetland (Stevenson 1986; summarised here in Table 7.2), are

Table 7.2: Single-finds of Viking-age coins from Orkney and Shetland.

Saevar Howe, Birsay: Burgred	Brough of Birsay: Edgar
Buckquoy, Birsay: Edmund	Brough of Birsay: Æthelred II (× 2)
Newark, Deerness: Anlaf (York)	Jarlshof, Shetland: Æthelred II
Newark, Deerness: Eadred	Brough of Birsay: Olav Kyrre (Norway)
Brough of Deerness: Edgar	

paralleled by coins in the Western and Northern hoards from the mid-10th to late 11th centuries.

None of the 10th/11th-century single coins has been pierced for suspension, perhaps because their mutilation would have been 'inhibited by a potentially monetary or exchange function', as Stevenson has suggested (Stevenson 1986, 339). At any rate, these excavated single-finds corroborate the impression that silver was in growing circulation in the Northern Isles from the mid-10th century (even if the amounts need not necessarily have been very large), by reinforcing the chronology of silver availability revealed by the contents of hoards.

An early ornament amongst the silver single-finds is the rather slight, plain arm-ring of Hiberno-Viking type, now lost (Fig. 7.4), from a female grave at Clibberswick on Unst, Shetland (Grieg 1940, 103–5, Figs 57a and b), together with a pair of Early Viking Period oval brooches (Berdal type) and a Middle Viking Period trefoil brooch (Borre style), which combine to suggest a burial of the later 9th century.[8] The arm-ring, which has parallels in the Cuerdale,

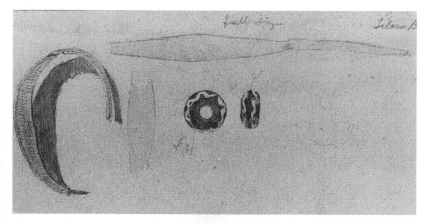

Figure 7.4: Plain silver Hiberno-Viking arm-ring (lost) found in a female grave at Clibberswick, Unst, Shetland (from the Irvine ms, Society of Antiquaries of Scotland): reduced.

Lancashire, hoard of *c.* 905 (e.g. Bjørn & Shetelig 1940, Fig. 9), presumably represents silver with an Irish Sea origin.

Another of the six single-finds from Shetland (see Appendix), likely to have been Irish (or at least Irish Sea) in origin, is the ornate silver 'thistle-brooch' from Gulberwick (Graham-Campbell 1983b). This is, however, of 10th-century date, to be compared with the magnificent collection of ball-type brooches from the Skaill, Orkney, hoard (*c.* 950).

The Skaill (Orkney) Hoard

The mixed hoard found in 1858 at the Bay of Skaill, on the west side of Orkney Mainland, is the largest Scandinavian-type hoard on record from Scotland, deposited *c.* 950 (Graham-Campbell 1984). It weighed somewhat over 8 kg making it similar in size to the largest known Viking-Age hoards that have been found in Scandinavia. At the same time, however, it is three times larger than any of the equivalent 10th-century hoards from Norway,[10] and four times heavier than any other Viking-Age treasure from Scotland.

On this relative scale, the Skaill hoard is *large*; it represents a great accumulation of portable wealth, which was concealed in a prime settlement location (Morris (ed.) 1985). It suggests the presence at Skaill by the mid-10th century of a wealthy family which had perhaps buried its capital for safety during a time of unrest, or which was in the habit of keeping it conveniently concealed near to, but away from the farm, until some disaster prevented its recovery.

In commercial terms, the Skaill hoard is to be classified as 'active' rather than 'passive' (Graham-Campbell 1989), for it contains hacksilver and 'ring-money', alongside a selection of prestige ornaments (for further discussion, see Kruse, this volume). How active its contents had been will only be determined by a detailed study of the hacksilver for evidence of economic transactions in the form of 'nicking', a practice that had clearly become well established in the Viking West before the beginning of the 10th century (Archibald 1990).

The hoard most similar to Skaill in its contents, from anywhere in Britain and Ireland, is the Ballaquale (Douglas) treasure from the Isle of Man. It was deposited *c.* 970 and so these two hoards were concealed within a generation of each other. There are strong stylistic reasons for supposing that the Skaill ball-type brooches were made on Man (Graham-Campbell 1983a). Taking both the general and the particular parallels, it seems reasonable to suggest that the Skaill hoard, at least in part, may represent the rewards of one of those 'many Vikings and war-kings' (as Snorri tells) who 'joined the army of King Erik', as he marauded in the Irish Sea and the Hebrides at the end of the 940s (Crawford 1987, 61–2).

'Ring-money'

'Ring-money' consists of plain penannular rings, normally of adult arm-ring size (but occasionally smaller), made from a single rod of circular or lozenge-shaped section (Graham-Campbell 1976, 125–6). It is first found in a datable context in Scotland as part of the Skaill hoard, but 'ring-money' dominates both mixed and coinless hoards in the Earldom of Orkney (as also in the West) from the late 10th and 11th centuries.

In Orkney, there are numerous examples and fragments awaiting full publication from the Skaill (*c.* 950) and Burray (*c.* 1000) hoards. The Caldale hoard (*c.* 1035), found in 1774, is reported to have consisted of two horns containing about 300 coins of Canute, 'on and near which were found several pieces of fine silver, in the form of crescents, or *fibulae*, differing from one another a good deal both in figure and dimensions. Some of them were flat, others angled; some round, some nearly met at the ends; others were wider at the extremities; one resembled in shape the staple of a door, and another a hook for hanging clothes upon'. (Barry 1805, 225). In addition, at the bottom of one of the horns 'were discovered some bits of apparently coarser silver, which, though they exhibited marks of being cut with an instrument, were manifestly the parts of crescents or *fibulae*, of the same kind with those already described'. (Barry 1805, 225). All the non-numismatic silver has been lost, but the presence of complete and fragmentary 'ring-money' suggested by this description is confirmed by an illustration in Gough (1777) of 'two of the *fibulae*, or crescents' (Barry 1805, 226). Finally, from Orkney, there is a lost coinless hoard found in a mound by the Ring of Brodgar which consisted of 'nine Silver Clasps shaped somewhat like a Horse's Shoe',[11] identifiable as 'ring-money' from the one illustrated specimen (Wallace 1700).

In Shetland, the Garthbanks/Quendale mixed hoard included both complete and fragmentary examples of 'ring-money' (Graham-Campbell 1976, pl. 13), as presumably did that from Dunrossness manse. There is a single example from the Norse settlement at Jarlshof where it was found 'adhering to peat ash on the lower face of a drain slab on the south side of the parent dwelling', attributed to Phase III (Hamilton 1956, 152, Fig. 60, 8).

On the Mainland, the only known hoard from Caithness consists of eight pieces of 'ring-money' (Batey 1987, 41), whilst the Tarbat, Easter Ross, mixed hoard from *c.* 1000 contained four examples (Graham-Campbell 1976, plate 12). It is noteworthy that both these hoards were buried in churchyards.

'Ring-money' weights seemed to Richard Warner (1976) to be related to a standard unit of 24 ± 0.8 g, although 'a large number of rings miss the target, often by a large amount' (Kruse 1988, 288). This would not, however, have seriously inhibited their use in making payments, but more detailed analyses remain to be performed on both the typology and the metrology of 'ring-money' to determine the nature of their probable role as currency. On the other hand, a vital consideration remains the fact that none of the Northern hoards consists exclusively of coins, whilst all those that are mixed seem to have contained 'ring-money'.

The arguments for the use of 'ring-money' as a form of currency (Graham-

Campbell 1976, 125–6; Morris 1985, 233–4) have been developed by Crawford (1987, 133–4), who comments that 'its existence points to an economic and trading system in the north which had no need of coins and which was independent to some extent of the Irish trading world', although its distribution also indicates 'continued contacts between Man and Norse Scotland during the eleventh century' (following Graham-Campbell 1983a). She suggests that it constituted 'a state currency' and introduces the 'possibility that ring-money was linked with the assessment system, based on the ounce, found in the Northern and Western Isles', although adding the caution that 'new hoards may change the known distribution of ring-money and make new explanations necessary' (Crawford 1987, 134). Her interpretation is criticised below by Kruse as 'overly elaborate' (p. 199).

CONCLUSIONS

Whilst new archaeological discoveries may always alter the balance of known evidence, it is apparent that the Viking-Age hoards which have come to light during the last decade or so, whether in Britain, Ireland, the Isle of Man or Norway, have all fitted into the currently perceived pattern of silver circulation in the Viking West, whilst augmenting it in detail (see also Kruse, this volume, for further analysis of the Scottish finds).

The Northern hoards of Scandinavian Scotland are few in comparison with those known from around the Irish Sea, but what they lack in number some make up in size and quality. These attributes of the Skaill hoard have already been commented on, but Orkney's second largest hoard, deposited *c.* 1000 on the island of Burray, weighs about 1.9 kg, placing it amongst Norway's heaviest (and equivalent in size to the native Pictish hoard from St Ninian's Isle).

Economic success in terms of portable wealth in the Earldom of Orkney was not only measured by weight of silver, but also in gold. There is a splendid gold arm-ring of plaited rods (Graham-Campbell 1980, no. 225) from the island of Oxna in Shetland (as well as a simpler gold finger-ring from Whalsay), whereas there is evidence from Orkney that two gold arm-rings were found in the Broch of Burgar (Graham-Campbell 1985, 242–4); a hoard of four gold finger-rings was discovered in a field by the Loch of Stenness, including an elaborately plaited example of 11th-century type (Graham-Campbell 1980, no. 238; Graham-Campbell 1988). Such plaited rings as those from Oxna and Stenness are amongst the finest standard types of prestige ornament that successful Vikings aspired to own and wear – as visible symbols of their wealth and status.[12]

Notes

1. References to material which have not been superseded (since Graham-Campbell 1976) are not normally repeated here; additional finds and new information have been published by Graham-Campbell (1982; 1983c; 1984; 1985; forthcoming), Hunter

(1986) and Stevenson (1986). A full account of all the Viking-Age hoards of Scandinavian character from Scotland, and related single-finds, is in preparation by myself and Olwyn Owen for the Royal Museum of Scotland. I am most grateful to Ms Owen and to Sir David Wilson for their helpful comments on a draft of this paper.

2. Hoards are classified as 'coin hoards' when consisting exclusively of coins, and 'coinless' when consisting exclusively of bullion (ornaments, ingots and/or hack-silver); 'mixed hoards' contain both coins and bullion (Graham-Campbell 1989).

3. I am grateful to Dr Donal Bateson, Mr Mark Blackburn and Mr Hugh Pagan for their advice in this connection.

4. Dr Alison Sheridan kindly made this mixed hoard available to me for inspection in the Royal Museum of Scotland. It consists of a cow horn found with some 40 pieces of hack-silver, mostly 'ring-money', and two fragmentary Norman deniers struck *c.* 990–1030/40 (information from Mr Mark Blackburn).

5. Information from Dr Donal Bateson.

6. I am grateful to Mr Brian Smith for drawing this letter to my attention (Shetland Archives: D.6/9/9).

7. This letter was located by Mr Alan Bell of the National Library of Scotland (Ms 3916, ff 62–3), thus resolving the problem alluded to in Graham-Campbell 1976, 128, note (iv). Scott received it as he was revising *The Pirate*, originally published in 1821, for the collected edition (1831), and was thus able to add a note referring to the hoard's discovery.

8. The drawing of the Clibberswick arm-ring, reproduced here (reduced) as Fig. 7.4, is by J. T. Irvine who recorded, in his *Sketches of a Collection of Antiquarian Remains from Shetland, etc.* (Library of the Society of Antiquaries of Scotland), that 'the silver bracelet, sketched in 1863, in the Shetland Museum, was quite plain'.

9. I am grateful to Alison Rosie of the Scottish Record Office for the information that the appropriate Letterbook (E806/10) contains no trace of the April 1831 correspondence referred to above, whilst their series of Treasure Trove Papers (E872) commences only in 1840.

10. There are only four 10th-century hoards from Norway that contain over 1 kg of silver, and of these only the coinless hoard from Vulu, Nord-Trøndelag, weighs over 2 kg (Grieg 1929, 254–6, no. 104 = 2.5 kg of gold and silver).

11. Quoted from a manuscript account of James Robertson's 1769 visit to Orkney and Shetland, pp. 39–40 (Shetland Archives: D.25/88/1), to which Mr Brian Smith kindly drew my attention.

12. In this connection, it is worth drawing attention to a lost Viking-Age gold neck-ring of twisted rods, found at the end of the 18th century at Braidwood Castle, Penicuik, Midlothian. This has generally been overlooked, despite its publication by Daniel Wilson (1851, 318), with a woodcut taken from a drawing said by him to be 'preserved in the Library of the Scottish Antiquaries'.

Appendix

CHECKLIST OF GOLD AND SILVER HOARDS AND SINGLE-FINDS OF SCANDINAVIAN CHARACTER FROM THE NORTHERN ISLES AND NORTH-EAST MAINLAND OF SCOTLAND

References as in Graham-Campbell 1976, Appendices A–C, unless otherwise noted. For single-finds of coins, see Stevenson 1986, Fig. 5.

Mixed hoards

Orkney: Skaill, deposited *c.* 950 (Graham-Campbell 1984)
                Burray, deposited *c.* 1000
                Caldale, deposited *c.* 1035

Shetland: Garthbanks/Quendale, deposited *c.* 1000
                Dunrossness manse, deposited *c.* 1065?

Mainland: Tarbat, Ross, deposited *c.* 1000

Coinless hoards

Orkney: Broch of Burgar (Graham-Campbell 1985, 242–4)
                Ring of Brodgar
                Stenness (Graham-Campbell 1980, no. 238)

Shetland: none

Mainland: Kirk o' Banks, Caithness (Batey 1987, 41)

Single-finds

Orkney: Brough of Birsay, 4 pieces (Hunter 1986, 186–7; Morris, forth-coming)
                Oxtro broch (Graham-Campbell 1985, 299–300)
                Westness, Rousay, 2 pieces

Shetland: Clibberswick, Unst
                Gulberwick
                Jarlshof, 2 pieces (Bruce 1907, 28)
                Marrister, Whalsay
                Oxna (Graham-Campbell 1980, no. 225)

Mainland: Freswick, Caithness, 2 pieces (Morris & Rackham 1992, 94)

Note: the ring from the Brough of Birsay, previously listed as silver (Graham-Campbell 1976, 131, Appendix C) and as bronze (Curle 1982, no. 447), is now known to be made of lead (analysis no. Fo771B, by J. Tate; information from T. Cowie).

REFERENCES

Archibald, Marion M. 1990. 'Pecking and bending: the evidence of British finds', in *Sigtuna Papers: Proceedings of the Sigtuna Symposium on Viking-Age Coinage, 1–4 June 1989*, eds Jonsson, Kenneth & Malmer, Brita. Commentationes de Nummis Saeculorum IX-XI in Suecia repertis, Nova Series 6, Stockholm-London, 11–24.

Barry, George 1805. *The History of the Orkney Islands*, Edinburgh.

Batey, Colleen E. 1987. *Freswick Links, Caithness: a Reappraisal of the Late Norse Site in its Context*, British Archaeological Reports British Series 179, Oxford.

Bjørn, Anathon & Shetelig, Haakon 1940. 'Viking antiquities in England', in Shetelig, Haakon (ed.), 1940, Part IV.

Blackburn, Mark & Pagan, Hugh 1986. 'A revised checklist of coin-hoards from the British Isles, *c.* 500–1100', in *Anglo-Saxon Monetary History: Essays in Memory of Michael Dolley*, ed. Blackburn, Mark A. S., Leicester, pp. 291–313.

Bruce, John 1907. 'Notice of the excavation of a broch at Jarlshof, Sumburgh, Shetland', *PSAS*, 41 (1906–07), 11–33.

Crawford, Barbara E. 1987. *Scandinavian Scotland*, Scotland in the early Middle Ages (Studies in the early history of Britain) 2, Leicester.

Curle, Cecil L. 1982. *Pictish and Norse Finds from the Brough of Birsay 1934–74*, Society of Antiquaries of Scotland Monograph Series 1, Edinburgh.

Dolley, R. H. Michael 1966. *The Hiberno-Norse Coins in the British Museum*, Sylloge of Coins of the British Isles, London.

Dolley, Michael & Skaare, Kolbjørn 1973. 'To penninger fra Harald Hardråde funnet på Vesterhavsøyene', *Nordisk Numismatisk Unions Medlemsblad* 8 (October 1973), 221–7.

Gough, Richard 1777. *Catalogue of the Coins of Canute, King of Denmark and England*, London.

Graham-Campbell, James A. 1976. 'The Viking-age silver and gold hoards of Scandinavian character from Scotland', *Proceedings of the Society of Antiquaries of Scotland* (=*PSAS*), 107 (1975–76), 114–35.

Graham-Campbell, James 1980. *Viking Artefacts: a Select Catalogue*, London.

Graham-Campbell, James 1982. 'An unpublished gold finger-ring of Viking-age date from the Isle of Skye, and new light on the 1850 Skye hoard', *PSAS*, 112, 568–70.

Graham-Campbell, James 1983a. 'The Viking-age silver hoards of the Isle of Man', in *The Viking Age in the Isle of Man*, eds Fell, Christine, Foote, Peter, Graham-Campbell, James & Thomson, Robert, London, pp. 53–80.

Graham-Campbell, James 1983b. 'Some Viking-age penannular brooches from Scotland and the origins of the "thistle-brooch"', in *From the Stone Age to the 'Forty-Five*, eds O'Connor, Anne & Clarke, D. V., Edinburgh, pp. 310–23.

Graham-Campbell, James 1983c. 'A Viking-age gold arm-ring from the Sound of Jura', *PSAS*, 113, 640–2.

Graham-Campbell, James 1984. 'Two Viking-age silver brooch fragments believed to be from the 1858 Skaill (Orkney) hoard', *PSAS*, 114, 289–301.

Graham-Campbell, James 1985. 'A lost Pictish treasure (and two Viking-age gold arm-rings) from the Broch of Burgar, Orkney', *PSAS*, 115, 241–61.

Graham-Campbell, James 1987. 'Western penannular brooches and their Viking-age copies in Norway: a new classification', in *Proceedings of the Tenth Viking*

Congress: Larkollen, Norway, 1985, ed. Knirk, James E., Universitetets Oldsaksamlings Skrifter, Ny Rekke 9, Oslo, pp. 231–46.

Graham-Campbell, James 1988. 'The gold finger-ring from a burial in St Aldate's Street, Oxford', *Oxoniensia*, 53, 263–6.

Graham-Campbell, James 1989. 'The coinless hoard', in *Coins and Archaeology*, eds Clarke, Helen & Schia, Erik, British Archaeological Reports International Series 556, Oxford, 53–61.

Grieg, Sigurd 1929. 'Vikingetidens skattefund', *Universitetets Oldsaksamlings Skrifter*, 2, 177–311.

Grieg, Sigurd 1940. 'Viking antiquities in Scotland', in Shetelig, Haakon (ed.), 1940, Part II.

Hamilton, John R. C. 1956. *Excavations at Jarlshof, Shetland*, Ministry of Works Archaeological Reports 1, Edinburgh.

Hunter, John R. 1986. *Rescue Excavations on the Brough of Birsay 1974–82*, Society of Antiquaries of Scotland Monograph Series 4, Edinburgh.

Kruse, Susan E. 1988. 'Ingots and weight units in Viking Age silver hoards', *World Archaeology*, 20:2, 285–301.

Morris, Christopher D. 1985. 'Viking Orkney: a survey', in *The Prehistory of Orkney 4000 BC–1000 AD*, ed. Renfrew, Colin, Edinburgh, pp. 210–42.

Morris, Christopher D. (ed.) 1985. 'Skaill, Sandwick, Orkney: preliminary investigations of a mound-site near Skara Brae', *Glasgow Archaeological Journal*, 12, 82–92.

Morris, Christopher D. & Rackham, D. James 1992. 'Excavations at Freswick Links, Caithness 1980–82: environmental column samples from the cliff-side', in *Norse and Later Settlement and Subsistence in the North Atlantic*, eds Morris, Christopher D. & Rackham, D. James, Glasgow, pp. 43–102.

Robertson, Anne S. 1961. *Hunterian and Coats Collections of the University of Glasgow, Part I: Anglo-Saxon Coins*, Sylloge of Coins of the British Isles 2, London.

Shetelig, Haakon (ed.) 1940. *Viking Antiquities in Great Britain and Ireland*, Parts I–V, Oslo.

Small, Alan, Thomas, A. Charles & Wilson, David M. 1973. *St Ninian's Isle and its Treasure*, Aberdeen University Studies Series 152, Oxford.

Smart, Veronica 1985. 'The penny in the pennylands: coinage in Scotland in the early Middle Ages', *Northern Studies*, 22, 65–70.

Stevenson, Robert B. K. 1966. *National Museum of Antiquities of Scotland, Edinburgh, Part I: Anglo-Saxon Coins (with associated foreign coins)*, Sylloge of Coins of the British Isles 6, London.

Stevenson, Robert B. K. 1986. 'The Anglo-Saxon silver penny and its context', in Morris, Christopher D. with Emery, Norman, 'The chapel and enclosure on the Brough of Deerness, Orkney: survey and excavations, 1975–1977', *PSAS*, 116, 301–74, 339–41.

Wallace, James 1700. *An Account of the Islands of Orkney*, London.

Warner, Richard 1976. 'Scottish silver arm-rings: an analysis of weights', *PSAS*, 107 (1975–6), 136–43.

Wilson, Daniel 1851. *The Archaeology and Prehistoric Annals of Scotland*, Edinburgh.

8

SILVER STORAGE AND CIRCULATION IN VIKING-AGE SCOTLAND

THE EVIDENCE OF SILVER INGOTS

SUSAN E. KRUSE

INTRODUCTION

The popularity of precious metals, particularly silver, in the Viking Age is attested by the many hoards and single finds. Hoards generally comprise wealth saved and circulated in four main forms throughout the areas influenced by the Scandinavians: in coins, ornaments, hacksilver and ingots. An examination of the composition of hoards can show different fashions current for storing silver in different times, which can be compared with preferences for storing silver in other areas.

For the Scottish finds, the studies by Graham-Campbell on hoards and single finds with non-numismatic items (Graham-Campbell 1976; this volume) and Stevenson on the coins (Stevenson 1966; 1986) provide an invaluable starting point.[1] These studies indicate how much silver and gold has been lost, even within the last few centuries. As a result, the quantification of artefacts is rarely meaningful in itself, and any studies which base conclusions on raw numbers of separate types of artefacts are based on incomplete foundations unless a sufficient number survive. Nevertheless, certain general trends can be isolated.

This paper stems from a study of one fashion for storing silver, in ingots, and the role these bullion preferences may have played in the economy. The evidence of preferred ways to store wealth in Viking-Age Scotland will be examined, with special emphasis on silver ingots, which have formed the subject of a larger study by the author (Kruse 1988b). Since no coinage was minted in Viking Age Scotland, the silver must have been used in a metal-weight economy, where any bullion would have passed according to weight. As a result, studies of the metrological basis of some of the silver will be outlined and correlated with findings elsewhere. Recent work on silver composition, which can help identify sources of silver used for some of the objects in the hoards, will also be discussed. Finally, all of these factors must be integrated to assess whether it is possible to determine the extent of wealth in Viking-Age Scotland, and its use in foreign and local exchange.

FASHIONS FOR SILVER STORAGE: INGOTS

Ingots provide the most obvious means of bullion storage in a metal-weight economy. They are a different type of object from others found in hoards, manufactured without any intent for ornamentation, generally with a primary purpose to store bullion in a convenient form. The use of ingots to store silver can be found in all areas of the Scandinavian world, with the exception of Iceland and Greenland, as well as around the East Baltic. In some areas they were more popular than others, for example, in Ireland, alongside Hiberno-Viking armrings, which indeed represent a worked state of ingot, and in Denmark (though excluding the southern Swedish provinces). In Scotland, although ingots appear in hoards, they are not common (Table 8.1).

The numbers of ingots listed in Table 8.1 must be viewed as minima. Find records are often vague, and when hoards were melted down, ingots were generally the first to go. Some attributions are questionable due to imprecise wording, whereas some records provide no details other than the fact some ingots were found. In addition, 21 unprovenanced ingots are in the National Museum of Ireland of which most, but possibly not all, are presumably from Ireland. The English material is overwhelmingly dominated by two finds, the Cuerdale, Lancashire hoard (c. 905) with over 350 ingots, and the Chester (Castle Esplanade), Cheshire hoard (c. 965) with 98 ingots (Kruse 1988b); the Irish finds by the recent ingot hoards from Loch Ennell, Co. Westmeath (Ryan et al. 1984).

Around a third of the hoards of Scandinavian character with non-numismatic silver from Scotland contain ingots (Table 8.2).[2] This is not as insignificant as first appears, since a number of finds are known only from records, which are themselves often incomplete. A large amount of recorded non-numismatic material has also been lost, including the ingots from Gordon and Machrie. On the other hand, in at least one case, the Tiree hoard, no ingots are recorded in the records, but can be demonstrated to have been present (Graham-Campbell 1976, 122).

Ingots are most common in the British Isles in finds from the first three quarters of the 10th century. Thus it is noteworthy that they appear in all Scottish hoards of Scandinavian character which can be dated to this period, with the exception of the St Helen's, Cockburnspath, Berwickshire and Port Glasgow, Renfrewshire, hoards, about which almost nothing is known (Graham-Campbell 1976, 118 & 122).

The incomplete find records for many of these hoards hinder detailed discussion, but it appears that the importance of ingots within the hoard changes with time. Only in the Gordon, Berwickshire, and Storr Rock, Skye, hoards do ingots appear to make up a significant part of the finds (Graham-Campbell 1976, 119 & 124). These two hoards are the earliest Scottish hoards of Scandinavian character, and have distinct Irish connections (Graham-Campbell 1976, 124);

Table 8.1: Known occurrences of Viking Age silver ingots in the British Isles.

	No. of Ingots	No. of Finds	Earliest	Latest
Scotland	36	7	late 9th/early 10th	*c.* 1000
England	484+	9	*c.* 872	*c.* 965
Wales	1	1	*c.* 925	*c.* 925
Isle of Man	1	1	*c.* 970	*c.* 970
Ireland	256+	42	late 9th/early 10th	*c.* 1030

given the propensity for ingots in Irish hoards, it is possible that the ingots from these two hoards also came from Ireland.

Ingots are not an important element in the later finds. Although the Skaill, Orkney, hoard has fewer ingots than the Storr Rock hoard, they consist of over twice the weight, *c.* 300 g. Nevertheless, this is an insignificant proportion of the total hoard, accounting for less than 4 per cent of the total weight. From the later Burray, Orkney, find, which contained close to 2 kg of silver, only two ingots (one of which may be a 'ring-money' fragment) weighing a total of 13.52 g are known.

Even in the early finds, the evidence suggests that the ingots had circulated. Many of the ingots, like much of the silver in Scandinavian hoards, have nicks (pecks), presumably made to check silver purity. As a result, analysis of nicking can provide a very rough indication of circulation, where one would expect the more utilised silver to have more nicks. Of the surviving Scottish ingots which have been examined for nicks,[3] most contain evidence of nicking: 48 per cent between 1 and 4 per ingot; 26 per cent between 5 and 9; and 23 per cent more than 10. One example from the Skaill hoard (IL 53) has 30 nicks. This pattern is greater than that for the ingots found in England, where only 14 per cent have more than 10 nicks per ingot, and far greater than Ireland where only 1 per cent have more than 10 nicks per ingot.

The distribution of the finds with ingots is almost entirely from the Northern and Western Isles, a distribution reflecting the entire corpus of hoards (Graham-Campbell 1976). The exception, the find from Gordon, Berwickshire, has been associated with Scandinavian activity through the area (Graham-Campbell 1976, 115). Thus, although no geographical significance can be associated with their occurrence in finds, a chronological distinction can be made, whereby (if one can generalise from two finds) ingots may have been a common way to store silver in Scotland at a time when they were popular in Ireland and the northern Danelaw. The evidence of the nicking suggests that many of the ingots may not have been manufactured in Scotland, but instead imported and saved in this form. A similar argument has been made for the 'ball' brooches, an ostentatious fashion of silver storage found in the Irish Sea area, but only in two Scottish finds, albeit in some numbers in the Skaill hoard (Graham-Campbell 1983a).

Table 8.2: Viking Age finds of ingots from Scotland.

Hoard	Date	No. of Ingots
Gordon, Berwickshire	late 9th/early 10th century	2
Storr Rock, Skye	c. 935	15
Skaill, Orkney	c. 950	10
Machrie, Islay	c. 970	4+
Tiree, Argyll	c. 970	1
Iona Abbey, Argyll	c. 986	1
Burray, Orkney	c. 1000	2

FASHIONS FOR SILVER STORAGE: 'RING-MONEY'

In the second half of the 10th century, ingots still circulated in small numbers, but silver resources in Scotland were now overwhelmingly stored in 'ring-money'. Over 62 complete and 150 fragments are known, most dating to the period between 950 and AD 1050. The distribution and number of finds suggest that 'ring-money' were made in Scotland (Graham-Campbell 1976, 125–6; 1983b, 62–3; this volume). Studies of nicking on 'ring-money', including comparisons with Scottish, Manx and Irish examples, could prove interesting.

A great deal of silver was stored in 'ring-money'. Total weights cannot be estimated, since many remain unpublished or no longer survive, but extant complete examples from Scotland weigh more than 2.5 kg, with complete examples from the Skaill hoard comprising over 15 per cent of the total weight of the hoard, and from the Burray hoard over 45 per cent.[4] The number of finds from this later period, and the amounts of silver, suggest that the Scandinavians in the Northern and Western Isles were managing to obtain more silver than their forebears a generation or two earlier, and developing distinct forms in which to store and circulate it.

COINS

Find records are particularly vague for recording numbers of coins, and the surviving examples are only fractions of the original numbers found (Stevenson 1966, xviii–xxiii). However, some finds included a large number of coins (e.g. the Tiree, Iona Abbey, and Caldale, Orkney, hoards) suggesting no great prejudice against storing silver in coin during the 10th and 11th centuries. The range of ultimate sources, including the Arabic empire, 10th-century Frankish kingdoms and Normandy, 9th- and 10th-century Northumbria (from both Anglo-Saxon and Viking rulers), 10th- and 11th-century Anglo-Saxon England, 11th-century Ireland, and 11th-century Norway show little preference for certain issues (Stevenson 1966; 1986; Smart 1985). These need not of course represent direct contacts, and are more likely in most cases to derive from coin stock floating around metal weight economies in the Irish Sea.

What does appear significant, and contrasts with the Isle of Man (Graham-Campbell 1983b) and Ireland (Kenny 1987), is the scarcity of hoards containing only coins. Again find records are vague, but only three very poorly recorded hoards, two from the Western Isles and one unprovenanced, may be purely coin hoards (Graham-Campbell 1976, 127). Unlike Man and Ireland, no minting of coins occurred, nor are many single finds known (Graham-Campbell 1983b, 60–2; Stevenson 1986). The two largest hoards, from Skaill and Burray, contained very few coins (21 and 3 respectively; Stevenson 1966, xviii, xxii). Altogether, the impression is that storage and circulation in an artefact form was preferable to coin.

METALLURGICAL ANALYSIS[5]

It is possible that many of the imported coins were melted down into forms more acceptable to their owners. In particular, the 'ring-money' is so prevalent in later hoards that one suspects coins may have formed the raw material. An important study by White and Tate analysed a number of pieces of 'ring-money' from the Skaill and Burray hoards (White & Tate 1983). In addition, almost all the ingots found in Scotland have also been analysed by x-ray fluorescence analysis (Kruse & Tate, forthcoming).

The analyses of 'ring-money' clearly showed different silver alloys, the Burray 'ring-money' being substantially more debased (White & Tate 1983). Almost all ingots were of pure silver, better than 90 per cent, although three of the Storr Rock ingots were less than 86 per cent silver, and one of the Burray ingots was very base, less than 70 per cent silver (and thus comparable to the 'ring-money'). The silver used for most 'ring-money' in the Skaill hoard, with one exception, was similar to the ingots, although the latter displayed some compositions not found in the 'ring-money'. Of the two ingots tested from the Burray hoard, one matched the debased 'ring-money', but the other was of much purer silver, consistent with other Scottish ingots.

When compared to contemporary Anglo-Saxon coins which have been analysed,[6] there is general conformance, although the lowest Storr Rock ingots are baser than most contemporary Anglo-Saxon coins. However, it is the comparison of the other elements in the alloy which allows a better idea of silver sources. Since the gold probably entered as part of the silver, the ratio of gold in silver can be a useful diagnostic feature. A wide range in the gold and silver ratios amongst objects tested would suggest a range of silver sources. A uniform range could indicate either a single source of silver, such as from one mine, or the gradual homogenization of alloys into a fairly uniform pattern (Metcalf & Northover 1986, 36 & 43).

The range of all the Scottish ingots analysed was basically similar, although four Skaill ingots and one Storr Rock ingot displayed a cluster below the rest of the material, and the Burray 'ring-money' was decidedly lower than most ingots. Contemporary Anglo-Saxon coins until the reform of Eadgar have a much wider range of gold in silver ratios than the ingots, but nevertheless higher than ratios in the Storr Rock and Skaill ingots and 'ring-money'. As a result, these objects were not formed exclusively from Anglo-Saxon coins. Recent work by Metcalf and Northover on late Anglo-Saxon coins suggests alloys varied from mint to mint (Metcalf & Northover 1986), and it may prove possible to localise some objects in the future.

Although few Arabic coins have been found in the British Isles, they occur in 20 hoards dating from the third quarter of the 9th century through the third quarter of the 10th century (Graham-Campbell 1987, 337). Some scholars have postulated that Arabic silver was introduced into the Irish Sea silver stock in the 10th century (e.g. Wallace 1987, 217). Fortunately, many Arabic coins are composed of a very distinctive alloy, with very pure silver, very little gold, and moderate bismuth (McKerrell & Stevenson 1972; Werner & Cowell 1975). No ingots can be confidently attributed to purely melted Arabic coins, although one ingot each from the Storr Rock and Skaill hoards have similar alloys, and three further ingots from the Skaill hoard have lower gold and higher bismuth than other ingots, overlapping the edge of the ranges from analysed Arabic coins.

A few ingots with similar alloy occur in the Irish Sea area. The Scotby, Cumbria, hoard, contemporary with the Storr Rock hoard, had one rod fragment with a similar composition, and the Cuerdale, Lancashire, hoard (c. 905) contained two rod fragments and two ingots with similarly low gold and high silver content, though less bismuth. Consequently, in a few cases, but not as a general rule, Arabic silver may have formed a major component in the silver cast into some ingots in the Irish Sea and Northern Isles. This is in stark contrast to analyses performed on 128 objects found in southern Swedish hoards dating from the 10th through 12th centuries, in which almost all were probably derived from Arabic silver (Hårdh 1976, 112–27).

A few analyses have been performed on ingots and hacksilver from 10th-century Irish hoards (Ryan et al. 1984, 356–61). The Scottish ingots and Skaill 'ring-money' displayed similar gold in silver ratios, much more similar than that found when comparing coins. Very few Hiberno-Viking coins have been found in Scotland (Smart 1985, 68–70), a puzzling gap since they are common on Man (Graham-Campbell 1983b, 61). In any case, only a few ingots are contemporary with Hiberno-Viking coins and none with Hiberno-Manx coins. Recent analyses of the early Hiberno-Viking coinages also indicate that the coins are unlikely to represent identical silver sources as the ingots, since the coins may well be re-used Anglo-Saxon coins, possibly from the Chester mint (Heslip & Northover 1990, 103–5).

As a result, it is likely that similar silver sources, coin and bullion, were being used for ornaments and ingots in different areas of the Irish Sea, though no one source was predominant. The similarities in the Skaill 'ring-money' and ingots suggest at least some of these ingots may have been manufactured in Scotland, or that the craftsmen had access to the same sorts of silver. Further analysis of the other trace elements in the Scottish material hopefully will render it possible to narrow down some of the possible options.

The finds of balances and weights in Scandinavian graves in the Western Isles (Grieg 1940, 29–30 & 79; Graham-Campbell 1980, no. 307) and indeed some native hoards (Graham-Campbell 1976, 117–8), indicate the existence of some metrological tradition. Without written records, two approaches are available to elucidate the underlying metrological basis: analysis of weights and analysis of objects which may have been weighed. Both approaches have methodological problems (Kruse 1988a, 286ff).

No analysis of the weights of gold finds from the British Isles has been undertaken, in part due to the limited number and in part due to the difficulties of integrating with analyses of the more common silver objects, without knowing the correspondence in value of gold to silver. However, such a study might prove valuable. A great deal of attention, on the other hand, has been addressed to the underlying systems for silver. In some cases, there have been assumptions that the same system underlay all Viking-Age finds, whether in Scandinavia or the British Isles; in other cases, the evidence from local areas has been analysed independently (Kruse 1988a, with references). This latter approach would seem the more promising, although it necessitates a large amount of data.

Ingots, without any possibilities of direct use as ornaments, present an obvious source for determining Viking-Age weight standards. Analysis of ingots from the hoards found in England revealed a clustering in the mid-20 g zone, but without any great precision (Kruse 1988a; 1988b). If one compares this to the weights of Scottish ingots, an entirely different pattern is evident (Fig. 8.1). No ingots weigh in the mid-20 g zone, nor is any clustering evident in the material. However, the numbers are undeniably small, and most of the ingots fragmentary and light-weight.

Unlike the ingots, the 'ring-money' shows some clustering in the low 20 g zone, but more strongly around 50 g (Fig. 8.1). Warner analysed the 62 complete examples from Scottish finds and 10 complete examples from the Isle of Man using quantum analysis, and postulated a unit of 24.0 ± 0.8 g. However, he also found a standard deviation of 5 g, which at the least suggests craftsmen 'were not too careful about their accuracy' (Warner 1976, 141). Quantum analysis presents some problems (Kruse 1988a, 293–4), and the standard deviation of 5 g is rather worrying. With such imprecision, it is difficult to interpret the 'ring-money', as Crawford has done, as currency (Crawford 1987, 134).

The lack of correspondence in ingots and 'ring-money' may be due to several factors. Half of the ingots in Figure 8.1 predate the 'ring-money'. The 'ring-money' are probably manufactured in Scotland, but the undiagnostic features of ingots do not allow any such localisation, although, as noted above, metallurgical analysis does not rule out the possibility. Thus the ingots may be imports,

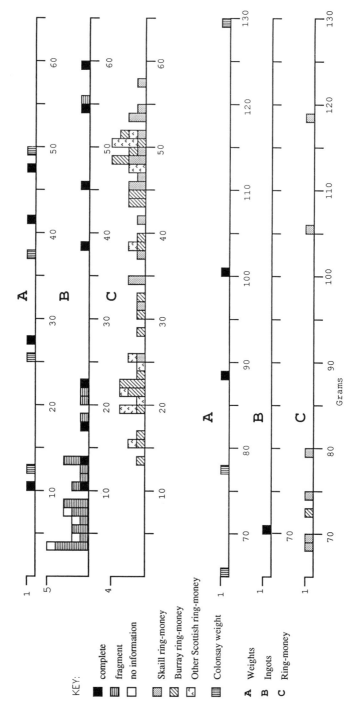

Figure 8.1: Weights of ring-money, ingots and weights from Scotland (Sample size: ring money – complete for whole examples; missing all fragments (over 150). Ingots: complete. Weights: missing Whithorn weight. Data: Warner 1975-6; Kruse 1988b; see also note 6).

KEY:

- ■ complete
- ▥ fragment
- □ no information

- ▨ Skaill ring-money
- ▨ Burray ring-money
- ▨ Other Scottish ring-money

- ▦ Colonsay weight

A Weights
B Ingots
C Ring-money

representing other systems or preferences. Moreover, most are fragments, again showing secondary use, while the 'ring-money' for which weights are published are all complete. The complete ingots for which figures are known are within the sprawl of 'ring-money' weights, though rarely near the target weights produced by Warner's analysis.

A third type of metrological evidence available for the Scottish finds consists of weight sets found in graves from Kiloran Bay, Colonsay (Graham-Campbell 1980, no. 307) and Gigha (Grieg 1940, 29–30), and single weights found in the Talnotrie, Kircudbrightshire hoard (Maxwell 1913, 13), and during excavations at Little Dunagoil, Bute (Marshall 1964, 52) and Whithorn (unpublished; personal communication P. Hill). The Talnotrie hoard was deposited *c.* 875 and may have belonged to a native craftsman rather than a Scandinavian owner (Graham-Campbell 1976, 118), which may best explain the unusual mixture of objects. No further details survive concerning the Gigha find, but the Colonsay owner was certainly Scandinavian, and the grave probably dates to the late 9th century. As a result, this evidence predates that of the hoards.

The Colonsay set in particular, has long featured in metrological literature (e.g. Brøgger 1921, 79; Kyhlberg 1980, 172–4, with references). Fundamental to the analysis of all the Scottish weights is their condition. All weights are visibly corroded or damaged, hindering fine metrological interpretation. Nevertheless, some correspondence with the 'ring-money' may be present (Fig. 8.1),[7] although the imprecision in the 'ring-money' and the condition of the weights prevent any more definite conclusion.

The majority of the weights have lead bases and gilt-bronze caps, many re-used from earlier insular metalwork. Nine similar weights were found in the Kilmainham/Islandbridge graves outside Dublin, possibly part of one set (Graham-Campbell 1980, no. 308), but the weights when compared to the Colonsay finds display some close correspondence and some distinct differences. Over 200 weights, most of lead and dating to the 10th century, were found during excavations in Dublin. Wallace analysed these lead weights by quantum analysis, concluding that a standard of 26.6 g can be found in the material. This, he argued, represents a change from a lighter Scandinavian standard of *c.* 24 g. The differences in the Kilmainham/Islandbridge weights, he suggested, are caused by having weights of both standards present in the material (Wallace 1987, 212–3). The Scottish weights can be correlated with both standards, with neither proving more convincing (Kruse 1988b, 161).

A fuller treatment of these weights is warranted, but awaits the full publication of the Dublin weights, and an integration with an assessment of Anglo-Saxon weights (Kruse 1992). For the purposes here, their general correspondence but lack of precision is the main point to note.

Together the analysis of 'ring-money' and ingot weights indicates that no great precision can be attached to the ornaments, and the evidence of Scottish weights cannot provide closer attributions. One possibility is that Viking-Age balances were not sufficiently sensitive to measure such differences, but this is generally thought unlikely (Sperber 1988, with references). It seems inescapable that the craftsmen were not concerned to reproduce 'ring-money', ingots, and probably other ornaments, with a great deal of accuracy.

This imprecision could have been due to several reasons. It may have been tolerated in a weight-money economy, with the expectation that hacksilver would always have been on hand to top up the scale pan. Alternatively, some objects may be from different areas or have been destined for different markets with other standards. Another, and complementary, explanation is that ornaments, and possibly ingots in some places as well, were manufactured with other purposes in mind than simply bullion standards, so that when found in mixed hoards they may have been serving a role different from that originally intended.

CIRCULATION OF SILVER IN THE ECONOMY

The remainder of this paper will briefly explore some of these' issues, although in many cases more questions than answers will be raised. The evidence available suggests some wealth reaching Scotland, though the extent is debated, with some fashions apparent in storing this wealth. The hoard evidence is limited for the early period, suggesting little silver reached Scotland. Some ingots may have been made in Scotland, but many, like the 'ball' brooches, may have been brought in that form to Scotland, and considered satisfactory to keep without remelting. The 'ring-money' on the other hand appears to be a Scottish fashion, developing when silver became more plentiful.

The interpretations concerning the mechanisms by which the silver reached Scotland, as other areas affected by the Scandinavians, have been subject to fashions of modern scholarship. Plunder and trade have been the two most often cited reasons, although other factors such as gift exchange and tribute have also been suggested (Grierson 1959; Sawyer 1971; Metcalf 1981; Wilson 1982). Similarly, the use of the silver in Scotland has been subject to fashions in interpretation. In the past, almost all researchers argued the silver represented wealth to purchase goods and services (e.g. Crawford 1987). However, recent studies using theories gained from economic anthropological approaches, have suggested this view is overly simplistic, and the other functions of money in primitive economies, such as to indicate and preserve status, should be considered.

The key question comes back to who used the wealth found in the hoards and why? What could the silver in particular be used for? It is evident that the wealth belonged to Scandinavian and colonial-Scandinavian, rather than the native population (Graham-Campbell 1976, 127). There is no evidence of a monetary economy in pre-Scandinavian Scotland (Spearman 1988, 99–101), although there was a tradition of craft activity using silver. Nevertheless, the debased alloy of the late Pictish silver, as revealed by analyses of some of the St Ninian's Isle treasure (McKerrell 1973) and a Pictish silver ingot found during excavations at Clatchard Craig, Fife (Close-Brooks 1986, 167-8), suggests perhaps silver supplies were not large.

The Viking-Age hoards are of a recognised Scandinavian character with affinities to other Viking hoards in Scandinavia and the British Isles. Although some differences between settlements in the Northern and Western Isles have been suggested (e.g. Crawford 1987, 121ff), the contents of hoards in both areas are similar, indicating participation in the same economic network for these items. The only diagnostic Scottish ornament, 'ring-money', shows silver moving to and from Scotland, both in the Northern and Western Isles, with a particular relationship to Man (Graham-Campbell 1983b, 62-3; Sheehan 1984, 89ff). It would be overly restrictive to see none of this as the result of trade. The hacksilver fragments, the evidence of weights and balances, and foreign objects from graves and settlements (Crawford 1987, ch. 5 with references) suggest some trading must have occurred.

However, the extent of this is the subject of some dispute. Graham-Campbell argued that the number of finds, particularly when contrasted with the evidence of hoards from Ireland, suggest that 'overseas trade, other than in basic commodities, did not play a central part in the economic life of the Norse settlers in Scotland' (Graham-Campbell 1976, 127). Wilson argued that during the 10th and 11th centuries the Scottish communities capitalised on their geographical position to take advantage of the increased trade from Dublin, and 'became richer than they were ever to become again' (Wilson 1976, 110-11). Wallace endorsed this view for the 10th but not the 11th century (Wallace 1987, 232-3). Crawford goes further, and has argued that the amount of silver indicates wealthy communities and a large, flourishing participation in trade (Crawford 1987, 134-5).

The interpretation of the extent of wealth is distorted by the very large Skaill and Burray hoards. They are indeed collections of great wealth, but exceptional in size compared to other hoards. The number of complete ornaments and size of the Skaill and Burray hoards suggest wealth of leaders, not simple traders, although such interpretations cannot be proven (Graham-Campbell, this volume). Nor need it represent wealthy communities as much as wealthy individuals (Morris 1985, 233). The latter may lead to the former, but only if a sustained supply of wealth occurs.

Without denying that some trade must have occurred, the available evidence on balance supports the more cautious conclusions of Graham-Campbell. Silver arrived into Scotland, but by no means it seems with regularity or as part of one mechanism. Gold too arrived, or was melted down from other objects, but in no great quantities (Graham-Campbell 1976; this volume). The Scottish finds have gold finger-rings, not armrings.

It is more difficult to assess the local circulation of silver in Scotland. What might the silver have been used for? To purchase subsistence goods and/or luxuries from one another? A savings deposit for use only in foreign markets? Or a mixture of the two, which is generally what is considered as characteristic of a fully fledged market economy? Or as wealth to enhance status and prestige?

How can one identify what was used in local purchases based on archaeological material alone, and in an area with few distinctive local objects? This problem has been addressed for other areas (e.g. see Hårdh 1978; Metcalf 1981; Kenny 1987), and various models proposed. The difficulty with assessing the Scottish material is simply that so little evidence exists with which to test any model. Although no consensus is available on the distinguishing characteristics, one would expect at least some of the following: widespread finds, a substantial number of finds in areas of settlement, many finds with silver in small denominations, and probably a large number of single coins or small amounts of silver. Exact quantification of these conditions is impossible, depending on population size and settlement patterns. One approach used to shed light on accumulation and circulation, the examination of the age structure of coins in hoards (Metcalf 1981; 1986), is unfortunately possible only with a small fraction of the Scottish hoards due to the incomplete find records, and cannot therefore be used to generalise about the nature of the economy.

The number of finds is not large and their distribution, as noted above, corresponds almost entirely to areas of Scandinavian settlement or movement. These facts, which were important when assessing foreign contacts, become crucial for interpreting local exchange. If many commodities were purchased with silver, a fair amount of silver must have been present and, although our find records are incomplete, one would nevertheless expect a reasonable amount of this to survive (the difficulty of course being to quantify 'fair' and 'reasonable' amounts). It is noteworthy how there has been only one hoard found in Scotland in the last decades, as compared, for example, with Ireland (Ryan et al. 1984; Kenny 1987) or Scandinavia (Sawyer 1971, 91). The silver in the hoards is generally not in light-weight pieces, although this feature corresponds in many respects to the Norwegian composition of hoards (Hårdh 1976, 133). Hoards are generally small, but when coupled with the small number of finds, this fact suggests a less than vigorous circulation.

Single finds of coins are often used to suggest local circulation (e.g. Stevenson 1966, xvi). Less than two dozen single coins are known, the majority from the Northern Isles. Ninth-century examples are pierced, unlike the 10th- and 11th-century examples, leading Stevenson to consider that these later coins might have had a monetary function (Stevenson 1986). However, the fact that many of this small sample occur from high prestige sites, such as the Brough of Birsay, cautions an interpretation of flourishing local exchange. Future archaeological finds throughout the Northern and Western Isles may modify this picture, but at present the evidence is ambiguous, leading Smart (1985, 70) to conclude that the acquisition and use of coins in Viking-Age Scotland 'cannot be answered by numismatic evidence'.

The small number of single finds, together with the hoard evidence, led Graham-Campbell (this volume) to conclude a small amount of silver was in circulation. Crawford, on the other hand, based on her perspective of a wealthy society, argued that a vigorous local economy existed, with the 'ring-money' operating as standardised metal currency (Crawford 1987, 133–4). Such a sophisticated local economy seems most unlikely. The imprecision of the 'ring-money' or other silver to a standard suggests such an interpretation is overly elaborate, unless one assumes the differences in weight were not important to those using the 'ring-money' as cash. Nor is her argument that the 'ring-money' may have kept out Hiberno-Viking coins from the economy convincing (Crawford 1987, 134), since other forms of coinage and object were accepted in hoards.

Moreover, if a flourishing local circulation of silver occurred, the gap in hoards after the Viking-Age remains very puzzling. The latest Viking-Age hoards are four dating to the 1020s and 1030s, and a poorly recorded find from Shetland of *c.* 1065 (Graham-Campbell 1976, 128). This is not that different from the situation elsewhere in the Irish Sea area, where hoards with non-numismatic material disappear during the course of the 11th century. What is unusual is that no native coinage developed, as in Ireland, or any other indication of new preferences in silver. There are no hoards, and almost no single finds of coins, until David I began to mint coins in *c.* 1136 (Metcalf 1977, 8).

Metcalf argued that no significance could be attached to this negative evidence (Metcalf 1977, 8–9), but the evidence he cited relates to the years just before minting began, and reveals money from English sources or ecclesiastical contacts. Other documentary evidence suggests a long use of in-kind rather than monetary payments (Spearman 1988, 105). Even after the introduction of minting, there are few Scottish hoards (Metcalf 1977, 9) suggesting that silver in local exchange took a long time to become established.

As a result, it can be argued that silver never had a great influence on the local economy in the Viking Age. This is not to say that it was not valued or had a potential for purchase. However, this is more likely to have been on an *ad hoc* basis and for external goods, rather than as an element in an established local trading system.

One of the functions of silver and gold, and perhaps one not always given enough credit, was as a measure of status. Recent studies making use of economic anthropological theories have stressed the different functions money could have, including very important social roles (Grierson 1959; Hårdh 1978; Doherty 1980; Hodges 1988, 1989; Thurborg 1988). In such a situation, where wealth was primarily collected to indicate status, one would expect certain artefact forms to appear, where silver resources were converted to socially acceptable forms. When manufactured with such roles in mind, exact metrological accuracy would be irrelevant. Instead, only a rough approximation to a standard and value would be necessary. These objects could be converted to hard cash when necessary, as the fragmentary forms of arm-rings and hacksilver suggest. Even ingots in some societies could fulfil such a social function. In Ireland, they are listed as one of the items rendered as tribute to kings (Doherty 1980, 74), and the large numbers of finds with only ingots, most without nicking, may relate to this situation.

When Scotland became silver poor, as it appears to have become after the mid-11th century, some adaptations would have been necessary, but whether more to the local economy or social structure remains open to question. If the population had been used to silver in local exchanges, the lack of silver would have provoked a crisis. Unfortunately, little evidence exists which can be brought to bear on this, but one does not find, for example, hoards with much debased silver. If, as I am arguing here, the role of silver in local exchanges was slight even in the Viking Age, the diminishing supplies would not have been a major economic issue. New commodities could be adapted for foreign export if necessary, but the local economy would have continued in its basically non-silver exchange. On the social side, the lack of silver would have necessitated some changes, with different artefacts emerging to indicate status.

Notes

1. My debt to the published works of James Graham-Campbell is obvious in this paper. I would also like to thank him for many useful conversations and generous access to unpublished work, and helpful comments on a draft of this paper.
2. Table 8.2 excludes the Plan Farm, St Blane's Church, Bute hoard, which although it contained a silver ingot, dates long after the Viking period, to *c.* 1150.
3. All ingots with the exception of one Skaill ingot (IL 516), an ambiguous object, completely hammered and tapering now into a pincer-like shape.
4. Ring-money weights from Warner 1976; totals of hoards from Graham-Campbell 1976, 119, 123.
5. Since this paper was written, new metallurgical analyses have refined many of the conclusions, particularly in regard to Arabic silver (see Kruse & Tate, forthcoming).
6. Major studies of coins contemporary with the hoards can be found in Harris 1962; McKerrell and Stevenson 1972; and Metcalf and Northover 1986.
7. Weights of the Colonsay weights and one Skaill ingot (IL 516) from a recent reweighing on a modern digital balance at the Royal Museum of Scotland; weights of the Gigha weights kindly supplied by Dr Euan Mackie, Hunterian Museum, Glasgow, weighed on a balance of unspecified accuracy; Talnotrie and Bute weights from Maxwell 1913 and Marshall 1964, respectively, both converted into grams; weight of the Tiree ingot weighed on a modern Digital balance in the British Museum.

REFERENCES

Brøgger, A. W. 1921. *Ertog og Øre. Den gamle norske vegt. Videnskapsselskapets Skrifter*, II, Hist.-filos. Klasse 3, Kristiania.
Close-Brooks, Joanna 1986. 'Excavations at Clatchard Craig, Fife', *Proceedings of the Society of Antiquaries of Scotland* (=*PSAS*) 116, 117–84.
Crawford, Barbara E. 1987. *Scandinavian Scotland*, Leicester.
Doherty, Charles 1980. 'Exchange and trade in early medieval Ireland', *Journal of the Royal Society of Antiquaries of Ireland* 110, 67–89.

Graham-Campbell, J[ames] A. 1976. 'The Viking-age silver and gold hoards of Scandinavian character from Scotland', *PSAS* 107 1975–6, 114–35.

Graham-Campbell, James 1980. *Viking Artefacts. A Select Catalogue*, London.

Graham-Campbell, James 1983a. 'Some Viking-age penannular brooches from Scotland and the origins of the "thistle-brooch" ', in *From the Stone-Age to the 'Forty-Five*, eds O'Connor, Anne and Clarke, David V. Edinburgh, pp. 310–23.

Graham-Campbell, James 1983b. 'The Viking-Age silver hoards of the Isle of Man', in *The Viking Age in the Isle of Man*, eds Fell, Christine *et al.*, London, pp. 53–80.

Graham-Campbell, James 1987. 'Some archaeological reflections on the Cuerdale hoard', in *Coinage in Ninth-Century Northumbria*, ed. Metcalf, D. M., Oxford (B.A.R. British Series 180), pp. 329–44.

Grieg, Sigurd 1940. *Viking Antiquities in Scotland* (Part II of Shetelig, H. (ed.), *Viking Antiquities in Great Britain and Ireland*), Oslo.

Grierson, Philip 1959. 'Commerce in the Dark Ages: a critique of the evidence', *Transactions of the Royal Historical Society*, 5th series, 9, 123–40.

Hårdh, Birgitta 1976. *Wikingerzeitliche Depotfunde aus Südschweden. Probleme und Analysen*, *Acta Archaeologica Lundensia*, series in 8° minore, No. 6, Bonn and Lund.

Hårdh, Birgitta 1978. 'Trade and money in Scandinavia in the Viking Age', *Meddelanden från Lunds Universitets Historiska Museum*, 1977–8, 157–71.

Harris, Edward J. 1962. 'Debasement of the coinage', *Seaby's Coin and Medal Bulletin*, 5–7.

Heslip, Robert & Northover, Peter 1990. 'The alloy of the Hiberno-Norse coinage', in *Sigtuna Papers. Proceedings of the Sigtuna Symposium on Viking-Age Coinage 1–4 June 1989*, eds Jonsson, Kenneth and Malmer, Brita, Stockholm, pp. 103–11.

Hodges, Richard 1988. *Primitive & Peasant Markets*, Oxford.

Hodges, Richard 1989. *Dark Age Economics. The origins of towns and trade AD 600–1000*, 2nd edn, London.

Kenny, Michael 1987. 'The geographical distribution of Irish Viking-age coin hoards', *Proceedings of the Royal Irish Academy*, 87c, 507–25.

Kruse, Susan E. 1988a. 'Ingots and weight units in Viking Age silver hoards', *World Archaeology* 20, 285–301.

Kruse, Susan E. 1988b. 'Viking Age Silver Ingots from England and Wales and their Economic Implications', unpublished Ph.D thesis, University of London.

Kruse, Susan E. 1992. 'Late Saxon balances and weights from England', *Medieval Archaeology* 36, 67–95.

Kruse, Susan E. & Tate, James, forthcoming. 'XRF analysis of Viking Age silver ingots', *PSAS* 122, 1992.

Kyhlberg, Ola 1980. *Vikt och Värde*, Stockholm Studies in Archaeology 1.

Marshall, Dorothy N. 1964. 'Report on excavations at Little Dunagoil', *Transactions of the Buteshire Natural History Society* 16, 1–69.

Maxwell, Herbert 1913. 'Notes on a hoard of personal ornaments, implements, and Anglo-Saxon and Northumbrian coins from Talnotrie, Kirkcudbrightshire', *PSAS* 47 1912–13, 12–6.

McKerrell, Hugh 1973. 'Appendix B. Chemical analyses of the silver objects', in *St Ninian's Isle and its Treasure*, eds Small, Alan, Thomas, Charles and Wilson, David M., vol. 1, London, pp. 174–5.

McKerrell, Hugh & Stevenson, Robert B. K. 1972. 'Some analyses of Anglo-Saxon and associated Oriental silver coinage', in *Methods of Chemical and Metallurgical Investigation of Ancient Coinage*, eds Hall, E. T. & Metcalf, D. M. London, pp. 195–209.

Metcalf, D. M. 1977. 'The evidence of Scottish coin hoards for monetary history, 1100–1600', in *Coinage in Medieval Scotland (1100–1600)*, ed. Metcalf, D. M., Oxford (B.A.R. Brit. Ser. 45), pp. 1–59.

Metcalf, D. M. 1981. 'Some twentieth-century runes. Statistical analysis of the Viking-age hoards and the interpretation of wastage rates', in *Viking-Age Coinage in the Northern Lands*, eds Blackburn, M. A. S. & Metcalf, D. M., Oxford (B.A.R. Int. Ser. 122), part ii, pp. 329–82.

Metcalf, D. M. 1986. 'The monetary history of England in the tenth century viewed in the perspective of the eleventh century', in *Anglo-Saxon Monetary History*, ed. Blackburn, M. A. S., Leicester, pp. 133–57.

Metcalf, D. M. & Northover, J. P. 1986. 'Interpreting the alloy of the later Anglo-Saxon coinage', *British Numismatic Journal* 56, 35–63.

Morris, Christopher D. 1985. 'Viking Orkney: a survey', in *The Prehistory of Orkney 4000 BC–1000 AD*, ed. Renfrew, Colin, Edinburgh, pp. 210–42.

Ryan, Michael *et al.* 1984. 'Six silver finds of the Viking period from the vicinity of Lough Ennell, Co. Westmeath', *Peritia* 3, 334–81.

Sawyer, Peter H. 1971. *The Age of the Vikings*, 2nd edn, London.

Sheehan, John G. 1984. 'Viking Age Silver Arm-rings from Ireland', National University of Ireland M.A. thesis, Galway.

Smart, Veronica 1985. 'The Penny in the pennylands: coinage in Scotland in the early Middle Ages', *Northern Studies* 22, 65–70.

Spearman, R. Michael 1988. 'Early Scottish towns: their origins and economy', in *Power and Politics in Early Medieval Britain and Ireland*, eds Driscoll, Steven T. and Nieke, Margaret R., Edinburgh, pp. 96–110.

Sperber, Erik 1988. 'How accurate was Viking Age weighing in Sweden?', *Fornvännen* 83, 157–66.

Stevenson, Robert B. K. 1966. *National Museum of Antiquities of Scotland. Part I. Anglo-Saxon Coins*, Sylloge of Coins of the British Isles 6, London.

Stevenson, Robert B. K. 1986. 'The Anglo-Saxon silver penny and its context', in Morris, Christopher D. with Emery, Norman, 'The chapel and enclosure on the Brough of Deerness, Orkney: survey and excavations, 1975–1977', *PSAS* 116, 301–74, 339–41.

Thurborg, Märit 1988. 'Regional economic structures: an analysis of the Viking Age silver hoards from Öland, Sweden', *World Archaeology* 20, 302–24.

Wallace, Patrick F. 1987. 'The economy and commerce of Viking Age Dublin', in *Untersuchungen zu Handel und Verkehr der vor- und frühgeschichtlichen Zeit in Mittel- und Nordeuropa. Teil IV. Der Handel der Karolinger- und Wikingerzeit*, eds Düwel, K. *et al.* (=*Abhandlungen der Akademie der Wissenschaften in Göttingen*. Philo.-Hist. Klasse 3, Nr. 156), pp. 200–45.

Warner, Richard 1976. 'Scottish silver arm-rings: an analysis of weights', *PSAS* 107, 1975–6, 136–43.

Werner, A. E & Cowell, M. 1975. 'Report on the compositional analysis of two groups of coins from the hoard', in Lowick, N.M. 'An early tenth century hoard from Isfahan', *Numismatic Chronicle*, 7th series, 15, 110–54, 123–4.

White, N. & Tate, J. 1983. 'Non-dispersive XRF analysis of Viking silver from

Orkney', *Proceedings of the 22 Symposium on Archaeometry, Bradford, 30 March – 30 April 1982*, 245–53.

Wilson, David M. 1976. 'Scandinavian settlement in the north and west of the British Isles – an archaeological point-of-view', *Transactions of the Royal Historical Society*, 5th series, 26, 95–113.

Wilson, David M. 1982. 'The Vikings and their use of wealth in the ninth and tenth centuries', *Saga och Sed*, 252–61.

9

ON THE WRITING OF *ORKNEYINGA SAGA*

FINNBOGI GUÐMUNDSSON

On 31 January 1989 a century had passed since the death of Guðbrandur Vigfússon, an event which was commemorated both in Iceland and Britain. In preparing an exhibition of his works in the National Library of Iceland, my attention was drawn to a short preface in the first of the two volumes of *Origines Islandicae* published in Oxford in 1905 and dedicated to the editors, Guðbrandur Vigfússon and F. York Powell, who did not live long enough to give the final touch to this last large work of theirs. In this preface, the anonymous author (who was in fact William Craigie) wrote:

> The Icelanders of the saga-age were not a secluded self-centred race; they were untiring in their desire to learn all that could be known of the lands round about them, and it is to their zeal for this knowledge, their sound historical sense, and their trained memories, that we owe much information regarding the British Isles themselves from the ninth to the thirteenth century. The contact of the Scandinavian peoples with the English race on the one hand, and the Gaelic on the other, has been an important factor in the subsequent history of Britain; and this is naturally a subject on which the Icelandic evidence, much of which is given in these pages, is of the highest value.

In these noteworthy words Craigie acknowledges the contribution made by the ancient Icelanders, who not only took an interest in their own history, but reached out and studied and wrote the history of their neighbours both west and east of the ocean, including the history of the Earls of Orkney.

Many British scholars have with Craigie acknowledged the Icelandic contribution. Quite recently Professor Peter Foote did so in a lecture given at a conference held in Kirkwall in 1987 on the theme of St Magnus Cathedral and Orkney's 12th-century Renaissance. In his paper Professor Foote wished 'to note a few points in the saga which seem to me to give some indication of what may be called, rather grandly, the mentality and moral stance of the author' (Foote 1988, 192). As an introduction he looks 'at two notably entertaining works from that period [around 1200], *Jómsvíkinga saga* and *Færeyinga saga*, which resemble *Orkneyinga saga* in dealing with the fringes of the Norwegian past'. Concerning the authors and audiences of these sagas he says (1988, 194):

The primary audiences lay among circles of prominent Icelanders; the leading families of the late twelfth century provided the collective establishment whose attitudes are reflected in these sagas. It may be worth recalling that the Icelanders were not a poor and isolated community but a substantial and self-confident nation, with little experience of major strife in the near two hundred years of their Christian existence, and certainly nothing of the scale of twelfth-century conflict in Norway, Denmark and Orkney. Some Icelanders were well connected abroad, and relatively many of them in the twelfth century were widely travelled.

These and many other most interesting things that Peter Foote points out indicate quite clearly what kind of a man the author was. In his portrayal of the main characters we learn to know him and his audience at the same time. 'It is clear,' as Peter Foote says, 'that the author had an overview and saw large themes in his history'. In other words: he had a feeling for the dramatic besides having a good sense of humour.

After having, for instance, in ch. 82 described the dispute between Sveinn Ásleifarson and Þorbjörn klerkr over the sharing of loot, a quarrel that ended with Þorbjörn, who got less than he wanted, complaining about it to Earl Rögnvaldr and finally divorcing Ingigerðr, Sveinn's sister, the author refers to the old saying: *Foruðin sjásk bezt við*, 'monsters beware best of each other'. The author is here more of an onlooker than a participant. He must in his life have known rude characters like Sveinn Ásleifarson and Þorbjörn klerkr: they were found in Iceland like anywhere else. We notice the same attitude at the end of ch. 66, when Bishop Vilhjálmr thanks Sveinn Ásleifarson for killing the rough Sveinn brjóstreip, something the bishop calls a *landhreinsun*, literally a cleansing of the country, or in other words a good riddance. This remarkable word, *landhreinsun*, is still used in Iceland in a similar context. But like Earl Rögnvaldr the author realizes that one day Sveinn will pay for his injustice (*Orkneyinga saga*, ch. 82).

The account in ch. 103 of the killing of Earl Rögnvaldr by Þorbjörn klerkr and his men at Forsie, and later the fall of Þorbjörn, after Earl Haraldr not unhesitatingly had refused to give him quarter, is undoubtedly the most dramatic point in the whole saga. The speeches of Þorbjörn and Magnús Hávarðsson disclose the rivalry between the two earls and show in what a difficult position Earl Haraldr really was. But the author was in no less difficult a position to end his account without humiliating the young earl, who had so suddenly become the sole holder of the Orkney earldom. 'Earl Haraldr and his men', he says, 'were standing on the edge of the morass. And when he saw the uselessness of giving peace, he leapt over the morass in full armour, and the morass was nine ells wide. His followers leapt after him, and no one made a clean jump; but most of them got hold of the bank and so floundered to land.' This is a striking picture and the author ends the chapter by showing us the earl making his own way down the valley towards Thurso, while his men, after having killed Þorbjörn, returned to Forsie to take care of Earl Rögnvaldr's body. Earl Haraldr was neither looking nor going back any more than the priest and the Levite in the story in the Gospel of Luke, who passed the man who had been attacked by robbers on his way from Jerusalem to Jericho.

Turning to when the *Orkneyinga saga* was written, I for one believe that the original version starting with the rule of the sons of Rögnvaldr Mærajarl (in the present ch. 4) and ending with the killing of Sveinn Ásleifarson (ch. 108), was written before 1190. Nothing really speaks against it. The account of Earl Rögnvaldr's translation (in 1192), mentioned in ch. 104, could just as well have been added to the saga later. It is noteworthy that the words put into Sveinn Ásleifarson's mouth, just before he was killed in Dublin, in which he speaks of Saint Rögnvaldr, are not in manuscript Þ, the 16th-century Danish translation of the so-called Codex Academicus, and must thus be classified as one of many clerical additions found in the *Flateyjarbók* version of *Orkneyinga saga*.

Many have in the past made a guess at who might have been the author of *Orkneyinga saga* or at least what sort of a milieu he came from. Even though Dr Jón Stefánsson argued long ago for Bishop Bjarni Kolbeinsson as the author, it is now generally accepted that the author must have been an Icelander.

Einar Ól. Sveinsson, in his monograph on the historical writings of the Oddaverjar (1937), the people of Oddi in the south of Iceland, argued that some member of that family had written *Orkneyinga saga*, pointing out that ties of communication and even of kinship existed between the Oddi family and the earls of Orkney, both being descended from Earl Rögnvaldr the Mighty.

Sæmundr, the son of the great chieftain Jón Loftsson of Oddi, who in his turn was the son of Þóra, an illegitimate daughter of King Magnús bareleg of Norway, wanted to marry Langlíf, the daughter of Earl Haraldr Maddaðarson. Sæmundr was however not willing to go abroad for the wedding nor would Earl Haraldr send his daughter to Iceland, so that nothing came of it.

Another attempt at arranging an Icelandic-Orcadian marriage was more successful, the marriage of Eiríkr Hákonarson and Guðný Þorvarðsdóttir. Eiríkr was the son of Hákon kló, who is often mentioned in *Orkneyinga saga* together with his brothers, especially Magnús and Þorsteinn. Hávarðr Gunnason, their father, who was married to Bergljót, a granddaughter of Earl Páll Þorfinnsson, was greatly involved in the events leading to the execution of Earl Magnús Erlendsson. Hávarðr was in fact one of the followers of Earl Hákon Pálsson when he sailed to Egilsey pretending to want reconciliation with Earl Magnús Erlendsson, but really intending to kill him. Hávarðr Gunnason, realising this in the last minute, left the boat before they reached Egilsey and swam to an uninhabited island nearby. It is evident that the author of the saga wanted to free Hávarðr of all guilt in this matter.

Before taking a close look at Guðný Þorvarðsdóttir it is worth noticing that her husband's mother, the wife of Hákon kló, was Ingigerðr, a daughter of Auðhildr, a member of the Moddan family, and Sigurðr slembir, with whom she lived for a while, a great adventurer and an alleged son of King Magnús bareleg of Norway. Auðhildr had been married to Eiríkr streita, their son being Eiríkr stagbrellr, the husband of Ingiríðr, the daughter of Earl Rögnvaldr kali. Auðhildr, Eiríkr Hákonarson's grandmother, and Margrét, Earl Haraldr Maddaðarson's mother, were first cousins, which shows that Eiríkr was closely related to both earls.

If we on the other hand look at Eiríkr's Icelandic wife, Guðný Þorvarðsdóttir, she was a member of the Reyknesingar family in the west, descendants of Þorgils Arason at Reykjahólar. His great-grandson was Ingimundr Einarsson the priest, a learned man, who gave his *goðorð* (chieftaincy) to a first cousin of his, Þorgils Arason at Staðarhóll. Ingimundr's sister, Hallbera, married Þorgeirr Hallason at Hvassafell in Eyjafjörðr in north central Iceland. They had many children. One of them was Þorvarðr, the father of Guðný, another Ari, the father of Bishop Guðmundr at Hólar, the third Ingimundr the priest.

At the beginning of *Prestssaga Guðmundar góða* (the saga dealing with Guðmundr's life until he became bishop at Hólar in 1203), Þorgeirr Hallason and his family are introduced (*Sturlunga saga* I, 116). The first mentioned of Þorgeir's children is Einarr. He died in Greenland. There are two versions of his death. According to the account of Styrkárr Sigmundsson, who was a 'great and reliable historian', their ship was later found in the wilds of Greenland, but the crew had divided into two factions and fought each other when one party had used up all its provisions. Einarr escaped with two companions in search of the settlements. He went up on the glacier, and there they perished, when they had only a day's journey left to the settlement. Their bodies were found a winter later. Einar's body was in fact undamaged and 'he rests now at Herjólfsnes'.

A second son of Þorgeirr was Þorvarðr (the father of our Guðný). He went abroad at the age of 18, and when he stepped ashore in Bergen he struck a courtier of King Ingi called Jón so that he never recovered and died the following winter. The reason was that this man had sailed away from him in Eyjafjörðr. Þorvarðr got passage on another ship right away and reached Bergen three days later than Jón. Þorvarðr went to see Ketill Kálfsson holding the axe and the shaft that had broken when he struck Jón. The end of the story was that Þorvarðr became King Ingi's courtier and was very dear to him. A rough customer, we see, who can easily be compared with some of the rude characters of *Orkneyinga saga*. It is further mentioned that after Þorvarðr gave up travelling he got married and had five daughters that survived childhood. 'One of them was Guðný, who married Þorgeirr, the son of Bishop Brandr, and later Eiríkr Hákonarson of the Orkneys, a grandson of Sigurðr slembir' (*Sturlunga saga* I, 117).

Ingimundr Þorgeirsson gets only two lines in this introduction: 'The fourth [son] was Ingimundr. He married Sigríðr Tumadóttir and had no child. He was a priest and a very noble man.' Then we hear about Ari, the fifth son of Þorgeirr: 'He was a big and strong man.'

Ari went to Norway in 1161 and became the follower of Earl Erlingr Kyrpinga-Ormsson, King Sigurðr Jórsalafari's son-in-law, who in 1151–3 went

on a crusade to the Holy Land together with Earl Rögnvaldr kali. Ari stayed two
years with Earl Erlingr. But after two more years in Iceland he returned to
Norway and this time together with his brother, Ingimundr the priest (*Sturlunga
saga* I, 118–20). When they a year later were prepared to sail to Iceland, Ari
decided to stay behind, challenged by men who blamed him for leaving Earl
Erlingr when he needed his support very badly. This was to cost him his life,
since he was later that year, 1166, felled in a battle after having saved the earl's
life. When the news of his death reached Iceland, we hear that Þorvarðr, his
brother, composed an elegy about him, thinking that he would forget his
brother's death more easily, if he turned his heroic deed into poetry that could be
carried far afield (*Sturlunga saga* I, 120–21).

Later in the saga we read about Ingimundr's second voyage to Norway, in
1185, this time together with Abbot Karl Jónsson of Þingeyrar and Ögmundr
Þorvarðsson, Ingimundr's nephew (*Sturlunga saga* I, 133). It is a fact that Abbot
Karl on his arrival in Norway began writing the saga of King Sverrir with the
king's consent and cooperation.

In my introduction to *Orkneyinga saga* in 1965 I was so bold as to suggest that
Ingimundr the priest, a man of learning and known for his love of books, had
something similar in mind, for instance writing the history of the earls of
Orkney, a work he might have started as early as 1165 on his first trip to Norway.
Turning again to Guðný, Ingimundr's niece, her first husband, Þorgeirr
Brandsson, died in 1186 shortly after he returned to Iceland after a year in
Norway. I have suggested that she may, for the sake of relief, have gone abroad to
stay in Norway with her brother Ögmundr and uncle Ingimundr and there and
then met her husband to be, Eiríkr Hákonarson, Orcadian chieftains being
frequent visitors in Norway. It may have happened either that she met the
Orcadian because of her uncle's involvement in writing the history of the Orkney
earls, or that this Icelandic Orcadian connection led to the writing if Ingimundr
first conceived the idea of writing our saga during his second trip.

It is however more likely that Ingimundr had been working on the saga for a
long time. He may already have written some chapters in Iceland and gathered
relevant material such as Icelandic and other poetry, in particular the stanzas
composed during the 1151–3 crusade that the Icelandic poets accompanying
Earl Rögnvaldr must have brought with them to Iceland. The poets seem to have
hailed from the west of Iceland, as I have tried to show in my edition, and it must
have been easy for Ingimundr, who had close connections in the west, to acquire
this material. It is interesting to note that Sigurðr slembir, when he spent a
winter in Iceland earlier in the century, stayed with Þorgils Oddason at
Reykjahólar in the west, the home of Ingimundr's forefathers on his mother's
side.

Ingimundr had intended to go abroad in 1180 and along with him his nephew,
Guðmundr Arason. They were however shipwrecked at Strandir in the
northwest of Iceland, Guðmundr breaking one leg and Ingimundr losing his

chest of books that was washed overboard. But Ingimundr made a vow and prayed that the chest should come ashore and so it did with one hasp holding and two broken off and the contents undamaged. Maybe some preparatory notes for *Orkneyinga saga* were in this chest. Who knows? But Ingimundr had to postpone his journey for five years.

Ingimundr stayed in Niðaróss in the winter 1185–6 and was given the prebend of St John's chapel in Christchurch, and during Christmas and Easter he stayed with the archbishop who held him in high esteem. In the spring Þorgeirr, Guðný's husband, who had stayed with the archbishop during the winter, left for Iceland, as mentioned before, but Ingimundr stayed on in Norway moving to Mary's church at Staðr (just across the fjord from Niðaróss) and serving there for two years. It shows how highly Archbishop Eysteinn thought of his learning when Bishop Jón, the first Greenlandic bishop of that name, who had the nickname knútr, died, Archbishop Eysteinn wanted Ingimundr to succeed Jón. But he would not accept that, which shows his modesty and caution, as it is put in the *Prestssaga*.

After leaving the north Ingimundr stayed in Bergen for some time, from where he made a journey to England in the spring of 1188, returning to Bergen in the autumn. On this journey he could easily have visited the north of Scotland and Orkney and acquainted himself with persons and places of interest over there, if what I am saying is not a mere fantasy. If my theory that Guðný Þorvarðsdóttir met Eiríkr Hákonarson in Norway during Ingimundr's stay there is valid, Ingimundr might just as well have been visiting with them in Orkney and then had Eiríkr as an expert guide over there.

It is evident that the author of *Orkneyinga saga* is well-informed about the Moddan family as we see in ch. 53 and onwards. The account of Earl Haraldr Maddaðarson's last meeting with Sveinn Ásleifarson in ch. 106 is so real that one would think the earl told the story directly to the author. Margrét, Earl Haraldr's mother, and Auðhildr, Eiríkr Hákonarson's grandmother, were first cousins as mentioned before, both of them granddaughters of Moddan. The members of the Moddan family are a different strand in the fabric of characters in the saga and add a considerable colour to it. It is evident that the author of the saga takes a special interest in these people and gives some very clear and striking pictures of them.

But, plausible as this may seem so far, how is it possible that Ingimundr the priest was the author, considering the fact that in the spring of 1189 he left Bergen for Iceland, never to reach it, since the boat he was travelling in came to some uninhabited area of Greenland with the result that everyone was lost? This was discovered 14 winters later (according to the *Prestssaga*, 11 winters according to the Annals) when their boat was found and furthermore seven bodies in a cave. One of them was Ingimundr the priest (*Sturlunga saga* I, 138):

Wax was found beside him [i.e. wax tablets] and runes describing how their death came about.

No books are mentioned in this shipwreck like the one of 1180, when they were saved in an almost miraculous way. But if they found wax tablets and a runic text, they could just as well have found Ingimundr's books and for that matter among them the original version of *Orkneyinga saga*.

We know for certain that Snorri Sturluson had a copy of the original version of *Orkneyinga saga* and that he was in one way or another involved in the composition of the revised version we know. I have gone so far as to suggest that he himself wrote the mythological introduction making the Orcadian earls descendants of the northernmost king he could find, King Fornjótr, instead of following the tradition of seeking their origin in the far south, as he had done in his *Edda* and *Heimskringla* for the royal families of Scandinavia.

According to the Icelandic Annals, Ingimundr's body was found in Greenland in the year 1200, or somewhat later, 1203, according to the *Prestssaga*. If Ingimundr's belongings, his books for instance, were brought to Iceland, one of the most likely ports was Hvítáróss in the west, close to Borg, where Snorri Sturluson was living 1202–6. Besides, it can be mentioned that Jón, the second bishop of that name in Greenland, came to Iceland in 1202 according to the Annals. He might of course have brought Ingimundr's things to Iceland.

If Ingimundr finished writing *Orkneyinga saga* in good time before he left for his final journey, a copy could have been made of the saga in Norway and Ögmundr Þorvarðsson, his nephew, for instance, might have been its owner. He returned to Iceland in 1192. He was a clever man, and somewhat unruly like his father. He was usually on good terms with the Sturlungs, so for that matter he could have given the saga to Snorri Sturluson.

You might say now or even earlier that I am in all my speculations taking things too far: it will never be possible to find the author. However, the more I think about this the more I am convinced that the author of the saga is to be sought among the members of the Hvassafell family. I have chosen Ingimundr the priest, because we know that he was a man of books and learning and that through his brothers, Þorvarðr and Ari, he had early contacts in Norway, and through the marriage of his niece, Guðný, important personal contacts with Orcadian chieftains.

One of the arguments for some member of the Oddi family having written the saga was that the family descended from Hrollaugr, the son of Earl Rögnvaldr of Mæri, who went to Iceland. But he was, as a matter of fact, also the forefather of Ingimundr the priest.

I should like to discuss an interesting variant in the text of ch. 90, where it says in ms 325 that Þórhallr Ásgrímsson, the captain who brought Earl Rögnvaldr and his men from Bergen to Orkney late in 1153, was an Icelandic man by birth and had an estate in Byskupstungur in the south (*hann var íslenzkr maðr at kynslóð ok átti bú suðr í Byskupstungum*). The manuscripts 332 and F have the reading: *ok kynstórr*, of noble birth. The 325 reading is the more difficult one (or *locus difficilior*) and thus more likely to be the original one, which could mean that the saga was at least partly written abroad and with foreign readers in mind. But even more interesting is the continuation saying that he had an estate in Byskupstungur in the south. If that is an original reading it points to the north, i.e. that the author was from the north of Iceland. The Norwegian scholar Anne Holtsmark made this point in a review of Einar Ól. Sveinsson's monograph (Holtsmark 1940). He took this for a later addition by a northern scribe, but considering that both 325 and 332 have this reading we are not able to discard it altogether. We must remember that Guðný Þorvarðsdóttir, the wife of Eiríkr Hákonarson, came from the north of Iceland and that their marriage must in one way or another be linked up with the writing of the original version of the saga in the 1180s.

The negotiations for a marriage between Sæmundr Jónsson of Oddi and Langlíf, the daughter of Earl Haraldr Maddaðarson, took place at least ten years later and were without a result as we remember.

If any one thinks that *Orkneyinga saga* is too worldly to have been written by a priest, we should not forget the opinion King Haraldr harðráði had of Gizurr Ísleifsson as a young man, that he was fitted to be a viking chief, king or bishop. We should also remember the reaction of Bishop Vilhjálmr of Orkney to Sveinn Ásleifarson's killing of Sveinn brjóstreip referred to earlier in this paper. Even though the men of the church in the 12th century did not usually take an active part in the feuds of their compatriots they watched them with a keen eye. And having in mind the close combat in such small communities as Iceland and Orkney the men of the church were more or less involved in the struggle and strife of their day.

REFERENCES

Foote, Peter 1988. 'Observations on *Orkneyinga saga*', in *St Magnus Cathedral and Orkney's twelfth-century renaissance*, ed. Crawford, Barbara E., Aberdeen, 192–207.
Holtsmark, Anne 1940. Review of Sveinsson 1937, *Arkiv för nordisk filologi* 55, 136–9.
Orkneyinga saga, ed. Guðmundsson, Finnbogi, Íslenzk fornrit 34, Reykjavík, 1965.
Sturlunga saga, ed. Jóhannesson, Jón, *et al.*, Reykjavík, 1946.
Sveinsson, Einar Ól. 1937. *Sagnaritun Oddaverja*, Studia Islandica 1, Reykjavík.
Vigfússon, Gudbrand & F. York Powell 1905. *Origines Islandicae*, Oxford.

IO

THE SEA, THE FLAME AND THE WIND

THE LEGENDARY ANCESTORS
OF THE EARLS OF ORKNEY

PREBEN MEULENGRACHT SØRENSEN

Orkneyinga saga opens with a story about the ancestors of the Orcadian earls (chs 1–3). They are traced back to the mythical king *Fornjótr*, who lived in the most extreme northern part of the Scandinavian peninsula 'east of the sea-gulf that leads to the White Sea' (ch. 3), i.e. in the extreme North, according to the geographical conceptions of the Northerners in those days.

Fornjótr, the saga tells us, had three sons. One of them was called *Hlér* – or, 'as we call him', *Ægir* –, the second son was called *Logi*, and the third one *Kári*. These three sons represent natural forces. *Ægir* is the name of a sea-god or sea-giant, and the word was also used as an appellative for 'sea'. *Logi* means 'flame', and *Kári* – which is rare in Old Norse – is a name for the north wind.

Kári was the father of *Frosti*, 'frost', and *Frosti* had a son by the name of *Snær hinn gamli* 'Snow the Old', whose son was *Þorri*, 'the Dry One'. *Þorri* had two sons, *Nórr* and *Górr*, and a daughter by the name of *Gói*. *Þorri*, we are told, was a great sacrificer *(blótmaðr mikill)*: 'He held a sacrifice each year at mid-winter' (ch. 3). And from him the winter-month *Þorri* got its name.

One winter, while the sacrifices were going on, it so happened that *Gói* disappeared. Having searched for her in vain for a month, they held a new sacrifice in order to learn where she was. This was called 'Gói's sacrifice' – and *Gói* became the name of another winter-month.

Three years later the two brothers set out in search for their sister, and *Nórr* was to search for her by land, while *Górr* should search by sea. *Górr* took off with his ships into the Sea around Åland and searched among the skerries and islands of the Baltic. He sailed to Gotland and afterwards came to Læsø in Denmark, where he met his kinsmen, the descendants of *Hlér*. But nowhere did he find any trace of his sister.

Nórr, his brother, waited until snow fell in the mountains and the skiing was good. Then he went around the gulf south to Finnmark and west to Kjølen. They lived out there for a long time without meeting other people, hunting animals and birds as a means of their subsistence. At last, they came to where the rivers fall westward, and descending from the mountains they followed them until they reached the sea. The area there was densely populated, and *Nórr* conquered the land and made himself king of Western Norway. After more travelling and fighting he finally met his brother. Neither of them had found their sister, but on their journeys they had subdued all the land, and now they divided it between themselves. *Nórr* got the mainland, and *Górr* got the islands.

From *Górr*, the sea-king, come the Earls of Orkney. According to the saga there were five generations between him and *Rǫgnvaldr* the Powerful and Wise, Earl of Møre, who obtained the Shetland Islands and the Orkneys from Harald Finehair as a compensation for his dead son.

Genealogical lore plays a conspicuous part in Old Norse literature right from the oldest scaldic poetry which we have to the prose literature of the 12th and 13th centuries, where the genealogies form an indispensable element of the historical narratives called the sagas.

In the sagas genealogy served, just as it did in real life, at least three important functions. First, it was of great practical consequence to know about family ties. Secondly, one's genealogy was indicative of one's social status, and for that reason genealogy was often developed as what Joan Turville-Petre (1978–9, 7) has called 'an imaginative art'.

Except for the closest degrees of kinship, a man's or a woman's pedigree was more or less an elaborate construction and the result of a choice between many possible links, whether real ones or invented. It is on this level, then, that the third function of genealogy comes into play: it was a means of historical interpretation and mythical thinking.

Obviously, the story about the ancestors of the Orcadian jarls serves both the second and the third function mentioned. Its aim is to account for the jarls' princely status as a quality which they had inherited from Scandinavian kings of prehistorical times. Its mythical form, however, also carries an ideological meaning. It is this ideological meaning I want to consider, and I begin by discussing the tradition about *Fornjótr* and his family as well as its connection with the history of the jarl dynasty. Then I shall compare this northern-oriented origin legend with the more familiar southern-oriented origin legend of the Norwegian royal dynasty.

The name-lists, the *þulur*, which were incorporated into some manuscripts of Snorri Sturluson's *Edda*, list *Fornjótr* among the names for giants, and most scholars agree with this classification found in Snorri. Otherwise we know nothing at all about *Fornjótr*. *Orkneyinga saga* euhemerizes the mythical figure by calling him 'king' and furnishing him with a kingdom; the mythical meaning of the names, which occur within this family, remains, nevertheless, intact. *Fornjótr* and his sons personify the nordic winter and northern nature.[1]

The meaning of the name *Fornjótr* is not entirely clear to us and the manuscripts in which it occurs show that the scribes did not quite grasp its actual meaning, either. Several explanations have been put forward, 'the old owner or usufructuary', 'the old destroyer', 'the receiver of sacrifices', 'the old howler, i.e.

the storm' and 'the old Jute' (Hellquist 1903; de Vries 1977, 138 f.). This last sense is how *Flateyjarbók*, the main manuscript of *Orkneyinga saga*, understands the name. Here we read of *Fornjótr* that 'he ruled over Jutland which is called Finland and Kvænland, the one that lies east of the sea-gulf that leads towards the White Sea' (*Flateyjarbók* I, 219). The word *jótr* means 'Jutlander', 'Jute'; it should, however, here be taken, in a broader and more general sense, simply to mean 'man', whereby the expression 'the old Jute' would become the name for a primeval being, which lived in a mythical Jutland, from where his sons set out and conquered the northern hemisphere.[2]

Flateyjarbók's conception of *Fornjótr* as a primeval human being agrees very well with his role as progenitor; however, it is unlikely that this had also been his role on an older, mythical level. On this level, he is a figure rather empty of meaning. He is the old giant, who serves as a nucleus for the forces of nature. If there ever existed a myth about how he became the procreator of his three dangerous sons at all, it has dissolved without leaving any traces behind it whatsoever.

The linking together of the hostile forces of nature by means of genealogy is a traditional device in Old Norse mythology. In the Norwegian Þjóðólfr's poem *Ynglingatal* from about AD 900, there are two kennings, which describe the 'fire' as *sævar niðr*, 'the sea's kinsman' (in strophe 4) and as *glóðfjalgr sonr Fornjóts*, 'the glowing-hot son of Fornjótr' (in strophe 29). Snorri Sturluson, in his *Skáldskaparmál* (ch. 36, *Edda* 118), quotes a strophe from a poem, *Norðrsetu-drápa*, by the otherwise unknown Sveinn, which Finnur Jónsson assigns, though only tentatively, to the 11th century. Here, the 'snowstorm' is called *Fornjótrs synir ljótir*, 'Fornjótr's hideous sons'. Taken together, these few examples suffice to show that the conception of *Fornjótr* and his sons goes back to pre-Christian times.

Despite this evidence, however, it has been called into doubt, most recently so by Claus Krag, that this *Fornjótr*-genealogy should date from such early days and should be of such venerable origin. In Krag's opinion, we should, instead of taking *Ynglingatal*'s examples as evidence for the antiquity of the *Fornjótr*-myth, rather view them as indicative of his hypothesis that *Ynglingatal* is not as old as it is generally held to be (Krag 1985; von See 1988, 77–9).

I shall dwell briefly on this new suggestion concerning the age of the *Fornjótr*-genealogy. It rests on the assumption that *Fornjótr* and his three sons represent the four elements and that their linking together in the Old Norse sources was inspired by the Greek doctrine about the four elements of nature, which was transmitted to the North through religious and didactic literature. The story of *Fornjótr* and his family are thus held to be a learned speculation from the High Middle Ages. Krag suggests the beginning of the 12th century as a possible date for its invention.[3]

The answer to this must be that *Fornjótr* and his sons do *not* represent the four elements of nature – earth, water, atmosphere and fire – but only the last three of them, and, what is more, they are not represented in a passive way as the elements of which nature consists, but actively as natural forces, i.e. the sea, the storm and the burning flame. Nor does the idea of kinship between these forces belong to the classical tradition of the four elements.

The ideas which lie at the bottom of this myth of *Fornjótr* and his sons are quite different from the conceptions that underlie the theory of the four elements. The myth implies the notion of the dangerousness of these natural forces, and the Northerners did not need to go back to the ancient Greeks for an understanding of the interplay of these phenomena, with which they were familiar from their own experience. Seafaring people need not read books in order to discover that there is an interplay between wind and sea, and he who has seen a blazing fire knows about the relationship between wind and fire. The smithy provided ample opportunity for anyone to speculate about the interplay of these three natural forces, of which Skalla-Grímr Kveld-Úlfsson around the year AD 900 had the following to say in a strophe, which is ascribed to him in *Egils saga Skalla-Grímssonar* (1933, 79). The strophe may be rendered in prose, as follows:

> Very early must the blacksmith rise, who shall demand richness from the wind-sucking clothes of Viddi's brother; I let the sledge hammer ring on the hot gold of the owner of the brilliance, while the wind-greedy turbulent dwellings of the storm howl.

'The wind-greedy turbulent dwellings of the storm' are the bellows in the smithy. 'The owner of the brilliance' is the fire on the forge, and 'the hot gold' of this fire is the red-hot iron. *Viddi* in the first half of the stanza is the name of a giant, and according to Björn M. Ólsen he is a sea-giant, that is, *Ægir* (Ólsen 1903, 99; c.f. Sigurður Nordal in *Egils saga Skalla-Grímssonar* 1933, 79, note). *Viddi*'s brother, then, must be either the wind or the flame, most likely the wind. 'The wind-sucking clothes' of the wind are the bellows.

Like the myth about *Fornjótr*, Skalla-Grímr's strophe is founded on a personification of natural phenomena and on their linking together by means of kinship relations. Mythological thinking of this sort is well-known from our oldest poetical sources, not least from the kennings of the skalds. Once the forces of nature had been personified as supernatural powers, it would immediately suggest itself to express the mythical relationship between these forces with the help of such concepts as kinship and marriage.

Let us return to the prelude to *Orkneyinga saga*. So far we can say that the oldest part of its genealogy has its roots in pre-Christian mythology and cannot be dismissed as merely being a learned speculation. The medieval contribution to this narrative is limited to its euhemerization of the mythical forces which are simply understood to be pre-historical kings.

The agnatic line of the Orcadian jarls may be divided into three different sections. Its historical section, i.e. the one whose members the saga links with specific historical events, begins with Rǫgnvaldr Earl of Møre. The three generations before Rǫgnvaldr establish a transition from historical back to legendary times. They are his father, Eysteinn glumra, his grandfather Ívarr Earl of the Upplanders, and his great-grandfather, Hálfdan the Old. From Hálfdan the Old back to *Fornjótr*, who is at the top of the pedigree, there are eight legendary and mythical generations. They are set off against the later generations through their unusual personal names. The three generations closest to the legendary-heroic section are represented by *Sveiði*, *Heiti* and *Górr*, who bear invented names, which we find also in the *þulur* of the *Edda* as names for sea-kings. They may be safely assigned to the realm of legend. The last four names leading back to *Fornjótr* are names of winter-phenomena.

The question arises: what sort of idea has formed the conceptual basis that underlies this connection between the historical Rǫgnvaldr and the mythical *Fornjótr*? And where did it get its inspiration from?

Apart from *Orkneyinga saga*, the narrative about *Fornjótr* and his descendants is also found in the chapter *Hversu Nóregr byggðisk* 'How Norway was settled', in *Flateyjarbók* (1: 21–4). The purpose of this tract is to show how the family conquered Norway and gave names to its various districts. For this reason, the focus is on the descendants of Norway's eponymous hero, *Nórr*, and the number of generations given in order to account for his descendants is considerably greater than in *Orkneyinga saga*. In a genealogical tract that follows *Hversu Nóregr byggðisk* in *Flateyjarbók*, one of the pedigrees leading back to *Nórr* is traced down to Halfdan the Old and his sons (1: 24; c.f. 1: 22). There is a similar account in Snorri Sturluson's *Edda* (181–4).

This Hálfdan is one of the key characters in the genealogy contained in *Orkneyinga saga*. Here, however, he belongs to the lineage leading back to *Górr*, the sea-king, and his descendants differ from those named in the *Flateyjarbók*-tract. In *Orkneyinga saga* he is the first ancestor who bears the name of a historical character, and he is the one who establishes the link between Rǫgnvaldr's closest forefathers and the mythical and legendary descendants of *Fornjótr*.

In the genealogical tract about Hálfdan contained both in *Flateyjarbók* and in *Snorra Edda*, his 18 sons are enumerated. It is also said that he arranged for a sacrifice in order to be granted a life-span of 300 years. This wish, however, was declined, but instead he was compensated with the promise that for 300 years in succession there would only be sons and no daughters born in his lineage.

In contrast to *Orkneyinga saga*, there is among the 18 sons who are named in this source none by the name of Ívarr. It is only in the saga, that we are informed about the pedigree from Hálfdan back to *Górr* and down from Hálfdan to Rǫgnvaldr, and we must ask ourselves why Hálfdan was introduced into this genealogy at all.

The earliest source which mentions Hálfdan's 18 sons is the mythological poem *Hyndluljóð*, which is also contained in *Flateyjarbók*, and only here. This

poem has the following to say about Hálfdan (in Henry Adams Bellows'
translations):

> His bride was Almveig, the best of women,
> And eighteen boys did Almveig bear him.
>
> (15, 5–8)
>
> Hence come the Skjoldungs, hence the Skilfings,
> Hence the Othlings, hence the Ynglings,
> Hence come the free-born, hence the high-born,
> The noblest of men that in Mithgarth dwell.
>
> (16, 1–8)

Hálfdan is the ancestor of the most noble dynasties in the North, and for this
reason also the Orcadian jarls descend from him. The author of the saga or some
other genealogist before him included Ívarr Upplendingajarl among Hálfdan's
18 sons – or identified a Hálfdan in Rǫgnvaldr's family with the Hálfdan of
Hyndluljóð, who is called Hálfdan the Old in other sources. The purpose with
this was to pinpoint the noble ancestry and status of the jarl kin.

The genealogy, which from Hálfdan leads upwards to *Fornjótr*, has a different
meaning. It provides the jarl's dynasty with a mythical origin that goes back to a
time beyond known history. The period around AD 1200 seems to have been
especially interesting in such origin-myths (Turville-Petre 1978–9, 12). It was
inspired by a conception of history which conceived of it as a continuous
development from the past to the present propagated by that new literacy, which
had established itself in the North, and influenced by foreign origin-stories and
aristocratic genealogies, and, behind that, by what the Bible tells about the
spreading of mankind over the world.

Origin-myths were already well-known in genuine northern tradition, and it
was there that the saga-authors found their models and material. *Ynglingatal*
gives the names of the legendary kings of Sweden, beginning with the first one,
Fjǫlnir, who according to *Heimskringla*, was a son of the god Freyr and the
giantess Gerðr. This myth is repeated in Eyvindr Finnsson's poem *Háleygjatal*
from about AD 985, which traces the earls of Hlaðir back to *Sæmingr*, who was the
son of Óðinn and the giantess Skaði.

These poems do not intend to tell us about the historical achievements of these
dynasties. Rather, they give, as Gro Steinsland has shown in her thesis about
'The sacred marriage and Norse kingship-ideology', expression to a central
northern myth about their origin and fate (Steinsland 1991). It is the Christian
authors who transform the mythical genealogies into history. At the beginning of
the 12th century, the Icelander Ari Þorgilsson has the Yngling genealogy start
with the Turkish king Yngvi and links it with the Norwegian royal dynasty of
historical times. The lost *Skjǫldunga saga* from the end of the 12th century,
which dealt with the Danish kings, was introduced by an account of their lineal
descent from Óðinn and of the immigration of the *Æsir* from Asia. And in the

beginning of the 13th century Snorri Sturluson combines in his *Heimskringla* the origin-myth contained in *Ynglingatal* with the immigration theory of foreign inspiration, and he has Óðinn and his three sons at the top of the northern royal genealogies.

The story about the prehistory of the dynasty of the Orcadian jarls must be seen in this context. *Orkneyinga saga* was first written around AD 1200, if we accept the dating agreed upon by the majority of scholars. In other words, it was written after *Skjǫldunga saga* and before *Heimskringla*, and the three sagas belong within all probability to a literary milieu whose members were familiar with each other's work and learning. These three sagas about foreign dynasties all begin with an origin-legend, which provides the kin with a mythical ancestry outside the Scandinavian countries and continues with generations that are taken from nordic prehistory, with which the historical members of the family are finally linked. The idea behind these three introductions was in all three cases the same: the princely houses were to have mythical origins.

However, the genealogy with which the Orcadian jarls were provided differs conspicuously from the other genealogies. After Snorri Sturluson had given the Norwegian royal dynastic genealogy and origin-myth its final shape, immigration from Troy was to become the authoritative explanation of the origins of the nordic peoples; at the same time, however, people realised that the North had been populated long before Óðinn and his followers arrived. It is to this aboriginal population that the Orcadian jarls trace their ancestry.

Strikingly enough, the account given in Snorri's *Edda* as well as in his *Heimskringla* as to how the three sons of Óðinn became the ancestors of the royal dynasties in the nordic countries, does not include the Orcadian jarls and the other powerful families which came of Jarl Rǫgnvaldr of Møre. Similarly, it seems strange that in *Orkneyinga saga* there is no attempt to construct a link between these families and Óðinn's famous descendants. It would have been easy enough to create such a link, and indeed, there is such a fabrication in *Hálfdanar saga Eysteinssonar*, which lets Eysteinn glumra, Rǫgnvaldr's father, be in lineal descent from Óðinn's son Sæmingr (89, 133–34), otherwise the ancestor of the Earls of Hlaðir in Norway. At the end of the saga it is explicitly stated that many noble families in Norway and in the Orkneys can trace their ancestry back to this family (139).

In *Orkneyinga saga*, the Orcadian jarls descend in direct agnatic line from *Fornjótr*, just as the other dynasties descend in direct line from the three sons of Óðinn. In the prologue to Snorri's *Edda* we read that the gods and the sons of the gods took wives in those countries to which they emigrated, and that their race then spread all over the northern countries (*Edda Snorra Sturlusonar* 1931, 7). This explanation of the relationship between the aboriginal population and the immigrants is unfolded more fully in the already mentioned genealogical tract about Hálfdan the Old in *Flateyjarbók* (1: 24–6). Here, the lineages of six of Hálfdan's sons are linked on the female side with Harald Finehair's agnatic line.

In other words, Harald and his forefathers marry women of those royal families that had existed in the North before the arrival of Óðinn and his people. The tract about Hálfdan represents, however, a mythical version, which modifies that of the prologue of the *Edda* in that it states that there were no female descendants born in Hálfdan's family for 300 years. During this period the aboriginal families remained independent of the immigrant dynasty with regard to kinship as well as social order. In *Orkneyinga saga*'s version of the oldest history of the Orcadian dynasty there is no union between the two. The jarl kin is traced back directly and uninterruptedly to the aboriginal ancestor.

What are the reasons for this obvious preference for a genealogy which differed so conspicuously from the rule which otherwise provided the northern – and other European – princely houses with a noble Trojan ancestry? A possible answer to this could be that this genealogy, which has *Fornjótr* at its top, gave expression to a specific Nordic self-esteem and pride in that it provided a counterpart to the immigration theory which got its inspiration from the continent. Its dynasties not only come from the extreme, frosty North, from fierce, uninhabitable quarters, which contrast sharply with the classical idea of an emigration from the centre of the world, where there was splendour and beauty. It chooses also the giants, the arch-enemies of the gods, as its ancestors. In a way, the descendants of these giants become the gods' equals in their role as culture heroes. They are sacrificers and wizards just like Óðinn was, and they travel by ship and introduce the art of skiing, both specific northern skills.

The generations that follow enhance this impression of distinctness. *Gór* is contrasted with his brother *Nórr* through his role as a sea-king, who will rule over the islands. With Hálfdan the Old the family becomes one of the great heroic dynasties, which rules for 300 years without marrying off their women to the dynasties that stem from Óðinn. Not until Hálfdan's son, Ívarr Upplend-ingajarl, is the Fornjótr-kin associated – though not explicitly – with the forefathers of Harald Finehair, who from Hálfdan hvítbeinn onwards ruled over Uppland as kings. The title of jarl anticipates the saga's later preoccupation with the relationship between king and jarl.

Let us return, now, to the sister who had disappeared, Gói, who had been the immediate cause for *Nórr* and *Górr* to set out and conquer Norway and the islands in the sea. She turned up again. At long last, *Nórr* found her in Uppland or, to be precise, in Heiðmǫrk, where *Hrólfr frá Bjargi* was king. 'He was the son of Svaði the giant from Dovre,' the saga tells us (5). It was Hrólfr who had abducted Gói from Kvænland. Now he went to meet *Nórr* and challenged him to single combat. They fought for a long time, and neither was wounded. Then they made peace, and Nórr married Hrólfr's sister and Hrólfr married Gói.

Strictly speaking, this happy ending to the story of Gói from the extreme North and of Hrólfr from that part of Norway which later was to become the first domain of the Yngling kings, does not belong to the laconic account of the forefathers of the Orcadian jarls. As a part of the dynasty's origin myth it is, however, of special relevance, because it underlines the exceptionality of the jarl kin.

Marriage between the king and a mythical woman from abroad is a well-known motif in Old Norse mythology and legend. The bride is characterised as coming from the 'outside' in one sense or another. Her extraction and nature are different from that of the bridegroom, and their marriage makes an alliance between opposites. Gro Steinsland shows that the alliance between the god and the giant-daughter, which takes the form of a *hieros gamos*, forms a constituent element of Old Norse kingship-ideology.

The main literary example is *Ynglingatal*. Here the *hieros gamos*-myth supplies not only the starting-point for the dynasty, but is, as Gro Steinsland shows (1991, 199–206), repeated in later generations of the poem's royal lineage. The third strophe deals with Vanlandi's death. In Snorri's prose commentary we read that Vanlandi married Drífa, 'Snowdrift', the daughter of king Snow of Finland, i.e. a member of *Fornjótr*'s family. They have a son, but Vanlandi deserts Drífa, and she takes revenge upon him through a sorceress, whom she employs to kill him. Strophe 10 deals with king Agni, who was killed by his wife Skjálf – *Logadís* – who managed to hang him by his neck in his own necklace. Snorri explains that Skjálf was the daughter of Frosti and sister of Logi, all of whom belong to *Fornjótr*'s family, though the names are arranged differently in *Orkneyinga saga*.

In these myths, the northern dynasties of giants and foreign tribes form the dangerous and at the same time indispensable counterpart of the kings who rule over the civilised countries. The kings marry the daughters of these giants, and these giant-daughters bear them children. The clans of these giant-women remain, nevertheless, enemies. This double relationship of alliance and conflict, of indispensability and dangerousness, is fundamental to Old Norse mythical thinking, and the historians later on make use of it in their accounts of the dynastic history.

Orkneyinga saga tells the same story, but does so from a different point of view. Here, the focus is on the 'others', on the dynasties of giants and Finns. Their sister is abducted, but they find her again, and they make peace with the abductor through an exchange of women, through intermarriage. Where the old *hieros gamos*-myth emphasises those aspects of intermarriage between antagonistic clans that lead to strife, deception and revenge, *Orkneyinga saga*'s mythical counterpart tells of a conflict, which is resolved by an alliance between equal partners. The story of Gói and Hrólfr of Bjarg seems to be intended as a counterpart of the otherwise prevailing origin-myths of the royal dynasties of Scandinavia.

We do not know how old the story about the forefathers of the Orcadian jarls contained in *Orkneyinga saga* actually is, and we do not know either, whether it was thought up in the Orkneys, or in Iceland or, maybe, in Norway. However, as an element in the historical account it has a specific meaning. It provides an explanation of the special status of the Earls of Orkney in relation to the Norwegian kings. They are independent from these through their ancestors, who belong likewise to a remote mythical past, and they are more deeply rooted in Norwegian history than Norway's royal dynasty; they are, in a way, more Norwegian than the kings of Norway. Just like the story of Torf-Einarr at the beginning of the historical section proper of the saga, the origin-myth of the Orcadian jarls is an expression of their independence in relation to those kings, to whom they owe their title of jarls, but by no means their aristocratic status. This is, I think, the meaning of the first three chapters in *Orkneyinga saga*.

Notes

1. These four figures are recently discussed in Clunies Ross 1983.
2. This interpretation of the name *Fornjótr* is in accordance with the information that Fornjótr's son, Hlér, settled on Hlésey, Læsø, from where we might imagine that he has extended his lineage to the historical Jutland. We can see this as a parallel to the story in Snorri's *Edda* about the emigration of the *æsir* from *Ásgarðr inn forni* to the new *Ásgarðr* in Sweden.
3. C.f. Anne Holtsmark 1958.

REFERENCES

Clunies Ross, Margaret 1983. 'Snorri Sturluson's use of the Norse origin-legend of the sons of Fornjótr in his *Edda*', *Arkiv för Nordisk Filologi*, 98, 47–66.
Edda Snorra Sturlusonar, ed. Jónsson, Finnur, København, 1931.
Egils saga Skalla-Grímssonar, ed. Nordal, Sigurður, Íslenzk fornrit 2, Reykjavík, 1933.
Flateyjarbók, vol. 1, ed. Vigfússon, Guðbrandur og Unger, C. R. Christiania, 1859.
Hálfdanar saga Eysteinssonar, ed. Schröder, Franz Rolf, Altnordische Saga-Bibliothek 15, Halle a. S., 1917.
Heimskringla, vol. 1, ed. Aðalbjarnarson, Bjarni, Íslenzk fornrit 26, Reykjavík, 1941.
Hellquist, Elof 1903. 'Om Fornjótr', *Arkiv för Nordisk Filologi* 19, 134–40.
Holtsmark, Anne 1958. 'Elementene', *Kulturhistorisk Leksikon for Nordisk Middelalder*, København, vol. 3, 593–94.
Krag, Claus 1985. 'Element-guddommene – mytologi eller skolelærdom', *The Sixth International Saga Conference 28.7.1985–2.8.1985*, *Workshop Papers* 2, 613–28.
Ólsen, Björn Magnússon 1903. 'Til versene i Egils saga', *Arkiv för Nordisk Filologi* 19, 99–133.
Orkneyinga saga, ed. Guðmundsson, Finnbogi, Íslenzk fornrit 34, Reykjavík, 1965.
See, Klaus von 1988. *Mythos und Theologie*, Heidelberg.
Steinsland, Gro 1991. *Det hellige bryllup og norrøn kongeideologi. En analyse af hierogami-myten i* Skírnismál, Ynglingatal, Háleygjatal *og* Hyndluljóð. Oslo.
The Poetic Edda, trans. Bellows, Henry Adams, New York, 1936.
Turville-Petre, Joan 1978–9. 'The genealogist and history. From Ari to Snorri', *Saga-Book* 20, 7–23.
Vries, Jan de 1977. *Altnordisches etymologisches Wörterbuch*, 2nd ed., Leiden.

II

ENGLAND AND *ORKNEYINGA SAGA*

JUDITH JESCH

THE ENGLISH CONNECTION

One of the themes to emerge from the St Magnús Cathedral 850th Anniversary Conference held in Kirkwall in 1987 was the importance of the English connection. The architectural derivation of the building from Durham cathedral has long been known, but other contacts were also discussed. Donaldson (1988, 5–7) noted that the 11th century saw the revival of English influence in Scotland and stressed the links the Scottish royal family had with Durham. Helle (1988, 47) suggested that Orkney may have been 'a bridgehead by which some of the early Christian and ecclesiastical impulses passed to Norway from the British Isles'. Fernie (1988, 156–9) noted links between Orkney and East Anglia and argued for a possible East Anglian derivation for St Magnús church on Egilsay. De Geer (1988, 249–51) noted musical affinities with the British Isles and France. We may perhaps connect ecclesiastical influences from England with the claims to authority over the islands by the Archbishopric of York in the late 11th and early 12th centuries (Crawford 1983, 105–11).

Two contributions where this aspect was lacking were those dealing with *Orkneyinga saga* (Foote 1988, Bibire 1988), since the saga has little to say about Anglo-Orcadian contacts. Thus, when the building of the cathedral is described in ch. 76,[1] there is no mention of where the masons came from or what models were followed. Yet the English dimension is not entirely absent. In ch. 59 we find Rǫgnvaldr kali as a young man in Grimsby and this is perhaps confirmed by his verse cited in ch. 60. While most of the miracles (ch. 57) performed by St Magnús after his death take place in the North Atlantic area, one concerns a dice-player in England who prays to St Magnús in desperation when his opponent throws two sixes. Moreover, it has been suggested (*OS* Finnbogi Guðmundsson, xlvi–vii; Foote 1989, 73) that the first life of St Magnús was written by Master Robert of Cricklade, also known for a life of Thomas Becket.

The cosmopolitan nature of 12th-century Orkney is indubitable and the English influence was one ingredient in the melting-pot. But no one has asked whether this influence had its origins in even earlier contacts. In this chapter I wish to explore what evidence there is for Anglo-Orcadian connections in the late 10th and 11th centuries, and how these connections are reflected in *Orkneyinga saga*.

REFERENCES TO ENGLAND IN *ORKNEYINGA SAGA*

There are the following references to England in the part of the saga describing the period in question (chs 11–42):

- *Ch. 12* notes that Óláfr Tryggvason was baptised in the Scilly Isles and spent some time in England and Ireland, before returning to Norway by way of Orkney, where he forcibly baptised Sigurðr jarl.[2]
- *Ch. 20* describes an attack launched by Karl Hundason on Þorfinnr jarl Sigurðsson from Berwick.
- *Ch. 23* tells how Þorfinnr, while raiding in the Hebrides and Scotland, but based in Galloway, sent a troop south to make shore-raids in England. The troop met with resistance from the English, who killed most of them and sent a few back to Þorfinnr to tell of their humiliation. He vowed to avenge himself on the English.
- *Ch. 24* begins by noting that Hǫrða-Knútr (Hardicanute) was the ruler of England and Denmark at the time. During his absence in Denmark, Þorfinnr and his co-jarl Rǫgnvaldr Brúsason raided widely in England, with two major battles and many minor skirmishes. The chapter is supported by two verses by Arnórr jarlaskáld.[3]
- *Ch. 31* has an ambiguous reference to England. The ambiguity is illustrated by giving two versions of the text and two translations of it:

OS Nordal:
> Þorfinnr iall red nu Orkneyium ok ollu rike sinu. Kalfr Arnason var ok longum med honum; stundum var hann i vestrviking ok heriade um Skotland ok Irland; hann var ok i Æinglande ok var um hrid firir þingamannalide.

OS Taylor:
> Earl Thorfinn now ruled the Orkneys and all [the rest of] his realm. Kalf Arni's son was also usually with him; sometimes he went a-roving in the west, and harried round the coasts of Scotland and Ireland; he also visited England and was for a time chief of the King's bodyguard [there].

OS Finnbogi Guðmundsson:
> Þorfinnr jarl réð nú Orkneyjum ok ǫllu ríki sínu. Kálfr Árnason var ok lǫngum með honum. Stundum var hann í vestrvíking ok herjaði um Skotland ok Írland; hann var ok í Englandi ok var um hríð fyrir þingamannaliði.

OS Pálsson/Edwards:
> Earl Thorfinn was now sole ruler of Orkney and the other territories he had

won. Kalf Arnason never left his side. From time to time the Earl would go on viking expeditions to the west of Scotland and to Ireland and also spent some time in England as leader of the King's bodyguard.

In Pálsson and Edwards' translation the sentence about Kálfr is parenthetical and all the other statements in the paragraph refer to Þorfinnr. Taylor's translation is not so decided, but his punctuation indicates a different interpretation: the paragraph is divided into two sentences – the first is about Þorfinnr, the second about Kálfr, and most of the statements in this passage must be taken as referring to the latter.[4]

- *Ch. 34* contains a brief summary of Haraldr Sigurðarson's expedition to England in 1066, including the fact that he stopped off in Orkney on the way there, leaving behind his wife and daughters, and that his son Óláfr returned to Orkney with Þorfinnr's two sons, Páll and Erlendr, and spent the winter there before going home to Norway.
- *Ch. 38* tells that Hákon Pálsson urged King Magnús berfœttr of Norway to invade England on an expedition to the west, 'thus to avenge your grandfather, Haraldr Sigurðarson'.
- *Ch. 40* tells that, on this expedition, Magnús Erlendsson escaped from the king's troop after a battle in Wales and spent some time in England.[5]

REFERENCES TO ORKNEY IN ENGLISH SOURCES

If the saga is sparing with its references to Anglo-Orcadian connections, English sources are even more so. The only obvious one for the relevant period is the annal for 1066 in the 'D' version of the *Anglo-Saxon Chronicle*. This tells us that, after winning the battle of Stamford Bridge, Harold of England gave *gryð* to Olaf, the son of the king of the Norwegians, to their bishop, and to *þan eorle of Orcanege*, along with the rest of their company, letting them leave once they had sworn oaths to keep the peace (*ASC*, I 199). This text of the *Chronicle* is thought to have reliable information about northern matters not found in other versions. A similar redaction may have been used by John (i.e. 'Florence') of Worcester, who also knows that the name of the earl of Orkney was Paul (*FW*, I 226). Further evidence of an Orcadian connection with the Norwegian invasion is provided by the Anglo-Norman verse chronicler Gaimar, who relates that Tostig had a supporter called Copsi who had been exiled to Orkney in 1065 and came from there to join Tostig with 17 ships in 1066 (*Gaimar*, 164).

Besides the accounts of 1066, there are two other references in the *Anglo-Saxon Chronicle* which have relevance to Orcadian affairs, although this is not apparent from the *Chronicle* entries themselves, but only when they are compared with other sources. Thus, an event unknown to *Orkneyinga saga* is mentioned in the 'C' version of the *Chronicle*, *s.a.* 1030. This time it is 'C' that is better informed than other versions and, after noting the killing of King Olaf in Norway and his subsequent canonisation, it states that earlier that year *forferde Hacun, se dohtiga eorl on sæ* ('Hacun, the valiant earl, perished at sea', *ASC*, I 157). John of Worcester, however, notes (*s.a.* 1030) alternative versions of Hákon's death, that he drowned at sea, or that he was killed in the Orkneys (*FW*, I 184–5). The entry for the previous year had noted that King Cnut, afraid of disloyalty by Hákon, had sent him into exile, although seemingly on an errand for the king.

Similarly brief is a reference in the 'D' version of the *Chronicle*, *s.a.* 1058. Ælfgar, son of the Earl of Mercia, had repeatedly been driven out of the country, sought allies in Ireland and Wales, and made attacks on England. On this occasion he soon returned with the help of the Welsh king, Gruffydd. The *Chronicle* goes on to say that *her com scyphere of Norwegan, hit is langsum to atellan eall hu hit gefaren wæs* ('in this year a fleet came from Norway, it is tedious to tell how it all happened', *ASC*, I 188–9). There is no indication in the *Anglo-Saxon Chronicle* that these two events are really one and the same, but Welsh and Irish chronicles confirm that they were. Thus, the *Annales Cambriae* (p. 25) tell us that the son of the Norwegian king was involved:

> Magnus filius Haraldi, vastavit regionem Anglorum, auxiliante Grifino rege Britonum. (Magnus the son of Harald ravaged the province of the English, helping Gruffydd king of the Welsh.)

Even more detail is provided by the *Annals of Tigernach* (Grabowski & Dumville 1984, 197), which record that in 1058 came:

> a naval expedition of the son of the king of Lochland [Norway?], with [the] foreigners of Orkney and of the Hebrides and of Dublin, to seize the kingdom of England, but God did not at all allow it.[6]

There is no indication in *Orkneyinga saga*, or any Icelandic source, that Þorfinnr was involved in this raid on England, indeed it is not even mentioned.

However, a similar expedition 40 years later, which also had Orcadian involvement, is better documented. Magnús berfœttr's expedition to the west in 1098 is widely reported in chronicles and annals from all over the British Isles and Ireland (Power 1986), but only *Orkneyinga saga* (chs 38, 40) mentions Hákon Pálsson's reason for inciting the king to undertake the expedition and Magnús Erlendsson's escape after the battle of the Menai Strait into England.

Thus English sources provide confirmation for the Anglo-Orcadian contacts noted in *Orkneyinga saga*, except those that took place in the lifetime of Þorfinnr jarl (chs 13–32). But when contemporary English sources are compared with other accounts, there are hints of such contacts in his lifetime, too. As we cannot fill out the picture that *Orkneyinga saga* gives of Anglo-Orcadian contacts in the 11th century by means of direct references in contemporary English sources, the question will have to be approached in a more roundabout way. This can be done using a variety of other sources, not necessarily either historical or

contemporary, that illuminate these contacts. This will involve considering first
some texts deriving from England and then some non-textual evidence, before
returning to Old Norse texts and, eventually, to *Orkneyinga saga*.

Some of the points already noted (12th-century contacts with Durham, the
Yorkshire setting of the events of 1066) suggest an Orcadian connection with
Northumbria and it is here that we may find further evidence to illuminate that
connection. The cycle of legends, historical, fantastical and hagiographical,
surrounding the earls of Northumbria, Siward and his son Waltheof, provide a
number of interesting parallels to episodes familiar from *Orkneyinga saga*.

Earl Siward is perhaps best known today for his role in Shakespeare's
Macbeth, but he is attested in contemporary English sources as the earl of
Northumbria from the last years of Cnut's reign until his own death in 1055.
Stenton (1971, 417) called him 'a Danish warrior of a primitive type', but little or
nothing is known for certain of his origins. We find him first witnessing a charter
as 'Siward Dux' in 1033 (Whitelock 1959, 83). He is mentioned several times in
the *Anglo-Saxon Chronicle* (*s.a.* 1043, 1048, 1052, 1054, 1055). His son Waltheof
is also attested in contemporary sources (Scott 1952) and is best known as one of
the few 'survivors from the Old English order' to make a career under William,
only to become 'the only Englishman of high rank whom King William
executed' after the attempted rebellion of 1075 (Stenton 1971, 610–12).

Waltheof came to be venerated as a saint and a number of post-Conquest
sources about him and his father provide some interesting material. Most of this
derives from traditions about Waltheof collected at the abbey of Crowland in
Lincolnshire, of which he was patron and where he was buried. These are
preserved mainly in a single manuscript now at Douai (Dehaisnes 1878, 598–
602). One of the sections of this manuscript deals with the 'Gesta antecessorum
comitis Waldevi' and tells a long and fantastic tale about Siward's origins and
youth.[7] This tale has frequently been discussed and, while some commentators
may have been over-enthusiastic in seeing a *Siwards saga behind the
Waltheofian material, there is little to add to their exposition of the Scandinavian
parallels.[8] Three points to note about this legend are:

(1) Siward is called *Dicre* (i.e. ON *digri*, 'stout').
(2) His first adventure is to sail to Orkney (*apud Orkaneiam portum invenit
    salubrem*) and there to drive out a dragon that had been terrorising the
    inhabitants.
(3) From there, he sails to Northumberland, where he hears of another dragon
    that needs dealing with. On the way to find it, he meets an old man who tells
    him to go to London where he will serve and be honoured by the king. To
    help Siward convince his companions of this prophecy, the old man gives
    him a banner called *Ravenlandeye*, meaning 'Raven, terror of the land'

(*Nomen autem vexillo imposuit idem senex Ravenlandeye, quod interpretatur corvus terrae terror*).

Previous commentators have noted similarities with Sigurðr jarl Hlǫðvisson of Orkney:[9] he also had the cognomen *digri* and owned a 'raven banner', although we do not know that he engaged in any fights with dragons. None of this is especially surprising. *Digri* is common in Old Norse nomenclature (Lind 1920–21, cols 60–61) and the raven banner is familiar from a number of Old English and Old Norse texts (see below); at a cursory glance the banners of Siward and Sigurðr are not very similar.

The literary relationship (if any) between these two namesakes is made difficult to determine by the fact that Earl Siward is not mentioned in any Norse sources. However his son Waltheof appears in many of the Norse accounts of 1066 and all that (where he is invariably mistakenly said to be the son of Godwine) and even had skaldic verse composed in his honour. Several of these accounts mention the death of Valþjófr, as he is called in Old Norse. In discussing the version found in *Fagrskinna* (which is the most detailed), Scott (1953-7, 91) notes its hagiographical tinge and suggests 'at least a reminiscence of an English or Norman account', quoting the version of Waltheof's death given by Orderic Vitalis (*Orderic*, II 320-22), which Orderic got from his friends the monks of Crowland.

It is of course not unexpected for the Norse accounts of Valþjófr's death to show similarities with English accounts of the same, but it becomes interesting when we find similarities between these English accounts and Norse descriptions of the death of St Magnús.[10] Besides the fact that both Waltheof and Magnús were killed as a result of a political power struggle, and besides the usual hagiographical commonplaces, the following points are worthy of note:

(1) Both are killed early in the morning in or near a church (Waltheof at St Giles' in Winchester, Magnús on Egilsay).
(2) Both give away their garment(s) to a person or persons on the spot (Waltheof to the assembled clergy and poor, Magnús to his unwilling executioner, Lífólfr).
(3) Both prostrate themselves on the ground, lamenting and praying, immediately before their execution, which is by beheading.
(4) Both are denied proper burial until the intervention of their wife (Waltheof) or mother (Magnús).

The similarities between the Norse accounts of the death of Magnús and Orderic's account of the death of Waltheof may not seem very great, but they are greater than those noted by Scott between the latter and the version of Valþjófr's death given in ch. 76 of *Fagrskinna*. In this, Valþjófr is killed on a heath by 12 of the king's knights. *Fagrskinna* has only the second, and part of the third, of the motifs listed above: Valþjófr gives away his *kyrtill* to one of the knights about to kill him and lies prostrate on the ground (though not praying) before being beheaded.

Precisely what significance there is in the admittedly superficial and perhaps circumstantial parallels between *Orkneyinga saga* (and related texts) and the Siward/Waltheof cycle is not easy to say. However, for the sake of argument, I would like to assume that they provide further evidence of cultural contacts between Orkney and England in the late 11th and early 12th centuries.

SEA-ROUTES AND NON-TEXTUAL EVIDENCE

A question that must be considered here is the route along which Anglo-Orcadian contacts could have taken place. Crawford (1986; 1987, 16–27) has suggested that, in addition to the well-documented route from Orkney around the northwest of Scotland to the Hebrides and thence down to the Irish Sea, Man, and Wales, another route was possible, into the Moray Firth, through the Great Glen, and then down past Kintyre. Either of these would be one way of coming to England, even to its eastern half.

Yet the route straight down the east coast of Scotland must also have been used. It is at any rate attested in the 12th century. In *Orkneyinga saga* ch. 86, one of the pilgrims in Rǫgnvaldr's company, the Icelandic poet Ármóðr, declaims a verse indicating that the company is sailing past the mouth of the Humber – the prose tells us that they sailed '. . . south to Scotland and then to England. And when they sailed past Northumbria, Ármóðr spoke a verse . . .'. Chapter 91 of the saga refers briefly to a raiding expedition to Scotland and England from Orkney by Eysteinn Haraldsson, the king of Norway, in 1152. Other sources referring to this expedition preserve a series of verses by Einarr Skúlason which show that Eysteinn sailed south along the east coast.[11] This is indicated by those place-names in the verses that can be identified: Aberdeen, Hartlepool and Whitby.

This eastern route may have been in regular use before the 12th century. The description in ch. 59 of *Egils saga* of Egill's voyage, via Orkney, to the mouth of the Humber may be fictional, but Binns (1968) has shown that it accords well with 10th-century conditions, in so far as we can deduce them. Early contacts along this route are suggested by the distribution of Scottish hogbacks, a type of monument which originated in North Yorkshire in the early 10th century and spread to Scotland, reaching Orkney by the 11th century. In his study of Scottish hogbacks, Lang (1972–4, 209) found that the majority of them were close to maritime routes, particularly along the east coast.

Besides the hogbacks, other archaeological evidence for Anglo-Orcadian contacts before the 12th century consists mainly of numismatic finds. The most spectacular of these is the hoard containing around 300 coins of Cnut found in Caldale and now thought to have been deposited around 1035 (Stevenson 1966, xviii; Graham-Campbell 1975–6, 128; Blackburn & Pagan 1986, 298). It may be possible to see this hoard in relation to two slightly earlier ones found in southeast Scotland, at Lindores in Fife and at Jedburgh. It has been suggested

(Dolley 1966, 15, 37 & 40) that these hoards were a result of Cnut's English and Norwegian activities in the 1020s rather than having any connection with the Norse inhabitants of northern and western Scotland. But if Orcadians, at least, became involved in those Anglo-Norwegian activities, then the two need not be mutually exclusive.

Other than the Caldale hoard, there are English coins in the Burray hoard, deposited *c.* 1000 (Graham-Campbell 1975–6, 123; Stevenson 1966, xviii; Blackburn & Pagan 1986, 297). Stray finds include half of a silver penny of Eadmund (940–46) found in a grave at Buckquoy, and a worn coin of the reign of Eadgar (959–75) found on the Brough of Deerness. In fact, eight of the nine coins found in Orkney since 1966 are English, mainly from the 10th century (Morris *et al.* 1986, 339–401).

A further suggestion of an English connection for the Northern Isles is provided by the small bronze strap-end decorated in the Ringerike style which was found at Jarlshof in Shetland and which may have been made in England (Fuglesang 1980, 51).

THE ANGLO-ORCADIAN AXIS IN OLD NORSE LITERATURE

Although there are frequent references to both England and Orkney in Icelandic sagas, few of these texts show any obvious awareness of direct contacts between the two countries. The interest in, and personal contacts with, Orkney that some Icelanders (in particular the Oddaverjar) had was demonstrated by Einar Ól. Sveinsson (1937). More recently, Helgi Þorláksson (1979, 62–70) has shown how political developments of the 12th and 13th centuries influenced Icelandic trade. In the late 12th and early 13th centuries, he argues, the Orcadians successfully competed with Norwegian merchants, probably in the import of luxury wares from England in particular. This is the period which saw the compilation of *Orkneyinga saga*. However, this Orcadian influence was relatively short-lived (*c.* 1175–1220). Norwegian influence reasserted itself with the political demise of the Oddaverjar and the growth of a strong monarchy in Norway, supported by Snorri Sturluson.

Although a later historical work such as Snorri's *Heimskringla* draws heavily on *Orkneyinga saga* with frequent references to Orkney and its jarls, it is therefore not surprising that it reveals no special interest in Orkney's connections with the wider world and with England in particular. The focus in *Heimskringla*, as in other kings' sagas, is naturally on the kings of Norway. Thus, while both *Morkinskinna* (p. 266) and *Fagrskinna* (ch. 63), as well as *Heimskringla* (*Haralds saga Sigurðarsonar*, ch. 83), note that Haraldr took one or two jarls of Orkney with him to England in 1066, none of these mentions the fact that the jarls returned to Orkney with Óláfr Haraldsson. Yet this fact cannot have been unknown to the authors of these texts for, in *Heimskringla* at least, Páll and Erlendr crop up again when Magnús berfœttr deposes them in Orkney at the beginning of his 1098 expedition (*Magnúss saga berfœtts*, ch. 8).[12]

In *Heimskringla*, the jarls of Orkney are a foil to the king of Norway, their subservience adding to his reputation. This is particularly evident in the saga of St Óláfr in *Heimskringla*, where we get the most extended references to Orkney, with a summary of Orcadian history in chs 96–103. This section develops to a climax when the rival jarls, Þorfinnr and Brúsi, travel to Norway so that King Óláfr can sort out their differences (chs 100–2). Once the two are back in Orkney, Snorri again resorts to summary, this time with reference to his source: *er þó þat sagt í Jarlasǫgunum* (ch. 103). Comparison of this summary with *Orkneyinga saga* is made difficult by the fact that the revised version of the saga that we have today is in turn based on Snorri at this point. But it is clear that once the quarrels of the jarls of Orkney no longer involved the Norwegian king, Snorri felt no need to include them in his account. That he knew about them and selected his material rather carefully is indicated not only by his source reference, but also by his separate saga of St Óláfr. It is believed that Snorri wrote this first and later used it as the backbone of *Heimskringla*. In ch. 270 of the separate saga, Snorri summarises the conflict between Þorfinnr and his nephew Rǫgnvaldr Brúsason (*Þessi urðu upphǫf til deilu þeira frændanna, ok er frá því lǫng saga*, 'this was the origin of the dealings between those kin, and there is a long saga about that') and briefly describes the final battle between them, citing a verse.[13]

Fagrskinna (ch. 48) has only a very brief reference to these events, saying of King Magnús Óláfsson that he helped Rǫgnvaldr to power in Orkney and that

> um hans daga gørðisk missætti milli Rǫgnvalds ok Þorfinns, fǫðurbróður hans, sem getit er í Jarla sǫgunum.
> (in his days was the conflict between Rǫgnvaldr and his uncle Þorfinnr, which is told in the Sagas of the jarls.)

Morkinskinna (pp. 31–2) has a nearly identical summary, followed by a more detailed account of the battle of Rauðabjǫrg.

As the source references indicate, all three of these texts derived their information (directly or indirectly) from an earlier (lost) version of *Orkneyinga saga* (called *Jarla sǫgur*, or 'Sagas of the jarls'). If that earlier version had as much information about the reign of Þorfinnr as the extant one does, then it is clear that the Icelandic historians of Norway were extremely selective in using this source and that they therefore cannot give us any more direct information about Þorfinnr's exploits in England than *Orkneyinga saga* can. What they can perhaps illuminate, however, is the ambiguity at the beginning of ch. 31 in *Orkneyinga saga*.

As noted above, this ambiguity consists in whether the statement *hann var ok í Englandi ok var um hríð fyrir þingamannaliði* refers to Þorfinnr or to Kálfr Arnason. If taken only in the context of *Orkneyinga saga*, the former (and hence Pálsson & Edwards' translation) seems to be more likely. Kálfr makes only brief appearances in the saga and then mainly as a supporter of Þorfinnr (chs 25 and 27). Þorfinnr, on the other hand, is frequently shown on viking expeditions and, as we have already seen, chs 23–4 indicate that these reached as far as England.

In contrast, ch. 31 later tells us that, after coming back from his pilgrimage, Þorfinnr

[l]ét . . . þá af herferðum, lagði þá hug á stjórn lýðs ok lands [ok] á lagasetning.
(then gave up raiding, and took an interest in governing his people and country, and in making laws.)

Þorfinnr is the great viking hero and the statements at the beginning of the chapter fit most easily with his description. But if we look at other texts, the situation is not so clear. Kálfr is a major character in the kings' sagas, infamous as the man who dealt St Óláfr his death-blow. The kings' sagas all tell of his cycle of reconciliation with Magnús Óláfsson, exile from Norway and reconciliation again; several of the texts note that he spent his exile with his niece's husband, Þorfinnr. Among the references to him, the closest to *Orkneyinga saga* ch. 31 is in *Heimskringla* (*Haralds saga Sigurðarsonar*, ch. 51):

Kálfr Arnason hafði verit í vestrvíking, síðan er hann fór ór Nóregi, en opt á vetrum var hann í Orkneyjum með Þorfinni jarli, mági sínum.
(Kálfr Árnason had been on viking raids in the west since he left Norway, and in the winters he was often in Orkney with his in-law, Þorfinnr jarl.)

Although *Morkinskinna* (p. 25) also knows that he went to stay with Þorfinnr, none of these texts makes any reference to England.

On the other hand, earlier in his career, Kálfr is presented as plotting with King Knútr in England to overthrow King Óláfr. *Ágrip* (ch. 26), *Heimskringla* (*Óláfs saga helga*, ch. 183) and *Fagrskinna* (ch. 34) all show the king promising Kálfr power in Norway in exchange for getting rid of Óláfr. The last two of these texts also emphasise that this plotting took place in England. It is possible that ch. 31 of *Orkneyinga saga* is thus a garbled reminiscence of this episode in Kálfr's life, put in its chronologically incorrect place in the saga, but to admit this means to give preference to the kings' sagas over *Orkneyinga saga*.

Is there then any evidence for the alternative explanation, that Þorfinnr, as well as raiding in England as recorded in chs 23–4 of *Orkneyinga saga*, might have spent some time at the court of the English king, with the high position of captain of the *þingamannalið*? Some light is shed on this question by the verse preserved in the saga, particularly that of Þorfinnr's court poet, Arnórr Þórðarson jarlaskáld.

Arnórr was a prolific poet and his verses are recorded in a large number of texts. As well as verses for Þorfinnr, we have compositions in honour of Rǫgnvaldr Brúsason, and the Norwegian kings Magnús góði and Haraldr harðráði. *Skáldatal* (*Edda Snorra Sturlusonar*, III 258, 262, 267) also tells us that he composed for the Norwegian king Óláfr kyrri as well as for Knútr, although no such verses are preserved. Arnórr's father Þórðr Kolbeinsson was also a poet. He composed in honour of the Norwegian jarl Eiríkr Hákonarson, who became earl of Northumbria under Knútr (and who was the father of *se dohtiga eorl* Hákon). It is thus not surprising that scholars have seen signs of

English influence in Arnórr's verses, both in his innovative use of the metre *hrynhent* and particularly in his vocabulary (Hofmann 1955, 101–5; Fidjestøl 1984, 241). Such influence is detectable throughout his poetry, but quite a lot of it can be found in his verses on the Orkney jarls. We know little about Arnórr's biography, but it seems reasonable to assume that the English influences on his poetry had their origins in the fact that he had spent some time in England, and why not in the company of Þorfinnr? If so, it would imply an extended stay rather than just raiding.[14]

This explanation might also illuminate the somewhat obscure verse by Arnórr cited towards the end of ch. 22 of *Orkneyinga saga*:[15]

Ymisst vann sás unni,	He who succeeded in attacking
írsk fell drótt, þás sótti,	overcame now men of 'baldr',
Baldrs eða brezkar aldir,	now men of Wales, the Irish
brá eldr Skota veldi.	troop fell, fire ravaged the realm of the Scots.

A problem here is the interpretation of the phrase *Baldrs aldir*. The verse names the peoples over whom Þorfinnr was victorious: the Irish, the Welsh and the Scots. We might be tempted to feel that *Baldrs aldir* ought therefore to mean the English. I wonder if it is not possible to connect the use of *Baldr* with Old English *bealdor*, meaning a prince or lord. The Norse god's name *Baldr* is common as a base-word in kennings, but Hofmann (1955, 76) notes three instances where it is the second element in a compound whose first element refers to troops (such as *fólkbaldr*), so that the whole compound means 'military leader'. He cites some Old English parallels to this construction, such as *winia bealdor, gumena bealdor*. *Baldrs aldir* is just the opposite of this particular construction, but might we not see a playful reference to Englishmen behind it? If a 'lord of men' is an Englishman, could not the 'men of a lord' be Englishmen?

If we accept the possibility that Þorfinnr spent some time in England, we can go on to ask when and where that might have been, although it is unlikely that such a question can be answered with certainty. Another literary-historical detour can hint at some more questions, if not a solution.

Earl Siward's *Ravenlandeye* is not the first appearance of a raven banner in an English source. This happens when four of five versions of the *Anglo-Saxon Chronicle* record, *s.a.* 878, the death in Devon of an unnamed viking, the brother of Ingwær and Healfdene, and 840 men with him (*ASC*, I 77):

> . . . þar wæs se guðfana ge numen þe hi ræfen [v.l. hræfn] heton.
> (. . . there the war-banner which they called 'raven' was taken.)

Further information on this banner is provided in 12th-century additions[16] to the *Annals of St Neots* (p. 78):

> Dicunt enim quod tres sorores Hynguari et Hubbe, filię uidelicet Lodebrochi, illud uexillum texuerunt et totum parauerunt illud uno meridiano tempore. Dicunt etiam quod, in omni bello ubi praecederet idem signum, si uictoriam adepturi essent,

appareret in medio signo quasi coruus uiuus uolitans; si uero uincendi in futuro fuissent, penderet directe nichil mouens — et hoc sepe probatum est.
(For it is said that the three sisters of Hynguar and Hubba, the daughters that is to say of Lodebroch, wove that banner, and made ready the whole of it in one noontide. People say also that in every battle in which this standard precedes [the warriors], if victory is to be theirs then there appears in the middle of the banner what seems to be a living raven flying; but if they are to be defeated, then it hangs down quite lifeless. And this fact has often been proved.)[17]

According to the *Encomium Emmae* (pp. 24–5), Cnut's army had a banner with similar properties when defending London from Eadmund:

Erat namque eis uexillum miri portenti, quod licet credam posse esse incredibile lectori, tamen, quia uerum est, uerae inseram lectioni. Enimuero dum esset simplissimo candidissimoque intextum serico, nulliusque figurae in eo inserta esset [i]mago, tempore belli semper in eo uidebatur coruus ac si intextus, in uictoria suorum quasi hians ore excutiensque alas instabilisque pedibus, et suis deuictis quietissimus totoque corpore demissus.
(Now they had a banner of wonderfully strange nature, which though I believe that it may be incredible to the reader, yet since it is true, I will introduce the matter into my true history. For while it was woven of the plainest and whitest silk, and the representation of no figure was inserted into it, in time of war a raven was always seen as if embroidered on it, in the hour of its owners' victory opening its beak, flapping its wings, and restive on its feet, but very subdued and drooping with its whole body when they were defeated.)

Although there have been attempts to associate these two Danish banners (as well as that of Earl Siward) with references to raven banners in Old Icelandic texts (e.g. *Encomium Emmae*, 96–7), the comparison is not straightforward and should be considered in more detail.

There are basically two Norse banners in question, one belonging to Sigurðr, jarl of Orkney, and one to the Norwegian king Haraldr harðráði (which is not recorded as having a raven on it). The latter is mentioned several times in both *Heimskringla* and *Fagrskinna*, although not much is said of it except that it was called *Landeyðan*. Snorri notes (*Haralds saga Sigurðarsonar*, ch. 22) that *sá myndi hafa sigr, er merkit er fyrir borit* ('he would have victory, before whom the banner was carried').

Sigurðr's banner is mentioned in *Orkneyinga saga* (chs 11–12), *Njáls saga* (ch. 157) and *Þorsteins saga Síðu-Hallssonar* (ch. 2), all referring to the Orkney jarl's participation and death in the battle of Clontarf. Indeed, there is almost certainly a literary relationship between these three texts, with *Þorsteins saga* based on *Njáls saga* and both sagas making use of a lost saga (often, but probably erroneously, called **Brjáns saga*) which was possibly a version of *Orkneyinga saga* (as argued by Jón Jóhannesson in *Þorsteins saga*, ci–ciii). Certainly a close comparison of the three texts confirms this literary relationship, with the two later sagas developing some of the details found in *Orkneyinga saga* and ignoring others. Both of the later sagas concentrate almost exclusively on the dramatic scene whereby the jarl's followers refuse to carry the banner knowing that it means certain death for the bearer. The deaths only make sense if we bear in mind the statement in *Orkneyinga saga* that *sigrsælt myni verða þeim, er fyrir er borit, en banvænt þeim, er berr* ('he, before whom it is carried, will be victorious, but he who carries it can expect death'). Not only is this not explained in the two later sagas, but they do not mention the image of the raven, either, although in *Njáls saga*, one of the men asked to carry the banner is called Hrafn! In sum, there is nothing in the two later sagas that cannot be derived from *Orkneyinga saga*.

Orkneyinga saga, on the other hand, concentrates more on the banner itself and on Sigurðr than on the drama on the battlefield. The battle of Clontarf and Sigurðr's death are dismissed in a few lines in ch. 12, but they are carefully prepared in ch. 11, where Sigurðr fights a battle in Scotland in which three of his flagbearers die before he gets his victory. The chapter also explains that Sigurðr's mother Eðna made the banner for him and describes it thus:

> Merkit var gǫrt af miklum hannyrðum ok ágætligum hagleik; þat var gǫrt í hrafns mynd, ok þá er vindr blæss í merkit, þá var sem hrafn beindi fluginn.
> (The banner was made with great skill and splendid workmanship; it was made in the shape of a raven and when the wind caught the banner it was as if the raven spread its wings.)

Orkneyinga saga is thus the only one of the Norse texts which mentions a *raven* banner, but the raven on Sigurðr's banner is quite different from that in the two English sources. There, the Danish banners only show a raven in time of war, the shape of the raven indicating either victory or defeat. The raven on Sigurðr's banner is described poetically rather than ominously: it looks as if it were flying when the wind catches the banner. The significance of the banner for victory applies to whoever it is carried before, rather than deriving from the appearance of the raven.

In the same way that the two later Icelandic sagas borrow the story of the raven banner and subtly change it, so I believe the version in *Orkneyinga saga* is also a variation on an original theme from elsewhere, possibly on a story of the type found in the two English sources quoted above. There are similarities which indicate such a connection, the most striking being that the banner was made for the hero by a woman or women using magical arts.

The progressive development of this legend of a raven banner from southeast England to Iceland seems clear, even if the details of how it happened are obscure, and the Orcadian version occupies an intermediate position. Thus it does not seem too speculative to suggest that the story of the raven banner came to Orkney from England and from there passed on to Iceland. The *Encomium Emmae* indicates that stories about raven banners were current at the court of Cnut. A sojourn by Þorfinnr in England either at his court or that of his successor Hardicanute could provide the link by which such stories found their way to Orkney.

Where Earl Siward's *Ravenlandeye* fits in is not clear, mainly because the text gives no information about this banner except its name. But it is not likely that this legend was 'borrowed' from that about Sigurðr jarl, as has been suggested. More plausible is the possibility that the legend about Sigurðr jarl was based on the same English stories that gave rise to the legend about Siward. However, in both cases we are dealing with texts at several removes from their historical background and it is difficult to evaluate them without any knowledge of their immediate sources. Siward's banner is also intriguingly similar in name to King Haraldr's *Landeyðan* (although this is nowhere said to be a raven banner). Again, we seem to be circling around Anglo-Orcadian connections in the 11th century without being able to pin them down.

CONCLUSIONS

Literary texts, even 'historical' texts in literary form, cannot be used to 'prove' historical facts. But they have suggestive powers. Close readings of such texts, careful attention to their sources and how they are used, to the historical and geographical contexts in so far as they can be discovered, and comparisons with other texts – all of these can, especially if taken together, suggest historical contours not immediately discernible from other sources. These historical contours can be particularly valuable when we suspect that the authors of the texts were not themselves aware of them. Thus, *Orkneyinga saga* shows no particular awareness of Anglo-Orcadian contacts, and certainly not of their significance. This is not surprising, given the date and the literary, political and geographical context in which the extant version was written. The earlier version is unfortunately not available for analysis. It is thus debatable whether the contours I have sketched above could have been discerned in the lost, original saga, or whether they were merely latent in the literary and historical traditions behind it.

I believe that the historical contours discernible from the evidence considered above amount at the very least to the possibility that there were extensive, frequent and direct contacts of a largely political nature between Orkney and England throughout the 11th century. But to demonstrate this to the satisfaction of sceptics will require further research on many fronts.

Notes

1. Unless otherwise indicated, all references to *Orkneyinga saga* are by chapter number to Nordal's edition (*OS* Nordal). Normally, these chapter numbers also apply to the edition by Finnbogi Guðmundsson (*OS* Finnbogi Guðmundsson) and to the translations by Taylor (*OS* Taylor) and Pálsson and Edwards (*OS* Pálsson/Edwards).

2. This chapter unfortunately exists only in the 16th-century Danish translation of the saga made (probably in Western Norway) from a manuscript now lost.

3. One manuscript, an excerpt of verses rather than of the whole saga, contains an additional verse (*OS* Nordal, 65).

4. It is clear that the translators are in each case basing their interpretations at least partially on editorial punctuation of the passage (Taylor on Nordal's edition, Pálsson & Edwards on that of Finnbogi Guðmundsson). The editors' punctuation is in turn based on their interpretations of the passage since, as far as can be seen from the facsimile (*Flateyjarbók*, col. 529), the manuscript has no punctuation at all in these sentences.

5. The *Legenda de Sancto Magno* adds that he stayed with 'king Henry, son of William' (*OS* Finnbogi Guðmundsson, 305).

6. I am grateful to David Dumville for help with this text.

7. The text of the *Gesta* is conveniently printed, with a translation, and discussed by Wright (1939, 129–35, 267–70).

8. Besides Wright (1939), see Olrik (1908–9) and Smith (1928–36, 225–6). The legendary material is expressly rejected as evidence by Scott (1952) in his historical study of Waltheof.

9. The similarities confused Anne Holtsmark (1956, 194), who assumed that the banner referred to was actually Sigurðr jarl's banner. Both Olrik and Smith assumed that Siward's youthful adventures were 'borrowed' from Sigurðr jarl. It should also be noted that, in the *Gesta*, *dicre* does not appear in the text, but only in a marginal comment (Michel 1836–40, II 105).

10. The accounts of *Orkneyinga saga* and the two sagas of St Magnús, all printed in *OS* Finnbogi Guðmundsson, are substantially the same and go back to a common source.

11. Johnsen (1965) gives a useful summary. He does not believe the verses give an accurate description of the events of this expedition, but does not doubt that it took place and went to the places mentioned. Attempts to identify the placenames in the verses can be found in Taylor (1965) and Poole (1980).

12. However, the Norwegian *Ágrip* ch. 41 notes both that Óláfr asked for *grið* from King Harold and that he returned to Orkney with Earl Paul. This is closer to the English chronicles than to the later Icelandic traditions.

13. Passages from the separate saga which Snorri did not include in *Heimskringla* are printed in *Heimskringla*, II 448–9.

14. It may be possible to glimpse the political context for Þorfinnr's sojourn in England: in a verse by Óttarr svarti (*Skjd* A I 299, B I 275), Cnut is called *konung Dana, Íra ok Engla ok Eybúa* ('king of the Danes, Irish and English and "island-dwellers" '). If the term *Eybúar* refers to the inhabitants of the Northern Isles, does this mean that their ruler acknowledged the overlordship of the king?

15. The text given here is that of *OS* Finnbogi Guðmundsson. The verse, although difficult, is not impossible to construe and there seems no justification for the extensive emendations of *OS* Nordal. It is clear that the adjective *brezkr* here means 'Welsh' and not 'English' (see Poole 1987, 292–4).

16. The editors of the *Annals of St Neots* note (pp. lxii–iii) this reference as an example of 'local East Anglian matter' from an unknown source. Since the *Annals* were compiled between 1120 and 1140 (p. lxv), these traditions were not necessarily current in the 9th century.

17. Translation by Wright (1939, 126).

REFERENCES

Ágrip: *Ágrip af Nóregskonunga sǫgum. Fagrskinna – Nóregs konunga tal*, ed. Einarsson, Bjarni, Íslenzk fornrit 29, Reykjavík, 1984.
Annales Cambriae, ed. Williams ab Ithel, John, Rolls series 20, London, 1860.

Annals of St Neots: *The Anglo-Saxon Chronicle 17: the Annals of St Neots*, eds Dumville, David & Lapidge, Michael, Cambridge, 1984.

ASC: *Two of the Saxon chronicles parallel*, eds Earle, John & Plummer, Charles, Oxford, 1892–9.

Bibire, Paul 1988. 'The poetry of Earl Rǫgnvaldr's court', in *St Magnus Cathedral and Orkney's twelfth-century renaissance*, ed. Crawford, Barbara E., Aberdeen, pp. 208–40.

Binns, Alan 1968. 'The navigation of viking ships round the British Isles in Old English and Old Norse sources', in *The Fifth Viking Congress*, ed. Niclasen, Bjarni, Tórshavn, pp. 103–17.

Blackburn, Mark & Pagan, Hugh 1986. 'A revised check-list of coin hoards from the British Isles, *c*. 500–1100', in *Anglo-Saxon monetary history. Essays in memory of Michael Dolley*, ed. Blackburn, M. A. S., Leicester, pp. 291–313.

Crawford, Barbara E. 1983. 'Birsay and the early earls and bishops of Orkney', *Orkney heritage* 2, 97–118.

Crawford, Barbara E. 1986. 'The making of a frontier: the firthlands from the ninth to the twelfth centuries', in *Firthlands of Ross and Sutherland*, ed. Baldwin, John R., Edinburgh, pp. 33–46.

Crawford, Barbara E. 1987. *Scandinavian Scotland*, Leicester.

De Geer, Ingrid 1988. 'Music and the twelfth-century Orkney earldom: a cultural crossroads in musicological perspective', in *St Magnus Cathedral and Orkney's twelfth-century renaissance*, ed. Crawford, Barbara E., Aberdeen, pp. 241–63.

Dehaisnes, C. 1878. *Catalogue général des manuscrits des bibliothques publiques des Départements VI, Douai*, Paris.

Dolley, R. H. M. 1966. *Sylloge of coins of the British Isles: Hiberno-Norse coins in the British Museum*, London.

Donaldson, Gordon 1988. 'The contemporary scene', in *St Magnus Cathedral and Orkney's twelfth-century renaissance*, ed. Crawford, Barbara E., Aberdeen, pp. 1–10.

Edda Snorra Sturlusonar, Copenhagen, 1848–87.

Encomium Emmae reginae, ed. Campbell, Alistair, London, 1949.

Fagrskinna: Ágrip af Nóregskonunga sǫgum. Fagrskinna – Nóregs konunga tal, ed. Einarsson, Bjarni, Íslenzk fornrit 29, Reykjavík, 1984.

Fernie, Eric 1988. 'The church of St Magnus, Egilsay', in *St Magnus Cathedral and Orkney's twelfth-century renaissance*, ed. Crawford, Barbara E., Aberdeen, pp. 140–61.

Fidjestøl, Bjarne 1984. 'Arnórr Þórðarson: skald of the Orkney jarls', in *The Northern and Western Isles in the Viking world: survival, continuity and change*, eds Fenton, Alexander & Pálsson, Hermann, Edinburgh, pp. 239–57.

Flateyjarbók, ed. Jónsson, Finnur, Corpus Codicorum Islandicorum Medii Aevi 1, Copenhagen, 1930.

Foote, Peter 1988. 'Observations on *Orkneyinga saga*', in *St Magnus Cathedral and Orkney's twelfth-century renaissance*, ed. Crawford, Barbara E., Aberdeen, pp. 192–207.

Foote, Peter 1989. 'Master Robert's prologue in Magnúss saga lengri', in *Festskrift til Finn Hødnebø*, ed. Eithun, Bjørn, *et al.* Oslo, pp. 65–81.

Fuglesang, Signe Horn 1980. *Some aspects of the Ringerike style*, Odense.

FW: *Florentii Wigorniensis Monachi Chronicon ex chronicis*, ed. Thorpe, Benjamin, London, 1848.

Gaimar: L'Estoire des Engleis by Geffrei Gaimar, ed. Bell, Alexander, Anglo-Norman Text Society 14–16, London, 1960.

Grabowski, Kathryn & David Dumville 1984. *Chronicles and annals of mediaeval Ireland and Wales*, Woodbridge.

Graham-Campbell, James 1975–6. 'The Viking-age silver and gold hoards of Scandinavian character from Scotland', *Proceedings of the Society of Antiquaries of Scotland* 107, 114–35.

Heimskringla: Snorri Sturluson: Heimskringla, ed. Aðalbjarnarson, Bjarni, Íslenzk fornrit 26–8, Reykjavík, 1941–51.

Helle, Knut 1988. 'The organisation of the twelfth-century church in Norway', in *St Magnus Cathedral and Orkney's twelfth-century renaissance*, ed. Crawford, Barbara E., Aberdeen, pp. 46–55.

Hofmann, Dietrich 1955. *Nordisch-englische Lehnbeziehungen der Wikingerzeit*, Bibliotheca Arnamagnæana 14, Copenhagen.

Holtsmark, Anne 1956. 'Vefr darraðar', in *Studier i norrøn diktning*, Oslo, pp. 177–97 [first published in *Maal og minne* 1939].

Johnsen, Arne Odd 1965. *Er Einar Skulesons fyrstedikt '. . . lutter historiske og historisk nøjagtige; . . .'?* Det kongelige norske videnskabers selskabs skrifter 2, Trondheim.

Lang, James 1972–4. 'Hogback monuments in Scotland', *Proceedings of the Society of Antiquaries of Scotland* 105, 206–35.

Lind, E. H. 1920–1. *Norsk-isländska personbinamn från medeltiden*, Uppsala.

Michel, Francisque 1836–40. *Chroniques Anglo-Normandes*, Rouen.

Morkinskinna, ed. Jónsson, Finnur, Samfund til udgivelse af gammel nordisk litteratur 53, Copenhagen, 1932.

Morris, Christopher D. with Emery, Norman 1986. 'The chapel enclosure on the Brough of Deerness, Orkney: survey and excavations, 1975–77', *Proceedings of the Society of Antiquaries of Scotland* 116, 301–74.

Njáls saga: Brennu-Njáls saga, ed. Sveinsson, Einar Ól., Íslenzk fornrit 12, Reykjavík, 1954.

Olrik, Axel 1908–9. 'Siward digri of Northumberland: a viking-saga of the Danes in England', *Saga-Book* 6, 212–37.

Orderic: The Ecclesiastical history of Orderic Vitalis, ed. Chibnall, Marjorie, Oxford, 1969–80.

OS Finnbogi Guðmundsson: *Orkneyinga saga*, ed. Guðmundsson, Finnbogi, Íslenzk fornrit 34, Reykjavík, 1965.

OS Nordal: *Orkneyinga saga*, ed. Nordal, Sigurður, Samfund til udgivelse af gammel nordisk litteratur 40, Copenhagen, 1913–16.

OS Pálsson/Edwards: *Orkneyinga saga*, trans. Pálsson, Hermann & Edwards, Paul, Harmondsworth, 1981.

OS Taylor: *The Orkneyinga saga*, trans. Taylor, Alexander B., Edinburgh, 1938.

Poole, Russell 1980. 'In search of the *Partar*', *Scandinavian studies* 52, 264–77.

Poole, Russell 1987. 'Skaldic verse and Anglo-Saxon history: some aspects of the period 1009–16, *Speculum* 62, 265–98.

Power, Rosemary 1986. ''Magnus Barelegs' expeditions to the west', *The Scottish Historical Review* 65, 107–32.

Scott, Forrest S. 1952. 'Earl Waltheof of Northumbria', *Archaeologia Aeliana* 30, 149–215.

Scott, Forrest S. 1953–7. 'Valþjófr jarl: an English earl in Icelandic sources', *Saga-Book* 14, 78–94.

Skjd: Den norsk-islandske skjaldedigtning, ed. Jónsson, Finnur, Copenhagen, 1908–15.

Smith, A. H. 1928–36. 'The early literary relations of England and Scandinavia', *Saga-Book* 11, 215–32.

Stenton, F. M. 1971. *Anglo-Saxon England*, Oxford.

Stevenson, Robert B. K. 1966. *Sylloge of coins of the British Isles: National Museum of Antiquities of Scotland, Part I*, London.

Sveinsson, Einar Ól. 1937. *Sagnaritun Oddaverja*, Reykjavík.

Taylor, A. B. 1965. 'Eysteinn Haraldsson in the west, *c.* 1151', in *The Fourth Viking Congress*, ed. Small, Alan, Edinburgh, pp. 119–34.

Þorláksson, Helgi 1979. 'Snorri Sturluson og Oddaverjar', in *Snorri: átta alda minning*, Reykjavík, pp. 53–88.

Þorsteins saga: Austfirðinga sǫgur, ed. Jóhannesson, Jón, Íslenzk fornrit 11, Reykjavík, 1950.

Whitelock, Dorothy 1959. 'The dealings of the kings of England with Northumbria in the tenth and eleventh centuries', in *The Anglo-Saxons: studies in some aspects of their history and culture presented to Bruce Dickins*, ed. Clemoes, Peter, London, pp. 70–88.

Wright, C. E. 1939. *The cultivation of saga in Anglo-Saxon England*, Edinburgh.

12

EARL ROGNVALD AND THE RISE OF
SAGA LITERATURE

OLE BRUHN

Of Friar Robert, who in 1226 translated *Tristams saga* and *Elis saga ok Rosamundu* from French, the Danish scholar Paul V. Rubow wrote 'There ought to be erected a statue to him somewhere, as he is in all probability the founder of Old Norse light prose literature'.[1] The idea does not seem at all unreasonable in that there are people who have been honoured in such a fashion for much less. One might, however, have one's doubts as to whether Friar Robert is the right man. Without necessarily developing it into a Vigelandspark, I would like to suggest at least one other obvious candidate, the Earl Rognvald Kali, d. 1158.

Rognvald Kali, Earl of Orkney, is remembered first and foremost as one of the main characters in *Orkneyinga saga*. He inherited the title of Earl through his mother who was the sister of St Magnus, patron saint of the Orkneys, d. 1117. The impression one gets in the saga of this earl, and descendant of a saint, is of a man liberally reciting skaldic poetry on every possible occasion. He is in fact a bit of a dandy and in his own opinion a man of many talents, warlike as well as peaceful. Among other things he could both read and write, decipher runes, play chess, etc. (*Orkneyinga saga* 1965, chs 58–60). The portrait of him is somewhat complex. On the one hand he acts like a veritable viking whilst on the other he is a studious modern prince finding the time to take part in a pilgrimage to the Holy Land. In connection with this journey he has a love affair with a French countess, all in a courtly fashion.

To perceive him as a transitional figure between Norse antiquity and the European Middle Ages, a viking and skald entering modern times, seems rather unsatisfactory. One is rather more inclined to think that there is something chic and modern about his skaldic and viking mannerisms, which are more a young man's acquired attitudes than a continuation of heritage and tradition. Earl Rognvald's character would thus seem to represent a fashionable revival, an over-elaboration of an otherwise contemporary way of life, with opinions and attitudes belonging to another period of history. This is well illustrated by the often quoted narrative of how he and his men, after having boarded and taken a foreign ship in the Mediterranean on the way to the Holy Land, discuss details of the fight and agree that the earl should immortalise the correct version in a skaldic strophe (*Orkneyinga saga* 1965, ch. 88). The incident has often been used as an example to illustrate how one in a non-literate society manages to preserve memorable events. The fact that the whole course of events was written down so soon after their occurrence should in itself be sufficient to arouse suspicion of such an interpretation. Moreover, there are at least two people present (the Earl and the Bishop) who can read and write. Finally, it is not the actual course of events that is to be established but rather the Earl's ability to compose a skaldic strophe in a certain situation, set in heroic viking style by a group of people, many of whom were skalds.

Rather than seeing the Earl as a representative of a nonliterate society, it would be more natural to assume that he, with his viking mannerisms and his untimely skaldic poetry, was something of a pain in the neck to his more level-headed contemporaries. That he at the same time had spiritual peers is illustrated by the fact that an account of him was written shortly after his death, probably because he was one of the most illustrious and prominent figures in a circle of likeminded men. There is a constant swarm of named skalds, many of whom are Icelandic, around Rognvald and the saga recounts that Rognvald together with the Icelander Hallr Þórarinsson composed *Háttalykill*, a poetological work, which was originally to have demonstrated the use of five different metres (*Orkneyinga saga* 1965, ch. 81). The title, copied from Latin, shows certain knowledge of contemporary Latin literary culture, but the actual idea of demonstrating the different metres could lead one to believe that they to a certain extent found it necessary to revive skaldic art. I would finally like to draw attention to the figure of Bjarni Kolbeinsson, later Bishop of Orkney, who was a poet himself and the author of *Jómsvíkingadrápa* and probably co-author of the saga (Holtsmark 1937, 1961 & 1962).

The tale of Earl Rognvald gives one, all in all, the impression of a setting, consisting mainly of folk from the North Atlantic Islands, in which a devotion to the past, including skaldic art, has become both a passion and fashionable. Peculiar to this milieu is a kind of formalised code of conduct which helps to accentuate it as something out of the ordinary relative to its surroundings. The like-minded members of this fraternity constantly behave as though they expect their every action, and especially the verse they compose, to be remembered and immortalised. For instance, Rognvald's fishing trip, referred to in ch. 85, gives the impression of being contrived and staged with the intention of making it appear as an accentuated story based on an ambiguous skaldic strophe. In the same chapter we are told that this was not the only occasion when Rognvald had such amusing ideas. It has been conjectured that this milieu has been influenced by courtly literature, or more precisely troubadour composition, in view of Rognvald's trip to France and the proximity of the Orkneys to Scotland (Andersson 1969, Einarsson 1961 & 1971, von See 1981). This does not seem at all improbable but at the same time we must keep in mind that any such interaction would take place between two independently established societies. Rognvald and the men around him were not troubadours, they were skalds. They were also warriors and vikings, not knights. They sought their inspiration and ideals in Norse antiquity and not in an imported culture.

This is all the more remarkable as Rognvald's world would seem to have been open and cosmopolitan. During the pilgrimage to the Holy Land, which brought Rognvald and his men into contact with a number of different and strange cultures, they had, if we are to believe the saga, no difficulty in making contact with local populations or in being judged on their merits. At Narbonne, they were invited in and their stay was a great success as they were recognised, in spite of all cultural barriers, as being men of high rank. By the same token their visit to the Emperor in Constantinople was also considered to be successful. This sense of rank, across cultural boundaries, also causes Rognvald to spare the captain of a ship they plunder in the Mediterranean. This kind of open world, with relatively easy access to a great number of diverse cultures, provides a basis for cultural interaction and harmonisation across borders. On the other hand, an opposite reaction can manifest itself from a confrontation with an open world, that is a deeper awareness of the distinctness of one's own cultural background and a demonstrative need to preserve it: one is a viking and a skald, that is a Norse knight and troubadour.

A consequence of such an interpretation of the milieu around Earl Rognvald is that the special Norse culture, from having been taken for granted, is transformed into something of value. It is only after exposure to an open and modern era that the Norse peculiarities become apparent and show their character through a concurrent experience of other ways of life. At the same time the Norse culture loses its traditional characteristics. It comes no longer as a matter of course, as something automatically adopted, but has been transformed into something which can be chosen from a number of alternatives. It has, to use a pointed phrase, become something consciously acquired, one lifestyle in a whole repertoire of lifestyles. Besides being Norse, this lifestyle can be characterised by the sense of history and individuality it exhibits. It maintains the presence of a historical continuity by asserting that present day skalds and warriors do not qualitatively differ from those of the past. This assertion is, however, only relevant against the background of an awareness of a historical discontinuity. The demonstrative postures are to revive and secure a past era's virtues and thereby bridge the gap across the intervening period, which is considered a break or a respite. At the same time a person adhering to such a way of life exposes his individuality by appearing as something extraordinary in the context of contemporary society. If everyone had been a skald and a warrior, hardly much importance would have been attached to the description of these qualities in Rognvald and his followers.

We cannot of course know with any certainty whether life in Rognvald's circle really was as conventionalised and as attitudinised as the saga suggests, or whether it is the author of the saga who is responsible for making things seem as such. In any case one thing is certain: Rognvald's life, relatively shortly after his death, became a lore which emphasised the aforementioned traits. We see therefore a relatively rapid fusion between the archaic traditional form of expression, that is skaldic art and viking mannerisms, and the, in this context, completely new and modern form, the written word. The way this coupling takes place is in itself interesting. We might for instance have imagined that the connection between traditional oral skaldic art and the new medium, text, was brought about by traditional means, that is through the solemn chronicling of the entire known skaldic tradition, in order to maintain and preserve it. A collection of skaldic poetry corresponding to the *Elder Edda*'s collection of Eddaic poetry is not however to be found in manuscript tradition. Here skaldic verse always appear in a prose context. Therefore one must have been acquainted with skaldic tradition otherwise one could not have used it in the sagas. On the other hand there was a lack of interest in the tradition for its own sake. On the contrary it has been broken down and used in the construction of a historical or biographical literary fiction. The old, viking mannerisms and skaldic tradition, and the new, the use of the literary medium to present oneself, were closely associated from the start and together define the characteristics of the new lifestyle.

In his book on the uses of literacy in England from 1066 to 1307, M. T. Clanchy (1979, 149) wrote: 'What is most evident is that literate habits and assumptions, comprising a literate mentality, had to take root in diverse social groups and areas of activity before literacy could grow or spread beyond a small class of clerical writers.' What applies to the English Middle Ages would also seem to apply to the Norse Middle Ages. However strange and tradition-bound Old Norse literature may seem to be when viewed in a European perspective, it is evident that here too the formation of a literate mentality must have preceded the creation of the literature and the literate culture of which the literature is a part. The figure of Rognvald fits very nicely into such a perspective that differentiates between literate mentality and literate creativity. This makes it, in part, possible to see him as evidence that a literate mentality has taken root in a particular social group, that is the secular aristocracy. By reason of this literate mentality it is relevant to associate him with the saga literature which began to take form in earnest 30–40 years after his death.

If we consider the development of Old Norse literary culture as far as it, at the present time, can be reconstructed, we would find, strangely enough, that it first assumes its Old Norse characteristics relatively late. If we accept that literary skills, reading and writing, date from *c.* 1050, then we must proceed to about the year 1200 before we see a reasonably well developed saga form. There can be many reasons for this. One could for instance point to the fact that the church, throughout the early Middle Ages, had a monopoly on literacy, and that it concentrated primarily on matters pertaining to the life of the church and religion. On the other hand, the enormous amount of translation which took place, for example in Iceland, shows that there was no lack of a broad literary foundation, nor of the ability to express oneself in one's native language.

What perhaps was absent was the ability to fuse literacy and one's own everyday surroundings. Works dealing with local conditions are few and far between. One could mention Ari's shorter history of Iceland, *Íslendingabók*, which was written in about 1130, but it was not until about 1170 that a history of Norway saw the light of day, Theodoricus' *Historia de antiquitate regum Norwagensium*. We can assume that during the same period works on local saints were published, especially Óláfr Haraldsson. When we consider the aforementioned works, we get the impression that the things written about had, in advance, to be considered suitable for literary exposition. Writing about a local saint was not at all problematic. A local saint does not differ qualitatively from any other saint and is therefore a good candidate for literary attention. On the other hand it must have been considerably more difficult for Ari to write the history of Iceland, as the Icelandic social structure and community life were too distinctive for a form of historical presentation which concentrates on institutions. There may therefore have been a reason for writing it so soon after the great reforms: the passing of the law of tithes, the writing down of certain laws. Co-operation between the church and the Althing was running very smoothly at that time and this could have given him the structure of the book. It could have inspired him to let, in an anachronistic sort of way, a well-functioning Althing be the institutional midpoint in Icelandic history and community life until the foundation of the church. In the same way it would be possible to regard the establishment of the archbishopric in Niðarós and St Olav's elevation to Norway's eternal saintly king as the immediate prerequisite for Theodoricus' work. Maybe it was first possible at this point in time to regard the list of Norwegian kings as a succession of monarchs in a certain office and not just a series of winners in a never settled struggle between members of a large family group to gain or hold power in a particular country.

If such a manipulation of reality, and a partial transformation of it according to the principles of a literary mentality, were necessary before it could be put onto parchment, then it is understandable that it was difficult transforming large portions of Old Norse tradition into articulate literature. It was simply not known what to do with them, as there was no reference of understanding within which they could meaningfully be articulated. At one time or another a usable model was found, because at the turn of the century the Old Norse texts appear in rapid succession, *Sverris saga*, *Orkneyinga saga*, *Færeyinga saga*, *Jómsvíkinga saga*, a possible *Hlaðajarla saga*, *Skjǫldunga saga*, sagas about Norwegian kings, in particular the two Olavs, and finally the first of the Icelandic sagas, the so called skald sagas.

When considered as a whole, this literary productivity displays a distinct pattern. First, the idea of the institutional antiquity of the Norwegian kingdom must have had a structural influence and made it possible to articulate large amounts of material which previously could not be used. The establishment of a wider historical universe became possible because the Norwegian royal lineage gave a perspective and a chronology to which other subject-matter could be related. This perspective and this chronology are present in virtually all of the saga material. Secondly, the writing of history relatively rapidly became a medium for the expression of a political ideological conflict. Sagas such as *Orkneyinga saga*, *Færeyinga saga* and the probable *Hlaðajarla saga* have one thing in common, that they within the framework of Norwegian history manifest the independence of their regions as power bases by pointing to the fact that they had had a relatively independent status from the time of the foundation of the Norwegian kingdom. The same manifestation of a primordial independence and autonomy is also found in the *Íslendingasǫgur's* repeated accentuation of the fact that the Icelanders had nothing against serving kings and remained on good terms with them, but that they would not tolerate tyranny. A more or less fictitious description of the past was used as an argument for the possession of ancient rights and if we were to ask who this argument was used against, then it would be natural to mention the strong and expansive kings of the House of Sverrir.

We know that *Sverris saga* was written at his own request. We also know that his descendants had contemporary historical sagas written about kings. On the other hand, we have no accounts of them having sagas written about early Norwegian kings. Added to this is the strange situation that none of the compilations of king's sagas from the 13th century go beyond 1177. It is not until the 14th century that we see compilations that include kings from the House of Sverrir in the long line of Norwegian kings (Bekker-Nielsen 1965, 42–71). It would appear that the civil war, and especially its outcome, was at the time and afterwards considered a turning point. It was in any case a catastrophe for the ruling Norwegian aristocracy who were either annihilated or, after the war, stripped of their privileges. This could explain why stories of the past, unlike those of the present, stress in such strong terms the historical role of the aristocracy. There is a tendency in these tales of the past, as in *Heimskringla* for instance, to show the aristocracy's idealised picture of society, the good old days. It is a society where kings rule in conjunction with the people, i.e. the aristocracy. If the present is the age of monarchy, then the past was the age of the aristocracy, an era populated by high-born, independent men who were the kings' loyal servants or worthy opponents and many of these men were skalds.

This is perhaps a good point to return to Rognvald. We know very little of the historical skalds in the time of, for instance, Earl Hákon or the St Olav. Therefore we cannot say whether they had such a prominent position and played such an important role as the impression one gets when reading the sagas. We cannot exclude the possibility of the skald figures being products of a tradition handed down together with the skaldic verses. On the other hand neither can one exclude the possibility that the skald character in the sagas is a result of posterity bringing its own norms and ideas into play. The prominent position of the skald and his aristocratic personality would then be a reflection of a later period's perception and evaluation of skalds, that is a literary mentality's moulding of the skald picture before it appears in the sagas. Where does this picture come from? We know that Snorri Sturluson considered himself a skald as can be seen in *Edda* and *Háttatal*. We also know that he belonged to the Old Norse aristocracy, which developed a complicated relationship to the kings of the House of Sverrir. He probably did not consider his role as an aristocrat incompatible with his role as a skald. On the contrary he almost certainly considered that skald role embellished the original historical and spiritual character of his aristocratic position. We know furthermore that Snorri grew up and was educated in Oddi where Jón Loptsson became the first and only Icelander to be paid tribute to in a skaldic poem, the *Nóregs konunga tal* (*c.* 1190). Finally, we know that the population of Oddi had close relations with the Orkneys and the Earls of Orkney (Sveinsson 1937). Is it not possible that in these surroundings the poetic Earl could have contributed to the rehabilitation of skaldic art and given it a new meaning in a new historical context?

Even though Earl Rognvald's lifestyle lent itself to the writing of sagas, he did not write any sagas himself. He is however by all accounts one of those chiefly responsible for transforming skaldic tradition from a state of stagnation in the first half of the 12th century into a means whereby an aristocracy in a specific historical situation could express in a meaningful way its historical, spiritual and political horizons. He has therefore to a substantial degree contributed to making the world of the Old Norse past, as we see it the saga, possible.

And what about the statue? I am well aware that I have only sculpted a coarse outline. The next step is the immense amount of work necessary to produce the finer details, and to give the statue a solid plinth.

Note

1. 'Der burde et Sted oprejses ham en Statue, thi han er efter al Sandsynlighed Grundlægger af den oldnordiske Underholdningslitteratur i Prosa' (Rubow 1928, 355).

REFERENCES

Andersson, Theodore M. 1969. 'Skalds and Troubadours', *Medieval Scandinavia* 2, 7–41.
Bekker-Nielsen, H. *et al.* 1965. *Norrøn Fortællekunst*, København.
Clanchy, M. T. 1979. *From Memory to Written Record*, London.
Einarsson, B. 1961. *Skáldasögur*, Reykjavík.
Einarsson, B. 1971. 'The Lovesick Skald: A reply to Theodore M. Andersson', *Medieval Scandinavia* 4, 21–41.

Háttalykill: *Háttalykill enn forni*, eds Helgason, Jón & Holtsmark, Anne, Bibliotheca Arnamagnæana I, København 1941.

Holtsmark, Anne 1937. 'Bjarni Kolbeinsson og hans forfatterskap', *Edda* 37, 1-17.

Holtsmark, Anne 1961. 'Háttalykill', *Kulturhistorisk Leksikon for Nordisk Middelalder*, vol. VI, col. 242-3.

Holtsmark, Anne 1962. 'Jómsvíkingadrápa', *Kulturhistorisk Leksikon for Nordisk Middelalder*, vol. VII, col. 606-8.

Orkneyinga saga: *Orkneyinga saga*, ed. Guðmundsson, Finnbogi, Íslenzk fornrit XXXIV, Reykjavík, 1965.

Rubow, Paul V. 1928. 'Den islandske Familieroman', *Tilskueren* 1928, 347-57.

von See, Klaus 1981. 'Mündliche Prosa und Skaldendichtung. Mit einem Exkurs über Skaldensagas und Trobadorbiographien', in *Edda, Saga, Skaldendichtung*, Heidelberg, pp. 496-505.

Sveinsson, Einar Ól. 1937. *Sagnaritun Oddaverja*, Íslenzk fræði I, Reykjavík.

13

THE ORKNEY EARL AND SCALD TORF-EINARR AND HIS POETRY

ELSE MUNDAL

Torf-Einarr was a bastard son of the Norwegian Earl Rǫgnvaldr Mœrajarl. He was the third or fourth earl in the Orkneys. The first one was his uncle Sigurðr who according to the sources received the earldom as a gift from his brother Rǫgnvaldr, who in his turn received the earldom in the Orkneys and Shetland from King Haraldr Fairhair as compensation for the death of his son Ívarr, killed in the King's war expedition to the western islands. The second earl was Guðþormr, the son of Sigurðr, who held the earldom for only one winter and died childless. Then, the sources say, Rǫgnvaldr sent another of his bastard sons, Hallaðr, to take over the earldom. But after a short time Hallaðr gave up because of the constant unrest caused by vikings.

Of what happened then, *Orkneyinga saga* (chs 5–7), Snorri (*Heimskringla*, *Haraldz saga ins hárfagra* ch. 27), who uses *Orkneyinga saga*, and *Landnámabók* (*Sturlubók* ch. 309, *Hauksbók* ch. 270), which seems to build on an older form of *Orkneyinga saga* than the one preserved, all give a vivid description. The texts are similar to each other, but have some differences. In *Heimskringla* and *Orkneyinga saga* Rǫgnvaldr was enraged when he heard of Hallaðr's behaviour. In *Orkneyinga saga* and *Landnámabók* he sent for his sons – *Landnámabók* mentions Þórir, Hrollaugr and Hrólfr, in *Orkneyinga saga* Hrólfr was out on a viking expedition – and asked who of them wanted to take over the islands, but Þórir left the decision to his father, *bað hann fyrir sjá*.

Rǫgnvaldr Mœrajarl seems to have had some sort of a vision, and took his decision on the basis of the knowledge he had gained. Þórir's destiny was to stay at home and Hrollaugr's fate was to go to Iceland. Then Einarr enters the scene and asks if his father wants to send him to the Orkneys. Rǫgnvaldr has no other choice. It is however emphasised that fate controls his brothers' lives. It must therefore also be fate that sent Einarr to the Orkneys and made him earl.

This emphasis on fate, which in my opinion makes the *Orkneyinga saga* text the most interesting one, since it harmonises so well with – and may be based on – Einarr's own poetry, is left out by Snorri. Snorri focuses not on Einarr's brothers, but on the conversation between Einarr and his father. In this conversation Einarr's family background on his mother's side is the main point in all the texts. Snorri has, typically sharpened the speech a little. According to Snorri, Einarr says to his father:

> 'You show me little respect, and I leave little love behind. I want to go west to the islands if you will give me some help. And I will promise you something that you will like very much. I will not come back to Norway.' Rǫgnvaldr answered that he would like him not to come back, 'for I do not think that you will be an honour to your family since the whole family on your mother's side are born slaves.' [1]

After this friendly conversation between father and son, Einarr set out for the islands.

Among Rǫgnvaldr's sons Einarr at first glance seems to have the least promising background. Rǫgnvaldr had, according to the sources, six sons. Three of these were with his highborn wife, Hildr Hrólfsdóttir: Þórir þegjandi, who succeeded his father as earl in Mœrir, Gǫngu-Hrólfr, who conquered Normandy, and Ívarr, who died in King Haraldr's war expedition to the western islands. Rǫgnvaldr's three bastard sons were Hallaðr, who gave up the earldom in the Orkneys, Hrollaugr, who settled in Iceland as a farmer, and Einarr, who both was a bastard son and whose mother was a slave.

But how is this interest in Einarr's slave mother actually to be understood? Do the authors who focus on her background intend to present Einarr as the least promising or as the most promising of Rǫgnvaldr's sons, that is to say: are Rǫgnvaldr's harsh words to be taken literally? In my opinion they are not. If we analyse the function of the conversation between father and son in the text, we see that what we have is a variant of a very common scene in Old Norse literature, a provocation scene. In the most common type of this scene a woman provokes one or more men – often sons – to avenge the death of a kinsman. Such a provocation is usually called by the Old Norse word *hvǫt*. However in other situations where the family honour is injured, women, and sometimes old men, also provoke young male members of the family to make them restore the former social order. Both in the *hvǫt* as in other provocation scenes, the actual provocation is an accusation of not behaving as is expected of an honourable man. The opening of the scene in Snorri's text is quite normal for a provocation scene. When Rǫgnvaldr got to know about Hallaðr he said that his sons would turn out to be very unlike their forefathers. The rest of the scene differs from the standard provocations by being based on a true statement. When Rǫgnvaldr in his provocation reminds his son of his mother's social status as a slave, this provocation is probably based on fact, and differs from the standard provocations where sons are accused of being like daughters and suitable to be married away – or things like that. But the function is the same whether the son has to prove that he does not act like a daughter or like the son of a slave.

Rǫgnvaldr's harsh words to Einarr are the sort of provocation which women and old men in Old Norse society were entitled to use in order to make their sons act according to the standards of honour. When Rǫgnvaldr reminds Einarr that his mother was a slave, he is probably referring to a fact, but when he bases his lack of faith in him on this fact, this is part of the provocation and not to be taken literally. In literature a provocation is usually directed to the most promising of the men in question, where there is most hope for a positive response. Such a provocation in fact proves that the person who provokes has faith in the young man in spite of what he or she says. When Einarr himself turns to his father and asks for the earldom, there is certainly hope for a positive response and Rǫgnvaldr takes the opportunity to send him away with a provocation strong enough to blow him at least half the way to the family's deserted bastions in the islands.

This understanding of the text seems to be identical with the interpretation of the author of *Vatnsdœla saga* who says in ch. 9: 'Then he sent his son Torf-Einarr, and said that he expected him to keep the land.'[2] Also in *Landnámabók* (1968, 316) the conversation between father and son seems to be understood as a provocation scene. After Rǫgnvaldr's harsh words, we find the laconic remark: 'Thereafter Einarr went westwards and conquered the islands, as his saga says.'[3] Einarr's unfriendly words to his father also imply a promise to succeed. He promises not to come back, but that also means that he promises to remain earl in the Orkneys and not act like Hallaðr.

In Old Norse literature a provocation scene will also always foreshadow that the young man in question will prove himself to be the opposite of what he is accused of. In Einarr's case he will have to prove that he does not act like the son of a slave, but like the son of an earl. And the very next thing that is told about Einarr is that he on his way to the islands killed two vikings. That indicates that he will gain the upper hand of the vikings to whom his brother gave in, and it promises the fulfilment of the good omen for his future, which is what his father's provocation actually is.

Thus it seems that it is not so bad to have a slave for mother if the father belongs to a princely house. It is a fact that Old Norse literature very often focuses on the slave background of the mother of a king's or an earl's son. What really deserves notice is that the slave background on the mother's side is not mentioned as a negative remark, on the contrary it seems to indicate a promising future, and in some cases it even seems that the author makes the most of the mother's humble background and presents her as a slave even if she was not. The typical example is Þóra, the mother of the Norwegian king Hákon inn góði, who is mentioned in several of the king's sagas. She is called *konungs ambátt*, 'the king's slave', but she was probably not only a freeborn woman, but of good family as well. Snorri obviously feels a need to explain this mysterious wording and he remarks that in those days it was the custom to call even women of good family *konungs ambátt* (*Heimskringla, Haraldz saga ins hárfagra* ch. 38).

But if women of good family were called *konungs ambátt*, that must indicate that in Old Norse culture the alliance between a slave woman and a man of princely family was not only tolerated, but could even be a lucky combination for the offspring. A possible explanation of this positive assessment of an alliance which in Old Norse society normally was looked upon as a misalliance, we can find in Gro Steinsland's doctoral thesis (1991): Here she points out what is obvious in the Old Norse sources, but has generally been neglected, namely that royal houses do not descend from the gods only, but from the giants as well. The prototype of a king is a descendant of a god and a giantess. *Jafnrœði*, that is to say: 'equal social status of husband and wife', which is the general rule in Old Norse society, seems not to be valid for the royal houses. Gro Steinsland argues that a different model, an alliance of socially opposite parties, which seems to be accepted in the royal houses, reflects the mythic model, the alliance of god and giantess; the departure from the principle of *jafnrœði* in the royal houses is to be understood in connection with central ideas in the ideology of kingship in Old Norse society, namely the prototype of a king must be a descendant of socially opposite parties.

Such an ideology may explain why it is promising for a king's or an earl's son to have a slave for his mother. When Rǫgnvaldr reminds his son of his mother's social status, he provokes him to prove that he is the son of an earl and not of a slave. But he also provokes him to prove that he is not an ordinary slave's son, but a slave's son who is the result of an alliance modelled on the mythic *hieros gamos* between god and giantess. That makes him a special type of a slave's son, a born ruler.

The author of *Orkneyinga saga* must have been aware of the Old Norse ideology of kingship which required a mythic origin for the ruler's family. The family of Rǫgnvaldr Mœrajarl is provided with such a mythic background in the Fornjótr episode in the opening of *Orkneyinga saga*. Whether the Fornjótr episode was part of the original saga or a later interpolation has been a matter of discussion. It follows from my view of the function of this episode that it most likely formed an integral part of *Orkneyinga saga* from the very beginning. In the decription of Einarr and his background the mythic basis for the Earls in the Orkneys is strengthened. Actually Einarr is not the third or the fourth Earl. He is the progenitor of the princely family in the Orkney islands. Einarr's uncle's family branch died out, and his brother gave up the earldom. The later Earls in the Orkneys are Einarr's descendants. Therefore the authors find reason to stress his special social background which conforms to the mythic pattern, that is: being the son of a slave mother and a princely father. Besides this pattern both *Orkneyinga saga* and Snorri underline a small detail. Einarr is one-eyed. The progenitor of the Orkney Earls has Óðinn's mark on him.

If the author of *Orkneyinga saga* and Snorri pictured Einarr as a born ruler on the grounds that he conformed to a mythic pattern, what about Einarr himself? What does his poetry reveal of his inner self? In his poetry, we meet a self-conscious, proud man with a firm belief in being chosen and successful, the best among his brothers, and a man in a position to humiliate the royal family; he even expresses a very unusual belief in having the fate-making norns on his side.

Einarr's attitude is surprising if we think of him as an ordinary bastard and slave's son, but easy to understand if Einarr too was conscious of the mythic pattern to which he alone among his brothers, the slave's son, conformed. If he understood his own life as modelled on a mythic pattern which appointed him ruler, and he interpreted his increasing success as ruler as proof that he was right, that may explain the belief in himself and the conceit close to arrogance in his poetry. Such a background could – I think – give a new dimension to his poetry, and in some cases a better and deeper understanding of the meaning in his stanzas. I will now continue to comment on his stanzas, and try out an interpretation which presupposes Einarr's understanding of himself as predestined to his position of a successful ruler.

Of Einarr's poetry only five stanzas are preserved, all of them dealing with the revenge on the killer of his father. The stanzas are here quoted from Finnur Jónsson's edition (1912–15, 1B, 27–8). In the different manuscripts there are variants of some lines in these stanzas. In Finnur Jónsson's edition these variants are to be found in 1A, pp. 31–2. I will comment on these variants in so far as they are relevant to my approach. The manuscripts also lay the foundation for different readings of some words and phrases. My translation follows Finnur Jónsson's reconstructed text except in a few cases where – in my opinion – a more correct reading of the text has later been achieved. Since scaldic poetry is in fact untranslatable, the translation is only to give readers an idea and a first impression of the content of the stanzas. The competence of Einarr as a scald should on the other hand be obvious from the comments on each stanza.

1. Sékat Hrólfs ór hendi
né Hrollaugi fljúga
dǫrr á dolga mengi;
dugir oss fǫður hefna;
en í kveld meðan knýjum,
of kerstraumi, rómu,
þegjandi sitr þetta
Þórir jarl á Mœri.

'I do not see spears flying from the hands of Hrólfr, nor from the hands of Hrollaugr, against the troop of enemies; it is proper of me to avenge my father/I will succeed in avenging my father; and this same evening while we make din of battle, Earl Þórir the silent sits silently drinking in Mœrir.'

2. Rekit hefk Rǫgnvalds dauða,
rétt skiptu því nornir,
(nú 's folkstuðill fallinn)
at fjórðungi mínum;
verpið snarpir sveinar,
þvít sigri vér rǫðum,
(skatt velk hǫnum harðan)
at Háfœtu grjóti.

'I have avenged my father for my fourth part, the norns arranged/shared it correctly/
fairly, now the prince has fallen; throw, good boys, since the victory is ours, stones at
Háfœta (Longlegg), I choose for him hard taxes.'

3. Ey munk glaðr, síz geirar
(gótt 's vinna þrek manni)
bǫðfíkinna bragna
bitu þengils sun ungan;
þeygi dylk, nema þykki,
(þar fló ár at sǫrum
hræva nagr) of holma
holunda val sem gœlak.

'After the spears of the men eager to fight hit the King's young son, I will always be
glad, it is good for a man to execute a heroic deed; I certainly do not hide that the King
is angry – there the eagle flew early over the island to the wounds.' [The translation of
the last part of this stanza does not correspond with the text of Finnur Jónsson.]

4. Eru til míns fjǫrs margir
menn of sannar deilðir
ór ýmissum ǫttum
ósmábornir gjarnir;
en þat vitu þeygi
þeir, áðr mik hafi feldan,
hverr ilþorna arnar
undir hlýtr at standa.

'Many men coming from different directions, and not lowborn, are because of [my]
true hostility eager to take my life; but they certainly do not know before they have
killed me, who will come under the eagle's claw.'

5. Margr verðr sekr of sauði
seggr með fǫgru skeggi,
en ek at ungs í Eyjum
allvalds sonar falli;
hætt segja mér hǫlðar
við hugfullan stilli;
Haralds hefk skarð í skildi
(skalat ugga þat) hǫggvit.

'Many a man is outlawed because of sheep [i.e., because of stealing and killing sheep],
man with the fair beard! but I because of the death of the King's young son here in the
islands. Men say that the brave King is a danger to me; I shall not be afraid of that, I
have made a cut in Haraldr's shield.'

The first stanza was, according to *Orkneyinga saga*, composed the same
evening as Einarr met Hálfdan háleggr, the son of the Norwegian king, and one

of the killers of Rǫgnvaldr Mœrajarl, in a battle which Einarr won, but Hálfdan escaped. That is to say that the revenge on Hálfdan had not been executed at the moment the stanza was composed. But Einarr in this stanza expresses a sure belief in his ability to carry out the revenge to the end – *dugir oss fǫður hefna*. This sentence has at least a double meaning. It means both: 'I will succeed in avenging my father', and 'It is proper of me to avenge my father'. The word *oss* refering to Einarr places Einarr in opposition to his brothers. Three of them are mentioned by name in the stanza. Ívarr is already dead. What has happened to Hallaðr, the brother who gave up the earldom, we do not know. But the fact that Einarr in his second stanza reckons with only four brothers committed to revenge may indicate that Hallaðr is dead too – or that he has acted so badly that he is no longer looked upon as a member of the family.

When Einarr says that he does not see weapons flying from the hands of Hrólfr, nor from the hands of Hrollaugr, against the troop of enemies, the interpretation of this has been that Einarr had expected these brothers to take the lead in the revenge, and that he here expresses his disapproval of them. And the disapproval of his brothers must be part of the message of the stanza, but not the whole message, as I will discuss below.

Some of the manuscripts have instead of *dolga mengi*, 'troop of enemies', *dœla mengi*, 'troop of *dœlir*, men from the inland'. Scholars who prefer that reading put forward the argument that Hálfdan háleggr was brought up in the inland of Eastern Norway. But *dolga mengi*, 'troop of enemies', is in my opinion much more to the point. What it is all about, is to know how to handle one's enemies.

Þórir is not mentioned together with Hrólfr and Hrollaugr. He sits in Mœrir, saying nothing. By picking him out, Einarr may want to direct attention to the one brother who succeeded their murdered father. What happens – or does not happen – in Mœrir, is focused by underlining the simultaneity of the din of battle in the Orkneys and the silence in Mœrir. (In my opinion the words *kveld*, 'evening', and *þetta*, 'this', belong together.) The decription of the silent Þórir is especially effective. He had brought himself into a position where he could do or say nothing. He had settled with the King's family, and had married the daughter of the King and the sister of the man who had killed his father. He was no longer in a position to take revenge. We do not know when Þórir got his nickname. If he already was called *þegjandi*, 'the silent one', before this event, Einarr uses his nickname in a very effective way. Besides being a nickname, it gives a decription of him in the situation, a situation where the silence around Þórir forms a contrast to the sounds of battle around Einarr, as already pointed out by Magnus Olsen in his work on Einarr's stanzas (1938 [1936], 191).

But the nickname *þegjandi* calls forth other associations. The silent beer or mead-drinking brother in Mœrir also forms a contrast to Einarr, the scald who drank Óðinn's mead, the poetic talent, and further the nickname *þegjandi* probably called forth associations to the mythic avenger, Víðarr, who avenged his father, Óðinn. His nickname was *inn þǫgli*, which means exactly the same as *þegjandi.* Þórir's nickname then reminds us that he did not do what was expected of him. In fact the nickname *þegjandi* is so well-chosen in the situation that it is tempting to belive that the use of the word *þegjandi* in this stanza occasioned Þórir's nickname, and if so, this stanza must have pursued him ever since.

There is no doubt that Einarr in this stanza mocks his brothers for not avenging their father. The stanza comes in fact very close to the Old Norse conception of *níð* and, by avenging, Einarr presents himself as the leading one among his brothers. It may be a correct interpretation that Einarr is disappointed in his brothers and had expected them to take the lead in the revenge. But the fact that his brothers did not do anything to carry out the revenge could be a sign to Einarr that he among his brothers was the one fate had appointed to avenge their father. The sentence *dugir oss fǫður hefna* indicates that Einarr's main reason to act is a feeling of being appointed to carry out the revenge. It is proper for *him* to do so, and only *he* will succeed.

According to normal practice in society Einarr, the slave's son, should not be the first in line to take on the burden of revenge. But in Einarr's second stanza, composed after he killed Hálfdan, Einarr says clearly that it was not his former prestige – compared to his brothers' – that appointed him avenger; it was the fate-making norns who assigned him that part and who secured him success.

Magnus Olsen (1938 [1936], 191) assumes that it is irony when Einarr says: *rétt skiptu því nornir,* 'the norns arranged/shared it correctly/fairly', or *en réðu því nornir,* 'the norns decided that', which is the wording in some manuscripts. He also understood this comment as referring only to the relationship between Einarr and his brothers. In my opinion this comment also refers to the fact that the revenge on Rǫgnvaldr's killer has been fulfilled, and that is in Einarr's view thanks to the norns. But the statement, of course, also refers to the fact that the revenge was executed by Einarr alone. That too, Einarr says, was a correct decision of the norns. But that need not be irony. On the contrary Einarr may consider his success in avenging his father a new sign that he was predestined to be the leading one among his brothers by virtue of the mythic pattern to which only he conformed. Einarr may have grasped with both hands the chance to avenge his father so as to prove himself fitted for his new position as earl in the Orkneys. The revenge was the chance he needed and which the norns gave him by sending the killer of his father straight into his arms.

The last part of the second stanza tells how Einarr asks his men to throw stones at the dead body of the King's son, Hálfdan háleggr. These stones Einarr calls *harðan skatt,* 'hard taxes'. The tax which Hálfdan wanted Einarr to pay him, symbolises the preeminence of the king's son over the son of the earl. But Einarr refuses to submit, instead he throws his taxes at Hálfdan's dead body. And if what he says about his brothers is close to *níð,* his mentioning of Hálfdan is certainly *níð.* Instead of his nickname *háleggr,* 'the one with the long legs', Einarr uses a feminine form, *háfœta,* which means the same. This feminine form is used in some medieval Norwegian texts, but as pointed out by Gustav Indrebø

(1922, 56), the source for this form was probably Einarr's stanza. Magnus Olsen has commented (1938 [1936], 192; 1942a, 40–1; 1942b, 151–2) on the feminine form of the nickname in his work on Einarr's poetry. He considers it to be a common name for a sheep, or even worse, for a goat. And if Einarr calls Hálfdan by the name of a sheep or a goat, this is certainly *nið*, also according to Old Norse laws.

In the third stanza Einarr gives expression to his happiness, and he says: *gótt es vinna þrek manni*, 'it is good for a man to execute a heroic deed'. As a slave's son he would have to prove himself worthy of princely dignity. Even though his special family background conformed to a mythic pattern that appointed him ruler, he would have to prove by executing a deed that he was that born ruler. Princely sons like Einarr must therefore have felt the pressure of expectations more heavily than other princely sons. And Einarr's satisfaction when he has met his test is proportionately greater.

The reading and the interpretation of the last part of Einarr's third stanza is somewhat disputed. The interpretation of Finnur Jónsson (1912–15, 1B, 28), 'I will not deny that people think I feed the raven well here on the islands',[4] is well-chosen in the situation since the verdict of the public must have meant a lot to Einarr in his situation. But Finnur Jónsson has no basis for the form *gœlak* – the last word in the stanza – in the manuscripts. Magnus Olsen (1942a, 36) gave the interpretation: 'I do not deny that this may look like bragging by him who makes the raven cry in ectasy'.[5] In my opinion it does not sound right for Einarr to have such a reservation. I cannot go into all the different readings here, but the interpretation which I prefer, since the interpretation of Finnur Jónsson has no basis in the manuscripts, is the interpretation of Finnbogi Guðmundsson and Bjarni Einarsson (Guðmundsson 1965, 14; Einarsson 1984, 293). In Bjarni Einarsson's reading the last line of the stanza has the form *holundavals gœli*, which is a kenning for 'warrior', and refers to the King, who is angry – *þykki*; and the meaning is: 'I certainly do not hide that the King is angry.' This interpretation also fits well since Einarr in the next stanza is preoccupied with the reaction of the royal family and of the King. There is another little detail which falls into place if the last part of this stanza, too, deals with the killing of Hálfdan and the King's reaction. The word *ár* in the sixth line means 'early'. Some of the manuscripts have instead of *ár*, 'early', the word *grár*, 'grey', an adjective which belongs to the kenning for eagle – *hrœva nagr* or *hrœva valr*. Some scholars prefer this reading, probably because the grey eagle is a common scaldic image. In my opinion the word *ár*, 'early', is to be preferred because it refers directly to the killing of Hálfdan and what happened then. According to the prose text in *Orkneyinga saga* ch. 8, and in *Heimskringla*, *Haraldz saga ins hárfagra* ch. 31, Hálfdan was killed early in the morning.

According to *Orkneyinga saga* Einarr composed the fourth of these stanzas after he had heard the news that the brothers of Hálfdan and the King himself would come for revenge. In this stanza Einarr says that a number of men coming from all directions want to see him dead, and he characterises these men, the members of the royal family, with the adjective *ósmábornir*, 'not lowborn'. This understatement shows that Einarr is preoccupied with the question of status. He now tries it out on the King's family. The adjective *ósmábornir* emphasises this, but at the same time the choice of this word, instead of a word meaning 'highborn', indicates in my opinion certainly not inferiority but, on the contrary, a certain amount of conceit, perhaps even a touch of humour in a serious situation. Einarr is equal to the situation. The understatement with the touch of humour demonstrates that he does not show much respect for the King's family.

The choice of the word *ósmábornir*, which focuses on social status and family, also activates the double meaning of *ǫttum* (dat. of *ǫtt/ætt*) which besides 'direction (one eighth of the horizon)' means 'family'. The men who come from different directions of the horizon, and gather to take the slave's son from Mœrir, are also the men from the different branches of the royal house and men allied to them.

But as Einarr states in the last part of the stanza, it is an open situation. Nobody can say who will come under the eagle's claw. The variants in the manuscripts make other, slightly different readings of the last part of this stanza possible, but the picture of the eagle's claw is central in all the possible readings. By mentioning the eagle's claw, Einarr perhaps wants to arouse associations to Hálfdan's manner of death. *Orkneyinga saga* ch. 8 tells that Einarr cut a blood eagle on Einarr's back and sacrificed him to Óðinn in order to obtain victory. To torture to death by cutting a blood eagle on someone's back, which means to loosen the ribs from the backbone and draw the lungs out through the back, seems to have been a ceremonial killing, and it must have been an even greater provocation to the victim's family than an ordinary killing. If the eagle's claw is meant to call forth associations to Hálfdan's death, this is a provocation and a double threat. He threatens to give them the same treatment and he reminds them that Hálfdan was not his goal, he sacrificed him like a slave to get Óðinn's help to go for someone higher. Magnus Olsen hints (1942a, 44) that by changing Hálfdan's nickname *háleggr* to *háfœta* Einarr produces a good omen for his final victory, since a dead goat forebodes more dead goats. The blood eagle on the back of an enemy may also forebode the killing of more enemies.

The man at the top, the King himself, who went to the islands in person to avenge Hálfdan on the slave's son from Mœrir, preoccupies Einarr's mind in the last stanza. According to *Orkneyinga saga* ch. 8, Einarr composed this stanza shortly after he had killed Hálfdan. According to Snorri (*Heimskringla, Haraldz saga ins hárfagra* ch. 32) the stanza was composed as the last of the stanzas dealing with the revenge on the King's family, and while Einarr was preparing himself for the final meeting with the King himself. This is the situation which in my opinion gives the best background for the understanding of the stanza.

Seggr með fǫgru skaggi have been understood as part of the subject – *Margr maðr með fǫgru skeggi*, 'many a man with a fair beard' is outlawed because of sheep, that is to say, because of stealing and killing sheep. Magnus Olsen (1942a, 37) interprets this stanza as referring to Einarr's brother Gǫngu-Hrólfr, whom the King outlawed because of robbery in his native country. But we do not know anything about Hrólfr's beautiful beard, and in my opinion this is not a reference to Gǫngu-Hrólfr or his stealing of sheep. The mention of sheep refers to Háfœta, who after all was not an ordinary sheep, but the King's young son. Therefore Einarr's situation is more dangerous than that of other men stealing and slaughtering sheep in the islands. And *seggr með fǫgru skeggi*, 'man with a fair beard', does not need to be part of the subject. It may be a person Einarr addresses, and it could be a paraphrase of the King's nickname, Fairhair. There is a variant in the manuscripts, *breiðu skeggi*, 'broad beard', which perhaps does not suport this interpretation, but the majority of the manuscripts have *seggr með fǫgru skeggi*. If Einarr addresses the King, it gives the stanza a more aggressive voice. Einarr is ready to meet the King face to face. He knows that he has injured the King, but as he says: *skalat þat ugga*, 'I shall not be afraid of that'. And his will to fight even the King himself is emphasised by the very last word of the stanza: *hǫggvit*, 'cut'.

Step by step Einarr makes his way up the social scale. He begins with his own brothers whom he humiliates in his first stanza. He continues with the King's son whom he kills and humiliates, and he goes on to the rest of the royal family and the King himself whom he addresses as his equal in the last stanza.

By his actions and behaviour documented in his own poetry, Einarr proves to himself and to anybody else that he is the born ruler his special background modelled on a mythic pattern indicated, and worthy of high rank as progenitor of a new princely house.

Notes

1. Þá svaraði Einarr: 'ek hefi lítinn metnað af þér, á ek við lítla ást at skiljask. Mun ek fara vestr til Eyja, ef þú vill fá mér styrk nǫkkurn. Mun ek því heita þér, er þér mun allmikill fagnaðr á vera, at ek mun eigi aptr koma til Nóregs'. Rǫgnvaldr segir, at þat líkaði honum vel, at hann kvæmi eigi aptr – 'þvíat mér er lítil ván, at frændum þínum sé sœmð at þér, þvíat móðurætt þín ǫll er þrælborin'.
2. Þá sendi hann Torf-Einar, son sinn, ok lézk vænta, at hann myndi halda ríkinu.
3. Eptir þat fór Einarr vestr ok lagði undir sik eyjarnar, sem segir í sǫgu hans.
4. . . . jeg nægter ikke, at man synes, at jeg føder (godt) ravnen her på Øerne; . . .
5. Men ikke nekter jeg at det kan ta sig ut som skryt av ham som får ravnene til å skrike av henrykkelse; . . .

REFERENCES

Einarsson, Bjarni (ed.) 1984. *Ágrip. Fagrskinna*, Íslenzk fornrit 29, Reykjavík.
Guðmundsson, Finnbogi (ed.) 1965. *Orkneyinga saga*, Íslenzk fornrit 34, Reykjavík.
Indrebø, Gustav 1922. 'Aagrip', *Edda* 17, 18–65.
Jónsson, Finnur 1912–15. *Den norsk-islandske skjaldedigtning*, København.
Landnámabók: *Íslendingabók. Landnámabók*, ed. Benediktsson, Jakob, Íslenzk fornrit 1, Reykjavík, 1968.

Olsen, Magnus 1938 [1936]. 'Torv-Einar og Hamðismál', in *Norrøne studier*, Oslo, 189–96.

Olsen, Magnus 1942a. 'Hild Rolvsdatters vise om Gange-Rolv og Harald Hårfagre', *Maal og Minne*, 1–70.

Olsen, Magnus 1942b. 'Torv-Einar og Kormak', *Maal og Minne*, 151–3.

Orkneyinga saga, ed. Guðmundsson, Finnbogi, Íslenzk fornrit 34, Reykjavík, 1965.

Snorri Sturluson, *Heimskringla*, ed. Jónsson, Finnur, Oslo, 1966 [1911].

Steinsland, Gro 1991. *Det hellige bryllup og norrøn kongeideologi: En analyse av hierogami-myten i* Skírnismál, Ynglingatal, Háleygjatal *og* Hyndluljóð, Oslo.

Vatnsdœla saga, ed. Sveinsson, Einar Ól., Íslenzk fornrit 8, Reykjavík, 1939.

14

CAROLINGIAN ORKNEY
AND ITS TRANSFORMATION

RAYMOND G. LAMB

Presented to the First Viking Congress at Lerwick in 1950 were studies of Iron Age brochs, and separately, of Norse topics in Shetland. They did not meet; even at Jarlshof, with both broch and Viking-Age occupation, little could be said about the transition between the two. Indeed, in looking for the beginnings of the Norse occupation of the Northern Isles, we have worked backwards from the High Middle Ages rather than forwards from the broch period; understandably so, for the brochs were perceived as belonging in the very early centuries of our era, being followed by some 500 years of vague uncertainty punctuated towards the end by the occasional Pictish symbol stone or dubiously dated Christian cross-slab. More recently, it became respectable to talk about a Pictish period, and two excavations, at Buckquoy by Anna Ritchie (1977) and at the Deerness Skaill by the late Peter Gelling (1984), revealed sites which spanned the Pictish-Norse transition. The results appeared contradictory; at Buckquoy a quiet transition was implied, at Skaill there was abandonment of Pictish buildings followed by establishment of strongly contrasting Viking ones.

We have now a better appreciation of the Pictish kingdom than was possible in 1950, and there is a group of sites – churches – which bear on the workings of Pictish royal administration in Orkney in the immediately pre-Viking period. These churches relate to brochs. Brochs in the Orcadian Iron Age have the same role as hillforts in Iron Age societies in mainland Britain, on the Continent, and in Scandinavia – they are enclosed and fortified places reflecting the social position of a military élite, who offer protection in return for some form of taxation and for privileged status. Warlords or chieftains, their enclosed fortresses, their gates, their tower-like redoubts become, like the medieval castle, symbolic of lordship. In this society and in these ideals are the roots of medieval kingship, of which the Pictish kingship was a successful early example. In medieval fashion, success depended on a symbiosis between King and Church, as developed in the Merovingian and early Anglo-Saxon kingdoms, but the retrospection of the High Middle Ages cast Charlemagne in the role of its archetypal achiever. Indeed, it was in the 8th century that the symbiosis between a King and the Church in his kingdom, with the King's rule sanctified by Divine authority, became perceived as fundamental – thus Offa's anxiety to do down Canterbury and up Lichfield (Godfrey 1964). It is unlikely that Offa's Pictish contemporaries, Oengus and his successors, would have been unaware of its significance.

In 714 Pippin II died and his illegitimate son Charles Martel was quick to develop his policies by endowing with substantial estates the newly-established see of Utrecht, as the base for the already successful Willibrordian mission in the Low Countries and the soon-to-be-embarked-upon Bonifacian mission into Germany – areas into which Frankish political power was to be extended in parallel with the structure of the Roman Church (Wallace-Hadrill 1967, 82–3). The following year, 715, is the likeliest date for the correspondence, a climax in Bede's History, between King Nechtan of the Picts and abbot Ceolfrid of Jarrow, which inaugurated the Roman reformation of the Pictish Church (Bede, HE, lib v, ch. 21; Kirby 1973; Duncan 1981). It will be suggested that Orkney now became absorbed into a Carolingian-style Pictish kingdom with a hierarchical Roman Church and an effective royal administration. Glancing ahead to the 11th century, we see Thorfinn the Mighty again representing that medieval world of church-endowing kings. What came in between the Pictish kingdom and Thorfinn's jarldom – the 9th century incursion of Vikings and the 10th century development of the rule of the jarls – remains ill-defined. But 8th-century Pictish Orkney is emerging as firmer ground, from which we now can try the experiment of looking forward into the Viking period, as a change from standing in the High Middle Ages and groping backwards.

In 1955 Stevenson published an important paper, 'Pins and the Chronology of the Brochs', which started with the National Museum's boxfuls of unstratified artefacts from old excavations. Evidently some brochs remained occupied long beyond the period to which they conventionally had been assigned. That late occupation now appeared more general than the few cases where it had been obvious, such as Burrian in North Ronaldsay, where finds from Traill's 1870 excavation had included a Pictish symbol carved on a bone, an ecclesiastical bell, and an ogham-inscribed cross-slab (MacGregor 1974). With brochs paralleling hillforts in social function, the occupation of some of them into early historical times need not surprise us. Such work as Alcock's at Dinas Powys and South Cadbury and Rahtz's at Cadbury-Congesbury, in the 1960s, established the post-Roman use of hillforts in England and Wales (Alcock 1963, 1972; Burrow 1982; Rahtz 1982), while in Scotland we are accustomed to finding strongholds such as Dunadd and Dunollie figuring in the early chronicles (Alcock 1981). The Orcadian counterpart of 7th century Dunadd would have been a broch, and brochs with artefactual evidence of late occupation are listed, alongside the forts, in a recent gazetteer of 'enclosed places AD 500–800' (Alcock 1988, 40–6). More recently still, a study in spatial analysis has emphasized the social distinction between the central 'tower' of a broch, and the surrounding buildings, suggestive of patron/client relationship (Foster 1989).

As centres of power, enclosed and fortified places, such as Irish raths or German hillforts, lent themselves to use by the Church. There developed a relationship between secular potentate and the evangelising Church, which is expressed in the location of early ecclesiastical centres within the enclosed space of the potentate's stronghold. In Orkney so far, no excavation has tested this relationship, but there are numerous cases of medieval churches or chapels which occupy sites showing signs of Iron Age settlement. It is most obvious when the church is associated with the big ruin-mound of a broch, as in the prominent case of the church of St Michael at Overbrough, the parish church of Harray (RCAHMS 1946, ii, 37, no. 39). Most striking are the Peterkirks, together with two quite exceptionally large sites in Papay (Papa Westray).

The pattern of Peterkirks emerged after the writer's routine field survey in Sanday, Westray and Stronsay revealed sites of that name which were remarkably similar both in appearance and in local historical circumstance (RCAHMS 1980, 26, no. 181; 1983, 38, no. 153; 1984, 29, no.153). In each case the dedication was to St Peter and the site was referred to locally as a kirk – not as a chapel as is normally the case with these long-abandoned sites which never had parish church status. In each case the site of the church stands atop the mound containing a broch – a substantial site of the same order of size as Gurness, with outbuildings surrounding the central 'tower'. The clearest Mainland example is Peterkirk in Evie (RCAHMS 1946, ii, 73, no. 257), where remains of a bicameral 12th-century church, quite a grand one by Orkney standards, stand on a mound which in the cliff-section can be seen to be an extensive broch site. This circumstance is repeated at other sites, resulting across Orkney in a very deliberate-looking pattern divorced from the parish system of the High Middle Ages – a system which probably was put in place during the later 12th and 13th centuries, after the establishment of the Norse Orkney bishopric (Fig. 14.1).

In Papay there is something special. Two sites of the same general style – extra-large broch-complexes with medieval churches on them – are dedicated to St Boniface and St Tredwell, or Triduana. The identities of these saints need lengthy discussion which is not appropriate here – the names are significantly associated in the late Life of Boniface in the Aberdeen Breviary (Skene 1867, 421–3), this Boniface being the one who has been conflated with a figure named Curitan and linked with Fortrose and Rosemarkie (Skene 1877, 229–33, but c.f. Henderson, I. 1971, 50–2). Rosemarkie with its impressive group of sculptures (Henderson, I. 1990) and its Petrine dedication evidently was an important centre of Roman Church influence in the Black Isle in the later 8th and 9th centuries. The direction of contact is Pictish and eastern. The site at St Boniface's Church is huge. The broch-type settlement covers a hectare of ground. There had been finds of 8th-century artefacts in the coastal section, and recently a limited-scale excavation has confirmed a sequence extending from a

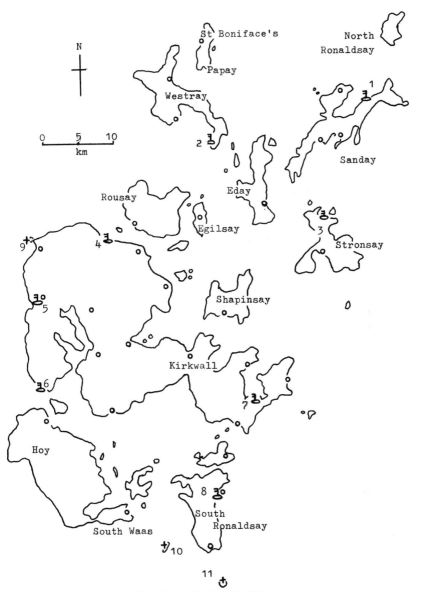

Figure 14.1: Distribution of Petrine dedications in Orkney.

Key symbol – Peterkirks, i.e. sites where the dedication is to St Peter and the place is locally referred to as a kirk. 1, Peterkirk, Sellibister, Sanday; 2, Peterkirk, Rapness, Westray; 3, site of St Peter's Church, Whitehall, Stronsay; 4, Peterkirk, Evie; 5, parish church of St Peter, Sandwick; 6, 'Monks' Green', site of old parish church of Stromness, probably dedicated to St Peter but this not certain; 7, Peterkirk, Campston, St Andrews; 8, St Peter's Church, North Parish, South Ronaldsay.

Cross – Sites known locally as chapels, with dedications to St Peter. 9, St Peter's Chapel, Brough of Birsay (with archaeologically attested high-status 8th-century occupation of the Brough, this site may belong among the Peterkirks); 10, site of St Peter's Chapel, Swona; 11, St Peter's Chapel, Muckle Skerry.

Open circle – Parish churches of the later medieval system.

broch into the early historical period (Lowe 1990). The site has yielded two early cross-slabs, and there is a Norse hogback monument still there (RCAHMS 1983, 18–19, no. 29). The impression is that this has been a centre of extra special importance, and that St Tredwell's (ibid., 19, no. 30) is another centre in some way associated with it.

The Peterkirk pattern in Orkney replicates the organisation put in place in Hessen and Thuringia during the extension of Frankish power into those regions under Charles Martel and Pippin III. In Hessen, St Boniface (this is St Boniface of Crediton, whose original name was Winfrith) cut down the sacred oak of Thor and with its timber built a church to St Peter. Parsons (1983) has identified four qualities characteristic of 8th-century ecclesiastical sites associated with the mission. These are: strategic position; elevated position – defensible sites which had become centres of local administration; pre-existing enclosure, defining the religious temenos; and royal ownership or ultimate control. Behind the choice of fortified sites lies also the Roman prejudice in favour of basing bishops in urban centres; a hillfort, oppidum, was the best approximation to a city within a rural society. Within a generation of the original mission, there were bishops established in suitable centres with Boniface as archbishop in Mainz before his martyrdom in 753 or 754. The whole operation was exceedingly well planned and efficiently executed, and it was the work of Anglo-Saxon churchmen co-operating with the expansionist Frankish royal power, working in an area in which the jockeying of rival local potentates gave openings for outside interference. Behind it is the figure of Egbert, and upon Egbert is the stamp of approval of Wilfrid.

Egbert, the instigator of the Continental missions, seems originally to have been a monk of Ripon, but early on he became established in an unlocated Irish monastery named by Bede as Rathmelsigi, which had Northumbrian connections and evidently became a centre of Romanising influence (Bede, *HE*, lib. iii, ch. 27; Ó Corráin 1984). Egbert originally intended himself to work among the Frisians, but he was warned through dreams that his real work was to 'go and give instruction in the monasteries of Columba' – that is, to bring the familia of Iona over to the Roman observance (Bede, *HE*, lib. v, ch. 9) – so he dispatched his pupils, Wihtbert, then Willibrord, and eventually Boniface, to the Continent instead. The role of Egbert in bringing Iona to accept the Roman Easter in 716, following which Nechtan expelled all non-conforming Columban clergy from Pictland, has been discussed by Kirby (1973) and elaborated by Duncan (1981). Probably it was Egbert at Nechtan's court who in 715 set up the Jarrow correspondence (he was a special friend of Bede's) and master-minded the change.

Bede indeed rates Egbert highly. He shows Egbert as healer of the old schism of the British churches, in bringing Iona to the Catholic observance, while presenting him also as instigator of a new and dramatically successful thrust of the Faith into the pagan heart of Europe. A recent art-historical study has brought him forward as a key personality at the centre of politics, whose ramified contacts, linking Ireland, Iona, Pictland, Northumbria and Frankish Europe, are expressed in the experimental and innovative qualities of the Gospel-book art which flourished in this exciting milieu. It is a context within which Pictish animal art has influenced scriptoria outwith Pictland, as revealed in the calf of Echternach and the eagle of Corpus 197B – the eagle which finds so immediately striking a parallel in Orkney's Knowe of Burrian stone (Henderson, G. 1987, 93–7).

Egbert died at Iona in 729. The influence of his circle at the Pictish court would account for the resemblance of the Peterkirk network in Orkney to the carefully-structured system in Germany. The background circumstances are parallel. Frisia and Germany had been peripheral to a Frankish kingdom, which now became culturally vigorous and physically expanded, taking these regions under its political control. Orkney was in the same relationship to the Pictish kingdom, which, some few decades after the decisive battle at Nechtansmere in 685, had become the dominant power in northern Britain. We have Class I stones (Wainwright 1962, 93–4 with plate x) which suggest that Orkney in the 7th century was within the Pictish cultural orbit. At that stage it probably still was ruled by one or more local potentates who had emerged successful from a power-struggle. The establishment of the Roman Church, clearly as a deliberate act, marks the absorption of Orkney into the Pictish kingdom, probably not long after the ecclesiastical reformation of 715–17.

In Orkney there is no sculpture nor other artefact bearing Christian symbolism, which need be dated earlier than the 8th century. This reflects the situation which Hughes (1980, 52) convincingly argued to have prevailed throughout the Pictish kingdom: 'among the Picts east of the spine of Britain, we should not think of a king and aristocracy giving Christianity their active support, nor of a Church commanding artistic patronage, until the beginning of the 8th century'. Although some earlier contact with Christians is probable, the condition of Orkney at that time would have been much like that of Germany – a pagan society ripe for conversion. In Orkney as in Germany the operation began at the top level and worked downwards, and enabled the king's power to pervade the countryside as the highly-structured and hierarchical pastoral system was put in place. On the German analogy, we should expect an established Pictish bishop in Orkney around the middle of the 8th century.

The likeliest seat of that bishopric is the St Boniface's complex in Papay. The name of the island is, of course, significant, but the sheer size of that site marks it out as exceptional. There are a number of enigmatic late references to early bishops in Orkney, assembled by Kolsrud (1913, 294), and Thomson (1986) has unearthed an intriguing reference in the late 9th-century Life of St Findan, which assumes the presence earlier in that century of a bishop on an Orkney island which, from the circumstantial details, seems to be Papay. The Pictish king as he consolidated his control over Orkney, was looking towards Shetland,

and the location of the main ecclesiastical centre is influenced by Papay's strategic position for sea communication between Orkney and Shetland. From the sheltered waters between Papay and Westray is direct access to a true sea, safer waters than those surrounding the dangerous low-lying coasts of North Ronaldsay and Sanday at the north-eastern corner of the archipelago. By steering west of Fair Isle, with Fitful Head on the starboard bow, Sumburgh Roost would be avoided and landing eventually made in one of the sheltered voes of the west coast, north of Fitful. It is in this area that we find early ecclesiastical centres, with important groups of 9th-century sculptures, at St Ninian's Isle and the Burra Papil (Wainwright 1962, 94–5 with plates xi–xiv; Thomas 1971, 153–60; 1973).

The papa placenames and the identity of the Shetland and Orkney *papar* are discussed at length elsewhere (Lamb forthcoming). *Íslendingabók* and *Landnámabók* clearly imply that the men the Norsemen called *papar*, and found in Iceland, were hermits – ascetics who had sought out desert places for their solitary contemplations. Applying this formula to Orkney and Shetland does not work. *Papa* names are not associated with the remote stack sites which in Shetland represent the ultimate in ascetic living (Lamb 1973, 1976). No medieval document attempts to tell us who the Orkney and Shetland *papar* were, except the *Historia Norvegiae*, which names two classes of inhabitant before the Norse in Orkney. These were the Picts and the Papar; the *Historia* tells us that 'all clerics are called *papar* in the Norse tongue' (in *Theutonica lingua omnes clerici papae dicuntur*) (Storm 1880, 89). For what it is worth, the *Historia* implies that the papar were sufficiently numerous, or at any rate, socially prominent, to be bracketed alongside the Picts, the ordinary people of Orkney. Among the *papa* names, the commonest forms are Papey (modern Papay or Papa) meaning the 'island of the *papar*', and modern Papil, which where we have early forms represents Papuli, which probably means something like 'at the estate of the *papar*'. The locations themselves – the Papils in Unst, Fetlar, Yell and Burra, the Shetland island of Papa Stour, Papay and Papa Stronsay in the north isles of Orkney, Papil in South Ronaldsay and the former parish of Paplay, now part of Holm – are characterised as tracts of prime-quality farmland. In 1046 jarl Rognvald Brusason personally went to Papa Stronsay to secure a supply of malt for his Yuletide ale (*Orkneyinga saga*, ch. xxix) – which we safely can take as a statement that Papa Stronsay grew the best barley in Orkney.

It is absurd to think of wandering hermits landing their curraghs on the beaches and discovering the best farmland in the islands unoccupied and not in use. We are dealing with whole islands – named Papa or Papay – and substantial estates – the Papils – which can only have come into the possession of the Church by the same mechanism which operated throughout Christendom. We are in the world of Charles Martel, his endowment of Utrecht, and the rich gifts of lands to the Bonifacian mission as it worked its way into Germany. Egbert followed in the tradition of Wilfrid, and Wilfrid knew all about kings as dispensers – and on occasion, when he fell out with them, as confiscators of revenue-yielding estates. In Orkney and Shetland it looks as if we arrive at a situation worthy of comparison with Frankish Gaul at the mid-point of the 8th century, when approximately one-third of all cultivated land had come into the hands of the Church (Roper 1974).

The *papar* in Orkney and Shetland were the pastoral hierarchy of the Roman Church, which acquired estates as part of the planned process by which the 8th-century Pictish kings consolidated their power in Orkney and extended it towards Shetland. Artist-craftsmen were patronised by the Church as well as by the secular power. The monumental sculptures are public statements of the way Churchmen perceived themselves and wished to be perceived. The equestrian cleric on the Burra Papil 'pony-rider' slab is certainly no ascetic, by appearing on horseback he is stating his privileged social and political position.

Stevenson's dating for the Christian sculpture in Shetland (1981) puts the Papil cross-slab earliest at around 800, the rest later – perhaps as late as around 900 for the Bressay cross-slab. From Orkney we have the Flotta slab (RCAHMS 1946, ii, 342–3, no. 1027) of similar date. We cannot ignore the implications relative to the Norse settlement. The *papa* placenames are Norse names, and they imply a recognition by the Norse, of estates held by the Church. However, compared with 8th-century Pictish sculpture, the Bressay stone is an unimpressive effort. We can expect the wealth and status of the Church by 900 not to have been what it formerly was. What follows is some ideas about what may have happened when the Vikings appeared, starting from the recognition that the Northern Isles by the end of the 8th century were part of a strong Pictish kingdom with institutions we fairly can call Carolingian. These are just questions for further research. Questions have to be asked, they cannot yet be fully answered but the act of asking is not without value.

The Pictish treasure hoards from St Ninian's Isle (Wilson 1973) and the Broch of Burgar (Graham-Campbell 1985) imply trouble – Viking raids – by 800. The Pictish kingdom was still very strong in the east of what now is Scotland – the Vikings found more scope in the West. Alongside the Church, the king would have the support of an aristocracy. The monumental sculptures of Angus and Perthshire (Cruden 1964), in the 8th century the heartland of the kingdom, show us how the Pictish aristocracy saw itself. Warriors are depicted in the aristocratic pursuits of hunting and fighting – on horseback. The Picts took pride in horsemanship and in the highly refined schooling of their horses. Only one stone, from Cossins in Forfarshire (Allen & Anderson 1903, iii, 216–18), in the whole corpus of Pictish sculpture shows a boat, and even on that stone, the focal point is occupied by horsemen. Compare the stones being erected around that time in Gotland (Lindqvist 1941–2). These likewise display the self-perceptions of a warrior élite, but even where we are shown the subject riding on horseback into Valhalla, pride of place is given to the Viking ship. The key to the transformation of Pictish Orkney is simply that whereas the Pictish kingdom at its height of power in the 8th century was able to take in Orkney, it was unable to hold Orkney when challenged by a new élite with superior nautical technology and, above all, pride in seamanship.

Facing this new force, and failing to organise successful resistance, the Pictish aristocracy in Orkney must have lost status. The key development leading to full Norse settlement would be the displacement of the Pictish aristocracy by Viking war-leaders and their war-crews. This would probably take place, at least in the initial stages, with some diplomatic concession towards the authority of the Pictish administration – the formal granting of an estate to a war-captain, confirming him in the possession of what otherwise he might have taken by force, in return for his oath of allegiance and his enlistment to repel subsequent raiders. Such war-leaders would take the place of the discredited aristocracy, exercising authority through the existing structure of power, of which the Church was a fundamental component. At the top levels of society, the social upheaval would be dramatic; at the level of those who farmed the land and paid taxes, it may have made little immediate difference. It happens that at the Deerness Skaill, a high-status site, there is a sharp break between Pictish and Norse settlement, whereas at Buckquoy, at the peasant level, there is gradual transition.

Kenneth MacAlpin overthrew the Pictish kingdom in 843. He had quite enough to do in securing his position in the old Pictish heartland. As heir to the Pictish kings he would have a claim over Orkney but he was in no position to exercise it: Orkney was left in the hands of the Norse. There are hints that Kenneth and his successors, feeling none too secure, deliberately set about dismantling Pictish culture and institutions (Henderson, I. 1967, 102), one of which was the special relationship between the Pictish dynasty and the Roman Church. Giric (c. 878–89) is credited with being 'the first to give liberty to the Scottish Church, which was in servitude up to that time after the custom and manner of the Picts' (Skene 1867, 151). The Church in Orkney had depended on its parent institution in the Pictish heartland, the character of which now was being changed. This, on top of the weakening of contacts, must have undermined the status and effectiveness of the Church in Orkney, and its usefulness to the new rulers would become harder to justify, while its rich estates would be a sore temptation. The establishment of the Orkney jarldom represents the stage when the Norse élite found that it no longer needed to rule through the old Pictish institutions; by then, the emerging kingdom of Norway was taking an interest. The Church continued to operate in an attenuated way. Its outside contacts now would be with the Scottish kingdom, and following the trend there, it would be likely to assume a more western, Irish-connected flavour. This may be the context of the stack sites.

Orkney did continue Christian. Evidence for Norse pagan worship is slight. What saga references there are – particularly with respect to Sigurd the Stout's death, wrapped in the raven banner, at Clontarf – indicate the aristocratic cult of Odin, and for what it is worth, the few Orkney placenames which may relate to

Norse paganism, if one believes in them, refer to Odin. Possibly at the stage when the Norse ruling élite broke its association with the Church (no doubt then purloining the Church lands), there was a limited revival of paganism at the top level of society. This also may be the context of the rich Viking graves, which, as exercises in conspicuous consumption, are public expressions of status. Eldjárn (1984, 7) pertinently observed the surprising paucity of pagan graves in the islands, and suggested that these belonged to first-generation settlers, who arrived as pagans, while the next generation became Christian. This is a plausible scenario, but it requires the burials to be dated early; some at least of burials of the first generation should belong in the early 9th century, but surely the grave-goods do not support such early dating? Is not a more probable historical context for these extravagant funerals, a self-conscious pagan revival at the time of the establishment of the jarldom?

The 9th-century breakdown of the Pictish kingdom can be likened to the contemporary decline of Mercia after the death of Offa, and indeed, to the disintegration of the Frankish empire of Charlemagne. Vikings came to Normandy and to eastern England and built there societies which owed much to the institutions of the 8th-century kingdoms of which those lands had formed part. The Vikings in Orkney likewise irrupted upon a province of a well-ordered kingdom which possessed recognisably medieval institutions. Questions which future research should address, are for how long and to what extent those institutions influenced the development of Norse culture here.

REFERENCES

Alcock, Leslie, 1963. *Dinas Powys*, Cardiff.
Alcock, Leslie 1972. 'By South Cadbury is that Camelot', *Excavations at Cadbury Castle*, London.
Alcock, Leslie 1981. 'Early Historic Fortifications in Scotland', *Current Archaeology*, 79, 230–6.
Alcock, Leslie 1988. 'The Activities of Potentates in Celtic Britain, AD 500–800: a positivist approach', in *Power and Politics in Early Medieval Britain and Ireland*, eds Driscoll, Stephen T. & Nieke, Margaret R., Edinburgh, pp. 22–46.
Allen, John Romilly & Anderson, Joseph 1903. *The Early Christian Monuments of Scotland*, Edinburgh.
Bede, *HE: Historia Ecclesiastica Gentis Anglorum*, ed. Plummer, Charles, Venerabilis Baedae Opera Historica, Oxford, 1896; also ed. and trans. Colgrave, Bertram & Mynors, Roger, A. B., *Bede's Ecclesiastical History of the English People*, Oxford, 1969.
Burrow, Ian 1982. 'Hillforts and Hilltops 1000 BC–1000 AD', in *The Archaeology of Somerset*, eds Aston, Michael & Burrow, Ian, Taunton, pp. 83–97.
Cruden, Stewart 1964. *The Early Christian and Pictish Monuments of Scotland*, Edinburgh.
Duncan, Archibald A. M. 1981. 'Bede, Iona and the Picts', in *The Writing of History in the Middle Ages: Essays Presented to Richard William Southern*, eds Duncan,

Archibald A. M., Davis, Ralph H. C. & Wallace-Hadrill, John M., Oxford, pp. 1–42.

Eldjárn, Kristján 1984. 'Graves and Grave Goods: Survey and Evaluation', in *The Northern and Western Isles in the Viking World*, eds Fenton, Alexander & Pálsson, Hermann, Edinburgh, pp. 2–11.

Foster, Sally M. 1989. 'Spatial Patterns in the Scottish Iron Age', *Antiquity*, 63 (1989), 40–50.

Gelling, Peter S. 1984. 'The Norse Buildings at Skaill, Deerness, Orkney', in *The Northern and Western Isles in the Viking World*, eds Fenton, Alexander & Pálsson, Hermann, Edinburgh, pp. 12–39.

Godfrey, Cuthbert J. 1964. 'The Archbishopric of Lichfield', in *Studies in Church History*, eds Dugmore, Clifford W. & Duggan, Charles, vol. 1, London, pp. 145–53.

Graham-Campbell, James 1985. 'A lost Pictish Treasure (and two Viking-age gold arm-rings) from the Broch of Burgar, Orkney', *Proc. Soc. Antiq. Scot.* 115, 241–61.

Henderson, George 1987. *From Durrow to Kells: the Insular Gospel-books, 650–800*, London.

Henderson, Isabel 1967. *The Picts*, London.

Henderson, Isabel 1971. 'North Pictland', in *The Dark Ages in the Highlands*, ed. Meldrum, Edward, Inverness, pp. 37–53.

Henderson, Isabel 1990. *The Art and Function of Rosemarkie's Pictish Monuments*, Groam House Lecture Series no. 1, Rosemarkie.

Hughes, Kathleen 1980. 'Early Christianity in Pictland' (Jarrow Lecture for 1970), revised in Hughes, Kathleen, *Celtic Britain in the Early Middle Ages*, Woodbridge, pp. 38–52.

Kirby, David P. 1973. 'Bede and the Pictish Church', *Innes Review*, 24, 6–25.

Kolsrud, Olav 1913. *Den norske kirkes erkebiskoper og biskoper = Diplomatarium Norvegicum* 17 part 2, Christiania.

Lamb, Raymond G 1973. 'Coastal Settlements of the North', *Scottish Archaeological Forum*, 5 (1973), 76–98.

Lamb, Raymond G. 1976. 'The Burri Stacks of Culswick, Shetland, and other paired Stack-Settlements', *Proc. Soc. Antiq. Scot.*, 107 (1975–6), 144–54.

Lamb, Raymond G. (*Forthcoming.*) 'The papar of Papil', in *Shetland Settlement: Past to Present*, eds Smith, Brian & Turner, Val, Lerwick.

Lindqvist, Sune 1941–2. *Gotlands Bildsteine* vol. 1 (1941), vol. 2 (1942), Stockholm.

Lowe, Christopher E. 1990. The St Boniface's Church and Monkerhoose Cliff-Section Site Assessment: Interim Report, Edinburgh.

MacGregor, Arthur 1974. 'The Broch of Burrian, North Ronaldsay, Orkney', *Proc. Soc. Antiq. Scot.* 105 (1972–4), 63–118.

Ó Corráin, Donnchadh 1984. 'Rath Melsigi, Willibrord, and the earliest Echternach Manuscripts', *Peritia*, 3 (1984), 17–49.

Orkneyinga saga, ed. Guðmundsson, Finnbogi, Íslenzk Fornrit vol. 34, Reykjavík, 1965.

Parsons, David 1983. 'Sites and Monuments of the Anglo-Saxon Mission in Central Germany', *Archaeological Journal*, 140 (1983), 280–321.

Rahtz, Philip A. 1982. 'The Dark Ages 400–700 AD', in *The Archaeology of Somerset*, eds Aston, Michael, and Burrow, Ian, Taunton, 97–107.

RCAHMS 1946. Royal Commission on the Ancient and Historical Monuments of Scotland, Twelfth Report with Inventory of Monuments in Orkney and Shetland, 3 vols, Edinburgh.

RCAHMS 1980. *Sanday and North Ronaldsay*, Archaeological Sites and Monuments of Scotland series no. 11, Edinburgh.

RCAHMS 1983. *Papa Westray and Westray*, Archaeological Sites and Monuments of Scotland series no. 19, Edinburgh.

RCAHMS 1984. *Eday and Stronsay*, Archaeological Sites and Monuments of Scotland series no. 23, Edinburgh.

Ritchie, Anna 1977. 'Excavation of Pictish and Viking-age farmsteads at Buckquoy, Orkney', *Proc. Soc. Antiq. Scot.*, 108 (1976–7), 174–227.

Roper, M. 1974. 'Wilfrid's Landholdings in Northumbria', in *St Wilfrid at Hexham*, ed. Kirby, David P., Newcastle-upon-Tyne, pp. 61–79.

Skene, William F. 1867. *Chronicles of the Picts and Scots*, Edinburgh.

Skene, William F. 1877. *Celtic Scotland*, vol. 2, Edinburgh.

Stevenson, Robert B. K. 1955. 'Pins and the Chronology of the Brochs', *Proc. Prehistoric Soc.* 21 (1955), 282–94.

Stevenson, Robert B. K. 1981. 'Christian Sculpture in Norse Shetland', *Fróðskaparrit* 28–9, 283–92.

Storm, Gustav 1880. *Monumenta Historica Norvegiae: latinske kildeskrifter til Norges historie i middelalderen*, Christiania.

Thomas, [Antony] Charles 1971. *The Early Christian Archaeology of North Britain*, Oxford.

Thomas, [Antony] Charles 1973. 'Sculptured Stones and Crosses from St Ninian's Isle and Papil', in *St Ninian's Isle and its Treasure*, eds Small, Alan, Thomas, [Antony] Charles & Wilson, David M., 2 vols, Oxford, vol. 1, pp. 8–44, with plates in vol. 2.

Thomson, William, P. L. 1986. 'St Findan and the Pictish-Norse Transition', in *The People of Orkney*, eds Berry, Samuel & Firth, Howie, Kirkwall, pp. 279–87.

Wainwright, Frederick T. 1962. 'Picts and Scots', in *The Northern Isles*, ed. Wainwright, Frederick T., Edinburgh and London, pp. 91–116.

Wallace-Hadrill, John M. 1967. *The Barbarian West 400–1000*, 3rd edn, London.

Wilson, David M. 1973. 'The Treasure', in *St Ninian's Isle and its Treasure*, eds Small, Alan, Thomas, [Antony] Charles & Wilson, David M., 2 vols, Oxford, vol. 1, pp. 45–148, with plates in vol. 2.

15

SOME ASPECTS OF EARLY VIKING
SETTLEMENT IN ORKNEY

JOHN R. HUNTER   JULIE M. BOND   ANDREA N. SMITH

It is hardly surprising, given the strength of the historical background, linguistic evidence and ongoing traditions, that the Orkney/Shetland area ranks as a key region of Britain where Scandinavian influences were most widespread and most enduring. It is thus a matter of logic to deduce that any difficulties encountered in understanding basic issues of Norse settlement in such a well-suppported region leave little grounds for hope of success in places where the colonial presence was less intense and less dynamic in character. Unfortunately the picture for Orkney and Shetland is less than desirable from this point of view, with settlement sites and burials seemingly at a premium; basic questions of date, place and infrastructure are still largely unanswered. Apart from the notable exception of the Birsay Bay area in Orkney (Morris 1989), research designs have stubbornly avoided overall themes and have traditionally concentrated instead on the excavation and interpretation of individual sites. Part of the reason for this is undoubtedly rooted in funding and organisational problems, but part is also a reflection of the nature of the archaeological landscape itself.

It is not the purpose here to review the progress and fortunes of Viking studies in the islands – an exercise which is best carried out by a comparison of Wainwright's pioneering paper of 1962 and Morris' update over 20 years later (1985). It suffices here to outline a few ideas developed from recent, post-Morris fieldwork which may, given further investigation, provide food for thought on at least one basic issue in any subsequent overview.

The starting place should suitably rest on a positive note, or at least on the most positive note available to students of Viking culture in the Northern Isles, namely the Earldom itself and the uneasy marriage between archaeology and history. This union implies an earldom seat on the Brough of Birsay, a small tidal island located off the north-west coast of Mainland Orkney and the focal point of relatively intense archaeological activity since the later 1930s. Excavations undertaken by the principal author (Hunter 1986), confined as they were to the peripheral area of the site affected by coastal erosion, identified some 12 Viking/Norse period buildings of various types – buildings whose arrangements, organisation, hierarchical features and interpreted economy, not to mention insular geographical position, did *not* conform to the accessible, sheltered and farm-based model of Norse settlement that viking scholars have grown to anticipate from the Atlantic colonies.

The site can be justifiably denoted as exceptional (avoiding evocative terms such as 'princely' or 'special'). Given the historical circumstances, an earldom seat is a reasonable interpretation (Hunter 1986, 115f), indeed the probability is greatly improved by the eventual construction of ecclesiastical and associated buildings. Despite this and the weight of the emerging archaeological evidence there is, nevertheless, a respected body of scholarly opinion which argues against the presence of a seat at this location and the debate has been well-aired (e.g. Thomson 1983). The fervour which the issue generates reflects not only the prevailing interest in the affairs of Nordic colonisation but also the extent to which even the most important settlement issues are still open to dispute. Birsay's current importance, however, is less to do with status than with cultural relationships; the site is one of the few where the impact of primary Scandinavian occupation has been interpreted – an issue largely irrelevant in other Atlantic colonies where native populations are unevidenced.

The Brough of Birsay site was occupied in pre-Norse times, one important aspect being that the relationship between the native population and the Norse incomers (although blurred by issues of monasticism) manifested itself both structurally and spatially, and conformed to some extent to Ritchie's findings at adjacent Buckquoy, where native (Pictish) traditions were seen to continue for a short time at least (Ritchie 1977). One point of particular interest, and one which merits specific attention, pertains to the nature of organisation of the incoming culture and, more critically, the extent to which this organisation was adopted. This interface period, whilst not entirely a matter for scholastic agreement (e.g. Crawford 1974), has since taken an important position in research designs. Birsay, according to argument, is atypical and, therefore, by definition is a less than valid model; although it generates observations which are stimulating, its evidence requires corroboration from other settlement locations within the overall framework of colonisation.

The imposition of an earldom structure is implicitly assumed by most viking scholars and, while relatively simple, the model is, with current knowledge, almost impossible to test. The Birsay debate highlights such a problem. However, one model worthy of attention here (although perhaps less through conviction than curiosity) is that of Steinnes (1959) whose work postulated the *huseby* or royal farm system, based on a Scandinavian prototype but using the Orkney *urisland* as a unit of measurement. More recent developments have perhaps made it less acceptable now than in the 1950s but its strength lies in the fact that the argument is based on land values. As a result it draws attention to the island of Sanday in the north-east of the Orkney group where later rentals show values as much as three times that of land in other parts of Orkney (see

Thomson, this volume). The valued land on Sanday is largely a consequence of the light, well-drained sandy soils (hence the placename) giving the island a justified reputation for fertility. The presence of a greater than average proportion of high status placenames might also be seen as a reflection of this wealth.

Steinnes postulated a Huseby site at the south end of the island on the west coast near a place called Braeswick – a region traditionally associated with the recovery of artefacts. His precise location matches a small dyked area with the name *Housy* according to a mid-18th-century chart by MacKenzie (1750). The name could equally be a corruption of other forms and to complicate matters a large mound lying approximately 1 km to the north is now known locally by the same name. Whether Steinnes' original location is a *huseby* settlement or not is certainly unprovable by archaeological means, but the point remains that the site of Pool, unlike the Brough of Birsay, conforms to the classic sheltered bay and fertile land locational model of the type originally postulated by Small (1968).

Opportunity to investigate this area arose as a result of coastal erosion when, during the course of routine sites and monuments recording, Dr Raymond Lamb was able to draw attention to the enormity of the landscape changes taking place (RCAHMS 1980) and identified an exposed archaeological section on the edge of the Bay of Pool, roughly in the area designated by Steinnes. The section, over 3 m deep and around 65 m in length, belonged to an eroding settlement mound (Hunter & Dockrill 1982, 570–3); excavation was subsequently undertaken on behalf of the Scottish Development Department (Historic Buildings and Monuments, now Historic Scotland). Work demonstrated that the settlement was multi-period with a lower zone of tip-like deposits dating to Neolithic times and a darker upper, more structural zone dating to the later Iron Age and Viking periods, effectively encapsulating the interface between native and Norse cultures, thus providing an opportune research focus.

The settlement remains had survived in the form of a broad low mound of a type not dissimilar to a number of other mounds uniquely located on Sanday and its immediate neighbour North Ronaldsay, several of which are now capped by modern farm buildings. Their distribution has been shown to be closely related to prime land (Davidson *et al.* 1983) and similar 'farm mounds' have been identified in parts of coastal Norway. Bertelsen (1984) and Davidson *et al.* (1986) in their respective countries have examined the dynamics of these monuments and have discussed the likelihood of exceptional economic circumstances causing their formation.

It would be satisfying to see these landscape phenomena as physical manifestations of the incoming Viking culture; however, a comprehensive programme of dating appears to place them in existence *before* the accepted onset of the Viking period (i.e. before *c.* AD 800). In some instances this interval is considerable (Bertelsen 1979, 50) and the mounds might equally be seen as being in some way attractive as settlement foci. Pool hence joins a small but growing number of sites in the Northern Isles where Norse settlement represents the final phase of multi-period occupation. The significance of this might be ascribed to a number of factors including the geographical importance of the location with respect to the proximity of good land, the availability of existing building materials or the likelihood of special political status. The significance of other, pre-Norse phenomena has been discussed elsewhere (Hunter 1990, 178) emphasising a group of sites (possibly including Pool) where Neolithic burial is a common primary element.

The Viking/Norse phase at Pool is therefore best viewed as part of a process of continuity rather than as a discrete entity of period culture. The 'colonial' Norse period subsequently becomes placed in a much broader context of social development; it gives the opportunity to consider, for example, the economic resources of a single location over lengthy periods of time with all the implications for material technology, trade and subsistence study. Pottery analysis, for example, has been able to demonstrate the traditional selection of local clays from Neolithic times onwards (MacSween *et al.* 1988, 105) while certain elements of animal husbandry seem equally unaffected (below). As a result it seems justifiable to treat the site as an entity rather than as a series of superimposed cultural units.

Briefly, the primary settlement at Pool belongs to the Neolithic with a complex sequence of small stone-built dwellings associated with discrete mounds of tip-like deposits. These contained domestic material, notably quantities of pottery of Grooved Ware tradition paralleled elsewhere in the Northern Isles. Abandonment around the end of the 3rd millennium BC was probably caused by a variety of sociological and climatic factors. On present evidence the period of desertion continued until the construction of a small sequence of buildings culminating in a simple roundhouse, probably in the 4th century AD. This had developed into a nucleated settlement by the 6th century AD and shows a thriving farming community housed in a series of sub-circular, cell-like dwellings with a common flagged exterior. It possessed, by way of a pointer to the dangers of structural typology, a courtyard-type component of rectangular form more in keeping with Norse architectural styles than with expected native traditions. Contraction of the settled area followed although without evidence of further total abandonment. Indeed, certain buildings and parts of buildings survived well into the Viking period; several of the components constructed in the 5th and 6th centuries AD were still being utilised over half a millennium later.

Scandinavian influences were interpreted from a series of observable shifts in structural morphology, material culture and subsistence economics. A clearly identifiable period of overlap was evident between the two cultural groups and this was denoted as the 'interface' period (phase 7 in the site chronology). This was further divided on the basis of structural change to an earlier (phase 7.1, structure 25) and later (phase 7.2, structure 27) phase. To the north of the Iron

Age complex a rectangular structure set on stone footings (structure 25) was established utilising an inner timber framework while to the south, in the residue of the part-abandoned Iron Age village, a less formal example (structure 27) was created using part-existing walling on a newly-levelled site.

The northern structure (structure 25, Fig. 15.1) had been built away from the main nucleus of the settlement, thus avoiding the need (or desire) to utilise extant walling and surfaces. Although not totally excavated the building is estimated to have been approximately 14.5 m in internal length with rounded ends. The maximum internal width was approximately 5 m, giving an internal area of some 72.5 m². Two phases of floor surface were identifiable although a combination of alteration, robbing and plough damage had left little of the original structure intact, the long south-west wall for example survived only as a sporadic line of inner facings.

The form of the building is best interpreted from the long north-east wall with its defined inner face, end curvature and surviving width of approximately 1.1 m. Centrally located between the two long walls was a line of three postholes each containing packing material. These were considered to have contained load-bearing supports and the middle example is argued to have been central to the structure as a whole. Unusually, however, the building also appears to have utilised an inner framework, identified from post sockets and slots set at intervals adjacent to the inner face of the south-west long wall but set at a distance of some

Figure 15.1: Structure 25 from the south-east showing likely inner timber framework supports (Crown copyright).

1.3 m from its north-east counterpart. The relatively small size of the features and the general imbalanced arrangement suggests that these timbers were not fundamental to the structural integrity of the building, and are best seen as purely internal elements dedicated to some specific function.

Burnt spreads and deposits were numerous across the primary surface and the absence of an obvious hearth suggests non- domestic use. Other overtly domestic features such as flagging and benching were also unevidenced. Some 10 m to the south a former Iron Age cellular building had been converted to a smithy, complete with an elevated hearth (G. McDonnell, personal communication), further suggesting a well-founded settlement with outbuildings and activities at this earliest identified phase of settlement.

There were relatively few finds from structure 25, particularly from the earlier floor level which produced only a handful of sherds of steatite as well as some pottery. The later surface produced slightly more material, although even there the amount of steatite was negligible in comparison to that found elsewhere on the site during this phase. Also recovered were two partially burnt yellow clay loomweights similar to those found at Saevar Howe (Hedges 1983, 103–6) and two nail-headed bone pins. However, the most significant find from the building was a fragment of a side-plate from an antler comb of Ambrosiani's A3 class, a common Viking type, usually dated to *c.* 850–950 (Ambrosiani 1981, 26–7). The finds from the structure were almost entirely Scandinavian in character, unlike other areas of the site at this time.

To the south, for example, a surface associated with the remnants of some curvilinear walling produced three hipped pins and two worked astragali. A further worked astragalus came from one of the remaining cellular buildings, and a phalange exhibiting Pictish symbols was recovered from a contemporary surface. Characteristic late Iron Age double-sided combs continued into this interface period (phases 7.1 and 7.2) alongside Scandinavian types, but were not recorded later.

The latter part of the interface (phase 7.2) saw the building of structure 27 (Fig. 15.2), probably the most oddly designed structure of its period known from Orkney, if not from the Atlantic islands as a whole. The internal dimensions of 9.5 × 3.5 m gave an area of some 33.25 m² which is comparable to that of the smaller structures on Birsay (Hunter 1986, 106) but less than half the size of structure 25 above. Unparalleled, however, was the nature of construction which appears to have been generated from a combination of residual, collapsed and newly-built lengths of stone footings of varying thickness, quality and stature. The short north wall was based on an extant length of the former Iron Age 'courtyard', while the southern part of the long east wall also appeared to have utilised an existing building line, the former outer face now providing a new inner face. Here, however, the construction was faced on both sides and was approximately 1 m wide with a fill of small rubble. Part of this wall line had been demolished in order to allow an access. The north and east walls were conjoined

Figure 15.2: Structure 27 from the south-east showing different wall structuring (Crown copyright).

by a length of irregular footings composed of large stones set in linear arrangement.

A similar method had been devised to produce the long west wall, although here the builder had found it opportune to incorporate remnants of curved walling from an earlier Iron Age cellular form into the overall design. A 'straightening' exercise was achieved by positioning large stones at suitably aligned points culminating in a freshly built length of double-faced walling some 1.2 m wide to complete the junction of the west and north walls. The short south wall merely closed off the space that was left in order to complete the enclosed area. This was faced on the inside only and was of indeterminable rubble width. Such was the variety of footings and levels that the walling itself, in the absence of any evidence to the contrary, seems almost certain to have contained a major turf component and is perhaps best envisaged as being of relatively low height.

Internally the main feature was a rectangular stone-sided hearth, open at the short south end and possibly flanked by two lines of coarse rubble. These may reflect some benching facility although they lacked the positive alignment of orthostatic types seen in later periods of occupation. The interior also lacked clear evidence for any internal timber support system either in posthole or plinth form, although examples of the latter might easily have been destroyed. Certainly the crude flagging which had survived at both ends of the building suggested that such features may have once existed.

Figure 15.3: Iron Age roundhouse reused in the Viking period (Crown copyright).

Structure 27 produced a most peculiar finds assemblage. Around 70 iron objects were recovered from a variety of contexts, and of the half of which were sufficiently well-preserved to be identified, most were nails, some with roves. Absence of slag deposits in the building suggested that rather than being made there, the nails belonged to the construction itself or to relevant internal fittings. Occupation surfaces and deposits within the building also produced finds of both Iron Age and Viking character, notably hipped pins, a needle-case, and a thistle-headed pin, together with a small quantity of steatite which included two spindle whorls. A specific concentration of sheep metapodials, seemingly collected for a particular purpose, was recovered, and there was also a considerable quantity of animal and fish bone. It seems possible that butchering or some form of meat processing was being carried out in this structure and it may be significant that a large cetacean bone chopping block was recorded among the finds.

A third structural form also merits attention in this interface period, albeit indirectly, namely the original Iron Age roundhouse. Subsequent alteration to structure 25 to the north included the cutting of a flight of five stone steps down to the roundhouse and the opening of a former blocking to allow access into the roundhouse from the north-east (Fig. 15.3). This building then became little more than a passageway; the hearth was flagged over to provide a thoroughfare across the central inner zone while the outer zone became a convenient dumping ground for rubbish. As far as the pottery evidence shows, native wares were still persisting on the site to this time; indeed it is conceivable that even until this point the primary roundhouse may still have been occupied by an indigenous population.

One of the problems in interpreting the pottery evidence rests with the appearance of grass-tempered pottery, normally accepted as being Norse in origin. At Pool, however, it can be shown (MacSween, personal communication) that grass-tempered vessels already appear in pre-Norse phases (phase 6) where they constitute approximately 10 per cent of the total sherd count. The proportion remains roughly the same in the interface period (phase 7) and increases only slightly in the final stages of Norse occupation (phase 8). This suggests that pottery appearing in the interface period indicates a continuation of pottery traditions already established in the Iron Age rather than evidence for a new cultural force. The quantity of material declines considerably during these later phases and this is almost certainly a reflection of the introduction of steatite.

Steatite deserves more than passing reference in that it represents the traditional diagnostic indicator of a Norse presence and is an import, presumably from the Norwegian homeland rather than from Shetland in the earlier years of occupation. Steatite cannot always be assumed to signify a Norse presence, as cremation vessels of steatite are known from Bronze Age funerary sites in the Northern Isles and several fragments have recently been recovered from domestic Bronze Age contexts at Tofts Ness on Sanday (S. Dockrill, personal communication). However, at Pool, no steatite other than in pottery temper occurs before phase 7.1, the bulk of the finds being recorded from later Norse contexts. The quantity of material recovered at Pool (over 66 kg) representing vessels, whorls and weights is impressive and implies a major shift in the availability and use of natural resources. Non-vessel forms were few, and the majority appear to have been fashioned from broken vessels and still exhibit sooting. The assemblage contains a number of repaired items as well as rare British examples of bakestones.

The likely date of the primary Scandinavian presence at Pool (phase 7.1 of the site chronology) can be interpreted from a sequence of radiocarbon dates derived from materials in associated contexts. Four dates were produced, the calibrated ranges being calculated according to Stuiver and Pearson (1986) to one standard deviation.

GU 1998   1505 ± 50 BP, cal. 531–608 AD
GU 2002   1250 ± 50 BP, cal. 681–852 AD
GU 2004   1270 ± 55 BP, cal. 671–788 AD
GU 1807   1105 ± 70 BP, cal. 882–1004 AD

These early dates are awkwardly located in the calibration curve where the period 1100–1300 BP offers a wide range of probable calibrated values. With the possible exception of the GU 1998 date which may represent earlier residual material from a levelling surface, all are from contextually secure materials which are unlikely to have been redeposited or aged at the time of deposition. Even by discounting GU 1998, the dates suggest a significantly early primary occupation in advance of the creation of the Earldom in the later part of the 9th century. The implications of this are important for settlement studies in North Scotland and the Atlantic islands generally and will be pursued more fully in the final excavation report. Five further dates were taken from the second part of the interface (phase 7.2), the values being calculated as above:

GU 1810   1270±50 BP, cal. 673–786 AD
GU 2003   1185±50 BP, cal. 778–893 AD
GU 2241   1160±50 BP, cal. 789–954 AD
GU 2006   1160±50 BP, cal. 789–954 AD
GU 2005   1090±50 BP, cal. 891–1000 AD

These generally confirm the site sequences and chronology and might be used not only to strengthen the relatively early date of Scandinavian influences but also to enable some assessment of the duration of overlap to be attempted.

As far as economic subsistence trends can be identified, preliminary work has shown a number of important developments, not least of which is the cultivation of flax. This first appears at Pool in the interface period, although other sites outside Orkney have produced flax at an earlier date (Bond & Hunter 1987, 175). The flax plant can be used to produce either linseed oil or fibre, or indeed both at a lower level of yield. Sanday's soil and climate are particularly appropriate for cultivation according to ethnographic parallels taken from Irish sources (Bradbury 1925, 23) where pre-technological cultivation in the 1920s seems in many ways analogous to Viking period Orkney.

As far as the overall agricultural picture is concerned, the traditional farming methods normally associated with Orkney life already seem to be in place in the interface period. Typical elements are the lax-eared six-row hulled barley like the traditional 'bere', a cultivated form of oat, and carbonised seaweed now being recognised on a number of Norse-period sites in the Northern Isles. The weed flora also seem to be much the same, although cereal culm bases appear to stand out more strongly in the record. If these are from crops their presence suggests possible uprooting during harvest as a result of the loose sandy soils. One find of particular note was a concentration of carbonised six-row barley representing whole heads and possibly stalks. With only 6 weed seeds to 126 barley grains it seems clear that some form of post-harvest preparation was in hand.

Seaweed (the wracks *Fucus vesiculosus*, *Fucus serratus*, *Ascophyllum nodosum*) occurs in small numbers of fragments throughout the interface and Norse period proper and infrequently in earlier contexts, but what is perhaps most interesting is its occurrence in concentrations. For example, a burnt lens found inside the doorway of a building, and beneath the bench line was found to consist entirely of burnt frond, stem and holdfast fragments. Carbonised seaweed seems to be relatively common on Norse sites and is variously explained as fuel, fertiliser or even fodder (e.g. Crawford 1979, 40; Donaldson *et al.* 1981, 78). Both volume and context are unfavourable for any of these explanations at Pool and no satisfactory answer has been produced. The specific use and function of basic local resources is therefore still to be identified.

Within the animal bone assemblage the character of the interface is partly formed by the presence of horses. Although the horse is also found in the Iron Age at Pool it is not until this period that any evidence of actual breeding is apparent (to be seen in the presence of young animals less than 18 months old at death). Butchery marks are found on horse bones from the interface onwards and while some of these probably relate to skinning, others suggest dismemberment of the carcass presumably for food purposes. None of these bones showed signs of canid gnawing thus discounting any notion of being ultimately used as animal food.

The story is rather different with cattle where the economics of stock-rearing conform more strongly to those of the Iron Age, and indeed to those of the Neolithic on the site. Only at the later end of life is there a significant change; animals now appear to show far more pathologies – eburnation, wear and infection of the pelvic joint, eburnation of the distal metatarsal, and extension of the articular surface are commonly associated with stress due to traction. Interestingly, none of these are found in the horse assemblage, indicating perhaps that the horse was too valuable for routine heavy labour. Pathologies were also evident on the sheep, including obvious dental problems. The few polycerate and polled examples suggest a fairly variable flock.

Mention should also be given to red deer which, although present only in small numbers, reaches its maximum (about 3 per cent of the total bone fragment assemblage) during this interface period. The bones are from all parts of the body and from most ages of the animal, arguing for a local source. If this source was not actually on the island itself (and the relatively small amount of rough land on Sanday seems inadequate for a breeding herd) considerable time and effort must have been expended in both travel and hunting, disproportional to the apparent food contribution. Deer also provided antler, a valuable raw material which was exploited at Pool throughout the Iron Age and into the Norse period, although there does seem to be a decrease in antler working in favour of animal bone in the later Norse phases, possibly paralleled by a similar decrease in deer bone numbers.

Pool is an important new site and has much to offer for the study of settlement continuity and subsistence economics in the early stages of Scandinavian settlement. The site gives the rare opportunity to consider viking colonisation within the context of longer term settlement and hence to identify in detail the character of cultural change. Pool addresses a number of issues: the character and significance of so-called farm mounds, the chronology of settlement, the development of agricultural economy and the concept of cultural assimilation perhaps being the most pressing. These are basic elements essential to the understanding of Scandinavian settlement in the Northern Isles and it is hoped that the findings will provide new impetus for research designs.

REFERENCES

Ambrosiani, Kristina 1981. *Viking Age combs, comb-making and comb-makers, in the light of finds from Birka and Ribe*, Stockholm Studies in Archaeology 2.
Armit, Ian (ed.) 1990. *Beyond the Brochs*, Edinburgh.
Bertelsen, Reidar 1979. 'Farm mounds in North Norway, a review of recent research', *Norwegian Archaeological Review* 12:1, 48–56.
Bertelsen, Reidar 1984. 'Farm mounds of the Harstad area', *Acta Borealia* 1, 7–25.
Bond, Julie M. & Hunter, John R. 1987. 'Flax growing in Orkney from the Norse period to the 18th century', *Proc. Soc. Ant. Scot.* 117, 175–81.
Bradbury, Frederick 1925. *Flax Culture and Preparation*, London.
Brothwell, Donald & Dimbleby, Geoffrey (eds) 1981. *Environmental Aspects of Coasts and Islands*, BAR 94.
Crawford, Barbara E. 1979. 'A progress report on excavations at "Da Biggins" Papa Stour, Shetland, 1978', *Northern Studies* 13, 37–41.
Crawford, Iain A. 1974. 'Scot(?), Norseman and Gael', *Scot. Arch. Forum* 6, 1–16.
Davidson, Donald A., Lamb, Raymond G. & Simpson, Ian A. 1983. 'Farm mounds in North Orkney: A Preliminary Report', *Norwegian Archaeological Review*, 16, 39–44.
Davidson, Donald A., Harkness, Douglas D. & Simpson, Ian A. 1986. 'The formation of farm mounds on the island of Sanday', *Geoarchaeology* 1:1, 45–60.
Donaldson, Alison M., Morris, Christopher D. & Rackham, James 1981. 'The Birsay Bay Project', in *Environmental Aspects*, eds Brothwell, D. & Dimbleby, G., pp. 65–85.
Hedges, John W. 1983. 'Trial excavations on Pictish and Viking settlements at Saevar Howe, Birsay, Orkney', *Glasgow Archaeological Journal* 10, 73–124.
Hunter, John R. 1986. *Rescue Excavations on the Brough of Birsay 1974–82*, Soc. Ant. Scot. Mon. Series 4, Edinburgh.
Hunter, John R. 1990. 'Pool, Sanday: a Case Study for the Late Iron Age and Viking Periods', in *Beyond the Brochs*, ed. Armit, I., pp. 175–93.
Hunter, John R. & Dockrill, Stephen J. 1982. 'Some Norse sites on Sanday, Orkney', *Proc. Soc. Antiq. Scot.* 112, 570–6.
MacKenzie, Murdoch 1750. *Orcades, or a geographic and hydrographic survey of Orkney and Lewis islands*, London.
MacSween, Ann, Hunter, John R. & Warren, Stanley E. 1988. 'Analysis of coarse wares from the Orkney Isles', in *Science and Archaeology*, eds Slater E. A. & Tate J. O., pp. 95–106.
Morris, Christopher D. 1985. 'Viking Orkney: A Survey', in *Prehistory of Orkney*, ed. Renfrew C., pp. 210–42.
Morris, Christopher D. *et al.* 1989. *The Birsay Bay Project Vol. 1*, Durham.
RCAHMS, 1980. Royal Commission on the Ancient and Historical Monuments of Scotland, *The archaeological sites and monuments of Sanday and North Ronaldsay*, Edinburgh.
Renfrew, Colin (ed.) 1985. *The Prehistory of Orkney*, Edinburgh.
Ritchie, Anna 1977. 'Excavation of Pictish and Viking-age farmsteads at Buckquoy, Orkney', *Proc. Scot. Antiq. Scot.* 108 (1976–7), 174–227.
Slater, Elizabeth A. & Tate, James O. (eds) *Science and Archaeology, Glasgow 1987*, BAR 196.

Small, Alan 1968. 'The Distribution of Settlement in Shetland and Faroe in Viking Times', *Saga-Book* 17, 145–55.

Steinnes, Asgaut 1959. 'The "Huseby" system in Orkney', *Scot. Hist. Rev.*, 38, 36–46.

Stuiver, Minze & Pearson, Gordon W. 1986. *Radiocarbon*, v 28, no. 2B, 805–38.

Thomson, William P. L. (ed.) 1983. *Birsay: A Centre of Political and Ecclesiastical Power*, Orkney Heritage 2, Kirkwall.

Wainwright, Frederick T. 1962. 'The Scandinavian Settlement', in Wainwright F. T. (ed.) *The Northern Isles*, Edinburgh, pp. 117–62.

16

THE BIRSAY BAY PROJECT

A RÉSUMÉ

CHRISTOPHER D. MORRIS

INTRODUCTION

Although the Brough of Birsay has received some attention in previous Congresses (Cruden 1958; 1965; Hunter & Morris 1981), there is far more to Birsay than simply the Brough, and an overall summary and up-dating of recent work by a number of researchers is to be seen in vol. 2 (1983) of *Orkney Heritage*. During the period of the 11th Congress in Orkney the monograph entitled *Birsay Bay Project Volume 1* (Morris 1989) was published. This volume is the final report on recent rescue excavations on the Mainland side of the Bay, on sites no longer visible along the road leading to the Point of Buckquoy, opposite the Brough. The excavations and surveys reported there formed part of a wider archaeological project of which the present paper is a summary of results as of 1990.

BIRSAY BAY: BACKGROUND AND HISTORY

The Bay of Birsay is a marked indentation on the NW coast of Mainland Orkney (see Fig. 1.21). It is, in fact, two bays, divided by a small promontory of land called the Point of Snusan or Snushan. The northernmost is the larger, bounded on the N by the Point of Buckquoy, which was originally attached to the Brough of Birsay, itself projecting out into the Atlantic. This tidal island is connected at low tide by a modern concrete track across the natural causeway of exposed rocks (see Fig. 16.1).

Inexplicably, Dr Hugh Marwick in his book on the *Place-Names of Birsay* (1970), did not include the name Birsay itself in his volume! It is clear, as both Marwick himself in 1952 (Marwick 1952, 130–1), and Crawford in 1983 (Crawford, B. 1983, 116–17) have emphasised, that the name 'Birsay' is a contraction of the form *Byrgisherað*, as found in *Orkneyinga saga*. The second element, *heraò*, refers to the administrative district, later parish, of Harray, while the first is derived from ON *borg*, a fortress or stronghold. Marwick quotes Matras for the use of the term in Faroese in relation to 'a place so shaped by nature that it can easily be shut off', and Dr Lindsay MacGregor states that 'in Faroe it is almost always used of narrow necks or steep cliffs or of enclosed places for sheep, e.g. Víkarbyrgi and Hambyrgi, Suðuroy' (personal communication). She has also noted a reference to a similar, but unpublished, definition by Jakobsen (quoted in Morris 1989 ch. 1.4). With such a definition, the apparent tautology of the Brough of Birsay is avoided, and an entirely appropriate description emerges for the first element of *Byrgisherað*. Such a narrow neck of land might well have originally existed – rather as had clearly existed at the Brough of Deerness (Morris with Emery 1986b, 309–10) – and perhaps represented on the 17th-century drawing of the Earl's Palace (RCAHMS 1946, II, Fig. 68, opp. 12).

In the past Birsay has been a centre of both political and ecclesiastical power in Orkney second only to Kirkwall in the later Medieval and early Modern periods, but forerunner to that place in the Viking period. However, it is only with the accounts in the *Orkneyinga saga*, written *c.* 1192-1206, of the exploits of the later Viking Earls of Orkney that Birsay itself enters the historical record. Two entries concern Earl Thorfinn:

> By now he was finished with piracy and devoted all his time to the government of his people and country and to the making of new laws. He had his permanent residence at Birsay, where he built and dedicated to Christ a fine minster, the seat of the first bishop of Orkney. (ch. 31, Pálsson & Edwards 1978, 71)
> He died towards the end of the reign of Harald Sigurdarson and was buried at Christchurch, Birsay, the very church he had built. (ch. 32, Pálsson & Edwards 1978, 71)

The first event was *c.* 1048, the second *c.* 1065 (Taylor 1938, 188–9, 368, n. 3), and they establish quite clearly that in Birsay was both the Earl's seat and the first Cathedral. Although the probability is that the location was in the Birsay Bay area of *Byrgisherað*, it need not necessarily have been so (see Lamb 1974, 201; 1983, 38–9; Crawford, B. 1983, 116–17, n. 13). As Birsay became the political and ecclesiastical power-centre of an Earldom, which extended N to Shetland, and S at the very least to Caithness, and at times probably far wider (c.f. *OS* ch. 32, Pálsson & Edwards 1978, 71), apart from the structures mentioned in the *Saga*, there would of necessity presumably be many other buildings belonging to retainers of both Earl and Bishop.

The description as a 'permanent residence' might indeed be taken to imply a previous impermanence, or peripatetic system of residence by the Earls, which was ended by Thorfinn (Lamb 1983, 37; Crawford, B. 1983, 99–101). Also, Adam of Bremen's account (Tschan 1959), in referring to previous rule by English and Scottish bishops, can be taken to imply the existence of Christian structures from before Thorfinn's time and, therefore, we *cannot* infer that the minster built by Thorfinn in the Birsay area was necessarily the first Christian building.

Archaeologically, earlier structural elements below the chapel excavated on the Brough of Birsay, have generally been associated with the pre-Norse 'Celtic' church (Cruden 1958, 160; Radford 1959, 5 & 18; Radford 1962a, 20; Radford

1962b, 167–9; Cruden 1965, 23–4), but they may, by analogy with Brattahlid in Greenland (Radford 1983, 31) and the Brough of Deerness (Morris with Emery, 1986), possibly be dated to the Norse period (Morris 1990). Similarly, the Christian cemetery at Saevar Howe, now no longer necessarily pre-Norse in date, but probably Christian Norse, may be either earlier than, or contemporary with the establishment of Thorfinn's minster (Farrer 1862; Hedges 1983). There is, thus, suggestive archaeological data from Birsay, although (as yet) no conclusive correlation with the historical data for a possible pre-Thorfinn Christian community here.

There has been much discussion as to the significance of the *Saga* entries for location and identification of these structures, and this has been well-rehearsed elsewhere (e.g. Cant 1983, 8–9; Lamb 1983, 41 and Radford 1983). Later, Birsay became an area particularly associated with Orkney's own martyr-saint, Magnus. The sequence of events concerned with his death, burial in the minster at Birsay and the subsequent miracles reported at his grave are re-told in some detail by the *Saga* writer, culminating in the translation of his relics to Kirkwall (chs 52, 56 & 57: Pálsson & Edwards 1978, 88–9 & 94–9). Thereafter, the focus of secular and ecclesiastical power shifted *from* Birsay to Kirkwall and, as Clouston observed, between then and the 16th century, Birsay was transferred from the hands of the Earl to the Bishop (1927, 142).

BIRSAY BAY: PREVIOUS ARCHAEOLOGICAL WORK (Fig. 16.1)

Archaeological work in Birsay Bay began in the mid-19th century, with work at the Knowe of Saverough or Saevar Howe (Farrer 1862; 1868; Soc. Antiq. Scot. 1864, 9–12). James Farrer found numerous full-length graves and slabs from two to ten feet below the surface, and the remains of ruinous buildings which he attributed to the 'broch-period'. A few feet away from this building he uncovered three burial cists and a setting of stones in the form of a cist, from which he recovered a fine bell. These graves have generally in the past been seen as pre-Viking, and Joseph Anderson saw the bell as buried deliberately to save it from invading Norsemen at the beginning of the Viking period (Anderson 1881, Lecture V, 167–73). Reassessment by Hedges presented a revised chronology for the site. The graves appear to be Christian Norse, and it could be seen that where Farrer had excavated, his trenches cut into, and through, two major phases of building construction from the Pictish and Early Viking periods (Hedges 1983a). This more recent work might suggest a later, and different, context for the bell, and Dr Anna Ritchie has pointed out that the idea of burying valuables in stone boxes is instanced from both pre-Norse and Norse times (1983b, 62–3). However, Farrer's information is insufficient for resolution of the point. What must be emphasised, though, is that there clearly are also major features below the Pictish and Viking structures. Indeed, the buildings represented only the uppermost levels of what is clearly a major mound-site, of a type whose existence is increasingly being recognised in Orkney (Lamb 1980; Davidson *et al.*, 1983;

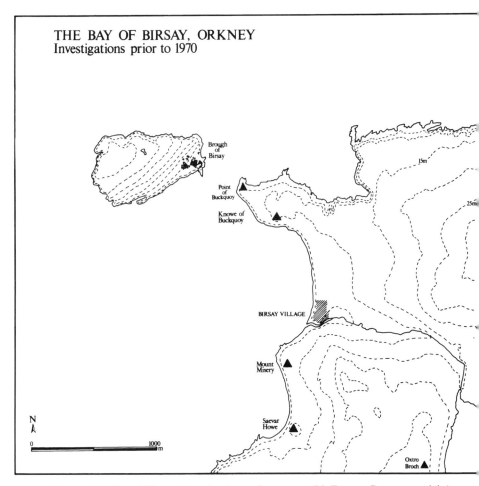

THE BAY OF BIRSAY, ORKNEY
Investigations prior to 1970

Figure 16.1: Bay of Birsay: Investigations prior to 1970 (N. Emery. Crown copyright)

Morris 1985, 226: Hunter & Dockrill 1982). As the placename Savaquoy was from this area, it may indeed be descriptive of this mound (see Morris 1989, 18).

A second site on the mainland side of Birsay was excavated some time before 1866, and possibly as early as 1849, when the Broch of Oxtro was cleared by Mr Leask of Boardhouse (Petrie 1873, 76–8; Hedges & Bell 1987, 55–8). The section drawing published then was clearly schematised, but it indicates unquestionably that there was a group of short cists, above the broch, which Petrie attributed to the Bronze Age. It would appear that a decorated stone covered one of the cists, with 'the figure of an *eagle* . . . boldly cut' (Petrie 1873, 76–8). This seems best explained as a Pictish symbol-stone (Wainwright 1962a, 93–4; Ritchie, J. N. G. 1969; Ritchie, A. 1985b, 188 & 190–1). Among the other finds listed was a brooch, which is perhaps pre-Norse, and a Viking period ringed-pin (Graham-Campbell, 1984b). Perhaps of more significance is an object of silver described as 'a plain cylindrical piece of silver like the head of a walking-stick' (Petrie 1873, 87). This was sold to a watchmaker and melted down. Graham-Campbell recently suggested that it was part of the pin shaft of a large 'ball-type' brooch similar to an example from the Skaill hoard (1984a), and was clearly Viking age and a piece of hack-silver (Graham-Campbell, 1984b).

In the 20th century, on the mainland side during these years three sites were investigated in a preliminary fashion. James Fraser looked at Mount Misery by the Point of Snushan, but his account seems to indicate that there was an absence of structures or graves and the conclusion seems to be that the mound was natural (RCAHMS 1946, II, 36). Fraser also examined a major mound known as the Knowe of Buckquoy. The large mound was dug into, and wall-faces discovered, together with peat-ash and burnt animal-bones, which led to its classification by the Royal Commission as a 'domestic structure' (RCAHMS 1946, II, 18–19). Later, Wainwright described it as a possible stalled cairn (unpublished notes on Orkney Survey 1960).

At the same time as his Orkney Survey, Wainwright carried out a small excavation at an eroding site on the Point of Buckquoy, opposite the Brough of Birsay. This exploratory excavation uncovered two adjacent circular structures with a common wall. It was particularly noted that 'food debris' or midden was present in the wall core, and animal bones and shell below the flagstones of the floor of one of the huts. Wainwright suggested the buildings were corbelled and of early Iron Age date although without specific reasons. Unfortunately, like the Survey, the results of the excavation were not published before Wainwright's untimely death: a summary, based upon the notes in the SDD archives has now been published (Morris 1989, ch. 4.1). A small excavation was carried out in 1980 to clarify several matters, especially as further erosion had been taking place regularly since Wainwright's day (see Morris 1989, ch. 4.4). F. T. Wainwright also drew attention to a number of other mounds during a survey in 1960 on the Point of Buckquoy. This work also has been summarised, based upon notes deposited in the archives of SDD, and amplified by the work of a follow-up survey in 1982 (Morris 1989, ch. 2.4).

In the 1970s (see Fig. 16.2), work in the Birsay Bay area began again with the rescue excavations of Dr Anna Ritchie at one of the mounds identified by Wainwright (no. 5). Although now known as the site of 'Buckquoy', it is possibly that referred to in the name Castra Geo. Erosion was severely affecting the mound, and in addition the road to the Point of Buckquoy lay across it. This mound was fully examined in 1970–1: burials were not entirely unexpected, but the presence of both Viking/Norse and Pictish farmsteads was perhaps surprising – although the placename for the peninsula (see Morris 1989, 16) has clear implications regarding Norse farming here. These results have been published elsewhere, and the excavations have, in many ways, revolutionised our picture of Pictish Orkney (Ritchie, A. 1974; Ritchie, A. 1977; Ritchie, A. 1983) although the Pictish buildings were quite unusual in form and have proved to be controversial in their interpretation.

When seen as an isolated domestic site in this area of Birsay, questions obviously arose as to its status in relation to the Brough of Birsay (Ritchie 1983b, 54); the excavator has postulated that 'it is possible that Buckquoy functioned as the home farm for the community living on the Brough' (Ritchie 1985b, 198). However, it has to be remembered that the Knowe of Buckquoy is nearby, and may also be domestic in nature – although of what period cannot be hazarded at present. Even so, in 1976, before monitoring of the coastal area, this excavated site was largely seen as an isolated site between the two well-known *foci* on the Brough and in the village area of Birsay.

THE BIRSAY BAY PROJECT (Fig. 16.2)

As the preceding section emphasises, this area has a number of archaeological monuments which have individually attracted attention: a remarkable concentration of archaeological wealth which serves to reinforce the picture of an area both of considerable importance in earlier periods as well as the Viking and Norse periods. The Birsay Bay Project was initially essentially concerned with coastal sites in the N part of the Bay of Birsay, beside the Brough Road, close by the site excavated by Dr Ritchie. The present author became aware of the considerable archaeological potential of the eroding cliff-faces of the Point of Buckquoy in 1975, and the first archaeological examination took place in 1976. After survey work in the following year, the 'Small Sites' project was initiated (Morris 1989, Ch. 2.5): as its name implies, the intention was to examine a number of apparently small-scale features within a restricted area. It is perhaps the work of coastal monitoring which has most changed the perception of archaeological reality in this area. Along an area of approximately 500–600 m, some 25 archaeological features have been identified (Morris 1989, ch. 2.5). Although some of these may not contain substantial elements, it is nevertheless the case that this represents a radically different picture. When allied with the evidence from the mound survey inland at the extreme W part of the Point of Buckquoy (Morris 1989, ch. 2.4), it indicates that there is a remarkable density of archaeological sites present. It is now very difficult to accept that any single archaeological site in this region can be viewed in isolation, for the whole area is an 'Area of Archaeological Importance'.

At an early stage in this monitoring exercise it was felt that some form of further investigation would be needed to assess the potential of each of the archaeological features concerned. Some, perforce, was of the nature of 'salvage' archaeology: the visible destruction of three very obvious archaeological features, putatively graves, led to the limited excavations in 1976 of Cuttings 1, 3 and 4 (Morris 1989, chs 3.2, 3.6 and 3.7). Where erosion created a section

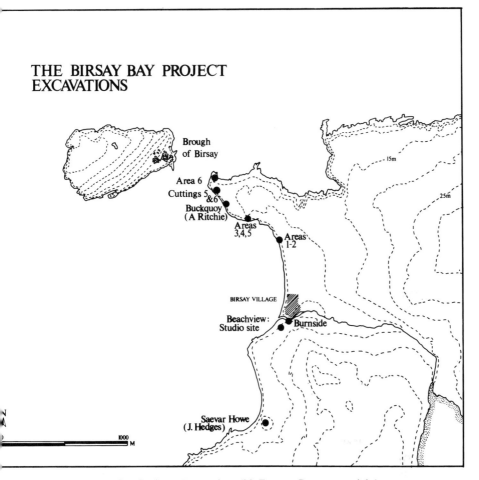

THE BIRSAY BAY PROJECT
EXCAVATIONS

Figure 16.2: Birsay Bay Project : Excavations (N. Emery. Crown copyright)

through various superimposed deposits, the technique involved was to clean and draw the section thus revealed – although even here another grave was salvaged in advance of destruction (Cutting 2/Area 2: Morris 1989, chs 3.3 & 3.4; Cutting 6: Morris 1989, ch. 4.8). Yet another technique utilised was that of geophysical survey to examine sub-surface features behind the cliff-face area (Morris 1989, chs 3.5, 3.8 & 3.9). Where obvious archaeological potential was clear, preliminary investigation and trial-work was kept to a minimum, in order that proper area excavation could be undertaken.

A further approach was that utilised in September 1978 when the destruction by 'Hurricane Flossie' of archaeological deposits currently under excavation paradoxically revealed other archaeological deposits below, which had not been apparent in the original exposed cliff-section (Cutting 5: Morris 1989, ch. 4.7). Here, due to the nature of the deposits – including red deer bones in the midden – in a basal position, it was decided to undertake block sampling for later laboratory analysis. The strategy (as described in Morris 1989, ch. 4.11) could be adapted to other similar situations. Further sampling of cliff-side deposits to characterise the environmental succession was subsequently undertaken (Morris 1989, chs 2.6 & 4.3).

While the sampling employed in relation to these earlier features at the particular site cannot be viewed as a structured strategy for the analysis of environmental and economic aspects (and indeed were never intended as such), the results have allowed us to consider in a preliminary manner these aspects of the archaeology (Morris 1989, chs 4.11 & 4.12). They certainly illustrate the potential for a more detailed approach – should excavation be possible in the future. Indeed, the samples have more than fulfilled their expectations, illustrating the obvious rich and interesting characteristics of the deposits surrounding this 'settlement'. The knowledge gained from such an exercise can be expected to produce significant rewards in terms of excavation/sampling strategies and requirements from the on-site excavation record and planning. Indeed, such a preliminary procedure can pose many questions that might otherwise not be raised until after excavation – and therefore would probably remain unanswered.

The trial excavations and resistivity surveys (Morris 1989, ch. 3) established the importance of some features sufficiently for large-scale 'rescue' excavations to be undertaken in 1978, followed by smaller-scale investigations in 1979 and 1980. The final (survey) work was carried out in 1982 (Morris 1989, ch. 2.4). The sites include Roman Iron Age/Pictish burials, Viking burials, Pictish and Viking period buildings and middens, Iron Age buildings and Bronze Age occupation and middens.

Red Craig (see Morris 1989, chaps 6 & 7.3–7.6)

This part of the Point of Buckquoy gains its name from the red sandstone bedrock and was investigated because erosion had revealed traces of stone walling in the cliff-face.

The earliest usage of the site appeared to be at the W (Area 5: Phase A), where a weathered clay surface was present, with debris from an adjacent domestic hearth. In this area, this was succeeded by the construction of a building (Phase B1), of which only the N end remained after coastal erosion. It consisted of a 'scoop' into the natural subsoil which had been lined with stones to create a circular room; this was divided off from what presumably was the main room by a partition represented by three 'socket' holes originally filled with vertical slabs. A shallow gulley ran in from the N, a curious feature, but the constructional method for the circular room, with vertical slabs, is reminiscent of the Late

Pictish building at Buckquoy (Ritchie 1977). No dating material was associated with its construction.

Since there was no further structural evidence to the W, it is logical to associate this building with one found at right-angles to it in Area 3. This building remained substantially intact, being eliptical in shape, with an internal figure-of-eight shape. Two rooms were thus created, and the entrance was in the S wall of the W room, stepping down from a flagged threshold to some internal flagging. There may have been a possible hearth at the E end of Room A, but there were clearly two fire-pits in Room B and a stone-lined gulley. Against the E wall of Room B was added what is interpreted as an oven. From the later phases of collapse, and the absence of internal roof-supports, it is deduced that the building was constructed in corbel-fashion, and in one area of the site – to the E – there was some evidence for the presence of a surrounding *annulus* (Area 4, Phase A). It would thus seem that, as with the building to the W, a hollow had been deliberately created in the natural subsoil, which was lined with stones. In this case, a substantial horizontally-coursed wall was created on the inside, and, despite later destruction, it would seem that there was then an encircling bank of clay with further walling forming a rim or edge to this.

Due to the absence of any further structural elements to the E of this building, it must be regarded as a dwelling unit to be associated with the second unit, whose character could not be determined from the fragmentary surviving evidence. However, it does not seem unreasonable to interpret the two together as a small farming-unit, with perhaps a yard to be implied to the S of the figure-of-eight shaped building, but now destroyed by erosion. Dating cannot be provided by the artefactual material, but fortunately carbonised seed from one of the fire-pits produced a radiocarbon date range of AD 600–915.

Usage of, and modification to, the figure-of-eight shaped building was distinguished: the fire-pits in Room A were replaced by a hearth constructed of upright flagstones, with an opening (for removal of the ash) at the N end; this hearth was later modified with a reduction in size. Perhaps more significant in structural terms was the construction of what appears to have been a solid stone partition wall between Rooms A and B, with a passage to both N and S. It may well have also had a structural function, as roof-support, but there was insufficient stratigraphical evidence to support the idea that it may have been a fire- or hearth-back at this period. In the next phase, C, usage of both rooms was marked by a number of organic soil-clay dumps and stones, and, surprisingly, the disuse of the hearth of Phase B. A radiocarbon date from a dump in Room B gave a date-range of AD 600–910, and is indistinguishable, statistically, from that derived from the fire-pit of Phase A. A number of artefacts were recovered from Phase C, including an iron knife-blade (RF 281), an iron needle (RF 284), a whetstone (RF 253) and, perhaps most significant of all, a stone gaming board (RF 280). This is particularly interesting as a further example of a type of board found three times on Dr Ritchie's site (and with an additional graffito – perhaps of a ship). It is perhaps the only artefactual evidence to go with the radiocarbon date-range, to suggest that this building-complex is perhaps to be seen as contemporary with Dr Ritchie's Late Pictish and Early Norse farmstead.

Hereafter, the phases distinguished relate to the disuse and collapse/ destruction of the buildings. The first episode of major deterioration in the building (Episode 9, Phase F) appears to have slight evidence for metalworking: 1.307 kg of fuel ash slag from context OI alone; only 0.123 kg from associated contexts, and 0.112 kg of fired clay from all contexts. The only metal artefact recovered was part of a blade, possibly from a sickle (RF 185). An interesting antler object is a possible wrest plank of a lyre (RF 191), but the other artefacts are fairly nondescript.

Subsequent phases consisted of heavy concentrations of collapsed stone. The buildings were clearly completely out of use and forgotten by Phase D in Area 5 to the W and Phase H in Area 3, for now there was a uniform deposit of sandy clay across the whole area. The most significant find is a glass bead (RF122). It is of a quite distinctive – although essentially unparalleled – form, and has yielded interesting evidence through scientific analysis, of both composition and technology. It is difficult to date precisely, but it would appear on balance to date to the 2nd half of the 1st millenium AD. Although there are respectable parallels in Viking Age Scandinavia for the applied decoration there is no precise parallel for the conjunction of this with the particular form involved. In theory, this find gives a *terminus ante quem* for the destruction of the building – and could be used to support the postulated Late Pictish date for its construction and usage. However, it must be remembered that such a single find could have been deposited at any time *after* the date of manufacture.

It is not very surprising that so few mammalian remains were recorded, since disposal was taking place *outside* buildings on rubbish heaps. Those that were and could be identified were most frequently sheep, with the usual collection of horse, cattle, pig, dog and cat, together with seal and vole. They were concentrated firstly, and as would be expected, in the occupation phase, but also, less explicably, when the building had gone out of use. Bird remains were almost entirely absent, but there was an interesting, if small, collection of fish bones (see Morris 1989, ch. 8.4). Notable was the presence of very small saithe in Phase B, along with common eel, the absence of ling, and, amongst the species found from Phase C, at least one cod that was over 1 m long.

The botanical remains (Morris 1989, ch. 8.6) occur from all early constructional and usage phases, and appear to reflect a variety of activities. Peat, heather and some other burnt organic material (? turf) would have provided fuel, along with other wood collected from local scrub (willow) or as driftwood (pine/ spruce). Chaff might well have been used as kindling for the fire, and heather and docks for basket and rope-making. Some species may represent wild plants deliberately collected for culinary usage (wild cabbage, wild radish, wild mustard) or medicinal (speedwell or henbane). None of this is inconsistent with a context of an occupied building, although a number of the other weed species are probably best explained as having been accidentally incorporated. Flax, although only present in a small amount, is consistent with the evidence from Saevar Howe, and it is clear that grain was grown in the vicinity – as would be expected from the placename of Buckquoy. Considerable numbers of bere barley (i.e. the 6-row form), and both wild and cultivated oats were recovered from samples from several phases.

It is to be noted that there is little by way of characteristically 'Pictish' artefacts to rely upon: indeed the only artefact from Red Craig that parallels the Buckquoy collection is the gaming-board from Phase C. Although it has been emphasised that such a game was as common among the Celtic peoples as the Scandinavians (Sterckx 1970, 1973a, 1973b; Ritchie 1983, 60), the Buckquoy examples were, arguably, part of the Norse cultural assemblage (Ritchie, 1977, 187), and so cannot be used to argue for a Late Pictish dating and cultural context at Red Craig. An alternative approach might be to argue from the absence of clearly identifiable Norse cultural attributes in the artefact assemblage from the early phases – no steatite, antler combs or bone pins. Negative evidence is always difficult to sustain in argument, however, at least it may be a pointer, for on the sites to the S, more characteristically Viking-age artefacts *were* present above the earlier phases.

While accepting that too much emphasis should not be placed upon one or two radiocarbon dates, the sequence would seem to be as follows:

Phase A   AD 600–915
Phase C   AD 600–910
Phase E   AD 875–1055

This would then imply that the construction and occupation of the structure should be dated to the Late Pictish and Early Viking periods, and its disuse clearly to the Viking period proper.

In the end, the cumulative circumstantial evidence has to be based on the nature and parallels of the structural forms involved. It is now a commonplace that Pictish-period house forms are cellular in form, be they 'radial' or 'axial' (Hunter 1986, 26) and that they contrast markedly with the buildings of the Scandinavian incomers (Crawford 1987, 140–6, esp Fig. 46). Despite the likely exterior form as an oval, it is quite evidently the case that the Red Craig building is related to this native 'cellular' tradition.

It is notable that the two date ranges accepted above for Phases A and C at Red Craig are consistent with the overall range obtained from Sites VII and IX on the Brough of Birsay (from AD 640±60 to AD 828±70). No radiocarbon dates were utilised at Buckquoy, but the Late Pictish period dating derived from artefacts and retrospective chronology relative to the Norse phases (Ritchie 1977, 192) is internally consistent and does not conflict with other historical or cultural considerations. Overall, the overwhelming probability is that all three sites are contemporary and reflect the same Late Pictish period cultural milieu.

South of Red Craig (see Morris 1989, chaps 5; 7.1–7.2; 7.6 & 9)

Excavations to the S of Red Craig had their origins in archaeological features salvaged in 1976 and the follow-up work of Easter 1978. Areas 1 and 2, originally excavated quite separately and with some quite different deposits, should be regarded as arbitrary divisions of one original entity whose sequences can be correlated (see Morris 1989, ch. 5.3 & illus. 102). Even so, the site extends both to the NW (i.e. beyond the limits of Area 2) and to the NE (i.e. under the Brough Road and into the adjacent field), where there is a rise in the road level to the side of Area 2, and a mound exists within the field; it is also possible that the site originally extended to the SE also.

On top of the naturally-deposited sand at the base of the excavations were set two stone cairns over human burials. Cairn 2, the more completely preserved example, demonstrated the construction method. A stone cist (in this case incomplete) had been set in the underlying sand, with an extended inhumation on a NNW-SSE orientation, placed on its side. Over this was heaped a layer of clean, barren sand, and then a mound of irregular stones and sand, which were faced with an outer kerbing of horizontally-coursed sandstone slabs, seven or eight courses high. No grave-goods were found in association with this burial, which was of a mature, possibly elderly, male. Some associated features, such as an area of cobbles, might come from the construction of the cairn.

Cairn 1, much less well-preserved, but apparently of similar form, covered a cist (of much better construction than that under Cairn 2) in which two burials had been placed. The lower was probably an adult male, the upper an individual of about 18 years of age, whose sex is unclear. Only the lower halves of the bodies remained, due to erosion, but it was nevertheless likely that the lower torso had been covered with a shroud, weighted down with pebbles; and that the upper lay upon a slab over sand infill above the lower body. No grave-goods were found with either skeleton. Some associated disturbed sands and stone accumulations were probably the result of the cairn-building activity.

In the absence of characteristic artefacts, dating is completely reliant upon the radiocarbon determinations. Three human skeletons were dated from this phase and are internally consistent, with date ranges of AD 55–570; AD 230–570 and AD 245–585. Clearly, the Roman Iron Age and earlier part of the Pictish period are involved here.

It now seems reasonable, in the light of the evidence from Cuttings 3 and 4, and the recovery of isolated human bones, some of which at least are earlier than, or contemporary with, these cairns, to describe this as a cemetery. It also seems reasonable to accept the implication of the radiocarbon dates in cultural terms, and to describe these as 'Pictish' burials. The dating fits in with those obtained by radiocarbon for comparable sites (see Close-Brooks 1984, Appendix 1), most recently those from Sandwick, Unst, Shetland (Bigelow 1984 & 1985). The circular form thus takes its place alongside those already so identified at Keiss, Ackergill and Watenan, Caithness; Garbeg and Whitebridge, Inverness-shire, and others. In the N Pictish area the Pictish tradition appears to have been that of long-cist burial below mounds surmounted by well-constructed kerbed cairns. There is some indication that the circular form may be earlier than the rectangular, and that the latter may have been in usage amongst the Picts when they came into contact with the Norse – perhaps prompting 'borrowing' of the form. The long-cist form of burial is also a contemporary tradition that was followed in cemeteries where no cairns were constructed.

The long-cist form is ubiquitous in relation to these cairns, and the mound of sterile sand a common feature. As long ago as 1926, A. J. H. Edwards had faced a similar problem in deciding whether the sand apparently below a cairn was the natural sub-surface or a covering for a burial (see Edwards 1926, 163–4; 1927, 198) and this problem clearly recurred at Tillytarmont (Ashmore 1980, 349). Even the 'double-cist' feature in Cutting 1 which contained two skeletons had been foreshadowed in Edwards' work (Edwards 1926, nos 4 & 5; 1927, nos 9 & 10), and he cites a number of parallels for the form in Orkney, which appear to have received little attention (Edwards 1926, 178). These double or multiple cists from Newbigging, Crantit and Isbister are the closest parallels, geographically, for the Brough Road example, and that from Newbigging at least, appears to have come from what would appear originally to have been a mound or cairn. Although some examples only have one burial, the form is clearly far from uncommon. In the light of the association of isolated long-cist burials with cairns at some of the sites now clearly identified as Pictish period cemeteries, it seems reasonable to interpret the feature from Cutting 3 in similar terms, and to assume that the isolated human bones found through the early deposits of Area 1 may have come from similar burials. The lack of associated artefacts is an obstacle, but it may be noted that a similar isolated cist grave was excavated by Dr Ritchie at her Buckquoy site (Ritchie 1977, 183–4; 1983b, 61–2), and recently Pictish period slab-lined graves, dated by radiocarbon, have been identified from Westness, Rousay (Kaland, this volume).

Phase B on Area 1 represents a period when the cairns may have partially collapsed. Further disturbance of burials other than those excavated is indicated by the presence of additional bones which cannot be explained in terms of bones missing from the excavated skeletons – as could other isolated bones from contexts in this phase. Over the two cairns, there built up a substantial deposit of sand, either windblown or sea-deposited.

The sands of Phase A in Area 2 were succeeded on two separate parts of the site by stone spreads and flagging, which is best interpreted as a pathway between buildings, or from a building out of the settlement area. Perhaps, in view of the existence of the aforementioned mound, a building to the N might be suggested. There could well have been a change in focus between what is represented by Phases B and C in Area 2; such movement is well-documented on Viking settlements, the most obvious example of this being Jarlshof (Hamilton 1956, Section VI). Indeed the different patterns of midden deposition in relation to domestic buildings on this major Viking farmstead in Shetland is most instructive and a warning against too simplistic a correlation betveen the two (see Fig. 44, 97 & Fig. 49, 101).

It is in Phase C of Area 2 that it becomes clearest that the fringes of a settlement-focus have been sampled in these excavations. Arguably, this is another mound-site, similar to those already located at Saevar Howe (see above) and Beachview (see below) to the S. Even if it is tantalising that no definite structural remains have been uncovered to associate with the occupation debris and midden, the opportunity was taken to sample and analyse these deposits at a level not hitherto attempted in the area. The major deposit was in Area 2, with an extension to the SE in Area 1. An earlier period of midden-dumping can be distinguished from a later period with stone and rubble dumps, in both Areas 1 and 2. Vertical distinction is complemented by horizontal, with rubble dumps to the E and W separated by dirty brown sands and more characteristically midden dumps. Radiocarbon determinations on the earlier period of the midden are AD 885–1245 (Area 2, Phase C1) and AD 620–890 (Area 1, Phase D1), with AD 855–1050, (Area 2, Phase C2) and AD 790–1035 (Area 1, Phase D2) from the later period.

The contemporary environment is perhaps indicated by the molluscan analysis (Cavanagh & Spencer in Morris 1989, ch. 2.6). Although there were, in total, much fewer snails from these samples than elsewhere, there is some indication of a change to the modern open rabbit-grazed dune pasture. In the latter, there is more indication of 'shade-loving' species such as *Discus rotundatus*, but they may well reflect an artificially created micro-habitat (shade from building collapse, etc.) as much as a naturally changing one.

The charcoal analysed (Donaldson & Nye in Morris 1989, ch. 8.6) does indicate the existence of a scrub woodland of willow and birch – a picture also derived from the material from other sites in the Bay area. Indeed it is likely that, for the Late Pictish and Viking periods, there would have been a patchwork of coastal habitats, heath, arable and scrub, affording a varied resource-base for exploitation on land – in contrast to the implied more extensive woodland in the earlier Prehistoric period. It is not surprising, therefore, that the picture derived from the middens is of a community looking to a resource-base of mixed agriculture with both arable and pastoral activity, exploitation of the fishes and molluscs of the seashore, some seasonal deep-water fishing and fowling from the cliffs. The range of resource is clear from the botanical remains, with heather, peat, turf, kelp and cow dung, all perhaps utilised in addition to driftwood and imports (pine, spruce, oak) for the fires, but with some of these also providing other uses – such as thatching or basketry from heather, fertiliser and fodder from kelp. Other locally-occurring species, such as sedges, could be utilised as a 'straw for thatching, floor covering or animal bedding, and some of the wild plants could be used to supplement the diet, such as corn spurrey, dock, brassicas and chickweed. The presence of flax, although not so emphatic as at Saevar Howe, is interesting as it can be used, for instance, as animal fodder as well as the more obvious fibre uses. The main dietary component was clearly the grain, which was essentially bere barley, with an admixture of oats, both wild and cultivated. The material has presumably come down to us because of accidents in the drying process, and it was clearly winnowed elsewhere, for there was an absence of chaff.

The mammalian material from the middens (Rackham in Morris 1989, ch. 8.1) is indicative mainly of the pastoral farming activities of those who disposed of refuse in these middens. Antler from red deer was clearly being utilised here for manufacture of artefacts, and this is also true of some other bone material, but otherwise we are looking at food debris. That this was based upon family or group use is indicated by the exploitation of the whole carcass of the three dominant species: cattle, sheep and pig. Only with the very large numbers of rib fragments from the lower midden in Areas 1 and 2 is there a hint of selection and/ or butchery away from the site. There is also an indication that there may be some spatial differences, for the correlation of the mammalian material from Area 1, Phases F1 and F2, and Area 2, Phases E1 and E2, is not good. Also the frequency of sheep remains in Area 2 is less than in Area 1, where they are as frequent as cattle.

However, although there may have been similar-sized flocks of sheep and cattle, the dominance of cattle in terms of meat weight or food supply is clear, and offers a contrast to other sites around the Bay. Similarly, this collection is in contrast with that analysed from the Brough (Seller 1982; 1986). Here there is little evidence of any of the three main species being kept until they were old: the pigs rarely reached over 2 years old; the sheep were apparently slaughtered generally between 12 months and 3–4 years; and the cattle, although killed at a variety of ages between 6 months and 10 years, tended to concentrate at 2.5–3.5 years and 4.5–6 years. Whereas the interpretation put upon the Brough material is for a concentration upon dairying, here it would seem likely most stock were raised for their value as meat and hide. [One *caveat* must be, however, that inability to sex the material is a significant limiting factor in relation to this interpretation.] One particular feature worthy of note is the trend to increasing abundance of pig in the later phases on the site. Although there was little contribution to the diet from wild animals, there are small numbers of seal bones through the phases (indeed the largest number come from Phase A in Area 2) and some red deer (although mainly in the form of antler). The presence of one or two juveniles, together with the chop-marks on some bones, indicate their utilisation for meat and blubber as well as their fur and skin.

Apart from a collection of bones representing four individual starlings from basal layers in Area 1, virtually all the bird bones could represent a food resource – albeit a small addition to the diet (Allison in Morris 1989, ch. 8.3). Gannet, manx shearwater, and six varieties of auk (including the now-extinct Great Auk) are in the collection – which is the range of traditional fowling species. This activity, presumably carried out on the cliffs of the Brough of Birsay or Marwick Head, would offer a welcome seasonal variety to the diet. Evidence also is present for the consumption of domestic fowl and goose.

The coast offered many resources to the inhabitants of the area, and some, such as kelp, have already been referred to. Indeed, it may be the collection of seaweed which has given rise to the presence of the less common mollusc species in the middens. There is a contrast in the overall collection, with the material from Red Craig (see Rackham in Morris 1989, ch. 8.5). Here the most common component in the phases up to E in Area 1 and D in Area 2 is limpet, which it is suggested were taken from their shells outside the buildings and deposited in the midden, in contrast to the periwinkles which were probably cooked inside in their shells as a food resource and then discarded. The periwinkle is the second most common mollusc, and may well have been for the human diet, in contrast to the limpets, perhaps used as fish bait. In later phases, flat winkles became much more significant, and this pattern is reflected in the collection from both Area 1 (Phases F and G) and Area 2 (Phases E and F). It is to be noted that this is a pattern unmatched on other sites around the Bay. All these molluscs would have been collected from the intertidal zone, but one or two of the less common species, such as scallop, would imply fishing.

The midden deposits examined in Areas 1 and 2 were assumed to be contiguous and clearly correlated. However, it must be remembered that the formation processes that were operational for the midden were, no doubt, many and varied. There could well have been selective dumping in particular areas of the midden for particular material and what appears at the time of excavation to be a uniform deposit, may well be the result of many small-scale actions by individuals. The broad phasing divisions of 'lower' or earlier, and 'upper' or later, are used for Phases C1 and C2, and D1 and D2 of Areas 2 and 1 respectively, and, as becomes evident from a study of the results of the biological analysis, there is an essential homogeneity to the material from all six phase-groupings (Area 1: Phase D1, D2 and F1; Area 2: Phase C1, C2 and E1).

Although the biological data is particularly noteworthy, the cultural material is far from negligible. The lower midden assemblage in Area 2, for example, includes a particularly large whetstone of probable Norwegian origin and sinkers or weights. Some very small-scale industrial activity nearby is implied by possible hammer-scale and fired clay from Area 1, together with fuel ash slag, possible cramp and fired clay from Area 2. Copper alloy is present, both as sheet metal and a large concave stud from Area 2, paralleled in both pre-Viking and, more particularly, Viking contexts. Iron artefacts from Area 2 include nails, plates, a fish hook, a knife blade and tang, a fragment of fastening strip and perhaps part of a hinge or lock mechanism. Antler comb fragments from Area 2 are apparently conjoining pieces of a comb similar to finds from Hedeby and Århus, and antler is found in some profusion, with a particularly noteworthy artefact being a possible hair ornament. A worked piece of flint from Area 2, and an amber bead (RF 19) from Area 1 are also of some interest.

Burials are, in fact 'a feature of the later usage of this site, for cist-graves were found cut into the midden deposits in both areas. From Area 1 comes, firstly, a rough-and-ready cist-grave apparently deposited in the developing midden, and subsequently much disturbed by animal burrowing, although there are also hints of human interference or late inhumation after death. The individual was male, possibly as old as late 50s/early 60s, who suffered severe infection of the mouth and periodontal disease, as well as osteoarthritis of the spine. Found with the body was a fine antler comb (RF 315), similar to Scandinavian examples of the mid-9th to mid-10th centuries; an iron knife-blade with traces of a haft. A radiocarbon determination on the bone from the skeleton gave a date range of AD 600–915: i.e. later Pictish and Viking periods; the comb would suggest the latter end of the range is more likely. A second skeleton of uncertain sex but aged *c.* 30–5, was found overlying the remnants of the stone Cairn 1, on an E-W orientation; no associated grave-goods were found. Bone utilised for radiocarbon dating gives a range of AD 850–1140: i.e. the Viking and later Norse periods.

From Area 2, a similar cist-grave cut into the midden was salvaged, which contained part of an extended inhumation orientated roughly E-W, with an iron knife (RF 1), but no other surviving finds. The individual here was a female, probably in her 50s, who probably died from a fracture to the base of the skull. However, she was in poor health from fairly severe arthritis of the spine and a badly infected mouth with abcesses and severe tooth attrition. The date-range from radiocarbon for this burial was AD 670–1020: i.e. the later Pictish and Viking periods. There is further evidence, from Area 1, of isolated human bone fragments from skeletons other than those excavated.

It is rather more unusual that burials should have been deposited in a developing midden, although it is clear that, as well as formal cemeteries, such as Pierowall, Westray (Thorsteinsson 1968), and Westness, Rousay (Kaland 1973; Kaland, this volume), a variety of final resting-places were utilised as well as a variety of forms (Morris 1985, 239–40). Secondary burials in mounds are far from uncommon: Skaill, Sandwick clearly was one such, a furnished male burial of the Viking period was placed in the top of the Buckquoy mound (Ritchie 1977, 190–1), and the Viking cemetery at Gurness was presumably inserted into the collapse of the buildings there. Perhaps when we reflect upon the fact that Viking burials are not infrequently placed into pre-existing cemeteries, with consequent disturbance of earlier 'occupants', one comes to the conclusion that sentiment for the *physical* remains of their relatives and forebears had little place in the Scandinavian outlook on life. Thus, it may not be entirely inexplicable, or apparently callous, that the burials should themselves have been covered over by the debris of everyday life.

Above the cist-grave in Area 2 was a series of loam-sand accumulations and stones in Phase E1. It had some midden-like characteristics, and was disturbed by rabbit-burrowing. It is likely to correlate with an upper midden deposit and sands in Area 1 in Phase F1. From the latter area, the date-range derived from a radiocarbon determination is AD 610–1020: i.e. the later Pictish and Viking periods. Artefactual material would indicate the latter end of that range. The most characteristic artefact is a fragment of steatite vessel (RF 337) from Area 1, which would best be explained in terms of a Viking-period and Scandinavian cultural milieu. Other finds include stone pot-lids, a possible stone gaming-counter (RF 203), a fragment of pumice (RF 86), and further small amounts of fuel ash slag and fired clay. The metal assemblage includes a number of iron finds, none particularly distinctive, a possible part of a decorated piece of copper sheet (RF 38), and a lead gaming piece (RF 35). The bone and antler assemblage includes two fragments of a pin with a splayed head (RFs 247 and 248) from Area 2, and two other crudely executed pins from Area 1 (RFs 215 and 294), an antler tooth plate (RF 210) from Area 1, and, most interesting of all, from Area 1, a possible needle case made from a bird long bone (RF 296). A number of these can be paralleled – although not exclusively – with Viking and Later Norse sites.

Above the upper midden and sands of Area 1, and the dirty brown sand and stones of Area 2, was a sand cover (Phase E2, Area 2; Phase F2, Area 1) which marks the termination of the deposition of human debris in midden-dumps. In Area 2, one artefact of particular note relates to this phase: the remains of a simple copper alloy ringed pin (RF 2), usually to be associated with a Viking context.

In view of the complexity of the sequence it is probably appropriate here to draw together the threads of argument concerning dating of the various phases. Radiocarbon has supplied a sequence which can also be supplemented and refined by artefactual dating. The lower phases are entirely dependent upon this scientific method, and clearly demonstrate a probable early Historic Pictish period date for the Phase A burials of Area 1, with a hint perhaps of a slightly earlier Roman Iron Age extension: the dates are AD 55–570; AD 230–570; AD 245–585. Phases B and C produced no diagnostic artefacts, but are given a *terminus ante quem* by the radiocarbon date-range of AD 620–890 for Phase D1 in this Area. There need, therefore, be no difficulty with accepting that essentially they date from the Pictish period. Such a probability is enhanced by the dating of AD 625–895 accorded to Phase A of Area 2, which was seen as broadly contemporary. The lack of characteristic artefacts precludes immediate refinement to either the later Pictish or earlier Viking periods, and the same chronological spread is implied by the *terminus ante quem* given by the overlying lower midden, Phase C1, dated to AD 885–1245. In between is Phase B, with little other than an antler comb bar with ring-and-dot design, usually, although not exclusively, associated with a Viking milieu.

There is a significant distinction between this date from Area 2, and that accorded to the midden of Phase D1 in Area 1: AD 620–890. Although they have been seen as broadly contemporary, it is possible therefore that the material from Area 1 represents an earlier dump, whose focus shifted to Area 2 as time passed. There is no doubt that the artefactual dating and cultural context for Phase C1 of Area 2, reinforces the radiocarbon range: an antler comb paralleled at Hedeby and Århus, and a concave copper alloy stud, best paralleled at such sites as Balladoole and in Viking contexts. There is no such possible chronological dislocation for the upper parts of this midden. Phase C2 of Area 2 has a radiocarbon date range of 855–1050, and Phase D2 from Area 1, a range of 790–1035. These are statistically indistinguishable, and are reinforced by artefacts such as a haunched hone with parallels on Norse sites, a curious antler handle paralleled in Iceland (and elsewhere), and a pin beater of Viking period form.

It has been observed above that the cist-grave burials of Phase D, Area 2 and Phase E, Area 1, appear to be placed in developing midden, and essentially it would seem that a relatively short time-period covers this whole process of early midden development-burials-late midden deposition. The burials themselves are given ranges of AD 670–1020 (Area 2) and AD 600–915 (Area 1). A comb from the latter, of 9th–10th-century form in Scandinavia, would suggest restriction to the end of the range (i.e. Viking period, rather than late Pictish) and is reinforced by the Viking period parallels for a knife from the same deposits. The apparently associated third skeleton (from Area 1) is clearly from the Viking period, dated AD 880–1140. It can be expected that in this last case the real date is likely to be at the early end of the range, for a *terminus ante quem* is provided by a radiocarbon date-range of AD 610–1020 for Phase F1 in Area 1. Equally the *terminus post quem* provided by the radiocarbon and artefactual evidence from Phase E strongly suggests that the latter part of this range is likely as the true reflection. This Viking period dating is reinforced by the finding of fragments of a steatite vessel, and a range of other finds, all to be best seen in Viking and Late Norse contexts.

Above this upper midden, in the sand-cover, was a characteristically Viking period copper-alloy ringed pin, emphasising again the relatively short time-scale involved for upper levels of the deposits in this area. This is, in any case, both logical and likely if they are viewed as coming from the edges of a 'farm-mound' to the N; the picture is essentially one of continuous dumping of refuse, of one form or another, away from the central focus, and encroaching over a quite separate earlier Pictish-period cemetery.

Beachview and the Village Area

The Birsay Bay Project was simultaneously extended to the village area of Birsay (see Morris 1983), and some other excavations have also taken place here. In the Village, the Earl's Palace is prominent (see a brief account in Ritchie & Ritchie

1986), and some small-scale excavation work by both John Lewis and Beverley Smith has been undertaken there. In 1978, the upper floors of the SE and SW towers of the 16th-century Earl's Palace were examined in advance of masonry consolidation (J. R. Lewis, personal communication). In 1989, further work was undertaken by Beverley Smith, examining deposits in the ground floor rooms of the W, S and E ranges, and several interesting differences between the ranges emerged. These will be explored in the Final Report (Smith in Morris, forthcoming b).

The Parish Church has been the subject of considerable debate in relation to the location of 'Christchurch', which is obviously of direct relevance to the results of excavations undertaken there by John Barber in 1982 (Radford 1958; Lamb 1974; Cant 1983, 8–9; Barber n.d.). In 1982, excavations also took place in advance of restoration of the Parish Church, under the direction of Mr John W. Barber. It has been suggested that the present building was preceded by a pre-Reformation, probably 12th century, church, perhaps of some sophistication – as judged by the presence of carved stones and architectural detail. In addition, a burnt mound deposit, presumably earlier, was found below the NW corner of the church (Youngs et al., 1983, 223; Barber n.d.; Barber, personal communication). The material for the Final Report will be published in volume 2 of the report on the Birsay Bay Project (Barber in Morris, forthcoming b).

Beyond the village to the south are the Links, at the southern end of which is Saevar Howe, another major multi-period mound-site, mentioned above (Farrer 1862; Farrer 1868; Hedges 1983). To the south of the Burn of Boardhouse running through the village, is a second such mound-site, investigated by the author in a preliminary manner at the 'Studio Site' at Beachview, and it could well be that there is a third such mound underneath the modern building itself. Thus, the Beachview area consists of one or two mounds composed of archaeological deposits, both remains of buildings and the debris of man's everyday life. A short account is presented in *Orkney Heritage* vol 2 (Morris 1983, 142–7), but these investigations, together with those of the other archaeologists mentioned above in this area, are the subject of the second report (Morris forthcoming b). As is discussed in the first monograph (Morris 1989, 18), it is possible that this site might be equated with the placename Tuftaback ('bank or slope of house-sites') on the S side of the Burn of Boardhouse. There is clearly much yet to be explored here.

CONCLUSIONS

In chronological terms, there have been essentially three periods of the prehistoric and historic past which have received attention in this project. Most unexpected was the addition of the early Prehistoric perspective where the late Neolithic to Bronze Age is represented by the examination of the lower levels at the Point of Buckquoy (see Morris 1989, chs 4 & 10.4). However, the major contribution is to our understanding of the archaeology of Birsay Bay in the

Pictish and Viking periods. At one level, it has been to widen the archaeological context for other sites, to 'create an archaeological perspective for the area' (Ritchie, 1983b, 63). These surveys and excavations have served to fill in the geographical gap between the Brough and the Village so that, as Anna Ritchie has said, 'Buckquoy can now be seen as neither so isolated nor so odd as it seemed in the early 1970s' (1983b, 63). It is now clear that there are archaeological features along the whole coastal margin of the area, and also quite a number inland at the Point itself.

This project has provided, it is argued, along with Saevar Howe (Hedges 1983a), some of the contemporary context for both the late Pictish and Viking periods at Buckquoy. Middens and occupation debris from the area S of Red Craig serve to provide evidence of a sort that was not available from the Norse domestic phases there. Similarly, the pagan Viking burials serve to show that the similar burial from Buckquoy was not an isolated example. The buildings and internal occupation debris from Red Craig provide a contemporary parallel for the Late Pictish settlement at Buckquoy. They also emphasise, along with Hunter's recent work on the Brough of Birsay, the variety of the cellular structural forms of this period. In addition, they suggest a different picture of the distribution of farming settlements at this time, for the two sites are barely 100 m apart. Hitherto, the main evidence from the Bay for Pictish period burials has been the (essentially unpublished) late Christian cemetery on the Brough. The cairn-burials and long-cists from S of Red Craig appear to date from the early Pictish period, rather than the later, and are, therefore, an addition to the archaeological database, widening the chronological range. The early Pictish burials and the later Pictish buildings have already had some input into more general discussions of the archaeology of that period both in Orkney and in Scotland more generally (see Ashmore 1980; Close-Brooks 1984; Ritchie A. 1985b).

Within the Viking period, the focus changes, with attention being given to the North Atlantic and Scandinavia as well as the British Isles (see Morris 1985). Of current concern is the nature of the economy of the Viking settlements, and the relationship of the incoming Scandinavians to the native peoples. In its modest way, the work S of Red Craig has certainly something to offer on this topic. The changed overall picture of Pictish and Viking settlement in the Bay that necessarily derives from the work of the project as a whole is of major importance to the latter question, as Birsay is so often seen as a key area (see Ritchie 1983b; 1985b, 191–8; Morris 1985, 216–21; Crawford B. E. 1987, 155–88). Similarly, the identification of the major Viking/Late Norse focus at Beachview has turned attention back to the village area – as indeed have the implications of the work under St Magnus Parish Church.

Several writers – including this author – have emphasised the degree to which the amount of work carried out in this one, relatively small, area may imbalance the picture as a whole. That is a danger, of course, but it is to be hoped that the benefits are seen as far outweighing the defects. Without the concentrated imput of work at a detailed level in particular localities, archaeology is always going to be subject to the charges of random selection and ill-founded generalisation. 'The whole is greater than the sum of the parts' is certainly applicable here, and the further work in the village area of the Bay (Morris, forthcoming b) should demonstrate this more. Additionally, it is to be hoped that the philosophy of 'rescue archaeology in a research context' can be seen to have borne fruit in Birsay Bay.

Acknowledgements

This project had its origins in small-scale work funded by Durham University – through both the Excavation Committee and the Vacation Grants Fund. Without these resources provided in the crucial initial stages, the project would never have developed further. The subsequent major funding was provided from the Rescue budget of the Inspectorate of Ancient Monuments, Department of the Environment (now Historic Scotland). The support and co-operation of the members of the Inspectorate – especially Mr Patrick Ashmore and Dr David Breeze for the excavation funding, and Dr Noel Fojut for the post-excavation project – is gladly acknowledged. Practical assistance with equipment, huts and miscellaneous requests in Orkney was – as ever – cheerfully provided by Mr John Drever and the Orkney D. O. E. maintenance squad. The permission to excavate was kindly given by the landowners, Mr Gilbert Comloquoy and Mr William Moar, and their support was welcome and much appreciated. Many others have contributed to the work of this project: the major contributions of three of these is duly acknowledged on the title-page of the monograph: Norman Emery, Colleen Batey, and James Rackham. Nicholas Pearson's sterling work as Assistant Supervisor on site 1978–80 was fundamental. It must not be forgotten that a large number of students and volunteers were the basis of the achievment, backed up in 1978 by an MSC scheme organised through Orkney Education Committee and Durham University.

REFERENCES

A very full bibliography is to be found in the monograph, and hence is not repeated here. All references, other than those specifically concerned with work at Birsay, will be easily found there. What follows is a selected listing of works concerned specifically with recent archaeological work in Birsay Bay.

Barber, John W. n.d. *Excavations at Birsay Parish Church. Interim Report*, Excavation CEU 48 Report 005, Scottish Development Department (Ancient Monuments), Edinburgh.
Crawford, Barbara E. 1987. *Scandinavian Scotland*, Scotland in the Early Middle Ages 2, Leicester.
Cruden, Stewart H. 1958. 'Earl Thorfinn the Mighty and the Brough of Birsay', in *Third Viking Congress, Reykjavík 1956*, ed. Eldjárn, Kristján, Reykjavík, pp. 156–162.

Cruden, Stewart H. 1965. 'Excavations at Birsay, Orkney', in *The Fourth Viking Congress, York, August 1961*, ed. Small, Alan, Edinburgh & London, pp. 22–31.

Curle, Cecil L. 1982. *The Pictish and Norse Finds from the Brough of Birsay 1934–74*. Society of Antiquaries of Scotland Monograph Series 1, Edinburgh.

Donaldson, Alison M., Morris, Christopher D. & Rackham, D. James. 1981. 'The Birsay Bay Project: Preliminary Investigations into the past exploitation of the coastal environment of Birsay, Mainland, Orkney', in *Environmental Aspects of Coasts and Islands*, eds Brothwell, Don & Dimbleby, Geoffrey W., BAR Internat. Ser., 94, Oxford, pp. 65–85.

Graham-Campbell, James A. 1984. 'A Lost Silver Object from Oxtro Broch, Birsay, Mainland, Orkney', *Proc. Soc. Antiq. Scot.* 114, 299–300.

Hedges, John W. 1983. 'Trial excavations on Pictish and Viking settlements at Saevar Howe, Birsay, Orkney', *Glasgow Archaeological Journal* 10, 73–124 & Microfiche 40–102.

Hunter, John R. 1986. *Rescue Excavations on the Brough of Birsay 1974–82*, Society of Antiquaries of Scotland Monograph Series 4, Edinburgh.

Hunter, John R. & Morris, Christopher D. 1981. 'Recent Excavations at the Brough of Birsay, Orkney', in *Proceedings of the Eighth Viking Congress, Århus 1977*, eds Bekker-Nielsen, Hans, Foote, Peter G. & Olsen, Olaf, Odense, pp. 245–58.

Lamb, Raymond G. 1974. 'The Cathedral of Christchurch and the monastery of Birsay', *Proc. Soc. Antiq. Scot.* 105, 1972–4, 200–5.

Morris, Christopher D. 1990. *Church and Monastery in the Far North: An Archaeological Evaluation*, Jarrow Lecture 1989, Jarrow.

Morris, Christopher D. & Rackham, D. James. 1989. 'Birsay Bay, Orkney: Human Exploitation of natural and agricultural resources', *Hikuin* 15, 207–22.

Morris, Christopher D. with Batey, Colleen E., Emery, Norman, Rackham, D. James, and others. 1989. *The Birsay Bay Project Volume 1*. University of Durham Department of Archaeology Monograph Series 1, Durham.

Orkney Heritage 2, 1983. Articles by Ronald G. Cant; C. A. Ralegh Radford; Raymond G. Lamb; Anna Ritchie; Cecil L. Curle; Peter D. Anderson; Barbara E. Crawford; Christopher D. Morris; John R. Hunter.

Radford, C. A. Ralegh. 1959. *The Early Christian and Norse Settlements at Birsay*. Official Guide, Edinburgh.

Renfrew, A. Colin (ed.) 1985. *The Prehistory of Orkney* BC 4000–1000 AD, Edinburgh, chs 3, 9 & 10.

Ritchie, Anna 1974. 'Pict and Norseman in Northern Scotland', *Scot. Archaeol. Forum* 6, 23–36.

Ritchie, Anna 1977. 'Excavation of Pictish and Viking-age farmsteads at Buckquoy, Orkney', *Proc. Soc. Antiq. Scot.* 108, 1976–7, 174–227.

Ritchie, Anna. 1986. *Brough of Birsay*. Official Guide, Edinburgh.

Ritchie, Anna & Ritchie, J. N. Graham 1986. *The Ancient Monuments of Orkney*. Edinburgh.

17

THE SETTLEMENT OF WESTNESS, ROUSAY

SIGRID H. H. KALAND

The western side of Rousay has a long continuous settlement history shown by the Stone age chambered tombs, the broch people at Midhowe in the early Iron age, and the cemetery of the Picts at Westness. This cemetery was later used by the Viking settlement.

Westness is mentioned in the *Orkneyinga saga* as the place of the kidnapping of Earl Paul. Svein Asleifarson sailed from the Hebrides to Scotland where he heard about the fight between Earl Paul and Rognvald Kolsson for the Earldom. With a cargo-boat and 30 men he sailed with a north-westerly wind along the west coast of Mainland Orkney to Eynhallow Sound and Rousay, where Earl Paul was visiting his friend Sigurd of Westness. Svein managed to kidnap the Earl while he and his men were out hunting otters. Svein took the Earl with him to the boat and sailed back to the Moray Firth in Scotland.

Archaeological surveying and excavations at Westness revealed a Viking farm with a noust (boat house) and cemetery close to the shore (Fig. 17.1).

THE FARM (Fig. 17.2)

The excavation of the farmstead at Westness has shown that it consisted of two parallel longhouses – house I, a dwelling house, and the two smaller houses II and III built together, situated to the south of the dwelling house. The area between the houses had slabbed paving. The houses were orientated NE–SW sloping across the sandy beach, and sheltered from the strong winds.

The living house was nearly 35 m long and 6.5–7.0 m wide with two large halls and a smaller room in between. Secondary walls showed rebuilding during its time of use. The entrance to the 15 m long north hall of the house was from the eastern side. Along the walls were earth-filled benches, and a stone-lined fireplace was in the middle, giving light, warmth and cooking facilities. The southern hall, 10 m long, had a curved entrance in the western long wall to protect it against the prevailing wind. The entrance was paved and led towards the central paved pathway. Artefacts from the houses included fragments of

Figure 17.1: The farm houses seen from SE.

knives, soapstone sherds, bone pins, combs, and pottery, together with animal bones and carbonised seeds.

Parallel with house I, on the southern side, were houses II and III built together. House II was 15 m long and 5.0–5.5 m wide with the long walls sweeping inwards at their extremities so that it was curved. The doorway in the north corner opened on to a paved sunken pathway about half a metre wide. On both sides of the pathway were edging stones framing the benches. This was a byre with room for about 18 cows. The third house – a byre for sheep – was joined to the southern wall of house II and was only 5 × 5 m. The floor was fully paved and sloped downwards to the east where it ended in a ditch. There was also a similar ditch along the western side of the floor. These ditches met in the corner where there was a narrow passage way. The sloping floor let the urine run down and kept the floor dry. The ditches were probably built in this way to ease the collection of the dung which was then shovelled out through the corner.

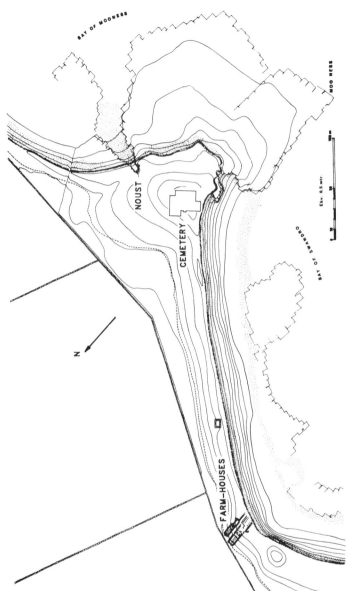

Figure 17.2: Map of the excavation area at Westness, Rousay.

Westness has yielded remains of carbonised grains: barley, rye and flax. Pollen analysis confirms that barley, rye and oats have been cultivated in the fields nearby. Bone material from the house foundations demonstrates the exploitation of different seabirds and also grouse. The bird colonies at the cliffs at Scabra Head on Rousay would have been the natural place for the trapping of birds. Bone fragments also show that whale, seal, deer and otters were hunted.

Evidence for fishing comes from shell and bone material which consisted of the remains of many varieties of fish, but mostly cod and ling. The artefacts from Westness support the evidence of the bone material by the occurrence in small boats of 'vadbein' for fishing-lines, as well as sinkers.

THE NOUST (Fig. 17.3)

The noust (boat house), 4.5 m wide and 8 m long, had been shortened by sea

Figure 17.3: The noust at very low tide seen from NW.

erosion. The building was situated at the eastern side of Moaness, orientated
SE–NW with the opening towards the sea. The choice of place is the best one on
the shore of Westness for shelter from the wind and the strong tidal currents in
the sound between Eynhallow and Rousay. At this place, the Vikings could have
their boats moored even at low tide because a depression of the rock, partly filled
in with sand, made the water somewhat deeper here than at other places. The
noust was dug down into the sand with an inner stone wall. There was room for
two small boats or a ship.

THE CEMETERY (Figs 17.4–17.9)

The excavation of the cemetery at Westness has revealed graves of both Picts and
Vikings. The cemetery contains graves of different types, and graves with and
without grave-goods. Graves that have been dated by the radiocarbon method
indicate that the cemetery was in use from the 7th to the 9th century. The burials
show that the Vikings respected the graves of the native population, since none of
them has been cut into. The graves were not visible on the surface, but the
excavation showed that, at the time of use, most of the graves had grave markers
in the form of a headstone. The Picts had no grave-goods. They were laid

Figure 17.4: Pictish, slab-lined grave, without grave-goods. Note the headstone which marked the
grave. The skeleton was dated by the radiocarbon method.

Figure 17.5: Oval-shaped, Norse grave of a woman. The woman was buried on her back with knees bent and her hands across her chest. By her hands is her sickle. The rest of her belongings were a bone comb, a bronze brooch and two spindle-whorls.

Figure 17.6: Oval-shaped, Norse grave of a young man. Note the stone setting of the grave with its higher prow-stone. The shape of the grave probably symbolises a boat. Grave-goods: shieldboss, sickle, arrowheads, ringheaded pin, comb and dice.

extended in narrow, full-length shallow graves. Some of these were completely or partly lined with slabs and with some slabs covering the body (Fig. 17.4). Other bodies were only put into a shallow trench.

The first Viking grave from Westness was accidentally found in 1963 by Ronald Stevenson of Westness farm. It was the burial of a young woman with her newborn child. Nothing is known about the grave form. The woman was provided with many grave-gifts, amongst which were two oval brooches, a beautiful ornamental ringed pin, beads, a weaving batten, bronze straps, the remains of a bronze bowl, and a pair of wool combs. The silver-gilt ringed pin, with gold filigree and inlaid amber, was most probably made in Scotland in the 8th century, but was still used in the Viking period in the 9th century.

The graves of the Vikings were of different types, rectangular without grave-goods, oval-shaped, or boat graves with grave-goods. The oval-shaped graves

Figure 17.7: A 9th century boat grave – the boat with the burial chamber constructed in the middle. A man was buried with his set of weapons and implements. The weapons and tools include: sword, axe, spear, arrows, shield boss, adze, sickle, shist hone, strike-a-light and flints. Note the slash on the Viking's shieldboss, which indicates that he has been fighting. The boat was 5.5 m long – a 'færing' (very similar to the modern Oselver-boat).

(Figs 17.5 & 17.6) were lined with slabs on edge, and could also have some covering slabs. Behind the head, the lining stone was higher, a 'stemstone' pointing towards the sea. The Viking men or women buried in such graves had different grave-goods – weapons: sword, axe, spear or arrows, shieldboss; jewellery; tools: sickle, adze, or weaving implements. The grave-goods showed whether they were warriors and/or farmers, or farmers' wives.

Two boat graves have been excavated, 5.5 and 4.5 m long respectively, but all the wood of the boats has decayed except around the rivets, where it has been preserved by the rust. The boats were clinker-built of oak, in the shape of a traditional Norwegian small boat. Both burials were made in the same way (Fig.

Figure 17.8: Another boat, a 'færing', 4.5 m long used for a 9th-century burial of a man, seen after the skeleton and the artefacts had been removed. The excavated boat is shown with its rivets – marked white – in position. All the wood of the boat was decayed except around the rivets.

Figure 17.9: A boat-shaped stone setting.

17.7): the boats were placed in a hole in the ground and stabilised with stones and clay outside. Then the burial chamber was made amidship by filling in the aft and the bow with flat stones. Next the body of the man was laid down outstretched in the chamber surrounded by his weapons and tools. Both graves contained swords and shields, arrows and axes, and one had a spear as well. Both had farming tools, such as a sickle and an adze, but one had a strike-a-light and a hone, and the other had a fishing weight and a bone comb. Both men showed signs of having been fighting (not with each other!). The shield boss of one was badly slashed, and the other man had been shot by four arrows in his back, arm, belly and thighbone, where only the broken tips were left.

The only remains of the boats in the Westness cemetery were rivets and impressions in the sand, but this information is sufficient to reconstruct the boats. They were both clinker-built with three and four strakes, similar to a 'færing'. The boat from grave II (Fig. 17.8) had a rowlock on the gunwale made from deer antler and a 'vadbein' of deer antler for the fishing-line on the other gunwale.

In addition to the graves, a big stone setting shaped as a boat, built of large slabs, was discovered on the edge of the beach (Fig. 17.9). However, only half of the stone setting was finished, and no grave was found within it.

Analysis of the skeletons showed that they represented the whole community of Westness from the newborn child to old people of about 50 years. There are men, women and children, and some of them bear traces of pathological conditions, e.g. having horizontal overbite, only 11 pair of ribs, trepanation, arthritis or tuberculosis. The tallest was 1.7 m high.

From: Sigrid Kaland, 1987. *The Norse Connection: Orkney-Norway, 800–1500*, Exhibition booklet, Tankerness House Museum, Kirkwall, 19–29, Bergen.

18

TUQUOY, WESTRAY, ORKNEY

A CHALLENGE FOR THE FUTURE?

OLWYN A. OWEN

INTRODUCTION

The infamous Orkney winds and stormy seas repeatedly batter and erode the coastline, here and there exposing and threatening ancient sites of all types and periods. The challenges for the archaeologist are twofold: first, to recognise and record such eroding sites; and, secondly, to ascertain which of them are sufficiently significant, and intact, to merit excavation in advance of their inevitable destruction. This chapter sets out to examine the case of Tuquoy, an eroding Norse and Medieval site, located on the northern Orkney island of Westray, on the S shore of the Ness of Tuquoy (NGR: HY 454 431; Fig. 18.1).

Orcadian sites often preserve unusually full structural, artefactual and palaeoenvironmental evidence and the site at Tuquoy is no exception. Identified as Norse in 1981 by Dr Raymond Lamb, it was instantly recognisable as the focus of a major settlement. Immediately to the E is the ruined, probably 12th-century church of Crosskirk, now in State care, its seaward side protected by a modern sea wall. Extending westwards from the wall for more than 80 m, a variety of archaeological deposits and associated structures were visible in the eroding cliff section, which stands 1.20 to 2.75 m high. Subsequently, survey and trial excavation, undertaken in 1982–3, were complemented by a full assessment of the settlement in 1988.

The aim of the project to date has been to place Tuquoy in its historical, archaeological and environmental context in order to define the site's potential. This paper sets out to present selected aspects of a broad-based, interdisciplinary study of Tuquoy.

HISTORICAL AND DOCUMENTARY EVIDENCE

The name 'Tuquoy' applies to a large and prosperous farm situated some 800 m to the N of the site (Fig. 18.1) and is ostensibly of low status within the social hierarchy of Norse farm-names, incorporating as it does the humble element, *kví*, with its original connotation of a sheepfold. The 'Tu-' element is less certain, possibly from *þúfa*, 'mound' (R. Lamb, personal communication). No

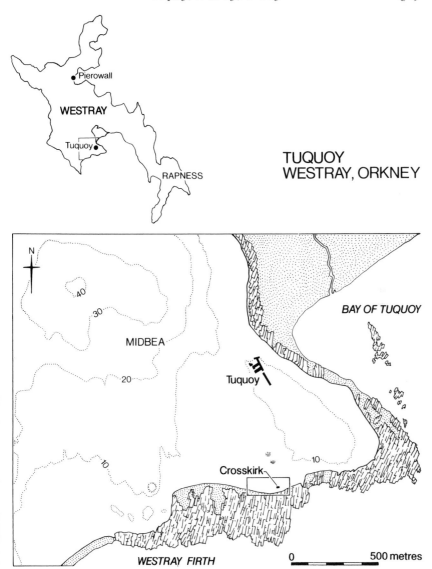

Figure 18.1: The context of the site (C. Unwin).

specific name survives for the site under investigation. However, Marwick, in his study of Orkney farm names, pinpointed the existence of an early 'tunship' called 'Midbea' (ON *mið-bœr*, mid-farm or settlement). This name applies to an area stretching from present-day Midbea to the Bay of Tuquoy and 'plainly indicates the middle portion of a larger unit' (Marwick 1952, 35, 245; Fig. 1).

It is likely that the 'larger unit' was a large, original settlement of ON *bœr* type, one of the oldest farm-names in Norway and which, in the English Danelaw, gave rise to town names now ending in -by, such as Whitby and Grimsby. The original sense was of a large and important farm-settlement. The terms *bú* and *bær* each occur some 30 times in *Orkneyinga saga* and are both used, for instance, of the earl's residence at Orphir. In Birsay, the old 'tunship' of Beaquoy demonstrates how the name of a secondary, outlying quoy-farm has supplanted the parent name, Beaquoy being the quoy-extension of an earlier *bær* farm which survives in name at Houseby. The latter occupies a better site for exploitation of agricultural resources and the old *urisland* chapel lies adjacent to it. As the original units gradually broke up into smaller farms, new (often secondary) names were applied to the component parts; the original name survived by chance or not at all, as at Tuquoy.

Crosskirk is situated within a district recorded in the Orkney rentals of the early 16th century as the *urisland* of Tuquoy and Air (Peterkin 1820, 79–80). In the Medieval period and later, it was the parish church of West (or Cross) parish and Marwick comments: 'Here was the seat of the most powerful family in the parish at the time parish churches were set up' (1952, 35). Marwick's fundamental work on the rentals (which date from 1492 onwards) demonstrated the great wealth of the three 'tunships' centred around Crosskirk, for its time a colossal value of 4.5 *urislands*, which prompted his assertion that it represents 'the "landtake" of one of the greatest of the early Norse settlers in Orkney' (1952, 35). Thus, Marwick first inferred that a wealthy, influential family lived in the vicinity of Crosskirk.

The subject of the earldom or odal *bu*s was first explored by Clouston (1927b) who described the characteristics of *bu* farms as their great size, the presence of *umbesetters* or 'attached farms', their location by the shore, and the presence of a chapel, in four cases the parish church. Marwick cites the presence of Crosskirk and the rental evidence (notably of the wealth of Tuquoy and Air, and of Midbea being a tunship composed of many small-holdings) as indicative that the Tuquoy area may represent one of the lost earldom *bu*s (1952, 34–5).

Unfortunately, but not surprisingly, *Orkneyinga saga* makes no reference to Tuquoy or Midbea by name. However, the politics of 12th-century Westray are vividly invoked in the Saga because of the importance that that island assumed when Rognvald came via Shetland from Norway in 1136 to challenge Paul for the Earldom (*Orkneyinga saga* chs 65–73: Taylor 1938). Lamb has interpreted the saga evidence to suggest that Thorkel Flettir and his family were prominent land-holders in SW Westray at that time (Lamb 1981; *contra* Clouston 1927a, 333), while Helgi and Kugi had named centres at Pierowall and Rapness respectively, both obvious settlement foci. Lamb has postulated, on the grounds of the apparent status of the archaeological site with its elegant church, that Thorkel Flettir, his heir Haflidi and their family were based at Tuquoy. Excavation can hardly confirm this association although trial work has confirmed the high status of the site (below).

There is an absence of historical or documentary evidence for Orkney for the period between the writing of *Orkneyinga saga* (*c.* 1192–1206) and the earliest surviving rental of 1492. This period is critically relevant to Tuquoy on the basis of the excavated evidence and William Thomson has kindly offered to attempt to 'bridge the gap' with a detailed study of the early estate of Tuquoy and Air of the sort which he so ably demonstrates elsewhere in this volume.

Thus, the historical and documentary evidence so far examined indicates that, as Marwick suggested, here might be the farm of one of the richest of the early Norse settlers in Orkney, someone whose work, good fortune and likely cunning laid the basis of the documented, colossal wealth centred on Crosskirk by late Norse times. Here was probably the home of one of Rognvald's most crucial allies during the tumultuous period which accompanied his succession to the Earldom in the 1130s; and here is a site which might illumine a little known period of Orcadian protohistory: the transition from late Norse to Medieval Orkney.

CROSSKIRK (Figs 18.2 & 18.3)

by Christopher Lowe

The settlement lies adjacent to the ruinous, 'Romanesque' chapel of Crosskirk (Radford 1962, 181), conventionally dated to the 12th century (MacGibbon & Ross 1896, 126; Dietrichson & Meyer 1906, 29; RCAHMS 1946, ii, 344). Folk memory describes the original building as 'the Danes' work' (MacGibbon & Ross 1896, 125; Westray islanders, personal communications). It fell out of use sometime between 1777 and 1823 (NSA 1842, 125; OSA 1799 (1978), 359; Lamb

Figure 18.2: Crosskirk.

1983, 38), although it may have been temporarily abandoned at an earlier date
(OSA 1799 (1978), 360).

Description

The kirk, of nave and chancel form, is built of schistose rubble laid in lime
mortar and traces of plaster still adhere to internal wall faces in the E part of the
building. The western half of the present nave (14.3 by 4.25 m internally) is a
later addition to an earlier, shorter, nave and is now much reduced, standing only
0.5 m high. Eroded sandstone roll mouldings in its S entrance indicate a 16th- or
17th-century date (J. Dunbar, personal communication; Lamb 1983, 37).

The original nave measured 5.65 by 4.15 m internally and its well-preserved
walls and those of the chancel still stand up to 2.25 m high. The nave was entered
through an unrebated, round-headed doorway in the S wall. A round-headed
window is located E of the entrance and a similar one may have existed in the
chancel's E wall (MacGibbon & Ross 1896, 124–6). The small, barrel-vaulted,
square-ended chancel, only 2.8 m E to W by 2.1 m, was entered through an arch
which had inclined jambs but was otherwise similar to the original doorway.

The present graveyard (75 by 40 m) is enclosed by a drystone wall. Traces of
an earlier, sub-rectangular enclosure are apparent to the N, E and, perhaps, W of
the church (Fig. 18.3), in the form of a turf-covered bank which enclosed an area
some 50 by 25 m.

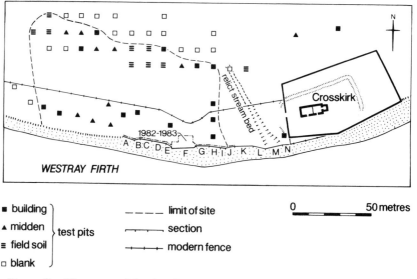

Figure 18.3: The extent of the site (C. Unwin).

Discussion

Crosskirk is a well-preserved example of a typically Orcadian nave-and-chancel church, similar to St Mary's chapel, Wyre and Linton chapel, Shapinsay, for example, but rare elsewhere in Scotland and differing in detail from those found in Shetland. Dedications to the Holy Cross or Rood are common in the Northern Isles and 12 are known today. The popularity of this dedication is generally associated with the Crusades and, locally, could be related to the visits to the Holy Land by the Orkney Earls, Haakon and Rognvald, in *c.* 1120 and *c.* 1152 respectively (*Orkneyinga saga* chs 52, 86–9: Taylor 1938).

The dating of the Northern Isles' churches, few of which have been excavated and all of which lack readily diagnostic, dateable features, is fraught with difficulties. The 'Romanesque' plan-form and arch-types (Radford 1962, 181) and the presence of lime-mortared and plastered masonry indicate a 12th-century date (RCAHMS 1971, 145) which is supported by several pieces of circumstantial evidence, notably the dedication and its possible association with the Crusades, the folk memory of 'the Danes' work', and the fact that Crosskirk was elevated to parish church status, a process commonly assumed to have been a feature of the late 12th or 13th century (Clouston 1932a, 155–6; Lamb 1981).

Ironically, confirmation may be found in the association of Crosskirk with the settlement site at Tuquoy. The association of farm and church is a well recognised phenomenon in areas of Norse settlement in Britain and elsewhere, although its origins are unclear where the incoming Norse encountered an indigenous Christian population (Clouston 1918; 1932a; Cant 1972; 1984; Lowe 1987).

Farm and church associations occur throughout the Greenland settlements (Krogh 1983; Roussell 1944) and the phenomenon has also been recognised in Faroe. At Sand, for example, excavation uncovered the remains of a small, timber, nave-and-chancel church, succeeded by a similar but slightly larger, stone-clad building. A hall-like building and other domestic structures were located immediately outside the churchyard (Krogh 1975; Diklev 1981). The primary settlement and church at Sand have been assigned to the 11th century on the basis of coin hoard evidence.

The widespread use of timber in early church construction, at Sand and throughout the North Atlantic province (Ahrens 1981, 571–630), and the discovery of timber chapels on the Brough of Deerness (Morris & Emery 1986) and at Kebister, Shetland (Owen 1987, 31–2; Owen & Smith 1989, 2), indicate that the Orcadian and Shetlandic stone churches may not be as early as they seem. It is conceivable that the present Crosskirk, too, was preceded by a timber phase.

The early 12th-century church at Orphir, which stood outside the Earl's 'drinking-hall' (*Orkneyinga saga* ch. 70; Dietrichson & Meyer 1906, Fig. 43; Taylor 1938, 385; RCAHMS 1946, ii, nos 483, 485, 174–5), is an obvious parallel to

Crosskirk in the context of its setting. Similarly, St Mary's chapel and Kolbein Hruga's (Cubbie Roo's) castle, Wyre (RCAHMS 1946, ii, nos 618–9, 234–9) provide another parallel, the castle dated on saga evidence to *c.* 1150 (*Orkneyinga saga* ch. 84). St Mary's chapel is believed to date to the late 12th century on the basis of an association with Bjarni Kolbeinsson, bishop of Orkney (1188–1223). Tammaskirk and the nearby Hall or Bu of Rendall have also been assigned a mid to late 12th-century date on the basis of saga evidence (Clouston 1932b; Lowe 1987, i, 75–7).

In short, the balance of the evidence is that the proximity of Crosskirk to the site at Tuquoy can hardly be coincidental. It is likely that these are intimately related monuments whose archaeological and historical association is parallelled by other sites of similar status in the North Atlantic province. The date of the kirk is likely to be illuminated by the dating and nature of the various phases represented on the adjacent settlement, where its builders probably lived.

THE EXTENT OF THE SETTLEMENT (Fig 18.3)

That the eroding site at Tuquoy was a likely candidate for the nucleus of the important settlement inferred by Marwick was apparent even from the two-dimensional glimpse of it which the low, sandy cliff section offered in 1981. Massive, lime-plastered masonry protruded from the approximate centre of the section exposure, prompting trial excavation here in 1982–3; extensive midden deposits surrounded and filled consecutive and abutting sequences of structures with flagged floors, hearths and underfloor drains; and artefacts could be found littering the beach.

In 1988, a detailed assessment of the site was undertaken which included determining its three-dimensional extent. Coring with a bucket augur took place on a 10 m grid, starting behind the excavated trench; and where archaeological deposits occurred, their depth, thickness and general character were recorded. Whenever two successive cores failed to locate archaeological material, coring on that gridline ceased.

The site survives up to 50 m inland and extends, in section, 150 m W of the churchyard wall, rather than the 80 m length first noted. An apparently 'blank' area from *c.* 15 m to *c.* 40 m W of the churchyard may represent the course of the stream bed which originally sprang from the, now drained, Loch of Tuquoy to the NW. This separates the churchyard and its adjacent archaeological strata from the core of the site to the W. It probably represents the fresh water source for the settlement.

W of the stream bed, archaeological deposits vary from sturdy masonry and rubble to middens and cultivated field soils. In general, structures abound close to the excavated area; further away, rich midden material and occasional structures were identified; beyond this, field soils surround the settlement. Other, probably unrelated, archaeological sites were also identified in the field immediately N of the Norse and Medieval settlement and further W and E along the cliff face.

By their very nature, eroding sites only survive partially and local memory suggests that as much as 40 m of land may have been lost in the past century or so at Tuquoy. Large, eroding sites offer ever diminishing returns to the archaeologist, until what survives cannot be considered to be representative of the site as a whole. Individual components of the site may still have intrinsic value in their capacity to address specific archaeological questions, but constant vigilance is needed against the possibility of over-interpretation of partial data.

Several factors are impeding erosion at Tuquoy. The site faces S to SE, from which direction gales and hurricanes are relatively infrequent, although when they do occur, they tend to be particularly fierce. Secondly, the exposure of blocks of masonry and hard-packed rubble has temporarily strengthened the face and slowed erosion. However, the real threat to the site lies not in steady and predictable erosion but rather in freak storms from the S, any one of which could remove several metres of ground overnight. It is thus not possible to determine the original extent of the settlement, nor to estimate the proportion represented by the surviving deposits.

However, the assessment exercise has revealed a linear settlement site, strung out along the shoreline. The impression is that the nucleus of the site gradually moved westwards with, very generally, new buildings being erected adjacent to the ruins of the old, a practice which is still prevalent in the Northern and Western Isles today. The nucleus of at least the 12th-century and Medieval site appears to be present. Several boat naust sites were located and surveyed to the E of the churchyard which, although they are undated, may indicate an inconsiderable erosion rate here. On balance, it seems likely that a large, though undefinable, proportion of the settlement is relatively intact. It would be prohibitively expensive to protect a monument of this size from marine erosion.

THE CLIFF SECTION

The formation processes of the deposits visible in section were ascertained by excavating a 0.50 m wide strip through the site over a length of *c.* 100 m from the modern sea wall westwards (Fig. 18.3). Beyond this point, the site is temporarily stable, with grass growing on the overburden, and its disturbance would probably have exposed it to erosion unnecessarily. Nonetheless, several apparent archaeological foci of the site lay within the examined section, in which every type of deposit identified through the coring programme was represented.

The section segments (labelled A–N; Fig. 18.3) were brought to straight and vertical faces; the section was drawn and photographed; and the separate contexts, their stratigraphic relationships and their field interpretations were recorded. Segment F represents the 1982–3 excavation area and no further work was undertaken here. Once cleaned, it could be seen that segments K–L contained no deposits earlier than the Post-Medieval period. Segments M–N, dislocated from the main site and disturbed by the modern sea wall construction, were drawn but not excavated.

Work was concentrated on the remaining segments, A–E and G–J (c. 54 m in length). For each soil context, the soil was described and sampled for routine analyses (pH, phosphates, loss on ignition, particle size analysis, pollen and calcium carbonate content). Additionally, a 20 kg sample of every soil context was floated and wet-sieved on site. Finally, the remainder of the deposit was coarse sieved until a predetermined weight of inclusions was recorded. In post-excavation, inclusions within all soil layers are being analysed and quantified as relative indices of the anthropogenic components of each deposit which, together with the results of the routine soil tests, are being used to test the field interpretations.

The section is clearly dominated by midden-site deposits (humic soils rich in anthropogenic materials which formed in the immediate vicinity of inhabited structures), cultivated soils and windblown sand. In some parts of the site, structures and structural debris predominate and, almost everywhere, stone is a major component of the contexts. As expected, the deposits are generally artefact rich.

The section segments can be broadly characterised as follows:

A–C – rich midden-site deposits with occasional structures;
D–E – complex structural sequence and associated strata;
G–H – some midden-site deposits and cultivated soils, almost no structural debris;
I–J – structures and distinctive fills (anaerobic, waterlogged, organic material overlain by burnt debris) within a substantial pit.

Publication of this work, aimed at characterising the nature, variety and formation processes of the site's deposits, is in preparation. The results will facilitate the formulation of a set of archaeological hypotheses to be tested at Tuquoy and, by implication, guide the selection of areas for further excavation.

THE TRIAL EXCAVATIONS

Trial work in 1982–3 concentrated on the massive, externally lime-plastered structures visible in section. An area of less than 100 m² was opened, in which the remains of a rectilinear 'hall' were uncovered (Fig. 18.4 & 18.5), aligned NW to SE, with an entrance in the centre of the SE wall (facing the sea). Nowhere were the walls less than 1 m thick and, at the entrance, they expanded to a massive 1.4 m wide. Its full extent was not revealed (although the rest of the building survives to the N of the excavated area); however, it was 3.75 m wide internally and at least 6.65 m in length. The interior of the building was paved over at least three times with large, well-laid flagstones; otherwise, internal features were rare, although a range of high quality artefacts was retrieved. The structure was partitioned on at least three occasions, indicating that the building served different functions at different periods.

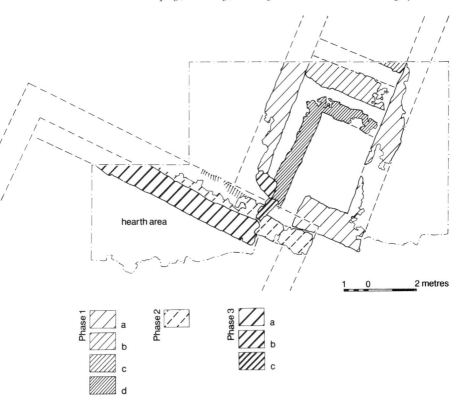

Figure 18.4: The late Norse 'hall' and other buildings (C. Unwin).

A large slab, incorporated into the latest partition wall, bore a complete runic inscription which reads:

þorstæin. æinarssunr. ræist. runar þesar

translated as 'Þorstein Einarsson carved these runes' (Owen & McKinnell 1989). It has not proved possible to identify this individual elsewhere, but the formula and spelling are exactly parallelled at Maeshowe, inscription XXII, which probably dates from the mid-12th century (Dickins 1930; Liestøl 1968). A complete, Irish-type, kidney-ringed pin from a slightly lower level is probably of late 11th- or early 12th-century date on typological grounds (T. Fanning, personal communication).

Analogies with Cubbie Roo's documented 12th-century castle on Wyre (*Orkneyinga saga* ch. 84; Marwick 1928; RCAHMS 1946, ii, no. 619, 235–9) which is also massive in structure and has externally plastered walls, prompted an initial suggestion that the Tuquoy building was defensive in character and might augment the small number of known, Viking fortified sites (c.f. Morris 1985,

224–6). However, the monumental nature of the edifice may well indicate the high status of the patron of the builders, rather than any serious defensive intention. In this, it may be more comparable to the putative earl's 'drinking-hall' at Orphir (*Orkneyinga saga* ch. 70, Taylor 1938, 385; Dietrichson & Meyer 1906, Fig. 43; RCAHMS 1946, ii, nos 483, 485, 174–5), where small excavations have confirmed the presence of buildings, though of uncertain date (Johnston 1903, 22–3; Morris 1985, 223).

Rather grander comparative monuments also occur. At the Wirk, Rousay, traditionally the site of a 'fortalice', a possible 'hall' is appended to a small, square tower (Clouston 1931, 27–33; RCAHMS 1946, ii, no. 550, 191–20). Ground surface indications are that the 'hall' is more than 26 m long and almost 7 m wide; it is not known whether the tower and 'hall' are contemporary. This 'hall' is reminiscent in scale to the surviving portions of the 12th-century Bishop's Palace, Kirkwall which was probably begun by Bishop William the Old (1102–68) in parallel with the earliest work on St Magnus' Cathedral. This apparent 'hall' had its main accommodation on the first-floor above an undercroft (*The Saga of Hacon*, chs 330–1, Dasent, 1894; MacGibbon & Ross 1887, i, 519–22, ii, 337–47; RCAHMS 1946, ii, no. 402, 145–8; Cruden 1960, 184; Simpson 1961, 65–71) and may be roughly contemporary with the Tuquoy building.

This group of Orcadian mortared, stone-built 'halls' represents a departure from the native Scandinavian tradition of the simpler, timber hall. Just as ecclesiastical architecture of the period (Kirkwall Cathedral, the round church at Orphir and Crosskirk, amongst others) reflects an essentially Romanesque tradition, so do edifices such as the Bishop's Palace and perhaps even the Tuquoy building, albeit the latter is a much cruder manifestation of that tradition. Nonetheless, its architectural aspirations do seem to indicate Continental, rather than Scandinavian, social and cultural connotations which are not out of place in the general context of 12th-century Orkney.

Another rectilinear structure, *c.* 13 m in total length by more than 5 m wide and aligned NE to SW, was appended at right angles to the 'hall', blocking access to the latter (Fig. 18.4). Stone building techniques were primitive and it had to be substantially re-built during its period of use. Amongst its many internal deposits and structural features, substantial areas of burning were predominant, demarcated by wall benches containing stone-lined boxes used for some industrial activity. Analysis of the quantities of metalworking debris recovered indicated that the building may have been a smithy (M. Spearman, personal communication).

All the excavated structures, though impressive in scale and conception, were poorly founded. In every case, phases of re-building and other modifications were evident. Abandoned buildings were blocked off and in time they filled with rich midden-site deposits, dumped by the inhabitants of the Medieval settlement which probably lies immediately to the W. Some 140,000 fish bones alone were recovered from midden levels filling into and over the 'hall'.

Other, probably Medieval, rectilinear structures of similar character were recorded in section immediately to the W. The structural nucleus of the late Norse and Medieval site is certainly represented in segments D–F (Fig. 18.3). The section here is so studded with masonry that there is little soil to excavate. The structures can be difficult to interpret two-dimensionally but the glimpse of Medieval Orkney they offer is tantalising, especially as the buildings all appear to be substantially intact behind the exposed face, albeit vulnerable to further erosion.

The archaeological record of Medieval Scotland as a whole remains deficient and 13th- to 15th-century settlements do not yet appear in the otherwise exceptionally rich archaeological record of Orkney. One such is intimated by small-scale excavations in Kirkwall in 1978 (McGavin 1982) where a Medieval waterfront perhaps comparable to those in Bergen and Trondheim may have existed (R. Lamb, personal communication), but opportunities to examine it further appear limited. Most excavated late Norse sites, such as Beachview, Birsay or the later phases of Pool, Sanday appear to have been abandoned by the 12th or 13th centuries (Morris 1983, 142–7; Hunter, this volume), whereas Tuquoy apparently continued to flourish until the 14th to 15th century. Most late Norse farmsteads were probably never abandoned; their descendants are still occupied today.

Thus, at Tuquoy, the importance of the Medieval site lies as much in its relationship to the preceding Norse settlement as in what it may reveal about the nature and basis of the Medieval settlement itself. The processes and effects of increasing 'Scottification' (Wainwright 1962, 190) are little understood and Tuquoy may offer a rare opportunity to examine them. It is likely that the succession of Scottish earls in the Orkney Earldom from 1231 began this process but Clouston was able to assert that, although there were Scottish householders in Kirkwall from the early 14th century, they appear to have had little impact on the Orcadian land-owning classes (1914, lvii, xlix). The Medieval pottery from Tuquoy, predominantly from middens filling into the 'hall', is a varied assemblage from Scottish and other North European sources, dating from between the 13th and 15th centuries. In general, it parallels the earlier phases of the assemblage from Kirkwall although the presence of sherds of Low Countries redwares at Tuquoy is 'exceptional' (S. Mills, personal communication). Finds of other materials, such as metalwork, also confirm the presence of the Medieval site, although, structurally, it was poorly attested in the trial trench. The indications are that its focus lies immediately W and N of the excavated area, a prime target for further excavation.

EARLY VIKING FEATURES

In common with most Orcadian sites, the soils at Tuquoy are predominantly sandy, conditions which preserve artefactual and ecofactual evidence well but not less durable, uncarbonised materials such as wood and leather. However, towards the E end of the cliff section and at its base (segments I–J; Figs 18.3 & 18.6), a substantial pit was discovered which contained waterlogged Viking deposits, unique in an Orcadian context. It was excavated where it occurred on the beach in front of the section face. It had a minimum cord of 7 m W to E and was *c*. 3.5 m wide N to S, although it was eroded along its S edge. In section, it appeared to have been dug 1.65 m into windblown sand in the E, but the original depth of its W edge had been obscured by the insertion of later walling and other deposits. The chronological sequence here was not unambiguously determinable in section but the most likely sequence of events is outlined below.

The butt end of a well-built wall, up to 1.1 m wide and standing to a maximum height of 1.6 m, was found within the pit, built on the lowermost, coarse gravel fill and protruding from the section face (Fig. 18.6). No associated walling was discernible in the section face and its function remains unclear. To the E, at the level of its base, stones surrounded by voids and waterlogged brown clay may represent a sump, draining water away from associated features which survive behind the present face.

The E edge of the pit was cut (possibly re-cut) to a depth of 1.65 m into windblown sand, which had probably accumulated against the E wall face. A 0.6 m depth of extremely compacted, waterlogged, organic material was discovered within the pit and butted against the wall, from which a radiocarbon determination of AD 885 ± 65 (GU-1650) was obtained. This material appears to be largely comprised of a mixture of animal dung, straw and grey ash. At

Figure 18.5: The late Norse 'hall'.

Figure 18.6: The waterlogged pit.

different levels, it also contained varying quantities of peat, unburnt wood, twigs, grasses, insects, marine shells and shell sand, and other microscopic remains.

The wood assemblage (examined by Dr Anne Crone) consists of artefacts, woodworking debris and roundwood. The sparse, natural woodland cover of Norse Westray probably consisted of local patches of willow scrub with, at most, some birch and hazel (Donaldson 1986a; 1986b). As corroboration, the willow component consists entirely of small twigs and branches which were fashioned into a variety of small domestic articles and used as twine, perhaps to hold down thatched roofs (Stummann Hansen 1988). Of only three pieces of birch, one was a carved handle, burnt at one end and covered with a crudely executed, geometric pattern (Owen 1988, 6, Fig. 4).

The sources of all other species must have been as driftwood or as traded imports. The quantity of pine recovered implies large-scale importation, the majority of the offcuts probably representing the trimming of radially split planks. The preliminary trimming of the trunks, possibly to squared cross-sections for ease of transportation, was done at source, probably in Norway. A single example of maple, a finely made handle, argues for the importation of ready-made objects, perhaps via Pierowall which both Brøgger (1929, 121) and Taylor (1938, 386) have identified with the *Höfn* of the *Orkneyinga saga*.

The small amounts of larch and spruce present probably arrived as driftwood since they exhibited boreholes of a marine bivalve mollusc (J. Sadler, personal communication). Since these pieces are offcuts, it seems that driftwood was used for constructional purposes as well as fuel (*contra* Small 1969). Oak and ash occur in small quantities and may have been imported given their suitability for particular purposes: oak for carpentry and ash for handles, hafts and shafts.

The assemblage also provides evidence of a range of tools: knives, spoon-bits, axes and adzes, and a re-used fragment of worked oak (whose rounded face has knife cuts which may be runic) shows probable evidence of the use of a plane with a blade 1.8 cm wide. The presence of roughouts and unfinished objects in the pit testifies to the presence of an active, domestic industry.

The field interpretation of the material in the pit was that it represents either redeposited byre-manure, the product of layers of animal bedding (grass and short heath, dry mould and household ashes) and dung accummulated in the byre from over-wintering animals; or occupational build-up, discarded ejecta from a structure; or some combination of both, household ejecta being transferred to the byre intermittently with other materials to provide animal bedding. Usually, byre-manure would have been transferred outside to a dunghill or compost midden for further fermentation; and its deposition here, in a waterlogged pit, would be anomalous. However, past peoples must have had an indefinite number of motives for their actions (as indeed present peoples do), many of which are not susceptible to archaeological interpretation. As just one such example, an outbreak of illness could have provoked a change in house and byre clearing habits.

This interpretation, that the material represents redeposited byre-manure, is being tested by a range of specialist analyses. The varying quantities of wood which occurred at different levels support the contention that the pit was filled intermittently with dumped deposits. The sedimentological, palynological and entymological analyses permit more detailed examination of the sources of these mixed dumps of material.

Amongst the insect fauna (examined by Jon Sadler, Sheffield University), insect pests, insects associated with rotting organic matter, aquatic and waterside insects, peatland insects and insects associated with the wider environment are prevalent. The presence of both synanthropic insects associated with decomposing material and human and animal ectoparasites implies that a considerable proportion of the material formed within some kind of structure, although whether this was a house or byre is unclear. The outdoor species, diverse and numerous, could have been incorporated into a building in a number of obvious ways, such as through doors and windows or brought in by constant human movement. Materials such as peat, hay and seaweed, brought into buildings for a variety of purposes, would have had breeding populations which would have mixed with indoor faunas if stored inside a building. The entomological evidence favours the interpretation that the material represents occupational build-up, with wool-processing and the collection of peat, seaweed and hay for various purposes all represented as likely activities.

The inhabitants at Tuquoy appear to have been infested with lice and fleas which might indicate a low level of hygiene, a suspicion reinforced by the numbers of species associated with large amounts of rotting organic material. Similar conditions pertained in near contemporary deposits from Iceland, Greenland, Oslo, Dublin and York and were almost certainly the norm throughout antiquity (Buckland, this volume). The insect assemblages are markedly similar to the faunas recovered from probable floor layer deposits on Viking sites in York with the same range of abundant species (Hall *et al.* 1983). This close comparison supports the contention that the materials found in the Tuquoy pit seem to have, in part, accumulated within a structure.

Sedimentological and palynological analyses (undertaken by Dr Richard Tipping) reveal a complex stratigraphic sequence, amongst which six major sediment types were identified, with an implied repeated disruption to the sedimentary processes (consistent with the hypothesis that material was repeatedly being added to the fill). Radiocarbon dating is being undertaken to attempt to identify the period of use of the pit for dumping, but the impression is of intensive use over some time. The organic fills are extremely pollen rich; and the pollen spectra successfully discriminate between the major sediment types and may also suggest their likely provenances.

Percentage pollen analysis of the basal silt shows this to be a freshwater deposit and high counts of microscopic charcoal imply its close proximity to areas of burning in the landscape. There are some indications that there was originally a silty clay lining to the pit which, since the stratigraphic and pollen preservation evidence suggest that the pit was waterlogged during and following deposition of the material within it, may have been created intentionally.

The source of cut, unburnt blocks of peat was probably high ground away from the settlement, probably Fitty Hill, the peat presumably intended as fuel when collected. The discrete bands of peat ash appear to have become intermixed with the matrix material away from the pit, at a time prior to the deposition of the ash lenses. The pit was certainly not intended primarily to contain ashes since these layers constitute only a small proportion of the deposits.

The bulk of the material is a variably humified, layered organic deposit extraordinarily rich in pollen of cereals (probably oats and barley) and arable 'weeds', together with a prominent background component of pastoral indicator species. It seems likely that the common oat (*Avena sativa*) was the most important crop and that either or both barley and bristle oat were also grown. Tuquoy was evidently a farming community whose economy relied on a mix of arable and pasture; in what proportions may become clearer from analysis of a pollen core extracted from the Loch of Tuquoy. A farm arranged into infield, outfield and pasture, as described by Fenton (1978) for later Orkney farms, seems a reasonable working hypothesis.

Several of the arable 'weeds' may have been encouraged, given their usefulness around the farm. Analysis of the charred plant remains from the late Norse site has indicated that certain types of herbs and weeds were used domestically in the later period (S. Nye, personal communication). Tipping has tentatively suggested that the high amounts of cereal pollen at the base of the main pit fill perhaps imply that the farm was flourishing prior to the digging of the pit and that the pit itself is relatively late in the sequence.

The problems of interpretation are compounded because it is not clear whether the deposit originally contained the heads of cereals and flowers of associated herbs or simply their pollen; and because of the combinations of two types of cereal and of cereals and arable weeds within the one deposit. The pollen of *Avena* and *Hordeum* type occur together, with the ratio of barley to oats varying markedly within the sample sequence examined. It is unlikely that the two crops would have been raised in the same field (Fenton 1978, 335) and there would have been no obvious advantage in mixing the two crops after reaping, storage in separate stacks being the usual option. The cereal pollen grains could have been mixed before or during deposition in the pit but the mixing makes it unlikely that grain storage was the purpose of the pit.

Reynolds (1981) has argued that mixed assemblages of cereals and weeds are more likely to represent the results of reaping the cereal stalks for straw. Accordingly, bedding material for stalled animals could be represented here, the straw from both barley and oats being bundled together. Straw was an integral part of manure derived from cattle dung in byres, necessary to absorb the high water content of such manure (Fenton 1978; Darling 1945). The making of manure was a sophisticated practice with preparation depending on the intended crop. Byre-manure was a 'sandwich mixture' (Fenton 1978, 281) of wild grass and heath, mould, dung and ashes, some of which can be recognised in the Tuquoy pit sediments. The addition of mown grass would explain the large quantities of wild grass and pastoral pollen types and it may be that some distinctive lenses of 'soil' correspond to Fenton's mould, the 'dry upper surface of peaty hill land where vegetation had not taken root' (1978, 281). Peat ash was certainly added.

Thus, the sedimentological and palynological evidence appears, tentatively, to bear out the field interpretation with one added complication. The removal of byre-manure would disrupt the sedimentological sequence; from the small sample examined, it can be inferred that this did not happen to the material within the pit. Could this therefore be an *in situ* byre floor with an intact accummulation of byre-manure whose constituents included household refuse incorporated as part of the animal bedding? The waterlogged nature of the feature would seem to argue against this interpretation though does not preclude it altogether.

Whatever the answer, (and the results of further specialist reports are awaited), somewhere in the immediate vicinity there is almost certainly a large, early Viking farm, perhaps the *bœr* farm first inferred by Marwick. The butt-ended wall which continues behind the section and the depth of the deposits here suggest that a substantial part of it survives unexcavated.

As a footnote, the pit was later re-used, its upper levels comprising a 1.4 m depth of burnt stones and peat ash, the debris from water heating activities on a substantial scale. This typical burnt-mound material definitely dates from the Norse period or later.

PRE-VIKING FEATURES

There are several pointers which hint at the possibility that some of the large manor farms had a pre-Norse origin, for instance, the *papa*-element in the name of the former earldom farm of Paplay (W. Thomson, personal communication). Pre-Norse features are of course well attested at Pool, Sanday (Hunter, this volume). The presence of a flourishing early farm, perhaps even pre-Norse, has been hinted at by the palynological evidence from the pit at Tuquoy (above); and by the evidence of burning in the locality recovered from microscopic charcoal in the basal silt in the pit.

In section segments E–F, a flagged passageway, 0.6 m wide and bordered by single-faced walls of coursed slabs, protruded 2.3 m in front of the section face. It lay 0.6 m below the floor of the putative smithy building (above) and was infilled with windblown sand. A massive upright slab, 1.2 m long and at least 0.85 m high, was butted against its W face. This slab, together with several large stone blocks found nearby, indicate that the passage leads into an earlier structure of unknown date, function and morphology, which, again, survives behind the section face. The glimpse of the structure currently available suggests that, architecturally, the feature is unlikely to be Viking in origin.

CONCLUSION

Morris, in his survey of Viking Orkney (1985) has urged that an interdisciplinary approach be taken to sites of the protohistorical period. At Tuquoy, the specific issue of the relationship of Crosskirk to the settlement, against the background of the historical, documentary and placename evidence, may offer a platform, or type-site, from which to explore farm and church associations, and the secular and ecclesiastical organisation of Norse and Medieval Orkney. Given the scarcity of archaeologically tangible, Medieval settlement in Orkney, the Tuquoy site takes on more significance than it may, perhaps, warrant in the fullness of time. The emphasis here must be on the examination of the processes of 'Scottification', as revealed by the structural, artefactual and ecofactual assemblages, viewed against all aspects of the historical backgound, but particularly the apparent political *floruit* of the 12th century. The pottery assemblage so far recovered is an especially encouraging indicator of the site's potential in this respect, with locally made pottery found alongside a rich collection of imported wares.

The apparent high status of several of the few excavated Norse sites in Orkney (i.e. Skaill, Deerness; Westness, Rousay; Birsay and Orphir, Mainland) could be seen as disadvantageous in that they are, perhaps, less representative of Viking settlement as a whole. However, the early Viking farm at Tuquoy may be fairly typical of a primary Viking settlement; and typicality in Viking Orkney may mean larger farms, or an agglomeration of farmsteads, than the simple farmstead excavated, for instance, at Underhoull, Unst, Shetland (Small 1966). Equally, in the late Norse and Medieval period, the high status 'hall' lies adjacent to a building currently interpreted as a smithy. There is every reason to believe that ordinary domestic and farm buildings are present in the vicinity, even if their proximity to the 'hall' implies some measure of patronage or political protection.

The wealth of the early Viking palaeoenvironmental evidence so far recovered is of particular importance given the dearth of waterlogged sites in Orkney and the consequent inadequacies of our understanding of the economic and environmental basis of these settlements. Tuquoy may allow us to move beyond a body of data biased by rich faunal and molluscan assemblages, and to embrace an interpretation informed by a fuller range of materials.

The emphasis of the 1988 assessment was on ascertaining the formation processes of the deposits at Tuquoy, particularly the midden-site deposits. Any further work will have to be keyed into work being undertaken in Orkney and Norway on the phenomenon of sites known as farm mounds (Bertelsen 1979). Here, it must be asked why Tuquoy is not a farm mound in the strict sense. It may be that the farm mound element of the settlement was in an area now eroded away; or that similar formation processes are represented but less intensively; or that they began much later than on sites such as Pool, Sanday (Hunter, this volume) and that the resulting accumulations are thus less extensive.

The question of whether this likely *bær* farm had a pre-Norse origin can only be addressed through excavation and, should this prove possible, there may be another opportunity to examine the interface between the Norse colonisers and their predecessors, a matter which continues to provoke considerable debate (Morris 1985, 216–17).

Complete excavation of the Tuquoy settlement would be prohibitively expensive and is probably unnecessary. The programmes of trial work and assessment so far undertaken can inform future selections of excavation areas, amongst which the likely foci of the early Norse and Medieval sites would be paramount. Already, the status and potential of the site have been established; now detailed strategies have to be formulated to ensure that any future excavations are directed towards those questions which Tuquoy seems particularly well suited to answer. In the longer term, the intention must be that a substantial, structured sample of the whole site be examined. This then is the challenge for the future. Meanwhile, the sea continues to encroach.

ACKNOWLEDGEMENTS

I am greatly indebted to Mr Tom Pottinger and his family of Tuquoy farm, for all the help they have given over the years; to the people of Westray for their kind welcome; and to individual islanders too numerous to mention for assistance and co-operation in many ways. The success of the project has relied on the hard work and skills of many people, excavators, colleagues and specialists, to all of whom I extend my thanks. This paper, in particular, has benefited from the contributions of Dr Anne Crone, Dr Christopher Lowe, Dr Jon Sadler and Dr Richard Tipping; and the illustrations were drawn by Christina Unwin. I am grateful to all those friends and colleagues who have discussed the site with me on many occasions over the years, but especially John Barber, Dr Barbara Crawford, Norman Emery, Dr Raymond Lamb and Professor Christopher Morris. The project is funded by the Scottish Development Department, Historic Buildings and Monuments (now Historic Scotland).

REFERENCES

Ahrens, Claus (ed.) 1981. *Frühe Holzkirchen im Nördlichen Europa*, Hamburg.
Bertelsen, Reidar 1979. 'Farm Mounds in North Norway. A Review of Recent Research', *Norwegian Archaeological Review* 12, 48–56.
Brøgger, Anton Wilhelm 1929. *Ancient Emigrants: A History of the Norse Settlements of Scotland*, Oxford.
Cant, Ronald Gordon 1972. 'The Church in Orkney and Shetland and its relations with Norway and Scotland in the Middle Ages', *Northern Studies* 1, 1–18.
Cant, Ronald Gordon 1984. 'Settlement, Society and Church Organisation in the Northern Isles', in *The Northern and Western Isles in the Viking World*, eds Fenton, A. & Pálsson, H., Edinburgh, pp. 169–79.
Clouston, Joseph Storer 1914. *Records of the Earldom of Orkney 1299–1614*. Scottish Historical Society Series 2, no. 7.
Clouston, Joseph Storer 1918. 'The Old Chapels of Orkney', *Scottish Historical Review* XV, 58, 89–105 and *Scottish Historical Review* XV, 59, 223–40.
Clouston, Joseph Storer (ed.) 1927a. *The Orkney Parishes*, Kirkwall.
Clouston, Joseph Storer 1927b. 'The Orkney Bus', *POAS*, V, 41–9.
Clouston, Joseph Storer 1931. *Early Norse Castles*, Kirkwall.

Clouston, Joseph Storer 1932a. *A History of Orkney*, Kirkwall.

Clouston, Joseph Storer 1932b. 'Tammaskirk in Rendall', *POAS*, X, 9–16.

Cruden, Stewart 1960. *The Scottish Castle*, Edinburgh.

Darling, Frank Fraser 1945. *Crofting Agriculture*, Edinburgh.

Dasent, George Webbe 1894. *The Saga of Hacon*, London.

Dickins, Bruce 1930. 'The Runic Inscriptions of Maeshowe', *POAS*, VIII, 27–30.

Dietrichson, Lorentz & Meyer, Johan 1906. *Monumenta Orcadica*, Christiania.

Diklev, Torben 1981. 'Ilska og Øska', *Mondul* 1, 14–25.

Donaldson, Alison 1986a. 'Charcoal Remains', in *Rescue Excavations on the Brough of Birsay 1974–82*, ed. Hunter, J. R., Society of Antiquaries of Scotland Monograph Series 4, Edinburgh.

Donaldson, Alison 1986b. 'Wood and Charcoal', in 'The Chapel and Enclosure on the Brough of Deerness', Morris, C. & Emery, N., *Proc. Soc. Antiq. Scot.* 116, 349.

Fenton, Alexander 1978. *The Northern Isles: Orkney and Shetland*, Edinburgh.

Hall, Richard *et al.* 1983. *Environment and Living Conditions at Two Anglo-Scandinavian Sites*, The Archaeology of York Series 14, York.

Johnston, Alfred W. 1903. 'Notes on the Earl's Bu at Orphir, Orkney, called Orfjara in the Sagas, and on the Remains of the Round Church there', *Proc. Soc. Antiq. Scot.* 37, 16–31.

Krogh, Knud J. 1975. 'Seks Kirkjur heima á Sandi', *Mondul* 2, 21–54.

Krogh, Knud J. 1983. 'Gård og Kirke', *Hikuin* 9, 231–44, 287–8.

Lamb, Raymond G. 1981. 'The Hall of Haflidi', *The Orcadian*, 23 July.

Lamb, Raymond G. 1983. *The Archaeological Sites and Monuments of Papa Westray and Westray, Orkney*, Royal Commission on the Ancient and Historical Monuments of Scotland List 19, Edinburgh.

Liestøl, Aslak 1968. 'The Maeshowe Runes. Some New Interpretations', in *Fifth Viking Congress, Tórshavn, 1965*, ed. Niclasen, B., Tórshavn. pp. 55–61.

Lowe, Christopher Edmund 1987. *Early Ecclesiastical Sites in the Northern Isles and Isle of Man: An Archaeological Field Survey* (2 vols), Unpublished PhD thesis, University of Durham.

MacGibbon, David & Ross, Thomas 1887. *The Castellated and Domestic Architecture of Scotland*, Edinburgh.

MacGibbon, David & Ross, Thomas 1896. *The Ecclesiastical Architecture of Scotland*, Edinburgh.

Marwick, Hugh 1928. 'Kolbein Hruga's Castle, Wyre', *POAS*, 6, 9–11.

Marwick, Hugh 1952. *Orkney Farm Names*, Kirkwall.

McGavin, Neil A. 1982. 'Excavations in Kirkwall, 1978', *Proc. Soc. Antiq. Scot.* 112, 392–436.

Morris, Christopher D. 1983. 'Excavations Around the Bay of Birsay', in *Birsay: A Centre of Political and Ecclesiastical Power*, Orkney Heritage 2, Kirkwall, pp. 119–51.

Morris, Christopher D. 1985. 'Viking Orkney: A Survey', in *The Prehistory of Orkney BC 4000–1000 AD*, ed. Renfrew, C., Edinburgh, pp. 210–42.

Morris, Christopher D. & Emery, Norman 1986. 'The Chapel and Enclosure on the Brough of Deerness, Orkney', *Proc. Soc. Antiq. Scot.* 116, 301–74.

New Statistical Account of Scotland 1842. Edinburgh.

(Old) Statistical Account of Scotland: 1799 (1978) (see Sinclair 1791–9).

Owen, Olwyn Anne 1982. 'Rescue Project at Tuquoy, Westray, Orkney Islands,

1982', in *Universities of Durham and Newcastle upon Tyne Archaeological Reports for 1982*, Durham, pp. 45–50.

Owen, Olwyn Anne 1983. 'An Interim Report on the Second Season of the Archaeological Rescue Project at Tuquoy, Westray, Orkney', in *Universities of Durham and Newcastle upon Tyne Archaeological Reports for 1983*, Durham, pp. 49–53.

Owen, Olwyn Anne 1987. 'Interim Report on the Survey and Excavations undertaken at Kebister, Shetland', in *Central Excavation Unit and Ancient Monuments Laboratory Annual Report 1987*, Edinburgh, pp. 28–39.

Owen, Olwyn Anne 1988. 'Tuquoy, Orkney 1988: Further Assessment and Tapestry Excavation of the Norse and Medieval Site', in *Central Excavation Unit and Ancient Monuments Laboratory Annual Report 1988*, Edinburgh, pp. 5–8.

Owen, Olwyn Anne (*Forthcoming*). *Tuquoy, Orkney: A Large Norse and Medieval Farm-Settlement*.

Owen, Olwyn A. & McKinnell, John 1989. 'A Runic Inscription from Tuquoy, Westray, Orkney', *Medieval Archaeology* xxxiii, 53–9.

Owen, Olwyn A. & Smith, Brian 1989. 'Kebister, Shetland: An Armorial Stone and an Archdeacon's Teind Barn?', *Post-Medieval Archaeology* xxii, 1–20.

Peterkin, Alexander 1820. *Rentals of the Ancient Earldom and Bishoprick of Orkney*, Edinburgh.

Radford, Courtenay Arthur Ralegh 1962. 'Art and Architecture: Celtic and Norse', in *The Northern Isles*, ed. Wainwright, F. T., London, pp. 163–87.

Reynolds, Peter 1981. 'Deadstock and Livestock', in *Farming Practice in British Prehistory*, ed. Mercer, Roger J., Edinburgh, pp. 97–122.

Roussell, Aage 1944. 'Farms and Churches in the Medieval Norse Settlements of Greenland', *Meddelelser om Grønland* 89, 1, 1941–4.

Royal Commission on the Ancient and Historical Monuments of Scotland 1946. *Inventory of the Ancient Monuments of Orkney and Shetland* (3 vols), Edinburgh.

Royal Commission on the Ancient and Historical Monuments of Scotland 1971. *Argyll: an Inventory of Ancient Monuments, vol. 1 Kintyre*, Edinburgh.

Simpson, William Douglas 1961. *The Castle of Bergen and the Bishop's Palace at Kirkwall*, Aberdeen University Studies no. 142, Edinburgh.

Sinclair, John (ed.) 1791–9. *The (Old) Statistical Account of Scotland, 1791–1799. Vol. XIX: Orkney and Shetland*. (Facsimile Reprint with Introduction by Thomson, W. P. L. & Graham, J. J. 1978, Edinburgh.)

Small, Alan 1966. 'Excavations at Underhoull, Unst, Shetland', *Proc. Soc. Antiq. Scot.* 98, 225–48.

Small, Alan 1969. 'The Distribution of Settlement in Shetland and Faroe in Viking Times', *Saga-Book of the Viking Society* 17, 145–55.

Stummann Hansen, Steffen 1988. 'The Norse Landnam in the Faroe Islands in the Light of Recent Excavations at Toftanes, Leirvik', *Northern Studies* 25, 58–84.

Taylor, Alexander Burt 1938. *The Orkneyinga Saga: A New Translation with Introduction and Notes*, London.

Wainwright, Frederick Threlfall 1962. 'The Golden Age and After', in *The Northern Isles*, ed. Wainwright, F. T., Edinburgh, pp. 188–92.

19

SOME SETTLEMENT PATTERNS
IN MEDIEVAL ORKNEY

WILLIAM P. L. THOMSON

Although the *Orkneyinga saga* has a great deal to say about the deeds of the leading men of the 12th century, it tells us much less about their lands and estates. Inevitably these places do receive many passing mentions, but seldom more than that. Regretfully we have to admit that the saga is of limited value as a source of information on settlement and farming patterns, and other contemporary documentation is entirely lacking. However, Orkney is fortunate in having a splendid series of skat rentals, the earliest dating from 1492, but incorporating much that was older (Sinclair 1492; Peterkin 1820). This chapter attempts to bridge the gap between saga and rentals, and it looks at some of the larger units of settlement which can be reconstructed.

Using the rentals it is easy to identify certain very big blocks of land. Fig. 19.1 shows one such block in Egilsay and the district of Sourin in the adjacent island of Rousay, the most obvious clue to its underlying unity being that it was all bishopric property. This reflected the natural unity of the two sides of the sound, and provides a good illustration of how, until the building of roads, the sea united communities rather than divided them. As late as 1678 it was complained that Sourin people attended services in Egilsay, to the neglect of their proper church which lay seven miles away across the island and, despite claims that Sourin was 'annexed to Egilsay without any law', the Egilsay connection was allowed to continue when it was established that the link went back 'past memory of man' (Craven 1893, 76–7).

It is interesting to note that the vanished farm-name, Husabae, is associated with this block (Marwick 1947, 38, 71). I do not intend to discuss Steinnes's theory that, in the early Norse period, Orkney was divided into six equal districts each controlled from a *huseby*, a great administrative farm which served as a base for peripatetic earls (Steinnes 1959; Thomson 1987, 28–9). Despite doubts about anything so regular as 'a huseby-system', it is clear that large blocks of land were to be found in association with these names. Note the symmetry – there were 36 pennylands on each side of the Sound, 72 pennylands, or four ouncelands in total (Peterkin 1820, 68–9; *RMS*, v, no. 836). By the date of the rentals, all this

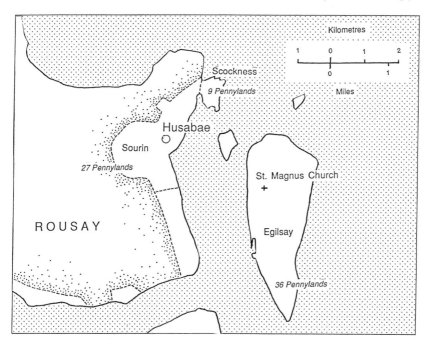

Figure 19.1: Egilsay and Sourin: a former 'Huseby'? This large block of territory, associated with Bishop William the Old, contained a *huseby*-name, and represents an estate detached from the earldom as an early endowment of the Bishopric of Orkney.

belonged to the Bishop of Orkney. The earl received no payment whatsoever, not even skat, and so it appears that the whole area represented a gift to the church by the king or one of the earls, since no one else had a right to give away taxation, and indeed it is unlikely that any lesser person would have had such a block of land at his disposal (Marwick 1947, 40–1). There is a distinct impression that, after the earls acquired a settled residence, one of their older *huseby*-properties had been used to endow the new bishopric.

This rental evidence links readily with what the *Orkneyinga saga* tells us about Bishop William the Old and his association with Egilsay. On three occasions he was recorded as residing in Egilsay, and twice the season was Yule – a time to be at home (Taylor 1938, 244, 258 & 261). The bishop's cathedral was at Christchurch in Birsay, but perhaps Egilsay was 'home'. Such were his links with Egilsay that it seems probable that the island was already bishopric property at the time of St Magnus's martyrdom and, for that reason, was intended to have been a neutral place between rival earls. If, as is supposed, Bishop William owed his appointment to King Magnus Barelegs (Crawford 1983, 108–9), perhaps he also received his lands from the king. We know that King Magnus, after he had dispossessed the joint earls, Paul and Erlend, detached the manor farm of Paplay from their forfeited earldom in order to provide a suitable dowry for the bride of Kol Kalisson (Taylor 1938, 203 & 204). What could be more natural than that he should take another ex-earldom property to provide for his new bishop?

Although the boundaries of the Egilsay–Sourin block can be mapped, little can be said about its internal organisation. Later Sourin was divided into a series of tenant farms or *dells* of very even three-pennyland size (Marwick 1947, 37–8). To see the structure of an estate it is better to go to Westray to look at the lands of Kugi of Rapness.

The *Orkneyinga saga* tells us quite a lot about Kugi, although he was not the owner of Rapness which was *bordland*, part of the 'table-lands' of the earls (Clouston 1924, 61–2; Winchester 1986, 129–39). From time to time the earls themselves were resident (Taylor 1938, 246 & 327), for example during rent-collecting circuits, and so, although not dignified by a *huseby*-name, perhaps Rapness performed the same function. Kugi was 'a wise man and wealthy' (Taylor 1938, 218), and he was one of Earl Paul's most important supporters. When Rognvald Kolsson invaded Westray *c.* 1136, Kugi was involved in a secret midnight plot and was put in fetters. However, Earl Rognvald apparently saw the comical side of the incident and, in his inimitable fashion, he marked the occasion with some light-hearted verses (Taylor 1938, 252–3).

The earliest rental reveals that in 1492 Rapness was occupied by a person of similar standing to Kugi. The Bu (*Bu*=big farm) was still bordland, and it was held by Lord Henry Sinclair's brother, Sir William Sinclair of Warsetter who, when Henry was absent at the Scottish court, acted as his manager. Sir William was the most important person in Orkney, and Rapness was only one of several properties which he held (Saint-Clair 1898, 138).

The great extent of the Rapness bordland, some five miles from north to south, is shown in Fig. 19.2 – no wonder the saga described Kugi as 'wealthy'. The area around the Bu was known as the Wasbister Bordland and it contained some 22 little holdings which formed a semi-circle of satellites (Sinclair 1492, 63–5; Peterkin 1820, 80–4). In Orkney these satellites of a big farm were known as *umbesetts* (Clouston 1927a, 42–3). Then, farther to the north and separated from the Bu by land only later brought into cultivation, was the Swartmeil Bordland with a further 9 holdings of slightly superior status. By the time of Sir William Sinclair and the rental of 1492 nearly all of these places in both bordlands were rented to small tenants as distinct holdings, but it is easy to see the former pattern of a very traditional manor with its division between *desmene* or *réserve* and the part allocated to individual holdings (van Bath 1963, 40–53). Perhaps the pattern also reflects social distinctions between a low status or servile labour force round the Bu, and people more remote from the farm who, although still decidedly subservient, had a more independent status. It was a pattern which would still have been recognisable to 18th and 19th century Orcadians. Big farms, although never so large as their medieval predecessors, continued to be surrounded by a superabundance of cottars, paid with scraps of land rather

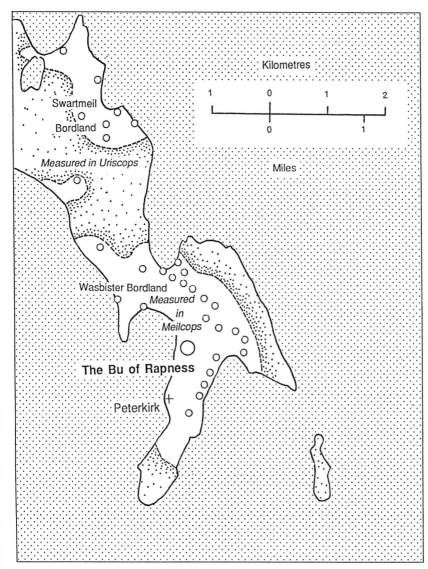

Figure 19.2: The Bu of Rapness. This huge manor farm was part of the Earl of Orkney's *bordlands*. It was surrounded by low status satellites in the immediate vicinity of the bu (the Wasbister bordland), and slightly larger and rather more independent places at a greater distance from the farm (the Swartmeil bordland).

than money in return for 'never-ending and ill-defined personal services' (*NSA* Cross & Burness, 94). These people in the apt Orkney phrase were *on ca'* (on call) whenever their services were needed, and they were still liable to render the kind of miscellaneous payments and services which would not have been out of place 1,000 years earlier (Thomson 1981, 40).

Farms in the Wasbister bordland were measured in *meilcops* and those in the Swartmeil bordland in *uriscops*. Both of these tiny units were one-sixth of a pennyland, the difference being the level of the rent. The term 'meilcop' derives from the Orkney weight, the *meil* (*c.* 72.5 kg.) and ON *kaup*, meaning 'a purchase or bargain' (Marwick 1952, 203–4). But a meilcop did not pay one meil – rather it paid 'in meils'. The meil was used to weigh grain, but not other commodities such as butter. To be allowed to pay 'in meils', that is entirely in grain rather than partly in butter, was always regarded as a valuable concession (Sinclair 1492, 60; Thomson 1987, 119–20). The uriscop (literally 'ounce-agreement') can be regarded as a special kind of meilcop, originally paying grain to the value of 20 skat-pennies. Since an ounce was one-eighth of a mark weight, it was possible to think of this payment as 'an ounce of money', 20 pennies being one-eighth of the 160 penny mark of money. By the date of the 15th-century rentals, the idea that money could be related to weight in this manner was an archaic concept, suggesting that the origin of the uriscops ought to be sought at a somewhat earlier date.

But what did the payment cover? That ought to be a rhetorical question since bordland, almost by definition, was supposed to be skat-free, and so the payment could only be rent. The authors of the rentals were not so sure. The 1492 rental noted that the whole bordland paid no skat 'the cause we watt not' (Sinclair 1492, 63 & 65). An investigation was carried out *c.* 1497, evidence was taken that skat was indeed due and the amount was recorded, but the tenants apparently successfully resisted its imposition (Peterkin 1820, 84). Then, nearly a century later in the rental of 1595, skat suddenly re-appeared on both bordlands although, amazingly, the addition of skat did not increase the total amount which tenants had to pay (Peterkin 1820, 71–3). The payment had simply been apportioned in somewhat rough-and-ready fashion partly to skat and partly to rent. It looks as if it had been decided that meilcops and uriscops had all along included skat as well as rent. But why, we might well ask, were tenants of supposedly skat-free bordland expected to pay skat?

Before trying to answer that question we should note that Rapness was far from unique – the same doubts about whether skat ought to be paid were to be found round nearly all the earldom farms. I will quote a few examples. The first is from the Overtoun in Burray (Peterkin 1820, 18), a community adjacent to the Bu of Burray and very similar to the Westray bordlands. Here the 1500 rental recorded that no skat was paid 'quia nescio' (I do not know why). In South Ronaldsay it was likewise noted that Brough and Tarland 'payis nane, we wait nocht quhy' (pays none, we do not know why), and the same comment was made with reference to Burwick (Peterkin 1820, 24; Sinclair 1492, 17). Again at Lyking it was recorded that skat was never paid 'quare nescio' – I do not know the reason (Sinclair 1492, 55). Whether expressed in good Scots or bad Latin, the non-payment of skat was regarded as a bit of a mystery.

The explanation seems to relate to a change in the use of the bordland. Its skat-free status was obviously a concession as long as the Earl of Orkney paid skat to the Norwegian king. It meant that the earl did not have to pay tax on his main properties. But earls of Orkney seldom paid skat to Norway, and latterly the right to collect skat was, by implication, granted to them at their installation. So when bordland was let to tenants its skat-free status became a positive disadvantage. Bordland had been intended to exempt the earl from paying tax, but it now exempted other people from paying tax to him – a complete reversal. Clearly it was potentially a source of landlord–tenant conflict; tenants of bordland were bound to maintain that their land had always been skat-free; on the other hand, the earl could argue that they were getting their land cheap and ought to pay the same rates as other people.

The unusual Westray land-units, the meilcops and the uriscops, must be seen in this light. They seem to date from the break-up of desmene farming and the letting of these satellite places as independent tenancies. The purpose was to charge rents which were much higher than traditional rates to compensate for the absence of skat. This payment could be viewed in either of two ways: a single grain payment from bordland was always likely to be regarded as rent, but the alternative view – and this is the view that prevailed – was that the reason payment was so high was because it 'contained' an element for skat as well as for rent.

A number of other places exhibit the same features as we have found at Rapness. For example, the former Earl's Bu at Orphir which figures so prominently in the *Orkneyinga saga* was, by the 15th century, like Rapness, a nine-pennyland farm and, although still large, it also was merely a shrunken remnant of its medieval precedessor. It too was surrounded by the same pattern of little tenanted farms (Sinclair 1492, 23–5; Peterkin 1820, 41–4; Johnston 1903, 174–214). These farms lay on bordland, either explicitly described as such or identifiable by its tax-free status, extending over a three-mile coastline throughout the townships of Orphir, Houton and Petertown. Once again the earl's right to skat was disputed, and once again the plaintive refrain of the tax-gatherer was to be heard – 'And quhy it is unpayit I know not' (Sinclair 1492, 24). Again, apparently to compensate for the absence of skat, rents were quite abnormally high, even higher than at Rapness. At both Orphir and Rapness it seems that desmene formed a fairly compact block centred on the principal residence, little inter-mingled with allotted lands. At both places satellite communities were differentiated – low status communities in the vicinity of the Bu and more independent people, although still of a lowly status, at a greater distance from the centre. It is tempting to speculate that this pattern reflects the one-time existence of free and servile populations.

The question remains – how common were these large manor farms? At least in the North Isles they seem to have been so common that they might be regarded as the norm. There was little room for anything else. Kugi of Rapness was not the only chieftain in Westray. The saga records the presence of two other important people, Helgi and Thorkel Flettir (Taylor 1938, 218 & 252). Helgi's territory included the *hǫfn*, the present Pierowall, and his estate was probably the forerunner of a huge block of bishopric territory. At the Reformation Bishop Adam Bothwell feued this property to Gilbert Balfour and on it Balfour built his immensely strong refuge of Noltland Castle (*RMS*, iv, no. 1668). The Orkney historian, Storer Clouston, was reluctant to locate the third chieftain, Thorkel Flettir, in Westray, and tried to remove him to Shapinsay on the dubious grounds that 'three chiefs in Westray are too many' (Clouston 1927b, 333n). Yet there is no real reason to doubt the saga and, by a process of elimination, Thorkel must be located in the west of the island where his family has been linked with the high-status late Norse site at Tuquoy and Cross Kirk (Lamb, 1981; RCAHMS 1983, 33 & 37). These sites are described in Olwyn Owen's paper elsewhere in this volume, and the whole of the surrounding area exhibits a Tuquoy-orientated pattern of settlement (Thomson, 1990, 1–16).

Sanday was similarly dominated by large farms. The rental of 1595 records no less than six bordland *bu*s, the Bu of Tofts, the Bu of Walls, the Bu of Lopness, the Bu of Tresness, the Bu of Brough and the Bu of Hacksness. All of them were 18 pennylands and none of them paid skate (Peterkin 1820, 77, 79 & 81). The three first-mentioned places lie close together in the extreme east of the island, and look like the result of the division of a single block of bordland. Hacksness was also the remains of a much bigger 72 pennyland block centred on Stove (Marwick 1952, 13–14 & 14–16). This huge farm was bordland, but it was also *kingsland*, and so it is possible that it was earldom property which passed into the hands of the King of Norway as a result of the 1194 forfeitures which followed the defeat of Earl Harald Maddadsson's ill-advised rebellion (Thomson 1987, 73–4). Two further very big, but somewhat shadowy units have been identified by a combination of rental and placename evidence in the districts of Bea and Overbister (Marwick 1952, 8, 11; Thomson 1987, 27–8). We cannot be sure that they were contemporaneous with the bordland *bu*s, but the picture begins to emerge of an island, some 13 miles in length, containing about six farms of manor-proportions. As in Westray they dominated the agrarian and social structure of the community in a way which makes it clear that the multiple estate rather than the family farm was the basic unit of settlement.

Finally, what can we say about dates? By the date of the earliest rentals (1492) the bordland *bu*s were already shrunken in size, and much of the former desmene was let to small tenants. From evidence elsewhere in Europe we might expect desmene farming to have reached its peak in the 11th and 12th centuries, but to have been in decline from about 1300 onwards, with the second half of the 14th century being the main period for dividing it into tenancies (Postles 1986; Dodgshon 1987, 185). Insular Orkney was not immune from the workings of wider economic forces – on the contrary its peripheral location resulted in change sometimes being experienced in acute form – so the break-up of Orkney desmene may well have followed the usual European chronology. The one pointer that this was indeed the case comes from Papa Stour, Shetland, where, at Easter 1299, an angry woman named Ragnhild appeared in the *stofa* of Duke Hakon Magnusson's farm to denounce the injustice of a disputed payment (Crawford 1985, 128–9). Although there is great difficulty in understanding the exact nature of Ragnhild's complaint, it had two features in common with the situation I have been describing in Orkney: first, there was a dispute about payments in the immediate vicinity of a prestigious farm and, second, the dispute somehow arose from the emergence of satellite places as independent farms in their own right.

In looking for the origins of these large blocks of land, Marwick suggested that they resulted from a series of 'landtakes' on the Icelandic model (Marwick 1947, 18–19). However, the Norse settlement in Orkney must have been a different process from the colonisation of empty Iceland. It has been argued that some of these blocks, like Bea in Sanday, may have a pre-Norse origin, and Paplay may be another example. This huge farm was former earldom bordland, yet it incorporates a *papa*-name and, like other *papa*-names, it shows that the clergy of the pre-Norse church had an eye for good land and were monastic as well as eremitic (Lamb, this vol.). Perhaps the earldom farm was a direct successor of a Pictish monastic estate. And to return to Rapness, we find that the Bu was adjacent to one of the Peterkirk sites which Raymond Lamb suggests were existing power-centres used for a network of 8th century head-churches (Lamb, this vol.). At Peterkirk, Rapness, 'a more than usually considerable chapel occupies the site perhaps of a broch' (RCAHMS, 38). Although hardly conclusive proof, these examples suggest that some manor farms were Pictish estates, taken over in their entirety and re-named by the Norse.

REFERENCES

Clouston, J. Storer 1927a. 'The Orkney "Bus"', *Proc. Ork. Ant. Soc.* 5, 1926–7, 41–9.
Clouston, J. Storer 1927b. *The Orkney Parishes*, Kirkwall.
Craven, J. B. 1893. *History of the Church in Orkney 1662–1688*, Kirkwall.
Crawford, Barbara E. 1983. 'Birsay and the Early Earls and Bishops of Orkney', *Orkney Heritage* 2, Kirkwall, 97–118.
Crawford, Barbara E. 1985. 'The Biggins, Papa Stour', in *Shetland Archaeology*, ed. Smith, Brian, Lerwick, 128–58.
Dodgshon, Robert 1987. *The European Past*, London.
Johnston, Alfred. W. 1903. 'The Round Church of Orphir', *Saga-Book* 3, Viking Society, 1901–3, 174–214.
Lamb, Raymond G. 1981. 'The Hall of Haflidi', *The Orcadian*, 23 July.
Marwick, Hugh 1947. *The Place-Names of Rousay*, Kirkwall.
Marwick, Hugh 1952. *Orkney Farm-Names*, Kirkwall.
NSA = *Statistical Account of Scotland; Orkney Islands* 1842. Edinburgh and London.
Peterkin, Alexander 1820. *Rentals of the Ancient Earldom and Bishopric of Orkney*, Edinburgh.

Postles, D. 1986. 'The Perception of Profit before the Leasing of Desmene', *Agricultural History Review*, 34, 1, 12–28.

RCAHMS=Lamb, Raymond G. 1983. *The Archaeological Sites and Monuments of Papa Westray and Westray*, Royal Commission on the Ancient and Historical Monuments of Scotland, Edinburgh.

RMS=Thomson, J. M. 1984. *The Register of the Great Seal of Scotland*, Edinburgh, London and Melbourne.

Saint-Clair, Roland 1898. *The Saint-Clairs of the Isles*, Auckland.

Sinclair, Lord Henry 1492. Mss rental (extant only as copy). Orkney Archives, D2/7.

Steinnes, Asgaut 1959. 'The Huseby System in Orkney', *Scottish Historical Review*, 38, 36–46.

Taylor, A. B. 1938. *The Orkneyinga saga*, Edinburgh and London.

Thomson, William P. L. 1981. *The Little General and the Rousay Crofters*, Edinburgh.

Thomson, William P. L. 1987. *History of Orkney*, Edinburgh.

Thomson, William P. L. 1990. 'Settlement Patterns at Tuquoy, Westray, Orkney', *Northern Studies*, 26, 1–16.

Van Bath, B. H. Slicher. 1963. *The Agrarian History of Western Europe*, London.

Winchester, Angus J. L. 1986. 'The Distribution and Significance of Bordland in Medieval Britain', *Agricultural History Review*, 34, 2, 129–39.

20

THE INTERPRETATION OF THE
RUNIC INSCRIPTIONS OF MAESHOWE

MICHAEL P. BARNES

In this chapter I review critically attempts to interpret the sense of the Maeshowe inscriptions. I touch only incidentally on their runological and linguistic interpretation since I shall be treating these aspects separately elsewhere (cf. Barnes 1989 on the orthography).

Maeshowe was opened in July 1861 by an amateur archaeologist, James Farrer, MP, in company with a number of prominent people gathered together for the occasion, and assisted by a group of local workmen. Among those at the excavation was the Orkneyman, George Petrie, a Corresponding Member of the Society of Antiquaries of Scotland.

The first notice of the discovery of runic inscriptions in Maeshowe appeared in *The Orkney Herald* on Tuesday, 16 July. It was anonymous, like the brief article about the chamber and its contents published in *The Orcadian* on the following Saturday. Both mention the inscriptions in general terms, and the *Orcadian* writer quotes a report that 'two female mummies had been discoveried [*sic*], and also the skeleton of a gentleman ten feet long'. With more than a hint of scepticism, however, the writer adds: 'no one, so far as I have heard, has been favoured with a sight of the lady mummies or the long gentleman.' The same issue of *The Orcadian* contains a longer article by George Petrie in which he furnishes a detailed description of Maeshowe and suggests that it pre-dates considerably the arrival of the Norsemen in Orkney (Petrie 1861a). An expanded version of this report appeared later in *The Archaeological Journal* (Petrie 1861b).

The very first attempt to interpret any of the Maeshowe inscriptions was by C. C. Rafn in a letter to Petrie published in Danish in *Berlingske Tidende*, 11 September 1861 and in English in *The Orcadian*, 14 September 1861. A much fuller account appeared three months later in the Norwegian *Illustreret Nyhedsblad* 48–9, this time by P. A. Munch. His interpretations are sober and shrewd, and he offers tolerably accurate versions of all the inscriptions except VII, XXII and XXIV (for working texts see the appendix). In VII and XXIV he found the runes too unclear to hazard an interpretation, while XXII was carved with 'nogle ganske egne, sammensatte Runer, der nu neppe tilfredsstillende kunne forklares, om de overhoved skulle forestille Bogstaver' 'some strange, composite runes, which can now scarcely be satisfactorily explained – if indeed they are meant to be letters at all' (Munch 1876, 527). The cryptic runes of VIII and XVIII, variously called palm, bough, tree or twig-runes, Munch also declares to be uninterpretable.

Rafn and Munch's swift response to the challenge of the Maeshowe inscriptions gained them no praise or gratitude. On the contrary, it unleashed a torrent of criticism and abuse. To recount in full this obscure but entertaining story would lead too far from the main subject matter of the present paper (see Barnes 1992). Briefly, it was assumed by some that Rafn and Munch were 'jumping the gun' and trying to rob Farrer of the honour and fame due to him as the discoverer of the inscriptions.

Farrer himself did not apparently share this view, but he seems nevertheless to have been annoyed at the speed with which Rafn and Munch went into print because he had intended all the scholars to whom he had sent copies of the inscriptions to produce readings and interpretations independently of one another. His aim was to publish all or some of these so that the scholarly world might have a chance to compare them. In the event he received manuscripts from Rafn, Munch and George Stephens, but apparently from no one else. It was these manuscripts which formed the basis of his book *Notice of Runic Inscriptions Discovered during Recent Excavations in the Orkneys* (Farrer 1862) – still the nearest thing we have to a full edition of the Maeshowe inscriptions.

It is clear from a perusal of the texts in Farrer's edition that Rafn and Munch were largely on the right track (Munch's readings and interpretations differ little from those he published in *Illustreret Nyhedsblad*). Stephens, on the other hand, frequently goes off the rails, as those who are familiar with his runic studies would expect. Inscriptions I and II furnish good examples of the three men's work, though they perhaps make Stephens appear more accurate than is in general the case (Farrer 1862, 25–6).

I   Rafn: THAT IR VIKINGR . . . A KOM UT IRHIRTIL.
                 This is a Viking . . . come out is hereto.
    Munch: THATIR VIKINKR . . . KOMUTIRHIRTIL.
                 That which the Wicing . . . came outerly here to.
    Stephens: THATIR VIKINKR . . . A, KOM, VTIR, HIR, TIL.
                 Thatir the Viking, came here to weary – (perhaps from the sea, or from battle.)

II Rafn: THOLFR KOLBEINSSONR REIST RUNAR THESSAR HATT.
                 Tholf Kolbeinsson carved these Runes on High.
    Munch: THOLFR KOLBEINSSONR RAEIST RUNAR THESA.
                 Tholf Colbanesson engraved these Runes.
    Stephens: MOLFR KOLBAINSSONR RAEIST RUNA THESA GHAUT.
                 Molf Kolbainsson carved these Runes to Gaut.

If we ignore slight oddities in the texts of the inscriptions, for which the three scholars may not be entirely responsible, and the strange English, which is not necessarily Rafn and Munch's own, it is clear that the two Scandinavians had a much clearer perception of what were likely to be the individual words in the inscriptions than Stephens. Stephens seems unaware of some of the basic rules of Norse phonology as well as of certain orthographic principles of runic writing, and this allows him to assume that word-initial ✱, for example, can represent /g/ (✱⌁⋔=*Ghaut*) or that ⋔ may stand for [ð] ('weary' apparently renders *mvtir*, which has thus been taken as a way of writing *móð(i)r*, cf. *lutin*=*loðin* in VIII). Nevertheless, Rafn and Munch have clearly not got it completely right either, and Stephens is the only one of the three to provide the proper interpretation of the cryptic runes in VIII and XVIII.

Of particular interest is Farrer's introduction to the readings and translations, which he says is based on information provided by 'the learned Professors' (1862, 21). From this introduction it is clear that all three scholars took what they supposed to be the content of the inscriptions at face value. On the basis of a partial misreading of the beginning of XIX–XX Rafn and Munch date the mound within the period of Norse settlement. Rafn suggests it was raised as a sorcery hall for a female magician called 'Lodbrok' and Munch that it was the burial place of a woman of the same name. Stephens considers the beginning of XIX–XX to be evidence that Maeshowe was used by the sons of 'Lodbrok' 'as a fortress and place of retreat' (Farrer 1862, 21). Although some of the more informative inscriptions are dated to the middle of the 12th century, and Munch seems to have thought they were all, or virtually all, from that period, Farrer's introduction claims that a number are considerably older. Stephens' speculations about the presence of the sons of Loðbrók in Maeshowe (he even suggests that parts of XIX–XX may have been carved by some of them) and his conviction that the final rune in IX is the ᛉ of the older alphabet (cf. his reading *Haelghis Raeisto*) are doubtless partly responsible for this, but Farrer also points to the worn state of some of the inscriptions.

The implausibility of many of Stephens' readings and interpretations pales into insignificance compared with what followed. The 1860s saw the publication of a large number of articles on Maeshowe and its inscriptions, as well as a further book, and although some of these contributions are sober and scholarly, three in particular (Barclay 1863; Mitchell 1863; Carr 1868) show such ignorance of runic writing and of Old Norse that one is astonished the authors were prepared to go into print and risk the ridicule they justly deserve. Nor can one easily understand the neglect of editorial duty which allowed two of these pieces a place in archaeological publications of repute. Barclay, Mitchell and Carr's method, if method is the word, consists in associating ill-read sequences of runes in the inscriptions with words or alleged words, mainly from Scandinavian languages but sometimes from Anglo-Saxon and further afield, and in attempting to string together into sentences the words they thus claim to recognise, with complete disregard for grammar, linguistic integrity or history. Their readings and translations of VIII show the results that such an approach can achieve (Barclay 1863, 11; Mitchell 1863, 49; Carr 1868, 74).

Barclay: INGIBJORG HIN FAGRA, AKKIA MORKA KONA, HEFIR FARIT: LYTR INGIR, MIKIL OFLATI, ÆRLIGR.
Ingiborga, pulchra dicta, Akki Morka (fusci) uxor, mortua est: vitiis expers, gestu decora, ortu honesta.
Ingiborg the fair, the wife of Akki the dark, is gone: a lady of faultless character, of graceful manners, and of honourable descent.

Mitchell: INGEBIORG HIN FÆGRA AHGIA.
MOERHK KOGA HÆFER FARET LURIN HIR MIHKIL OFLATE.
Ingeborg den smukke i Far,
Seilede i det mörke Kogende Hav,
Luren her i stort Haab.
Ingebiorg the fair in distress.
(After) sailing on the dark raging waves,
(We are) lurking here in great hope.
The six tree Runes form the word *Arrier*, or the time-roll, and represent the year A.D. 1063.

Carr: INGEBORG HIN FAHRI ÆHKIA.
MORHK KONA HAFER GARIT LUTRIN HER MIHKIL OFLATE.
Ingeborga pulcra vidua,
Tenebrarum Domina hanc demissè se gerentem magnificam auguravit futuram.
Ingeborg the fair widowe;
The Mirk-Quene hath here decreed the depressed to become greatly exalted.

Carr offers four further readings and translations, all equally improbable (1868, 74–6). The date 1063 given by Mitchell is arrived at by assuming that the cryptic runes have the golden number values of the runes they represent. Thus $a = 10$, r, confused with the sixteenth rune, so-called palatal R or y, $= 16$, $r = 5$, $i = 9$, $3:6$, which seems to be taken as *árlaug*, $= 17$, $r = 16$. By ignoring the first rune, we obtain a total of 63; if we then place the 10 in front of it, we arrive at 1063. Mitchell claims that the first rune has a value of 1,000, but I think he must have reckoned more or less along the lines I suggest here (cf. 1863, 67–8). With the inscription thus firmly anchored in the 1060s, Ingebiorg is identified as the wife of Earl Þorfinnr (1863, 59). Some may feel that this procedure foreshadows ominously the work of Alf Mongé and O. G. Landsverk (e.g. 1967).

Before doing these three scholars the kindness of returning them to the obscurity in which they have languished for the last 100 years, I cannot forbear to mention Carr's treatment of the beginning of XIX–XX. His reading and English translation are:

SIA HOUHR VAR FYRLATHIN HAELLR LOTHBROKAR SYN(D)AR HÆN(D)AR
The how was a forsaken vault (or cavity) of shag-behosed swimming harpooners

From his understanding of this alleged sentence he draws the conclusion that the Norse carver was trying to spread information about earlier inhabitants of Orkney: 'And they [the words] point to a race of kilted harpooners, who, leaving their boats on approaching the marine animals, swam forward to inflict the deadly harpoon-cast' (Carr 1868, 79–80).

Obviously, not all or even most of the books, monographs and articles that touch on the Maeshowe inscriptions can be mentioned here. A full, but by no means complete, bibliography can be found in Marquardt 1961. Having surveyed the beginnings of Maeshowe scholarship, I want in the following to concentrate on what appear to me the most important contributions to the subject – those works which have altered or sought to alter our conception of individual inscriptions or the inscriptions as a whole.

The remainder of the 19th century saw little fresh thinking about Maeshowe and its runes. A few new ideas did emerge, but not as a result of major studies of some or all of the inscriptions. They come in the form of incidental remarks in general descriptions of the site or as the by-product of research into other topics. Several writers express the view that many or all of the inscriptions are graffiti – mere idle scribbles – although they seem happy enough on occasion to accept at face value what the inscriptions say. One such writer, for example, connects the stories of missing treasure with the Skaill Bay hoard (Fergusson 1872, 252–3). Various attempts are also made to identify the names in the inscriptions with characters known from *Orkneyinga saga* and other sources. Urging strongly the view that the inscriptions are mere graffiti carved by Earl Rǫgnvaldr Kali's crusaders (Finnbogi Guðmundsson 1965, 194, 204–39), Sir George Dasent casts doubt on such attempts at identification (1894, xxxvi–vii):

There has always been a tendency to make more of runic inscriptions than they deserve. They were as often as not the production of whim or caprice, and no more meant to be serious than the scrawlings of modern tourists after their own names on national monuments. Thus when we read in one of these inscriptions 'Ingigerð is the loveliest woman,' this may mean earl Rognvald's only child Ingigerð; but then Ingigerd is not at all an uncommon name, and just as when we read 'Mary is a pretty girl' on the Pyramids we do not think it means a Princess Mary, but some Mary whom the tourist knows, it is probable that this Ingigerd was another maiden than the earl's daughter.

Dasent goes on to suggest, as the first I think, that the reference in Maeshowe XVI to Gaukr Trandilsson's axe is not necessarily to be taken literally. It reflects knowledge of Gaukr and his axe, but 'it was probably only scored as a joke or hoax on generations to come' (1894, xxxvii). If this is true, the hoax must be judged very successful.

Other topics widely debated were:

(1) the origin of Maeshowe; a few argued that it was Norse, but the majority that
     it was older;
(2) the date of the inscriptions; were they carved over a long or a short period or
     all on the same occasion?
(3) Orkahaugr (cf. Finnbogi Guðmundsson 1965, 247–8); was it identical with
     Maeshowe, or a different mound, or even a farm – the elusive Orkhill
     (Munch 1876, 523, cf. Marwick 1931, 13)?

In the discussion of all three questions one can see as the 19th century moved to a
close a gradual shift towards the views that are held today: that Maeshowe is
much older than the Norse settlement of Orkney, that the inscriptions are from
the 12th century and almost certainly its middle decades, and that Orkahaugr
and Maeshowe are indeed one and the same place. In support of a mid-12th-
century dating of the inscriptions, Joseph Anderson (1886, 279) suggests not
only (following P. A. Munch) that 'the forms of the letters accord with the style
used in Norway in the first half of the twelfth century', but also that 'the
orthography almost exactly resembles that of the earlier Icelandic MSS. from
about 1150'.

   In the course of a discussion about whether Loðbrók was the hero Ragnarr's
nick-name or the name of the mother of the famous 'sons', Gustav Storm (1878,
84–5) brings in Maeshowe XIX–XX. The anaphoric use here of *hennar* is taken
as evidence that Loðbrók was the mother's name, and the first sentence of the
inscription is deemed to indicate that she was buried in Orkney and therefore
must have accompanied her sons on their Viking expeditions. Whatever one may
feel about the validity of Storm's conclusions, it is worth noting that he is the first
scholar to give what must be the correct rendering of the beginning of XIX–XX,
although the interpretation of what was then read *hælr* as *heldr*, 'than', is
attributed by him to Sophus Bugge. Storm translates: 'Denne Haug blev før
opreist end Lodbroks (Haug)', 'This mound was raised earlier than Loðbrók's
(mound)'.

   The early years of the 20th century saw the first of Magnus Olsen's major
contributions to Maeshowe scholarship. In his monograph *Tre orknøske
runeindskrifter* (Olsen 1903), he discusses at length XVI, XVIII and XXII,
beginning with the last. XXII had previously been declared uninterpretable by
all but the rashest scholars. Olsen, dismissing the earlier notion that its unusual
characters are bind-runes (see Fig. 20.1), starts from the assumption that runes
4, 5, 8 and 18 can be transliterated in the usual way, i.e. h, r, i, s; he also identifies
rune 9 as s, on the grounds that it does not reach down as far as the others and
that that is the distinguishing feature of s 'i den almindelige yngre futhark', 'in
the usual younger *fuþark*' (1903, 6). Next he notes that runes 2, 6, 11, 15 and
probably 20 have the same form, while 7, apart from the fact that one of its
branches crosses the stave, is identical to 14 and 19. These two symbols are
temporarily designated *x* and *y*, which letters are then inserted in the appropriate

Figure 20.1: Maeshowe XXII (based on the drawing in Farrer 1862, Plate XI).

places together with **h, r, i** and **s**. Comparison of what emerges with one of the most common formulas in Maeshowe and in runic inscriptions in general leads Olsen to postulate the text *tryhr ræist runar þesar*: $x=\mathbf{r}$, $y=\mathbf{a}$, and, with the crossing branch, **æ**. Explanations are offered for the particular shapes of these and the other cryptic runes in the inscription, and there is a discussion of the principles on which they are constructed. Particularly important for Olsen is the identification of rune 3 as **y** which he arrived at because of its similarity to the ordinary **y**-rune and the principle he sees in Maeshowe XXII of carving additional branches to create symmetrical shapes. Once this rune is accepted as **y**, the first rune can hardly be read as anything but **t**, he claims, since only in that way will a familiar Old Norse name emerge.

After brief speculation about the age of the runic cryptography he had thus identified, in the course of which comparison is made with the baffling runes on the Manx inscription Andreas 5, Olsen goes on to connect Maeshowe XXII with XVIII and XVI, a pair which most people read as a single text and which he claims form a piece of continuous verse. Attention is drawn to the shape of the **h**-rune in XVIII with its double crossing branches, reminiscent of rune 4 in XXII (see Figs. 20.1 & 20.2), and to the fact that the three Maeshowe inscriptions with cryptic runes are all located to the left of a different side-chamber. But the clincher for Olsen is that between the lower halves, roughly speaking, of the ⚔ and **ᚿ** of **ko̜ukr** in XVI there are two much smaller runes (see Fig. 20.3), the

Figure 20.2: The **h**-rune in XVIII.

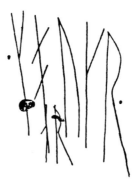

Figure 20.3: The word kǫukr in XVI with the additional, smaller runes between ⚹ and ᚾ.

second of which is clearly ᚱ and the first of which he takes as ᛏ. If the **ukr** of the
main inscription immediately following this **tr** is read in conjunction not just
with **kǫ** but also with the **tr**, the name Tryggr as well as Gaukr emerges. In
Olsen's view this provides compelling evidence that XVI, XVIII and XXII were
carved by the same man, one Tryggr, possibly son of someone called Trandill
and just possibly a descendant of Gaukr. He does not consider these three
inscriptions were made by an Icelander, however, in spite of the widespread
assumption by earlier scholars that XVI was Icelandic because of the reference
to Gaukr and the occurrence of the phrase *fyrir sunnan land,* 'in the south of
the country [i.e. Iceland]': the denotation of sounds, he maintains, is like
that in the other Maeshowe inscriptions, which linguistically must be taken
as a group representing early Island dialect. In the last part of Olsen's
monograph an attempt is made to show that the runes in XVI and XVIII are
deliberately divided into groups of 16 or 24, and a connection is made between
the spread of the short-twig runes to the Norwegian colonies in the west and
the richness and similarity of the cryptography on the Rök stone and in
Maeshowe.

Olsen's contribution was well received by contemporary reviewers. Only
Finnur Jónsson demurred a little, dismissing out of hand the idea that the text of
XVI and XVIII is verse (Finnur Jónsson 1904–5, 33). Serious criticism did not
come for over 20 years, when Bruce Dickins pointed out in a brief note (1924)
that the **tr** Olsen had read as part of Maeshowe XVI was in fact the final **ar** of
XVII; these two characters complete the word *rúnar* for which the carver of
XVII clearly had insufficient room on the slab he was using. Dickins softens the
blow by pointing out that Olsen had not visited Maeshowe when he wrote his
monograph and had thus had to rely on the drawings in Farrer 1862.
Furthermore, he seems content to accept Olsen's interpretation of XXII, even
down to the name Tryggr. For my own part I think it highly unlikely that rune 4
in XXII, if it really is **h**, can denote plosive [g:]. Two Swedish parallels quoted

by Olsen turn out to be worthless, and I know of no convincing substitutes. Whether, after the loss of the name Tryggr in XVI, Dickins believed XVI, XVIII and XXII were carved by one and the same man is not clear. Equally unclear is what he or the contemporary reviewers thought about Olsen's views on the language of the Maeshowe inscriptions, the importance of the numbers 16 and 24 and the possible connection with runic cryptography in 9th-century Sweden, for to a man they pass these matters by in silence. The question what type of language we have in the Maeshowe inscriptions is a tricky one. An analysis I have undertaken suggests Icelanders, Norwegians and Orkneymen may all have been involved (Barnes 1991). Olsen's numerical speculations have rightly been dismissed as unwarranted by Bæksted (1952, 186–90), while the similarity between the cryptography of Rök and Maeshowe is surely evidence of nothing other than a common runic tradition.

Olsen returned to Maeshowe twice more. In a lengthy article on the inscriptions of Urnes stave church (1908), he brings in Maeshowe XI, XVIII and XXII because in each of them, as in some of the Urnes inscriptions, the h or m-runes are highlighted in one way or another. Attention is drawn to the similarity between runic ✸ and Greek χ, the first letter in the Greek form of the name Christ, and to the fact that 'm' is the first letter in the name Mary. Maeshowe XI (see Fig. 20.4) with its seven crosses, its ↑ and the sequence I✸ᚿ, perhaps inspired by the manuscript abbreviation *iħu*, is declared to be replete with Christian symbolism, while the occurrence of 'highlighted' h, m or

Figure 20.4: Maeshowe XI as it is depicted in Farrer 1862, Plate IX. This inscription scaled off the east buttress on which it was carved, shortly after the excavation of Maeshowe in 1861, and only parts now survive (cf. Barnes 1988).

r (hr suggesting the first two characters in the name Christus) in XVIII and XXII may simply reflect a desire to increase the complexity of the inscriptions or possibly stem from the fact that the carver was used to seeing these characters highlighted in 'magiske indskrifter', 'magic inscriptions' (1908, 155).

The main conclusions of this article and the 1903 monograph are reiterated in Olsen 1932. The theme this time is the use of the word rýnn in two Swedish inscriptions (Sö 56 Fyrby and U 729 Ågersta) and in Maeshowe XVIII. An attempt is made to show that the runic skill denoted by the adjective is to be found not least in the 'tilsiktede tallforhold', 'deliberate numerical proportions' (1932, 187), which, according to Olsen, characterise all three inscriptions. His claim is that the runes in these inscriptions for the most part fall naturally into groups of 16, 24 or other products of 8 and he sees clear evidence that such divisions were intended by the carvers and were of deep significance. I refer once again to Bæksted – to his general critique of Olsen's method and in particular to his dismissal of the case for 'deliberate numerical proportions' in Maeshowe XVI and XVIII (1952, 186–90). The extensive numerical speculations aside, there is little new in Olsen's final attempt to wrestle with some of the problems of Maeshowe. One thing we learn is that he visited the mound in 1911 and made a careful examination of the runes. He thus realised long before Dickins pointed it out in 1924 that XVI cannot contain the name Tryggr. Nevertheless Olsen still maintains that there is a connection between XVIII, XVI and XXII. If Tryggr was not responsible for all three, then it must have been the runic skill displayed by the carver of XVIII that inspired him to go one better in XXII. But the similar appearance of the h-rune in XVIII and XXII points rather to a single author, Olsen feels, even though no attempt seems to be made in XXII to divide the runes into groups of 8, 16 or 24. In the Christian context of Maeshowe the embellished h-rune, because of its association through Greek χ with Christ, was a powerful symbol, and that is why Tryggr used it not only in haf, but more unusually for geminate g in his own name.

No doubt in an effort to provide some relief from these airy speculations, Olsen included a brief note about Gaukr Trandilsson in his 1932 paper (180–81). It is suggested (following Guðni Jónsson 1931, 164) that Gaukr's family may have moved to Orkney after his death, since his grandfather seems to have hailed from the Norwegian colonies in the British Isles and the family might well have sought refuge there. This could explain the unexpected form trænilson for Icelandic Trandilsson. The existence of such a form, which was probably Orcadian, must at the very least indicate that traditions about Gaukr had existed for a long time in Orkney before they were recorded in Maeshowe XVI.

To summarise the good and the bad in Olsen's work is not easy. Having already ventured negative comments on some of his conclusions, let me say that I find his interpretation of most of XXII appealing. The positions of the runes and their shapes give the rendering ræist runar þesar definite plausibility. Tryggr, however, is another matter. Apart from the unlikelihood that 💥 denotes [g:], already mentioned, we would have to accept that in this script the runes t and r can have two completely different forms; I cannot see why this should be, and I would not assume automatically, as Olsen does, that runes 4 and 5 are simply 'highlighted' variants of ✳ and R. A further problem is the otherwise late appearance of the name Tryggr in West Norse sources. The earliest example after Maeshowe XXII quoted in Lind 1915 is 1346, and Lind 1931 has just one example, from 1472. On the assumption that the second rune of this inscription is r, and that 1, 3, 4 and 5 are to be read as runes which otherwise do not feature in the inscription (since they have different shapes from the others), the only one of the 1,680 possible combinations that emerge which gives an obvious Norse name is **hrolf**. I do not suggest that this is a more likely interpretation than Tryggr. I simply note that it is what one comes up with using a less imaginative and more rigorous method than Olsen. If we accept, regarding initial **hr-**, that one or more Icelanders were involved in the carving of the Maeshowe inscriptions, and that rune 6 denotes both the nominative -*r* of Hrólfr and the initial consonant of *reist*, there are fewer problems with this name than with Tryggr. Whatever the correct interpretation of the first five runes of XXII, I see no compelling reason to assume that the carver of this inscription was also responsible for XVIII and XVI. The only thing which connects the trio is the embellishment of the h-rune, and that is a feature also found in XI, carved by one Óframr Sigurðarsonr. About the reasons for the embellishment of ✳ and certain other runes Olsen is doubtless right. Further evidence and arguments supporting his views can be found in Liestøl 1948.

While Magnus Olsen had been promoting his theories about parts of the Maeshowe corpus, other scholars had not been inactive. Of the many contributions which touched upon one or more aspects of the runes or the texts between the beginning of the century and the mid-1930s, I will single out for mention Dietrichson 1906, von Friesen 1918–19, Dickins 1930, Marwick 1931 and Clouston 1933.

Dietrichson's work is almost entirely secondary. He presents P. A. Munch's texts (in Norwegian translation) and interpretations from 1861 and 1862, together with a number of comments given to him orally by Sophus Bugge and Magnus Olsen. Among the more important of the latter is Bugge's suggestion that the name of the carver of II be taken as 'Eyolv' rather than 'Tholf' (Dietrichson 1906, 111). This sensible observation does not seem to have attracted the attention it deserved. The first time it was taken up in a discussion of the Maeshowe runes, as far as I can see, was by Aslak Liestøl in his 1967 article. The two principal impressions the reader gains from Dietrichson's contribution are first how adept Bugge was at reading and understanding runic inscriptions and second how confused Dietrichson (like many earlier scholars) seems to have been in his thinking about the comings and goings in medieval Maeshowe. Von Friesen (1918–19) introduces the Maeshowe inscriptions, especially XVI and XVIII, into a general discussion about the development of the dotted runes. He seems to view them as typifying the stage in the development reached by the mid-1100s. Marwick 1931 provides the interesting information that there is no place with the name Orkhill in Orkney. This means that Munch's view (1876, 523, cf. Farrer 1862, 36), repeated by others, that the Orkahaugr of Maeshowe XIX–XX (and by implication of *Orkneyinga saga* ch. 93) probably refers not to Maeshowe but to the farm Orkhill three to four miles south-east of the mound, must be incorrect.

Of particular importance is Dickins 1930, because this represents the best substitute for a modern edition of the Maeshowe runes. Although his treatment is brief, Dickins gives a proper transliteration, a normalised text and an English translation of all the inscriptions except VII and XXIV. His transliterations, moreover, unlike the 'readings' and texts of most earlier scholars, are based on careful and repeated study of the originals. The detail is preceded by a short introduction which sets out the principal facts and most plausible suppositions about the Maeshowe inscriptions as they appeared to scholars in 1930. Magnus Olsen's interpretation of XXII is accepted, XVIII and XVI are declared to belong together and to have enough rhythm and alliteration to qualify as poor verse. XIII and XIV are also taken as a single text, and so, oddly enough, are XIX and XX. How Dickins reached this last conclusion after careful examination of the runes is a mystery, but it leads him to describe what is obviously a series of different inscriptions as 'lacking in continuity of thought' (1930, 28). However, he seems to have hit upon the most likely reading and interpretation of the runes between **lif** and **iarls** in XIX–XX and to have seen that the three words which emerge here: *Líf matselja jarls*, should be connected with the verb **ræist** which occurs lower down on the same slab. Dickins' views about the sequence of visitors to Maeshowe in the 1100s are only a little less confused and contradictory than those of earlier scholars. The crusaders stated by two of the inscriptions to have broken into the mound are tentatively identified with the followers of Eindriði ungi and Earl Rǫgnvaldr, who were in Orkney during the winter of 1150–1. Then XIII and XIV, which in Dickins' translation state, *inter alia*, that 'Treasure was carried off before those Crusaders broke into the howe', are taken literally: 'We cannot be sure whether this is an expression of disgust from one of the Crusaders, or of glee from an Orcadian who resented their vandalism' (1930, 28). But if the crusaders had to break into the mound, how was the treasure carried off before their arrival? Perhaps Dickins assumed that it lay outside Maeshowe, but reading his account as a whole I do not think this is very likely.

An attempt to set up a rigorous chronology of the comings and goings in Maeshowe was made by Clouston in his 1933 article. Study of the inscriptions themselves and of ancillary sources suggested to him that the true sequence of events was the following:

(1) a certain Hákon, probably the Hákon kló of *Orkneyinga saga*, carried treasure from Maeshowe in the course of three nights, presumably entering through the passage;

(2) crusaders broke through the roof in 1150–1;

(3) Earl Haraldr and his men took shelter there 'in the winter of 1153–4' (Clouston 1933, 9; actually early in 1153, cf. Finnbogi Guðmundsson 1965, lxxxix, 247).

No one could have opened the mound before Hákon (a) because if they had, he would not have found treasure, and (b) because local superstitions and the impossibility of entering in secret would have ensured that Maeshowe remained inviolate. Clouston also considers that the central chamber filled up with debris soon after the crusaders broke through the roof. That is why the inscriptions, which otherwise would have been exposed to the Orkney weather, are so well preserved, and it is also the reason why some of the inscriptions are carved high up on the walls. Maeshowe XIX–XX are said to provide confirmation of the idea that the mound was only opened twice. While the first part of these inscriptions gives us 'a mixed bag of information, legendary and fact, finishing with the statement, "Away to the north-west is a great treasure hidden"', the second part, someone's ironic commentary on the spiriting away of the treasure, tells us *inter alia* that 'nobody but Hakon took treasure out of this howe': Hákon was there first, ensuring that the crowd who broke in after him drew a blank (1933, 11–12).

Many objections can be raised against Clouston's theories.

(1) It is still not clear why the crusaders broke in through the roof if Hákon had burrowed his way in through the passage a short while before.

(2) The crusaders may not have entered Maeshowe until their return from the Holy Land in late 1153.

(3) The fact that some of the inscriptions were carved high up in the chamber does not necessarily mean that they were made by persons standing on a pile of debris.

(4) The positioning of the lines of XIX–XX that form Clouston's ironic commentary makes it virtually certain that we have here not one but three separate inscriptions.

But there is a more fundamental objection than these. How do we know that what the inscriptions tell us is true – or even that it was meant to be taken seriously? If Hákon had been the first person to enter Maeshowe since the Stone Age what sort of treasure might he have carried away? The image of him as an early archaeologist melting into the night with a prize collection of bones and stone implements is an appealing one, but difficult to sustain. I am afraid that Clouston's attempt to set up a chronology of events in 12th-century Maeshowe must be deemed a complete failure, and the same goes for similar efforts by other scholars. If he had stopped to ask himself a few commonsense questions of the kind I have suggested here, he must have seen that the conclusions he draws either do not or cannot follow from the limited information at our disposal.

Since the 1930s interest in Maeshowe has subsided, to judge from the small number of publications that deal with the mound and its runes. I know of only two further studies of the inscriptions that add substantially to our knowledge (apart from my own modest contributions), those by Hermann Pálsson (1962, revised and reprinted 1970) and Aslak Liestøl (1968, see also Liestøl 1967 & 1984).

Hermann, after a somewhat confusing and contradictory account of the various visits to Maeshowe in the 1150s (better, but vaguer, in Hermann Pálsson 1970), makes a plausible case for the assumption that the Þorhallr Ásgrímsson who carried Earl Rǫgnvaldr and his fellow crusaders back to Orkney from Norway late in 1153 was the great-great-great-grandson of Ásgrímr Elliða-Grímsson, the man who according to *Njáls saga* slew Gaukr Trandilsson in Iceland in the late 10th century (Einar Ól. Sveinsson 1954, 72–3, 371). Less tenable in my view is the assumption that Maeshowe XVIII and XVI were carved with Gaukr's axe, which according to Hermann had remained in the possession of Ásgrímr's descendants through five generations. His belief is that Þorhallr took it with him on his voyage to Norway and that it thus came to be in Orkney during the winter of 1153–4. In the revised version of his article Hermann goes so far as to suggest that Maeshowe XVIII and XVI were carved by Earl Rǫgnvaldr himself, who wandered into the mound one day in the company of Þorhallr (1970, 53–4); originally he had attributed them to Þorhallr or a fellow Icelander because of the phrase *fyrir sunnan land* (1962, 42). If XVI and XVIII really are to be taken together, there are of course linguistic difficulties both in attributing them to an Icelander and to an Orkneyman (whether or not Norwegian-born). Attribution to Earl Rǫgnvaldr carries the added problem that, according to Dickins (1930, 28), they were made by a bad poet. More serious than these conundrums, though, is the fundamental question I posed in connection with Clouston's speculations: to what extent are these or any of the Maeshowe inscriptions to be taken literally? There seems no sensible reason to doubt that the kǫukr·trænilsonr of Maeshowe XVI and the Gaukr Trandilsson of the Icelandic sources are one and the same, but all Maeshowe XVI then tells us for sure is that the carver knew about Gaukr and his axe. We readily dismiss most of what we read in modern graffiti. Why should we give unusual credence to what seems to be its 12th-century counterpart?

A much less ethereal contribution is provided by Aslak Liestøl in his 1968 paper. In the mid-1950s Liestøl made a careful study of all the inscriptions except XI, and as a result was able to suggest a number of new readings and interpretations. He provides a transliteration of most of the previously undeciphered VII; he recommends that XIV be read as a separate inscription and III be taken instead as the continuation of XIII; and he draws attention to an inscription next to and partially disfiguring XIV, which no one before him seems to have noticed. In addition he offers a new interpretation of the enigmatic sequence **slituǫro·mæn** in XIX–XX: in his view it is a compound noun 'smooth-hide men', and a pun on the name Loðbrók. My own examination of the inscriptions in 1987–8 revealed in VII more or less the same runes as Liestøl had read, but how far I was seeing what he had led me to expect to see is hard to say. (Interestingly enough, Liestøl's drawing of VII (1968, 57) is very similar to one of George Petrie's, cf. Carr 1871, 141.) The runes are extremely faint and many of them can no longer be discerned at all. Liestøl's text of VII is as in the Appendix, and he assumes that VI provides the continuation. VII (in as far as it can be read) and VI would then run in English: '...[adverb] it is told to me that treasure is hidden here extremely well. Few say as Oddr Orkason said in the runes he cut.' Even if we accept this text and translation, the two inscriptions are not without their residual problems. I will mention four.

(1) The initial part of VII is illegible, but the runes at the beginning are undoubtedly much larger than the rest; this is possibly a different inscription.

(2) The final verb in VI looks more like **ristu** than **risti**.

(3) Orki may well have been a familiar name in 12th-century Orkney, but it seems otherwise to be extremely sparsely documented.

(4) The phrase *á rúnum* is an unusual way of saying 'in runes'; some scholars translate *sagði á* 'dictated', but that appears no less problematic.

Liestøl's suggestion that III rather than XIV forms the conclusion of XIII seems to me well motivated. XIV can more easily stand on its own than III, and III begins more or less where XIII breaks off (at right-angles to it), while XIV is on the other side of the chamber. XIII and XIV, it is true, are the only inscriptions in Maeshowe that run from right to left, but whereas all the non-symmetrical runes in XIII face left, only half do so in XIV. To have continued the vertical XIII as a right-to-left inscription where III now stands would have been impossible unless the carver had hung from the roof or cut the runes upside-down. The question whether XIII and III are more likely to be by the same hand than XIII and XIV I will leave open. Of Liestøl's other two principal suggestions in his 1968 paper, I accept one, but am considerably less sure about the other. The inscription that runs into XIV almost certainly does read **ristormrinyri**, 'Ormr the ? cut', but it is less clear, I think, that **slituǫro · mæn** means 'smooth-hide men' – orthography and punctuation seem to militate against this interpretation (Barnes 1989, 32).

At the beginning of his 1968 article, Liestøl draws attention to the wealth of literature which exists about the Maeshowe inscriptions. He points out in particular that the list of titles under Maeshowe in Marquardt 1961 'covers 25 columns' (1968, 55). In fact, Liestøl is guilty of a slight deception. Because each inscription is allotted a separate entry, Marquardt's Maeshowe bibliography is unusually repetitive. Nevertheless, there is no denying that over the 130 years since their discovery, the Maeshowe inscriptions have excited great interest. Their meaning has been sought by sober and imaginative scholars, by charlatans and cranks. What further contributions, then, can usefully be made? Where do we go from here?

A fair number of the individual inscriptions are still imperfectly or poorly understood. I would include in that category: I, III, V, VI, VII, X, XXII and XXIII. In addition, the various groups of runes that now go under the headings XIVb–d and XXIb lack a satisfactory interpretation, as do certain words in XIX–XX and other inscriptions. In several cases there is doubt about whether we are dealing with one or more inscriptions, and about what belongs with what. In this connection, it is clear that the numbering of the inscriptions, which goes back to Farrer, is in need of drastic revision.

Equally important are the broader questions. How close can we come to determining the age of any or of all of the inscriptions? What kind of language are they written in: colloquial, literary, or both? Norn, Norwegian, or Icelandic, or all three? Is the orthography native runic or influenced by that used when writing Norse with the Latin alphabet? While most of these questions can be investigated independently of an overall view of the context of the Maeshowe inscriptions, it seems to me sound method to proceed on the basis of a hypothesis about the general nature of the texts and to see whether the results of one's investigations confirm or invalidate the hypothesis. We have seen the kind of conclusions less rigorous methods lead to: Stone-Age treasure being carried out of the mound before it was broken into; Earl Rǫgnvaldr Kali writing poetry so bad that Finnur Jónsson refused to accept it as such; and a carver unable to get far down into the mound for all the rubble claiming he was writing runes on high.

For my own part, I think that most if not all the Maeshowe inscriptions are light-hearted medieval graffiti and that what they say is to be taken with a large pinch of salt. As I have made clear, I am by no means the first to think this, but few who have reasoned along similar lines seem to have realised that the adoption of such a hypothesis limits the range of admissible arguments. I cannot easily base theories about how and when the mound was opened on XIX–XX because my hypothesis renders suspect a literal interpretation of these inscriptions. I cannot, like Hermann Pálsson, date XVIII and XVI to the winter of 1153–4 and attribute them to Þorhallr Ásgrímsson or Earl Rǫgnvaldr because this dating and these attributions rest largely on the presence of Gaukr Trandilsson's axe in Maeshowe, and my hypothesis casts doubt on the veracity of XVI's claim that it was carved with that axe.

Much work remains to be done on the Maeshowe inscriptions. I do not know whether I shall be able to shed further light on them, but I hope at least to avoid the pits into which some of my predecessors unwittingly tumbled.

Acknowledgement

Part of the research for this article was supported by a grant from The British Academy, to whom I should like to record my gratitude.

Appendix

WORKING TEXTS OF THE MAESHOWE INSCRIPTIONS, WITH SUGGESTED ENGLISH TRANSLATIONS

Only those inscriptions in which a coherent text can be discerned are included here.

I	Þat er víkingr…rákum(?) undir hér til.
	'That is a viking(?)…[we] drove under to here.'
II	Eyjólfr Kolbeinssonr reist rúnar þessar hótt.
	'Eyjólfr Kolbeinssonr carved these runes high.'
III	Bre(?) haug þenna.
	'? this mound.'
IV	Vémundr reist.
	'Vémundr carved.'
V	fuþorkhniastbynu
	(The younger fuþark; the last three characters are problematic.)
VI	Orkasonr sagði á rúnum þeim, er hann risti.
	'Orkasonr said in the runes he cut.'
VII	…iga er mér sagt at fé er hér folgit œrit vel. Segja fáir sem Oddr–
	'…[adverb] it is told to me that treasure is hidden here extremely well. Few say as Oddr–'
VIII	Ingibjǫrg hin fagra ekkja. Mǫrg kona hefir farit lút inn hér. Mikill ofláti. Erlingr.
	'Ingibjǫrg the fair widow. Many a woman has gone bowed in here. A great show-off. Erlingr.'
IX	Þorný sarð. Helgi reist.
	'Þorný fucked. Helgi carved.'
X	Þórir fomir(?).
	'Þórir ? [nickname?].'
XI	Reist rúnar þessar Óframr Sigurðarsonr.
	'Óframr Sigurðarsonr carved these runes.'
XII	Óttarr fila(?) reist rúnar þessar.
	'Óttarr ? [nickname?] carved these runes.'
XIII	Þat man satt, er ek segi, at fé var fœrt á brott. Þrim nóttum var fé brott fœrt heldr enn þeir–
	'That will be true which I say, that treasure was carried away. Treasure was carried away three nights before they–'
XIVa	Jórsalamenn brutu haug þenna.
	'Crusaders broke this mound.'

366

XIVb	Reist Ormr inn ýri(?).
	'Ormr the ? [epithet] carved.'
XV	Arnfiðr matr reist rúnar þessar.
	'Arnfiðr food carved these runes.'
XVI	–með þeiri øxi, er átti Gaukr Trennilssonr fyrir sunnan land.
	'–with that axe which Gaukr Trennilssonr owned in the south of the country.'
XVII	Hermundr harðexi(?) reist rúnar.
	'Hermundr hard-axe(?) carved runes.'
XVIII	Þessar rúnar reist sá maðr, er rýnstr er fyrir vestan haf.
	'These runes carved that man who is most skilled in runes west of the ocean.'
XIX–XXa	Sjá haugr var fyrr laðinn heldr Loðbrókar. Synir hennar þeir vǫru hvatir. Slíkt vǫru menn, sem þeir vǫru fyri sér.
	'This mound was built before Loðbrók's. Her sons, they were bold. Such were men, as they showed themselves to be.'
XIX–XXb	Jórsalafarar brutu Orkhaug. Líf matselja jarls reist.
	'Crusaders broke Orkhaugr. Líf, the Earl's steward, carved.'
XIX–XXc	Útnorðr er fé folgit mikit.
	'In the north-west is great treasure hidden.'
XIX–XXd	Þat var lǫngu, er hér var fé folgit mikit.
	'That was long ago that great treasure was hidden here.'
XIX–XXe	Sæll er sá, er finna má þann auð hinn mikla.
	'Happy is he who can find that great wealth.'
XIX–XXf	Hǫkon einn bar fé ýr haugi þessum.
	'Hǫkon alone carried treasure out of this mound.'
XIX–XXg	Símun.
	'Símun.'
XIX–XXi	Sigríð.
	'Sigríð.'
XXIa	Arnfiðr reist rúnar þessar sonr Steins.
	'Arnfiðr carved these runes, son of Steinn.'
XXII	? reist rúnar þessar.
	'? carved these runes.'
XXIII	Ingigerð er kvinnanna(?) in vænsta.
	'Ingigerð is the most beautiful of the women(?).'
XXIV	Benedikt gerði kross þenna.
	'Benedikt made this cross.'

REFERENCES

Anderson, Joseph 1886. *Scotland in Pagan Times. The Bronze and Stone Ages*, Edinburgh.

Barclay, T. 1863. 'Explanation of the inscriptions found in the chambers of the Maes-Howe', *Collectanea Archæologica* 2:1, 9–17.

Barnes, Michael P. 1988. 'Two Maeshowe rediscoveries', *Nytt om runer* 3, 12–13.

Barnes, Michael P. 1989. 'Runic orthography west of the ocean: an analysis of some unusual spellings in the Maeshowe inscriptions', in *Festskrift til Finn Hødnebø 29. desember 1989*, Oslo, pp. 19–37.

Barnes, Michael P. 1991. 'Norwegian, Norn, Icelandic or West Norse? The language of the Maeshowe inscriptions', in *Festskrift til Ottar Grønvik*, Oslo, pp. 70–87.

Barnes, Michael P. 1992. 'The gentlemen *v.* the scholars: An early Maeshowe controversy', in *Eyvindarbók. Festskrift til Eyvind Fjeld Halvorsen*, Oslo, pp. 20–28.

Bæksted, Anders 1952. *Målruner og troldruner*, København.

Carr, Ralph 1868. 'Observations on some of the runic inscriptions at Maeshowe, Orkney', *Proceedings of the Society of Antiquaries of Scotland* 6, 70–83.

Carr, Ralph 1871. 'Note on No. VII of Mr Petrie's copy of the Maeshow runes', *Proceedings of the Society of Antiquaries of Scotland* 8, 139–42.

Clouston, J. Storer 1933. 'Something about Maeshowe', *Proceedings of the Orkney Antiquarian Society* 11, 9–17.

Dasent, Sir G. W. 1894. *The Orkneyingers' Saga*, The Chronicles and Memorials of Great Britain and Ireland during the Middle Ages, Icelandic Sagas 3, London.

Dickins, Bruce 1924. 'Note on Maeshowe inscriptions, XXII. and XVI.–XVIII., *Proceedings of the Orkney Antiquarian Society* 2, 59.

Dickins, Bruce 1930. 'The runic inscriptions of Maeshowe', *Proceedings of the Orkney Antiquarian Society* 8, 27–30.

Dietrichson, L. 1906. *Monumenta Orcadica*, Kristiania.

Einar Ól. Sveinsson (ed.) 1954. *Brennu-Njáls saga*, Íslenzk fornrit 12, Reykjavík.

Farrer, James 1862. *Notice of Runic Inscriptions Discovered during Recent Excavations in the Orkneys* [Edinburgh].

Fergusson, James 1872. *Rude Stone Monuments in All Countries, their Age and Uses*, London.

Finnbogi Guðmundsson (ed.) 1965. *Orkneyinga saga*, Íslenzk fornrit 34, Reykjavík.

Finnur Jónsson 1904–5. Review of Olsen 1903, *Nordisk tidsskrift for filologi* 3. række, 13, 32–3.

von Friesen, Otto 1918–19. 'Runenschrift', in *Reallexikon der Germanischen Altertumskunde* 4, Strassburg, pp. 5–51.

Guðni Jónsson 1931. 'Um Gauk Trandilsson', *Skírnir* 105, 149–74.

Hermann Pálsson 1962. Öxi Gauks Trandilssonar, *Samvinnan* 56: 11–12, pp. 4–5, 42–3.

Hermann Pálsson 1970. 'Farmaður frá Bræðratungu', *Tólfta öldin*, Reykjavík, pp. 44–54, 154.

Liestøl, Aslak 1948. 'Det norske runediktet', *Maal og minne*, 65–71.

Liestøl, Aslak 1967. 'Der var megen uro på øerne den vinter', *Skalk* Nr. 1, 18–25.

Liestøl, Aslak 1968. 'The Maeshowe runes: some new interpretations', in *The Fifth Viking Congress*, Tórshavn, pp. 55–61.

Liestøl, Aslak 1984. 'Runes', in *The Northern and Western Isles in the Viking World*, Edinburgh, pp. 224–38.

Lind, E. H. 1915. *Norsk-isländska dopnamn ock fingerade namn från medeltiden*, Uppsala.

Lind, E. H. 1931. *Norsk-isländska dopnamn ock fingerade namn från medeltiden.* Supplementband, Oslo.

Marquardt, Hertha 1961. *Die Runeninschriften der Britischen Inseln.* Bibliographie der Runeninschriften nach Fundorten 1, Abhandlungen der Akademie der Wissenschaften in Göttingen, philologisch-historische Klasse, Dritte Folge, Nr 48, Göttingen.

Marwick, H. 1931. 'Modern views of ancient Orkney', *Proceedings of the Orkney Antiquarian Society* 9, 9–16.

Mitchell, J. M. 1863. *Mesehowe*, Edinburgh.

Mongé, Alf & Landsverk, O. G. 1967. *Norse Medieval Cryptography in Runic Carvings*, Glendale.

Munch, P. A. 1861. 'Om de ved Steinsnes paa Orknøerne nysopdagede Runeindskrifter', *Illustreret Nyhedsblad* 48–9, 201–2, 206–8.

Munch, P. A. 1876. 'Om de ved Steinsnes paa Orknøerne nys opdagede Runeindskrifter', in *Samlede Afhandlinger* 4, Christiania, pp. 516–29. (An almost exact reprint of the article in *Illustreret Nyhedsblad.*)

Olsen, Magnus 1903. *Tre orknøske runeindskrifter*, Christiania Videnskabs-Selskabs Forhandlinger for 1903, No. 10, Christiania.

Olsen, Magnus 1908. 'Runeindskrifterne i Urnes kirke i Sogn', *Foreningen til norske fortidsmindesmærkers bevaring* 63, 118–75.

Olsen, Magnus 1932. 'Rúnar er ristu rýnastir menn', *Norsk tidsskrift for sprogvidenskap* 5, 167–88.

The Orcadian 20 July 1861.

The Orkney Herald 16 July 1861.

Petrie, George 1861a. 'The excavations in "Maeshow", Stenness', *The Orcadian*, 20 July.

Petrie, George 1861b. 'Notice of the opening of a tumulus in the parish of Stenness, on the Mainland of Orkney', *The Archaeological Journal* 18, 353–8.

[Rafn, C. C.] 1861. 'Runeindskrifter paa Orknøerne', *Berlingske politiske og Avertissements-Tidende* 11 September. (English version of the same, *The Orcadian*, 14 September.)

Storm, Gustav 1878. *Kritiske Bidrag til Vikingetidens Historie* 1, Kristiania.

21

TWO RUNIC INSCRIPTIONS FROM ORPHIR, ORKNEY

JAN RAGNAR HAGLAND

In 1953, during the demolition of the 18th-century parish church which stood at the west side of the old Round Kirk (Church) at Orphir, Orkney, a stone with a runic inscription on it was found. The precise circumstances of its discovery seem not to have been recorded. It is agreed, however, that part of the material for the parish church was taken from the Round Kirk, a fact which, of course, still leaves the possibility that the runestone was brought from elsewhere. The stone, which is presently kept in Tankerness House Museum, Kirkwall (exhib. N 690), measures 25 by 12 by 6.4 cm. The inscription is 20.5 cm long and the runes, which are the full height of the narrow longitudinal side on which they are cut, read as follows (cf. Fig. 21.1):

    i k i r g i r g i a k o þ l i u f s u̩ [--

Notes

Runes 4 and 7 have a shape of r which is particularly frequent in Greenlandic inscriptions (Stoklund 1981, 144f): almost parallel side twigs which do not touch each other. Rune 7 slightly differs from rune 4 as its lower side twig does not border on the stave. This type of r is known also from an inscription on Holy Island, Hebrides, cut by *Vigleikr stallare* apparently in 1263 (NIyR V: 231).

    Runes 5 and 8 are distinctly dotted ks. The upper side twig of rune 12 is damaged to the extent that it is hardly distinguishable. The remains of a twig can, however, be observed with certainty through a magnifying glass.

Figure 21.1: Tracing of runic inscription from Orphir (Tankerness House Museum, Kirkwall, ref. N 690).

Figure 21.2: Runestone from Orphir (photo: E. J. Brundle).

The side twig of rune 14 leaves the stave about 1 cm below the top and almost touches rune 15 which has a slight bend due to the uneven surface of the stone at this level. The top of rune 16 has weathered away so as to separate the stave and the twig. The upper half of rune 19, at the edge of the existing stone, is missing. The lower half, however, displays the remains of a **u**. The stone, as illustrated by Fig. 21.2, seems to have been trimmed into its present shape after the runes were cut, which implies that part of the original inscription is now missing.

In runic inscriptions from the Viking Age onwards an undotted **k** may represent the unvoiced palatal stop /k/ as well as its voiced counterpart /g/. The dotted **k**, however, when it appears late in the 12th century is only known to represent the voiced palatal stop in inscriptions. Thus a dotted **k** should represent /g/, and the undotted **k**, /k/, when occurring in the very same inscription, as is the case here. A straightforward reading of runes 1–19, then, does not produce any linguistic sense, mainly because of the distribution of dotted and undotted ks. The inscription on this stone from Orphir has, in consequence, been regarded as nonsensical and has until now remained unpublished, apart from a short presentation by Liestøl (1984, 236).

There is, however, a possibility that the carver of runes in this particular case has been unskilled and inexperienced to the extent that he has got his dots all wrong and dotted his ks where he should not and left out his dots where he ought to have kept them. Parallel cases are known in several inscriptions from Norway, e.g. NIyR no. 291 (Bergen V, cf. also NIyR III, 129 no. 1). A possible, but nevertheless somewhat speculative, emendation on this point might, in consequence, render a reading like the following: i k i r k i r k i a g o þ l i u f s u [––. A reading like this would allow an identification of runes 5–10 as *kirkia*, f. 'church', 11–13 as *góð*, adj. f. 'good', and 14–17 as *liúf*, adj. f. 'mild', 'gentle'. The noun and the adjectives agree in gender and case (fem. nominative), which would support the suggested interpretation up to this point.

Runes 1–4 represent, however, a problem even in this context. A possible interpretation would be to identify the first two runes as one segment which might be taken to signify the personal pronoun 1st pers. sg. *ek*, 'I'. The next two would then have to be understood as a verb: *er*, 'am'. A problem here is that the verb and the pronoun do not agree. The 1st person sg. form of the verb 'to be' in Old Norse, except in rather late texts, is *em*. The form *er* equals the 3rd person sg. and does occur in the 1st person from the 1280s in Norwegian source material, in Icelandic considerably later – from 1350 (Noreen 1970, §531,1). Independently of this, runes 18 and 19 most probably represent the adv. or conj. **su(a)** = *svá*, 'as'. However, an interpretation like *ek er kirkia góð liúf sv(á) —*, 'I am (the) church good, mild as —', does not seem very probable. The church speaking in the first person singular has no parallel in the religious texts from the Middle Ages that we know of, and the idea does not seem likely from a theological or dogmatic point of view either.

An alternative to reading **i k i r** as *ek er* might be *ekki (e)r*, 'not is'. This would imply that the rune **i** has the value of /e/ as well as of /i/, which is rather common. In the present inscription, however, in which punctuation is used, although with some confusion, such an interpretation cannot be taken for granted. The suggested interpretation would also imply that rune 3 has the double function of representing the final vowel in the negative adverb as well as the initial vowel of the verb. These vowels might in fact sound rather alike in this position, and double functions like that are not at all uncommon in medieval runic inscriptions from elsewhere. An illustrative parallel, also from an inscription found in a church, is NIyR no. 393 (Hopperstad church IV Sogn, Norway): – **þæimane** = *þeim manne*, 'that man' (dative case). The **m** here serves the double function of representing final /m/ in the pronoun and initial /m/ in the noun. There is, then, a possibility that the inscription be interpreted as *ekki er kirkia góð, liúf sv[—* which might be glossed as 'not is the church good, mild, as[—'.

An audacious interpretation like the one presented above seems to produce a rather impious or frustrated statement about the church, as an institution or perhaps as a building. The word *kirkja*, f. in the sense of *ecclesia*, is sufficiently well recorded particularly in legal usage to support the former (cf. Kahle 1890, 324 and Astås 1989, 18). Moreover, the use of the adjective *liúfr* seems to make the latter less probable as it is an abstract notion which normally would not occur as a qualifier of inanimate countables. The adjective is known from constructions like *minn liúfi herra* – 'my gentle Sir!' The adj. *liúfr* is frequently known also as part of the idiom *liúft eða leitt* – 'nice or nasty'. A statement about the Holy Church of a kind suggested above is, of course, intriguing and open to various interpretations. Implying a wider heretical context for an impiety of the kind which we may have to deal with here would, however, be even more audacious than the steps towards an interpretation already ventured.

The fact that the inscription was made prior to the final reshaping of the runestone from the parish church at Orphir and the probable reference to the

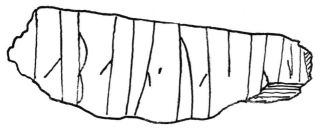

Figure 21.3: Tracing of runic inscription from Earl's Bu, Orphir (ref. EB 85 DF, small find 314).

church as an institution, seem to support the already established opinion about the provenance of the materials of the building which was demolished in 1953 and provide evidence to include even the runestone in this material from the old Round Kirk.

There is, consequently, reason to believe that the present runic inscription originates from Orphir, as does the one discovered on a bone from Earl's Bu (McKinnell 1989, cf. Fig. 21.3 & Fig. 21.4). McKinnell reads -?a·bain· uas·iþu[??- '. . . bone was in . . .', and suggests that the next word might be **þuisti**, ON *þvesti*, 'flesh'. As he rightly observes, the Bu inscription shows runological and linguistic evidence to suggest a date earlier than the 12th century. The inscription on the runestone suggests a somewhat later date than that. As we have seen, the particular shape of the rs has been recorded in this part of the world as late as 1263. The uncertainty about dotting, however, might be indicative of an early stage of this medieval refinement of the runic script, making the late 12th century a possible date. This goes well with the history of the Round Kirk, first mentioned in the written sources in 1135 (cf. Clouston 1932, 374).

Figure 21.4: Rune-inscribed bone (EB 85 DF, small find 314) from Earl's Bu, Orphir (photo: T. Woods).

Together, the two inscriptions from Orphir, then, seem to cover a timespan of a century or more, providing evidence for the use of runes in the Orkneys well into the Scandinavian High Middle Ages.

REFERENCES

Astås, Reidar 1989. *Kirkelig/skolastisk terminologi i et morsmålsverk fra middelalderen*, Oslo.

Clouston, J. Storer 1932. *A History of Orkney*, Kirkwall.

Kahle, Bernhard 1890. 'Die altnordische Sprache im Dienste des Christentums', I.Teil: Die Prosa, *Acta Germanica. Organ für deutsche Philologie* I, 307–441.

Liestøl, Aslak 1984. 'Runes', in *The Northern and Western Isles in the Viking World: survival, continuity and change*, eds Fenton, Alexander & Pálsson, Hermann, Edinburgh, pp. 223–38.

McKinnell, John 1989. 'A new find from Orkney', *Nytt om runer. Meldingsblad om runeforskning* 4, 15.

NIyR: Norges innskrifter med de yngre runer 1941–90. I-VI, Oslo.

Noreen, Adolf 1970. *Altnordische Grammatik. I. Altisländische und altnorwegische Grammatik* 5, unveränderte Auflage, Tübingen.

Stoklund, Marie 1981. 'Greenland Runic Inscriptions', *Michigan Germanic Studies* VII, 138–48.

22

ORPHIR CHURCH IN ITS
SOUTH SCANDINAVIAN CONTEXT

IAN FISHER

Orphir Church, with its intact apse and surviving fragment of the circular nave that was largely destroyed about 1758, is of outstanding architectural interest as the only medieval church of circular plan known to have existed in Orkney, or indeed in Scotland. Moreover the saga account of the 'fine church' standing in front of the door of the earl's great drinking-hall, 'just a few paces down from it', gives a vivid picture of a seigneurial church on a great manor where Earls Harald and Paul held their Christmas feasts. Indeed the repeated visits of Earl Paul and his entourage to services in the church form a remarkable counterpoint to the violent events of his Christmas feast in 1136 (Pálsson & Edwards 1978, 99, 124–6).

The church was of modest scale, only 5.8 m in diameter within a wall 1.2 m thick and with a barrel-vaulted apse measuring 2.2 m in both width and depth. In the context of early 12th century Orkney, however, it was a remarkable building, and the 18th century masons who attempted to demolish it for building-material testified to the strength of its mortar. Detailed descriptions and drawings have been provided by Dryden in 1855 (Dryden 1896) and by the Royal Commission in 1929 (RCAHMS 1946, (2), 174–5, Figs 260–1). These accounts also reproduce three 18th-century descriptions of the church, of which those by Pope and Pococke were written shortly after the demolition of the nave. Although they differ in the dimensions given, these contemporary descriptions are agreed that the interior was lit by a central opening in the roof, and Pope's mention of a 'cupola' corroborates Pococke's description of a vault above the nave. While the possibility of post-Reformation alterations to the structure cannot be ruled out, it is clear that there was no central pillar in the nave, and the more plausible records of the height of the walls, Pococke's '15 feet' (4.6 m) and Liddell's '20 feet' (6.1 m), hardly allow for an upper storey above the vault.

Most scholars are agreed that the round church at Orphir belongs to the period following the success of the first crusade in 1099, when Western Europe saw a resurgence of interest in circular church-plans inspired by the church of the Holy Sepulchre in Jerusalem. Dryden (1896, 145), Dietrichson and Meyer

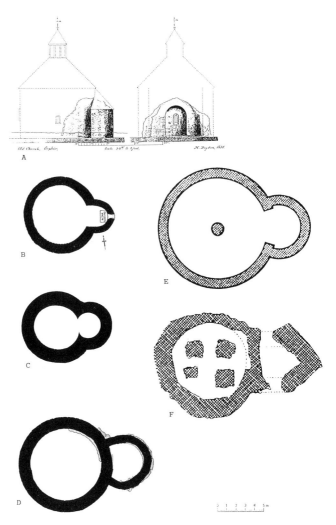

Figure 22.1: *A.* Orphir Church, reconstructed section and elevation by Dryden. Comparative plans of round churches (scale 1: 400): *B.* Orphir (after RCAHMS 1946); *C.* Levý Hradec (after Sláma 1988); *D.* St Michael, Hälsingborg (after Mårtensson 1934); *E.* St Michael, Schleswig (after Vellev 1973a); *F.* Søborg, Zealand (after Johannsen & Smidt 1985).

(1906, 21), and Cant (1973, 5) have pointed to Earl Hakon's pilgrimage to Palestine about 1120 as providing a specific link between Orkney and the Holy Sepulchre. There is no general agreement on the direct source of the Orphir design, however. Dryden discussed the small group of surviving Anglo-Norman round churches (Dryden 1896, 145; for other examples see Pevsner 1961, 313–14), most of which have pillared peripheral aisles and bear no stylistic resemblance to Orphir. Radford (1964, 181-2) preferred a Central European origin, drawing attention to a group of early 12th-century churches in Prague which appear from his description to be very similar to Orphir in plan and scale. The resemblance may indeed be closer than he states, since the roughly-formed apse window at Orphir is double-splayed like those of the Bohemian churches rather than single-splayed and 'typologically later'. No mechanism for the transfer of the design to Orkney was suggested, however. A very close parallel for the Orphir plan, only 4.8 m in internal diameter, was illustrated by Dr Martin Gojda in his 1990 Rhind lectures on Slav archaeology. This round church, whose excavated wall-footings underlie the Gothic and Baroque church of St Clement at Levý Hradec on the northern outskirts of Prague, was erected by Prince Borivoj beside a major stronghold of his Premyslid dynasty in the last decade of the 9th century, and is celebrated as the earliest church in Bohemia (Sláma 1988). Although this example is too early to be directly relevant to Orphir, it is clear that circular plans were well established in Bohemia long before the crusading period.

The possibility of a Scandinavian source for the Orphir design, although raised by the Royal Commission (RCAHMS 1946, (1), 43), has received surprisingly little consideration, no doubt because the best-known group of round churches in the Nordic area, the fortified churches of Bornholm with their massive central piers and capacious upper storeys, are so obviously different in character from the modest Orcadian building. The question deserves to be raised again, and this brief consideration is offered in the hope that it will arouse the interest of a scholar with better access to the Scandinavian literature than the present writer.

Most of the round churches in South Scandinavia fall into one of two main groups (Eriksson 1977, 76-7, 81; Frölén 1911; Johannsen & Smidt 1981, 53-61). The Bornholm type, with a central pier from which a tunnel-vault springs, has been discussed by some scholars purely in terms of the development of fortification, so that one standard work (Anker & Andersson 1970, (2), 141-7) has the section-heading 'Round or Fortress Churches'. This emphasis on defence seems less appropriate to the first phase of St Michael's Church, Schleswig, excavated in 1971-2 and dated to about 1130, where a central pier in the 10.6 m diameter nave was assumed by the excavator although no remains of it were found. It is of interest to note that this church may have been erected as a chapel associated with a Danish royal residence (Vellev 1973a; 1973b). Another recently-excavated church, All Saints' in Roskilde, was almost identical in diameter with St Michael's and had a central pier of slight dimensions compared with the Bornholm examples. A second type is derived from Charlemagne's palace chapel in Aachen, with four ground-floor pillars framing an aperture through which the potentate in the upper gallery could view the altar. This type is found with square, octagonal and circular naves, and there are at least a dozen examples in Denmark, including the excavated remains of the chapel of about

1150 at the bishop's castle of Søborg in north Zealand, as well as others in Sweden.

The excavated evidence for round churches of moderate scale built during the first half of the 12th century can be supplemented by the records of the excavations of 1899 and 1932 on the terrace adjoining the late medieval tower of Karnan in Hälsingborg, which identified the footings of St Michael's Chapel with its 7.5 m diameter nave and a three-quarter circular apse (Mårtensson 1934, 26–43). As at Søborg, this chapel rose as a tower which was incorporated in the enceinte, but its modest interior space is comparable with that at Orphir, and there was no excavated evidence of a central pier. The report on this building mentions two other Swedish churches with circular naves less than 8 m in internal diameter, at Himlingöje and Tjärestad (Mårtensson 1934, 33). The chronology of these small round churches deserves examination to establish whether potential models for Orphir, perhaps themselves inspired by the Bohemian examples, existed in the South Scandinavian area in the early 12th century. *Pace* Radford, the apse window at Orphir is of double-splayed form, a type of opening common in 12th-century Scandinavia. The Orphir plan also has local elements, for the straight opening through the plain chancel-arch into the stilted apse corresponds closely, when allowance is made for the curved nave-wall, with the chancel opening at St Magnus's Church, Egilsay, and other simpler Orcadian nave-and-chancel churches. In contrast, the 9th century Bohemian church at Levý Hradec, and the Scandinavian ones at Hälsingborg and Schleswig, had apses greater than a semicircle, whose entrances were narrower than their internal widths.

The possible Nordic context suggested here for Orphir Church is one that may also be appropriate for Egilsay itself. Fernie's discussion of round-towered churches in a North Sea setting, with links to Norfolk and North Germany, including the Schleswig area (Fernie 1988), may be extended further east, where examples occur in Skåne, close to the archiepiscopal city of Lund, which until 1154 was the centre of the ecclesiastical province that included Orkney (Cant 1973, 4). The four Scanian churches, Hammarlunda (Gustafsson & Weidhagen 1968), Hammarlöv, Blentarp and Bollerup, are all considerably larger than Egilsay and are probably of mid- or late-12th-century date but may be derived from lost earlier churches. However both Egilsay and Orphir allow ample scope for discussion as to whether the 12th century earldom of Orkney was receiving architectural ideas from South Scandinavia, or contributing them.

Finally, it will be obvious even from the few examples cited above that many round or centrally-planned churches and chapels were originally intended for private rather than parochial use, and others of this form include the Romanesque castle chapel at Ludlow and one on the ground floor of a circular keep at Starhemberg in Austria. In this and other examples, such as Søborg, the overall plan-form was evidently controlled by the needs of defence, while the resonances of Charlemagne's chapel at Aachen no doubt accounted for the popularity of the type in royal and aristocratic circles which might lack the direct connection of the Orkney earls with the Holy Land. In the case of the simpler buildings such as Orphir, moreover, their restricted scale was more appropriate to a congregation of limited size than to the assembled lay population of an area. We may be sure that the 'people' who attended vespers with Earl Paul in the 'fine church' of Orphir in December 1136, and returned to the hall to find one man dead and another dying, were not the common people of Orphir but the great men of the earldom.

Acknowledgements

I am grateful to Lars Kærulf Møller, Bornholm Museum, and to Ebbe Nyborg of the National Museum, Copenhagen, for discussion of the Scandinavian material; to Dr Barbro Sundnér, University of Lund, for providing plans of the Swedish round-towered churches; to Dr Martin Godja of Prague for information about Levý Hradec; and to friends including Colleen Batey, Ronald Cant, Barbara Crawford, Eric Fernie and Chris Morris for discussing the Viking Congress site-talk and a subsequent lecture on which this paper is based. None of them is to be held responsible for the views expressed.

REFERENCES

Anker, Peter & Andersson, Otto 1970. *The Art of Scandinavia*, London.
Bååth, L. M. (ed.) 1934. *Hälsingborgs Historia*, Hälsingborg.
Cant, Ronald 1973, 'The church in Orkney and Shetland and its relations with Norway and Scotland in the middle ages', in *Northern Scotland*, 1 (1972–3), pp. 1–18.
Crawford, Barbara E. (ed.) 1988. *St Magnus Cathedral and Orkney's twelfth century renaissance*, Aberdeen.
Dietrichson, L. & Meyer, Johan 1906. *Monumenta Orcadica* (English abridgement), Kristiania.
Dryden, Sir Henry 1896. 'Church at Orphir, Orkney', in *Ecclesiastical Architecture*, MacGibbon, D. and Ross, T., 1, pp. 141–5.
Eriksson, Torkel 1977. *Konsten i Sverige: Medeltiden*, Stockholm.
Fernie, Eric 1988. 'The church of St Magnus, Egilsay', in *St Magnus Cathedral*, ed. Crawford, Barbara E., pp. 140–61.
Frölén, Hugo F. 1911. *Nordens befäster rundkyrkor*, Stockholm.
Gustafsson, Evald & Weidhagen, Margareta 1968. 'Investigations in Hammarlunda Church', in *Res Medievales Ragnar Blomqvist Kal Mai MCMLXVIII oblata (Archaeologica Lundensia*, 3), pp. 154–68.
Johannsen, Hugo & Smidt, Claus M. 1985. *Danmarks arkitektur: kirkens huse*, Copenhagen.
Liddell, Rev Mr 1797. 'Parish of Orphir', in *Statistical Account*, ed. Sinclair, Sir John, 19, pp. 394–419.
MacGibbon, David & Ross, Thomas 1896–7. *The Ecclesiastical Architecture of Scotland*, Edinburgh.
Mårtensson, Thorsten 1934. 'Helsingborgs slott under medeltiden', in *Hälsingborgs Historia*, ed. Bååth, L. M., vol. 2: 2, 3–150.

Pálsson, Hermann & Edwards, Paul 1978. *Orkneyinga saga: the history of the Earls of Orkney*, Penguin Classics, London.

Pevsner, Nikolaus 1961. *The Buildings of England: Northamptonshire*, London.

Radford, C. A. Ralegh 1964. 'Art and architecture: Celtic and Norse', in *The Northern Isles*, ed. Wainwright, Frederick T., pp. 163–87.

RCAHMS 1946. Royal Commission on the Ancient and Historical Monuments of Scotland, *Twelfth Report with an Inventory of the Ancient Monuments of Orkney and Shetland*, Edinburgh.

Sinclair, Sir John (ed.) 1791–9. *The Statistical Account of Scotland*, Edinburgh.

Sláma, Jiří 1988. *Levý Hradec*, Prague.

Vellev, Jens 1973a. 'Vor tabte rundkirke', in *Skalk* 2, pp. 3–9.

Vellev, Jens 1973b. 'Die Ausgrabung der rundkirche "St Michaelis" in Schleswig', in *Beiträge zur Schleswiger Stadtgeschichte* 18, pp. 5–15.

Wainwright, Frederick T. (ed.) 1964. *The Northern Isles*, Edinburgh.

23

ORKNEY NORN

A SURVEY OF 'TABOO' TERMS

ALEXANDER FENTON

At the Viking Congress in Lerwick, my friend David Murison spoke on 'Scots Speech in Shetland' (Murison 1954, 255–60). When working with him on the Scottish National Dictionary, from 1955 till 1959, I compiled a glossary of the sea-language of fishermen in the Northern Isles. I am now patiently feeding this into my computer. My intention in this chapter is to further analyse this data, and to see what it could say for itself in terms of everyday life.

The first difficulty quickly presented itself. This Viking Congress is concerned with Orkney, but the bulk of the assembled data is from Shetland. Overall nearly 500 words have been labelled by the lexicographers Jakobsen and Marwick (1908; 1929) as fishermen's taboo words, used at sea but not on land. But of this number, I have identified only 20 Orkney examples, or 4 per cent of the alleged total for the Northern Isles. There was no category of 'taboo' words in Per Thorsen's analysis of Caithness Norn in 1950 (Thorsen 1954, 230–38). Examples are found in Caithness but these are essentially the same as those used amongst fishermen around the coasts of Scotland and on into England, the Isle of Man and Ireland (cf. Roeder 1904; Megaw 1941; O'Floinn 1980), namely terms relating to old taboo faithfuls such as the salmon, pig, rabbit, hare and minister. How is this apparently extreme difference between two groups of islands, not particularly remote from each other, to be explained? In any satisfactory explanation, if such can be found, will lie one of the keys to the interpretation of a set of words that scholars have made into something special.

First of all let me set out and classify the Orkney Norn terms that Marwick has entered in this Dictionary, including examples only tentatively labelled taboo by him.

Geographical Features

From Birsay, that once most primitive of parishes, comes *bairn*, a little hill, no doubt from ON *barn* but in form matching the Lowland Scots word for a child; and *hog*, a larger hill, from ON *haugr*, a mound. A Scottish National Dictionary informant from Sandwick, Stromness, recorded in 1933, that 'wir fishing-grund is seven hogs aff Marwick Heed', meaning that the boat was so far out to the west that the seven hills of Birsay were in sight in succession to the north. Both of these names were used by fishermen at sea in pinpointing fishing grounds.

Since the more general Orkney form of the word is *how* (as in Maeshowe), so recorded from the 18th century, the survival of a form with *g*, corresponding to the Shetland word, may be taken to go back at least to an 18th century or earlier form of speech in Orkney (*SND* s.v. Hog, *n.*2, and How, *n.*2).

Atmospheric Conditions

Two words, both from Sanday, come into question. They are *fair-weather* and *guid(s) weather*, thunder. Marwick (1929, 39) thinks they must be taboo words – 'evidently a relic of the old superstitious days when it was considered risky at sea to refer to things by their ordinary names'. For the second word, he compares Danish *guds-vejr*, and Low German *goddes-wedder*, a furious storm. The first word is not Norn and the second has at least a fifty-fifty chance of having a Low German origin, perhaps as a hangover from the Hanseatic traders or from Dutch fishermen. 'Geudwather' was first recorded in Orkney in 1889 (*SND* s.v. Guid). This raises the question of whether or not it is a simple equivalent of 'fair' weather, i.e. 'good' weather. The addition of the *-s-* in the middle is what appears to relate it to the Danish and Low German words, and allows Marwick to add (1929, 64): 'One is naturally prone to associate the "God" here with the Thundergod – Thor, the "Thunderer".' The lack of any Shetland equivalent, indeed, may tell against a Norn origin; there is, by the way, no word for thunder in the list of 323 meteorological terms recently gleaned from Jakobsen's *Dictionary* by the Swede, Greger Nässén (1988).

Religion

Religion is represented by three terms: *burly-hoose* and *munger-hoose*, a church, and *white-throat*, a minister. *Burly* probably derives from ON *byrligr*, promising a fair wind, Norwegian *byrleg*, favourable, propitious. *Munger* stems from ON *munka-hús*, a monastery, and may just point to pre-Reformation days. *White-throat* is clearly of younger vintage. In 1909 the *Old-Lore Miscellany* noted that the 'men of Rackwick in Hoy must not speak of a minister when in a boat. They call him a "white-throat"' (II, ii [1909], 107). Shetland fishermen used the same term, amongst others: 'The Minister was the Upstander, or the Beniman, or the Whitetrot (from his white collar)' (*Scots Magazine* August 1956, 341). This descriptive name, therefore, is common to the Northern Isles, though not recorded for the Scottish mainland, as far as I know.

Human Beings

Human beings are represented only by the word *pirren*, children. Its first recording is in the form *pirraina* in 1825 (Jamieson), meaning a child, generally a little girl, and in this sense is common to Orkney and Shetland according to

Edmondston's *Glossary* of 1866. In Orkney it is used in the plural, of children in general. Jakobsen claimed it in 1908 as a taboo term for a 'stunted, sickly child'. Though of unclear origin, it is almost certainly from the word *peerie*, that kenmark of the Northern Isles, i.e. *peerie ane*, parallel to Lowland Scots *littlin*, little one. It is likely, therefore, to be a Lowland Scots type compound, though the first element may well be connected with Norwegian dialectal *piren*, niggardly, feeble, Swedish dialectal *pirug*, slender, little, Norwegian *pir*, small fish, Faroese *pira*, a miser, *pirra*, a little creature (see *SND* s.v. *Peerie*). Even if still obscure in origin, it nevertheless appears in its present form as a blend of Scots and Norn.

Sea Creatures

Three words appear here: *hide*, a seal, and *himsel* and *kleppy*, a halibut or turbot.

Marwick thinks *hide* may be a taboo name, the name of the skin being used by synecdoche for the creature as a whole. He notes also that the North Ronaldsay people are nicknamed *selkies* or *hides*. 'Hide' is generally used in English for the skin, and jocularly for the human skin. If this is really a taboo name – and Marwick only supposes this – then it may be connected with the Orkney belief that seals could discard their skins and return to their original human state from time to time (see *SND* s.v. Hide, *n*.2).

Himsel is a Sanday term for the turbot or halibut, obviously Scots rather than Norn, for which I have found no parallels outside Orkney.

Kleppy is also a one-off term. It is likely to derive from Norwegian *klepp*, a gaff for hoisting a big fish into a boat, but since Old Scots has *clip*, a device for seizing or grasping, from the 15th century, influence from Scotland cannot be excluded.

Fishing Tools and Equipment

Two terms for a knife are included here: *biter*, from Rousay, and *ragger*, from Westray, the latter not included in Marwick. If not from the English or Scots 'bite', *biter* will be from ON *bita*, with the same sense. Though noted as a taboo word by Marwick (1929, 14), he added that such words were 'now used in a whimsical sense usually'. There is no Shetland equivalent, though attention may be drawn to *benibiter*, a word used in the Northern Isles of Shetland for a dog, i.e. 'bone-biter' (Jakobsen s.v.).

It was recorded in 1890 that if a fisherman called the knife he used for cutting the throat of a cod a knife, he had to throw it overboard. 'It had to be called a "ragger". That was to keep the devil away' (*Old-lore Misc.* II, ii [1909] 106). Omond noted the same name, later on (Omond 1911, 6). It is an agent noun from English *rag*, to make ragged, to tear. Though Shetland has no direct equivalent, Jakobsen records the verb *rag*, to hook a fish accidentally with a slanting stroke, which seems to encapsulate a comparable concept of tearing.

The end of a piece of line, especially of a long-line, is the *damp*. In joining two ends together, you would say, 'Hand me the damp' (Marwick 1929, 29). It is also used in Shetland for the lower end of a line, and sometimes for an end-piece in general. It was first recorded by Edmondston in 1866. Shetland also has a verbal use of the word, meaning to wear off the end of a fishing hand-line, or long-line, as in: 'de line is dampet (dampet op)', i.e. the end has been torn off (Jakobsen 1908, 96–7). There is also the Shetland name *arvi* for the same thing. It can be said that Shetland has both more names for this item and also a more differentiated range of senses for the work *damp* itself. For once, Jakobsen was inclined to consider it of fairly modern origin. Marwick was less certain. There are apparent Norwegian, Danish and Swedish parallels in the word *tamp*, a stump of rope or a rope-end, and Low German and Dutch have *tamp* also; but as Falk und Torp point out (1910, 1245), the sense of these points to something thick and lumpy. Probably the modification in sense, if the same word, and the spread over both island groups, argues for greater age than Jakobsen allowed.

Old Stronsay fishermen sometimes used *klaran* for an anchor. This has no clear parallels, nor is the etymology clear. Marwick compares Icelandic *klara*, a rake for spreading dung, with suffixed article; Norwegian *klorene*, claws, may also be relevant.

The final two in this group are the very odd terms *horse-leg-been* and *keel-root*, the right hand and left hand oars in a boat. Both are from one Rousay man, who related that if the skipper wanted the right oar to pull harder, he would say 'Up, *horse-leg-been!*' (Marwick 1929, 75). It is over 30 years now since the Norwegian Svale Solheim drew attention to the remarkable coincidence that these Orkney words translate the names of Folafoten in Hisøy, and Kjølrota, an off-lying skerry in the Sognefjord area. He argued for a transference of place names to the names of oars or rowing positions by suggesting derivation from navigational directions by Norwegians sailing these waters (Solheim 1947, 1–14). But a single source is a weak base for an argument. Furthermore, Marwick has heard the terms *owse-room* and *backber* for men rowing on the starboard and port sides, using the names for the parts of the boat where they sat. Perhaps *horse-leg-been* and *keel-root* are corruptions of names of parts of the boat, or jocular terms of purely local significance. I find it hard to see anything else in all this but the long arm of sheer coincidence (Fenton 1968–9, 118; 1978, 619).

Fishing

There is a curious fishing term from Rousay. As Marwick noted: 'A man would say, "We're gettan naething; I'm gaan tae run me line this time on Nellie o' H-'s *kan*." "Rin thee line this time on R-'s *kan*; thoo'll maybe hae better luck."' Marwick heard the phrase used jocularly, but was in no doubt that it was earlier used in all seriousness. The same word is found in Lowland Scotland as well as in Shetland in the sense of skill, knowledge, and also supernatural power. The verb *can*, meaning to have knowledge of or skill in, goes back to the 15th century in Old Scots. There is no obvious Norse parallel. The word is therefore likely to come from Scots, and is not so much a taboo word in itself as part of a phrase that touches on the possibility of superstitious knowledge.

Daily Life on Land

The only word in this category is *after-burn*, which in Birsay means the last 'wort' drawn off the malt. According to Marwick (1929, 2): 'there was a superstitious fear of calling the water used in brewing anything but the "burn", otherwise the ale might be spoiled'. This is not a sea word, but a land superstition. The name evidently comes from Scots *burn*, the water used in brewing, usually warmed up but not boiling. In this sense it is especially common to the northern counties of Scotland. In old Scots, it is recorded as water used in brewing from 1509, and is the same word as *burn*, a brook or stream, OE *burna*, a spring, well (*SND* s.v. Burn, *n.*).

There could well be other Orkney examples, even if they have not survived or have not been recorded with taboo implications. Orcadians were as superstitious as anyone else in earlier times. In 1633, it is recorded that Marrioun Layland washed a cat's feet into a fisherman's bait water. She cast the water after him when he went to sea:

> 'David Jok -was making mone that he had not luck to get fisch that zeir: The said Marrioun answerit and said, that that might be eassilie mendit, and callit for the thing that geid about the fyre, quhilk was the cat, and said that scho wold wasch the cat his head and feit into the watter quherin the bait was to be keipit, and said that scho wold take that watter and cast it about him and wpon him, and into his sea caschie, and into his bait coubbie, and quhen he came to the sea he schould get fisch'.
>
> (*Misc. Abbotsford Club* I [1837], 151)

This makes the welcome role of the cat clear for Orkney, and its name is not known there as one to be avoided at sea; yet Shetland fishermen had no fewer than 22 names for this little pet, and a superstitious feeling against the cat was widespread in the British Isles and Ireland, the Faroe Islands, Iceland, Sweden and Norway, and France (cf. O'Floinn 1980, 137–39).

As I said earlier, the Orkney inventory of items amounts to less than 4 per cent of taboo words noted as such in the Northern Isles. If we consider the Norn words in Jakobsen's and Marwick's *Dictionaries*, we get 10,000 for Shetland and Orkney has 3,000, or only 30 per cent of the total. Even if we take into account the greater influence of Lowland Scots on Orkney due to its greater proximity to the Mainland, and the much greater and continuing importance of fishing and all things associated with it in Shetland, the disparity between these percentages remains striking. In fact only 5 of the 20 Orkney examples can be certainly related to Norse, though there are 6 other possibles. The intermixture of Scots is marked, and there are 2 possible Low German words.

As the introductions to Jakobsen's and Marwick's *Dictionaries* show, the 18th century saw the end of Norn as a consistent language, though survival was longer in parts of Shetland than in Orkney (see also Fenton 1978, 616–18). Analysis of the total 'taboo' word hoard shows the majority of the recorded terms to be Norse, especially in Shetland, with a relatively thin scatter of Scots, Dutch and

Low German words. If we forget the taboo concept and think in terms of Norn words, even though still restricting ourselves to those marked as taboo, we see that analysis can tell a great deal about culture contacts, material culture, social and work organisation, and even forms of land holding (Fenton 1968–9, 121). Above all differences between the Shetland and Orkney island groups are emphasised. What the taboo inventory in Shetland represents is, I am certain, a fine example of an old vocabulary surviving long in the very special conditions of sea-fishing, in a man's working world. A recent study by Reginald Byron of Burra Isle in Shetland has shown well how fishing crews were physically isolated for substantial lengths of time, interacting only with their fellows on board. Many were related to each other, or came from the same close-knit community (Byron 1986, 96). The nature of such communities was such that there was little or no question of acculturation processes of the kind that lead to linguistic assimilation through intergroup interaction (cf. Hechter 1975, 192).

The old Norn ways of speech and especially work-related words remain much more intact under these special conditions. We are dealing with the concept of taboo to only a minor degree. The bulk of what remains is the working vocabulary, and I am reasonably sure that the real reason for the disparity in numbers of 'taboo' words between Shetland and Orkney is the 200 years of rarification, continual restriction in spheres of use, that in the end has given rise to a mystique. There is no word in the sources of any taboo language before the 17th century. Eighteenth-century sources speak only of Norn (and of its penetration by Scots). The taboo language of the Northern Isles appears to be in a great degree an academic concept of Victorian times and later, and, as Karl Sandred has pointed out also, is a vocabulary rather than a language, a fact which gives further support to my argument.

And there is a further message. I have said precious little about the Orkney Earldom, though I have been keeping in my mind the need to interpret back from known factors of a late date. A comparative viewpoint is necessary as well, and the obvious comparisons for Orkney are Shetland and Scotland. Shetland is so different from Orkney in so many ways, often small, that this needs much explanation. This paper is in fulfilment of a modest part of this need.

REFERENCES

Byron, Reginald 1986. *Sea Change. A Shetland Society 1970–79*, St Johns, Newfoundland.

Edmondston, Thomas 1866. *Etymological Glossary of the Shetland & Orkney Dialect*, Edinburgh.

Falk, Hjalmar S. und Torp, Alf 1910 *Norwegisch-Dänisches Etymologisches Wörterbuch*, Heidelberg.

Fenton, Alexander 1968–9. 'The Tabu Language of the Fishermen of Orkney and Shetland', *Ethnologia Europaea* II–III, 118–22.

Fenton, Alexander 1978. *The Northern Isles: Orkney and Shetland*, Edinburgh, 618–22.

Hechter, Michael 1975. *Internal Colonialism. The Celtic fringe in British national development, 1536–1966*, London

Jamieson, John 1825. *An Etymological Dictionary of the Scots Language*, Edinburgh.

Jakobsen, Jakob 1908 [1985]. *An Etymological Dictionary of the Norn Language in Shetland*, Shetland Folk Society, Lerwick.

Marwick, Hugh 1929. *The Orkney Norn*, Oxford.

Megaw, Basil R. S. 1941. 'Early Manx Fishing Craft', *Mariner's Mirror* 27:2, 103.

Misc. Abbotsford Club: Miscellany of the Abbotsford Club I, Edinburgh 1837, 151.

Murison, David 1954. 'Scots Speech in Shetland', in *Viking Congress Lerwick, July 1950*, ed. Simpson, W. Douglas, Aberdeen, pp. 255–60.

Nässén, Greger 1988. *Norn Weather Words. 323 Meteorological Terms in Jakobsen's Dictionary and Their Extent in Present-Day Shetland Dialect*, Department of English, Stockholm University, typescript.

O'Floinn, Bairbre 1980. *Cold Iron and the Cast. A Study of the Naming Prejudices of Irish Fishermen*, Unpublished MA thesis, Department of Irish Folklore, Dublin 1980.

Old-lore Misc.: Old-Lore Miscellany of Orkney, Shetland, Caithness & Sutherland II, ii (1909) 107/106.

Omond, James 1911. *Orkney Eighty Years Ago*, Kirkwall.

Roeder, Charles 1904. *Manx Notes and Queries*, Douglas, Isle of Man.

Scots Mag.: Scots Magazine August 1856, 341.

SND: Scottish National Dictionary.

Solheim, Svale 1947. 'Folafoten-Kjølrota', *Maal og Minne*, 1–14.

Thorsen, Per 1954. 'The Third Norn Dialect – That of Caithness', in *Viking Congress Lerwick, July 1950*, ed. Simpson, W. Douglas, Aberdeen, pp. 230–8.

24

THE LORD'S PRAYER
IN ORKNEY AND SHETLAND NORN

LAURITS RENDBOE

Mr Chairman, ladies and gentlemen, members of the Eleventh Viking Congress – I nearly added 'brothers and sisters', owing to the theme to which we will give our attention for the next half hour, for even though we may not constitute a Church assembly or a congregation as such, we are here assembled to discuss a prayer of great importance, not only to us latecomers, but also to the Norn-speakers of long ago who used to say it in their native tongue.

So, let us for a short while abandon the outer accoutrements of Norse life in this northern area which our beloved historians and archaeologists have described so well, the old houses, walls, arms and tools, the bones of man and beast, yes, even the mice and lice which plagued them in those days, and instead turn our attention to the inner man of the old *Orkneyingar* and *Hjaltlendingar* who communicated with their Maker in Norn, by means of the Lord's Prayer in that venerable tongue.

Now, about Norn as a language I do feel a few words need to be said, of that I became acutely aware yesterday when I heard one of our very distinguished scholars call Norn a 'debased' language – something which it, to my knowledge, never was. Basically, what we call Norn nowadays developed in the most natural way from the West Norwegian language brought to Shetland, Orkney, Caithness and the other areas 'west over sea' to which the Vikings came, and the very designation 'Norn', which may have a somewhat mysterious sound in the ears of some, is merely a natural contraction of the word *Norrœna*, which means 'northern'. The word itself is an apt illustration of the development of the language, which by means of contractions, loss of endings and other linguistic material, etc., developed into a West Norse dialect quite close to Faroese and to the dialects of Western Norway.

As far as the idea of its being 'debased' goes, this seems to derive from an old misunderstanding based, at least in part, on the admittedly poor state of the altogether too few Norn texts which have survived till modern times, but here we must remember that the majority of these texts which were taken down by Jakob Jakobsen in the 1890s, were not transmitted to him by Norn-speakers, but by people who merely remembered their parents or even their grandparents speaking Norn long years ago, and so, quite naturally, these informants were not able to give him a precise rendering of the old, half-forgotten rhymes and sayings.

There are a few texts, however, which apparently were handed down by Norn-speakers, namely those collected in 1774 by George Low, who wrote down the so-called 'Coningsburghen Phrase', a short word list, the *Hildina*-ballad, and the Lord's Prayer, the latter ones collected on his tour to Foula, where Norn was still spoken at that time (Low 1879, 104–14). The last-mentioned of these texts, the Lord's Prayer, is one of the most important Norn texts found, both because it is one of the longest continuous texts of its kind, and because of its excellent state of preservation – and, moreover, it is the only Norn text found in both Orkney and Shetland, and thus it forges a strong linguistic link between the two island groups. Now, Low took down the Shetland version in 1774, but we do not know exactly when and where the Orkney variant was found; it was published however, in the year 1700 in James Wallace's *An Account of the Islands of Orkney*, 2nd edn., pp. 68–9. No doubt it was taken down from the lips of a native speaker (Wallace died in 1688, and Norn was spoken in various places in Orkney at least until the 1750s, Marwick 1929, 225–7). I know of no manuscript copy of Wallace's version, but Low included it with the Foula version for the sake of comparison (cf. Fig. 24.1 which is taken from page 87 of Low's manuscript). There are at least two other handwritten versions of the Shetland variant, one of them purportedly from Unst, about 1800, and the other, which is virtually identical, is dated Lerwick 1884, but since both of them are of dubious origin and seem to be rather faulty copies, they are not included in this short study.[1]

Now when tackling such a text, which – according to Low – seems a bit 'corrupted', we need to apply a little textual criticism, having for our first principle the rule: *This made sense when spoken!* Maybe it did not make sense to Wallace or to Low, for they were Scotsmen who apparently knew little or no Norn from actual practice – but to the native Norn speakers it did. No doubt they had learned that old and dear prayer in early childhood from their Norn-speaking parents, and now they were able to recite it by heart. Let us just consider the steps of transmission:

(1) *The reciter*: No doubt he or she was a native Norn-speaker who knew the meaning and who could 'say' it in the usual manner, probably somewhat hurried and not too loud.

(2) *The writer*: A Scotsman who did not understand the language and who would easily miss the finer points, to say the least. Also, he would have to write down a recital in Norwegian dialect with his own Scoto-English spelling and, later, when he made his 'fair copy' for the printer, there would be more room for errors.

(3) *The printer*: Printers set what they see or believe they see, and when they do

Ki. — *The Norse Language is much worn out here, yet there are some who know a few words of it, it was the language of the last age, but will be entirely lost by the next. The Lords Prayer in Foula Norse is as follows.*

"Fy vor o er i Chimeri. Halaght vara nam det. La Koningg :dum din cumma. La vill din vera guerde i vrildin sunda wi chimeri. Gav vus dagh u dagloght braee. Forgive sin: corwara sin vi forgiva gem oo sinda gainst vus. Lia vus che o vera tempa, but delivra vus fro adlu idlu for do i ir Konungdum, u guri, u glori, Amen."

To compare this with Wallace's specimen of Orkney Norn.

"Favor i ir i chimeri. Hellour/rather Hellent/ ir i nam shite, filla cosdeum thite cumma, veya thine mota vara gort o yurn sinna gort i chimeri, ga vus da on da daught brow vara, forgive vus sinna vora sin vee firgive sindara mutha vus, lyu vus ye i tumealion min delivra vus fro olt ilt, Amen. or On aa meleth vera.

It is probable they are both corrupted, however I imagine the Foula specimen comes nearer the original language, and that so seems to be mixed with English more than the distant cou= :inship of the different tongues will allow. None of them can write their ancient language and but very few speak it, the best phrases are all gone and nothing remains but a few names of things and two or

Figure 24.1: Low's handwritten version of the Lord's Prayer as noted down by him in Foula, to which he added Wallace's Orkney version for comparison (Edinburgh University Library, Special Collections).

not know the language and work from handwritten material they are very prone to errors.

Of course we do not need to consider the third step in connection with Low's specimen, because we have his own manuscript, but we do not have Wallace's, so there we must make allowance for the full 'complement of errors', from the spoken word to the printed page.

Turning now to Wallace's text (it is the older one of the two), remembering that it was spoken in Norn, i.e. in West Norse, we may transcribe it in an approximation to Norwegian dialect spelling (which has never been standardised), somewhat like this:

Fa' vor e er i hjim'ri, Hellet[a] vere nam þit.
Gy' la kosdum[b] þit koma, a velja[c] þin mota vara gort o jor'n, sen 'a e[d] gort i hjim'ri.
Gæv vos da o da daligt brau vort[e].
Fyrgæv vos sinna vora sen vi fyrgæv sindara moða vos, lai vos '(k)je i *tumtation*[f], *min*[g] *delivera*[h] vos fro olt ilt.
Amen – o sa mæteð vera[i].

In this transcription I have used two letters no longer employed in the writing of Norwegian, namely 'þ' and 'ð', corresponding to unvoiced and voiced 'th' in English (Wallace spells these words with 'th'), but they are still used in Old Norse texts, as well as in Modern Faroese and Modern Icelandic, so I felt it appropriate to use them here, where they no doubt are better representations of the Norn sounds used than Wallace's English spelling. My notes are explanatory:

(a) Low corrects Wallace's 'Helleur' to 'Helleut', and no doubt he is right. The vowel of the second, unstressed syllable probably is a schwa-like sound [ə].

(b) 'Kosdum' (in Wallace's text, 'cosdum') no doubt represents 'kongsdóm', and the vowel of the first syllable probably was strongly nasalised, to compensate for the missing 'ng'.

(c) In Wallace's 'veya' the central consonant most likely was the long, palatalised l-sound so common in Norwegian dialects [ʎ] (Stemshaug 1978, 55).

(d) This 'e' represents 'er' ('is') and I guess that this is one of the finer points missed by the writer.

(e) Wallace had 'brau vora', which I take for an error for 'brau vort'. ON *brauð* and its modern Scandinavian variants are all neuter.

(f) Here is a Scoto-English word, most likely derived from the English Bible versions then used in the churches.

(g) This word, *min*, is Dano-Norwegian ('men'=but), and may have been derived from the then current Dano-Norwegian Bible translation.

(h) Once again, the Scoto-English intrudes; 'delivera' is from the English Bible then in use.

(i) The last four words are pure Norn, and as early as in 1860 the Danish dialectologist K. J. Lyngby diagnosed them to mean 'and so may it be' (ON *ok svá mætti þat vera*), i.e. it is a plain rendering of the word *Amen* into Norn.

This, then, is a very passable Norwegian dialect text, even though, for reasons unknown to us, a few Scoto-English words have sneaked into the last clause of the prayer proper, also a Dano-Norwegian one.

Now, let us get on to Low's Shetland version, which in a similar transcription would come out somewhat like this:

Fai vor o er i hjimmeri, heilagt vara nam dit.
La konungdom din koma, la vill' din vera gerð i vrildin sen da er i hjimmeri.
Gæv vos dag o [dag]ᵃ daglegt brau.
Fyrgæv sindar vora, sen vi fyrgæva djem å sinda *genst*ᵇ vos.
Laie vos ekki å vera *tempa*ᶜ, *but delivra*ᵈ vos fro adlu idlu, for 'dor er konungdom, o *puri*, o *glori*ᵉ. Amen.

Despite the obvious differences (mostly of a minor nature) it is easy to see that this is, indeed, the same prayer. The points referred to in the notes are these:

(a) The second 'dag' has been added on the strength of the Orkney version; most likely it was omitted because of the following 'daglegt'.

(b) This curious word, never found elsewhere, may well be a mixture of ON *gegnst* and English 'against'.

(c) Another *hapax legomenon*: 'tempa' looks as though it were derived from Shetlandic 'temba' ('tension', even 'danger') under the influence of English 'tempted'.

(d) Here we again have some Scoto-English words, but the ending of the verb has been nornicized (-*a*), a feature it shares with the same verb in the Orkney version (see above).

(e) This last line, the so-called doxology, is no doubt also an addition from the English Bible, as it was not found in the ON versions preserved (from which the Norn versions may well have derived), nor is it found in the slightly older Orkney variant. In my reconstruction of this part of the text I have taken the spelling 'do i' for a corruption of 'dor', the genitive of the polite personal pronoun 'di' (2nd person plural, used to address individuals of high standing, cf. its use in the *Hildina*-ballad). Here it is apparently used to render the archaic 'thine' of the English Bible.

As for the two words 'puri' and 'glori', they are also from the English Bible, but somehow the endings have been harmonised, maybe even nornicised, as -*i* corresponds to ON weak masculines in the nominative singular, a feature still found in the substratum of Norn in Shetland in Jakobsen's day (Gordon & Taylor 1957, 288; Jakobsen 1897, 101).[2]

A question of great importance which has hitherto been all but neglected by scholars is this: Whence did the Orcadians and Shetlanders get this old form of the prayer? It would appear that both variants derive from one source, most likely one of the early Norse renderings from the Latin into the vernacular, of which a few are still extant. These ancient Norwegian and Icelandic versions of this may be studied in detail in Ian J. Kirby's *Biblical Quotation in Old Icelandic-Norwegian Religious Literature* (1976–80), from which the following abbreviations are taken:

IsHom.: Old Icelandic Book of Homilies
NoHom.: Old Norwegian Book of Homilies
Leif.: *Leifar fornra kristinna fræða íslenzkra*

In Figure 24.2 you will see a syntactic comparison of the ON and its underlying Latin with the two Norn versions. While this comparison makes it even more probable that the Norn versions of this prayer derived from one of the early renderings into Old Norwegian, we also see clear evidence for changes in the various petitions, but (except for the Scoto-English intrusions) they all seem to be quite natural and may simply reflect the spoken language and its changes during the centuries, when Old Norwegian turned into Middle Norwegian and finally into Modern Norwegian; of course, the form of Norwegian spoken in the islands gradually became isolated and finally died out, also it was then a mere dialect with no written form, and so lacked the written or printed memory aids found in the homeland, Norway. Let us now take a look at some of the changes.

No doubt the basic form of the prayer still reflects faithfully the original ON form transmitted to the islands in the early days of Christianity in the North, and from the Dano-Norwegian sphere of influence we find the word 'min', which no doubt is DaNo 'men' (but), probably derived from one of the early Dano-Norwegian New Testaments in the 16th century.

Other words seem to reflect a local Norn development, such as 'tempa' and 'gainst' in the Sh variant, while the strengthening vocative 'Gilla' ('Gu' la', ON *Guð, lát* = 'God, let') in the Or variant is quite unique. Sh 'vrildin' ('the world') for ON *jǫrðunni* 'the earth' and Or 'chimrie', Sh 'chimeri' (ON *himinríki*, 'the kingdom of the heavens') give a rather different contrast in the third petition. The use of the imperative 'la' (ON *lát*='let') is Norn, of course, and it is paralleled in No dialect and elsewhere in the Scandinavian languages.

The influence from the English Bible is seen, first in the words 'delivra' (Sh) and 'delivera' (Or), also 'tumtation' (Or) and 'puri' and 'glori' (Sh), even in the inclusion of the final doxology; then, its influence is also seen in the verbal forms in the third petition, where Or 'vara gort' and Sh 'vera guerde' probably reflect the English 'be done' of the Authorised Version of 1611. And the same version's 'as it is' probably contributed to Or's 'sinna gort' and Sh's 'sin da er'. Of course, when the English Bible was used exclusively by the Scottish clergy and the Norn-speakers had no printed or written memory aids, such encroachments were hardly to be avoided over the centuries.

Indeed, it is nothing less than marvellous that this ancient prayer survived long enough to be written down in both island groups, and maybe its common use in private life and especially at funerals played a part in this. There is an old story from Orkney which may illustrate this: There, an old man on his deathbed called his minister to pray for him, but when this gentleman of the cloth started out in his normal Scottish manner, the old man stopped him:

> Awa', awa', wi' your sly Scotch tongue! I want you tae pray i' the Danska tong. Hid s'all never be said that ony een prayed ower me i' the ferry-lupper's jabber!

A. *The address*

Or	Fa	vor	i	ir	i	chimrie
Sh	Fy	vor	o	er	i	Chimeri
ON	Faþer	vár	es	ert	a	himnom (IsHom. 33)
					i	himenríki (Leif. 159)
Lat	Pater	noster	qui	es	in	celis

B. *First petition*

Or	Helleu(t)	(v)iri	nam	thite
Sh	Halaght	vara	nam	dit
ON	Helgesc		nafn	þitt (IsHom. 33)
		Verði	nafn	þitt heilagt (NoHom. 133)
Lat	Sanctificetur		nomen	tuum

C. *Second petition*

Or	Gilla	cosdum	thite	cumma
Sh	La	konungdum	din	cumma
ON	Til kome	ríki	þitt	
Lat	Adveniat	regnum	tuum	

D. *Third petition, first part*

Or	(a')	veya	thine	mota vara gort	o	yurn
Sh	La	vill	din	vera guerde	i	vrildin
ON	Værði	vili	þin	sa	a	iarðu
Lat	Fiat	voluntas	tua	sicut	in	celo

second part

Or	sinna	(e') gort	i	chimrie
Sh	sinda	er	i	chimeri
ON	sem		i	himnum
Lat	et		in	terra

Figure 24.2: A syntactic comparison of the Orkney, Shetland, Old Norse and Latin versions of the Lord's Prayer.

. *Fourth petition*

Or	Ga(v)	vus	da ou da	dalight	brow vora
Sh	Gav	vus	dagh u (dagh?)	dagloght	brau
ON	Gef	oss	í dag	brauð vort dagligt	
Lat	Panem nostrum cotidianum da nobis hodie				

. *Fifth petition, first part*

Or		Firgive	vus	sinna	vora
Sh		Forgive		sindor	wara
ON	Oc	fyr gefþu	oss	synþer	órar
Lat	Et	dimitte	nobis	debita	nostra

    second part

Or	sin		vee	firgive	sindara	mutha	vus	
Sh	sin		vi	forgiva	gem ao sinda	gainst	wus	
ON	sem		vér	fyr gefom	þeim er	viþ	oss	hafa misgert (IsHom. 33)
					skulderom órom (IsHom. 34)			
Lat	sicut	et	nos	dimittimus	debitoribus	nostris		

. *Sixth petition, first part*

Or		ly(v)	vus	ye	i	tumtation
Sh		lia	wus	eke	o	vera tempa
ON		leið	oss	eigi	i	freistni
Lat	Et	ne nos inducas		in	tentationem

    second part

Or	min	delivera	vus	fro	olt	ilt
Sh	but	delivra	wus	fro	adlu	idlu
ON	heldr	leys þv	oss	fra	öllu	illu (IsHom. 34; Leif. 161)
Lat	sed	libera		a		malo

. *The conclusion*

Or	Amen. *OR* Ou sa meteth vera.
Sh	For dor ir konungdom, u puri, u glori, Amen.
ON	(No equivalent)
Lat	(No equivalent)

As the minister was unable to comply with the wishes of the old man he was dismissed, because the only proper prayer in this situation apparently was the 'Danska' or, no doubt, Norn prayer, to which the old man evidently had been accustomed throughout his long life (Dennison 1880, x-xi). Indeed, this may well have been the very final function of the Lord's Prayer in Norn, to lay to rest the last ones belonging to the last Norn generation and, in a way, could there have been a better and more fitting way for it to go?

Notes

1. See my fuller treatment of this prayer elsewhere (Rendboe 1989–90).
2. See also the reconstruction of the Orkney form of the prayer (into Middle Norwegian) and the notes offered to both Norn versions by the Norwegian scholar Gustav Indrebø (1951, 285–6).

REFERENCES

Dennison, W. T. 1880. *Orcadian Sketchbook*, Kirkwall.

Gordon, E. V. & Taylor, A. R. 1957. *An Introduction to Old Norse*, 2nd edn., Oxford.

Indrebø, G. 1951. *Norsk Målsoga*, Bergen.

Jakobsen, J. 1897. *Det norröne sprog på Shetland*, Copenhagen.

Kirby, I. J. 1976, 1980. *Biblical Quotation in Old Icelandic-Norwegian Religious Literature*, I–II, Reykjavik.

Low, G. 1879. *A Tour through the Islands of Orkney and Schetland*, Kirkwall.

Lyngby, R. J. 1860. 'Om Sproget på Hjaltlandsøerne', *Annaler for Nordisk Oldkyndighed og Historie*, 201–16.

Marwick, H. 1929. *The Orkney Norn*, Oxford.

Rendboe, L. 1989–90. 'The Lord's Prayer in Orkney and Shetland Norn', *Nowele* 14, 77–112 and 15, 49–111.

Stemshaug, O. 1978. *Språkleg Tradisjon*, Oslo.

Wallace, J. 1700. *An Account of the Islands of Orkney*, 2nd edn, London.

25

SOME ORKNEY PERSONAL NAMES

GILLIAN FELLOWS-JENSEN

It has long been a commonplace of personal-name research that there are personal names which are in some way typical of the Northern and Western Isles (cf. Lind 1905–15, 976; Björkman 1912, 28–29; *DR* col. 718; Adigard des Gautries 1954, 268–69; Fellows Jensen 1968, 271). No attempt seems to have been made, however, to list or classify the names which have been thought by various scholars to be characteristic of the Viking settlements on the islands. This, of course, is chiefly because the body of names current in the islands does not differ radically from the names current in Norway and Iceland in the Viking period and most of the names are also recorded in Danish sources. It is my aim therefore, to discuss a few of the names which have been assumed to be characteristic of Orkney.

To gain an idea of the names brought to Orkney by the first settlers, I have chosen to look at the personal names contained in placenames in -*staðir* in the islands. From among these names, *Bersi, Fleinn, Geirmundr, Grímr, Haddr, Kollr, Tannr, Þórir* and *Þormóðr* are all also recorded independently or in placenames in Yorkshire and Lincolnshire, counties which were settled by Danes in the Viking period. These names and several of the others are well evidenced in Norway and Iceland. It is really only *Jaddvǫr* in a lost **Jaddvararstaðir* and **Kjarrekr* in Cairston that would seem to be peculiar to Orkney (Marwick 1952, 97 & 162). *Jaddvǫr* or *Játvǫr* was the name of an illegitimate daughter of the 11th-century Orkney earl, Erlendr, and the 16th-century Danish translation of *Orkneyinga saga* records the name of the place where she lived with her son as *paa Jadvarstodum*, where the text in *Flateyjarbók* reads *á Knarrastǫðum*, which must be erratic (*Orkneyinga saga* 86, 121 & 171; cf. Marwick 1952, 236–7). It is not, however, certain that **Jaddvararstaðir* was a genuine Orkney placename, for later in the saga Játvǫr's son was said to be living at *Geitabergi*, which is probably to be identified with Gaitnip. The name **Jaddvararstaðir* may have been invented as a replacement for an obviously erratic name-form on the basis of the feminine personal name. This personal name is not recorded in any other source. The spelling *Ját-* occurs in other

Scandinavian personal names, where it represents a scandinavianised form of the Old English (OE) element *Ēad-* (cf. *Játmundr* and *Játvarðr* for *Eādmund* and *Eādweard*) and *Játvǫr* is probably to be looked upon either as a scandinavianised version of an unrecorded OE **Ēad-waru* or as a hybrid compound of *Ját-* < *Eād-* and the Scandinavian (Scand) element *-vǫr*. No explanation has hitherto been offered for the name **Kjarrekr* in *Kjarreksstaðir* (Cairston). It might be tentatively explained as a variant of *Kjallakr*, which is a loan from Celtic *Ceallach* and sometimes occurs in Scandinavian sources in the form *Kjarlakr* (Lind 1905–15, 687–8). Alternatively, it may be a hybrid compound of the Celtic element *Ciar-*, recorded in other Celtic loan-names in Scandinavian such as *Kiaran* (< *Ciarān*) and *Kiarvall* (< *Cerball*), and the Scand element *-rekr*. Neither **Kjarrekr* nor *Jaddvǫr/Játvǫr* would seem to have taken root in Orkney or elsewhere. The most interesting fact about the two names in the context of the present survey is that they both reflect contact with the languages of earlier arrivals in the British Isles, **Kjarrekr* with Celtic and *Játvǫr* with English.

Of greater significance for the isolation of personal names typical of Orkney than these two rarities, however, are a number of names which are not only well evidenced in Orkney but also recorded in many other areas where Scandinavian was spoken in the Viking period. A good example to begin with is the name *Sumarliði*, which has been generally assumed to have arisen in the Atlantic islands. The first recorded bearer of the name in Orkney is Sumarliði, the eldest son of Earl Sigurðr digri. He received a third part of the Orkney earldom on the death of his father in 1014 (*Orkneyinga saga* 27–8). Other men called Sumarliði also appear in *Orkneyinga saga*: Sumarliði Óspaksson, Sumarliði, the father of Þorkell fóstri, Sumarliði Kolbeinsson, Sumarliði, the friend of Sveinn Ásleifarson, and Sumarliði hölðr, a chieftain from the Scottish fiords (*Orkneyinga saga* 85, 116, 193, 268 & 274). The name became popular in the Atlantic islands and, in gaelicised form *Somhairle*, it remains in use in the Hebrides to the present day. It will be familiar to some readers because of the works of the great Gaelic poet Somhairle MacGill-Eain, which in English translation have been published under the anglicised form of his name, Sorley Maclean.

The generally accepted explanation of the name *Sumarliði* is that it must have originated as a by-name, 'summer traveller', referring to men who took part in Viking expeditions in the summer months. Assar Janzén, however, seemed to prefer the explanation which takes the name to be a variant of the name *Vetrliði*, which in turn he assumed to be identical with the appellative *vetrliði*, 'a one-winter-old bear' (Janzén 1947, 45, 150 n.7). The fact that the name *Sumarliði* occurs in the Viking colonies in the west rather than in the Scandinavian homelands, together with the use of *-liði* as a second element in other personal names with associations with Viking travellers, e.g. *Hafliði*, *Sæliði*, *Vestliði*, combine to convince me that *Sumarliði* developed into a personal name from being a by-name for a roving Viking rather than as a variant of a term for a young bear. That this assumption is correct is supported by the fact that *somarlidius* in the sense 'Viking' occurs as a loanword from Scandinavian in a Latin account in a 14th-century manuscript of the defeat of a Viking fleet near Buchan in Aberdeenshire in the middle of the 10th century (Anderson 1980, 252). In this context it is worth noting that the Old English word *sumorlida* is only recorded in the *Anglo-Saxon Chronicle* s.a. 871 and that it there seems to have the meaning 'fleet'.

Although the name *Sumarliði* has been thought to have arisen in the Atlantic islands, it is recorded earlier in other areas. Several men with this name are mentioned in Icelandic sources, including a 10th-century Hrappr Sumarliðason, who was said to be Scottish on his father's side but all his mother's family came from the Hebrides and he was born there (*Laxdœla saga* 19; *Landnámabók* 142). Hrappr also had a son called Sumarliði. *Landnámabók* reveals further that the fifth son of Ketill Hœngr was called Heriolfr, that his son was called Sumarliði and his grandson Vetrliði. The intriguing fact from an onomastic point of view about this family is that they lived in a farm which, according to *Landnámabók*, was once called *í Sumarliþabœ* but at the time of the compilation of that work was known as *undir Brekkum* (*Landnámabók* 348). The Icelandic scholar Þórhallur Vilmundarson suggested in a lecture in London in 1975 that the specific of the placename Sumarliðabœr might be the Scandinavian compound appellative **sumar-hlíðar*, 'summer slopes', referring to pastures originally only employed in the summer. This explanation is formally acceptable but in the light of the frequent occurrence of the personal name *Sumarliði*, it does not seem necessary to look further than the personal name for the specific of the placename. There is nevertheless something slightly unusual about the placename in an Icelandic context and this is the fact that it is the only Icelandic placename consisting of a personal name plus the generic *-bœr* to be recorded in early sources (Kuhn 1966, 262; Bandle 1977, 61–2). In an attempt to explain the coining of the name *Sumarliþabœr*, Hans Kuhn has suggested that Sumarliði Heriolfsson's mother may have come from the Danelaw and that it might be her influence which is reflected in the choice of farm-name, since placenames consisting of a personal name plus *-bý* were much commoner in the areas of England settled by Danes than in the Scandinavian homelands (Kuhn 1972, 392). A placename formally identical with Icelandic *Sumarliþabœr* occurs no less than five times in the Danelaw, four times as Somerby and once as Somersby, and the multiple occurrence of this name led me to claim several years ago that the specific was more likely to be the genitive plural of the appellative *sumarliði*, 'summer traveller', referring to the Vikings, rather than the related personal name or the topographical compound proposed by Þórhallur Vilmundarson (Fellows Jensen 1978, 70). The personal name does, however, occur independently in the Danelaw so it may well be the personal name that enters into the five placenames (Feilitzen 1937, 377–8; Fellows Jensen 1968, 270–1).

The earliest recorded occurrence of the personal name in England is in anglicised form *SVMERLEDA* as the name of a moneyer on the coinage of King Edgar (959–75) and it reappears both in anglicised form and in forms closer to the original Scandinavian one, e.g. *SVMERLEÐI*, on later coins from York, Lincoln and Thetford (Smart 1981, 69). It is probably simply in imitation of these coins that the name appears in forms such as *SVMERLED* and *SVMERLETH* on Danish coins of Hardeknud, Magnus the Good and Svend Estridsen, for the name is otherwise unrecorded in Denmark, although Kristian Hald may be correct in assuming that moneyers from the Danelaw were actually brought to Denmark by the Danish kings (Hald 1934, 186–7). Tenants by the name of *Sumarliði* or perhaps a strong side-form, *Sumarliðr*, are recorded in the Domesday Book of 1086 for the counties of Devon, Suffolk, Huntingdonshire, Yorkshire and Lincolnshire. The tenant in Devonshire, which lies at a considerable distance from the Danelaw, is most likely to be an 11th-century arrival from Denmark, who had been rewarded for his services to the crown with a grant of land there by King Knut or his successors. The same may also be true of the other Domesday tenants. In the four Danelaw counties, however, the tenants may alternatively be descendants of Danes who had settled there at the end of the 9th century or later. The name *Sumarliði* is of fairly common occurrence in Norfolk and is twice compounded with the Old English placename generic *-tūn* in Suffolk (Insley 1980, 693–7). Since there would not seem to have been many new arrivals from Denmark in Suffolk after the year 903, when the Danes were driven out by the English, there must have been men bearing the name *Sumarliði* in England before the end of the 9th century. At least one Viking by the name of Sumarliði settled in Normandy in the 10th century and gave his name to the now-lost farm *Summelleville*, which has been located to St-Germain-le-Gaillard in Manche (Adigard des Gautries 1954, 141–2, 417). It was, incidentally, a Norman called William de Somerville, whose family must have originated here but who had lands in Staffordshire and the West Riding of Yorkshire, who brought the surname *Somerville* to Scotland, when David I granted him lands in Roxburghshire and Lanarkshire in the first half of the 12th century (Black 1946, 737; Barrow 1980, 193–5).

The surviving onomastic evidence suggests that the name *Sumarliði* had achieved a wide currency in the areas of Viking colonisation long before it came to be bestowed upon the son of an Orkney earl. All that can be said with certainty, however, is that the name arose in one of the colonies and not in the Scandinavian homelands.

The situation is quite different with the next name I intend to discuss, although it, too, is renowned as the name of an Orkney earl – *Kali*. Kali was the son of Kolr Kalason and Gunnhildr, sister of Earl Magnús. He grew up in Agder in Norway but was appointed Earl of Orkney in 1136 and on that occasion assumed the name *Rǫgnvaldr* (*Orkneyinga saga* 140; Lind 1905–15, 673–4). *Orkneyinga saga* says that King Sigurðr of Norway gave Kali this name at the request of Kali's mother Gunnhildr, who considered that Earl Rǫgnvaldr

Brúsason had been the most accomplished of all the Earls of Orkney and therefore that the name would be a portent of good fortune. The name *Kali*, which would seem to be an original by-name related to the verb *kala*, 'to freeze', does not occur very frequently in Norway or Iceland but it is a name with a long history in the British Isles. At the Viking Congress in Man, our much-lamented friend and colleague Aslak Liestøl described a memorial stone from Iona which has an inscription in Norse runes (Liestøl 1983). The inscription is slightly damaged but Ian Fisher has kindly confirmed that runologists and archaeologists agree that the most plausible interpretation of it is as a statement that the stone had been placed by Kali Qlvísson in memory of his brother Fugl (see Figure 25.1) (cf. RCAHMS 1982, 17, 21 & 190). In his discussion of the stone and the background for the inscription, Liestøl demonstrated how Earl Rǫgnvaldr Kali, who had himself taken part in several raids on the British Isles before he became earl, came from a family with connections in the west. His paternal grandfather, Kali Sæbjarnarson, had accompanied the Norwegian king, Magnús berfœttr, on his expedition to the Isles and Man in 1098, been wounded in Anglesey and died in the Hebrides (*Orkneyinga saga* 95–100).

The inscription on the Iona stone can be dated on stylistic and runological grounds to the latter part of the 10th century. Aslak Liestøl pointed, however, to one linguistic feature in the inscription which is incompatible with this date, if the compiler is to be considered as a Norwegian, namely the form **þensi** instead of regular **þenna**. Liestøl suggested that the form **þensi** might 'show a direct or indirect connection with Danes', for this form is very common in 10th-century inscriptions from Denmark. In support of Liestøl's tentative suggestion, it might be mentioned that the name *Kali* occurs more frequently both independently and in placenames in East Scandinavia than in Norway (cf. Lind 1905–15, 673; Hjorth Pedersen 1960, 28–9; *DR* no. 130; *SRU* nos 102, 660 & 708). Even more significantly, the name *Kali* enters into a number of placenames in the Danelaw which have been assumed to have been coined by Danish settlers. It is found in two or three Cawthorpes in Lincolnshire and Calthorpe in Norfolk (Fellows Jensen 1978, 124). The personal name does not seem to have become popular in the Danelaw, for it is not recorded independently in English sources. It is therefore unlikely that the placenames containing the name *Kali* were coined much later than the beginning of the 10th century. In Norfolk, from most of which the Danes were driven out in 903, the placename is almost certain to have been coined before this date, for Calthorpe does not lie in the enclave in the hundreds of Flegg, where Danes would seem to have remained longer. The name *Kali* would also seem to enter into a number of placenames in *-toft* in Normandy, which must have been coined in the 10th century (Adigard des Gautries 1954, 400–01).

The name *Kali*, then, arose in Scandinavia, possibly in Denmark, and was brought to the Danelaw and Normandy by Danish settlers in the Viking period. It may have spread to the Atlantic islands from England. Earl Rǫgnvaldr Kali

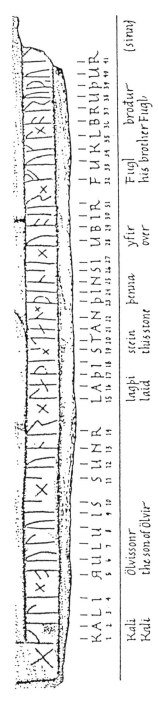

| Kali | ᚮlvissonr | | | | | lagþi | stein | þenna | yfir | Fugl | broður | (sinn) |
| Kali | the son of ᚮlvir | | | | | laid | this stone | | over | Fugl | his brother Fugl | |

Figure 25.1: Detail of the inscription on a cross-slab in the Abbey Museum, Iona (Copyright RCAHMS).

was, of course, born in Norway but his family connections with Orkney, the Hebrides and Man might well have led to his being given a name that was more popular in the west than in the Norwegian homeland.

The next name I should like to consider was borne not by an Orkney earl but by an earl's daughter. Earl Haraldr Maddadarson's second wife Hvarflöð (a Gaelic name in -*flaith?*) was the daughter of Malcolm macHeth, Earl of Ross. Earl Haraldr himself was the son of Earl Maddad of Atholl and his claim to the Orkney earldom was through his mother, who was a daughter of Earl Hákon Pálsson, but she, too, was partly of Scots descent on her mother's side. It is therefore not surprising that the children of the partly Scots Haraldr and the wholly Scots Hvarflöð should not all have been given Scandinavian personal names. Two sons were called *Davíð* (David) and *Jón* (John) and a third *Þorfinnr*, while the three daughters were called *Gunnhildr*, *Herbörga* and *Langlíf* (*Orkneyinga saga* 289). *Gunnhildr* is one of the commonest feminine personal names in Norway and Iceland (Lind 1905–15, 408–11) and *Herbörga* is not unprecedented among the members of the family of the Orkney earls (Lind 1905–15, 514), but there are only two recorded instances of *Langlíf* in sources from Norway and Iceland, the one being Langlíf the daughter of Earl Haraldr and the other the metronymic of *Ión Langlífar son* (Lind 1905–15, 729). E. H. Lind considered that this Ión was probably a son of the earl's daughter and in the light of the fact that she had a brother John, called Jón in *Orkneyinga saga*, this is very probable.

The name *Langlíf* is not uncommon elsewhere, however. A woman called *Langliva* assumed the name *Móðir* when she entered the convent at Lund in the middle of the 12th century (Hornby 1947, 205, 230). Her death is recorded in *Necrologium Lundense* fol. 129 with the words: *[Obiit] Langliua. mother dicta.* There is no way of knowing whether or not Langliua was a Dane. That the name may have been current in Denmark at an earlier period, however, is suggested by its fairly frequent occurrence in England. It appears as the specific of two placenames: Langthorpe in the North Riding of Yorkshire (*Langliuetorp* 12th century) (Smith 1928, 180) and Langley in Cumberland (*Langliuerh'* c. 1225) (Armstrong *et al.* 1950, 365). It is particularly interesting that the generic in the Cumberland name is the Gaelic loanword in Scandinavian *ærgi*, which is assumed to have been brought to Cumberland by Vikings from the Gaelic-speaking colonies. Independently, the name *Langlíf* occurs particularly frequently in Norfolk, Suffolk and Cambridgeshire (Seltén 1975, 45; Insley 1980, 568–69). This suggests that the name was current in eastern England in the late 9th century. The possibility must therefore be borne in mind that it may have been ultimately from the Danelaw that the name came to Orkney in the 12th century. It is known that many men from the Danelaw were introduced into Scotland by the Scottish kings and other great landowners at this period (Barrow 1973, 321; 1980, 48).

The last name that I have to consider in detail was not borne by an Orkney earl or even by a relation of an earl. It is a name whose only known record in West Scandinavian sources is that in one of the runic inscriptions at Maeshowe, which is probably to be dated to the middle of the 12th century. The inscription was recorded by James Farrer in 1861 but shortly afterwards it scaled off the east buttress on which it was inscribed and most of the inscription was lost. Five contiguous pieces of it came to light in 1983 and have recently been discussed by Michael Barnes (1989 and this volume). They confirm the general accuracy of Farrer's drawing, which is fortunate for my purpose, as the portion of the inscription containing the forename is still missing. Barnes confirms that **ræist runar þæsar oframr sihurþarsonr** is likely to be the correct reading. The name that is of interest in the context of the present study is the forename **oframr**. This has been interpreted as *Óframr*, an original by-name meaning 'shy', a side-form of the recorded by-name *Óframi* (Lind 1905–15, 810; 1920–1, 271). It would, however, be possible to explain the name as **Oframmr*, which would be an original by-name meaning 'very strong' or 'too strong'. I am not aware of any other instances of this name in Scandinavian sources but it may well have been brought to the Danelaw by the Vikings. There is a man who held several estates in Lincolnshire in 1065 and still retained one of these in 1086. His name is recorded in Greater Domesday Book ff. 358c, 368a–b, 370c, 371a and 377b–c as *Offram*, *Offran* and *Offrā*. These forms were explained by Olof von Feilitzen (1937, 339) as reflecting an OE **Ōsfram*, a name that is apparently not recorded in any other sources. Since all except one of the estates held by *Offram* lie in vills with Scandinavian names (Kirkby Underwood, Dowsby, Keisby, Bulby, Avethorpe, Southorpe, Elsthorpe) and the only exception is Little Lavington, it is very likely that he is a descendant of the original Danish settlers in the area. Alternatively, he may have been brought to England from Denmark by King Knut or one of his successors. At all events, I consider it more likely that the spellings of his name in Domesday Book reflect a Scandinavian **Oframmr* rather than an OE **Ōsfram* and hence that the name found in the Maeshowe inscription is one which was already in use in the previous century in Lincolnshire and may have been brought there a century and a half before that. It is possible that the name spread to Orkney from the Viking settlements in England.

If space had allowed, I should like to have discussed a few other personal names associated with Orkney, for example the by-name *Skotakollr*, which is attributed by *Flateyjarbók* to a man called Þorgeirr, who accompanied Earl Rǫgnvaldr on a voyage from Orkney to Norway in the 12th century (*Orkneyinga saga* 204, n. 2) and which was borne a couple of centuries earlier by one of the ancestors of Bishop Þorlákr Runólfsson, namely Þorkell Skotakollr, a man who was born in Iceland but was a neighbour there to Þorbjǫrn Jarlakappi, a settler who had come to Iceland from Orkney (*Byskupa sǫgur* 93; *Landnámabók* 382–3). Hans Bekker-Nielsen (1970) has argued persuasively that the by-name *Skotakollr* may originally have been given to a man whose bald head or characteristic hairstyle recalled the Celtic form of tonsure and that the name is to

Some Orkney Personal Names 405

be attributed to the Atlantic cultural sphere. At least one Yorkshire tenant in Domesday Book of 1086 bears the name *Scotecol* and I have argued elsewhere that he probably came to Yorkshire from one of the Viking colonies in Ireland or the Western Isles, perhaps in company with his neighbour *Glunier*, whose name has been explained as an Irish adaptation of the Scandinavian by-name *Jarnkné* (Marstrander 1915, 45; Fellows-Jensen 1991). A parallel formation to the by-name *Skotakollr* is **Bretakollr*, a name which is not recorded in West Scandinavian sources but is borne by a man living in Yorkshire in the 11th century (Fellows Jensen 1968, 64), by a moneyer of King Knut at York (Smart 1981, 21), and by a Viking settler in Normandy (Adigard des Gautries 1954, 96–7).

It would also have been interesting to delve deeper into the forename of one of the grandsons of Somerled of Argyll, the man referred to in *Hákonar saga Hákonarson* (ch. 163) as *Óspakr...son Dugals* but in a section of the Latin *Cronica Regum Mannie & Insularum* that was probably compiled in Man about 1257 as *Husbac filium Owmundi* (*Cronica* fol. 44v). He was, in fact, the son of Dubhgall or Dougal and it has been suggested that *Óspakr* is a Scandinavian substitution for Gaelic *Gilleasbuig*, 'the bishop's servant', and *filium Owmundi* an attempt to represent his lineage name from his great-grandfather *Macgilleadh-amhain*, 'son of Saint Adamnan's servant' (Barrow 1973, 110 & 108 n. 2). If this suggestion is correct, the question must be asked whether the Vikings replaced the name *Gilleasbuig* by one of their own forenames which resembled part of the Gaelic name in sound or whether the name *Óspakr*, which has hitherto been explained as an original by-name 'unruly' (Janzén 1947, 123), originated in the Orkney earldom as a Scandinavian rationalisation of a Gaelic name of whose lexical content the Vikings were ignorant.

Finally, I should like to have discussed a name which remains something of an enigma to me in spite of much anguished speculation. The only man to bear the name *Dolgfinnr* in the West Scandinavian sources originally excerpted for his dictionary by E. H. Lind is a Dolgfinnr, Bishop of Orkney 1286–1309 (Lind 1905–15, 201), while a reference in an Irish source to a *Dolfinn mac Finntuir*, who was killed in a battle between the Scots and the English in 1054, has been included in the supplementary volume (Lind 1931, 197). In 1092 Carlisle was in the possession of a man called Dolfin. It has been generally assumed that this was Dolfin, the son of Earl Gospatric of Northumbria, but an alternative suggestion has been made by William Kapelle (1979, 151) that he may have been a descendant of the Dolfinn mac Finntuir who was killed in 1054. The name *Dolfinn* occurs fairly frequently in Yorkshire and North-West England and it seems that it may have arisen on British soil. Its etymology is doubtful but its form would seem to reflect confusion with the term for the aquatic mammal and association with one or both of the unrelated personal-name elements, Scand *finnr* and Celtic *find*.

My scattered and inconclusive comments on a handful of Orkney names are not a firm enough base upon which to erect a theory involving a specifically colonial personal nomenclature but I would claim that they do reflect a greater degree of contact between the various areas of Scandinavian settlement and the Scandinavian homelands in the Viking period proper and the immediately succeeding centuries than has earlier been acknowledged.

REFERENCES

Adigard des Gautries, Jean 1954. *Les Noms de Personnes Scandinaves en Normandie de 911 à 1066*, Lund.

Anderson, M. O. 1980. *Kings and Kingship in Early Scotland* (rev. ed.), Edinburgh & London.

Armstrong, A. M. *et al.* 1950. *The Place-names of Cumberland*, English Place-Name Society, vols XX–XXII, Cambridge.

Bandle, Oskar 1977. 'Die Ortsnamen der Landnámabók', *Sjötíu Ritgerðir helgaðar Jakobi Benediktssyni*, Reykjavík, pp. 47–68.

Barnes, Michael 1989. 'Two Maeshowe Rediscoveries', *Nytt om runer* 1988 (1989), 12–13.

Barrow, G. W. S. 1973. *The Kingdom of the Scots*, London.

Barrow, G. W. S. 1980. *The Anglo-Norman Era in Scottish History*, Oxford.

Barrow, G. W. S. 1981. *Kingship and Unity. Scotland 1000–1306*, The New History of Scotland 2, London.

Bekker-Nielsen, Hans 1970. 'Skotakollr', *Fróðskaparrit* 18, 145–50.

Björkman, Erik 1912. *Zur englischen Namenkunde*, Halle.

Black, George 1946. *The Surnames of Scotland*, New York.

Byskupa sǫgur: Byskupa sǫgur I, ed. Jón Helgason, Copenhagen, 1938.

Cronica: Cronica Regum Mannie & Insularum, ed. George Broderick, Manx Museum and National Trust, 1979.

DR Danmarks Runeindskrifter, ed. L. Jacobsen & E. Moltke with A. Bæksted & K. M. Nielsen, Copenhagen, 1941–2.

Feilitzen, Olof von. 1937. *The Pre-Conquest Personal Names of Domesday Book*, Uppsala.

Fellows Jensen, Gillian 1968. *Scandinavian Personal Names in Lincolnshire and Yorkshire*, Navnestudier 7, Copenhagen.

Fellows Jensen, Gillian 1978. *Scandinavian Settlement Names in the East Midlands*, Navnestudier 16, Copenhagen.

Fellows-Jensen, Gillian 1991. 'Of Danes – and Thanes – and Domesday Book', in *People and Places in Northern Europe 500–1600*, ed. Wood, I. & Lund, N., Woodbridge, pp. 107–21.

Hákonar saga: Hákonar saga Hákonarsonar, ed. Marina Mundt, Norsk Historisk Kjeldeskrift-Institut. Norrøne Tekster nr. 2, Oslo, 1979.

Hald, Kristian 1934. 'Om Personnavnene i de danske Møntindskrifter', *Studier tilegnede Verner Dahlerup*, Copenhagen & Århus, pp. 182–7.

Hjorth Pedersen, Birte 1960. 'Bebyggelsesnavne på -by sammensat med personnavn', *Ti Afhandlinger*, Navnestudier 2, Copenhagen, pp. 10–46.

Hornby, Rikard 1947. 'Fornavne i Danmark i Middelalderen', *Personnamn*, Nordisk Kultur VII, Stockholm, Oslo, Copenhagen, pp. 187–234.

Insley, John 1980. *Scandinavian Personal Names in Norfolk*, unpublished Ph.D thesis for the University of Nottingham.

Janzén, Assar 1947. 'De fornvästnordiska personnamnen', *Personnamn*, Nordisk Kultur VII. Stockholm, Oslo, Copenhagen, pp. 22–186.

Kapelle, William E. 1979. *The Norman Conquest of the North. The Region and its Transformation, 1000–1135*, Chapel Hill.

Kuhn, Hans 1966. 'Die Ortsnamen der Kolonien und das Mutterland', *Proceedings of the Eighth International Congress of Onomastic Sciences*, The Hague, pp. 260–5.

Kuhn, Hans 1972. 'Die Anfänge der isländischen Ortsnamengebung', *Kleine Schriften* III, Berlin, New York, pp. 385–96.

Landnámabók: Íslendingabók, Landnámabók, ed. Jakob Benediktsson, Íslenzk Fornrit I, Reykjavík, 1968.

Laxdæla saga: Laxdæla saga, ed. Einar Ól. Sveinsson, Íslenzk Fornrit V, Reykjavík, 1934.

Liestøl, Aslak 1983. 'An Iona rune stone and the world of Man and the Isles', in *The Viking Age in the Isle of Man*, ed. Fell, C. *et al.*, London, pp. 85–93.

Lind, E. H. 1905–15. *Norsk-Isländska Dopnamn ock Fingerade Namn från Medeltiden*, Uppsala.

Lind, E. H. 1920–1. *Norsk-Isländska Personbinamn från Medeltiden*, Uppsala.

Lind, E. H. 1931. *Norsk-Isländska Dopnamn ock Fingerade Namn från Medeltiden. Supplementband*, Oslo.

Marstrander, C. J. S. 1915. *Bidrag til det norske sprogs historie i Irland*, Oslo.

Marwick, Hugh 1952. *Orkney Farm-Names*, Kirkwall.

Necrologium Lundense: Necrologium Lundense, ed. L. Weibull, Lund, 1923.

Orkneyinga saga: Orkneyinga saga, ed. Finnbogi Guðmundsson, Íslenzk Fornrit XXXIV, Reykjavík, 1965.

RCHAMS 1982. The Royal Commission on the Ancient and Historical Monuments of Scotland: *Argyll. An Inventory of Monuments, vol. 4, Iona*, Edinburgh.

Seltén, Bo 1975. *Early East-Anglian Nicknames. Bahuvrihi Names*, Lund.

Smart, Veronica 1981. *Cumulative Index of Volumes 1–20*, Sylloge of Coins of the British Isles 28, London.

Smith, A. H. 1928. *The Place-Names of the North Riding of Yorkshire*, English Place-Name Society vol. V, Cambridge.

SRU: Sveriges Runinskrifter. Upplands Runinskrifter I–III, Stockholm, 1940–51.

26

SHRIEKS AT THE STONES

THE VIKINGS, THE ORKNEYS AND
THE SCOTTISH ENLIGHTENMENT

ANDREW WAWN

The summer of 1989 marked the 200th anniversary of a remarkable British expedition to the Orkneys, to the Faroes and, eventually, to Iceland. It was on 31 May 1789 that the brig *John*, en route for Hafnarfjörður and Reykjavík at 66°N, dropped a rather uncertain anchor in the Orkneys, at Mill Bay, on the east of Hoy (West 1970–6, I, 8). Its passengers were a party of young Edinburgh University scientists and scholars, led by a then newly graduated Cheshire physician John Thomas Stanley (Wawn 1981); and the *terra firma* of Orkney was welcome relief for travellers who were already queasy of stomach and, literally and metaphorically, increasingly cold of feet. This brief scheduled stop in the Orkneys perhaps allowed them the chance to acknowledge that the motives behind their northern expedition had seemed clearer and more compelling to them viewed from the well-upholstered drawing-rooms of Edinburgh than they now seemed, four blustery days later, on the windswept outcrops of the Orkneys. The party had left Leith broads in a ship whose sails were filled by several heady intellectual breezes of the moment: medical research; geological field-work; Adam Smithean economic liberalism, highlighting the possibilities of commercial exploitation of such mineral resources as seaweed and sulphur; a fascination with the antiquities of the Viking North; and, underpinning everything, there was certainly also a good measure of youthful, muddle-headed, fashionable, armchair-primitive eagerness to flee from the 'follies of our polish'd Capitals' (Stanley's phrase; CRO MS DSA 7/3, letter to Charles Scot, dated 5 October 1789), and to embrace instead the wild, the terrific, the primitive, the sublime, the gothic, the romantic (Wawn 1989).

In view of the central theme of the 1989 Viking Congress it would be gratifying to confirm that the early pages of the manuscript journals kept by Stanley's colleagues – James Wright, Isaac Benners and John Baine – and as copied by Stanley in later years (Lbs MSS 3886–8 4to; see West 1970–6, I, III; the original of Benners' diary is NLS MS 6318, edited in West 1970–6, II; all subsequent references are to West 1970–6, I–III) throughout their four months of travel pulse excitedly with sharp-eyed observations about the Vikings in the

Orkneys: it would be gratifying but it would also be untrue. The Orcadian observations of the travellers concentrate rather on the local gin (I, 9), mineralogy (II, 21–2), economic recession caused by backwash from the American civil war (III, 19), the possibility of commercial exploitation of Orcadian kelp (III, 23), the absence of trees in Orkney (more planting, patriotism and perseverance required; III, 20), the presence of 'a most elegant assemblage of Beautiful & Fashionable Females' (I, 15), the 'uncommon Fatness and Jollinesss of the Male part of the better sort of inhabitants' (I, 11), 'the No. of Ideots of both sexes which appeared on the Street' (ibid.), and on the 'knavery & Rascality of the Orkney people' (I, 12), such as the local parson, up to his clerical collar in contraband from Tórshavn, whom they christened the 'sacerdotal smugler' (I, 23). There is comment, too, in each of the Stanley copies of the 1789 expedition journals, on Orcadian medieval remains: the Cathedral, the Earl's Palace (I, 18); and, more importantly in the context of this essay, on puzzling structures from a mistier and more remote past – the stone circles at Stenness. The stones themselves were measured, sketched, and rather perfunctorily reflected upon by Stanley's colleagues: 'a very curious Gothic structure, erected here in former times by the Druids' (II, 28). On the heart and mind of the expedition leader, however, the same stones made a rather deeper impression. For Stanley, as a result of his fondness for the immensely popular (throughout Europe) poetical works attributed to an ancient Highland bard called Ossian, the stones of Stenness had become indelibly associated with three related phenomena: an heroic Scottish king, a repellent Viking spirit and a single heart-stopping shriek. These elements make up the first of the two literary scenes, both set at the Stenness stones, which will serve in this paper to focus and define the theme of the presentation of Viking Orkney to British Enlightenment enthusiasts of Northern antiquity.

In his own fair copies of the expedition journals, annotated and illustrated 40 and more years after the 1789 voyage, can be found the fruits of an extraordinarily retentive memory dwelling on deeply felt experience. It was, quintessentially, emotion recollected in tranquillity. Some of this annotation has been edited and discussed (West 1970–6, passim) but not, until now, the Cheshire explorer's revealing comments on the shriek at the stones of Stenness, monuments now best viewed from the top of, appropriately, Stanley Hill (Ritchie & Ritchie 1988, 38). Stanley begins his discussion (Lbs MS 3886 4to, 40–2, 296f.) by considering the origins, the form and the significance of individual stones at Stenness, the stone of power, the stone of sacrifice, and the significance of their circular formation. They were, he felt sure, pre-Scandinavian in origin; of a size intended to impress those who frequented them with 'awe & fear of a divine power' (42), and with their remote situation ensuring that, once seen, these structures

> would leave him [a spectator] an Impression he never would dismiss from his Mind, of
> something supernatural & what he remembered to have heard in a wilderness where,

almost so much more than human art & labour could produce ... he would deam [*sic*] and ponder over as oracular.

(ibid.)

When he turns to the 'great Circle at Stenhaus' (Lbs MS 3886 4to, 295; Stanley is apparently referring to the Ring of Brodgar) it soon becomes quite clear what supernatural and oracular impression has been left on Stanley's mind by his 1789 visit there and his subsequent ruminations over half a century. He identifies this larger Stenness stone circle as the Circle of the Odinic Viking spirit Loda, the same Circle of Loda as that spoken of in the English translations (the first of which was published in Britain in 1760) – by the highland Scot James McPherson – of the extraordinary range of epic poems and lyric fragments attributed to an ancient Gaelic bard called Ossian (Omberg 1976, 26–33; Greenway 1977, 119–38; Stafford 1988). Initially made famous by the Ossianic literary works, the Circle of Loda soon took on a life of its own through paintings such as John Frederick Miller's 'The view of the Circle of Loda at a distance' (1775; Ritchie & Ritchie 1988, cover picture). There is no evidence that Stanley knew Miller's pastoral evocation of Stenness, untouched as it is by the spectral presence of Loda, save perhaps in the concerned expressions of the three foregrounded peasant folk, seated a respectful distance from the mysterious stones, as if uneasily aware of and awed by the possibility that these stones had, in Stanley's words, 'stood where they are defying the Storms in the midst of the deserts chosen for their occupation long before Druids or Woden or Thor were known or spoken of' (Lbs MS 3886 4to, 288); but of the Cheshire explorer's intimate knowledge of the hypnotic Ossianic texts which generated the painting there is no doubt. He had long before learnt to draw emotional support from them, in the desolate days after the death of his fiancée in 1791, as his manuscripts reveal (CRO DSA MS 5/6, 7–8, 11–13 & 17–18). Annotating his Iceland journal copy years later, the voice of Ossian speaks again to Stanley, this time telling of the Circle of Loda in what the Cheshire explorer claims to be 'the most striking & beautiful Episode in the whole of Ossian's Poems' (48). At that time, with this poet, these were striking claims.

It is a scene in the poem *Carric-Thura* (first published 1762, 276–97) set on the island of Inistore (the Ossianic term for the Orkneys). Frothal, a hostile Scandinavian king, is encamped near Carric-Thura, the palace of Carthulla, the native king; Frothal seeks revenge for an earlier defeat at the hands of the king. Fingal, father of Ossian the bard, and the king of West Scotland, arrives in the Orkneys and takes up the cause of the besieged and vulnerable local monarch. On the night before the battle, Fingal's young followers feast and then slumber; as the fires fade, and the warriors rest, their leader lies uneasily awake; the ancient forest echoes (Orcadian trees clearly grew more readily in McPherson's imagination than in 18th-century reality, or in John Frederick Miller's unwooded painting; 'McPherson probably never saw the place', Stanley in Lbs

MS 3886 4to, 302), the 'wan cold moon' casts its eerie light, the 'lonely blast of ocean' sighs in the distance. Suddenly an airborn spirit approaches, born on the wind, with flaming eyes and nostrils, shaking a spear. It is the spirit of Loda which takes up its position in the stone circle, the father of the vengeful Frothal, and identified by McPherson's editorial notes (1762 edition, 269n.; Thomson 1951, 51–3) as 'supposed to be the ancient Odin of Scandinavia'. There is a statuesque exchange of chill unpleasantries between the steadfast Fingal, an emanation of the defiant independence of the Gaelic homelands in the face of Viking incursion and invasion, and the Odinic spirit, all Viking bravado and truculence, threatening doom and defeat in the next day's conflict:

> Fly to thy Land ... receive the wind and fly. The blasts are in the hollow of my hand: the course of the storm is mine. The king of Sora [Frothal] is my son, he bends at the stone of my power. His battle is around Carric thura, and he will prevail. Fly to thy land, son of Comhal, or feel my flaming wrath.
>
> (1762 edition, 278; Lbs MS 3886 4to, 303)

The two champions then clash and Fingal runs his sword through the ghostly Óðinn-Loda figure. Loda, reduced to acrid smoke, rises into the air, and lets out a piercing, fearsome, island-shaking, ocean-stilling shriek. So it is that this moment, 'the most extravagant fiction in all Ossian's poems' (1762 edition, 290n), marks a crucial defeat of Viking power in the Orkneys; the confrontation at Carric-Thura acting as a macabre mythic anticipation of the fateful confrontation of similar forces at the Battle of Largs. Fingal has nothing to fear in his single combat next day against the defeated spirit's son, Frothal, whose life is eventually spared only after the intercession of his beloved, the beautiful Crimora.

From the point of view of the late 18th- and early 19th-century perceptions of Orkney and the Vikings, three features of particular importance emerge from Stanley's interest in the Ossianic Circle of Loda and the Orcadian Stones at Stenness.

First, it is important to appreciate that Ossianic poetry in its assorted Gaelic balladic forms (Christiansen 1931, passim) and, more pervasively, in its English prose manifestations from the early and mid-1760s (Stafford 1988, 185) was at least as influential as any other contemporary vernacular publication of a more ostentatiously Norse nature, in familiarising Enlightenment Scottish readers with the Vikings in general; and was by some way the most influential in establishing a sense of the Vikings in Orkney, as the invaders challenged, pillaged and murdered their way around the islands. It is true that the publication of Thomas Percy's *Five Pieces of Runic Poetry* (1763; Preface notes that publication, due in 1761, had been 'delayed by an accident') projects a more rugged, non-Ossianic glimpse of Viking literary activity in the Orkneys through Percy's translation ('The Dying Ode of Regner Lodbrog') of *Krákumál*, a poem of likely Orcadian composition. However, it is unlikely that any 18th-century reader would have been aware of this Orcadian provenance; and, in any case, as Percy's 1763 Preface makes clear, Ossianic poetry had itself been a major impetus behind the initial appearance of *Five Pieces of Runic Poetry*, through the publication in Edinburgh of a modest 70-page volume entitled *Fragments of Ancient Poetry translated from the Galic or Erse Language* (1760), in which austere prose translations of 15 short, (allegedly) Gaelic pieces prepared the way for the main Ossianic corpus published in the following five years. The rapturous reception enjoyed by the *Erse fragments* is as difficult to exaggerate as it is easy to explain. The scenes depicted are set against a haunting background of mountain gloom and mountain glory, of shaggy hills, fatal rocks, sounding shores, mossy streams, nodding rushes, dark waves, troubled lakes, blasted oaks and crumbling tombs – Orkney with trees. Spectral voices recall tumultuous passions and desperate deeds: they tell of grieving fathers, ardent sons, steadfast daughters, star-crossed lovers, rival suitors, and villainous (often Viking) foes, all victims of a universe governed by inescapable heroic obligation, hideous ill-chance, vengeful malevolence and eagerly embraced sacrificial self-destruction. The ache of aged memory and the nag of frustrated inactivity taunt the venerable narrators, but not beyond the limits of endurance bred by long experience of disciplining feelings which can then be recreated intensely in the distillations of poetry. These tales of Fenian heroes and Viking villains constantly strain the limits of literary form as, in an almost surreal but seductive way, past invades present, dialogue dissolves into monologue, the barrier between life and death is momentarily lowered and then cruelly re-established, and multiple perspectives are offered on individual events within and between fragments. Small wonder that the *Erse fragments* were popular; much wonder that they are not still popular. Thus, for several generations of enthusiasts up to and including John Thomas Stanley, Loda at Stenness was not to be thought of as isolated malignity expressed in a single poem; he was rather the personification in an Orcadian setting of that Viking evil to be found diffused and dramatised throughout the Ossianic corpus.

Secondly, though the Ossianic depiction of the Orcadian Vikings would have been influential whenever the texts had been first published, their impact was certainly amplified because major Ossianic texts appeared in print before the publication of Norse texts and translations of equivalent importance, including those texts which specifically address Viking Orkney. By 1763 two substantial volumes of Ossianic works had been published, each fleshing out the background to the *Erse fragments*. This was, thus, a time before the publication of Thomas Gray's two ubiquitously popular Norse odes, *The Descent of Odin* and *The Fatal Sisters* (written in 1761, published in 1768; Lonsdale 1969, 210–28; Bodleian MS Percy c.7 contains two English translations by Percy of the same Bartholinus-Torfæus [Þormóður Torfason] Latin version of the Norse *Darraðarlíoð* which Gray had used when composing *The Fatal Sisters* [Lonsdale 1969, 215–16]: the manuscript makes clear that Percy had intended there to be several more than five Runic pieces), each with its curious fusion of wild Gothic fantasy and sedate neo-Augustan propriety, the latter poem with its allusion (l.8) to Sigurður, Earl of Orkney, at the Battle of Clontarf and its eery Caithness Valkyrie vision (Lonsdale 1969, 215–16). It was also a time 20 years before the translated (into English) Orkney-based extracts from the *Hákonar saga Hákonarsonar* were prepared and published by the indefatigable James Johnstone (Johnstone 1782); and it was a time 20 years before the publication in Copenhagen under the auspices of the Arnamagnæan Commission of the first scholarly edition of *Orkneyinga saga* (Jón Jónsson 1780), with its Latin facing-page translation. It was certainly a time some 70 years before the first known English translation of any substantial part of the saga (Scottish Registry Office, Heddle MS GD 263/ 124, unidentified translator 'Mr W. W.', only the first third of the saga was translated); and it was certainly a century before Torfæus's *Orcades* was made available in the English translation prepared by the splendidly eccentric Reverend Alexander Pope (Pope 1866; written 1780; initially published in the 1840s in John O'Groats), flamboyant scourge of his Scottish parishioners' weekday lechery and Sabbatical intoxication, whose motives in laying the Nordic past of Caithness and the Orkneys in front of Enlightenment antiquarians seem not to have been wholly those of a disinterested humanist and scholar:

> I would recommend the perusal of these sheets to all classes … wickedness and daring villainy seldom pass unpunished even in this world … they will be convinced that they live in happy times, compared with those mentioned in this history, when murders, massacres, pyracies, invasions, and intestine divisions were so common. Who takes this view of it will see good cause to fall prostrate before God, and praise His name for the happy and quiet time in which we live.
>
> (Pope 1862, 5–6)

The third point arising from Stanley's Ossianic annotation in his Iceland journals, is the question of compatibility between the literary worlds of the invading Viking and the indigenous Scottish Gael. *Carric-Thura* dramatises the Orcadian destruction of Loda by Fingal – the rejection of alien Scandinavian values; yet, in the feast scene at the castle, the same poem also dramatises the subsequent reconciliation of Fingal with Loda's son Frothal. This apparent paradox finds important expression in the literary history of late 18th- and early 19th-century Britain; and finds reconciliation in John Thomas Stanley's Orcadian recollections. We have noted that the *Erse fragments* (1760) and Percy's *Five pieces of Runic Poetry* (1763) were in one sense complementary; the one paved the way for the other with the bleak lyricism of Ossianic elegy set against the jagged violence of the Runic vision. Taken together they could be seen as striking illustrations of the 18th-century sense of literary evolution: the Runic texts with their barbaric ferocity of spirit, and wild and animated language, full of syntactic inversion, and sinewy metaphor; the Ossianic texts with their Biblical sonorities, their taut understatedness, their 'tenderness and even delicacy of sentiment' (Blair 1763, 11). Yet in Sir Walter Scott's novel *The*

Antiquary (1816), the relationship is neither evolutionary nor complementary but adversarial. The avuncular but pedantic Jonathan Oldbuck (the antiquary of the novel's title), clashes with the hot-blooded young highlander Hector McIntyre, with their duel representing the opposition of maturity and youth, Hanoverian and Jacobite, phlegm and bile, and, crucially, Jonathan's comically-obsessive addiction to Norse antiquity versus Hector's fiery attachment to the Ossianic canon:

> 'I don't pretend to much skill, uncle; but it's not very reasonable to be angry with me for admiring the antiquities of my own country more than those of the Harolds, Harfagers, and Hacos you are so fond of.'
> 'Why, these, sir – these mighty and unconquered Goths – *were* your ancestors! The bare-breeched Celts whom they subdued and suffered only to exist, like a fearful people in the crevices of rocks, were but their Mancipia and Serfs!'
>
> (ch. 30, 1910 edition, p. 339)

It is, surely, in the figure John Thomas Stanley himself that Jonathan Oldbuck and Hector McIntyre are reconciled. It was Stanley, as we have seen, whose personal grief had responded to the understated sadness of Ossianic elegy, and who had rejoiced at Loda's destruction as he reflected on the twin images of the Stenness circle created by his Ossianic reading and by his own 1789 experience of wandering amongst the silent stone slabs. Yet, if Stanley's admiration for the Ossianic corpus made him a man of his time, so did his enthusiasm for Icelandic Eddic poetry. It was Stanley whose youthful published translation in 1786 of Burger's macabre German ballad 'Leonora' includes on its title-page a telling quote from the Poetic *Edda* (Wawn 1981, 54–5); it was the same Stanley whose encounter with the stones of Stenness took place on an expedition to Iceland; and it was the same Stanley who, at the very end of his life, copied out, in the frailest of hands, lines in Old Icelandic from the Eddic *Baldrs draumar*, the poem which underpins Thomas Gray's *The Descent of Odin* – these lines about the region of death, whence no traveller save Óðinn returns (Cheshire Record Office MS DSA 5/6, loose sheet in the back of a notebook; Wawn 1981, 70–1). They are touchingly appropriate lines for a frail and aged Icelandophile to ponder over in the final months of his life. Thus, whilst the shriek at the stones of Loda, as recalled by Stanley in the Iceland journal copy, tells of the rejection and destruction of the Viking spirit in Orkney, *Carric-Thura* also identifies images of ultimate reconciliation and accommodation between the Gaelic and Viking cultures. It was in that latter spirit that Stanley lived his life, and so did many another amateur enthusiast of the Vikings in the century after the Ossianic ballads helped to arouse interest in them.

The second literary scene to be examined in this essay which was influential in establishing images of the Vikings and the Orkneys for Scottish Enlightenment readers also takes place at the great Stenness Circle of Loda. Its author Sir Walter Scott was, of course, a committed enthusiast of Norse antiquity; witness his work on *Eyrbyggja saga* (Wolf & D'Arcy 1987) and his narrative poem *Harold the Dauntless* (Palsgrave 1884, 379–413), not to mention the accumulated holdings of the library at Abbotsford with copies of the major Latin quarto volumes of Viking narrative sources edited and codified by scholars such as Olaus Magnus or James Johnstone (notably the Orcadian material in his chronicle digest *Antiquitates Celto-Scandicæ*, 1786; Lieder 1920, 10–11) and with several volumes of the great Copenhagen series of Arnamagnæan Commission editions of the Icelandic sagas, all lavishly annotated with facing page Latin translations and scholarly introductions. This series of texts was of the greatest importance in tracing the growth of interest and knowledge in Viking culture in late 18th-century Enlightenment Britain. Two brief instances serve to make the point in the context of this essay: in Reykjavík some 12 years ago, the present writer purchased a copy of the 1786 first edition of the Copenhagen Arnamagnæan edition of *Víga Glúms saga*, the same edition as that owned by Scott: it was gratifying and also illuminating to note that the bookplate identified the volume's first owner as John Thomas Stanley. In 1810 a copy of the same saga was in the possession of Stanley's Cestrian protégé, and fellow Orkney and Iceland explorer Sir Henry Holland (Wawn 1987, 34–5). Two earlier editions in the Arnamagnæan series had provided British readers lucky enough to beg, borrow or buy them with edited primary texts about the medieval Scandinavian kingdom of Orkney. Most obviously there was Jón Jónsson's 1780 edition of *Orkneyinga saga*; there was also the Jón Eiríksson's 1775 edition of *Gunnlaugs saga ormstungu*, also in Scott's Abbotsford library – its British scenes (never mind its brief Orkney scene) may not loom large in the process of the saga as understood today, but a note written by the early 19th century antiquarian Francis Douce in his copy of the volume (now in the Bodleian library; a gift from Grímur Thorkelín) describes the saga thus:

> The Gunnlaugs saga … a chronicle contains matter relating to England and Scotland during the reign of Ethelred and Canute: a poem on an expedition to Ireland: an account of trial by battle: and a disputation on the Danish and other languages.

The tone could scarcely be more relentlessly antiquarian, less imaginatively engaged. Others, however, with access to the same saga reacted far more extravagantly. In 1812 in Edinburgh there was an absurd production of an absurd play based upon the saga of Gunnlaugr. The playwright was Sir George Mackenzie, Iceland explorer, collector of Gaelic Ossianic texts (Christiansen 1931, 59) and eccentric mineralogist (Wawn 1982). The preface and epilogue were written by Sir Walter Scott, but happily the 'author of Waverley's' imaginative engagement with the Viking world finds its fullest expression not in Mackenzie's ludicrous play but in his own splendid novel, *The Pirate* (1822), set in the Orkneys and Shetlands.

In outline *The Pirate* bears the familiar shape of a rationalised medieval romance, whether English or Icelandic, with the hero's *rite de passage* struggle for his own identity and for that of his parents, and his search for an appropriate bride. In the bridal quest Mordaunt Merton has to choose between two sisters, Brenda and Minna. One (Brenda) is blonde, the other is dark; one is full of sense, the other of sensibility; one embodies rationality, the other romanticism; one has little or no sense of the Viking past of the Orkneys, the other wallows insatiably in it. For the romantic and sentimental Minna the Viking Orcadian past is a golden age whose values represent a stinging challenge, rebuke even, to the enfeebled Orcadian and Shetlandic present. Minna's frequent strictures on the subject are reminiscent of the tone and attitudes of poems such as Jónas Hallgrímsson's poem 'Ísland' (1835) or, rather earlier, of Adam Oehlenschläger's 'Guldhornene' (1803; Greenway 1977, 158–9), this latter made available to Victorian readers in an 1843 English translation by the peppery Scandophile George Borrow (Borrow 1923–4, VII, 172–7; Lieder 1920, 10, notes the presence of 20 volumes of the Danish poet's works in Scott's Abbotsford library).

Certainly for Minna and for Scott's readers, the ancient Viking spirit echoes loudly around the landscapes and society of the Orkneys and Shetlands, no matter that the novel is ostensibly set in the late 17th century. It can be heard in the oaths constantly sworn to St Ronald (Rögnvaldr kali; 20, 35, 73: these and all subsequent page references are to the *Waverley Novels*, Centenary edition, XIII, 1871) and St Olaf (21) and St Magnus the martyr (159, 175 & 324); it can be noted in the dreams (39), and the dwarfs (328) and the Norse coins (70) and the rune-sticks and the superstitions; it can be heard in the ancient Norse rhymes (67–9, 163 & 235–9) and 'nursery stories of King Erick' (223), and 'dismal tales concerning the Trows or Drows (the dwarfs of the Scalds)' (21) which the old are ever eager to pass on to the young; it is to be heard in the Norn vocabulary deployed by Scott; it can be seen at the Yule-tide sword dance (167–9); it can be heard in the drinking songs (152) or the rowing chants (242–3); it can be seen more broadly in the clash between the Norse-derived odal values of the indigenous population (as represented by Magnus Troil, father of Minna and Brenda), and the alternatively mean-spirited or comic encroachments of Scottish trade and fashionable notions of agrarian improvement (exemplified by Triptolemus Yellowley); it can be seen in the name and Valkyrie-like presence of the eerie and ubiquitously manipulative mother-figure of Norna of the Fitful-Head (eventually revealed to be the mother of Minna's glamorous piratical lover Clement Cleveland, her illegitimate son by Mordaunt Mertoun's reclusive father); it can be noted in the literary references, both medieval and more modern (to Gray's Norse odes, 163, 230; to *Eyrbyggja saga*, 471; to Göngu-Hrolfr, 152; to Olaus Magnus, 314, 462–3; to Bartholinus, 470); Minna promises loyalty to her beloved Cleveland by 'the promise of Odin', linked in the text with the Stenness 'Stone of Power', with its hole through which pledging lovers must hold hands, and linked in Scott's notes with the massive silver ring as described in Chapter four of *Eyrbyggja saga* (Scott must have been amongst the last to see the Stone of Power upright during his 1814 visit to the Orkneys: later the same year it was knocked down, apparently deliberately, by a farmer who objected to young lovers crossing his land to approach the monument: West 1970–6, III, 25,197; Ritchie & Ritchie 1988, 39). It can be noted, too, that in the novel there are scenes and motifs based on or drawn from familiar Eddic or saga scenes, notably Norna and her fortune-telling rhymes (235–9), based on a scene from *Eiríks saga rauða* (via Bartholinus; 469–70), and Norna seeking a piece of metal from the buried coffin of an ancestor of Magnus Troil (282–3), with its strong though unacknowledged echoes of the *Hervarar saga* poem known all too well to Scandophiles in late 18th-century Britain as 'The waking of Angantyr'; known from the days of George Hickes' pioneering and oft-reprinted late 17th-century translation, and latterly from Percy's *Five pieces of Runic poetry* and the torrent of new English paraphrases and adaptations of the poem which followed in Percy's wake (Omberg 1976, 150–1). Scott's surreptitious use of this poem's central motif in *The Pirate* may well be an echo of his earlier intention to work on *Hervarar saga*, abandoned in favour of work on *Eyrbyggja saga* because of the 'Angantyr' poem's over-exposure (Harvey-Wood 1972, II, 467–8).

Most of all, however, is the spirit of the ancient Vikings to be found in the voice and values of Minna, daughter of Magnus Troil, the avuncular Shetland odaller. She rides a Norwegian bred pony (290); she is an outstanding performer at the sword-dance (167–9); in anthropological terms very much a hunter rather than a gatherer, Minna favours fighting over fishing ('no whale-striking, bird-nesting for me; my lover must be a Sea-King', 227), and admires modern piracy as a noble expression of independence against England, a latter-day emanation of the Viking spirit (256–7); she believes native superstitions without trembling, unlike her sister who trembles at them without believing (210); Minna, a Shetlander, suspects the Orcadians of being closer to Scotland, tamer of spirit, and 'dead to the throb of heroic Norse blood' (198); she sees herself as a direct ancestor of the formidable women of the sagas, 'a daughter of the old dames of Norway, who could send their lovers to battle with a smile, and slay them with their own hands, if they returned with dishonour' (227). Minna is as intoxicated with these ancient values as (for a time) the Englishman Edward Waverley was with romantic Highland values in Scott's first novel of 1814; and the crucial scene (435–8) of her disillusion and maturation marks the climax of *The Pirate*. It also represents a uncanny anticipation, never it seems previously remarked upon, of Thomas Hardy's use of the Stonehenge setting at the end of *Tess of the d'Urbervilles*. The setting is the Circle of Loda at Stenness, and the reader is reminded (437) of the Scandinavian and pre-Scandinavian forms of sacrifice which had taken place at the Orcadian stones, points which feature prominently in John Thomas Stanley's annotation of the Stenness stones journal entry. The Vikings sacrificed their fellows at the stones; now Minna must sacrifice her Viking delusions one by one. It is, in a sense, another (though more silent) shriek in the presence of the stones, another defeat for ancient Viking values at the hands of modern notions of rationality, and community and compromise with

Hanoverian England. One by one the romantically deluded confess, retract, and realign their lives. Minna, confessing now to the 'delusions which the credulity of early youth had flung around me' (438) and subsequently to 'the delusions which a solitary education and limited acquaintance with the modern world had spread around me' (453) finally rejects her pirate lover Clement Cleveland, at this final meeting at the stones. Cleveland in turn is denied a Grettir-like heroic outlawry (Grettir who was to become, for Victorian visitors to and writers on Iceland an exemplary, heroic reference point; Wawn 1990, 49–50; 1992); he ends up, unthinkably for the Minna of early in the novel, joining the hated British navy, whilst the real hero Mordaunt Merton, originally excluded because of the absence of Norse blood in his veins (225), marries the blonde and sensible Brenda, as her father's prized sense of 'Norse blood' yields 'to the natural feeling of the heart' (456). The Troil family's loyal retainer Claude Halcro retains a sympathy for Norse values to the end, but his invariably comic presentation undercuts their validity and guides the reader towards rejection. Norna of the Fitful Head, previously all runes, rhymes and revelations, retreats to a study of the Bible (456); and Minna herself does not marry a latter-day Viking sea-king of Norse stock: she does not marry at all. The Viking values she has espoused, and the unreasoning intensity with which she has espoused them, are not passed on to her children, for she has no children on to whom to pass them. The narrator insists (457) in the closing pages of the novel that Minna lived out her years happy and fulfilled, but the reader is not easily convinced.

In *Harold the Dauntless* (1816) Scott had examined a similar transformation, tracing the young Harold's uncomfortable *rite de passage* from compulsive berserker to responsible monarch. In many ways *The Pirate* is a more complex re-examination of this same process: a theme and variations. Scott's insistent rejection of the youthful values of Minna and Harold represents, on the surface at least, a rejection of feelings and attitudes which, however seductive, could not be seen to transcend the urbane sense of Hanoverian wholeness and compromise which breathes through the closing pages of *The Pirate*. British Scandophiles tended to be Whigs (Wawn 1981, 61; 1991, 177), and Sir Walter Scott was not politically of their number. Yet, if Scott's Hanoverian head knew that the renunciatory conclusion to *The Pirate* was the proper one for him, a restatement of the underlying truths of *Waverley* (1814), an acknowledgement of the destructive pastness of the Viking past, the suspicion remains that Scott's heart still thrilled uneasily to the 'throb of the Vikings'. The sterility of Minna's later life cannot serve as a ringing endorsement for the mature wisdom of what Scott's favourite medieval English poets might have called Hanoverian 'high elde' (see Wilt 1985, 119–23 & 143–6 for an alternative reading of the role of Minna and Norna).

The popularity amongst 19th-century readers of *The Pirate*, with its recreation of the Orcadian Viking spirit, was remarkable: most of the mid-century British chroniclers of Icelandic travel seem to have read it, and some feel able to refer frequently and without explanation to characters from the novel in the apparently confident belief that readers will be as familiar with Claude Halcro as with Hamlet and Horatio (for example, Metcalfe 1861, 37 & 70; Lock 1879, 74–5). References to *The Pirate* crop up in the most unlikely 19th century places, such as the copy of the 1862 first edition of Jón Árnason's *Íslenzkar Þjóðsögur og Ævintýri* collection of Icelandic folktales in the Turville-Petre Icelandic collection housed in the English Faculty building in Oxford; the volumes had belonged to Guðbrandur Vigfússon, the indefatigable Oxford-based Icelandic lexicographer, the centenary of whose death was marked in 1989 (McTurk & Wawn 1989). Guðbrandur, noting an Icelandic folktale motif relating to the good luck which can accrue to those responsible for saving a drowning man, adds in his own handwriting a note on the fly-leaf to remind himself of the contrast with the tradition of ill-luck said to accompany equivalent heroism in the Orkneys and Shetlands, as exemplified in the apparently ill-fated rescue of the shipwrecked anti-hero Clement Cleveland by the hero Mordaunt Merton in *The Pirate* (86–7). But it is to another immensely gifted British-based Icelandic philologist, also familiar with and fond of *The Pirate*, who almost certainly knew Sir Walter Scott in Edinburgh, and who shared temperamentally many of the best and worst Viking characteristics as revealed in Scott's novel – it is to him that this essay now turns for a third and final image of Vikings, the Orkneys and the British Enlightenment.

Thus far, both the scenes set at the stones of Stenness have dramatised the defeat or abandonment of ancient Viking values in the face of determined opposition from the British or Scottish mainland. In the 11 extraordinary years which the remarkable Icelandic philologist Þorleifur Repp spent in Edinburgh, as Assistant Keeper at the Advocates' Library (one of whose distinguished members was Sir Walter Scott), we can see the same conflict played out in bizarre 19th century reality (Ólason 1916; Wawn 1991; unless otherwise indicated, the remarks on Repp in the remainder of this essay derive from a study of Repp's unpublished, and individually unnumbered manuscripts, in Lands-bókasafn MSS ÍB 88–90 fol., and Acc.Repp 6.7.1989 fol.). Repp arrived in Edinburgh as unquestionably one of the most gifted philologists in Europe, a disciple of Rasmus Rask, already the recipient of what passed for glittering prizes at the University of Copenhagen, a fanatical Britophile, well-connected in high London and Copenhagen society, astonishingly widely read in English literature (needless to say, he knew his Scott and he knew his Ossian), the master of some 20 languages, an innovative theoretical contributor to the debates which marked this heroic age of comparative philology, responsible for the Latin translation of the Arnamagnæan Commission 1826 *Laxdæla saga* edition, and charged indeed on his arrival in Edinburgh with presenting a copy of the volume to Sir Walter Scott. By any normal standards Repp arrived in Edinburgh with a great future in front of him. Eleven years later he left Edinburgh with a great future behind him: ignominiously dismissed, penurious, humiliated, the respected friend of many in

Edinburgh literary society and further afield in Britain, but having fallen
irretrievably foul of the powerful governing forces of the Advocates' Library, led
by their inadequate and prickly Keeper of Books, David Irving. If ever there
were a latter-day philological spirit of Loda it was Repp, the 19th-century
Viking, whose writings so frequently glow with pride at the achievements of his
Viking ancestors. Repp's virtues – his learning, energy, skill as a teacher,
unquenchable curiosity about the antiquities of his new homeland, and
proselytiser's zeal towards celebrating and publicising Old Norse culture in
Britain – have to be balanced against negative qualities of temperament. He was
paranoid, vindictive, mischief-making, worm-tongued, a man invariably worthy
of the favoured 19th-century translation for the *Íslendingasögur* adjective *óðæll*
['difficult to have dealings with']. There is much that could be said of Repp's
complex and fascinating relationship with the Scottish Enlightenment (Wawn
1991), but one brief aspect must suffice: Repp's connection with the Vikings and
Orkney.

There is ample evidence of Repp's interest in the Orkneys. First, as we have
already noted, there was his championing of Scott's novel *The Pirate*, which is
frequently praised in Repp's writings, published and unpublished. Second, he
prepared in 1846, at the command of Queen Caroline Amalie of Denmark, an
account (Bodleian MS Add. C. 56, never published) of the last days of James
Bothwell, the maverick Scottish earl, lover of Mary Queen of Scots, driven out
by (in Repp's account) the forces of blimpish Scottish reaction, latterly
imprisoned and dying in Danish custody, his heart still in Scotland. Before his
fateful and futile flight from Scotland, Bothwell had been appointed Duke of
Orkney and Shetland by his queen, and Repp's account reveals a considerable
interest in the islands over which Bothwell was granted temporary sway.
Thirdly, Repp prepared, with the aid of the Scottish philologist Robert
Jamieson, a collection of Norn language documents, deeds of conveyance and
charters of land sale from Orkney and Shetland from the 15th and 17th centuries
(Repp 1840). Lastly, Repp's unpublished manuscripts in Landsbókasafn show
that around 1834, whilst still in post at the Advocates' Library, he had proposed
to the Bannatyne Club a revised edition of Jón Jónsson's 1780 Copenhagen
edition of *Orkneyinga saga*.

There is no record of this proposal being taken up at the time but in 1846 Repp
resurrected the project and named his price: he would require payment of £8 per
eight quarto pages, and such was the extent of the revision contemplated that his
estimated total fee was £250. There was indeed a rival bidder for financial
support for a revised edition: one of Repp's Copenhagen English language pupils
had offered to revise *Orkneyinga saga* for £100 (Goudie 1913, 287–8): it was Jón
Sigurðsson, no less, the father of the 19th-century Icelandic independence
movement. Both bids were turned down by the Bannatyne Club. The fate of this
project merely underlines the fact that if 19th-century Britain knew little of
Orkneyinga saga in the years before the 1873 English translation by Gilbert

Goudie and Jón Hjaltalín, or the greatly delayed Sir George Dasent translation for the Rolls Series (Knowles 1963, 119–23), it was no fault of Þorleifur Repp.

There were, thus, times in Victorian Britain when knowledge of the Orkney Vikings was sorely hampered by latter day Fingals still eager to take the sword to at least one latter day Icelandic spirit of Loda. Ultimately, Repp left Scotland not in a puff of smoke with a piercing shriek, but on a boat with a prolonged growl. There is perhaps one particular source for lament. In 1834, under pressure from his Scottish scholarly hosts who had been insulted half a century earlier by Grímur Thorkelín's reluctance to speculate, Repp attempted to decipher the runic lettering on the Ruthwell Cross. The result is splendidly and amusingly mistaken (Wawn 1991, 122–32). It is a pity that the Icelandic philologist's premature return to Denmark prevented his undertaking a trip to examine and decipher the Maeshowe runes, as his Edinburgh philological friend and colleague Ralph Carr was later to do with results of joyous absurdity (Barnes, present volume). I am sure Repp would not have disappointed us.

REFERENCES

Bartholinus, Thomas 1689. *Antiquitatem Danicarum de Causis a Danis adhuc gentibus Mortis*, Copenhagen.
Blair, Hugh 1763. *A Critical Dissertation on the Poems of Ossian, the Son of Fingal*, London.
Borrow, George 1923–4. *The Works of George Borrow*, ed. Shorter, Clement, 16 vols, London.
Cadell, Patrick & Matheson, Ann (eds) 1989. *For the encouragement of learning: Scotland's National Library 1689–1989*, Edinburgh.
CRO. Cheshire Record Office.
Christiansen, Reidar Th. 1931. *The Vikings and the Viking wars in Irish and Gaelic tradition*, Oslo.
Erse Fragments 1760. *Fragments of Ancient Poetry translated from the Galic or Erse Language*, Edinburgh.
Goudie, Gilbert 1913. *David Laing, LL.D: A Memoir*, Edinburgh.
Gunnlaugs saga 1775. *Sagan af Gunnlaugi ormstungu ok skalld-Rafni, sive Gunnlaugi vermilingvis & Rafnis poetæ vita*, ed. Eiríksson, Jón, Copenhagen.
Greenway, John L. 1977. *The Golden Horns: Mythic Imagination and the Nordic past*, Athens, Georgia.
Harvey-Wood, E. H. 1972. *Letters to an Antiquary: The literary correspondence of G. J. Thorkelin (1752–1829)*, Doctoral dissertation, University of Edinburgh.
Johnstone, James 1782. *The Norwegian account of King Haco's expedition against Scotland A.D.MCCLXIII*, [Copenhagen].
Johnstone, James 1786. *Antiquitates Celto-Scandicæ*, Copenhagen.
Jón Jónsson 1780. Jonas Jonaeus, *Orkneyinga saga, sive Historia Orcadensium...*, Copenhagen.
Knowles, David 1963. *Great Historical Enterprises*, London.
Lbs. Landsbókasafn Íslands. Lbs MSS ÍB 88–90 fol. and Acc.Repp 6.7.1989 fol. are the principal collections of Repp manuscripts.
Lieder, P. R. 1920. 'Scott and Scandinavian literature', *Smith College Studies in Modern Languages* 2, 8–57.

Lock, C. W. G. 1879. *The home of the Eddas*, London.

Lonsdale, Roger (ed.) 1969. *The poems of Gray, Collins and Goldsmith*, London.

McTurk, Rory & Wawn, Andrew (eds) 1989. *Úr Dölum til Dala: Guðbrandur Vigfússon centenary essays*, Leeds Texts and Monographs, New Series 11.

Metcalfe, Frederick 1861. *An Oxonian in Iceland*, London.

NLS. National Library of Scotland.

Ólason, Páll Eggert 1916. 'Um Þorleif Guðmundsson Repp', *Skírnir* 90, 121–57.

Omberg, Margaret 1976. *Scandinavian themes in English poetry, 1760–1800*, Uppsala.

Orkneyinga saga 1873. *The Orkneyinga saga*, transl. Goudie, Gilbert & Hjaltalín, Jón, ed. Anderson, Joseph, Edinburgh.

Palgrave, F. T. 1884. *Poetical works of Sir Walter Scott*, London.

Percy, Thomas 1763. *Five pieces of Runic poetry*, London.

Pope, Alexander 1866. *The ancient history of Orkney, Caithness and the North*, Wick.

Repp, Þorleifur Guðmundsson (transl.) 1826. *Laxdæla saga*, Copenhagen.

Repp, Þorleifur Guðmundsson 1840. *Deeds relating to Orkney and Zetland, 1433–1631*, [?Edinburgh].

Repp, Þorleifur Guðmundsson 1846. *Life of Bothwell*, Bodleian MS Add.C.56.

Ritchie, Anna & Ritchie, Graham 1988. *The ancient monuments of Orkney* (3rd edn). HMSO, Edinburgh.

Scott, Sir Walter 1816 (1910 edition). *The Antiquary*, Edinburgh.

Scott, Sir Walter 1822 (1871 edition). *The Pirate*, Edinburgh.

Stafford, Fiona J. 1988. *The sublime savage: a study of James McPherson and the poems of Ossian*, Edinburgh.

Thomson, Derrick S. 1951. *The Gaelic sources of McPherson's 'Ossian'*, Edinburgh.

Torfæus [Þormóður Torfason] 1697. *Orcades seu rerum Orcadensium historiæ*, Copenhagen.

Víga-Glúms saga: Viga-Glums saga sive Vita Viga Glumi, ed. Pétursson, Guðmundur, Copenhagen, 1786.

Wawn, Andrew 1981. 'John Thomas Stanley and Iceland: the sense and sensibility of an eighteenth-century explorer', *Scandinavian Studies* 53, 52–76.

Wawn, Andrew 1982. '*Gunnlaugs saga ormstungu* and the Theatre Royal, Edinburgh: melodrama, mineralogy and Sir George Mackenzie', *Scandinavica* 21, 139–51.

Wawn, Andrew (ed.) 1987. *The Iceland journal of Henry Holland*, Hakluyt Society, Series II, London, 168.

Wawn, Andrew 1989. 'The Enlightenment traveller and the idea of Iceland: the Stanley expedition of 1789 reconsidered', *Scandinavica* 28, 5–16.

Wawn, Andrew 1990. 'The silk-clad Varangian: Þorleifur Repp and *Færeyinga saga*', *Saga-Book of the Viking Society* 23, 46–72.

Wawn, Andrew 1991. *The Anglo Man: Þorleifur Repp, philology and nineteenth-century Britain*, Studia Islandica 49, Reykjavík.

Wawn, Andrew 1992. 'The spirit of 1892: Sagas, Saga-steads and Victorian philology', *Saga-Book of the Viking Society* 23, 213–52.

West, 1970–6. John F. West (ed.), *The journals of the Stanley expedition to the Faroe Islands and Iceland in 1789*, 3 vols, Tórshavn.

Wilt, Judith 1985. *Secret leaves: the novels of Sir Walter Scott*, Chicago.

Wolf, Kirsten & D'Arcy, Julian (1987). 'Sir Walter Scott and *Eyrbyggja saga*', *Studies in Scottish literature* 22, 30–43.

27

VIKING-AGE SKETCHES AND MOTIF-PIECES FROM THE NORTHERN EARLDOMS

UAININN O'MEADHRA

INTRODUCTION

In this chapter I wish to present further views on the significance of some of the more important Viking-Age sketches and motif-pieces which survive from the area of the Northern Earldoms, namely Caithness, the Orkneys and Shetlands, placing them within the NW European sketching tradition to which they belong. I will discuss this material under three headings (as treated in O'Meadhra 1987, 90ff): (1) free sketches, (2) designers' sketches and (3) motif-pieces.

The sketches to be dealt with in this paper occur on small slivers of slate or unworked bone (at Jarlshof, Shetland and Birsay, Orkney), on raised slabs of existing prehistoric monuments (at Burrian Broch and Maeshowe, Orkney), and on metalwork (at Birsay and Skaill, Orkney).

On Chronology and Terminology

Close dating of these Scottish sketches and motif-pieces is unfortunately impossible, but this situation is not uncommon in archaeological matters and broad dating must be tolerated. There is one outstanding exception, the group of sketches on the Skaill jewellery which come from a coin-dated hoard with a deposition date of *c*. 950 (Graham-Campbell 1976, 119 & 130; 1984, 289). The sketches and motif-pieces from Jarlshof and Birsay come from archaeological excavations of settlement sites with meagre stratigraphical contexting. The other sketches are stray finds lacking datable contexts. Stylistic analysis of the sketches themselves provides some further dating criteria, but neither dating method – whether stratigraphical or stylistic – is very secure.

In my use of the term Viking Age, I am being deliberately general. While the limits of the period are continuously under scrutiny, and there is a tendency for modern scholars to place the beginning of the period in Scandinavia within the second half of the 8th century, and its end in the early 11th century, I am concerned with Viking activity and resulting Scandinavian influence in the Northern Isles which continues on into the 12th century and even later. Rather than deal in real years, I shall content myself in this paper with allocation to two main cultural rather than chronological contexts: pre-Norse and Norse as applied to the Scottish area. My main concern is whether or not the material I am dealing with has been affected by Viking intervention into the political, social and cultural aspects of northern Scotland and the Isles. The term 'Insular' will be used with the specific meaning of non-Scandinavian pertaining to Great Britain and Ireland. The term 'medieval' is reserved in this paper for the period after AD 1200.

The Viking-Age sketches that survive in Scandinavia and in NW Europe have been recently surveyed in an attempt to place them in a historical context (O'Meadhra 1987, 90–129, Figs 64–89. See also O'Meadhra 1991, 45–7). A seminar was held in Oslo in 1979 (cf. Varia 1980) and included papers by Martin Blindheim (on stave-church graffiti), Arne B. Christensen (on late medieval farm-building graffiti) and Signe H. Fuglesang (on Viking-Age graffiti, sketches and designs). Already in the 1950s, Blindheim began gathering material for a major monograph on Norwegian stave-church graffiti of the period c. 1150–1350 (Blindheim 1985), while Christensen has worked since the 1960s on ship graffiti including that found during the excavations of Viking Dublin (cf. Christensen 1988). Other major studies of Scandinavian sketches have been published variously by U. Linder Welin, M. Hammarberg and G. Rispling (on coin-graffiti), E. Roesdahl and E. Munksgård (on miscellaneous Danish Viking graffiti), O. Crumlin-Pedersen (on ship graffiti) and E. Møller (on Danish medieval tile and church wall graffiti) (full bibliographical references in O'Meadhra 1987, 90ff; 1991, nn14–25). Some of the more significant English church-graffiti of the medieval period has been published in an illustrated analysis by Mrs V. Pritchard (Pritchard 1967). Swedish work on the medieval graffiti/sketches inscribed into the wall-plaster of the 13th–14th-century churches on the Baltic island of Gotland, has already been variously published by Erland Lagerlöf (e.g. Lagerlöf 1977; 1978; 1981). I am myself working together with Lagerlöf on a joint project documenting and analysing this graffiti which consists of designers' preparatory sketches, magical devices and represen-tational figures or scenes. Runic inscription-graffiti and ship drawings in these churches are being studied by specialists from the Swedish Central Board of Antiquities including Runverket.

For the Viking Age, the major area outside of Scandinavia where sketches abound is Scotland: in areas of Dalriadic and Pictish settlement in the west and in Pictish/Norse settlements in the Northern Earldoms. This could be the result of chance survival since the material used is stone, and of the relatively unexploited nature of the Scottish landscape which must assist survival and recognition of such enigmatic objects as artisans' sketches. The Scandinavian sketches are mainly on wood, which survives well in the northern climate. It is interesting to contrast the distribution of sketches with that of motif-pieces in

NW Europe. While numerous slate motif-pieces are recorded for Ireland for this period, no free sketches have been found there. From among all the Scandinavian sketches so far recorded, none can be classified as motif-pieces until about AD 1000, when true urban sites become established there (O'Meadhra 1987, 78–83, Figs 57–9). It is thus possible that in some similar way there is a cultural reason behind the concentration of sketches in Scotland. Since, as I argue below, most of the so-called Norse sketches there would seem to be non-Norse, sketching in Scotland might well be a Pictish characteristic.

Furthermore, graffiti in the Nordic world seem to be a reaction to contact with a literate world, met through pirating and trade. The most important graffiti from the Oseberg ship-furniture occur on a wooden writing-tablet base (cf. Fuglesang in Varia 1980), which must have been an exotic import into the non-literate court of the royal Norwegian personage buried at Oseberg. Graffiti become widespread in Scandinavia just at the time when these countries first come into contact with writing as a general practice, through the legends on coins, through trips abroad, and through visiting traders and Christian missionaries, or even through imported literate slaves. While runic writing had been introduced to Scandinavia many centuries before, little evidence survives for its common usage until later, when town life establishes itself (see for example the 11th century and later material from Lödöse and Bergen; cf. Svärdström 1982; Liestøl 1980). It may be no coincidence that some of the earliest graffiti known from Scandinavia take the form of runic inscriptions on metalwork and graffiti on coins (cf. O'Meadhra 1987, Figs 67 & 89). Perhaps echoing this trend is the fact that one of the three most popular motifs in West European manuscript-graffiti comprises the letters of the alphabet running across margins, even in manuscripts with illumination which should have attracted art-motifs (see preliminary list in O'Meadhra 1987, Fig. 66).

It is possible that we have a similar trend in operation in N Scotland, since Pictish sketches occur at a time when an illiterate group with an interest in graphic representation – as witnessed by the symbol stones – first came into contact with the literate West – in this case the Romans of Britain and the Insular Church. (Note, however, that some would argue that the Pictish symbol stones as well as cross slabs are themselves the result of contact with these sources; compare Henderson 1967; Stevenson 1971; Ritchie 1989.)

These Pictish symbol-stones present a special case with regard to the topic of this paper. Besides standing-stones (the so-called symbol stones and the later cross slabs) and portable artifacts such as discs, counters and metalwork decorated with symbols, the N Scotland area has also produced a number of cave-wall drawings, and unworked small pieces of stone and bone bearing symbols (cf. e.g. RCAHMS 1946, 5 and nos 21, 193, 345 & 842; Thomas 1963, 44–8, Figs 2–3). These include the curious stone from Portsoy, Banffshire, with carved human heads at either end and between these sketched fish and other figures, which Thomas (1963, 48, pl. II) included in his survey of Pictish art mobilier, and ox phalanges bearing a symbol on each face (gaming pieces?) from Burrian Broch, N Ronaldsay, Orkney (Mitchell 1902, 30, Fig. 51; MacGregor 1974, 88, Fig. 16 nos 210–12). While the correct interpretation of the significance of Pictish symbols is much debated, they do seem to hold more ritual value than do art motifs in general (cf. Thomas 1963; Henderson 1967; 1971; Stevenson 1971; Jackson 1984). Therefore the cave walls, pebbles and bones bearing symbols are considered in this paper to be a special category of decorated objects rather than sketches or motif-pieces. The same applies to the twenty-odd painted pebbles ('charm-stones'?) found on settlement sites from before and during Pictish times with a repertoire of motifs considered related to Pictish symbols (Thomas 1963, 46–8; Ritchie 1972, 299; 1989, 50). However, a stone pebble from Burrian Broch incised on one face with a pentagram ('pentacle') embellished with spirals and dots and on the other a hexagram, deserves further mention. The pentagram and hexagram, though common in medieval graffiti, do not belong to the true Pictish-symbol repertoire, although other examples considered to be Pictish are known from the cave walls at Covsea, Morayshire (a craft-working site), and on a painted pebble from Keiss, Caithness (Ritchie 1972; MacGregor 1974, 95–6, Fig. 20; I am grateful to Isabel Henderson for these references). Insular-Scandinavian examples of the pentagram occur at Late Viking (11th century) Dublin on a tiny antler-plate incised profile cut-out head found during excavations of the Christ Church Place site and on a rib-bone motif-piece from the Fishamble Street site (O'Meadhra 1991).

FREE SKETCHES

One of the freest sketches found in N Scotland is an undated chance surface find from a neolithic tomb at the Bridge of Brogar, Stenness, Orkney (described and illustrated in Noble 1887, 266–7). The stone has been divided on one flat face into four quadrants by incised framing, within two quadrants is a possible pictorial scene representing what might be a river and its rocky bank with an otter catching a fish. On one of the shorter sides of the stone, five(?) fish, two represented with scales and fins, are positioned as if biting at the one bait. The stone is not dated by its find-context since this has no stratigraphical reliability, and far from being of Viking-Age date, it is possible that this is a relatively modern sketch as scenes are unknown in Insular graffiti (though not in sculptural art) before the late medieval period (cf. Blindheim 1985; O'Meadhra 1987).

At Chapel Knowe, Burness Broch, Orkney, a slab measuring 100 × 20 × 6 cm was found in wall-filling material (Marwick 1924, 295–7, Fig. 1; RCAHMS 1946, 91–2, Fig. 72). This slab contains intensive markings from which can be deciphered a 6 cm-high human figure, a possible ship, and a grid for a game or ship's sail (Fig. 27.1). The human figure, dressed in a long cowled gown or cloak with decorated hem, is related to Pictish portraits showing local dress as found in slab/cross art which seem to be a feature of the N Scottish area. These shed an

Figure 27.1: Sketched slab from Broch of Burness (interpretative drawing by author).

interesting light on Pictish dress-traditions. The closest parallel to the Burness man is to be found in the foremost of three warriors (an Orcadian chief with retinue?) in ceremonial procession on a symbol stone from the Brough of Birsay (good photographic reproductions in RCAHMS 1946, Fig. 57 and Curle 1982, ill. 4; good analysis with line drawing in Ritchie 1989, 54).

Other human-figure sketches of the Viking Age found in our area, are the well-known men's portraits (Fig. 27.2a,b) on both sides of a slate fragment from the Pictish/Norse settlement at Sumburgh, Shetland, known popularly as Jarlshof, where over 100 fragments composing at least 50 slates were found (Curle 1935, 308–17 Figs 48–54; Hamilton 1956, 114–15, 121 pl. xvii & xxi). Most of these slate drawings are considered to be the idle product of moments of leisure (cf. comprehensive discussion by Fuglesang in Varia 1980). Those few that might be considered as motif-pieces are discussed later below. The Jarlshof sketches were found on different occasions and are usually understood as Viking work, depicting Norse themes and coming from the Norse levels, according to the excavators (Curle 1935; Hamilton 1956, 114). But I would like to suggest, as also independently remarked by Ritchie (1989, 50), that these are instead Pictish themes and Pictish renderings. As often observed, the heads have the hair curls typical of Pictish figures and the beard-detail is also found on Pictish slab art. These heads are quite unlike any known Scandinavian portraits of the Viking Age (O'Meadhra 1991). I would argue that none of the other slate-motifs is neccessarily Viking either. This is especially important for the ship drawings which are usually taken for Norse work.

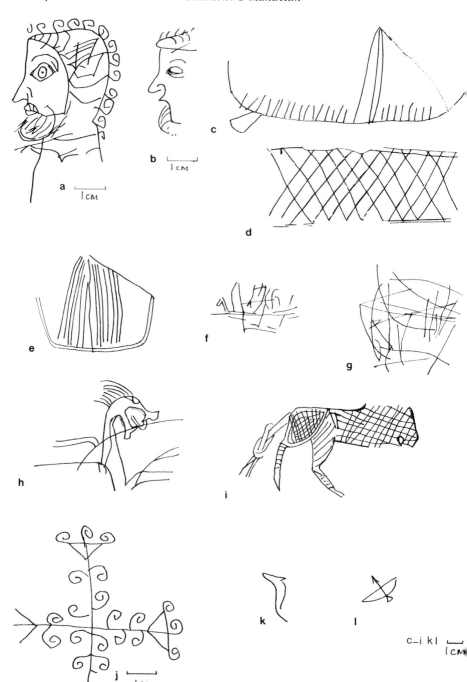

Figure 27.2, a–l: Men, ships, animals and cross-motif on slate fragments found at Jarlshof (interpretative drawings by author).

Two sketches undoubtedly represent ships (Fig. 27.2c, e), some other slates with confused markings have been interpreted as representing a ship sail (Fig. 27.2d) and ships, one even with a Viking tent (Fig. 27.2f, g), but these identifications are less certain. The most famous ship drawing (Fig. 27.2c) has often been compared to the Kvalsund boat (Curle 1954a, 28; Hamilton 1956, 114), but such a comparison does not indicate Norse identity since Kvalsund is pre-Viking and is furthermore similar to Anglo-Saxon ships of the Sutton-Hoo type. Thus this drawing could be of either an Anglo-Saxon or a Norse ship, or even of a Pictish ship, of which we know very little. In any event it could have been drawn by a Pict and I would argue that even if the ship represented is nonetheless a Viking ship, the drawing is characteristically non-Viking for the following reasons. The usual way that Vikings render a ship shows an awareness of ship-technology, portraying the overlapping plank construction of the body of the vessel and often indicating the special notched stern-timber for joining the strakes together at the prow – a construction typical of Viking ships, while a short slanting cut usually demarcates the prow tip. Some sketches indicate only the stern (as in the Viking-period Ranveig graffiti discussed below and early medieval Norwegian stave-church graffiti. cf. Blindheim 1985; O'Meadhra 1988). Others indicate the whole ship, rigged and often with men on board (as in the late Viking/early medieval sketches from Scandinavian Dublin and Löddeköping; cf. Christensen 1988). The Jarlshof drawings have none of these characteristics but concentrate on the overall image, illustrating both stem and stern with raised prows, but only impressionistically indicating the line of the ship and possibly its passengers. That there are no good Scandinavian parallels for the Jarlshof sketches became obvious in the preparation of an article (O'Meadhra 1988) on the ship graffiti cut into the metal baseplate of a pre-/early Viking-period Insular house-shaped shrine found in Norway, known as 'Ranveig's casket' (NMC reg. no. C9084). The shrine ships are cut in a different style from, and lie beneath the well-researched Ranveig ownership-inscription graffito in so-called Manx-Jaeren runes on the same baseplate, so the ships must have been sketched before the runes. This raised the interesting possibility that the ships might have been cut by an Insular sketcher before the shrine fell into Viking hands. This possibility, however, could be dismissed after it became evident from a comparative study of Scandinavian and Insular ship-depictions that the shrine ships adhered to the Scandinavian norm. If we look to the N Scottish area for parallels to the Jarlshof ships, we find that the only boat/ship known on a Pictish cross slab is the carving at Cossans, Angus, usually dated late 8th/early 9th century (good illustration in Ritchie 1989, 30–1). This seems to be a boat with high prow and stern, holding 5 persons, lacks a sail but has a clear rudder placed as in the slate drawing. The other major group of Insular representations, those on the Irish high crosses, show influence of classical Roman prototypes, apparently the result of artistic convention rather than drawing from real life.

The drawing of an animal head on another slate (Fig. 27.2h) is usually interpreted as a Viking ship's prow-figurehead. But the head lacks the sweep of line required for a boat prow. Furthermore the eye of the animal is distinctly Insular, with the triangular additive placed behind the circle of the pupil. This eye form is not found in Viking-Age Scandinavian art but does appear in the 12th century (Blindheim 1985). Distinctive too are the clearly defined snout endings and sharp teeth. These are features of Insular metalwork. An Insular copper-alloy mount in the shape of a striding lion found at the Viking cemetery of Kilmainham/ Islandbridge, Dublin (Boe 1940, 52, Fig. 35) exhibits a head quite similar in detail to the Jarlshof sketch. But it is difficult to find good analogies for the curve of the animal neck and body. The usual comparisons with Pictish-type penannular brooches such as from Ninian's Isle, Freswick and the Birsay moulds (Wilson 1973, pl xxxiv:a; Curle 1982, ill. 14; Curle 1954b, Fig 23) and sword chapes such as Ninian's Isle chape no. 16 (Wilson 1973, 65–7, pl. xxx) are not convincing.

The reverse of the same slate contains a different animal sketch (Fig. 27.2i). This seems at first glance to be roughly sketched without adherence to any stylistic norms, but in fact follows very specific conventions. The hindhip hatching stops short of the double contour surrounding the hip, and the tail knot ends in a bifurcation. The forehip area, unfortunately damaged by the broken edge of the slate, has a loop-feature which, being respected by the cross-hatching of the body, seems to be deliberate. This loop feature resembles the inner upper contour of crossed forelegs, typical of Anglo-Scandinavian sculpture.

Another slate (Fig. 27.2j) might show ecclesiastic affiliations and it should be remembered that Hamilton (1956, 88) suggested evidence for 8th century missionary activities at Jarlshof. The slate is filled with an embellished cross-motif which is unusual for this period but resembles medieval ironwork such as door-mountings or weathervanes. However, it also recalls the unusual motif decorating an initial letter in an early Bobbio manuscript (Milan, Biblioteca Ambrosiana MS S. 45. sup. (Atala Codex) p. 2, initial N). There are differences though, the manuscript motif is formed of C-curls neatly arranged around a cross in contrast to the irregular single curls and triangular terminals which extend off a linear cross on the slate. The manuscript, a palimpsest over a text in 6th century Gothic uncial, is considered to have been written in Bobbio rather than Ireland, and is dated to the early 7th century on the evidence of an inscription on the same page as our initial. This reads 'Lb DE ARCA DOMNO ATALANI', which, by connecting the manuscript with Atalanus who was abbot of Bobbio 615–22, dates it to before 622 (Lowe 1938, no. 365; Alexander 1978, cat. 2, ill. 8). There is other complementary evidence for contact between Pictland and Bobbio. The name of a Pictish monk is recorded in another Bobbio manuscript (Turin Lactantius. Uncial, 6th/7th century. Cf. Lowe 1947, 10, no. 438). This reads 'DE ARCA DŌM UORGUSTI ABBI', and uses the same formula as the Atala inscription just mentioned. The name Uorgustus is Pictish;

unknown from any other records, he almost certainly was a 7th-century abbot of Bobbio since this formula seems to be a 7th-century Bobbio feature (these are two of the three known examples). With regard to Pictish-Italian contact in the 8th century, a Pictish bishop, 'Fergustus, Episcopus Scotiae Pictus', is recorded as attending a Council held in Rome in 721 (Haddan & Stubbs (eds) 1873–8,116) (I am indebted to David N. Dumville for these references to Pictish ecclesiastics in Italy and for the Pictish identification of Uorgustus). This is the only possible decorative art motif on the Jarlshof slates. The remaining slates with less specific scratches will be discussed below when dealing with possible motif-pieces from Jarlshof.

To end this section on free sketches, I turn to perhaps the most famous sketch in the Orkneys – that of a lion-like beast cut into the north-eastern buttress of the central-chamber of the neolithic tomb at Maeshowe (Fig. 27.3) (Cochrane (ed.) 1899, 90; Clouston 1933; Mackenzie 1937; RCAHMS 1946, 309, Fig. 383; Pritchard 1967, 168–9, Figs 219–20; O'Meadhra 1987, 91–2, Fig. 65). This is cut apparently at the same time as a looping snake- or vegetal-interlace and unfinished walrus or seal-like creature (Clouston 1933, Fig. 3; RCAHMS 1946, Fig. 403), both on the same slab face as the lion, and possibly cut by the same hand. These are usually considered to be contemporary with some at least of the large number of Norwegian runic inscriptions which cover the inside of the central chamber of the tomb. The runic inscriptions seem to belong to various phases of

I CM

Figure 27.3: Lion-graffiti on the tomb at Maeshowe (interpretative drawing by author).

cutting within the mid-late 12th century, dated by a boast that some are the work of crusaders, or names of identifiable historical figures (according to *Orkneyinga saga*, in 1150–1 Norwegian crusaders wintered in Orkney before travelling to Palestine, and Earl Harold with his men were caught in a traumatic snow-storm in January 1153 when visiting Maeshowe) (RCAHMS 1946, 309–13) (see Barnes, this volume).

The lion-graffiti would fit a 12th-century stylistic date, showing a combination of Romanesque and late-Viking features. As in the case of all graffiti, the cutting of the Maeshowe lion could be symbolic – though the ingenious interpretations put forward by Clouston (1933) and Pritchard (1967, 168) are rather extreme. There is, however, no reason why this cannot be an idle sketch by a member of one of the rune-carving parties which might well have included an artistically skilled person versed in style norms. Body-piercing occurs in Scandinavian Viking and Romanesque contexts and has been traced to Romanesque France and 10th century Anglo-Scandinavian sculpture in N England (Belling 1984). The stance of the animal with backturned head and raised forepaw can be traced back to Hedeby coins of *c.* AD 900 through to the Bayeux tapestry and later. Surface-patterning in the form of scales has been identified as a Viking tradition by Mackenzie (1937, 171–2), and the foliated tail attributed to late Viking Ringerike-style influence (Mackenzie 1937; Shetelig in RCAHMS 1946, 313). Though the tail lacks the usual Romanesque manner of following the hindhip contour and ending in a single leaf-tip, a Continental(?) Romanesque rather than Scandinavian Viking milieu is indicated by the realistic legjoints and paws, and the parallel lines marking the animal's belly and the specific way in which the scales give way to hip-feathering with the resulting lack of spiral hipjoints. 'Lion'-graffiti is not uncommon in Romanesque Scandinavia: examples include a range of 'lions' among the late 12th-century Norwegian stave-church graffiti at Ål, Fortun, Kaupanger, Kvikne, Lom and Urnes (Blindheim 1985, pls I–IV, XIV, XV, XIX, XXXVI, XLI, XLVI & LXXII), and one in Romanesque style, cut into the original plaster of the 13th-century church at Lojsta, Gotland (Lagerlöf 1977).

DESIGNER'S SKETCHES

One of the most certain examples of a designer's sketch in the Northern area comes from excavation of the pre-Norse levels of the Pictish and Norse settlement at the Brough of Birsay, Orkney (Fig. 27.4). This is a lead disc which, being unfinished work, is furthermore important because it localises the manufacture or design of such discs to this site which provided much evidence of Pictish decorative metalworking during the 7th–9th centuries. The design is for Insular metalworking, being a trumpet-spiral motif of 6th–8th/9th-century type (cf. Curle 1982, 49; Stevenson 1983). I have previously argued (O'Meadhra 1987, 114–5, Fig. 75 :a–c) that this lead disc is clearly a designer's sketch utilising the malleable quality of lead, rather than being a finished negative master-

l____l
I CM

Figure 27.4: Unfinished spiral design (designer's sketch) on lead disc from Birsay (after O'Meadhra 1987).

pattern for impressing either sheet-metal or a metalcasting-mould as argued by Mrs Curle in her first detailed analysis of this disc (Curle 1974, 301–6, pl. 24). However, in her later discussion included in the site-analysis report (Curle 1982, 49, ill. 30), she admits the possibility that the disc was a trial piece. Curle's 1974 view has been supported by other specialists (most importantly Wilson 1976, 508 and Stevenson 1983, 452) who have interpreted the disc as a casting matrix used for shaping the wax patrix for cast metal decoration of the 'hairline spiral' type. But the disc is unequally finished on each of the three similar sections of the pattern (Curle's published drawings omit the multitude of sketch-lines covering the surface). This is most unlike a casting blank which would require all sections to be equally cut (finished or unfinished). It is much more reasonable to interpret the disc as a designer's sketch in the process of being worked out: as soon as one unit was fully developed, the design would be clear since all units are identical. In a finished state, certainly, such a disc could have served as a matrix master pattern for impressing foils or casting-moulds. (I wish to record my debt to the late Mrs Curle for stimulating discussions on the Birsay material, especially the disc and the motif-pieces.)

Another example of a Viking-Age Insular metalworker's design from our area occurs on the reverse of a stone amulet from the Inverness area – a small perforated flat pebble with one face covered by a neatly cut, framed cross surrounded by fields of geometric interlace. The sketched design on the reverse consists of an interlaced animal which despite the carelessness of the cutting, adheres to style-norms typical of one of the 8th/9th-century Insular types of animal interlace with which it must be contemporary. Since this pebble is being fully published by Isabel Henderson and others, it will not be discussed further here.

The only sketches that show clear Viking-Age Scandinavian influence in our area, are those occurring on a newly published silver brooch pin-head from the Skaill hoard (Graham-Campbell 1984, ill. 6) and that scratched onto the slightly expanded terminals of a silver brooch (Shetelig 1954a, Fig. 78) (Fig. 27.5a–c). These sketches seem to be unfinished designs perhaps originally intended to be finalised into decoration of the brooches but left in the designing stage. The designs echo the finished decoration on the other brooches from this hoard. Graham-Campbell has convincingly argued, from the occurrence of similar Insular Jellinge / Mammen-style animal ornament on the Kirk Braddan crosses (to which should be added Andreas 121), that the animal decoration of the Skaill brooches is most likely Manx or Manx-influenced work under the influence of the Scandinavian style (Graham-Campbell 1983, 70, n14, Fig. 11; cf. Shetelig 1954b, 139, Fig. 50). Related brooch decoration occurs on a fragment from the late-Viking Dublin excavations (P. Wallace, personal communication) and the most famous example is the silver and gold ball-type brooch from Møllerløkken, Denmark (NMC reg. no. 16370. Graham-Campbell 1980, no. 217), which is of Scandinavian manufacture to judge by the different techniques employed. Of relevance to our discussion of these sketches on the Skaill brooches is the secondary sketch on a Hiberno-Norse silver bossed penannular brooch found on a farm-site in Sandmúli, Iceland (NMR reg. no. 5884. Shetelig 1954b, 121, Fig. 38; O'Meadhra 1987, 117, Fig. 79). This Scandinavian or Insular-Scandinavian sketch is in a related style and was presumably cut when the brooch had become

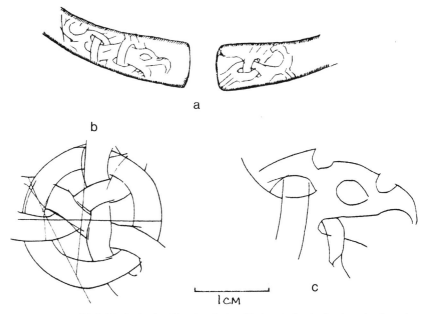

Figure 27.5, a–c: Unfinished animal and interlace designs (designer's sketches) on brooches from the Skaill hoard (a, after Shetelig; b–c, after Graham-Campbell).

scrap silver and thus might have been executed before reaching Iceland, and in that case could be a product of the Northern Earldoms or the 'Skaill' sketcher. (I am indebted to James Graham-Campbell for additional information on the sketches from Sandmúli and Skaill, which he intends to publish in more detail.)

MOTIF-PIECES

It is now time to turn to the motif-pieces from the Northern Earldoms. Motif-pieces are a particular category of sketch, probably chiefly connected with teaching and designing of decoration, and sometimes with the manufacture of fine metalwork (O'Meadhra 1979; 1987). There is every likelihood from the evidence of the overall NW European distribution of the motif-pieces so far recorded, that the antler motif-piece from Dooey, Co. Donegal (O'Meadhra 1979, no. 20; O'Meadhra 1987, 36–8) is the earliest, dating to the 5th/6th century AD and that motif-pieces represent an Ireland-originated activity (O'Meadhra 1987, 78–83). Despite this, their strongest concentrations per site occur in Viking urban contexts (O'Meadhra 1987, Figs 57, 59). Analysis of the situation in our Northern area, suggests that motif-pieces are too few there to be a feature of these Norse aristocratic rural settlements, even though such must have had contact with urban Dublin, the largest motif-piece site known in the Viking world.

The Scottish motif-pieces have a very specific distribution, breaking down into two clear groups: (1) Scottish Dalriada (the most prolific group), (2) Pictish/Norse in the Orkney and Shetland area. The Dalriadic motif-pieces relate to those Irish stone pieces of the 7th–9th (–10th?) centuries at Garryduff, Co. Cork, Nendrum, Co. Down and Gransha, Co. Down (respectively O'Meadhra 1979 nos 66–73, nos 74–112, nos 134–57; O'Meadhra 1987, 56–8, 58–9 & 71–4). (A detailed corpus and discussion of the non-Irish motif-pieces is in preparation by the present author, as Motif-pieces vols 3 and 5.)

Let us now return to the Northern area and the motif-pieces at Jarlshof, Shetland and Birsay, Orkney. At Jarlshof, as we have already seen, most of the slates contain miscellaneous scratches rather than art-motifs. These were queried on discovery by A. O. Curle as possibly learners' attempts at 'the elements of design', but more likely 'meaningless scribbles of an idler' (Curle 1935, 316). The latter interpretation is the more likely, as there is no evidence for animal or geometric interlace, or even of guidelines for interlace, on the Jarlshof fragments. This observation is based on analysis of the published drawings and photos of the less decipherable scribings (Curle 1935, 309–16, Figs 46–54; Hamilton 1956, pls xvii, xxi), and on my own detailed examination of the slates in 1972. Comparison with the apparently equally enigmatic scratchings at Nendrum and Gransha emphasises this lack of art motifs, since at the latter sites, the bases of various interlace and geometric patterns were discernible after careful examination. At the Scottish Dalriadic motif-piece site of St Blanes, Bute, free sketches occur alongside motif-pieces.

Figure 27.6: Motif piece: sliver of slate from Jarlshof (interpretative drawing by author).

There is, however, one fairly certain motif-piece from Jarlshof. This is a sliver of slate with deeply incised foliage ornament of Scandinavian form (Fig. 27.6). The closest parallels occur in the foliage ornament on the late 11th/early 12th-century silver bowls from Uppland, Sweden (e.g. Holmqvist 1963, Fig. 38 and Blomqvist 1971, Fig. 5. For best conclusions on the coin-dating of these bowls, see Blomqvist). A further parallel is with the Ringerike-style foliage scroll on the inner lip of the Irish drinking horn from Tongeren now in Brussels (Ryan 1985, Fig. 7). It is difficult to attribute any function to this slate sliver other than as part of a motif-piece. The foliage is very skillfully worked and all style norms are adhered to. Another Ringerike-style object was found at Jarlshof. This is the copper-alloy mount considered by Fuglesang (1980, cat. 55, pl. 32:A) to be the product of a workshop in the British Isles on close comparisons with the technique used on a copper-alloy disc (Fuglesang 1980, cat. 51) from St Martin le Grand, London. A Swedish connection for the slate is interesting when we remember that there are Swedish Late Viking-Age finds from the Northern Earldoms: two strap-ends of late 11th/12th-century Gotlandic type from the settlement at Freswick, Caithness (Curle 1954b, Figs 22, 24). (The Gotlandic animal-headed brooch of similar date, reportedly from Perthshire (Shetelig 1954a, Fig. 79) is now considered as of uncertain provenance and even to have reached Scotland through a modern collector.)

At Birsay we have two good motif-pieces, the only definite ones found so far in the Northern Earldoms (Curle 1982, 24, 70, ill. 11: 267, ill. 45: 606; O'Meadhra 1987, Figs 57, 58: b) (Fig. 27.7a, b). The question is, whether these belong to the Pictish or Norse settlement on this site. Stratification on the site was not unproblematic, but on the whole the two settlements were distinguishable by the

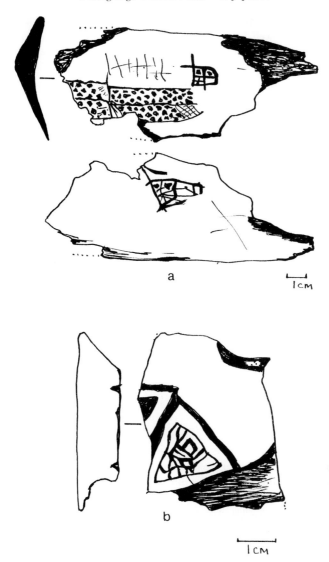

a

1 cm

b

1 cm

Figure 27.7, a–b: Motif pieces: carved bone and stone pieces from Birsay (interpretative drawings by author).

nature of the find assemblages and their horizontal and vertical stratigraphy, since the Pictish settlement clustered closer to the coastline. There are no good reasons for dismissing Mrs Curle's stratigraphical conclusions which place the bone piece in the Pictish horizon and the stone piece in the lower Norse horizon. The bone piece lay close to the area of intensive fine-metalworking debris around the Pictish well. High-quality brooch moulds, an interlace-decorated bone mount and the good quality of the chip-carving on the bone motif-piece, together with the well-known Pictish symbol-slab with warrior procession (discussed above) though not from an excavated context, further indicate high quality Pictish artwork on the site.

Both Birsay motif-pieces belong to mainstream types as found in Ireland, rather than those found so far in Anglo-Saxon/ late Saxon contexts in England (O'Meadhra 1987, Fig. 58). The bone piece (Fig 27.7a) shows the beginnings of two joined triquetras on one face and chip-carved plaitwork and the beginnings of a square knot-motif on the other. Mrs Curle argues (1982, 24–5) that the plaitwork is not typical for Pictish art because it is in chip-carved technique, and she turns to the Lagore motif-pieces (O'Meadhra 1979, nos 119–23) for parallels. I believe this is unnecessary. We know too little about Pictish metalwork to reject this piece as itself evidence of Pictish use of chip-carving. But the matter is not without problems. Better parallels than Lagore for the Birsay piece's type of chip-carving, are to be found in motif-pieces from mid–late 10th-century levels at Dublin (e.g. O'Meadhra 1979, no. 30). This means that the bone piece could fit in with a Norse settlement context if the published stratigraphical dating is found to be faulty. The stone piece (Fig 27.7b) shows a complex triquetra-like motif within a frame and lying against this a corner of the beginnings of what seems to be a similar motif, but broken away. An almost identical rendering but without a frame occurs on the coin-dated early-11th century stone motif-piece from Beal Boru (O'Meadhra 1979, no. 15; 1987, 31–2), while closely-packed frames are common on the late-10th/ early-11th century bone motif-pieces from Dublin (e.g. O'Meadhra 1979, no. 60)

REFERENCES

Alexander, J. J. G. 1978. *Insular Manuscripts from the 6th to the 9th century*, A Survey of Manuscripts Illuminated in the British Isles 1, gen. ed. Alexander, J. J. G., London.

Belling, Dorte Lorentzen 1984. 'Gennemstukne dyr', *Romanske Stenarbejder 2*, 155–76, Højbjerg (Hikuin).

Blindheim, Martin 1985. *Graffiti in Norwegian Stave Churches c. 1150–1350*, Medieval Art in Norway 2, Oslo.

Blomqvist, Nils 1971. 'Fem uppländska silverskatter', *Tor* 14, 7–32, Uppsala.

Boe, Johs 1940. 'Norse Antiquities in Ireland', in *Viking Antiquities in Great Britain and Ireland* 3, ed. Shetelig, H., Oslo.

Christensen, Arne-Emil 1988. 'Ship Graffiti and Models', *Fascicule 3* in *Miscellanea 1*. *Medieval Dublin Excavations 1962–81*, Ser. B, vol. 2 *(1988)*, ed. Wallace, P. F., Dublin, pp. 13–26.

Cochrane, R. (ed.) 1899. *Programme of Excursion and Illustrated Descriptive Guide to the Places to be visited [by Royal Society of Antiquaries of Ireland] in the Western and Northern Islands and Coast of Scotland*, Dublin.

Clouston, J. Storer 1933. 'Something about Maeshowe', *Proceedings of the Orkney Antiquarian Society* 11, 9–17.

Curle, Alexander O. 1935. 'An account of the excavation of a dwelling of the Viking Period at "Jarlshof", Sumburgh, Shetland', *Proceedings of the Society of Antiquaries of Scotland* 69, 1934–5, 265–324.

Curle, Alexander O. 1954a. 'A dwelling of the Viking Period at "Jarlshof", Sumburgh, Shetland', in *Viking Antiquities in Great Britain and Ireland* 6, ed. Shetelig, H., pp. 11–30.

Curle, Alexander O. 1954b. 'A Viking settlement at Freswick, Caithness', in *Viking Antiquities in Great Britain and Ireland* 6, ed. Shetelig, H., pp. 31–63.

Curle, Cecil L. 1974. 'An engraved lead disc from the Brough at Birsay, Orkney', *Proceedings of the Society of Antiquaries of Scotland* 105, 1972–4, 301–6.

Curle, Cecil L. 1982. *Pictish and Norse Finds from the Brough of Birsay 1934–74*, Society of Antiquaries of Scotland Monograph Series 1, Edinburgh.

Fuglesang, Signe H. 1980. *Some Aspects of the Ringerike Style*, Medieval Scandinavia, Supplement 1, Odense.

Graham-Campbell, James A. 1976. 'The Viking-age silver and gold hoards of Scandinavian character from Scotland', *Proceedings of the Society of Antiquaries of Scotland* 107, 1975–6, 114–35.

Graham-Campbell, James A. 1980. *Viking Artefacts: A Select Catalogue*, London.

Graham-Campbell, James A. 1983. 'The Viking Age silver hoards of the Isle of Man', in *The Viking Age in the Isle of Man. Select Papers from the Ninth Viking Congress, Isle of Man, 4–14 July 1981*, ed. Fell, C. *et al.*, London, pp. 53–80.

Graham-Campbell, James A. 1984. 'Two Viking-age silver brooch fragments believed to be from the 1858 Skaill (Orkney) hoard', *Proceedings of the Society of Antiquaries of Scotland* 114, 1984, 289–301.

Haddan, Arthur W. & Stubbs, William (eds) 1873–8. *Councils and Ecclesiastical Documents relating to Great Britain and Ireland* 2,1: *The Churches of Ireland and Scotland 350–1188*, Oxford (1964 reprint).

Hamilton, John R. C. 1956. *Excavations at Jarlshof, Shetland*, London.

Henderson, Isabel 1967. *The Picts*, London.

Henderson, Isabel 1971. 'The meaning of the Pictish symbol stones', in *The Dark Ages in the Highlands*, Inverness Field Club, pp. 53–68.

Holmqvist, Wilhelm 1963. *Overgångstidens metallkonst*, Kungl Vitterhets Historie och Antikvitets Akademiens Handlingar. Antikvariska serien 11, Stockholm.

Jackson, Anthony 1984. *The Symbol Stones of Scotland*, Stromness.

Lagerlöf, Erland 1977. 'Medeltida ristning i Lojsta kyrka', *Gotlands Allehanda* 12/4, Visby.

Lagerlöf, Erland 1978. 'En uppmättningsritning från medeltiden', *Gotländskt Arkiv* 1978, 33–42, Visby.

Lagerlöf, Erland 1981. 'Ristat och målat i Boge kyrka', *Gotländskt Arkiv* 1981, 81–6, Visby.

Liestøl, Aslak, 1980. *Bryggen i Bergen*, Norges inskrifter med de yngre runer 6/1, Oslo.

Lowe, Elias A. 1938–47. *Codices Latini Antiquiores* 3–4, Oxford.

MacGregor, Arthur 1974. 'The Broch of Burrian, North Ronaldsay, Orkney', *Proceedings of the Society of Antiquaries of Scotland* 105, 1972–4, 63–118.

Mackenzie, W. Mackay 1937. 'The dragonesque figure in Maeshowe, Orkney', *Proceedings of the Society of Antiquaries of Scotland* 71, 1936–7, 157–73.

Marwick, Hugh 1924. 'Two sculptured stones found recently in Orkney', *Proceedings of the Society of Antiquaries of Scotland* 58, 1923–4, 295–9.

Mitchell, Arthur 1902. 'The prehistory of the Scottish area', *Proceedings of the Society of Antiquaries of Scotland* 36, 11–65.

Noble, James 1887. 'Notice of a stone, apparently a sinker, with incised figures of animals, from a tumulus at Bridge of Brogar, Stennis, Orkney', *Proceedings of the Society of Antiquaries of Scotland* 22, 266–7.

O'Meadhra, Uaininn 1979. *Early Christian, Viking and Romanesque Art: Motif-pieces from Ireland. A descriptive catalogue of the so-called 'trial-pieces' from c. 5th–12th centuries AD, found in Ireland c. 1830–1973*, Theses and Papers in North-European Archaeology 7, Stockholm.

O'Meadhra, Uaininn 1987. *Early Christian, Viking and Romanesque Art: Motif-pieces from Ireland. 2: A discussion on aspects of find-context and function*, Theses and Papers in North-European Archaeology 17, Stockholm.

O'Meadhra, Uaininn 1988. 'Skibe i Ranveigs skrin', *Skalk* 1988/5, 1, 3–5, Højbjerg.

O'Meadhra, Uaininn 1991. 'A medieval Dubliner's talismanic portrait? An incised profile cut-out head from Christ Church Place, Dublin', *Cambridge Medieval Celtic Studies* 21, 39–53.

Pritchard, Violet 1967. *Medieval English Graffiti*, Cambridge.

RCAHMS 1946. Royal Commission on the Ancient and Historical Monuments of Scotland, *Inventory of the Ancient Monuments of Orkney and Shetland* II: *Inventory of Orkney*, Edinburgh.

Ritchie, Anna 1972. 'Painted pebbles in early Scotland', *Proceedings of the Society of Antiquaries of Scotland* 104, 1971–2, 297–301.

Ritchie, Anna 1989. *Picts*, Edinburgh.

Ryan, Michael 1985. 'The horn-reliquary of Tongre/Tongeren: a 12th century Irish object', in *Bulletin des Musées Royaux d'Art et d'Histoire* 56/2, Bruxelles, 43–56.

Shetelig, Håkon 1954a. 'Notes Supplementary to Viking Antiquities Parts I–V, in *Viking Antiquities in Great Britain and Ireland* 6, ed. Shetelig, H., pp. 235–46.

Shetelig, Håkon 1954b. 'The Norse style of ornamentation in the Viking settlements', in *Viking Antiquities in Great Britain and Ireland* 6, ed. Shetelig, H., pp. 115–49.

Stevenson, Robert B. K. 1971. 'Sculpture in Scotland in the 6th–9th centuries AD', in *Kolloquium über spätantike und frühmittelalterliche Skulptur, Heidelberg 1970*, Mainz, pp. 65–74.

Stevenson, Robert B. K. 1983. 'Review of Curle 1982', *Antiquaries Journal* 63, 452.

Svärdström, Elisabeth 1982. *Runfynden från Gamla Lödöse*, Lödöse-Västsvensk medeltidsstad 4/5, Stockholm.

Thomas, Charles 1963. 'The interpretation of the Pictish symbols', *The Archaeological Journal* 120, 31–97.

Varia 1980. *Ristninger i Forhistorie og Middelalder. Det norske Arkeologmøtet Symposium, Voksenåsen, Oslo 1979*, Universitetets Oldsaksamling, Varia 1, Oslo.

Wilson, David M. 1973. 'The treasure', in *St Ninian's Isle and its treasure*, eds Small, A., Thomas, C. & Wilson, D. M., Aberdeen University Studies Series, 152, Oxford, pp. 45–148.

Wilson, David M. 1976. 'The Borre style in the British Isles', in *Minjar og Menntir. Afmælisrit helgað Kristjáni Eldjárn*, Reykjavík, pp. 502–9.

28

ARCHAEOLOGICAL AND ETHNOHISTORIC EVIDENCE OF A NORSE ISLAND FOOD CUSTOM

GERALD F. BIGELOW

Excavations of a Norse farmstead at Sandwick, Unst, Shetland have revealed a previously unreported type of artefact made from sheep legbones (Bigelow 1984, 107–110). Subsequent research has been directed towards determining the presence or absence of the artefacts at other Scandinavian sites in the North Atlantic region, and as discussed below, at present it appears these finds have a very limited distribution restricted to only part of the North Atlantic Norse world. The functions of the artefacts have also been investigated, and a behavioural model for their production and use is proposed.

BI-PERFORATED SHEEP METAPODIALS

The animal bone collections from the Late Norse site at Sandwick, Unst, Shetland (Fig. 28.1) contain over 50 whole and fragmentary examples of sheep (*Ovis aries*) metacarpi and metatarsi, also known as cannon bones, that have been humanly modified in several distinctive ways. The most common types of modification are multiple perforations and abrasion and polishing of localised surface areas. Many bones exhibit one or two of these modifications, but some combine a whole repertoire of specialised perforations and wear.

One of the basic traits which are most common in these artefacts is a perforation of the posterior or anterior side of a metapodial's distal diaphysis (Fig. 28.2). A small foramen is located in that area approximately 5 mm below the epiphyseal suture, and the perforation is usually, but not always, centered on the foramen. The bone is pierced on only one side, and the hole is always just below the epiphysis. Often quite irregular in shape, the perforation was frequently accomplished by punching or breaking through the compact bone wall, or by expanding the foramen through rotary abrasion with a pointed instrument. No wear or marks are present around the margins of these perforations.

The other most common trait in the modified metapodials is a perforation of the proximal articular surface (Fig. 28.3). In common with the distal openings, the proximal perforations are frequently irregular in shape and never bear signs

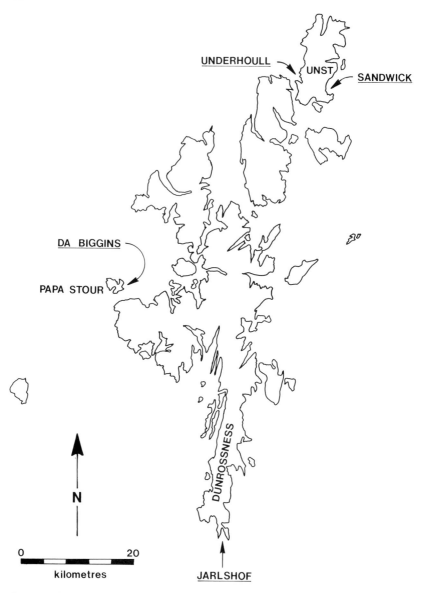

Figure 28.1: Excavated Norse settlements in the Shetland Islands.

of wear. In some cases the entire articular surface has been broken and removed (e.g. Fig. 28.4c).

Localised wear and surface polish in primarily three areas comprise the remaining traits that reoccur in many Sandwick sheep metapodials. The presence of surface modification is quite variable. Many of the perforated bones

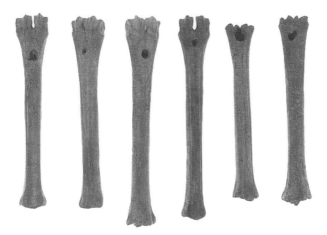

Figure 28.2: Bi-perforated sheep metatarsi from the Late Norse Site at Sandwick, Unst, Shetland. Only transverse perforations are visible in this view (Photograph by G. F. Bigelow).

lack any traces of wear or abrasion (e.g. Fig. 28.4a), some exhibit wear in only one area, some are worn or polished in three primary areas, and some *unperforated* metapodials are worn (e.g. Fig. 28.4d), and clearly were subjected to the same mechanical stresses that altered the perforated bones.

Polish and surface wear is most commonly observed on the edge of the proximal articular surface (Fig. 28.4). On fresh bones this well-defined articular boundary forms an abrupt, right angle with the diaphyseal shaft. On worn metapodials the edge has been rounded.

The distal articular surfaces of sheep metapodials were worn down and abraded in a smaller number of specimens. Again, a general rounding and smoothing of prominent areas, especially the verticelli and the epiphyseal junction, is observed (Fig. 28.5).

The least common place for wear traces is the midshaft of metapodials. In that area wear from usage generally takes the form of a pronounced surface polish or patina. Midshaft polish is usually accompanied by wear traces in the proximal and distal articular areas.

Figure 28.3: Proximal articular perforations in sheep metatarsi from the Late Norse site at Sandwick, Unst, Shetland (Photograph by G. F. Bigelow).

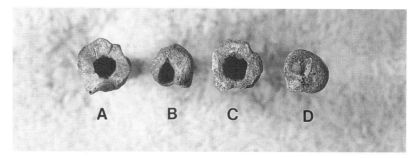

Figure 28.4: Variable wear on the proximal articular surfaces of sheep metatarsi from Sandwick, Unst, Shetland. Specimen A is unworn; B and C are severely abraded; D is unperforated, but very worn (Photograph by G. F. Bigelow).

Approximately 60–70 per cent of the sheep metapodials from the Sandwick site have been subjected to one or more of the modifications described above. For lack of a better term, the author refers to these artefacts as *bi-perforated metapodials* (Bigelow 1984).

Regional and Temporal Distribution

Bi-perforated metapodials were found in contexts dating from all phases of the Sandwick site's occupation, which has been dated securely to *c.* 1100–*c.* 1400 AD (Late Norse Period) through artefactual and architectural comparisons with other Norse sites in Shetland and neighbouring Norse regions, and through

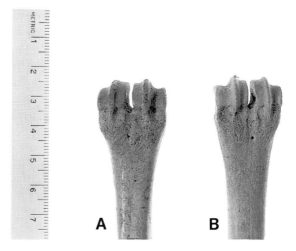

Figure 28.5: Variable wear on the distal articular surfaces of sheep metatarsi from Sandwick, Unst, Shetland. Both specimens have transverse perforations on their reverse sides; A is worn, B is unworn (Photograph by G. F. Bigelow).

radiocarbon analyses (Bigelow 1985; 1987; 1989). The numerous similarities between the Sandwick artefact assemblage and those recovered at the contemporary sites of Jarlshof and The Biggins, Shetland (Hamilton 1956; Crawford 1985 and in press), and from high medieval Norwegian contexts, particularly Bergen, Trondheim and Oslo (Herteig 1969; Høeg *et al.* 1977; Schia 1979; 1987; Christopherson 1987 and personal communication), suggested that bi-perforated metapodials may have been produced in those places as well. In the early 1980s, when the author first recognised the metapodials as a potential artefact type, there were no published descriptions of them from other North Atlantic sites.

It should be emphasised that bi-perforated metapodials may frequently escape identification in post-excavation studies. As rather 'minimal' artefacts, they would often be classified as animal bone refuse by most excavators and consigned to the zooarchaeological collection. In turn, while focusing on the biological aspects of their study sample, some zooarchaeologists might well overlook the frequently subtle modifications that have been discussed. Thus, the absence of these finds in a site's published excavation report is not always clear evidence that they were missing from the artefact assemblage.

The Shetland Islands

With this problem in mind, the author began researching the regional and temporal distribution of bi-perforated metapodials by examining the animal bone and artefact collections from Jarlshof, Shetland, the Norse site most similar to Sandwick in terms of material culture (Hamilton 1956; Bigelow 1984; 1985). A systematic survey of the Jarlshof bone artefacts at the Royal Scottish Museum (Queen Street), in Edinburgh, revealed no examples of bi-perforated metapodials, although legbones pierced in midshaft were present. In most of the latter specimens the proximal and distal ends of the bones had been removed completely, and the resulting bone 'tubes' have been interpreted as needle cases (e.g. Hamilton 1956, Fig. 57).

A similar survey of Jarlshof's faunal collection, housed at the Royal Scottish Museum (Chambers Street), in Edinburgh, was more successful. After examining 156 whole and fragmentary sheep metapodials from the Pre-Viking, Viking, Late Norse and Medieval levels, as well as some unprovenanced material, the author identified two definite bi-perforated metapodials. One, a metacarpus, displays wear along the edge of the proximal articular surface. The other, a metatarsus, is worn on both proximal and distal articular surfaces. These wear patterns are totally consistent with those observed on specimens from the Sandwick site, which is located 75 km to the north of Jarlshof (Fig. 28.1).

Both of the Jarlshof specimens were discovered in the faunal sample from Midden C, a deposit that overlay the 10th–11th-century Lower Slope Communal Red Peat Ash Midden. This deposit was very likely contemporary with a major portion of the Sandwick site's occupation. Thus, it is apparent that some Late Norse Shetlanders, in both northern and southern areas, were employing identical and very specific methods of processing and using sheep metapodials. The significance of the much smaller proportion of modified metapodials at Jarlshof, and their absence from the Viking Period deposits, is unclear because the animal bone collections were not recovered using more recently developed systematic, controlled methods; the collections should not be assumed to be fully representative of the site's architectural and midden contents.

The original presence or absence of bi-perforated metapodials at the other excavated Shetland Norse farmsites, The Biggins, Papa Stour (Crawford 1991) and Underhoull, Unst (Small 1966), cannot be assessed because animal bone was poorly preserved at both sites.

Orkney and Caithness

In view of the close proximity and shared history that link Shetland, Orkney and Caithness, one would expect to find many similarities in the material cultures of all three areas, and some have been documented for the post-medieval period (see Fenton 1978). Earlier parallels include a general change in artefact assemblages which seems to have occurred in both archipelagos and part of Caithness between the 11th and 12th centuries AD; the preceding three centuries are considered as the 'Viking Period', and the later medieval centuries are increasingly referred to as 'Late Norse' (Hamilton 1956; Batey 1987; Bigelow 1985).

However, bi-perforated metapodials have not been reported from Orkney and Caithness sites, and if present in faunal samples currently under analysis, they must be scarce (J. Rackham, personal communication; C. Batey, personal communication; C. D. Morris personal communication). This rather surprising distributional trend is another that may be considerably revised in the future, as there are at present few sites of late Viking Period/Late Norse age which have been investigated, e.g. Freswick Links (Batey 1987; 1989), the Beachview Site at Birsay (Morris 1983, 142–147), Tuquoy (Owen 1984), and parts of the Brough of Birsay (Hunter 1986; Seller 1986), and their substantial faunal collections are not yet fully analysed.

Norway

Late Norse Shetland artefact assemblages and architecture contain many attributes characteristic of contemporary Norwegian material culture (Bigelow 1985; 1987). Artefacts such as combs made from antler, schist baking plates and whetstones, copper alloy metalwork, and professionally produced ceramics were clearly imported into Shetland from Norway, or from the same sources that supplied Norway (Bigelow 1984, 212–215). On the other hand, some finds common in both areas were made locally, their production influenced by mutually held paradigms of artefact form and function. Many types of steatite technology probably fall into the latter category (Buttler 1989; 1991).

Given these similarities in material culture, which are substantive evidence of close economic as well as political and religious ties between Shetland and the motherland (Bigelow 1989, 188), one would expect that bi-perforated metapodials would also be present in Norwegian medieval sites. At the time of writing bi-perforated metapodials had not been mentioned in any Norwegian excavation reports. Discussions with zooarchaeologists and archaeologists familiar with Norwegian faunal and bone artefact collections also failed to reveal any knowledge of bi-perforated metapodials in Norwegian material culture (S. Perdikaris, personal communication; Ch. Keller, personal communication; R. Bertelsen, personal communication). Further analyses of existing faunal collections, and future excavations of additional medieval domestic sites, may alter this unexpected pattern.

Faroe Islands

Relatively few farm sites have been excavated in Faroe, and bone preservation tends to be poor in the archipelago's acidic soils. Thus, the lack of finds of bi-perforated sheep metapodials on Faroese sites is presently not of great significance. If that trend continues as more sites in a variety of environmental contexts are investigated, it will raise many questions about the origins of the artefact type and its possible diffusion into different regions.

Iceland

Although bi-perforated sheep metapodials have not yet been published in Icelandic excavation reports, numerous animal bone collections now under analysis contain hundreds of examples (T. H. McGovern, personal communication; T. Amorosi, personal communication). The earliest historically dated specimens, probably from the 12th century, appear in a faunal sample from the small inland farm of Aðalbol, in the Hrafnkelsdalur, Northeast Iceland (T. H. McGovern personal communication; 1982; Amorosi 1989, 212). Preliminary analysis of the faunal collection from the extensive stratified midden, dating from *c.* 11th–19th centuries, at Svalbarð, Þistilfjörður, northeast Iceland, indicates that bi-perforated metapodials are also common there in all levels except the earliest (Amorosi & McGovern 1989).

The author has had the opportunity to examine bi-perforated metapodials from the large faunal collection of Stóraborg, a manor farm on the south coast of Iceland (Snæsdóttir 1987 and 1991; Perry *et al.* 1985). The specimens were from levels dating from the late medieval period to the 19th century, and although many bones were perforated and worn according to the patterns found in 12th–14th-century Shetland, a considerable number had instead been split longitudinally. There were also extensive numbers of unmodified metapodials in the collection.

Therefore, it appears that bi-perforation of sheep metapodials was carried out

in many locations throughout the medieval and post-medieval centuries in Iceland, but metapodials were also processed in other ways.

Greenland

Among many analysed animal bone collections from Norse Greenland, there are
no reports of finds of bi-perforated metapodials (Degerbøl 1929; 1934; 1936;
1941; 1943; McGovern 1979; 1985; McGovern & Bigelow 1984). The author has
personally examined faunal collections from several Greenland farms and has
never observed bi-perforated metapodials, although other forms of modification,
particularly longitudinal splitting, are common. Other zooarchaeologists and
artefact specialists familiar with Greenland Norse material also report that these
artefacts have not appeared in studied collections (T. H. McGovern, personal
communication; J. Arneborg, personal communication; Ch. Keller, personal
communication).

Other Scandinavian Areas

Artefacts that resemble bi-perforated metapodials have been noted in faunal collections from Anglo-Scandinavian contexts (i.e. late 9th–11th centuries) in York,
Lincoln and Beverley (T. O'Connor, personal communication), but their abundance and possible patterns of utilisation await investigation.

Non-Norse Areas

In discussing the bone modifications described here with zooarchaeologists working in a wide variety of European, Asian and North American areas, only one
report of similar finds outside distinctly Scandinavian cultural contexts has been
received: bi-perforated metapodials may be present in late Anglo-Saxon archaeo-
faunas in East Anglia (P. Crabtree, personal communication). However, that area
also experienced much Scandinavian, if not identifiably Norse, influence in the
9th century (Jones 1984, 219–23).

Distribution Summary

At present it seems that the practice of opening sheep metapodials through transverse perforation of the distal diaphysis and breakage of the proximal articular
surface is restricted to Norse Shetland and Iceland. The available evidence also
indicates that bi-perforated metapodials may have been produced largely during
post-Viking times in both places. This apparent temporal trend is probably most
susceptible to revision through further work because relatively few early farms
with good bone preservation have been excavated, systematically sampled for
zooarchaeological remains, and analysed.

INTERPRETATION

Bi-perforated metapodials are particularly interesting finds because their formal
characteristics suggest their creation involved more than simple butchering or

food processing. Their appearance in both midden and house floor deposits, in both worn and abraded, and relatively fresh states, implies that the bones were primarily food refuse, but also that some were later utilised as tools.

Artefact Preparation

Any regular, frequently *repeated* pattern of breakage of land mammal long bones usually results from attempted consumption by scavengers, disarticulation of carcasses during butchering, or marrow extraction after cooking (see studies by Binford & Bertram 1977; Binford 1981; Behrensmeyer & Hill 1980). The author's first impression of bi-perforated metapodials was that they must represent artefacts of a marrow extraction technique. However, the simple act of breaking sheep metapodials, along with other bones having well-defined marrow cavities, was a ubiquitous practice in the Norse North Atlantic. It was accomplished by snapping the bones in half, or more commonly, by splitting the bones longitudinally; the resulting long splinters, still bearing segments of the articular termini, are very common finds in Greenlandic and Icelandic Norse faunal collections (McGovern 1979; personal communication). Such splinters are unusual in the Sandwick, Shetland collection, further suggesting that perforation was the basic marrow recovery technique there.

The making of two perforations in a small bone would seem to be a relatively labour-intensive method of removing a rather limited amount of marrow. However, an account by R. Angus Smith provides clear evidence of this practice in 19th century Iceland, and suggests a reason for its adoption:

> On opening this latter cairn, a bone was found of about 7 inches in length, having an aperture through its diameter, carefully made, *at one end near the joint*, whilst the whole had been carefully cleaned, – the core cleared out the whole length. It was not old, and had not been buried in the cairn, but it was a novelty to me, and I took it down to the town. Inquiring of a gentleman there, his wife said nothing, but went out, and brought one exactly the same with thread wound round it. Wood is scarce here, and so we have bone instruments. But why the hole? Mr. Jon Hjaltalin kindly writes an explanation: '*Usually they have two holes* – one in the end, and *another right through the bone near the joint*. These holes are made to suck out the marrow, which is taken out at one end. The *transverse hole is merely to make a draught*. Sometimes also they use the bones for needle cases, putting the needles in through the hole in the end, and then putting a stopper in it. There is a superstition connected with these sheep bones. You must get the marrow out either by sucking it or by splitting the bones longitudinally; but if you break them right across, your sheep will break their legs'.

> (Smith 1874, 153–4; emphasis added)

Although the 19th-century Icelandic method differs from the Late Norse procedure in utilising a *full* transverse piercing of the distal diaphysis, rather than opening just one wall, the idea is the same. Indeed, if the second hole was needed only for creating a draught, than any break in the bone's exterior would suffice. This minimal requirement is expressed in some of the Sandwick specimens in which the transverse hole is simply a slight enlargement of the small foramen

naturally present below the distal epiphysis, while the proximal end has been virtually knocked out to provide an exit for the marrow.

The functional explanation of bi-perforated metapodials as products of specialised food processing and consumption, with an intent to conserve the bones for
technological purposes, fits the Sandwick and Icelandic patterns. The frequent,
but not constant, bi-perforation of leg bones could easily reflect an eating habit – a
food custom – which prescribed a specific marrow extraction method originally
preferred over other methods because it ensured a steady supply of a useful technological resource. Judging by the frequent wear marks on the Shetland and Iceland specimens, this food custom retained its relevance in the technologies of
medieval Shetland and in medieval and post-medieval Iceland.

The loss of the custom in post-medieval Shetland perhaps may be attributed to
a change in the demand for prepared, intact metapodials, or may have been part of
general changes in food preparation and consumption related to the increased
Scottish influence in those centuries.

Artefact Use

The author has not found any ethnohistoric accounts which describe the use of
sheep metapodials in ways that would produce the whole range of wear patterns
observed on Shetlandic and Icelandic specimens. However, the folk life holdings
of the National Museum of Iceland contain numerous artefacts of various types
made from metapodials; down to the 20th-century sheep metapodials have served
many functions in Icelandic material culture, ranging from needle cases and fishing netweights to children's toys. None of the Icelandic tool applications would
create the specific pattern of articular surface wear that has been observed on
archaeological finds, but the use of metapodials as yarn or line bobbins could have
produced polish on the mid-diaphyses. The irregular shapes of the proximal aper-
tures, and the lack of wear on their margins, argues against the hypothesis that the
metapodials were used largely as needle cases.

In the absence of more detailed comparative ethnographic evidence, or other
possibly associated specialised elements in Late Norse Shetlandic and Icelandic
material culture, it is difficult to reconstruct the post-marrow extraction use or
uses of these carefully prepared bones.

CONCLUSION

From the evidence presented in this paper it is apparent that in Late Norse Shetland and medieval and post-medieval Iceland the metacarpi and metatarsi of
sheep were frequently subjected to an unusual and somewhat laborious marrow
extraction procedure during food preparation and/or consumption. Ethnohistoric information from Iceland suggests that this food custom was adopted in
order to preserve the bones for technological uses. Stereotyped patterns of surface
wear and abrasion on archaeological specimens from both Shetland and Iceland

indicate that bi-perforated metapodials were often conserved for use as tools, and that they seem to have served a rather narrow range of wear-producing functions.

It is hoped that further information from zooarchaeological and artefactual studies in progress, from additional excavated sites, and from folk life studies will confirm and help to explain the presence or absence of metapodial bi-perforation in various Norse North Atlantic settlements at different periods. At present it is difficult to explain why Iceland and Shetland shared this food custom, why it apparently died out in Shetland, and why it was not employed elsewhere. The possible practice of the custom in the Faroe Islands is another intriguing question: in view of Faroe's close proximity and early political ties with the islands to its southeast and northwest, it seems likely that metapodial bi-perforation also occurred there, but at present there is no supporting evidence.

This paper was written in part to enhance the recognition of one element in the anthropology of food in the North Atlantic region. It is also presented as a small example of a growing type of comparative multidisciplinary inquiry, linking evidence from material culture, history and the natural sciences, that is encouraged by the rich archaeological and ethnohistoric resources of the Norse North Atlantic settlements.

Acknowledgements

Excavations at Sandwick, Unst, Shetland were supported by the Scottish Development Department (HBM), now Historic Scotland; British Petroleum Development Ltd; and the Research Foundation of the City University of New York. The author would like to thank those who have provided personal communications, for their willingness to discuss work in process, and in some cases, for permission to cite unpublished reports. Thomas H. McGovern and Thomas Amorosi deserve special recognition for supplying interim information on key Icelandic faunal collections. The assistance provided by Drs. Joanna Close-Brooks and Alison Sheridan, Royal Museum of Scotland (Queen Street), and Dr A. S. Clarke, Royal Museum of Scotland (Chambers Street), in allowing access to Jarlshof artefact and bone collections, is also greatly appreciated. Finally, the author gratefully acknowledges the support of the Bowdoin College Fund for Course Development and The Peary-MacMillan Arctic Museum and Arctic Studies Center which underwrote travel to European institutions where this paper was in part researched.

REFERENCES

Amorosi, Thomas 1989. 'Contributions to the zooarchaeology of Iceland: some preliminary notes', in *The Anthropology of Iceland*, eds Durrenberger, E. Paul & Pálsson, Gísli, Iowa City, pp. 203–27.

Amorosi, Thomas & McGovern, Thomas H. 1989. 'Archaeological investigations, Svalbard 6706–60, Northeast Iceland, 1987–88: a preliminary report', privately circulated unpublished report.

Batey, Colleen E. 1987. *Freswick Links: A Re-Appraisal of the Late Norse Site in Its Context*, 2 vols, British Archaeological Reports 179, Oxford.

—— 1989. 'Recent work at Freswick Links, Caithness, Northern Scotland', *Hikuin* 15, 223–30.

Behrensmeyer, Anna K. & Hill, Andrew H. (eds) 1980. *Fossils in the Making: Vertebrate Taphonomy and Paleoeconomy*, Chicago.

Bigelow, Gerald F. 1984. *Subsistence in Late Norse Shetland: An Investigation into a Northern Island Economy of the Middle Ages*, Unpublished PhD dissertation, University of Cambridge.

—— 1985. 'Sandwick, Unst and Late Norse Shetland economy', in *Shetland Archaeology*, ed. Smith, Brian, Lerwick, pp. 95–127.

—— 1987. 'Domestic architecture in Medieval Shetland', *Review of Scottish Culture* 3, 23–38.

—— 1989. 'Life in Medieval Shetland: an archaeological perspective', *Hikuin* 15, 183–92.

Binford, Lewis R. 1981. *Bones: Ancient Men and Modern Myths*, New York.

Binford, Lewis R. & Bertram, Jack B. 1977. 'Bone frequencies and attritional processes', in *For Theory Building in Archaeology*, ed. Binford, Lewis R., New York, pp. 72–153.

Buttler, Simon 1989. 'Steatite in Norse Shetland', *Hikuin* 15, 193–206.

—— (1991). 'Steatite in the Norse North Atlantic', in *The Norse of the North Atlantic*, ed. Bigelow, Gerald F., *Acta Archaeologica* 61, 228–232.

Christopherson, Axel 1987. *Trondheim: En By i Middelalderen*, Trondheim.

Crawford, Barbara E. 1985. 'The Biggins, Papa Stour – a multi-disciplinary investigation', in *Shetland Archaeology*, ed. Smith, Brian, Lerwick, pp. 128–58.

—— 1991. 'Excavations at The Biggings, Papa Stour, Shetland', in *The Norse of the North Atlantic*, ed. Bigelow, Gerald F., *Acta Archaeologica* 61, 36–43.

Degerbøl, M. 1929. 'Animal bones from the Norse ruins at Gardar, Greenland', *Meddelelser om Grønland* 76(3), 183–92.

—— 1934. 'Animal bones from the Norse ruins at Brattahlid, Greenland', *Meddelelser om Grønland* 81(1), 149–55.

—— 1936. 'Animal remains from the West Settlement in Greenland', *Meddelelser om Grønland* 88(3).

—— 1941. 'The osseous material from Austmannadal and Tungmeralik, West Greenland', *Meddelelser om Grønland* 89(1).

—— 1943. 'Animal bones from inland farms in the East Settlement', *Meddelelser om Grønland* 90(3).

Fenton, Alexander 1978. *The Northern Isles*, Edinburgh.

Hamilton, John R. C. 1956. *Excavations at Jarlshof, Shetland*, Edinburgh.

Herteig, Asbjørn E. 1969. *Kongers Havn og Handels Sete*, Oslo.

Høeg, Helge I., Liden, Hans-Emil, Liestøl, Aslak, Molaug, Petter, Schia, Erik & Wiberg, Christina 1977. *De Arkeologiske Utgravninger in Gamlebyen, Oslo. 1, Feltet "Mindets Tomt"*, Oslo.

Hunter, John R. 1986. *Rescue Excavations on the Brough of Birsay 1974–82*. Society of Antiquaries of Scotland Monograph Series 4, Edinburgh.

Jones, Gwyn 1984. *A History of the Vikings*, 2nd edn, Oxford.

McGovern, Thomas H. 1979. *The Paleoeconomy of Norse Greenland: Adaptation and Extinction in a Tightly Bounded Ecosystem*, Ann Arbor (USA).

—— 1982. 'Preliminary report of the animal bone collections from Aðalbol, Hrafnkelsdalur, Eastern Iceland'. Unpublished report on file at the National Museum of Iceland.

McGovern, Thomas H. 1985. 'Contributions to the paleoeconomy of Norse Greenland', *Acta Archaeologica* 54, 73–122.

McGovern, Thomas H. & Bigelow, Gerald F. 1984. 'The archaeozoology of the Norse site 17a, Narssaq, Southwest Greenland', *Acta Borealia* 1(1), 85–102.

Morris, Christopher D. 1983. 'Excavations around Birsay Bay, Orkney', *Orkney Heritage* 2, 119–51.

Owen, Olwyn A. 1984. 'The archaeological rescue project at Tuquoy, Westray, Orkney', *University of Durham and University of Newcastle Upon Tyne Archaeological Reports for 1983* 7, 49–54.

Perry, David W., Buckland, Paul & Snæsdóttir, Mjöll 1985. 'The application of numerical techniques to insect assemblages from the site of Stóraborg, Iceland', *Journal of Archaeological Science* 12, 335–45.

Schia, Erik (ed.) 1979. *De Arkeologiske Utgravninger i Gamlebyen, Oslo. 2, Feltene "Oslogate 3 og 7"*, Øvre Ervik.

—— 1987. *De Arkeologiske Utgravninger i Gamlebyen, Oslo. 3, "Søndre Felt"*, Øvre Ervik.

Seller, Timothy J. 1986. 'Animal bone material', in J. R. Hunter, *Rescue Excavations on the Brough of Birsay 1974–82*, Appendix 4. Society of Antiquaries of Scotland Monograph Series 4, pp. 208–16.

Small, Alan 1964–66. 'Excavations at Underhoull, Shetland', *Proceedings of the Society of Antiquaries of Scotland* 98, 225–48.

Smith, R. Angus 1874. 'On some ruins at Ellida Vatn and Kjalarnes in Iceland', *Proceedings of the Society of Antiquaries of Scotland* 10, 151–77.

Snæsdóttir, Mjöll 1987. 'Archaeologists delve down through centuries at Storaborg farm', *Icelandic Review* 25(2), 19–22.

—— 1991. 'Stóraborg – an Icelandic farm mound', in *The Norse of the North Atlantic*, ed. Bigelow, G. F., *Acta Archaeologica* 61, pp. 116–119.

29

PROBLEMS CONCERNING THE EARLIEST
SETTLEMENT IN THE FAROE ISLANDS

HANS JACOB DEBES

INTRODUCTION

In recent years it has become more difficult to be a Faroese historian. Old solutions of difficult and fundamental questions and problems in our history have been undermined, so as to make the traditional historian less self-confident than he or she was earlier. However, in my opinion, this has not been a destructive development. On the contrary, this is an indication that there is growth in research in our country, not only in the discipline of history, but also in related sciences, especially in archaeology and the natural sciences, particularly botany.

Research in our field is not only going on in our new university, Fróðskaparsetur Føroya, but also in institutions with which we co-operate, especially the National Museum, Føroya Fornminnissavn, and the Museum of Natural Science, Føroya Náttúrugripasavn. Also we are in close co-operation with Danish institutions and scholars.

In this chapter I will provide a broad outline of the research and discussion of one of the main themes, perhaps the most interesting one, in our history: the problems concerning the dating of the earliest settlement in the Faroe Islands. I give first my own presentation of the sources at our disposal; then – divided up into different (and simplified) categories – the general views of historians, archaeologists and natural scientists, stressing not only different views, but also the different starting-points resulting from different methods of working. Finally, I shall attempt a provisional conclusion as to the present state of research in the field.

THE SOURCES

'The Irish Question'

It was only in the Romantic days of the 19th century that the Faroese began to try to find roots that were not Faroese. It was not enough just to be Faroese, members of a small and historically insignificant people, in the midst of their national awakening. They had to find some other and more exotic points of identification. Perhaps everyday life over the centuries had been too tedious – some 'grandeur' was necessary!

In or about 825 an Irish scholar, learning and teaching at the court school of Charlemagne at Aachen (Aix-la-Chapelle) finished a learned compilation of the most advanced knowledge of geography of his time, *Liber de mensura orbis terrae*. The only new knowledge he had to add was the information of some obscure islands situated in the ocean north of Britain. They had been deserted ('deserta') since the beginning of the world. After having described a country that must have been Iceland, he relates:

> There are many other islands in the ocean north of Britain which can be reached from the northern islands of Britain in a direct voyage of two days and nights with full sails filled with a continuously favourable wind. A devout priest told me that in two summer days and the intervening night he sailed in a two-benched boat and entered one of them.
>
> There is another set of small islands, nearly all separated by narrow stretches of water; in these for nearly a hundred years hermits sailing from our country Scotia (Ireland) have lived. But just as they were always deserted from the beginning of the world, so now because of the Northern pirates ('causa latronum Normannorum') they are emptied of anchorites, and filled with countless sheep and very many diverse kinds of sea-birds. I have never found these islands mentioned in (the books of) the authorities ('in libris auctorum memoratas').
>
> (Tierney transl. 1967, 71–4)

These are the words of the learned Dicuil who may have come from Northern Ireland or from Northern Scotland (*op. cit.* 12).

There are, however, other Irish sources that can, if not prove, then make likely Dicuil's statements. There exist also pre-Dicuilian indications of Irish discoveries in the ocean to the north of Scotland, making at least likely that they had, as the first seamen of the World, discovered the islands which were later to become known as the Faroe Islands, i.e. the sheep islands (Storm (ed.) 1880, 92; Marcus 1980, 7–32).

In a sensational lecture, at least for his time, presented before a learned audience in 1891, the German professor of Greifswald, Heinrich Zimmer, gave his views 'Über die frühesten Berührungen der Iren mit den Nordgermanen' (Zimmer 1891). What is interesting in his lengthy elucidation is that the contact between 'die Germanen', in our sense the Nordic peoples, with peoples not only of Celtic/Gaelic descent, but also with an amalgamation of peoples of Gaelic or Pictish descent, began much earlier than later historians have imagined. His statements have been severely criticised, first by Finnur Jónsson, later by F. T. Wainwright as 'unsupported speculation', having confused 'several subsequent writers' (in Sigurðsson 1988, 15).

It has been a commonplace in North Atlantic history that the Irish – who otherwise in no way were a seafaring people – nevertheless developed a tradition for sailing. One wonders whether most of the voyages related, many of them totally legendary and far from any believable reality, are not invented to illustrate sinful man's search for Heaven and Paradise. To the concrete-thinking medieval man such Promised Lands must have some geographical location in order to give any meaning. Christian life as a troublesome journey towards eternity survived the Middle Ages. To what extent this legendary material can be used as historical evidence has to be carefully re-considered, especially in this context. Adamnan and Brendan cannot be used as historical evidence in any real sense, while Dicuil's sober information, without any religious mission, belongs to quite a different category of historical sources.

On the other hand, according to early medieval historical sources, at least some Irish became seafarers, not pursuing the golden things of this World, but peace and solitude for the adoration of their Lord, conceived as a physically existing phenomenon, and, perhaps also as results of secular sentences, having to leave their native lands and to find some other places to live (Zimmer 1891, 298).

So, was it piety or necessity – or was it banal inquisitiveness – that called the newly-Christianised Irishmen to the sea? I shall give no answer. But at least some of them sailed. Zimmer talks of 'ein Hang zum Anachoretenthum. Was den egyptischen und syrischen Christen die Wüste war, das wird den Iren die See um Irland' (*op. cit.* 280–2).

Of course, the basic logical assumption for Zimmer's theory of pre-Viking contacts between Norsemen and peoples of Irish origin before the explosion of the Viking expansion can be doubted. The turning-point of his theory is the attack on Eigg and Tory Island in AD 617 recorded in the *Annals of Ulster*, and credited to the Christian Picts. To Zimmer the assailants are not likely to have been Picts, who may well not have been in possession of a fleet of the size described, and were not unknown to the Irish. In Zimmer's conception, such a 'Meerflotte' can hardly have been a Pictish, but rather a Norwegian one, especially as linguistic indications can, or must, be interpreted that this fleet was 'übers Meer gekommen'. To him a Pictish attack could have been no surprise to the Irish, since they had known them since the middle of the 4th century, so they had become 'vollkommen vertraut' to them. Therefore, this shocking attack must have been made by some other, unknown, people: in this case obviously Scandinavians, or rather Norsemen, thus proving, or at least making likely a much earlier date of the beginning of the Norse expansion than was generally believed at his time.

Heinrich Zimmer mentions several incidents from Irish sources which indicate that Irish seafarers, also according to Dicuil, might have landed in the Faroe Islands (Debes 1990). There can be little doubt that sources which Dicuil did not know can contribute – even if everything cannot be proved – to a story ranging farther back than that of Dicuil. Adamnan's *Vita Sancti Colombae* from the beginning of the 7th century, mentioned in the great work of the Venerable Bede, may make this assumption likely (Sherley-Price transl. 1968, 299–303,

326–7; Attwater 1965, 30–1, 73; O'Donoghue & Arnfelt 1893, 125–8), although nothing can be proven. This specific Faroese case is not a unique one in early Medieval history.

On the other hand, all these possibilities can be discussed as far as their historical importance is concerned. Anchorites are not supposed to produce new generations. So Irishmen, forsaking the pleasures or the evils of this World of sin, cannot be suspected of being the forefathers of the people that eventually became the Faroese nation! Consequently, an eventual Irish settlement in the Faroe Islands can hardly have left any mark upon our history. A recognised Gaelic element in medieval culture, especially manifest in the language, must be considered to be of a later date, and without any connection with the 'Imrama', the voyages of devout Christians seeking solitude for contemplation while awaiting arrival to a better World in the sense of eternity (Zimmer 1891, 290), or searching for Paradise in its physical, earthly sense. The presence of Basque fishermen or whalers, at this point of time, must be left for further research (cf. Yraola 1983).

Færeyinga Saga

Until recently traditional works on the early history of the Faroe Islands have connected the first Norse settlement with king Harald Hairfair's seizure of power in the last years of the 9th century. The main source for this supposition was *Færeyinga saga*, written in Iceland, probably on the basis of old oral tradition, at about 1200, preserved and handed down to the present as fragments of other sagas (Halldórsson 1961; transl. 1987). *Færeyinga saga* relates nothing about any earlier Irish settlement – as do, in the case of Iceland, *Íslendingabók* and *Landnámabók* (Benediktsson (ed.) 1968, 5 & 31–4).

The main theme in *Færeyinga saga* is not the question of the Faroese Landnam, but the efforts made by Norwegian kings to extend their powers to the Faroe Islands, practising a talented divide and rule policy among the families of chiefs. But the saga mentions by name the first man who settled in the islands, Grímr Kamban – the first name significantly being of Norse, the second of Scottish Gaelic origin (Matras 1939). The fact that *Landnámabók* counts Grímr's grandson among the first colonists in Iceland spoils the chronology of the saga (Halldórsson 1987, introduction and summary).

Recent studies in the saga material have made new interpretations possible and credible, thus eliminating all sure evidence of simultaneous Norwegian settlement in the Faroe Islands and Iceland (Debes 1990, 55–113). It has been pointed out by Dr Ólafur Halldórsson, in his masterly new edition of *Færeyinga saga*, that this saga had been preserved for a long time in oral tradition before it was written down (Halldórsson 1987). Nevertheless, there are so many correct references, especially geographical terms, to the Faroe Islands, that it must somehow have had a Faroese background. Chronologically it can date the coming of the first Faroese Landnam-man back to about or a little after AD 800. We are then in good harmony with Dicuil's dating of the coming of the first

Norse or Norwegian 'latrones'. Dr Halldórsson's well-founded choice of the version of *Óláfs saga Tryggvasonar* instead of that of *Flateyjarbók* as the source about the first settlement, has thus eliminated a logical historical vacuum, with allowances for traditional inaccuracies in medieval historical chronology. So, from the point of a historian, the coming of the Norsemen can still be dated to about AD 800.

As in most, perhaps all, countries, what might be called archaeological interest in the 19th century began among persons, amateurs, in the Age of Romanticism and awakening nationalism (cf. Winther 1985). Perhaps things were done, from idealistic and nationalistic inspiration, that were better never done (Dahl 1968, 188–92). Professional Faroese archaeology was only started in the early 1940s by the late Sverri Dahl, whom so many of us remember with reverence. By his research, especially at Kvívík and Tjørnuvík, archaeology moved from myth to science (Dahl 1951; 1958; Dahl & Rasmusson 1956). Dahl was not only an excavator, his outlook made him also a historian, and a man of culture in the broadest sense of the term. With him Faroese archaeology became professionalised, even if he, in so many senses of the word, was a self-made man. His intuition, his talent, cannot be doubted.

From the beginning, Dahl was influenced by A. W. Brøgger (Brøgger 1937), who fully accepted Dicuil and Zimmer's theory, when stating: 'There can be no doubt that Irish hermits had been in the Faroe Islands before the Norsemen came' (*op. cit.* 26). Also Dr Jakob Jakobsen had already, perhaps under the influence of Sophus and Alexander Bugge (*op. cit.* 28; Bugge 1905, 353–9), taken Zimmer as an unquestionable authority when speaking of 'the famous celtologist, professor Zimmer in Germany' (Jakobsen 1957, 73), concluding from him philological evidence and by analogy (especially *papa*-words in Shetland and Iceland, and historical sources, Dicuil and Icelandic saga) that a pre-Viking settlement in the Faroe Islands was more than likely (*op. cit.* 72–80). In his dissertation Professor Christian Matras was much more sceptical as to Celtic-Gaelic linguistic influence than he later became (Jakobsen 1909, n. 25).

So, Sverri Dahl had many 'authorities' to rely on, and this must have made it difficult to reject the possibility that cross-slabs showing clear Celtic-Irish influence might be relics of a 'Papa' period. He also found some support among archaeologists (Radford 1962; Kermode 1931) and historians (Steining 1958, 169–70; Jones 1968, 270; Jóhannesson 1969, 5–6; Ólafsson 1987, 69–78). After Sverri Dahl others continued his work – Thorsteinsson, Arge, Krogh, Diklev, Mahler and Stummann Hansen amongst others.

THE HISTORIANS

Since the earliest editions of Dicuil's work, the first of them nearly 200 years ago (Dahlmann 1841; Tierney transl. 1967), historians have put much confidence in his account of the islands north of Scotland. As alluded to earlier, his source of information, the islands of which he gives descriptions related to him by others as 'semper deserta' cannot be Shetland, cannot be Iceland (which has a separate description); they can only be the Faroe Islands. Consequently, since Dicuil first became known his work has constituted the basis for historians in the question of the first settlement of the Faroe Islands.

I am fully convinced that the statements of Dicuil are reliable. His compilation of the highest knowledge of traditional geography, his personal addition about the islands to the north of Scotland, especially of those which must be the Faroe Islands, is original information which he, who otherwise only refers to established authorities, has never seen or heard of amidst 'auctoritates' (Tierney *op. cit.* 75–7).

When we remember that Dicuil wrote his work, far from his native lands, perhaps after 30 years of voluntary physical and intellectual exile (*op. cit.* 11–17), there should be no insuperable discrepancy as to the chronology. It must be important that in the Bibliothèque Nationale in Paris the oldest preserved version can be dated back to about 845, i.e. not many years after the death of Dicuil. The fate of the other manuscripts is discussed elsewhere (*op. cit.* 37–40).

THE ARCHAEOLOGISTS

Sverri Dahl was a devout believer in an early Irish settlement and used the term 'Papa Age' (*Papatíð*) in his historical periodisation about the 'time' that to him, at least in 1968, preceded the Norse settlement, even if he had never found any concrete evidence of Irish settlement in the Faroe Islands (Dahl 1970; Debes 1990). Nor have his younger successors succeeded. The Icelanders have faced the same problem. We meet here the classical problem of 'e silentio' – evidence, not in its historical, but in its archaeological sense.

In his work as an archaeologist, Dahl tried to unite the results of archaeological research with historical evidence and more visionary concepts or beliefs in a pre-Viking Irish settlement. This 'Holy Historical Trinity' was an intellectual reality to him, even if not objectively proven.

The gravestones with engraved 'sun-crosses', showing Irish features, found at the village of Skúvoy, where, according to *Færeyinga saga*, the first Christian church was built and the first Christians buried; or mystical cornfields ('akrar') on the island of Mykines (and some other remote places in the islands), to him offering some resemblance with Irish phenomena, more than indicated to him a pre-Viking Irish settlement as related by Dicuil.

Both of these aspects of the evidence are now sources of dispute, and modern archaeologists tend to be far from convinced in his optimistic view of historical interpretation. At least to me, the most cautious and sceptical response so far has been made by Arge in his MA thesis, stating the archaeological fact that human settlement cannot be proven farther back than the middle of the 10th century, thus being close to the old Icelandic tradition (Arge 1986, 32–34; 1987; 1990; this volume), and Thorsteinsson in various articles (1976; 1981).

Dicuil may not be a problem for the archaeologists since they have not been able to find any settlement confirming Dicuil's story. From his excavation of the Viking-Age farm at Leirvík (Toftanes), Stummann Hansen has drawn the preliminary conclusion that he has reached as far back as 900 or perhaps some years before the turn of the century (1986; this volume). The 'ærgi' (shielings) excavated by Mahler at Eiðisvatn have been dated to the traditional Viking-Age time and early Middle Ages (Mahler 1986; this volume). Krogh's inspiring excavation of the six churches of Sandur relate logically to Christian times, and can hardly contribute to our problem: the first settlement in the Faroe Islands as churches are Christian institutions (Krogh 1986).

So the archaeologists can, at most, go back to about AD 900 as the earliest settlement. They are not able to fill the gap back to Dicuil. Consequently, to them what I have called the 'Irish Question' has not yet gained any importance.

THE BOTANIST(S)

Until recently, natural sciences, such as botany, have not been regarded as historical disciplines. Today, all historians and archaeologists are fully aware of the scientific interaction between the humanities and natural sciences, if only in terms of the dating of historical relics. From a scientific point of view we are, so far, on-lookers or listeners. Historians and archaeologists are not capable of being 'burglars' into the natural sciences! In the last resort, all science is a question of common sense, not of prejudice and fanaticism. So, we must listen to all who can contribute to our understanding of the past, particularly concerning the problems in question. A scholar can never feel too secure.

The peaceful two-fronted academic war between historians and archaeologists was spoilt some years ago when a third intruder invaded the field: the natural scientist, embodied in the botanist. This represents the necessary interaction between disciplines formerly entirely separated, but now interdisciplinarily dependent. During the 1970s the Faroese botanist Jóhannes Jóhansen carried out his pioneering research in pollen analysis in the Faroe Islands. In brief, his main thesis was that at about AD 600–650 oats had been cultivated. As corn-plants cannot grow wild in the islands, this presupposed the existence of human beings. For him it was natural to refer to Dicuil's account, in which Irish anchorites might have landed in the islands as early as about 700 (Jóhansen 1985). Fifty or 100 years do not spoil any early Medieval chronology. In reality it was a revolutionary theory, disturbing even the old gap between history and archaeology: the vacuum of 100, or perhaps 200, years.

Jóhansen's dissertation was of interest to the historians, but provoked the scepticism of archaeologists, already at their defence. Also the presumption – in accordance with the Sverri Dahl and P. V. Glob intuitive tradition – that the 'fields' on Mykines might be relics of a pre-Viking settlement there met with scientific resistance among archaeologists as they had found no evidence that confirmed the 'mythology' of any 'Irish Question' (Diklev 1981; Krogh 1986). Logically, an Irish hermit who had not been physically located could not have existed. Whether this is practical science or intellectual nihilism shall not be discussed in this paper.

In this context, it must be interesting that Jóhansen in his research in Shetland was able to unite the results of his own studies in vegetational history with accepted archaeological and historical facts (Jóhansen 1985, 61–88). But still more alarming is an article by Jóhansen, in the Faroese scientific journal *Fróðskaparrit* (1989), asserting that his demonstration of the presence of the plant *Plantago lanceolata* in the Faroe Islands as early as about BC 2300, according to a generally accepted theory, not only indicates, but rather makes likely the inhabitation of some kind of human beings (Jóhansen 1989, 68–75).

It is important to note that Jóhansen is always careful to give historical explanations. He sticks to his own subject, and his hints to history and archaeology are only allusions as to the origin of these early pre-Viking settlers (Jóhansen 1985, 58; 1989, 74). Having stated an 'Irish' settlement early in the 7th century, he finds some kind of a change at about 950, reflected in a shift from the cultivation of oats to that of barley. To him this fact might indicate a shift from Irish to Norse settlement, even if this change may have taken place over time (cf. Paasche 1938, 290).

In my opinion, this theory is not quite satisfactory to explain the 'gap' between a supposed early Irish and a later Norse settlement – at least only if we accept an idea of two Norse 'Landnams', one from the south at about 800 and one direct from Norway at about 900, possibly connected with King Harald Hairfair's seizure of power, sustained by the Icelandic tradition and Faroese archaeological research. The 'Dicuilian' Norsemen should then have carried on the already existing cultivation of oats, while barley was introduced by their Norwegian kinsmen 100 or 150 years later (Jóhansen 1985, 48–60). But the question arises: were two Norse Landnams possible in this small country? Could there have been space for a massive new colonisation more than 100 years after the first one? Had not the first settlers already divided the land among themselves over this span of three or four generations when the effect of inheritance must have been an active social force in the Faroese community?

So, temporarily leaving out of account the possibilities of a Stone Age settlement, it still remains to connect or to disconnect three hypothetical phases of Landnam in the Faroe Islands: one 'Irish anchorite' phase, one 'Dicuilian' phase and one period of change to permanent Norse settlement. At least natural science has provoked much interesting and inspiring disturbance in the study of our history.

PHILOLOGY AND PHILOLOGISTS

I have deliberately chosen to put subject and scholars under the same item, finding it necessary not to leave out this field of science, but at the same time stressing that it has had little to say about the question dealt with here: the dating of the first settlement. But, as a matter of fact, the philologists were the first to touch upon early Irish-Faroese relations.

In his studies Jakobsen pointed out that several placenames in the Faroe Islands were of Gaelic origin (1909). Matras continued his work, widening the spectrum also to language elements other than placenames. On the island of Mykines he maintained to have found an interesting placename, 'Korkadalur', meaning the 'oats valley', thus linking together Dahl's assumption concerning the 'fields' and Jóhansen's pollen analysis.(The Gaelic origin of the word 'korki' and the meaning of the word had already been observed by Jakobsen (1909, 94), but not in Matras' interpretation.) Matras also pointed out that the first part of two placenames, 'Papurshalsur' and 'Paparøkur', might relate to an early Irish settlement (Matras 1932; 1934; 1981 *inter alia*). But that such locations should have been the remote abodes of distressed Irish hermits has been made unlikely by the work of Arge (1987, 13–14). From pure logic it can hardly be possible that invading Norsemen should have adopted placenames from the enemies they had either killed or driven away. Gaelic cultural, also linguistic, influence after the permanent Norse settlement has been proven by irrefutable evidence.

A CONCLUSION

In this article I have tried to touch upon some of the main problems concerning the earliest settlement in the Faroe Islands. What has been attempted, in broad outline, is not to point out solutions, but to present a personal view of the state of research today (Sólstein 1987; Debes 1990). One may ask if there exists any state at all, or rather a state of confusion, with so many parties involved and with so many gaps in our knowledge. At least, no final synthesis is possible.

But many questions must naturally be asked. For example, how could it be that human beings had been living in Shetland almost 5000 years before the Faroe Islands were discovered? It must be accepted as a matter of fact that they were known by people in 'Scotia' early in the 8th century. Can it be possible that the Norse expansion to the West, beginning shortly before AD 800 should have been 100 or 150 years 'old' when Norse people settled in the islands, considering their geographical position? Only the future can tell us if it will be possible to bridge the gap, by means of the results of archaeological research, back to Dicuil, and eventually from him to early settlers – not to speak of those still more obscure peoples that might have visited our islands about 4000 years ago.

Some of the answers may be slumbering in the patient earth, and may some day be given a voice – either as a result of research, or by mere accident.

REFERENCES

Arge, Símun 1986. *Landnamet på Færøerne*, Århus.
Arge, Símun 1987. *Om landnamet på Færøerne. Beretning fra det sjette tværfaglige vikingesymposium*, København, pp. 11–25.
Arge, Símun 1990. 'Om landnamet på Færøerne', *Hikuin* 15, pp. 103–28.

Attwater, Donald 1965. *The Penguin Dictionary of Saints*, Harmondsworth.

Benediktsson, Jakob (ed). 1968. *Íslendingabók. Landnámabók*. Íslenzk fornrit 1, Reykjavík.

Brøgger, A. W. 1937. *Hvussu Føroyar vórðu bygðar. Inngongd til løgtingssøgu Føroya*, Tórshavn.

Bugge, A. 1905. *Vesterlandenes Indflydelse paa Nordboernes og særlig Nordmændenes ydre Kultur, Levesæt og Samfundsforhold i Vikingetiden*, Christiania.

Dahl, Sverri 1951. 'Fornar toftir í Kvívík', *Varðin* 29, pp. 65–96.

Dahl, Sverri 1958. 'Fornminni', *Føroyar* 1, Keypmannahavn, pp. 119–53.

Dahl, Sverri 1968. *Fortidsminder. Trap Danmark. Færøerne*, København, pp. 188–92.

Dahl, Sverri 1970. 'The Norse Settlement of the Faroe Islands', *Medieval Archaeology* 14, pp. 60–73.

Dahl, Sverri & Rasmusson, Jóannes 1956. 'Víkingaaldargrøv í Tjørnuvík', *Fróðskaparrit* 5, pp. 153–67.

Dahlmann, F. C. 1841. *Danmarks Historie indtil Reformationen*, 2 vols, Copenhagen.

Debes, Hans Jacob 1990. *Føroya soga 1*, Tórshavn, pp. 55–113.

Diklev, Torben 1981. 'Ilska og øska', *Mondul* 1, pp. 14–25.

Halldórsson, Ólafur 1961. 'Um landnám Gríms Kambans í Føroyum', *Fróðskaparrit* 10, pp. 47–52.

Halldórsson, Ólafur (ed.) 1987. *Færeyinga saga*, Reykjavík.

Jakobsen, Jakob 1909. 'Strejflys over Færøernes Stednavne', *Nordisk Tidskrift for Filologi III*, København. Reprinted 1957 (ed. Davidsen, John).

Jakobsen, Jakob 1957. 'Keltisk Indflydelse paa Færøerne', *Tingakrossur* January 1902. Reprinted in Jakob Jakobsen: *Greinir og ritgerðir*, (ed. Davidsen, John), Tórshavn.

Jóhannesson, Jón 1969. *Islands historie i mellomalderen*, Oslo, Bergen, Tromsø.

Jóhansen, Jóhannes 1985. *Studies in the vegetational history of the Faroe and Shetland Islands*, Tórshavn.

Jóhansen, Jóhannes 1989. 'Jóansøkugras (*Plantago lanceolata*) og forn búseting í Føroyum', *Fróðskaparrit* 34–35, pp. 68–75.

Jones, Gwyn 1968. *The Vikings*, New York and Toronto.

Kermode, P. M. C. 1931. 'Notes on Early Cross-Slabs from the Faroe Islands', *PSAS* LXV, 1930–1, pp. 373–9.

Krogh, Knud 1986. 'Seks kirkjur heima á Sandi', *Mondul* 2, pp. 21–54.

Mahler, Ditlev 1986. 'Ærgi undir brekkuni', *Mondul* 3, pp. 6–17.

Matras, Christian 1932. *Stednavne paa de færøske Norðuroyar*, København.

Matras, Christian 1934. 'Papýli í Føroyum', *Varðin* 14, pp. 185–7.

Matras, Christian 1939. 'Færøerne', *Nordisk Kultur v. Stedsnavn*, Stockholm, Oslo, 'København', pp. 53–59.

Matras, Christian 1981. 'Korkadalur', *Fróðskaparrit* 28–9, pp. 78–80.

Marcus, G. J. 1980. *The Conquest of the North Atlantic*, Woodbridge.

O'Donaghue, Denis & Arnfelt, P. P. 1893. *St Brendan the Voyager in Story and Legend*, Dublin.

Ólafsson, Haraldur 1987. *Íslensk þjóðmenning I*, Reykjavík.

Paasche, Fr. 1938. *Landet med de mørke skipene*, Oslo.

Radford, C. A. Ralegh 1962. 'Art and Architecture. Celtic and Norse', in *The Northern Isles*, ed. Wainwright, Frederick T., Edinburgh, pp. 163–87.

Sherley-Price, Leo (transl.) 1968. *Bede: A History of the English Church and People*. Revised by R. E. Latham, Harmondsworth.

464   HANS JACOB DEBES

Sigurðsson, Gísli 1988. *Gaelic influence in Iceland. Historical and Literary Contacts. A Survey of Research*, Reykjavík.

Sólstein, Andras 1987. 'Trupulleikar viðvíkjandi ti fyrstu búsetingini í Føroyum', mss submitted for Exam. Art. degree in History at Fróðskaparsetur Føroya.

Steining, J. 1958. 'Søgan í eldri tíð', *Føroyar* 1, Keypmannahavn, pp. 169–70.

Storm, Gustav (ed.) 1880. *Historia Norvegiae*, Monumenta Historica Norvegiae, Kristiania.

Stummann Hansen, Steffen 1985. 'Leirvík var við frá byrjanini', *Dimmalætting* nr 81.

Thorsteinsson, Arne 1976. 'Forn búseting í Føroyum', *Fróðskaparrit* 26, pp. 54–80.

Thorsteinsson, Arne 1981. 'On the development of Faeroese settlements', in *Proceedings of the Eighth Viking Congress, Århus 1977*, ed. Bekker-Nielsen, Hans, *et al.*, Odense, pp. 189–202.

Tierney, J. J. (transl.) 1967. *Liber de Mensura Orbis Terrae*, Scriptores Latini Hiberniae, vol. VI, Dublin.

Winther, N. C. 1985. *Færøernes Oldtidshistorie*, København 1875. Facsimile edition Tórshavn 1985, introduction by Hans J. Debes.

Yraola, Aitor 1983. 'Um baskneska fiskimenn á Norður-Atlantshafi, *SAGA. Tímarit sögufélags* XXI, pp. 27–38.

Zimmer, Heinrich 1891. 'Über die frühesten Berührungen der Iren mit den Nordgermanen', *Sitzungsberichte der Königlichen Preussenischen Akademie der Wissenschaften zu Berlin*, pp. 279–317.

30

ON THE LANDNAM OF THE FAROE ISLANDS[1]

SÍMUN V. ARGE

THE TRADITIONAL VIEW

The traditional view of who first came to the Faroes and when this was, has in particular been based on two written sources: *Færeyinga saga* and an older source written by the Irish monk, Dicuil *De Mensura Orbis Terrae*.

What we today know as *Færeyinga saga* is a collection of various texts, which describe events that mainly took place in the Faroes in the decades before and after the year 1000. Here it is said, that a man called Grímur Kamban settled in the Faroes first in the days of Harald the Fairhair. Until 1832 these texts were found scattered in different versions of the great Icelandic sagas. The philologist, C. C. Rafn collected these texts into one work and published them under the title *Færeyinga saga*. Whether there ever was a saga with this name and if so what it was like, is impossible to say today.

Dicuil's work was presumably written about the year 825. The writing contains, amongst other things, information about the voyages made by Irish clergy in the sea north of Ireland and Scotland, where they sought refuge to devote themselves to their religion as hermits.

From the short description in Dicuil's work of the appearance of the islands and the sailing distance to them from the British coast, scholars were readily agreed that the islands referred to were the Faroes, and that the Faroes were therefore inhabited by Irish hermits prior to the coming of the Norsemen.

Discussion and Evaluation of the Written Sources

By comparing Dicuil's account, in which it appears that the Irish hermits were driven from the islands, with the text of the saga, Rafn believes that the arrival of Grímur Kamban – and thus the first Norse settlement of the Faroes – can be fixed to the year 825, a view which on the whole still prevails.

It is presumed that the text of the accounts in *Færeyinga saga* was written about the year 1200. It is likely that the author based them on Faroese traditional stories. The accounts may therefore contain a grain of historical truth, although this is impossible to identify. Neither runic inscriptions nor archaeological evidence can be connected with the accounts in the saga. The fact that the text relates events that took place 200–400 years prior to its known date of writing, and that it on the whole ought to be regarded as fiction, render it rather useless as a historical source for the study of the earliest history of the Faroes.

The oldest preserved manuscript of Dicuil's work is from the second half of the 9th century. Regarding the authenticity and origin of the work itself there is apparently no doubt. But how far Dicuil is applicable as a historical source in the investigation of the earliest history of the Faroes is another matter. Here it must be pointed out that as far as this particular question is concerned, Dicuil's work contains a number of uncertainties. Not least the very important factor that the islands, which posterity has decided are the Faroes, are not given any placename. Likewise the sailing distance to the islands may very well be uncertain.

Moreover, an examination of the remains of activity or settlement, which have been connected with the passages dealing with the Irish settlement – i.e. some cross-slabs and some relics from cultivated areas, fields – makes it far from possible to prove that the islands that Dicuil talks about really are the Faroes. But on the other hand this possibility cannot be excluded. Verification must depend on the material remains.

Legends

Legends about so-called 'Holy men', and which are meant to have given proof of an Irish settlement, appear to be connected to actual relics in the landscape – namely the aforementioned evidence of cultivation in some remote locations.

These legends are typical examples of explanatory legends, which of course are quite unacceptable as historical sources.

PLACENAMES

By far the majority of Faroese placenames are of Norse origin. Since the turn of the century philologists have drawn attention to the fact that there are also placenames that must be of Celtic origin. The philological discussion – characterised by the two Faroese scholars Dr Jakob Jakobsen and Dr Christian Matras – that has taken place, has in short especially dealt with the question of whether the Celtic name-elements found in Faroese reflect influence from the south, or whether they are reminiscences of a local pre-Norse Irish population.

Evaluation of the Placenames

In my opinion the placenames do not provide a philological basis for the postulation of an Irish settlement in the Faroes. The very few Celtic placenames which are found here are presumably names which a Norse population gave them. That placenames have been used which are also known in the Irish-Scottish region south of the Faroes, and which also spread to Iceland, only emphasises the fact that there must have been contact with these regions. Such contact must be regarded as quite natural when considering the geographical position of the islands and the distance to the nearest neighbours: Shetland and Orkney.

In recent years it has been claimed, that pollen-botanical studies have proved a pre-Norse Irish habitation. These investigations have been carried out by the botanist, Dr Jóhannes Jóhansen, the leader of the Faroese Museum of Natural History. Peatbog samples have been radiocarbon-dated to ca. AD 600–50 in some sites and to ca. AD 850–900 at one site.

Discussion and evaluation

It must be stressed that none of Jóhansen's samples were taken in connection with archaeological investigations. As far as possible the counted sample and the radiocarbon-sample must be taken in an open profile, in which such important questions as the deposition of the various strata can be clarified both from a geological and archaeological point of view. With regard to the assertion that it has been demonstrated that there were two landnams, I feel it is important to point out that those are not shown in the same diagram.

Consideration ought to be given to the suitability of peat as sample material. The results of pollen investigations in Iceland in which peat samples were used, have also given dates that are relatively early, and this method of dating has there, too, resulted in significant deviations from the archaeological dating. This raises the question of radiocarbon datings of North Atlantic samples in general.

Summing Up

When it is claimed that these botanical investigations have proved an early, pre-Norse Irish habitation in the Faroes, I feel that the early dates, which Jóhansen put forward, should be applied with the greatest reservation. Further, it is evident from the foregoing discussion that the notions which in the course of time have been put forward concerning an early Irish settlement in the Faroes, cannot be maintained on the basis of the available sources of information. Whether there ever was such a settlement in the Faroes, can only be revealed by future examination and investigations.

I shall now turn attention to the archaeological evidence of Norse settlement in order to give an estimate of when the landnam could have taken place.

The earliest settlement was first discussed in greater depth when the book *Hvussu Føroyar vórðu bygdar* ('How the Faroes were settled'), written by Professor A. W. Brøgger, was published in 1937. At that time, however, there was very little to go on, and no proper comparative studies. It was not until Sverri Dahl's investigations during the Second World War that the collection of the material Brøgger had lacked really began. From the time of his appointment as curator of Føroya Fornminnissavn (The National Museum of the Faroes), which was founded in 1952, investigations began, revealing remains of habitation, which were dated to the Viking period: Kvívík, Fuglafjørður and Sørvágur.

Despite the considerable increase in archaeological material from 1937, when Brøgger's book was published, Dahl – as Brøgger – drew attention to the lack of items that could be dated to the 9th century. Arne Thorsteinsson too has pointed out that the earlier Viking period, the 9th century, is archaeologically completely unknown.

The Archaeological Material

Despite the fact that the archaeological remains which have been dealt with were dated to the Viking Period, there is a lack of more precise dating. Some years ago, in order to examine whether it was possible to achieve a narrower dating band, and thereby put us in a better position to evaluate the established concept of when the landnam in the Faroes may have taken place, I chose, from the available archaeological material, to study settlement remains from 15 selected sites and from one burial place. This was primarily based on material which had been published and had formed part of the archaeological debate, supplemented with material from the archives of Føroya Fornminnissavn. Furthermore, emphasis was lain on selecting material which represented the oldest finds and also those which were best documented.

Common to all the material is the fact that the investigations with which they are associated have never been published in their entirety. The material also suffers from not having been systematically examined, which of course has given a considerable factor of uncertainty, not least in regard to the problem of dating.

Since this examination took place some more recent excavations have been carried out, which have produced better documented artifacts. These shall be referred to below.

The Material and Dating

What, then, is the dating evidence for this material? The archaeological material in the Faroes is partly of Faroese origin and partly of foreign origin. The category of artefacts which is characteristic for Faroese archaeology is undoubtedly the locally produced pottery. The local earthenware is coarse and unglazed, shaped by hand without a potter's wheel. There appears to be a wide variety of both size and shape: vessels that are bowl-shaped, hemi-spherical, and bucket-shaped.

Other articles of Faroese origin are, for example, spindle whorls of tuff or basalt, line or net sinkers, which are pebbles about the size of a fist with a groove all the way round, lamps of tuff or stone.

On the whole these articles are very simple and uniform in their shape. But even although there is now a large collection, there has been no thorough examination of the separate categories of artefacts.

Amongst the imported assemblage, there are articles of soapstone, particularly large and small pots, weights for upright looms, and spindle whorls. These last are often re-utilised fragments of pots. In addition there are lots of whetstones of mica schist and clay slate, baking slabs of a slate-like soapstone, and grinding or quern stones.

Amongst the finds there are also wooden bowls and buckets, and metal articles – often in the form of rusty lumps, which as a rule have not been given a closer examination, but there are also small bronze fragments, sheet bronze, and occurrences of slag.

The above articles can mostly be described as household goods, which have been used in daily life. It is rare that one finds archaeological artefacts which can be described as personal belongings or ornaments, such as combs of bone or antler, beads, buckles or jewellery.

It was possible to classify some of the above mentioned articles as imported because they are made of materials which are not found in the Faroes. It must be assumed that the first people who came to the islands brought a lot of things with them. But from our present-day knowledge of the production of these goods and trade in them both in and out of Norway, there is little doubt that many of the imported articles came to the Faroes as a result of trading connections.

Discussion

Although there is a great deal of local pottery, it has not been analysed in detail, and therefore there is at present no chronology of this pottery. Despite this fact, however, it is reasonable to establish that the local production of earthenware is, in the main, medieval/early medieval. To what extent it commences as early as the Viking period is at present not known, but these are found in the earliest dated sites.

Concerning the fact that the artefacts of domestic origin are characterised by simplicity and uniformity, it must be acknowledged that – as far as dating is concerned – the main emphasis must today be laid on these imported goods, parallels for which are found in archaeological excavations in their country of origin, or in some other place, in the context of which they can be dated. It must therefore be stressed that traditional archaeological material in the Faroes only allows for relatively broad dating.

C-14 Dating

In recent excavations it has become more common to take samples of organic material for radiocarbon-dating. The sample material which was dated from the sites discussed here consisted of pine, fir, larch and juniper.

As there have never been forests in the Faroes, dates from timber are somewhat uncertain. Samples of juniper however are more suitable, pollen analyses having shown that juniper grew in the Faroes in the early period of habitation.

When this factor of uncertainty is taken into account, it appears that the radiocarbon-dating agrees fairly well with the archaeological dating, although in a few cases they seem to be a bit too old.

With regard to the application of radiocarbon-dating in the Faroes, I would like to draw attention to the fact that in other places in Scandinavia, a change in date in relation to the archaeological date has also been observed. Moreover, there has been no way of checking, for example by other methods of dating. Therefore Faroese radiocarbon-datings must be applied with caution; they ought only to be used as a guide.

Dating – Summing Up

The result of my attempt to date the selected settlements and burial place more exactly is that the oldest dated settlement remains can be traced back to about the year 1000 – or in broad terms, to the late Viking or Early Medieval period. However, the dating of the burial place at Tjørnuvík points back to the 10th century.

These dates fall a good bit later than the time it is claimed that the landnam took place. My own view is, however, that because the Faroese archaeological material has not been sufficiently analysed, the question of whether some sites belong to a somewhat earlier time ought to be left open in the meantime. This is particularly true of Kvívík and Fuglafjørður. But it is very obvious that the archaeological material lacks evidence of the earliest Viking age.

THE LANDNAM – AN EVALUATION

In the light of the foregoing, the question naturally arises as to whether these settlement sites and the burial place which have been studied, and which are the oldest existing evidence of the settlement of the Faroes, do in point of fact represent the landnam situation.

It is necessary to stress the haphazard nature of the collection of this material: most of the investigations were started by chance. It was not scientific questions that decided what was examined. The present investigations were not carried out with a view to clarifying the landnam situation, and it is therefore questionable whether the material is representative in that context.

Another matter is the effect subsidence has had on the preservation of the early settlement sites, and on the overall picture of the earliest settlement. It is reckoned that the islands have sunk towards the east by about 1 m in the course of the last 1,000 years.

It would also be natural to consider the landnam in the Faroes in the context of the population movements that took place in the Atlantic regions in the Viking period. On the basis of investigations carried out in recent years, there appears to be broad agreement that the Norse settlement of the Scottish islands took place in the beginning of the 9th century; in Iceland, about the year 900 and the following years.

There is therefore reason to wonder why the settlement of the Faroes, according to the archaeological material in question, can only with difficulty be dated back to the 10th century.

Considering this, I take the view that, in the meantime, this material ought not to be regarded as representative of the landnam period in the Faroes and thereby contribute to dating it late in relation to the initial settlements in the surrounding regions.

This view is now strengthened by the investigations which have been carried out in recent years of the settlement at Toftanes in Leirvík (see Hansen, this volume) and the summer pasture settlement at Argisbrekka in Eiði (see Mahler, this volume). On the basis of the archaeological material and radiocarbon-dating these are provisionally dated to AD 900–50 and early 10th century, respectively.

The archaeological evidence at Toftanes and Argisbrekka and the appearance in 1989 of an apparently pagan burial place at the church site in Sandur, thus fuels a continued discussion on when the landnam in the Faroes took place. But it seems clear to me, that from an archaeological point of view, it must be stressed that with regard to the dating of the landnam, the archaeological results and the botanical ones are still far from speaking the same language.

CONCLUSION

As written material from the earliest history of the Faroes is lacking, it must be the archaeological material which may be obtained in future investigations that will shed light on the landnam in the Faroes.

Systematic recording of fixed historic remains, which are scattered over the landscape, both in the in- and outfields, ought to be planned. Such a registration would contribute to giving a more varied picture of the early settlement.

Co-operation with people working in related fields is needed, for instance in solving the problems connected with the dating of the archaeological material and the radiocarbon-dating. It is crucial to obtain other methods of dating, for example, thermoluminescence, in order to evaluate and check the dating from several points of view.

In connection with archaeological investigations, suitable sites for pollen analysis should be selected, so that the results, along with the archaeological material, could give a more complete picture of the landnam. Not only is a closer co-operation with pollen analysts desirable, but the latest results from this science, which Jóhannes Jóhansen published in 1989, make it quite clear how urgent it is to get a critical debate within this science itself – a debate which I feel has been missing. On the basis of radiocarbon datings of the occurrence of *Plantago lanceolata* Jóhansen stresses that the habitation of the Faroes now can be dated back to *c.* BC 2300.[2]

Notes

1. A fuller version of this chapter with references is published in *Hikuin* 15, 103–28: 'Om

landnamet på Færøerne', and an English version in *Arctic Anthropology*, vol. 28, no. 2, 1991: 'The Landnám in the Faroes', 101–20.

2. Jóhansen, J.: Jóansøkugras (Plantago lanceolata) og forsøgulig búseting í Føroyum. *Plantago lanceolata* in the Faroe Islands and its significance as indicator of prehistoric settlement, *Fróðskaparrit* 34–5, bók (1986–87), 1989, 68–75.

31

VIKING-AGE FAROE ISLANDS
AND THEIR SOUTHERN LINKS

IN THE LIGHT OF RECENT FINDS
AT TOFTANES, LEIRVÍK

STEFFEN STUMMANN HANSEN

INTRODUCTION

According to tradition, the Norse settlers of the Faroe Islands originated from Western Norway. This strong tradition in Scandinavian history is mainly based on the evidence given in the Norse sagas recording relationships between Norway and the colonies in the North Atlantic.

However, there is still discussion on the situation the Viking settlers encountered when they first arrived on the islands. Were the islands unhabited or were they already occupied by Irish hermits when the settlers arrived? According to the work *De mensura orbis terrae*, written about AD 825 by the Irish ecclesiastic Dicuil, Irish hermits were in the Faroes in the 8th century and were later to be thrown out by the in-coming Norsemen. This tradition of a pre-Norse *landnam* has recently been supported by pollen analysis (Jóhansen 1971; 1979; 1982; 1985), but we still lack the supporting archaeological evidence (Arge 1989).

The interpretation of early Faroese history was originally entirely based upon written sources, and although archaeological excavations conducted during the last 50 years have produced important fresh archaeological material, only limited attention has been paid to the question of Irish influence in the Faroe Islands during the Norse period.

NORSE ARCHAEOLOGY IN THE FAROE ISLANDS

In the 1940s the late State Antiquary of the Faroe Islands, Sverri Dahl, commenced a series of archaeological excavations in the Faroe Islands. This pioneer work was to become the initial step in establishing archaeological science in the islands. These investigations gradually produced evidence of the Norse landnam in the Viking Age, thus supporting in general the information of written sources such as the so-called 'Saga of the Faroe Islanders'. Sites such as Kvívík, Tjørnuvík and Fuglafjørður are today inextricably bound up with the name of Sverri Dahl (Dahl 1951; 1958; 1971a; 1971b; Dahl & Rasmussen 1956).

Dahl held the opinion – in keeping with the tradition – that the settlers came from Western Norway, but at the same time he paid attention to information in

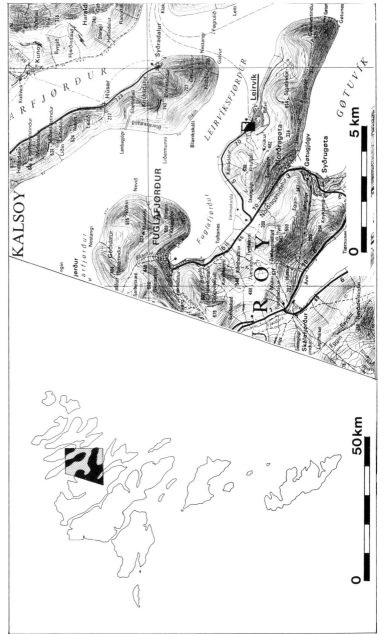

Figure 31.1: Location map of Toftanes (after an idea of Norman Emery).

the sagas that some of the first settlers had Irish or Christian names, thus indicating connections to the south. Dahl stressed the evidence of the written sources regarding the Celtic personal names of the settlers, and stated:

> Hence it is clear that settlers came to the Faroe Islands from Norse settlements to the south of the islands. This, of course, does not mean that all settlers came thence, although it is quite likely that the most noble ones and those most important for the saga did; indeed, we know that a number certainly came direct from Norway, from the regions of Sogn, Rogaland and Agder.
>
> (Dahl 1971a, 60)

Likewise, the linguistic studies of Christian Matras (Matras 1957) pointed to the Faroese 'ærgir' names, which were regarded as Celtic terms for Norse 'sæter' settlements (Dahl 1971a, 71).

For this historical concept of the 'southern link' Dahl found support in specific archaeological finds from different Faroese sites. The find of a bronze ringed pin of Hiberno-Norse type at the Viking cemetery in Tjørnuvík on Streymoy (Dahl & Rasmussen 1956, 165–6) made Dahl state:

> Although there is not much to build on, it is reasonable to suppose that this pin gives a hint of communication between the Norse settlements in the west during the first centuries of their colonization.
>
> (Dahl 1971a, 65)

A grave-slab ornamented with a wheeled cross discovered at the churchyard in the village of Skuvoy on the island of Skuvoy, Dahl found to be either evidence of Dicuil's Irish hermits or of Celtic influence in the Viking-Age Faroe Islands (Dahl 1971a, 62). Finally a wooden board with ribbon ornament of Hiberno-Norse type found at the site 'heima á Oyrini' in the village of Fuglafjørður on Eysturoy again gave occasion for mentioning the southern influence (Dahl 1958, 143–4).

Since Dahl's article of 1971 this question of a southern influence has only been discussed to a rather limited degree, partly due to the fact that little fresh archaeological material has been produced until recently.

In the following pages the finds from the recently excavated site, 'Toftanes', in the village of Leirvík on Eysturoy will be discussed in order to shed new light on the concept of the 'southern link' in Viking-Age Faroe Islands.[1]

EXCAVATIONS AT TOFTANES

During the 1980s Føroya Fornminnissavn conducted excavations of a Viking-Age farmstead at the site Toftanes in the village of Leirvík on the island of Eysturoy (Fig. 31.1). The excavation uncovered four contemporary buildings, all being part of the same farmstead.

The village of Leirvík is situated on the north-eastern shore of the peninsula of Gøtunes, in one of two low soft coastal areas (Fig. 31.2). These two areas are surrounded by three tall peaks, the tallest of them being 640 m high. The shores

Figure 31.2: General view from the north-west over the village of Leirvík. Note the wide infield areas surrounding the village and the indicator of Toftanes (photo: S. Stummann Hansen).

around the village are generally rather flat. The settlement of Toftanes is located around a small stream flowing down the slopes of one of the peaks. The settlement area of the Viking Age was located on the southern side of the stream.

In his article of 1969 Alan Small attempts to give a description of the 'primary Norse farmstead' in both Shetland and the Faroe Islands (Small 1969). He creates a model for the settlement based upon a division of the land into settlement area, infield area and outfield area. This model is still valid in the Faroe Islands today and can hardly be open for discussion. We can instead look at the specific requirements on which the model settlement is based. As the most important, Small lists:

1. access to the sea, with a reasonably flat or safe place to pull up the boat;
2. a patch of fairly flat, reasonably well drained land suitable for the construction of a farmstead and with the potential for some grain cultivation;
3. extensive grazing areas, since the number of animals which the poor vegetation of the islands could support would be rather low.

(Small 1969, 149)

Also one might add the necessity for access to fresh water.

The four buildings excavated at Toftanes have been tentatively interpreted as an outhouse (house I), dwelling house (house II), additional outhouse (house XI) and fire house (house XII) (Fig. 31.3) (Hansen 1989; 1990; 1991). On the

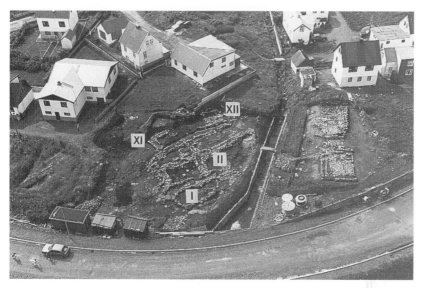

Figure 31.3: General view from the north-east over the excavation of Toftanes. I: outhouse; II: dwelling-house; XI: additional outhouse to building II; XII: fire-house (photo: Føroya Fornminnissavn/S. Stummann Hansen).

basis of the finds the settlement can be dated to the Viking period (Early Norse). A corroboration of the archaeological dating is available so far from three C-14 determinations from floor-layers in building I providing the following dates in conventional C-14 years: AD 865±65, AD 835±65 and AD 800±50 (calibrated years – according to M. Stuiver 1982 – AD 900–75, AD 895–940 and AD 890). The C-14 determinations have been provided by the Copenhagen Carbon-14 Dating Laboratory (K-4441, K-4442 and K-4443).

The shape and construction of all the buildings at Toftanes fits very well into the general picture of the Norse building customs in the North Atlantic during the Viking Age (Hansen 1989; 1990; 1991). Further, this settlement agrees perfectly with Small's model. Placed on a small headland and by a stream, its topographical location is almost classic, the Viking-Age sites in Kvívík and Fuglafjørður being situated in identical topographical conditions. With regard to infield and outfield facilities, the village of Leirvík is very well endowed. The village has a very extensive and rather flat infield area. Coming in by boat through Leirvíksfjørður, this place would probably have been the most attractive location to Norse settlers in this region.

THE FINDS FROM TOFTANES

A large proportion of the several thousand finds were found in the floor-layers of the buildings, but the layers outside the buildings also revealed several objects. The massive deposits – in some places covering the buildings to a depth of over

1 metre – have yielded optimum conditions for the preservation of wooden objects, and this group of finds is indeed very well represented. In the following section only a short résumé will be given, presenting some of the more important finds.

More than 700 objects of steatite have been recorded during the excavation (Hansen 1989, Fig. 9). They are mainly fragments of different bowls and saucepans of well-known West-Norwegian types (Skjølsvold 1961, Fig. 4a–b). A total of more than 50 spindle-whorls – including unfinished examples – have been recorded. There is a certain variation in the shape of these objects, but whorls of a flat or just faintly conical shape are most common. Line- or net-sinkers for fishing of an equally well-known Norse type have also been found. In quite a few cases sherds of broken vessels have been used for secondary purposes – for instance spindle-whorls, line-sinkers or tuyères.

Hones and querns of schist have been found especially in the floor-layers of the four buildings (Hansen 1989, Fig. 10). Several of the hones have been provided with a perforation for suspension. The schist used is of at least two different types, as both a light, coarse-grained type as well as a more fine-grained, dark schist is represented. The first one is of the Norwegian Eidsborg-type (Myrvoll 1985; Mitchell *et al.* 1984). Special attention should be paid to a 25 cm long mullion of the dark fine-grained schist, as this object must be regarded as an imported semi-manufactured piece, probably from Norway.

Two upper parts of querns made of schist have been recorded in the floor-layers in two different buildings (House II and XI). One of them has a diameter of 50 cm and was furnished with two holes for insertion of a wooden handle (Hansen 1991, Fig. 8). The other one – having a diameter of 40 cm – has only a single hole for a handle, with a groove for insertion of iron bars in the underface.

While all the stone-implements of steatite and schist have been imported (as these types of stone do not originate in the Faroe Islands), only very few artefacts produced of local material were found at Toftanes. Local materials, such as tuff and basalt, were used for such objects as spindle-whorls, loom-weights and line or net-sinkers. Of special note is a fragment of a bracelet of jet or lignite, which is the first of its kind found in the Faroe Islands.

Very few objects of metal have been unearthed at Toftanes, although three bronze objects deserve some consideration. One of them is a small circular brooch with a diameter of 2.6 cm. On the surface, the brooch has been furnished with an ornament of three animal-heads in Borre style (Hansen 1989, Fig. 11). Comparative finds have been made at Birka in Sweden (Arbman 1940, Tl. 71:11 & 1943, 211), Trelleborg in Denmark (Nørlund 1948, 128, Tl.XXV,7) and Haithabu in Northern Germany (Capelle 1968, Tl. 11:9). The brooch can be dated by these parallels to the 10th century. Two ringed pins, one of them intact, have been found in layers outside the buildings. The pins are of the same type as the one found in the 1950s in Tjørnuvík. The pins will be described in detail below.

About 30 beads, mainly of glass but also of amber, were found at Toftanes. Most of these belong to the segmented type, in colours of mainly blue and yellow. Other types of rounded beads are also represented at Toftanes.

Wooden items were, as mentioned above, preserved in huge numbers. Many of these, of course, would be waste from the construction of the buildings, but several artefacts were also found. Among these was a presumed doorplank with a carved wooden handle, spindle-whorls, a small box, tallies and small carved model-boats. Parallels to the last mentioned – which must be interpreted as toys – have been found at other Viking settlements in the Faroes (Dahl 1979, Fig. 1:c). Of domestic utensils, bowls, spoons and barrel staves with carved grooves for the bottom should be mentioned (Hansen 1989, Fig. 12; Hansen 1991, Fig. 11).

Special attention may be paid to a gaming-board with the old Norse game of 'Hneftafl' carved on the underside, while on the upperside was carved the game of 'Nine Men's Morris' (Hansen 1989; 1990 & 1992). The nearest parallel to the gaming-board from Toftanes derives from the famous boatgrave at Gokstad in Norway, where a fragment of a wooden gaming-board contained evidence of the same two games on the upper- and underside (Nicolaysen 1882, 46, Tl. VIII).

A very comprehensive group of wooden objects consists of cords of twined juniper branches. They are preserved in lengths of up to 2 m, and altogether more than a hundred metres of these have been found. Among other things they might very well have served the purpose of ropes for the roof-stones (Hansen 1989; 1990 & 1991; Larsen 1991). These cords may alternately have served a number of different purposes, just as they do even today in Western Norway, e.g. keeping the barrel staves together (Larsen 1991).

EVIDENCE OF THE SOUTHERN LINK

While the vast majority of the above mentioned finds by any reasonable argument may well have had Norwegian origins, a few finds clearly represent another origin. This group of finds includes, first of all, the two ringed pins, the jet-bracelet and one of the quern-stones.

The pins belong to the polyheadral headed type whose distribution is linked to the western part of the Viking world (Fig. 31.4), as they have virtually only been found in Ireland, Isle of Man, Scotland, The Hebrides, Orkney, Shetland, Faroe Islands, Iceland and Newfoundland (Fanning 1969; 1975; 1983a; 1983b; 1988). For the development of this type of pin one probably has to look to Dublin, where excavations during the last decades have produced substantial numbers of these Hiberno-Norse dress-fasteners (Fanning 1988, 7). The type is mainly dated to the 10th century. Previously only one pin of this type had been found in the Faroe Islands – in one of the graves at the Viking-Age cemetery in Tjørnuvík, Streymoy (Dahl & Rasmussen 1956, 162–6).

One of the ringed pins is only representated by a fragment of the shank (Fig. 31.5). The fragment is 6.8 cm in length and has a square section. On its four sides

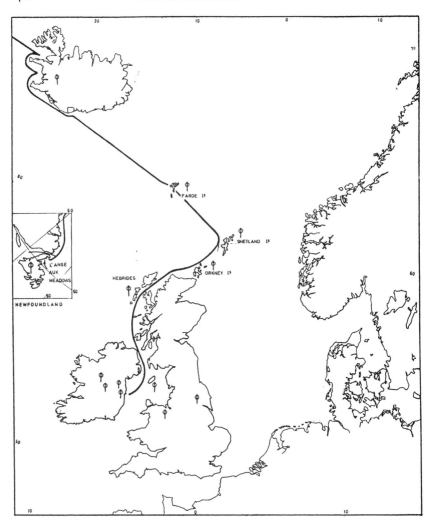

Figure 31.4: The western sea-route of the Vikings (after Gwyn Jones), with the distribution of plain-ringed polyhedral headed pins (after T. Fanning 1983a).

it is decorated with an incised step pattern delimited by two vertical lines. This step pattern is identical to that on a ringed pin found in a 10th-century grave at Buckquoy, Orkney (Fanning 1977, 223–4, Fig. 11) and on several other pins of this type found in Ireland, Scotland and the North Atlantic (Fanning 1969, Fig. 1; 1975, Fig. 2; 1983a, Fig. 141).

The other pin is complete, 12.5 cm in length (Fig. 31.6). The upper shank is circular in cross-section while the lower part is square. The polyhedral head has outlined lozenge-shaped panels ornamented with a simple interlaced knot on one

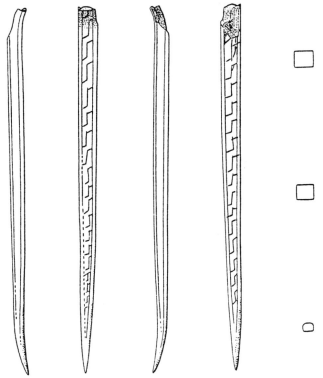

Figure 31.5: Fragment of ringed pin found at Toftanes (drawn by Aa. Andersen; scale 1:1).

side and a saltire motif on the other. The combination of these two ornaments is represented on other specimens of this type of pin found in the western part of the Viking world – for instance that from Buckquoy (Fanning 1977, 223–4).

The jet-bracelet is only represented by a fragment (Fig. 31.7). The fragment represents about one third of a ring, which has had an outer diameter of 7.8 cm, whilst the thickness has been 1.6 cm. The fragment had been split, so that only

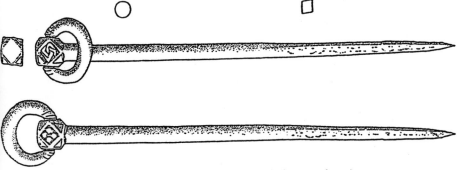

Figure 31.6: Ringed pin found at Toftanes (drawn by Aa. Andersen; scale 1:1).

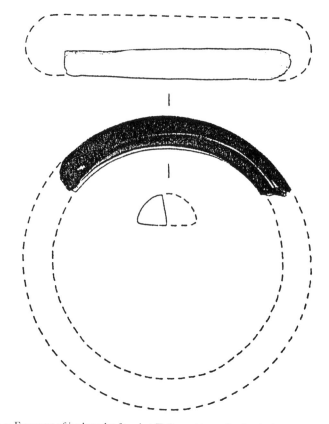

Figure 31.7: Fragment of jet-bracelet found at Toftanes (drawn by Aa. Andersen; scale 1:1).

half of the original fragment has been found. Objects made of jet are rather rare in the North Atlantic, but similar pieces have been found in Iceland (Eldjárn 1956, 332, Fig. 148), Shetland (Hamilton 1956, 121, Fig. 56) and Orkney (Curle 1982, 66, Fig. 42). However, jet is common in Viking-Age York and Dublin, where the recovery of hundreds of fragments and intact bracelets and finger-rings indicate that these were very common and popular objects in the Viking Age. The huge number of finds in Viking-Age Dublin indicates that it was either an important producer or distributor of jet-objects during the Viking Age. These finds from Toftanes may very well have originated from here.

As mentioned above, one of the quern-stones was furnished with a groove for the insertion of iron bars in the underface (Fig. 31.8). This feature seems to be common in the western part of the Viking world (Krogh 1982, 105; Hamilton 1956, pl. XXXV:10–11). To the author's knowledge it is not known in Scandinavia during the Viking Age. The origin of this object therefore may probably be looked for to the south.

These finds, although few in proportion to the total amount of finds from

Figure 31.8: Upper part of quern-stone of schist found at Toftanes (photo: Føroya Fornminnissavn/ A-C. Larsen).

Toftanes, certainly provide further archaeological evidence that Norsemen in the Faroe Islands had contacts to the south.

CONCLUSION

How then do we interpret the evidence of the finds from Toftanes? The vast majority of the finds from Toftanes represent imported materials. Daily life in the Viking-Age Faroe Islands seems to have been virtually impossible without imports. The word import may, in this connection, be regarded as a misleading term as it could imply a more or less continuous contact with other parts of the Viking world. Instead of regular import, for which we have no certain documentation, the objects thus may just represent an initial cargo brought during the phase of colonising the country. There is actually some slight evidence in the material from Toftanes that even the most simple things necessary for daily life were scarce and thus of very important value to the settlers (Hansen 1990). Contacts with the homeland (Norway) may not therefore have been as common as one would normally suppose.

What about their contacts to the south? The finds from the Faroe Islands recorded by Dahl supplemented by the artefacts from Toftanes are few, and can hardly be taken as an indicator of strong connections between the settlers and the areas to the south. But there certainly were contacts, as also demonstrated by the written sources. Probably the finds in the Faroes do not represent any sort of import or developed trading system, but rather are to be regarded as personal objects belonging to settlers coming from the south or brought to the islands by people who had visited Dublin or exchanged personal goods with people who had been there themselves. The exchange goods brought from the Faroe Islands would probably be imperishable materials such as skins and wool.

The excavations carried out in Viking-Age Dublin during the last decades have convincingly demonstrated the important role that this town must have played in Viking-Age Western Europe and in the North Atlantic in general. However, its influence in the North Atlantic – maybe with Orkney as an important transit area (Morris 1985) – must not be overestimated, but Dublin certainly contributed to the development of the Norse colonies in the North Atlantic. The excavations in Dublin thus raise some important questions concerning our understanding of the Norse communities in the North Atlantic. Did the Faroe Islands become an integrated link in trading systems or networks in the North Atlantic and did the established networks remain in existence or even develop throughout the Viking-Age and Medieval period? And what role did Dublin play in building up economic and cultural identity in the Norse communities in the North Atlantic?

The history of the Norsemen in the Faroe Islands and in the North Atlantic in general is thus probably an amalgam of events and processes, the existence of which is still difficult to quantify. Hopefully further examination of the material from Toftanes as well as future excavations in the Faroe Islands will help to throw new light on the history of the western part of the Viking world.

Acknowledgements

I want to express my thanks to Dr Patrick F. Wallace, Ard-Mhúsaem na hÉireann, who kindly permitted me to study the jet objects and ringed pins found during the excavations of Viking-Age Dublin. Further I want to thank Debbie Caulfield for her kind assistance during my stay in Ard-Mhúsaem na hÉireann in June 1990. Finally my thanks to Dr Thomas Fanning, Coláiste na hOllscoile Gaillimh, for his critical comments on this paper.

Note

1. For a more general preliminary presentation of the excavations at Toftanes see Hansen 1989; 1990; 1991.

REFERENCES

Arbman, Holger 1940. *Birka I. Die Gräber. Tafeln*, Stockholm.

—— 1943. *Birka II. Die Gräber. Text*, Stockholm.

Arge, Símun V. 1989. 'Om landnamet på Færøerne', *HIKUIN* 15, 103–128.

Capelle, Torsten 1968. *Der Metallschmuck von Haithabu. Studien zur wikingischen Metallkunst*, Neumünster.

Curle, Cecil L. 1982. *Pictish and Norse finds from the Brough of Birsay 1934–1974*, Society of Antiquaries of Scotland. Monograph No. 1, Edinburgh.

Dahl, Sverri 1951. 'Fornar toftir í Kvívík', *Varðin*, 65–96.

—— 1958. 'Toftarannsóknir í Fuglafirði', *Fróðskaparrit* 7, Bók, 118–46.

—— 1971a. 'The Norse Settlement of the Faroe Islands', *Medieval Archaeology* vol. XIV (1970), 60–73.

—— 1971b. 'Recent Excavations on Viking Age Sites in the Faroes', *Proceedings of the Sixth Viking Congress*, Uppsala, 45–56.

—— 1979. 'Forn barnaleiku í Føroyum', *Mondul* 1979:3, 3–13.

Dahl, Sverri & J. Rasmussen 1956. 'Víkingaaldargrøv í Tjørnuvík', *Fróðskaparrit* 5, Bók, 153–67.

Eldjárn, Kristján 1956. *Kuml og haugfé úr heiðnum sið á Íslandi*, Akureyri.

Fanning, Thomas 1969. 'The Bronze Ringed Pins in the Limerick City Museum', *North Munster Antiquarian Journal*, vol. XII, 6–11.

—— 1975. 'Some Bronze Ringed Pins from the Irish Midlands', *Journal of the Old Athlone Society*, vol. 1:4 (1974–1975), 211–17.

—— 1977. 'The bronze ringed pin from Buckquoy, Orkney', in Ritchie, A. 'Excavations of Pictish and Viking-Age farmsteads at Buckquoy, Orkney', *Proceedings of the Society of Antiquaries of Scotland*, vol. 108 (1977), 223–4.

—— 1983a. 'Some Aspects of the Bronze Ringed Pin in Scotland', in *From the Stone Age to the Forty-Five*, eds O'Connor, A. & Clarke, D. V., Edinburgh, pp. 324–42.

—— 1983b. 'The Hiberno-Norse Pins from the Isle of Man', in *The Viking Age in the Isle of Man*, ed. Fell, C. et al., London, pp. 27–36.

—— 1988. 'Three Ringed Pins from Viking Dublin and their Significance', in *Settlement and Society in Medieval Ireland*, ed. Bradley, J., Kilkenny, pp. 161–75.

Hamilton, John R. C. 1956. *Excavations at Jarlshof, Shetland*, Edinburgh.

Hansen, Steffen Stummann 1989. 'Toftanes–en færøsk landnamsgård fra 9–10. århundrede', *Hikuin* 15, 129–46.

—— 1990. 'The Norse Landnam in the Faroe Islands in the Light of recent Excavations at Toftanes, Leirvík', *Northern Studies* 25 (1988), 58–84.

—— 1991. 'Toftanes: A Faroese Viking Age Farmstead from the 9–10th Centuries AD', in *The Norse of the North Atlantic*, ed. Bigelow, Gerald F., *Acta Archaeologica* 61, 44–53.

Jóhansen, Jóhannes 1971. 'A Palaeobotanical Study Indicating a Previking Settlement in Tjørnuvík, Faroe Islands', *Fróðskaparrit* 19, 147–57.

—— 1979. 'Cereal cultivation in Mykines, Faroe Islands AD 600', *Danmarks geologiske Undersøgelsers Årbog 1978*, 93–103.

—— 1982. 'Vegetational development in the Faroes from 10000 BP to the present', *Danmarks geologiske Undersøgelsers Årbog 1981*, 111–36.

Jóhansen, Jóhannes 1985. *Studies in the vegetational history of the Faroe and Shetland Islands*, Annales societatis scientiarum Færoensis supplementum XI, Tórshavn.

Krogh, Knud 1982. *Erik den Rødes Grønland*, København.

Larsen, Anne-Christine 1991. 'Norsemen's use of juniper in Viking Age Faroe Islands', in *The Norse of the North Atlantic*, ed. Bigelow, Gerald F., *Acta Archaeologica* 61, 54-9.

Matras, Christian 1957. 'Gammelfærøsk ærgi'. *Namn och Bygd*, Årgang. 44, Hefte 1-4 (1956), 51-67.

Mitchell, J. G., Helge, Askvik & Heid, G. Resi 1984. 'Potassium-argon Ages of Schist Honestones from the Viking Age Sites at Kaupang (Norway), Aggersborg (Denmark), Hedeby (West Germany) and Wollin (Poland), and their archaeological Implications', *Journal of Archaeological Science* 11, 171-6.

Morris, Christopher D. 1985. 'Viking Orkney: A Survey', in *Prehistory of Orkney BC 4000-1000 AD*, ed. Renfrew, C., Edinburgh, pp. 210-42.

Myrvoll, Siri 1985. 'The Trade in Eidsborg hones over Skien in the Medieval Period', *Iskos* 5, 31-47.

Nicolaysen, Nicolay 1882. *Langskibet fra Gokstad ved Sandefjord*, Kristania.

Nørlund, Poul 1948. *Trelleborg*, København.

Skjølsvold, Arne 1961. *Klebersteinindustrien i vikingetiden*, Oslo-Bergen.

Small, Alan 1969. 'The distribution of settlement in Shetland and Faroe in viking times', *Saga-Book of the Viking Society* 17, 145-55.

32

SHIELINGS AND THEIR ROLE
IN THE VIKING-AGE ECONOMY

NEW EVIDENCE FROM THE FAROE ISLANDS[1]

DITLEV L. D.MAHLER

As known from the study of European, and especially Norwegian shielings, the importance of their role in their respective economies has long been recognised. The Norwegian 17th–18th-century *seter*-system was in many ways essential to the spreading and maintenance of a monetarian economy, and thus part of what could be called a 'cash-crop-economy'(Borchgrevink 1977, 22). The Scottish *eary*-system played a similar role in the 18th century, by functioning as intensive feeding stations for black cattle intended for export to the English market (Fenton 1976, 124f). Obviously one should be careful not to transfer later market-dependent mechanisms from reasonably well known historical shieling economies to older types.

The shieling economy or decentralised farming economy in general comprises a long list of advantages, which are roughly summed up in the following: by using the shieling system, the livestock was removed from the main farm as early in the spring as convenient, to avoid summer exploitation of the coming winter fodder. In their footsteps followed all related activities from the actual milking of cows, sheep and goats to the processing and preparation of the various dairy products. Additional winter fodder could be collected on the shieling site, helping to secure a stable milk yield during the winter months, as well as augmenting the number of animals the farm could support throughout the year. By using the dung accumulated during the shieling season or moving the pens around, certain areas could be fertilised, thus increasing the grazing potential as well as the eventual harvest of winter fodder. Expansion into hay cultivation would seem a natural extension of these activities (Reinton 1969; Borchgrevink 1977, 6).

Depending on the resource area in question, the main activity on the site could be supplemented by a range of activities. These may vary from the collecting of winter fuel, peat cutting, charcoal/iron production, fishing, the working of wool and other materials into semi-manufactured articles.

Shielings can be divided up into three or four categories, depending on the various degrees of importance attached to grazing and the production of fodder, the milking of the livestock and the location of the manufacturing of dairy products. A common denominator exists though, which is the specific way in which areas surrounding the main farm's arable land are utilised. A system which in respect to the catchment areas, can be described as *the spatially restricted but intensive exploitation of a topographically limited resource area in order to maintain and utilise the livestock*. Furthermore, the decentralised farming economy is incompatible with a broader exploitation of the area, by, for instance, common sheepgrazing unless strict herding is supervised. This also means that the presence of shielings constitute a main factor in characterising an agrarian economy, where farm and shieling(s) make up a complex whole.

How widespread then was the decentralised farming economy in the North Atlantic area, during the Viking Age or Norse Period? During the last 10–15 years, Norwegian mountain surveys and excavations among others in the Sognefjord area and in Friksdal have established the relative importance of *setre* to the agrarian economy, from the Iron Age and onward (Magnus 1986). It has even been suggested that the need of mountain pastures grew in importance during the settlement expansion from BC 500 to the end of the Viking Period (Bjørgo 1986). Although the historically well documented *sel* economy of Iceland has, as far as I know, never been archaeologically dated to the Landnam Period, it seems likely that the system may have its origin here (Hitzler 1979, 45f; Sveinbjarnadóttir 1989, 69). The interesting surveys in the Qordlatoq valley in Østerbygd, Greenland, show the shieling system to be a well established part of the Norse economy here. Although we again lack firm archaeological dates, the system is presumed to be as old as the Landnam (Keller 1983; Albrethsen & Keller 1986).

Concerning the areas already populated before the arrival of the Norse – Orkney-Shetland, the Scottish coast and Isles, and the Isle of Man – the situation is far more complex, as there existed a shieling system both before and after the domination of the Norse (Macsween 1959, 75; MacSween & Gailey 1961, 77; Megaw 1978, 327–46; Higham 1978, 347–55). Investigations on the Isle of Man have registered a multitude of sites which mirror a widespread and complex economic system presumed to date from the Iron Age to the post-Norse Period.[2] The Manx material is typically problematic. It is unlikely that the decentralised farming economy remained unchanged throughout the whole time span. Certain factors may indicate that the economy of the post-Norse Periods was based on transhumance rather than on a main farm/shieling system. In general the question of affinity, specially in relation to the presumed older mounds and structures, is a problem – specifically for the Viking Age as only a few clear Norse elements can be isolated[3] (Gelling 1961, 123–5; 1964, 156–72).

The list of surveys is a long one, especially if the question of placename evidence is taken into consideration and the re-evaluation of former interpretations, e.g. in Orkney (Thomson 1987, 30–1) and Shetland. However, these surveys do seem to suggest the decentralised farming economy as a very widespread part of the Viking-Age Landnam economy in the North Atlantic cultural area. In this respect the new evidence from the Faroes fits into this pattern.

As early as in the 1950s, Sverri Dahl pointed out the possibility of remains of a Viking-Age shieling economy on the islands. As a result of Matras' linguistic studies in the mid 1950s (Matras 1956), Sverri Dahl pinpointed 18 different sites, where the placenames indicated a possible shieling – many of these sites had ruins; one of these was Ergidalur on Suðuroy where in 1965 Sverri Dahl carried out a small excavation (Dahl 1970a, 362–8; 1970b, 71; 1971, 71–3). Here the remains of a small 5 by 3.5 m building very likely belonging to an *ærgi*, were uncovered. The building can be archaeologically dated to the late 10th or early 11th century. When surveying the area, another ruin was discovered of (approximately) the same size as well as the remains of foundations in the edge of the brook running between the two houses.

Then in the early 1980s a powerplant was planned at Eiði (Fig. 32.1) using Eiðisvatn as a reservoir, and from 1985–7 Føroya Fornminnissavn excavated the remains of a considerable *ærgi* site at Argisbrekka on Eysturoy. The area around Argisbrekka is to the West bordered by Eiðisvatn and to the East dominated by the two mountains Vaðhorn and Slættratindur. The latter is the highest mountain on the Faroes. South of the excavation-areas, the present landscape bears impressions of peat cuttings used right up to modern times. Excavations at Eiði have shown that this village goes back to the Landnam period, and the head farm of Argisbrekka is very likely to be found here.[4]

In all the remains of 18 buildings have been totally excavated, 17 dating from the Viking-Age/Earliest Middle Ages – and one undated but probably fairly recent. Among the traces of activity which is hard to date was a 'field system', Area XIII, which consisted of a limited area, criss-crossed by furrows created by a systematic turning over of the soil. In one of the furrows a corroded iron artefact was found, which may be the actual remains of an iron hoe. The so-called field has been stratigraphically dated to being contemporary with or slightly younger than the Viking-Age settlements. Pollen-analysis has so far been unable to turn up any trace of barley or oats – only grasses have been identified.[5] The many fragments of dried and carbonised peat found in the furrows, as well as heat-affected stones and traces of ash, may all indicate deliberate fertilisation of the area, although the actual dung can no longer be traced. Grains of naked barley have been found in connection with occupation deposits, but it is of course impossible to say where the barley came from.

The 17 Viking-Age houses are mainly divided into two large settlement areas (Fig. 32.2): an Eastern and a Western area containing respectively seven and ten houses each. Within these two areas are two to three smaller settlement units containing a dwelling house and one to two outhouses.

Three types of buildings emerged: dwelling houses, work hut and storage buildings. Regardless of function the houses were all built with walls of turf, sand, clay and gravel. Here and there stones were placed within the walls for

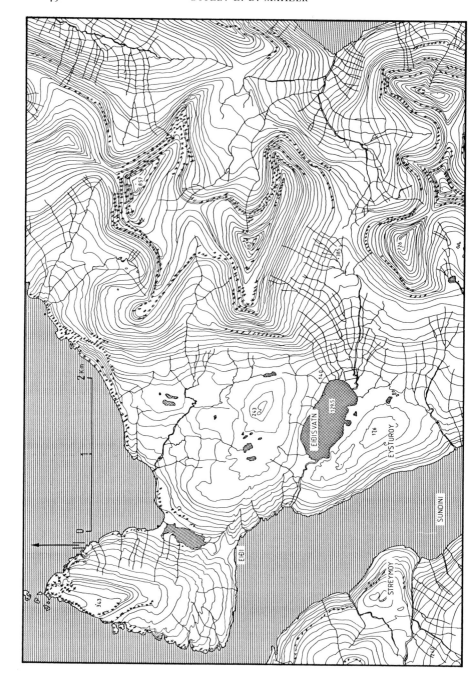

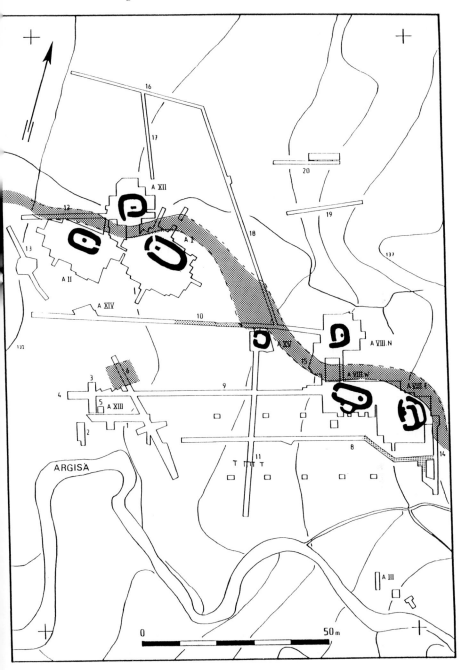

Figure 32.2: Map of the central excavation areas with the latest ruins roughly sketched into each area. The ruins are thus not contemporary but give a picture of the Western area (Area I, II and XII) and the older Eastern area (Area VIII, XV and XVI).

further stability. Although turf-built houses are very common in Iceland and Greenland, Argisbrekka is so far the only known Faroese settlement with houses entirely built in this technique.

Most of the houses are oriented east-west with an entrance through the western gable or placed near a corner. Typical of the dwelling houses are two rows of roof-bearing posts, stonebuilt fireplaces, smaller pits and one to two turf-built benches. The cultural deposits are fairly thick, but the actual floorlayer is often restricted to an area around the fireplace. These houses are generally 7–8 m long and 3.5 m wide, although smaller dwellings between 3.5–4 m long were also found. Preliminary drawings of a dwelling house and a connected storage house from Area VIII, House 1 and 2 have been published (Mahler 1989, 154; 1991, 65).

The smaller outhouses, although outfitted with fireplaces and a bench, lack the thick cultural deposits typical of the dwelling houses. Few, if any, artefacts were found, and presumably these structures have functioned as work huts. The roof bearing posts are restricted to either a post in each corner of the room, or to a single post near the gables. The work huts are about 3 m long and 2–2.5 m wide (Fig. 32.3).

The storage buildings are built along the same general lines as the outhouses/work huts. These however lack fireplaces and have almost no floor deposits. In one instance an air channel was found leading into a house under its entrance, apparently with the object of keeping stored products cool.

In several cases, dwelling houses and storage houses or houses with a more complex function not yet fully understood were built as a pair, joined by a common turf-built long wall. These units are invariably built on the edge of a brook, now fossilised, for maximum drainage effect. Other small outhouses lie separated from the dwelling houses and only the archaeological interpretation links them to a unit. Each unit thus consists of a dwelling house and one to two outhouses. This compares well with the 13th-century *Laxdæla saga* describing the Icelandic *sel* as consisting of a dwelling house and storage house, 'selin váru tvau, svefnsel ok búr', while an 18th-century source describes three buildings, adding a kitchen house (*eldhus*) to the 'svefnsel ok búr' (Hitzler 1979, 66 and 70; Sveinbjarnardóttir 1989, 70). Several of the units in each settlement area overlay older units, which supports the assumption that, possibly with a single exception, only one unit was functioning at a time.

Altogether we have six to seven units. Assuming that a single unit was in use for a generation, the duration of the settlement as a whole can be put to *c.* 200 years. However many of the houses bear evidence of several major alterations, which could indicate a period of use beyond a generation per unit.

The later settlements at Argisbrekka (in the Western area) are the ones that are best dated archaeologically as well as by 6 C-14 datings. Both indicate that activity in the Western area ended sometime in the mid-11th century. The horizontal stratigraphies as well as the C-14 dates (K4896: 860±70, cal., ±1 stand.dev.: 725–895; Ua-1456: 900–950±95 cal., ±1 stand.dev. 790–1015)

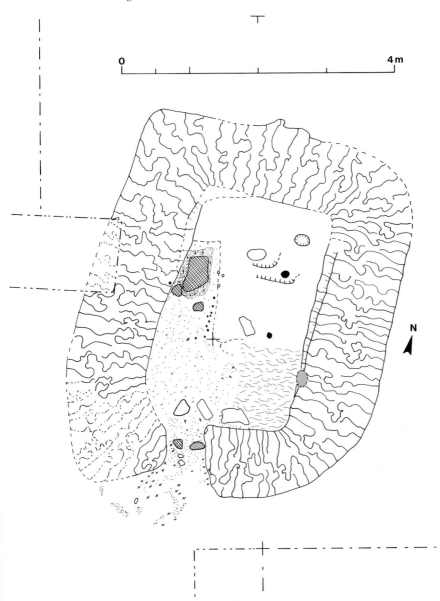

Figure 32.3: A 2 × 3 m² turfbuilt house from Area VIII, House 4, phase B, the second phase of three. The small two-aisled house contained a fireplace placed on the floor beneath a supposed bench, which was lined by small rafters. The entrance is towards the South, and *c.* 2 m south of this a brook, now fossilised, was found. Drift wood from phase A's entrance is C-14 dated, Ua-1456, but gives, unfortunately, an unacceptably high age (640 ± 100 cal.).

indicate a start of activity in the Eastern settlement area sometime in the 9th century, although this is a preliminary date.

A section between two units, A.I and A.XII, in the Western area points to the possibility of two shielings functioning simultaneously during the final stage of the Viking-Age use of the area. So far the C-14 dates from Argisbrekka are the earliest dates of human activity directly linked to archaeological material in the Faroe Islands (compare Jóhansen 1985, 55). However the chronology of Argisbrekka is far from finalised, and further C-14 dates are needed before we can be sure of the early start of the Eastern settlement area.

Unfortunately there are no artefacts from the Eastern area which can be more specifically dated, than to the Viking Age/Early Middle Ages. While the house types may give some pointers, we will have to rely on the natural sciences for more specific information.

Apart from the many finds of organic material such as wood (Mahler 1986a; Mahler & Malmros 1990) and leather, found due to the excellent preservation conditions in the Western area, very few artefacts were present at Argisbrekka. Only a fraction of the amount of artefacts that could be expected were found, compared to farmsteads such as Toftanes (Hansen 1987; 1989, 136–42; Larsen & Hansen 1984) and Kvívík (Dahl 1951), which is surprising, considering the numbers of structures excavated and the many square meters of earth removed. Furthermore, we found extremly few broken and therefore discarded objects, which points to a different pattern of behaviour than on the coastal farmsteads. Besides the many finds of wooden objects, we do have a cross section of the usual artefacts found on the Faroese Viking-Age sites. These include whetstones, steatite bowls, spindlewhorls of steatite and local tuff, round-bottomed clay vessels, as well as various metal objects such as knives, shears, locks and slag. Several glass beads and some metal ornaments such as rings of silver or bronze, a circular brooch (Mahler 1986b) and a bronze ringed pin of polyhydral type (Mahler & Malmros 1990) complete the picture.

In other words while the actual composition of artefacts is typical, the suprisingly small numbers found were one more indicator of the alternative function of the site.

The location of the site of Argisbrekka is atypical of the known Faroese Viking-Age settlement pattern – which is coastal – apart from the above mentioned Ergidalur (Thorsteinsson 1981a, 190; Arge 1989, 114). Furthermore, the houses differ partly by being turf-built, a technique which seems well-developed on Argisbrekka, and partly by their size, specifically that of the dwelling houses (much smaller), and the position of their entrances. Although so far unique for the Faroe Islands these characteristics have many parallels among shielings and smaller dwelling houses in Norway and Iceland, and fit well within the frame of the Viking period (Myhre 1980, 347 & 355; Bakka 1965, 121f; Lillehammer 1971, 20; Magnus 1986, 49).

The artefacts do not suggest a lower social status for the settlement as a cause of the aberrant site location. On the contrary, a different behaviour or function is indicated, resulting in the leaving of fewer artefacts. The placename may in fact indicate the actual function of the settlement. The old Nordic word *ærgi* is interpreted as meaning 'summer pasture', eventually including the presence of buildings from which the animals may be supervised.

How to interpret Area XIII in this context is somewhat uncertain. However it seems logical to see the 'field system' as a means of exploiting the manure produced on the site. No cultivation is known on the Icelandic *sel* (Sveinbjarna-dóttir 1989,70), but as the North Atlantic shielings are so little known, I think it would be unwise to exclude the possibility (cf. Gelling 1964, 156–72).

From the placenames Matras suggested that during the 9th century the Gaelic word *airge* was adopted into the Norse language and is seen widely distributed in those areas settled by western Norsemen during the Viking Age. One would think that the existing Norse words were more than enough to cover the phenomenon and related activities, and it is odd that this word was adopted into old Norse (cf. Pearsall 1961; Fellows Jensen 1980, 67f). The Faroese landscape, while variable, is far more compressed than its Norwegian counterpart and lacks the great differences in vegetation zones. Due to the shorter distances, different vegetational zones of a far less varied character are to be found close to the main farmsteads. None of the surveyed Faroese sites, with traces of house structures interpreted as *ærgir*, exceed a distance of 4–5 km ($\bar{x}$: 3.0 km) from the supposed winter farm, and the average altitude is only around 76 m above sea-level (see Table 32.1). Its closeness to the coast/main farm, notwithstanding the material from Argisbrekka, places it into the archaeologically defined group of shielings that can be classified, according to Reinton's typology, as a full-seter. That is used throughout the summer for the milking of animals, treating and storing of milk and other dairy products, as well as for the harvesting or collecting of winter fodder (Albrethsen & Keller 1986, 96).

In other words while Argisbrekka and maybe the other Faroese *ærgir* are, as far as their activities are concerned, 'full-*seters*', their location close to their supposed main-farms places them in the category of '*heim-seters*'. This contradiction might have been one of the reasons for applying a 'new' word for a known activity, but which differed in certain aspects. This suggestion does not necessarily apply to the whole Norse area where some kind of *ærgir* were used, and the different geographies and exsisting economic systems may well have had another impact on the adaption of the Norse economies there.

When Sverri Dahl mapped the *argir/ergir* placenames of the Faroes, he indicated the presence of structures on seven of the 18 sites. My fieldwork during 1989 was aimed partly at surveying some of the known placename connected sites, and partly at other areas where the topography might indicate *ærgir* sites or where unexplained house structures were known in the present outfields.

The ten sites are divided into two groups (Table 32.1), a simple and a complex group each consisting of five sites (Fig. 32.4). The first group consists of small

Table 32.1: Ærgir sites and presumed *ærgir* sites surveyed during 1989[6] (compare Fig. 32.4). The water supply is vital for any *ærgi*, and local information on the stability of the water supply, especially during spring time, has been used as a guideline. In the case of Argisgjógv, the running water in the near-by 'wadi' was very sparse. This, however, would not neccessarily mirror the situation when the site was in actual use. The location of the site within the presumed catchment area is meant as a guideline for the surveying of other areas, but unfortunately no clear pattern has yet appeared. The most likely position, though, is the central one. With accessibility, I have tried to estimate how easy or difficult it would be to reach the *ærgi*. Crossing high mountains and deep ravines are considered as

Location and Føroya Fornminnissavn's registration number, SNR	no. on fig. 32.4	Map number, location and structure	Number of ruins. (n)umber of divisions visible	Type of ærgir		Prescence of banks	Location in supposed catchment area	
				Complex	Simple		Central	Periphery
Argisbrekka, Eiði SNR: 4765	1	M0601/I-XVI	>17	●	●		●	
Argisá, Skúvoy SNR: 4937	3	M4001/I	>1	●	●	●	●	
Argisgjógv, Selatrað SNR 4952	2	M2004/I-II	>2	●	●	●	●	
Ergidalur, Hove SNR: 4050	4	M4901/I-II	>2(2)	●				●
Ergibyrgi, Sumba	5	M5201/I-VI	>5	●	●			●
Argisá, Havnabøur SNR: 4960	10	M1301/I	>1(5)	●		●	●	
Argisfossar, Kvívík	11	M1902/I	>1(2)	●			●	
Kvíngadalur, Klaksvík SNR: 4961	6	M1501/II-VI	>4(2-3)	●		●	●	
Í Hópinum, Norðoyrar SNR: 4250	7	M2202/I	>2(2)	●		●		●
Borðoyavík, Klaksvík Uppsalahagi 2 SNR: 4973	8	M2205/I	>1(2)	●				●
Borðoyavík, Klaksvík Uppsalahagi 1 SNR: 4974	9	M2204/I	>1(3)	●			●	

major obstacles. For daily or weekly communication with the farm and for transporting various dairy products the possible use of boat must have been of importance. As in the case of the accessibility of the *ærgir*, the distance from the supposed farm is measured along the old tracks. Where serious doubt may be raised, both locations of a supposed main farm have been shown. In several cases the *ærgi* is located at or near a present outfield border. These borders must be younger than the *ærgi*, and the presence of a parish border could indicate an old age for the *ærgi* (Thorsteinsson 1981b, 200–1).

Water supply			Accessibility			Communication by boat possible		Distance over land from supposed farm	Location of presumed head farm	Altitude of supposed ærgir	Outfield border near by	
Ample and steady	Medium	Unknown	Easy	Medium	Difficult	By sea	By fresh water	Km		m.a.s.	Farms	Between Villages/Parishes
●			●				●	3,1	Eiði	130–136	●	
●			●					1,8	Skúvoy	180		
	●		●			●		1,6	Selatrað	40–60		
●			●				?	3,7	Hove	180		●
	●			●				2,4	Vikarbyrgi	30–50	●	
●			●			●		2,3	Oyndafjørður	15–20		●
					●			3,6	Fuglafjørður			
●				●			●	4,7	Kvivik	80		●
●					●	●	●	4,0	Gerðar	20–30		
	●			●		●		3,0	Norðoyrar	10		
	●			●				4,5	Uppsalar	60		
	●			●				4,1	Uppsalar	60		

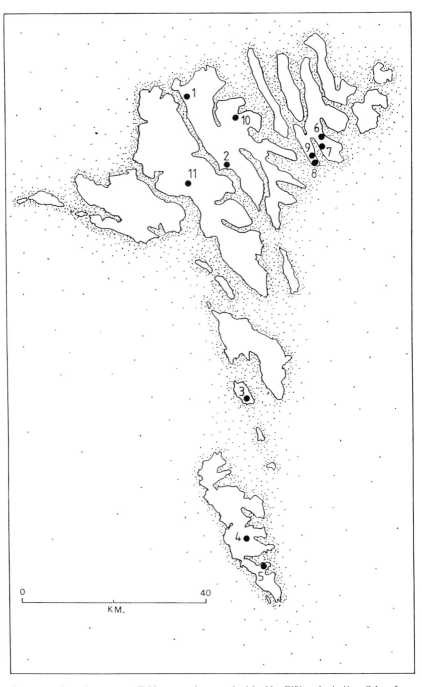

Figure 32.4: Location map, see Table 32.1 and text. 1: Argisbrekka, Eiði. 2: Argisgjógv, Selatrað. 3: Argisá, Skúvoy. 4: Ergidalur, Hove. 5: Ergibyrgi, Sumba. 6: Kvíingadalur, Klaksvík. 7: Í Hópinum, Klaksvík. 8: Uppsalahagi 2, Klaksvík. 9: Uppsalahagi 1, Klaksvík. 10: Havnarbø by Argisá, Hellunum. 11: Argisfossar, Kvívík. 12: Nesvík. 13: Argisdalur, Mula. (Locations in no. 13 have been surveyed but with no result.)

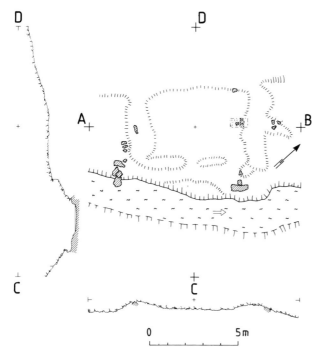

Figure 32.5: Argisá, Skúvoy. The small ruin measures internally 3 × 4 m². On the opposite side of the small brook a short dyke was found, presumably of the same age as the ruin. Local stories from recent times tell of cattle often falling from the bird cliffs while eating of the rich grass on the steep slopes. Herding the cattle could be another reason for using the *ærgi* system at Skúvoy.

4.5–5 × 3 m² house structures (internal measurement) as exemplified at Argisá on Skúvoy (Fig. 32.4, no. 3) where the walls were built of turf (Fig. 32.5). Just north of the ruin lies a depression from a fossil waterfall. The depression could very well have served as a pen during the site's use as an *ærgi*. These can also be stone-built, as at the houses at Ergibyrge (Fig. 32.4, no. 5). The simple group fits very well with the *ærgi* interpretation and the surface structures could in fact mirror minor dwelling houses like those at Argisbrekka, Area VIII, House 3 or Area XII, House 1 (both as yet unpublished).

The latter group consists of complex structures showing two to three transverse partitions or, as at Havnarbø (Fig. 32.4, no. 10 and Fig. 32.6) with structures also added to the western longside. The average internal length is 9 m – as far as this was possible to measure on the surface – the longest ruin being at Havnarbø (13.5 m). In several cases the ruins have been reused in recent times for building sheep shelters, adding further complications to the surface interpretation. The group of complex structures are more difficult to interpret, especially at Havnarbø and Kvíingadalur, whereas indications of a farm interpretation cannot be ruled out. During the late 17th-century farmers were

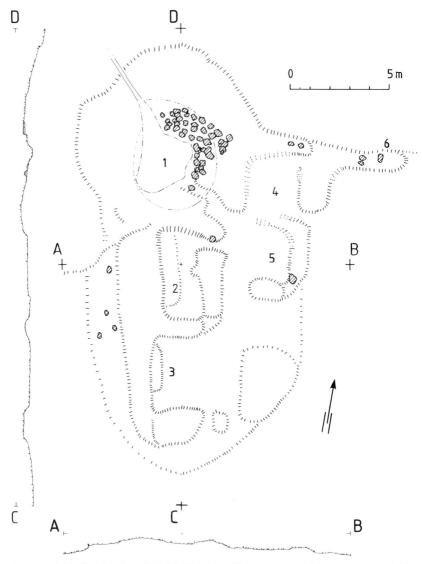

Figure 32.6: Surface drawing of Argisá, Havnarbø. The present Argisá runs 10 m east of the structures but has presumably eroded the area closer to the structures. Between 10 and 20 cm below the present surface east of room 3, stones can be felt, which suggest that the area could have been a kind of courtyard. A short dyke, 6, runs east from structure 4. Recent disturbances are very clear in structure 1, where stones have been taken from below. Modern drainages are seen visible in two places.

sought to settle in Kvíingadalur on certain conditions (Hansen 1981, part 7, 16; Joensen 1962, 4–5). It is unknown, but considered unlikely, that anybody accepted the offer, however the possibility cannot be excluded. Havnarbø at Argisá is situated in the fertile bottom of Oyndafjørður, and the man who 60 years ago drained the area in order to (re)cultivate it, reported the presence of traces of old agricultural activity (*teigar*). On the other hand Havnarbø seems to have a fairly close parallel in the *sel* site Brennigil in Austurdalur, Iceland (Sveinbjarna-dóttir 1989, 70, Fig. 6). One of the Faroese parallels to the group of complex *ærgir* ruins is found at Nesvík, where a three roomed building, with an internal length of 18.2 m has been surveyed.[7] The building remains at Nesvík are considerably longer than any of the presumed *ærgir* sites and it is interpreted as the remains of a Medieval farmstead.

All the non-excavated sites are undated except for the fact that most of them must be of a considerable age. Often a mythology has grown up around the sites in order to place them in an acceptable time frame. Í Hópinum was earlier called Íslendingatoftir (Bruun 1929, 41; Matras 1933,124; Hansen 1980, 6. partur,144) and Icelanders were thought in former times to have weathered out the winter here. In other cases the ruins have rested in total oblivion as on Skúvoy. The differences between the two groups of ruins could be functional, chronological or geographical, and in this respect it is interesting that the group of complex ruins are so far found only on the Northern Islands. We know that the Medieval dwelling houses are shorter than their Viking-Age counterparts (Thorsteinsson 1982), and some of the structures in the complex group could in fact be the remains of Medieval farms. However whether this chronological-functional factor is a reality cannot be determined on the basis of the present surveys. On the other hand it is highly unlikely that the ruins on the southern side of Borðoyavík were proper farms because of their aberrant location in relation to the known early settlements on this part of Borðoy and because of the bad harbour conditions here.

Until further surveys and excavations can determine the extent to which the use of *ærgir* was integrated in the Faroese Viking-Age economy, any speculation is limited by the sparse factual archaeological evidence. However our present knowledge points to the likelihood of a certain level of integration giving rise to the following model based on the two main themes of diffusion and adaption: During the expansion period, the Norse agrarian economy was based where necessary and possible, on a dualistic resource exploitation centered on the main farm/shieling system. The decentralised farming economy was as much part and parcel of the luggage brought by the Norse to their new homes, as their distinctive material and building traditions.

However the decentralised farming system was not just directly transposed to the new homelands, but was itself subject to adaption. Three major factors are relevant here: the local topography in question, indigeneous cultural influences and the internal development of the economy of which the system itself was a part. The local response to different kind of stress and economic/ecological pressure determined whether the decentralised farming economy could survive – which it clearly could not for long on the Faroe Islands (compare Hastrup 1989).

The historically known Faroese agrarian strategy can be briefly described as the infield-outfield system (Thorsteinsson 1981b) – the infield being intensively cultivated, while the outfield, also in extensive use, was mainly grazed by sheep. As mentioned in the beginning, a shieling economy cannot exist in the same areas used for extensive sheep grazing, unless the animals are strictly herded all the time.

The first Medieval lawcode, concerning the Faroe Islands alone, is the Seyðabrevið dictated in 1298 (Matras 1971). This code reflects the historically known system, and dwells mainly on the establishment of property rights in outfields (number of sheep, etc.) shared by two or more owners.

According to the Seyðabrevið and available archaeological evidence, then, the *ærgi* economy must have been superseded by the historically known infield/outfield system by the 12th or 13th century. It is therefore suggested as a model, that the two systems exclude one another chronologically, and I will postulate that the two systems seem topographically incompatible, too.

Notes

1. This paper was presented in a modified version at The 11th Viking Conference August 1989. Support from Knud Højgaards Fond and the Faroese Government made it possible for me to participate, for which I am very grateful. The paper has been translated by Susan Dall Mahler.
2. Fundings from the Faroese Vísindagrunnur gave me the opportunity to visit the Isle of Man. I am very grateful to Dr G. Quine for showing me some of the sites during my short stay on the island.
3. See also Gillian Quine: 'The use of the Uplands in the Norse Period in Man and the Isles' (Handout), 11th Viking Congress, Caithness-Orkney, 1989.
4. The author was responsible for the excavations, which lasted more than 12 months in all. The expenses were covered by the electricity company for Streymoy-Eysturoy-Vágar (S.E.V). Over 30 scholars and students participated in the excavations and related activities during the period and I am grateful for the overall enthusiasm shown by everyone connected with the project.
5. Dr Scient J. Jóhansen has analysed the pollen series from Argisbrekka, and I am grateful for the information gained hereby.
6. All sites have been surveyed by the author besides M2204 and 05, which have been surveyed by Anders Horsbøl Nielsen.
7. Nesvík was surveyed and registered by S. V.Arge, 1985, and I am grateful to S. Arge for letting me use the material.

REFERENCES

Albretchsen, Svend Erik & Christian Keller 1986. 'The use of the "saeter" in Medieval Norse Farming in Greenland', *Arctic Anthropology* vol. 22, no. 2, 1985, Wisconsin.

Arge, Símun Vilhelm 1989. 'Om landnammet på Færøerne', *Hikuin* 15, eds Christensen, K.-M. B. & Vilhjálmsson, V. O., Højbjerg, pp. 103–28.

Bakka, Egil 1965. 'Ytre Moa, Eit gardsanlegg frå Vikingetida i Årdal Sogn', *Viking* XXIX, Oslo, 121–45.

Bjørgo, Tore 1982. 'Oppsiktsvekkende arkeologiske funn i Nyset-Steggjevassdraget', *Verksposten* 1982:2, Oslo, 18–21.

—— 1986. 'Mountain Archaeology', *Norwegian Archaeological Review* vol. 19, no. 2, 122–7.

Borchgrevink, Anne-Berit Ø. 1977. 'The "seter"-Areas of Rural Norway, a Traditional Multipurpose Resource', *Northern Studies*, 1977:9, Edinburgh, 3–24.

Bruun, Daniel 1929. *Fra de Færøske Bygder. Samlede afhandlinger om gammeldags sæd og skik*, København.

Dahl, Sverri 1951. 'Fornar Toftir í Kvívík', *Varðin* vol. 29, 65–96, Tórshavn.

—— 1970a. 'Um ærgistaðir og ærgitoftir', *Fróðskaparrit* vol. 18, 361–8, Tórshavn.

—— 1970b. 'The Norse settlement of the Faroe Islands', *Medieval Archaeology* vol. XIV, 60–73, London.

—— 1971. 'Recent Excavations on Viking Sites in the Faroes', *Proceedings of the Sixth Viking Congress*, Uppsala 3–10 August, Bonäs, Dalarnar 10–12 August 1969, The Viking Society for Northern Research, 45–56, London.

Fellows Jensen, Gillian 1978. 'The Manx Place-Name Debate: A View from Copenhagen', in *Man and Environment in the Isle of Man*, Part ii., ed. Davey, P., British Archaeological Reports, no. 54, 315–25.

—— 1980. 'Common Gaelic Áirge, Old Scandinavian *Ærgi* or *Erg?*' *Nomina* vol. 4, 67–73.

—— 1983. 'Scandinavian settlement in the Isle of Man and Northwest England: The placename evidence', in *The Viking Age in the Isle of Man. Select papers from the Ninth Viking Congress*, eds Fell, C., Foote, P., Graham-Campbell, J. & Thomson, R., Isle of Man, 4–14 July 1981. University College London, 37–52.

Fenton, Alexander 1976. *Scottish Country Life*, Edinburgh 1977, 2nd. edn.

Gelling, Peter S. 1958. 'Recent Excavations of Norse Houses in the Isle of Man', *The Journal of The Manx Museum*, vol. VI, nr. 75, 54–6.

—— 1961. 'Shielings in the Isle of Man', *The Journal of the Manx Museum*, vol. VI, nr. 77, 1960–1, 123–6.

—— 1964. 'Medieval Shielings in the Isle of Man', *Medieval Archaeology* vol. 6–7, 1962–3, London, 156–72.

—— 1964. 'The Braaid Site', *The Journal of the Manx Museum*, vol. VI, nr. 80, 200–5.

Hansen, L. Símun. 1981. *Tey Byggja Land* 7, Partur. Klaksvík sókn, Klaksvík, 1981.

Hansen, Steffen S. 1987. 'Toftanes. Nýggj tíðindi frá útgrevsterinum', *Mondul* 1987 vol. 1, Tórshavn 1987, 4–6 & 24–6.

—— 1989. 'Toftanes – en færøsk landnamsgård fra 9–10. århundrede'. *Hikuin* vol 15. K.-M. B. Christensen & V. Ö. Vilhjálmsson (eds) Højbjerg 1989, 129–46.

Hastrup, Kirsten 1989. 'Saeters in Iceland 900–1600. An Anthropological analysis of economy and cosmology?' *Acta Borealia* 1–1989, Båstad, 72–85.

Higham, Mary C. 1978. 'The "Erg" Place-names of Northern England', in *Man and Environment in the Isle of Man*, Part ii., ed. Davey, P., British Archaeological Reports, no. 54, 1978, 347–55.

Hitzler, Egon 1979. *Sel-Untersuchungen zur Geschichte des isländischen Sennwesens seit der Landnahmezeit*. Institut for Sammenlignende Kulturforskning, Skrifter 60, serie B. Oslo.

Joensen, Robert 1962. 'Kvíingadalur', *14 September*, lørdag d. 2. juni 1962, no. 39, Tórshavn, 4–5.

Jóhansen, Jóhannes 1985. *Studies in the vegetational history of the Faroe and Shetland Islands*, Annales Societatis Scientarum Færoensis Supplementum, XI, Tórshavn.

Keller, Christian 1983. 'Gård og seter på Grønland – et forsøk på å analysere ressurstilgangen i middelalderen ved hjælp af satelitbilder', *Hus, Gård og Bebyggelse. Föredrag från det XVI nordiska arkeologmöte, Island 1982*, Guðmundur Ólafsson, Reykjavík, 59–66.

Lillehammer, Arnvid 1971. 'Ytre Moa i Årdal. Ein mangbølt gard frå Vikingetida', *Arkeo* nr. 1, 20–1, Hist. Museum Bergen.

Larsen, Ann-Christine & Hansen, Steffen S. 1984. 'Toftanes', *Mondul* 1984 no. 1, ed. Jákupsson, B., Tórshavn, 3–10.

Macsween, Malcolm D. 1959. 'Transhumance in North Skye', *Scottish Geographical Magazine* 75, 75–88.

Macsween, Malcolm D. & Gailey, Alan 1961. 'Some shielings in North Skye', *Scottish Geographical Magazine* 5, 77–84.

Magnus, Bente 1983. 'Seterdrift i Vest-Norge i yngre jernalder? En foreløpig rapport om en undersøkelse', *Hus Gård og Bebyggelse. XVI nordiske arkeologmötet, Island 1982*. Reykjavík, 93–103.

—— 1986. 'Iron Age Exploitation of High Mountain Resources in Sogn'. *Norwegian Archaeological Review*, vol. 19, no. 1. 44–50.

Mahler, Ditlev 1986a. 'Hvatt eit rekapetti eisini kan brúkast til'. *Mondul* no. 1. B. Jákupsson (ed.) Tórshavn, 12–27.

—— 1986b. 'Ærgid undir brekkuni'. *Mondul* 1986 no. 3. ed. B. Jákupsson, Tórshavn, 6–17.

—— 1989. Argisbrekka: Nye spor efter sæterdrift på Færøerne'. *Hikuin* vol. 15. V. Vilhjálmsson & K.-M. B. Christensen (eds.) 147–70.

—— 1991. 'Argisbrekka: New Evidence of Shielings in the Faroe Islands'. *The Norse of the North Atlantic*, ed. Bigelow, G. F., *Acta Archaeologica* 61, 60–72.

Mahler, Ditlev & Malmros, Claus 1990. 'Nýtt tilfar um ærgið undir Argisbrekku'. *Mondul* 1990, vol 2. B. Jákúpsson (ed.) Tórshavn, 10–32.

Matras, Christian 1933. 'Stednavne Paa De Færøske Norduroyar. *Aarbøger for Nordisk Oldkyndighed og Historie*, 1932. Kjøbenhavn.

—— 1956. 'Gammelfärøsk ærgi, n., og dermed beslægtede ord'. *Namn och Bygd*. Årg. 44, Hæfte 1–4. 51–67.

—— 1971. *Seyðabrævið*. With J. H. W. Poulsen & U. Zachariasen. Fróðskaparrit Føroya, Gøtu.

Megaw, Eleanor 1978. 'The Manx "Eary" and its Signifiance'. *Man and Environment in the Isle of Man*. Part ii. P. Davey (ed.) British Archaeological Reports, no. 54, 1978. 327–46.

Myhre, Bjørn 1980. *Gårdsanlegget på Ullandhaug I*. Arkeologiske Museum i Stavanger, Skrifter vol. 4, Stavanger.

Pearsall, W. H. 1961. 'Place-names as clues in the pursuit of ecological history'. *Namn och Bygd*, 72–89.

Reinton, Lars 1969. *Til Seters. Norsk seterbruk og seterstell*, Oslo.

Sveinbjarnardóttir, Guðrun 1989 'Tolkningsproblemer i forbindelse med ødebebyggelse i Austurdalur i Skagafjørður i Island'. *Hikuin* 15. Karen M. B. Christensen & V. Ö. Vilhjálmsson (eds) Højbjerg, 59–74.

—— 1991 'Shielings in Iceland – An Archeological and Historical Survey'. *The Norse in the North Atlantic*, ed. Bigelow, G. F., *Acta Archaeologica* 61, 73–96.

Thomson, William P. L. 1987. *History of Orkney*, Edinburgh.

Thorsteinsson, Arne 1981a. 'On the Development of Faroese Settlements'. *Proceedings of the Eighth Viking Congress 1977*. Hans Bekker-Nielsen, Peter Foote & Olaf Olsen (eds) Odense, 189–202.

—— 1981b. 'Jordforholdene i det gamle landbrugssamfund'. *Landinspektøren* vol. 30, hæfte 10, 90. årgang. 664–78.

—— 1982. 'Færøske huskonstruktioner fra vikingetid til 1800–årene. AmS-Skrifter 7'. *Vestnordisk byggeskik gjennom tusen år*. B. Myhre, B. Stoklund, P. Gjærder (eds) Stavanger, 149–61.

33

AN INSECT'S EYE-VIEW OF
THE NORSE FARM

PAUL C. BUCKLAND   JON P. SADLER   DAVID N. SMITH

INTRODUCTION

History rarely concerns itself with the details of everyday life (Fig. 33.1) and, whilst much can be gained from the careful analysis of near contemporary sources (cf. Foote & Wilson 1970), many problems of interpretation remain. Archaeology has added to the picture derived from documentary sources and its use in combination with regional ethnographic parallels, pioneered in the work of Roussell (1934; 1941; 1943a & b) in Iceland and Greenland, has fleshed out the bare bones of history and saga. There remains, however, a further layer, covering many aspects of human subsistence, which the conventional techniques of archaeology are unable to solve. The form, function and environmental conditions within a settlement and the nature of its catchment are areas where archaeological and historical sources remain, at best, ambivalent. The contrasting reconstructions from the description of the burning of Flugumýri in 1253 in *Sturlunga saga* provides a pertinent example (Guðmundsson 1889; Roussell 1941).

A refinement of the approach to archaeological excavation, involving the recovery of invertebrate remains from suitable sediments, provides an additional means of addressing such problems. Research upon fossil insect faunas has been carried out on Norse and later sites in Greenland, Iceland, Faroe, Norway and the British Isles and ranges from the urban centres of Oslo (Griffin *et al.* 1988), York (Hall *et al.* 1983) and Dublin (Coope 1981) to the farms and shielings of Iceland (Sveinbjarnardóttir 1983) and Greenland (McGovern *et al.* 1983). Many insects have very particular habitat requirements and exploit materials and conditions indicative of human and domestic animal living conditions. Some species, like the lice, are host-specific, whilst others only survive in the North in the artificially cushioned habitats created by humans. The presence of these species in archaeological sediments can reveal much about the provenance of the material, its mode of formation and the conditions under which it was deposited.

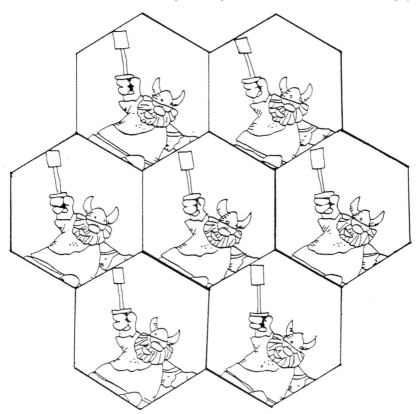

Figure 33.1: An insect's eye-view of the Norse farm. The essential artefactual evidence, the fly-swat, has yet to be recognised in the archaeological record. (For the 'un-natural historians', most insects have compound eyes with multiple lenses, each seeing an image, which is integrated by the central nervous system) (Drawing: R. J. Buckland).

THE NORSE FARM

The abandoned remains of isolated farm complexes that formed the cornerstone of the Norse subsistence economy, have long attracted the interest of archaeologists and historians and there has been much debate over the interpretation of plans. Early work in Iceland and Greenland, in particular the excellent survey work of Daniel Bruun (cf. 1898; 1917), was characterised by site survey and limited excavation and offered little in the way of interpretation. Excavations in both the Western (Roussell 1936; 1941) and Eastern (Nørlund & Roussell 1929) Settlements of Greenland produced data facilitating a better understanding of the Norse farm, indicating a rural economy based primarily upon the rearing of domestic animals and the utilisation of local resources. This research was followed by one of the first multidisciplinary research projects, the

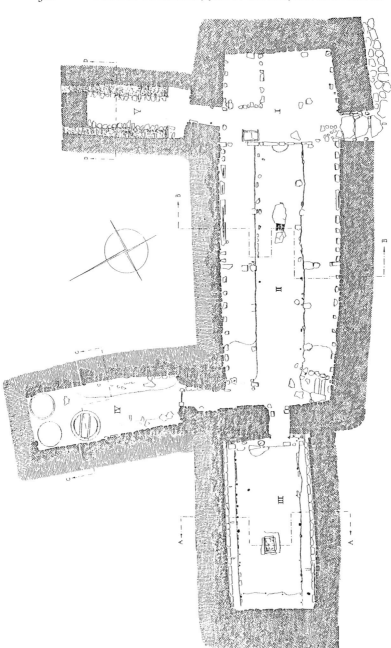

Figure 22.2. Plan of the farm house at Stöng in Þjórsárdalur, Iceland, reproduced from Stenberger 1943, Fig. 28.

joint Scandinavian expedition to Þjórsárdalur, Iceland (Stenberger 1943), where farms were preserved beneath the tephra of the 1104 eruption of Hekla (Þórarinsson 1967, 50–2; see, however, Vilhjálmsson 1989). Aage Roussell (1934; 1943b), who initially trained as an architect, applied his expertise to the interpretation of the excavated remains, drawing widely on the regional ethnography, and Nilsson (1943) discussed later Icelandic farm buildings and their usage. Animal bones were studied by Degerbøl (1943) and Steffensen (1943) reported upon the human remains. Subsequent pollen analysis by Þórarinsson (1944) indicated the cultivation of cereals and of two plants with uses in brewing and medicine, bog myrtle, *Myrica gale* and wormwood, *Artemisia* sp. The farmhouse at Stöng, excavated during this project, has become the type specimen for much subsequent discussion of the Norse farm (e.g. Foote & Wilson 1970, 154–7) and a full-scale reconstruction has been built close to the excavated site (Ágústsson 1983). The main structure consists of a hall (skáli), with a central long fire, a living room (stofa), placed in line, and two outshots (Fig. 33.2). One outshot, with stone-lined drains down either side, was interpreted initially as a cold room for the storage of meat over ice (Roussell 1943a, 90) and later, in Eldjárn's (1961, 32–5) study of another Þjórsárdalur farm, Gjáskógar, as a latrine; the other, containing the outlines of three barrels in the floor, was thought to be the dairy (búr) (Roussell 1943a, 87–91). Traces of a white substance in a similar barrel excavated at Bergþórshvöll have been interpreted as the residue of a dairy product, *skýr* (Eldjárn 1952), an interpretation also taken up in Greenland (Vebæk 1958, p.118). In view of its seminal position in the study of the Norse farm, it is unfortunate that the limited re-excavation of Stöng by Vilhjálmur Vilhjálmsson (1989) failed to locate well preserved organic sediments.

Historical and saga sources give some confirmation of archaeological evidence and the hypotheses derived from it. The account of the burning of the Flugumýri farm in 1253 may describe the internal form of the longhouse (Roussell 1943b, 207–9), and a passage in the *Laxdæla saga* gives a brief description of a shieling (sel/sæter) (Magnusson & Pálsson 1969, 185–6). Points of detail, like the occurrence of head lice, find occasional passing mention (Sveinbjarnardóttir & Buckland 1983). The conditions under which individuals and their animals lived in the past are rarely duplicated at the present day and careful use of travellers' accounts of the 18th and 19th centuries (cf. Boucher 1989) serves to remedy at least part of this deficiency. Henderson's description of a turf-built house in Iceland in the early 19th century could equally apply to the excavated evidence from Stöng:

> The walls which may be about four feet in height by six inches in thickness, are composed of alternating layers of earth and stone and incline a little inwards, when they are met with a sloping roof of turf, supported by a few beams which are crossed by twigs and boughs of birch.
>
> (1819, 87)

In the absence of well-preserved organics, it is often difficult to assess levels of hygiene when piecing together the archaeological evidence and, perhaps understandably, it is the niceties of life that tend to dominate site reports. It could be argued that poor preservation leads to the sanitisation of the archaeological record. Documentary records are also rare and, in part, this probably reflects a failure to notice the commonplace. Henderson notes:

> Foreigners always complain of the insupportable stench and filth in Icelandic houses, and, certainly, not without reason; yet I question much if these evils do not exist nearly in the same degree in the Highlands of Scotland, the country hamlets of Ireland, or the common Bauer huts in Germany.
>
> (1819, 88)

Surviving buildings, particularly in Iceland (Nilsson 1943) and the Western Isles (Fenton 1986, 83–95), and recent ethnological sources (e.g. Fenton 1978, 110–205; 1985; 1986; Jónasson 1961), provide valuable data regarding building structure and fabric. This forms an essential part of any attempt to reconstruct the detail of the Norse farm. The paucity of suitable timbers for building is a widespread feature of much of the region colonised by the Norse and it is a factor affecting the types of construction techniques adopted by the settlers. Walls are frequently constructed of interlocking layers of turves, sometimes placed upon stone foundations (Fig. 33.3). The extent of stone versus turf in wall construction varies as to the availability of materials and local building

Figure 33.3: The herring-boned turf walls of the hay store of a sheep house (beitarhús) at Skuggabjörg, NW of Skatastaðir in Austurdalur, Skagafjörður, N. Iceland. Vertical scale: 2 m (Photo: P. C. Buckland, 1982).

Figure 33.4: Roof structure of a sheep house at Kalmanstunga, Hvításíða, W. Iceland. Interleaved turf and stone walls support a roof of unworked birch branches overlain by turves (Photo: P. C. Buckland 1989).

traditions. Roofing materials also vary across the region but turf, sometimes over stone slabs, may be supported by driftwood timbers and birch branches (Fig. 33.4); where resources were sufficient to allow it, the whole may have been capped by a waterproofing layer of thatch (cf. Þórarinsson 1958, 23). In some areas, separate from the dwelling house, byres provided accommodation for at least some of the cattle, horse and sheep and it is these for which recent parallels exist (Fig. 33.5), although surviving examples represent a rapidly diminishing resource. The Stöng example, with an apparent clear separation between human and animal living accommodation, provides the basis for an interpretative account of the input and output of resources, and their residues, to a farm.

Palaeoecology and the Norse Farm

The dynamic elements of the farm community, including the movement of materials in and out of the complex, can be represented by a flow diagram (Fig. 33.6). The materials selected have distinct faunas of parasites, beetles (Coleoptera) and flies (Diptera) and are, therefore, 'visible', if not easily interpreted in the palaeoecological record. Driftwood, local timber, and materials such as seaweed, hay, dung, moss, peat, grain and other food stuffs may be introduced into the farm for a variety of purposes (Table 33.1). The nature of the settlement may dictate variations in this pattern, allowing distinction to be made between, for example, farm and shieling (Buckland & Sadler, 1991).

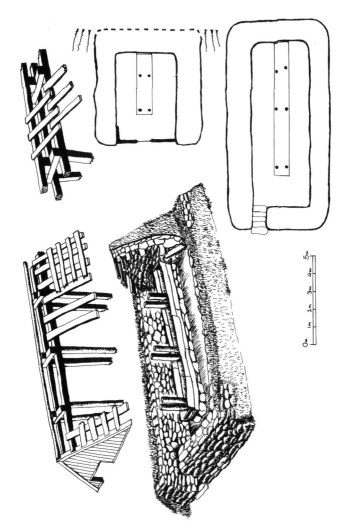

Figure 33.5: Sheep houses at Seljaland, Eyjafjallasveit, S. Iceland. The walls are of interleaved turf and stone and roof of driftwood spars, overlain by irregular, unsecured stone slabs, capped with turf. The central feeding trough rests on a drystone base and supports driftwood roof supports (Drawing: T. Addyman, 1983).

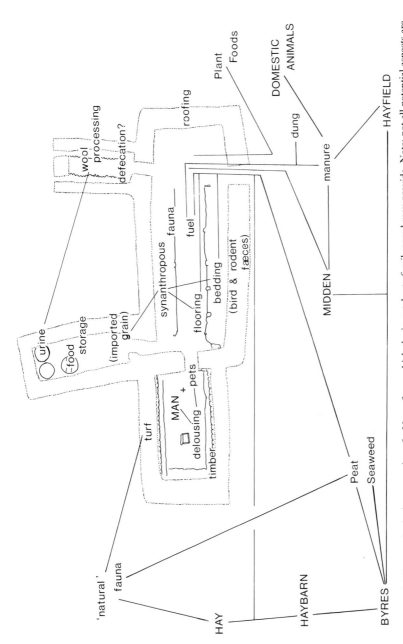

Figure 33.6: Elements in the interpretation of a Norse farm, which the invertebrate fossil record may provide. Note: not all potential aspects are included.

Table 33.1. Resource utilisation and ethnographic information.

Resource	Region	Usage	References
Peat	UK, Ireland, Orkney, Shetland, Western Isles	Fuel, fertiliser, litter	Evans (1957), Fenton (1978; 1986, 105–132)
Seaweed	Greenland, Iceland, Orkney, Shetland, Ireland, UK	Fodder, food, fuel, bedding, manure	Evans (1957), Fenton (1978; 1986, 48–92), Henderson (1819, 88), Kampp (1964, 68–72), Kristjánsson (1980, 105)
Dung	Denmark, UK, Western Isles, Shetland, Orkney, Ireland	Fuel, manure	Fenton (1985, 96–111), Knox (1985, 160), O'Danachair (1968, 117–20)
Hay	Orkney, Shetland, Greenland, Iceland, Western Isles	Fodder, flooring, bedding, fuel	Fenton (1985, 100–101)
Turf	Orkney, Ireland, Greenland, Iceland, Western Isles	Building material, fuel, manure	Evans (1957), Fenton (1978; 1986, 105–132), Roussell (1934)
Moss		Bedding, toilet paper	Seaward & Williams (1976)

Materials moving out of the farm mainly consist of waste material (*ejecta*), which is either thrown on to the midden, or used as manure to fertilise the homefield.

Limitations of the Data

Limitations on interpretation are considerable and the evidence pertaining to a Norse farm here adduced represents a best-fit scenario based on the results of previous and on-going studies. In general, suitable preservation of invertebrate remains is largely restricted to sites where waterlogging or permafrost has inhibited decay. It could be argued that the preservational bias towards waterlogged sites provides an inadequate sampling framework. Where suitable sites or their middens have been examined, however, a consistent picture of the nature of farm life has emerged which is apparently common across the entire social spectrum. Problems of differential preservation and mixing of material and faunas during deposition, fossilisation and sampling further complicate matters. For example, the fabric of the farm will have a fauna introduced along with the materials used in its construction and there are also major contributions of insect fragments casually introduced in bird, amphibian and small mammal faeces (cf. Kenward 1975). These faunal elements must be teased apart from other insect assemblages introduced in to the farm with resources such as peat and hay.

The Structures

Even in the 'over-hygienic' society of the late 20th century, a cursory examination of any building, either for storage or occupation, will reveal several *in situ* communities of insects which are exploiting various microhabitats provided by the structure and the materials used in construction. The importance of these faunas for the reconstruction of past human environments should be stressed since they represent the baseline from which any interpretative account of the past can be built. The biogeography of species introductions and native taxa inevitably leads to variations across the Norse world (Buckland 1988; Sadler, 1991), but the synanthropic elements in assemblages are surprisingly consistent from Dublin to York, from Orkney to Iceland and on to Greenland.

The fauna of decaying structural timbers, wickerwork and other small woodwork, inherited from natural forest during prehistory (cf. Buckland 1975), is widespread in the urban environments of Viking Dublin (Coope 1981) and York (Hall *et al.* 1983), but work upon rural sites has so far been restricted to relatively treeless areas where timber was at a premium and the wood fauna absent. The absence of woodworm, the furniture beetle, *Anobium punctatum*, from the numerous samples examined from Iceland suggests that its presence in medieval woodwork preserved in the National Museum collections in Iceland provides a clear indication of import of pieces of timber already infested. Elsewhere where timber is preserved, the large burrows, often with a calcareous lining surviving, of the various species of shipworm provide evidence of the use of driftwood. Eventually, the insect fauna of timber from the New World may identify imports from Markland to Greenland.

Studies on farms in the Outer Hebrides, with architectural antecedents that have been traced to Norse longhouses (Roussell 1934, but cf. Fenton 1985, 83–95), indicate that certain building materials appear to have distinct faunas of Coleoptera (Smith 1988). In particular, straw thatch contains a group of species, in which *Mycetaea hirta*, a species associated with moulds, is a common inhabitant. The turf layers of roofs and walls appear to contain a relatively high proportion of species associated with the open peatland vegetation from which they were derived. Comparable faunas have been recorded in straw and turf roofing materials from a barn at Pow Bank in Cumbria (Hall *et al.* 1983) and in the surviving turves of walls at the Norse and post-medieval farms at Bessastaðir and Reykholt in southern Iceland.

The House Interior

The preservation *in situ* of floor deposits in Iceland and Greenland within farms offers a rare opportunity to investigate aspects such as the function and interior environment of the buildings. Most samples are time averaged, but, occasionally, a particular activity may be recognised. Human lice, *Pediculus humanus* and *P. capitis*, are extremely common in Norse deposits where preservation conditions admit of their identification. The recovery of nearly 100 individuals in one sample from Reykholt, Iceland, is atypical and probably reflects a single event of delousing, a common practice in many human societies (Busvine 1976, 67–85). Familiarity with the louse is demonstrated by several near contemporary references. One is reminded of the fate of Stigandi in *Laxdæla saga*, betrayed by his bondswomen's offer to delouse his hair (Magnusson & Pálsson 1969, 137). Ectoparasites are no respecters of station, occurring from the smallest Greenland farms, such as Niaqussat (V48) in the Western Settlement (Sadler 1990), to the Danish Governor's residence at Bessastaðir in Iceland (Amorosi *et al.* 1992), and Earl Thorfinn's farm in Orkney (Sadler 1989). The two species of louse are particularly difficult to separate, but the body louse, *Pediculus humanus*, was recovered from the church farm site at Sandnæs (V51-Kilaersarvik) in Greenland (Sveinbjarnardóttir & Buckland 1983). The human flea, *Pulex irritans*, probably Europe's first gift from the Americas, appears in Norse Greenland, Orkney (Sadler 1989), Dublin (Rothschild 1975) and York (Hall *et al.* 1983), but arrived in Europe much earlier than the Vikings. It seems likely that Beringia and Asia provided the route, and the largescale movement of animal pelts in the Siberian fur trade the species' means of dispersal from America (Buckland & Sadler 1989).

The presence of human ectoparasites in Norse cultural deposits is not that surprising, but it is important to note that the Norse migrations involved the export of not only people but also a means of subsistence and the biota inevitably associated with it. The sheep ked, *Melophagus ovinus*, a wingless parasitic fly, and the sheep louse, *Damalinia ovis*, appear in the earliest deposits in Greenland and Iceland and have also been recorded in contemporary Coppergate, York (Hall & Kenward 1990, 349). In the absence of bones, such as in the acidic sediments of the post-medieval house excavated by Guðrún Sveinbjarnardóttir at Reykholt, Iceland, their presence may be used to prove what in that particular case is the obvious, that sheep husbandry was practised (Buckland *et al.* 1992). As an initial interpretational hypothesis, it might be expected that high ectoparasite frequency in samples would indicate sheep houses, but several factors militate against this. The intimate association between host and parasite means that casual losses from free-ranging and stalled animals are very low and the probability of appearance in samples is therefore equally low. The ked puparia, like the eggs (nits) of lice, are glued to the wool and the adults of both tend to remain on the fleece, or move to a position where they can acquire a new host after the death of the former one. Their presence is therefore more likely associated with shed fleeces and wool processing than directly with the animals. Large numbers of ked and lice in a sample from a late medieval drain at Stóraborg, Iceland, can be explained in terms of a process involving the use of stale urine as a cleansing agent for wool. The disposal of the spent liquid after use would lead to a concentration of parasites (Buckland & Perry 1989). This piece of interpretation has an interesting feedback into site interpretation since the use of urine necessitates receptacles for long-term storage. The barrels in the outshot at Stöng (Fig. 33.2) need not have been solely for the storage of milk products (*contra* Roussell 1943a, 87–91), but urine, and the white residue found in the barrels may be a result of the precipitation of salts. In view of this, it is possible to reconsider the apparently contradictory evidence from Nipaitsoq (V54), in the former Western Settlement of Greenland, where the palaeoecological evidence suggests foul conditions in the farm's putative larder. Analysis of this residue, however, indicates that this at least is not from urine (Arneborg, personal communication). Modern sensitivities should not preclude the proximity of functions in the past now regarded as insanitary, such as the storage of urine and food in the same room; it is less than a century since Yorkshire women used the chamber pot contents to wash their face and hair (Stead 1981; 1982). The outshot interpreted by Eldjárn (1947) as a latrine at Stöng has, despite his several parallels, a number of problems. There is no apparent facility for flushing out the channels constructed along opposing walls and, in the subsistence-based economy of a remote farm, it is tempting to suggest that the structure may have had some function related to the processing of materials. Discussion with Vilhjálmur Vilhjálmsson and Elsa Guðjónsson in the National Museum of Iceland has raised the possibilities that either dyeing or fulling of woollen cloth might be involved; only adequate environmental samples can answer the question.

The presence of ectoparasites has been taken as an indicator of low levels of hygiene and further species of insects, particularly the Diptera (true flies), recovered from the same deposits, tend to reinforce this assertion. Hamilton (1956, 97) suggests that the Viking floors (areas of minimal growth) at Jarlshof, Shetland, were kept relatively clean and that the majority of material would accumulate in pits and middens (areas of maximum growth), or be spread over the farmyard, if not used as manure. In the better preserved floor layers from Viking York (Hall *et al.* 1983), Dublin (Coope 1981), Oslo (Kenward 1980) and a number of Icelandic and Greenland sites (Buckland *et al.* 1983; McGovern *et al.* 1983; Perry *et al.* 1985), palaeoecological investigations have shown that such floors were frequently covered with a mass of decomposing and fermenting vegetation, carrion and faecal matter and other detritus of life, thereby providing habitats for a wide range of invertebrates.

The fly, *Heleomyza serrata*, occurs in some abundance at several farms in Iceland. It commonly breeds in accumulations of human faeces and is characteristic of localities where hygiene is lacking. At Nipaitsoq (site V54) in Greenland, where cold winters might have precluded a visit to the midden, occurrence of fly puparia shows a trail of faecal material through all rooms of the small centralised farm (Buckland *et al.* 1983). One element in the insect faunas is associated with decomposing vegetation, primarily hay, utilised for a variety of purposes (Table 33.1). It was not only used as fodder but as flooring material, where the sweet smell of its decomposition would mask the stench of other decaying organics. The recognition of the hay fauna also provides a potential means of discrimination between a farm and a shieling, where the winter storage of hay is likely to have been insufficient to maintain synanthropic insect communities (Buckland & Sadler, 1991).

Peat formed a major element of resource in both urban (Hall & Kenward 1990, 413–14) and rural contexts and the scale of its past exploitation is frequently forgotten. Both York and Hull took large quantities of turves from Thorne Moors, some 35 km from each, during the medieval period and, between 1316 and 1326, Norwich Cathedral's chamberlain was buying half a million turves annually (Beresford 1986, 154). This raises a serious potential problem in palaeoecological reconstruction, first noted by Hall *et al.* (1980, 128) in their study of a Roman well in Skeldergate, York. The frequent occurrence of assemblages of acidophile insects, which are associated with moorlands and raised mires, in a wide range of archaeological deposits, indicates that peat was not only used as fuel. Turf-Einar is credited with introducing peat cutting for fuel to the Northern Isles (*Orkneyinga saga*, ch. 7; Pálsson & Edwards 1978), and direct archaeological evidence of its extraction has been noted at Ketilsstaðir in Iceland, where the *c.*1357 Katla ash infills cuttings (Buckland *et al.* 1986). It is apparent that peat often supplemented hay on the floors in both human and animal habitation. Within recent memory, the Yorkshire Moss Litter Company sent peat from Thorne Moors in South Yorkshire to London, and even Eire, to be used as stable litter for horses (Limbert 1986; R. W. Buckland, personal communication), and similar uses were once widespread. The fossil faunas associated with any peat have to be carefully considered in site interpretation. Rarely are they distinguishable from contemporary structural turf and, on rural sites, the fauna of the unimproved hayfield is likely to differ little from that of the growing peat surface. The presence of larval water beetles and caddis-fly larvae are useful indicators of peat in anthropogenic deposits but the occurrence of the already fossil fauna from the peat may restrict the analysis of the remainder of any fauna.

In Greenland, Roussell (1936, 45; 1941, 24 & 173) had suggested that layers of twigs and wood chip in middens and floors of farms in the former Western Settlement are roofing or flooring material. The presence of a suite of synanthropic insects, that could not survive long outdoors, indicate that the material initially accumulated indoors (Sadler 1988). Several benefits would accrue from the spreading of twigs and other vegetation on the floor of the house. The mix of hay, moss, peat, twigs and wood chip would have been absorbent and Coope (1981) has suggested that such an apparently fortuitous accumulation might have been deliberate since the decomposition of the material would have provided an additional source of warmth. The Western Settlement farms lie directly over permafrost and it would have been essential to insulate against it, or floors would quickly become quagmires. The latter might seem a specific adaptation to life in the arctic but similar deposits appear in the earliest levels beneath Reykjavík (Ólafsson, personal communication) and have been noted in farm mounds in Norway, where they are interpreted as evidence of birch and willow foddering (Griffen 1985).

In the harsh environment of the North, survival of essential stock through the winter necessitated the collection of sufficient hay for animal feed and it is the insect fauna associated with this winter storage which dominates the assemblages from most rural sites. Hay also provided bedding, flooring materials and insulation, as well as fodder, and its fauna alone does not separate human from animal dwellings. Storage in large amounts, however, either in ricks or barns, provides a particularly warm habitat; as fungal decay sets in, insect faunas become dominated by the rapidly breeding feeders upon fungal hyphae and their predators. At Reykholt, where the main post-medieval dwelling house has been excavated, there are clear differences in the faunas from house floors. The identification of human from animal house is based not only on the presence of suitable ectoparasites but also upon a range of breeding flies, represented by their puparia in the floor deposits and a high frequency of beetles, particularly the spider beetle, *Tipnus unicolor*, associated with slightly drier, less foul conditions. Combined with the other lines of evidence, it is often possible to take the evidence further and suggest putative uses for particular rooms (cf. Buckland *et al.* 1983).

Farms close to the sea were able to utilise marine and littoral resources as well as those of their terrestrial hinterland, although the failure to exploit effectively the fish, whale and seal resources in Greenland is particularly noteworthy; the many hundred kilograms of samples processed from the Sandnæs midden failed to produce sufficient fish-bone to fill a guillemot's gullet, a contrast with contemporary Icelandic deposits. Further evidence suggests that sealing might have been restricted to certain areas. The penis bone of the seal is removed when an animal is gutted (Coope, personal communication) and these bones are absent from Greenlandic farms, indicating that the animals were taken and gutted on the pupping grounds. There is similarly an absence of specialised equipment for these activities in the archaeological record from the farms (McGovern 1981). Littoral resources, however, were employed throughout the North Atlantic. Some of the flies and beetles from Bessastaðir, Iceland, indicate the utilisation of seaweed, and a similar indication is provided by the fragments of a small colonial marine Hydrozoan, *Dynamaena pumila*, present from all the sites investigated so far in Greenland. Dehydrated seaweed is used as fodder for sheep in Greenland (Kampp 1964) and in post-medieval Iceland it was used for food, animal fodder, fuel and bedding (Henderson 1819; Kristjánsson 1980). Similar usages have been noted on the Hebrides, Orkney, Shetland and in Ireland (Evans 1957; Fenton 1978, 274; Table 33.1), although there it was primarily used for the production of manure.

Aside from faunas associated with local resources, other more transient imports are evident. At medieval Bessastaðir, the saw-toothed grain beetle, *Oryzaephilus surinamensis*, and the grain weevil, *Sitophilus granarius*, occur in all samples examined from the midden, indicating the presence of grain, although it is probable that the fossils arrived on the midden through the intermediary of human faeces (cf. Osborne 1983). It is doubtful whether the minimum temperature requirements for maintaining breeding populations of these species were ever attained in the small stores of grain in Icelandic medieval farms, and frequent importation with meal or cereals from the Continent seems probable. At the three other Icelandic farms examined, grain pests only occur in occasional samples, perhaps an indication of the primal status of Bessastaðir, a point further emphasised by the recovery of two grape pips. Remains of barley from Bergþórshvóll (Fridriksson 1960) and Gröf in Öræfi (Fridriksson 1959) may belong to locally grown cereals. Although a passage in *Eirik's saga* refers to the import of grain, malt and flour to Greenland (Magnusson & Pálsson 1965, 92), the grain fauna is absent from the several sites investigated in the Western Settlement, including the high status farm at Sandnæs (V51). This might be attributable to the infrequency of direct contacts with the European mainland, or simply sampling problems. A fragment of a hazel nut shell recovered from deposits adjacent to Erik's farm at Brattahlíð in the Eastern Settlement of Greenland is evidence of other food imports (Fredskild 1978, 9). The depauperate nature of island faunas allows imports to be recognised more readily and suitable mechanisms for their arrival considered. Reykholt provides an interesting example. Iceland lacks ants and yet two specimens were recovered from post-medieval deposits on the house floor. One species, *Hypoponera punctatissima*, is essentially a warm temperate species and probably a recent introduction to northern Europe (Buckland, 1976, 20). It seems probable that it had been introduced in straw packing around commodities and it is tempting to relate its occurrence to the import of a luxury item, perhaps fortified wine or spirits, on the return voyage from the stockfish trade with Iberia, a successor to the medieval trade (Carus-Wilson 1967, 122).

The Animal House

Animal houses, when mucked out on a regular basis, offer a variety of microhabitats for a range of insect species, although there has been little detailed research which might be applied to archaeological interpretation. Dugmore (1981; Buckland, Dugmore & Sadler 1991), working in Iceland, however, has carried out some detailed studies of barns and byres. Once the fauna associated with the building materials and the insects which are purely adventitious are removed, the predominant assemblages are the stored hay element and a group of insects found in animal manure and dung. When dealing with archaeological deposits, the situation is complicated by the introduction of fossils with peat used for litter. A suitable starting point may be to examine remains of ectoparasites which can be used to show what stock were housed in the structure, although only those of sheep have so far been noted and not in byres. It is also possible that the fly puparia may be used to differentiate which species of animal were stalled (Skidmore 1985; 1990). At the Norse and medieval site at Tuquoy on Westray, Orkney, a substantial amount of material from a ditch seems to have been waste from an animal house. The sheep ked and louse attest the presence of their host but unfortunately there was insufficient evidence to suggest what other animals were stalled. Faunas associated with peat and stored hay also occur and indicate the use of peat as litter and hay as bedding and fodder (Sadler 1989).

Recent ecological work indicates that this simple pattern may be more complex. The practice of deep littering, where large beds of straw and hay are allowed to build up over winter and only mucked out in early summer, poses some problems. A deep litter bed was examined over the winter of 1989 at Conisbrough Park Farm in South Yorkshire and few insect species were active. The bed was found to contain fragmented remains of mould-feeding species associated with the nearby hay stores (Smith, unpublished). Under such circumstances, the pooling of ammoniacal materials probably restricts the development of faunas associated with decaying vegetation and animal waste products. Although this evidence serves as a caution, it need not be applicable to all situations in the past. On the present evidence, it would seem, for example, that the animal house at Tuquoy was regularly mucked out.

The Midden

It has long been recognised that middens, rather than merely being structureless features, offer a great source of archaeological information (Simonsen 1954). Studies have shown that middens vary in both age and structure and consist mostly of occupational debris and the remains of buildings (Bertelsen 1979; Davidson *et al.* 1983; Holm-Olsen 1981). Hypotheses concerning the cause, mode and rates of accumulation have implicated economic factors such as the number of cattle (Bertelsen 1984) or a change in the subsistence base from farming to stockfishing (Stamsø Munch 1966), but the key area involves the factors which cause a surplus of waste material over that required for manuring. A number of species of insect, able to withstand the outdoor winter climate, partly buffered by the heat of decay in the midden, were widely introduced in the dunnage and ballast of ships around the Norse Atlantic (Sadler 1991) and there is the potential of using these, with the household's uninvited guests as a tracer upon the origins of colonists. Several of the introduced insects rapidly become widespread in the new environments created around the farms and are as clear an indication of Landnám as is possible to obtain. The presence of the dung beetle, *Aphodius lapponum*, in sediments, apparently belonging to the earliest phase of settlement in the Faroe Islands has been used to argue a northern, rather than Irish origin for these colonists (Buckland 1992).

The contents of a midden reflect a dynamic relationship between natural and man-made habitats and provide the evidence for the transition from farm to hayfield and beyond. Entomological studies from the Western Settlement of Greenland at Niaqussat (V48) and Sandnæs (V51) show that there is a certain unsavoury continuity of insect faunas from living floors inside and refuse heaps outside Norse farms in Greenland (Sadler 1988). The discontinous layers and lenses of twigs, characteristic of these middens are interspersed with layers of turf. The former probably represent clearings from the house floor, and it seems that the major phases of deposition occurred intermittently, when the gap between floor accumulation and roof became too slight. The turf layers have faunas with very few synanthropic species and probably represent the regrowth of grass on the midden when dumping ceased, although they might also include turves discarded during rebuilding phases. The middens seem to have accumulated in 'patch-work quilt' fashion. This highlights the haphazard nature of deposition, some areas of the midden becoming grass-covered as deposition moved elsewhere. In terms of modern analogue, it is interesting to note that the mix of faunas so typical of midden deposits is similar to assemblages recovered from well saturated and decayed byre material lying in the open yard of a working farm.

CONCLUSION

The potential of entomological studies in the reconstruction of Norse farms and their economies is considerable, but it is important that such research forms part of an integrated study. It should further be stressed that palaeoecological studies have several limitations and that the paper is purposefully optimistic attempting to highlight the promise of this type of work. The interpretation of faunas relies upon elucidating pertinent questions in the light of the archaeological, historical and ethnographic records. Equally important is continuing research into habitat requirements of the various components of fauna and flora. Such can only be satisfactorily achieved through problem orientated and multidisciplinary studies.

Acknowledgements

The application of palaeoecological techniques to a wide range of sites across the North Atlantic region would not have been possible without the ready cooperation of many archaeologists and other scientists. In Greenland, Claus Andreasen and Thomas McGovern were the prime movers in the research, in Iceland, Guðmundur Ólafsson, Mjöll Snæsdóttir, and Guðrún Sveinbjarnardóttir, and, in Orkney, Olwyn Owen. In other fields of research, particular thanks are due to Tom Amorosi, Andrew Dugmore, Jóhannes Jóhansen, Elsa Guðjónsson, Erling Ólafsson, Peter Skidmore, Vilhjálmur Vilhjálmsson, and Cindy Zutter. The project was initiated by a major award from the Leverhulme Trust in 1979, with later funding from the National Museums of Iceland and Greenland, NATO, SERC, and the Scottish Development Department. Credit rests with all these individuals and organisations; the errors remain with us.

REFERENCES

Ágústsson, Hörður 1983. 'Rekonstruktionen af Stöng', in *Hus, Gard och Bebyggelse. Föredrag från det XVI nordiska arkeologmötet, Island 1982*, ed. Ólafsson, Guðmundur, Reykjavík, pp. 13–20.

Amorosi, Thomas, Buckland, Paul C., Ólafsson, Guðmundur, Sadler, Jon P. & Skidmore, Peter 1992. "Site status and the palaeoecological record: a discussion of the results from Bessastaðir, Iceland', in *Norse and Later Settlement and Subsistence in the North Atlantic*, eds Morris, Christopher D. & Rackham, D. James, University of Glasgow Dept. of Archaeol. mon. ser. no 1, pp. 169–91.

Beresford, Maurice W. 1986. 'Inclesmoor West Riding of Yorkshire. Circa 1407', in *Local maps and plans from medieval England*, eds Skelton, R. A. & Harvey, P. D. A., Oxford, pp. 147–161.

Bertelsen, Reidar 1979. 'Farm Mounds in Northern Norway', *Norwegian Archaeological Review*, 12(1), 48–57.

Bertelsen, Reidar 1984. 'Farm mounds of the Halsted area: quantitative investigations of accummulation characteristics', *Acta Borealia*, 1(1), 7–26.

Boucher, Alan 1989. *The Iceland Traveller*, Iceland Review, Reykjavík.

Bruun, Daniel 1898. 'Nokkurar eyðijarðir í Árnesýslu, Skagafjarðardölum og Bárðardal. Rannsakaðar sumarið 1897', *Arbók hins íslenzka fornleifafélags 1898*, 49–77.

Bruun, Daniel 1917. 'Oversight over Nordboruiner i Godthaab of Frederikshab Distrikter', *Meddelelser om Grønland* 56(3), 55–147.

Buckland, Paul C. 1975. 'Synanthropy and the Death-watch: a Discussion', *The Naturalist* (Hull), 37–42.

Buckland, Paul C. 1976. 'The Environmental Evidence from the Church Street

Roman Sewer System', *Archaeology of York* 14/1, Council for British Archaeology, London.

Buckland, Paul C. 1988. 'North Atlantic faunal connections – introductions or endemics?', *Entomologica Scandinavica, Suppl.*, 32, 7–29.

Buckland, Paul C. 1992. 'Insects, Man and the earliest settlement of the Faroe Islands: a Case not-proven', *Fróðskaparrit*, 38–9 (1989–90), 107–14.

Buckland, Paul C., Dugmore, Andrew, J. & Sadler, Jon P. 1991. 'Faunal Change or Taphonomic Problems? A Comparison of Modern and Fossil Insect Faunas from South East Iceland', in *Environmental Change in Iceland*, eds Caseldine, Chris & Maizels, Judith, Kluwer Academic Publishers, pp. 127–46.

Buckland, Paul C. & Perry, David W. 1989. 'Ectoparasites of Sheep from Stóraborg, Iceland and their palaeoecological significance (Piss, parasites and people: a palaeoecological perspective)', *Hikuin* 15, 37–46.

Buckland, Paul C. & Sadler, Jon P. 1989. 'A biogeography of the human flea *Pulex irritans* L. (Siphonaptera : Pulicidae)', *Journal of Biogeography* 16, 115–20.

Buckland, Paul C. & Sadler, Jon P. 1991. 'Farm or Shieling? an entomological approach', *Acta Archaeologica* 61 = *The Norse of the North Atlantic*, ed. Bigelow, Gerald F., 93–6.

Buckland, Paul C., Sveinbjarnardóttir, Guðrún, McGovern, Thomas H., Savory, Diane, Skidmore, Peter & Andreasen, Claus 1983. 'Norsemen at Nipaitsoq, Greenland: A Palaeoecological Investigation', *Norwegian Archaeological Review*, 16, 86–98.

Buckland, Paul C., Perry, David W., Gíslason, Gísli M. & Dugmore, Andrew J. 1986. 'The pre-Landnám fauna of Iceland: a palaeontological contribution', *Boreas* 15, 173–84.

Buckland, Paul C., Sadler Jon P. & Sveinbjarnardóttir, Guðrún 1992. 'Palaeoecological investigations at Reykholt, Western Iceland', in *Norse and Later Settlement and Subsistence in the North Atlantic*, eds Morris, Christopher D. & Rackham, James, University of Glasgow Dept. of Archaeol. mon. ser. no. 1, pp. 149–67.

Busvine, J. R. 1976. *Insects, Hygiene and History*, Athlone Press, London.

Carus-Wilson, E. M. 1967. *Medieval merchant ventures: collected studies* (2nd edn.), Methuen and Co. Ltd, London.

Coope, G. Russell 1981. 'Report on the coleoptera from an eleventh-century house at Christ Church Place, Dublin', in *Proceedings of the Eighth Viking Congress*, eds Bekker-Nielson, H., Foote, Peter & Olsen, Olaf, Århus 24–31 August 1977, Odense University Press, pp. 51–6.

Davidson, Donald R., Lamb, Raymond & Simpson, Ian 1983. 'Farm mounds in north Orkney, a preliminary report', *Norwegian Archaeological Review*, 16(1), 39–44.

Degerbøl, Magnus 1943. 'Nogle Bemærkninger om Husdyrene paa Island i Middelalderen', in *Forntida Gårdar i Island*, ed. Stenberger, Mårten, E. Munksgaard, Copenhagen, pp. 261–8.

Dugmore, Andrew J. 1981. *Insect Faunas from South-West Iceland*, Unpubl. B.Sc. Diss., University of Birmingham.

Eirik's saga (transl. Magnusson, Magnus & Pálsson, Hermann, 1965) Penguin Books, Harmondsworth.

Eldjárn, Kristján 1947. *Rústirnar í Stöng*. Reykjavík.

Eldjárn, Kristján 1952. 'Rannsóknir á Bergþórshvoli', *Árbók hins íslenzka fornleifafélags*, 5–75.

Eldjárn, Kristján 1961. 'Bær í Gjáskógum í Þjórsárdal', *Árbók hins íslenzka fornleifafélags*, 7–46.

Evans, Estyn 1957. *Irish Folk Ways*, Routledge & Kegan Paul, London.

Fenton, Alexander 1978. *The Northern Isles: Orkney and Shetland*, J. Donald, Edinburgh.

Fenton, Alexander 1985. *The Shape of the Past 1. Essays in Scottish Ethnology*, J. Donald, Edinburgh.

Fenton, Alexander 1986. *The Shape of the Past 2. Essays in Scottish Ethnology*, J. Donald, Edinburgh.

Foote, Peter G. & Wilson, David M. 1970. *The Viking Achievement*, Sidgewick & Jackson, London.

Fredskild, Bent 1978. 'Palaeobotanical Investigations of Some Peat Deposits of Norse Age at Qagssiarssuk, South Greenland', *Meddelelser om Grønland* 204(5).

Fridriksson, Sturla 1959. 'Korn frá Gröf i Öræfum', *Árbók hins íslenzka fornleifafélags* (1959), 88–91.

Fridriksson, Sturla 1960. 'Jurtaleifar frá Bergþórshvoli á soguöld', *Árbók hins íslenzka fornleifafélags* (1960), 64–75.

Griffin, K. 1985. 'Stratigraphic studies of farm mounds in north Norway', *Iskos* 5, 191–204.

Griffin, K., Okland, R. H., Jones, Andrew K. G., Kenward, Harry K., Lie, R. W. & Schia, E. 1988. 'Animal bones, moss, plant, insect and parasite remains', in *De Arkeologiske utgravninger i Gamlebyen, Oslo* 5, ed. Schia, E. Øvre Ervik, pp. 115–40.

Guðmundsson, Valtýr 1889. *Privatboligen på Island i Sagatiden*, Copenhagen.

Hall, Alan R. & Kenward, Harry K. 1990. 'Environmental Evidence from the Colonia', *Archaeology of York 14/6*, Council for British Archaeology, London.

Hall, Alan R., Kenward, Harry K. & Williams, Dorian 1980. 'Environmental Evidence from Roman deposits in Skeldergate', *Archaeology of York 14/2*. Council for British Archaeology, London.

Hall, Alan R., Kenward, Harry K., Williams, Dorian & Greig, James R. A. 1983. 'Environment and Living Conditions at Two Anglo-Scandinavian Sites', *Archaeology of York 14/4*, Council for British Archaeology, London.

Hamilton, John R. C. 1956. *Excavations at Jarlshof, Shetland*. HMSO, London.

Henderson, Ebenezer 1819. *Iceland or the journal of residence in that island during the years 1814 and 1815*, Edinburgh.

Holm-Olsen, Inger M. 1981. 'Economy and settlement pattern 1350–1600 AD based on evidence from farm mounds', *Norwegian Archaeological Review* 14(2), 86–102.

Jónasson, Jónas 1961. *Íslenzkir Þjóðhættir*, Ísafold, Reykjavík.

Kampp, Aage H. 1964. 'Sheep farming in Greenland', in *Collected papers, Denmark*, ed. Jacobsen, N. K., Københavns Universitets Geografiske Institut, Copenhagen, pp. 68–72.

Kenward, Harry K. 1975. 'Pitfalls in the interpretation of insect death assemblages', *Journal of Archaeological Science* 2, 85–94.

Kenward, Harry K. 1980. 'Insect remains', in *Feltene 'Oslogate 3 og 7'. De Arkeologiske Utgravninger i Gamlebyen, Oslo*. 2, ed. Schia, E., 134–37.

Knox, Susan A. 1985. *The making of the Shetland landscape*, John Donald, Edinburgh.

Kristjánsson, Leo 1980. *Íslenskir sjávarhættir*, Reykjavík.

Laxdæla saga (transl. Magnusson, Magnus & Pálsson, Hermann, 1967) Penguin Books, Harmondsworth.

Limbert, Martin 1986. 'The Exploitation of Peat at Thorne', *Old West Riding* 6, 9–16.

McGovern, Thomas H. 1981. 'The Economics of Extinction in Norse Greenland', in *Climate and History*, ed. Wrigley, T. M. L. *et al.*, Cambridge University, pp. 404–34.

McGovern, Thomas H., Buckland, Paul C., Savory, Diane, Sveinbjarnardóttir, Guðrún, Andreasen, Claus & Skidmore, Peter 1983. 'A Study of the Faunal and Floral Remains from two Norse farms in the Western Settlement, Greenland', *Arctic Anthropology* 20, 93–120.

Nilsson, Albert 1943. 'Den Sentida Bebyggelsen på Islands Landsbygd', in *Forntida Gårdar i Island*, ed. Stenberger, Mårten, E. Munksgaard, Copenhagen, pp. 269–310.

Nørlund, Poul & Roussell, Aage 1929. 'Norse ruins at Gardar, the episcopal seat of Medieval Greenland', *Meddelelser om Grønland*, 76(1).

O' Danachair, Caoimhin 1968. 'Animal droppings as fuel', *Folk Life*, 6, 117–20.

Orkneyinga saga (transl. Pálsson, Hermann & Edwards, Paul, 1978) Penguin Books, Harmondsworth.

Osborne, Peter J. 1983. 'An insect fauna from a modern cesspit and its comparison with probable cesspit assemblages from archaeological sites', *Journal of Archaeological Science* 10, 453–463.

Perry, David W., Buckland, Paul C. & Snæsdóttir, Mjöll 1985. 'The Application of Numerical Techniques to Insect Assemblages from the Site of Stóraborg, Iceland', *Journal of Archaeological Science* 12, 335–345.

Rothschild, Miriam 1973. 'Report of a female *Pulex irritans* in a tenth century Viking pit', *Proceedings of the Royal Entomological Society* 38(7), 29.

Roussell, Aage 1934. *Norse Building Customs in the Scottish Isles*, Copenhagen.

Roussell, Aage 1941. 'Farms and churches of the Medieval Norse settlement in Greenland', *Meddelelser om Grønland* 89(1), 1–354.

Roussell, Aage 1943a. 'Stöng, Þjórsárdalur', in *Forntida Gårdar i Island*, ed. Stenberger, Mårten, E. Munksgaard, Copenhagen, pp. 72–97.

Roussell, Aage 1943b. 'Komparativ Avdelning', in *Forntida Gårdar i Island*, ed. Stenberger, Mårten, E. Munksgaard, Copenhagen, pp. 191–224.

Sadler, Jon P. 1988. *The analysis of insect remains from Norse sites in the former Western Settlement of Greenland*, Unpubl. M.Sc. thesis, Department of Geography, University of Birmingham.

Sadler, Jon P. 1989. *Insect assemblages from the Viking and post-medieval site at Tuquoy, Westray*, Manuscript Report on file, Archaeological Operations and Conservation, Scottish Office, Edinburgh.

Sadler, Jon P. 1990. 'Records of ectoparasites on humans and sheep from Viking age deposits in the former Western Settlement of Greenland', *Journal of Medical Entomology* 27, 628–31.

Sadler, Jon P. 1991. 'Beetles, Ballast and Biogeography: insect invaders of the North Atlantic', *Acta Archaeologica* 61 = *The Norse of the North Atlantic*, ed. Bigelow, Gerald F., 199–211.

Seaward, Mark R. D. & Williams, Dorian 1976. 'An interpretation of mosses found in recent archaeological excavations', *Journal of Archaeological Science* 8(3), 14–27.

Simonsen, P. 1954. 'Middelalderens og Renessansens Kulturminner i Nordland', in *Norges bebyggelse: Fylkesbindet for Sør-Trøndelag, Nord-Trøndelag og Nordland fylker*, eds Fiskaa & Myclan, Oslo.

Skidmore, Peter 1985. *The Biology of the Muscidae of the World*, Series Entomologicae, The Hague.

Skidmore, Peter 1990. *Dipteran Remains from the Pit at Tuquoy*, Manuscript Report on file, Archaeological Operations and Conservation, Scottish Office, Edinburgh.

Smith, David 1988. *Fossils and modern analogue: Insects from black houses*, Unpubl. M.Sc. thesis, Department of Archaeology and Prehistory, University of Sheffield.

Stead, Jennifer 1981. 'Uses of Urine, part 1 (with assistance from Arthur Saul)', *Old West Riding* 1, 12–17.

Stead, Jennifer 1982. 'Uses of Urine, part 2', *Old West Riding* 2, 1–9.

Steffensen, Jón 1943. 'Knoglerne fra Skeljastaðir i Þjórsárdalur', in *Forntida Gårdar i Island*, ed. Stenberger, Mårten, E. Munksgaard, Copenhagen, pp. 227–60.

Stenberger, Mårten (ed.) 1943. *Forntida Gårdar i Island*, E. Munksgaard, Copenhagen.

Stamsø Munch, Gerd 1966. 'Gardshauger i Nord-Norge', *Viking* 30, 25–59.

Sveinbjarnardóttir, Guðrún 1983. 'Palæoekologiske undersøgelser på Holt i Eyjafjallasveit, Sydisland', in *Hus, Gård och Bebyggelse. Föredrag från det XVI nordiska arkeologmötet, Island 1982*, ed. Ólafsson, Guðmundur, Reykjavík, 241–250.

Sveinbjarnardóttir, Guðrún & Buckland, Paul C. 1983. 'An Uninvited Guest', *Antiquity* 48, 25–33.

Þórarinsson, Sigurður 1944. 'Tefrokronologiska Studier på Island', *Geografiska Annalen* 26, 1–217.

Þórarinsson, Sigurður 1958. 'Iceland in the Saga Period. Some Geographical Aspects', *Þriðji Víkingafundur, Reykjavík 1956. Árbók hins íslenzka fornleifafélags*, 13–24.

Þórarinsson, Sigurður 1967. 'The Eruption of Hekla in Historical Times, a tephrochronological study', in *The Eruption of Hekla 1947–48*, I. Reykjavík.

Vebæk, C. L. 1958. 'Topographical and Archaeological Investigations in the Norse Settlements in Greenland', *Þriðji Víkingafundur, Reykjavík 1956. Árbók hins íslenzka fornleifafélags*, 107–122.

Vilhjálmsson, Vilhjálmur Ö. 1989. 'Stöng og Þjórsárdalur-bosættelsens ophør', *Hikuin* 15, 75–102.

34

GREENLAND RUNES

ISOLATION OR CULTURAL CONTACT?

MARIE STOKLUND

The Norse settlement on the south-west coast of Greenland existed for around 500 years from about 985 to about 1500. Some 75 runic inscriptions are known from Greenland, most of them medieval, the majority found on loose items of wood, soapstone, bone or baleen; five stones seem to have had connection with burials, none of them erected rune stones. Many of these inscriptions seem haphazard and without linguistic sense (or at least uninterpretable to us, some are too fragmentary, some are just markings): a couple of runes, rune-like scribbling, bind-runes, or decided owners' marks (Stoklund 1981, 1982). Most of the longer inscriptions were published early – the one on the Kingittorsuaq stone already by Rasmus Rask (1827), the majority by Finnur Jónsson (1914, 3–11; 1916, 63–6; 1924, 273–90; 1929, 173–9) and Erik Moltke (1936, 223–32; 1941, 249–50; 1961, 401–10).

It is important to stress that the Greenland inscriptions were thus mainly dealt with before most of the corresponding material from the Northern world. When Moltke wrote about the inscriptions from the Western settlement (1936) the main reference was Magnus Olsen's survey (1933, 83–113) and the same was the case when Anders Bæksted published the Icelandic runic inscriptions (1942). No doubt the Greenland inscriptions were considered to be much more unique than we would say today in the light of the hundreds of Medieval runic inscriptions, especially from the urban excavations in Bergen, Trondheim, Oslo, Lödöse and elsewhere. But our view of the Greenland inscriptions is still to a very great extent based on the early analyses and results of Finnur Jónsson (1924, 289–909) and especially Magnus Olsen (1932=1949, 51–71). It seems to have been generally accepted 'that the Greenlanders had their own local dialect, and in fact some rune forms of their own; in particular, they were more conservative than Icelanders and Norwegians in preserving forms used in the first Landnam period and long abandoned by others' (Nørlund 1936, 51). The majority of inscriptions has been dated to about 1300 (Jónsson 1924, 289; Olsen 1960, 233).

However, the dating as well as the position of the Greenland material as a whole ought to be reconsidered. The question whether we are able to define

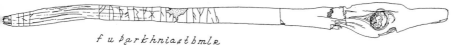

f u þ a r k h n i a s t b m l ʀ

Figure 34.1: The Narsaq futhark. The stick measures 42.5 cm, the *f*-rune 1.3 cm (Drawing: H. W. Schmidt, 1961).

some characteristics as peculiar to Greenland has recently become relevant, since these Greenland characteristics play an important role in the current discussion of the provenance of some of the merchants' labels in Trondheim and Bergen. The theory has been put forward that we can trace Greenland merchants in Norway (Johnsen 1981, 121–25), or that some of these labels were simply made in Iceland or Greenland to follow the export-goods to Norway (Hagland 1988, 145–57; 1989, 89–102). Without entering into the discussion of the Iceland trade (cf Johnsen 1987, 735–36; Seim 1989, 333–47; Nedkvitne 1989, 348–50; Hagland 1990, 106–9), I shall confine myself to the problem of the so-called Greenland characteristics which have been discussed in this debate. Of principal interest are the linguistic and/or runological problems of the representation of /o/, /ǫ/ by the *u*-rune, dotted *u*, or the *óss*-rune; the use of *b* instead of *f*, and *t* for (original) *þ*; and the question of a special variant of the *r*-rune (Fig. 34.2).

By giving a survey of most (not all) of the Greenland inscriptions which make sense, I hope not only to throw some light on the actual occurrence of the 'Greenland' peculiarities, but also to give an impression of the types of inscriptions and the general nature of this material, with special regard to the problems concerning isolated tradition versus variation reflecting cultural contacts.

SURVEY OF INSCRIPTIONS (cf. Appendix)

The Narsaq stick 1 came to light in 1953 (Moltke 1961); though all the riddles of this inscription by no means are solved, its short-twig futhark (Fig. 34.1) and use of ᛆ for nasalised /a/ and ᛒ for /b/ (retrograde) make it clear that it must be dated

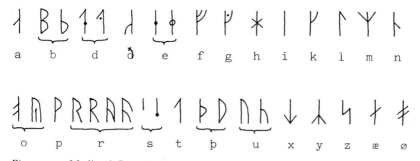

Figure 34.2: Medieval Greenland runes (Drawing: Elise Stoklund).

to the time around the millennium, and it proves that Greenland belonged to the short-twig area around the North Atlantic (Olsen 1954; Johnsen 1968, 96–7, survey of inscriptions). Related rune types without further qualifications (cf. Page 1983, 134–5) have been used on the Isle of Man, the Scottish islands, the Faroe Islands (cf. the futhark found in Eiði, Andreassen 1980, 28) and in Norway. In all these areas the runic tradition dates back to the Norse settlements. The view, set forward by Anders Bæksted (1942, 52), that the Icelandic settlers had no real runic tradition, and that the Icelandic runes were borrowed from the late Medieval Norwegian runes, ought no doubt to be questioned (Hagland 1989, 89–90). It seems very possible that no rune stone tradition spread at the time of settlement, but that does not imply that the settlers did not know and use runes for other purposes.

Probably the Narsaq inscription was made for some magic (protective?) purpose, it seems to be rooted in pagan mythology if we follow Erik Moltke's interpretation (1961), which he put forward with much hesitation: 'On the sea, sea, is the ambush of the Ases, Bibrau is the name of the maid, who is sitting on the blue (firmament)'. Though other attempts at interpretation have been made this is still very uncertain (Liestøl 1980, 46 with references) and the line consisting of cryptic runes is still uninterpreted, though the type as such is known from elsewhere.

A few other inscriptions might also turn out to be genuine early short-twig inscriptions, but otherwise the Greenland inscriptions are Medieval. If we compare the Narsaq transliteration with the later material in the Appendix it is quite evident that the general development from a traditional Viking-Age use of only 16 polyphonic symbols (the futhark) towards a much more nuanced system is reflected (Fig. 34.2). The orthography of the majority of the Greenland inscriptions comes very close to the West Norse system, which is represented in the Bergen inscriptions and described by Karin Fjellhammer Seim (1988, 17–20).

The use of Roman letters for vernacular inscriptions on two tombstones from Herjolfsnes/Ikigaat (one of them fragmented, the other with the inscription: DOMINUS HER HUILIR HRO . . . KOLGRIMS:S . .) shows that at least some people in Greenland could use Roman letters (Nørlund 1924, 193–5). Incidentally, one of the soapstone moulds for spindle whorls from the bishop's seat in Garðar/Igaliku has a Latin owner's inscription in Roman letters (Nørlund 1929, 147–9).

As it appears from the Appendix, in other rune-written inscriptions Latin and the vernacular are mixed (Herjolfsnes/Ikigaat VI and VII). Other inscriptions seem to be based on the rich supply furnished by the liturgical texts of the Roman Catholic church, but rather garbled, so that only some of the elements can be recognised: *adonay*, *lux*, *elon*, *(tetra)grammaton*, as expressions for God, or the names of the Archangels: *Michael*, *Gabriel*, *Rafael* (Sandnes/Kilaarsarfik 11). The same kind of inscription is Vesterbygd 53 d, also made in wood, but elsewhere this very common type of inscription is often found on lead (for instance Stoklund 1987, 198–208 with references). As demonstrated by Aslak Liestøl, some of these inscriptions copy rune-written patterns. On the fish-shaped Umiiviarsuk piece a dotted *i* with ring, ♦, has been copied as a reversed *þ*-rune in a garbled version of Psalm 119 v. 49 (118 in the Vulgate): *Memor esto verbi tui servo tuo, in quo mihi spem dedisti* (Liestøl 1980, 45–6). On the other hand the model of a cross-limb from Herjolfsnes/Ikigaat, which has been re-used in cross V (according to Finnur Jónsson's (1924) numbering), seems to have been written in Roman letters with abbreviations, (according to Liestøl: Revelation v. 8 on the outer panels, *p(rincipiu)m a et finis o* – i.e. *Alpha-Omega*), but in the main text only some of the elements are recognisable, for instance, *agla*, *tetragramma(ton)* (Liestøl 1980, 82).

This kind of inscription – presumably for some sort of magic protection – shows conclusively that Greenland belonged in a European-Scandinavian context. One could add the *Ave-Maria* inscription from Sandnes/Kilaarsarfik – numerous finds from the last decades have shown that religious-magic inscriptions form an important part of the Medieval Scandinavian runic material.

As a whole, the types of inscriptions found in Greenland are in many ways representative of what we find elsewhere in Scandinavia, with an important exception: there are no merchants' labels, they have only been found in Trondheim and Bergen.

The type of inscription that names itself I have found on a re-used piece of soapstone from Anavik/Ujarassuit, which has previously been dismissed as without sense. It has the inscription: *k l i ãr̂*, *kljár* 'loom-weight', besides *m r a ?* – Maria (?) (Fig 34.3).

On a piece of bone from the East settlement, Ø 167 (Vatnahverfi?) we should probably read *b æ n* as 'bone', though the spelling with *æ* is remarkable. A newly found inscription from Orphir, Mainland, Orkney, seems to have *b a i n* (McKinnell 1989, 15). A fine example of this type is found on the wooden spoon from Narsarsuaq, Uuntoq, where *s b o n*, 'spoon', is written twice, in 'knot-runes' (with a correction from *s b o a*) as well as in normal runes. Exactly the same kind of ingenious 'knot-runes' are found – as demonstrated by Aslak Liestøl – on a walrus tusk, which ended up in Florence, and on a rune stick in Bergen (Liestøl 1979, 228–34). But they are also found on a Viking-Age rune stone in Gästrikland in Sweden (Jansson 1981, 162–75; Stoklund 1982, 204–5) – a fact which bears witness to the close contact and mobility within the whole rune-writing community.

From Ø 71 two owner's inscriptions are known, +g͡unnarã+ with an elaborate bind-rune *gu* (earlier read +g͡unnar+, Stoklund 1981, 145 with references), and on a piece of soapstone *m a g n e*, no doubt a man's name, not as first assumed a woman's name (Vebæk 1952, 112), cf. *b a ñn e*, Bjarni, on the Kingittorsuaq stone. Including verb and object we find *l i o f̂r m k*, Ljótr á mik, on

Figure 34.3: Fragment of weight-stone, soapstone *c.* 11 × 10 cm, from Anavik/Ujarassuit with the inscriptions, *mra?* and *kliâr̂, kljár,* 'loom-weight' (Photo: National Museum, Copenhagen).

a meat-fork from the Western settlement, V 54, Nipaatsoq, and . . . *l : dur : a : mik,* '(Ha)lldur(or . . .(hi)ldur) owns me' – man or woman – possibly with svarabakhti *u*-vowel (cf. Icelandic), written retrograde on a soapstone mould for a spindle whorl from Garðar/Igaliku (cf above) (Jónsson 1929, 173).

The inscriptions on stones have probably all had connections with graves, though the *þurfinna* stone from Herjolfsnes/Ikigaat (?) was found in a house, partly built of material from Herjolfsnes, in Frederiksdal opposite the fjord (Vebæk 1964, 18–19), and the Napassut fragment was found on a little island off Ivittuut without any cemetery or church. The inscription 'Ingibjǫrg's grave' marked a stone-set grave at the head in the Brattahlid/Qassiarsuk cemetery (Nørlund 1929, 60; Jónsson 1929, 179). Until the Narsaq stick was found, it was considered to be the oldest of the Greenland inscriptions and dated to *c.* 1200 (Olsen 1932, 53) while the Garðar/Igaliku inscription, 'Vigdis M's d(aughter) rests here, God gladden her soul' was considered to be considerably younger. The rather indistinct runes on a small fragment also found here seem very similar to those on Vigdis' stone, especially the *r*-runes (Jónsson 1929, 176–9).

No doubt the 58 small wooden crosses – predominantly of deal – found in the Herjolfsnes/Ikigaat cemetery were burial crosses. Eight of them have runic inscriptions, in three cases only *Maria (Maia)* inscriptions, but the inscriptions on five of them form a very important part of the whole linguistic material: 'God Almighty protect Gudleif [a woman] well' (II, according to Finnur Jónsson's numbering), 'Thorleifr made this cross in praise and worship of God the Almighty' (III), the Latin-Norse: 'Jesus Christ help, Christus natus est nobis' (VII, Fig. 4) and VI with the Norse part, 'Father, Son and Spirit'. The already mentioned re-used cross-limb on V (made of juniper) has got a new shaft, with *Maria, Michael á mik Brakil* (or Brigit?) – *t o r i r* is written upside down – an inscription which must be secondary to the horizontal 'copy'-inscription.

Generally the runic crosses have been dated to about 1300, but the question is whether these cross inscriptions should be seen as a rather homogeneous group although they differ from each other in rune forms as well as orthography. This could be an indication of an extended period of production, especially if these crosses were used as devotional crosses before they were buried (Stoklund 1984, 101–13). The fact that similar wooden crosses with inscriptions have been found in Bergen, apparently without any connection with church or cemetery, might indicate this interpretation (Liestøl 1980, 90; Seim 1988, 59–60). Recently in Greenland a cross-arm with a *Maria*-inscription has been found in midden deposits far from any church (Stoklund 1989, 6–7).

Another question to be discussed is the provenance of the inscriptions found in Greenland. For instance the re-used cross-limb might have been brought to Greenland, or possibly a rune-written model; the same conditions must be true for the 'copy'-inscriptions from the Western Settlement.

It seems very likely that the little stick found in the bottom of a coffin in the churchyard of Herjolfsnes/Ikigaat got its inscription from a Norwegian: 'This woman, who was named Gudveg, was put overboard in the Greenland sea'. Its orthography – *h* for [ɣ] (the only Greenland example), symbols for /æ/ and /ø/; *i* for /i/ and /e/; *l a z* for *lanz*, *lands* – is quite in accordance with Norwegian orthography (Jónsson 1924, 274–5; Olsen 1932=1949, 55) but in all probability it was made in Greenland.

A message of quite another kind was found in 1824 and first interpreted by Rasmus Rask (1827), the Kingittorsuaq inscription is written on a little Greenlandic phyllite stone, only *c.* 10 cm long, and found far north of the settlements, probably connected with the *Norðrseta* expeditions. The inscription has been dated to about 1300, 'Erlingr Sigvatsson and Bjarni Thordarson and Endridi Oddson the Saturday before Rogation day made this (these) cairn(s) and *r y d u . . .*' – the last cryptic runes have not yet been interpreted with certainty, though the type is well known elsewhere, for instance on the Norum baptismal font from Bohuslän (Olsen 1960, 222–4) and the Andreas V inscription from the Isle of Man (Olsen 1954, 185–9). Parallels to the language and orthography can be found in late Norwegian inscriptions, the definite article in *l a͡u k a r d a k · i n*, cf. for instance N 170 Vinje I *l o͡u g a r : d a g e n* (*c.* 1200; Olsen 1951, 264–8, 301–5; 1960, 245) or *b o n d a n͡n* on N 648 from Bergen (*c.* 1300; Johnsen 1987, 739). The use of bind runes, *n͡n* and *l͡l* (and assimilation) is dominant in another Bergen letter, N 650 (*c.* 1300) *æiñnripi, æinndripi, giaĩlda, eĩlihar* (Johnsen 1987, 739) cf. N 564 Hurum *ællingr* and *ærlinkr* (*c.* 1180; Olsen 1960, 169–75), *râññar* N 148 Atrå I (*c.* 1180; Olsen 1951, 192–7).

LANGUAGE AND RUNE-FORMS

It has generally been accepted that the Greenland inscriptions (except Narsaq, Ingibjǫrg's stone – and Gudveg's stick as probably Norwegian) could be analysed as a rather uniform group from about 1300 or a little later (Olsen 1932, reconsidered 1949, 52–3). Inscriptions found since (except Narsaq) have not changed the picture of the language much, but as already mentioned, the corresponding material from the Northern world has grown enormously, and, especially, the urban excavations have given far better possibilities for archaeological dating. No doubt the dating of the Greenland inscriptions needs reconsideration, for instance some of the parallels to the Kingittorsuaq inscription noted above have been dated about 100 years before the assumed date of the Greenland inscription.

No doubt the use of runes in Greenland from Narsaq to Kingittorsuaq follows the general development from the Viking-Age to the more elaborate Medieval systems, and just like other contemporary rune-writing communities, with a certain competition and inspiration from the manuscript writing tradition. The occurrence of these novelties, and the spread of similar cryptic runes and 'knot-runes', say something about the interactive mobility and docility of rune-writers. The Greenland material, however, definitely belongs in the West Norse context (cf. Olsen 1960, 242–5; Seim 1988, 17–20) with the short *s*-rune for /s/, unlike the Danish system where this sign corresponds to *c* and *z*.

Like other Medieval runic inscriptions the Greenland examples still reflect the original runic orthography: there is for instance no double-writing of *n* in *henar*, 'her', on the grave slab from Garðar/Igaliku, but cf. *purfinna* on the ashlar from Herjolfsnes and *+gûnnarâ+* (Ø 71). The nasal *n* has been omitted before homorganic plosive in *eĩlikr* on the Kingittorsuaq stone, the *k*-rune is used for /g/, cf. *lâukardak·in*, but *g* (and *k*) in *gakndag*. In this carefully cut inscription in excellent condition it must be an example of an obvious preference for the symbol belonging to the futhark, *k*, to the dotted sign, *g* (cf. the discussion in Seim 1988, 18). Norse *andi* and Latin *deus meus* are rendered *a n t i* and *tius mius* on Herjolfsnes VI, but *deus meus* (V 53 d). Herjolfsnes VII has *istnubis* for *est nobis* and *hialbi, hialpi*, the Narsarsuaq spoon *sbon*. The occurrence of such features might indicate an earlier stage in the relative chronology. But archaic phonemic features found in fairly late inscriptions seem to be a rather common general phenomenon. In any case, this does not prove a special Greenland conservatism or isolated development. The use of the runes belonging to the futhark instead of the less ambiguous variants (as described above) cannot be phonetically based, although this could be considered for *o* instead of *u*, which might be a special Icelandic 'west-over-sea' feature (Hagland

1988, 148–9; 1989, 93–4; cf. Seim 1989, 340–2; Hagland 1990, 107–8). On the crosses from Herjolfsnes we find forms like *þurlibr* : *koþ*, 'God', *koþi*, *koþlibar*, and *þurfinna* on the ashlar, *guþuih* on the stick (which is probably Norwegian), *guþ* on the grave slab from Garðar/Igaliku.

The evaluation of the so-called 'Greenland' characteristics is essential to the debate about a special Greenland development and, in the discussion of the provenance of the merchants' labels found in Trondheim and Bergen they have, as already mentioned, become significant. I shall therefore focus on them and their position in the Greenland material.

'Greenland' r

In the Greenland runic inscriptions various *r*-types are used (Stoklund 1981, 144), but a certain preference for the 'Greenland' *r* is evident. It has two long, nearly parallel, sloping branches, the upper one can touch the lower one, but very often this is not the case (Fig. 34.2). No doubt it originates in cursive forms, designed for wood, and in its less distinct variations it is common in the Norse material (Seim 1989, 344–5 with references). In Greenland it is found in fourteen inscriptions, many of them very fragmentary, and it is also found in stone inscriptions (the two Garðar/Igaliku slabs) and on soapstone.

We might speak of a 'Greenland' *r* in the same way as a 'Gotland' *s*, which though common in the Gotland inscriptions, can be found elsewhere without indicating a Gotland carver. I am not convinced that Greenlanders made all the examples outside Greenland, which are found sporadically. But Aslak Liestøl ascribed the St Nicholas, Orphir, inscription to a Greenlander only because of the shape of the *r*-rune (1984, 236); several others have not been considered to be of Greenland origin, for instance Maeshowe VI, or *Vigleikr Stallari's* inscription 1263, due to Magnus Olsen's tracing (1960, 231; Liestøl 1984, 237; Stoklund 1981, 144 with references). The examples – not very marked – in nine inscriptions from Trondheim and Bergen (Hagland 1989, 99–100 with references) cannot be taken as clear evidence of Greenland origin (Johnsen 1987, 736; Seim 1989, 344–5). Even the theory of this *r*-shape as a special 'west-over-sea' feature combined with a dating of the Norwegian examples to the 12th century (Hagland 1989, 99–100) needs further consideration, since 'Greenland' *r* in inscriptions such as Sandnes/Kilaarsarfik 11 and 2, Vesterbygd 53 d, the Garðar/Igaliku slab, combines with special symbols for *ð*, *þ*, *x* (Latin *lux*) which are generally considered to be later. There are no traces of 'Greenland' *r* in the Icelandic material, except for the two (imported) soapstone spindle whorls (Bæksted 1942, 207–8, 16, 26 & 43–44). They may be of Greenland origin, but the soapstone could also originate from Norway or Shetland (Ritchie 1984, 59–84).

t : *þ*

In only one case is 'Greenland' *r* found together with one of the other

'Greenland' characteristics. On the Herjolfsnes/Ikigaat cross V three marked *r*-runes of this shape are found together with *t* for original *þ* in *torir*. The other examples are Herjolfsnes III *ſāna* (pronoun) (but *þurlibr* and *t* for /d/ in *ſy̆rkūnᶏr*, *Þórleifr*, *dýrkunar*, and in medial position: *þ*), and Kingittorsuaq: *te*, 'this' or 'these', and *tortᶏr*, in medial position both *þ* and *d* are used. Probably this use of *t*- reflects a sound development, which is also found in Norway and in other West Norse dialects or languages except Icelandic (Olsen 1932=1949, 65–9, Seim 1989, 338; but cf. Jónsson 1924, 289 & 279).

We might have a parallel in the Maughold V-inscription from the Isle of Man in *liktinniftr*, according to A. M. Cubbon and Aslak Liestøl: *leg penna eptir* (Johnsen 1968, 238–9, but otherwise Page 1983, 146, note 33). It must be a matter of dispute whether *t* for *þ* in a few cases in the Bergen material indicates Greenland provenance (Johnsen 1981, 121; Hagland 1989, 91; Seim 1989, 339).

Dotted u

This use of *t* instead of *þ* in only one case has been combined with the dotted *u* for /o/, /ǫ/, which has also been considered a Greenland peculiarity, though it is only found in three of the cross-inscriptions from Herjolfsnes/Ikigaat. In all other Greenland inscriptions, *óss*, **⁴**, or *u* denotes /o/, /ǫ/, but in the three cross-inscriptions the distribution of the symbols varies. Cross II has only dotted *u*; *koþ, koþlibar*; III has *u*: *þurlibr*, *Þórleifr* or *Þúrleifr?*, *tilūſs, til lofs*; dotted *u*: *koþi, Goði, kros, kross*; **⁴** – *óss*: *ōlmokkum, korþi, ōk*, 'almighty, made, and'; VI has dotted *u*: *ok* (twice), *iloi, iloiḥiṃ*, and *iǫᵃ̃nis, Johannes*. In this inscription 'son' is written *sunr*, Napassut and Kingittorsuaq (three times) have *son(r)*. In addition it should be mentioned that VII has only *u*, /u/, and /o/ (-Latin *nobis*). In III the *y*-rune is found: *ſy̆rkūnᶏr, dýrkunar*. The rather garbled 'copy'-inscription Vb has a 'normal' distribution of *u* and *o*, Va has only an example of *óss* in *torir*.

It is difficult to find any consistent system in this distribution, however, the use of *óss* versus dotted *u* cannot depend on a nasal : oral distinction (Hagland 1989, 96–7). What these inscriptions have in common are the remarkable long strokes instead of normal points in the dotted *u*-runes (except *iǫᵃ̃nis* (or *iṵᵃ̃nis?*). It seems relevant to ask whether the model was the Anglo-Saxon dotted *u* with this shape, which, however, denotes /y/. This *y*-value is out of the question in the Greenland inscriptions, but seen in a wider perspective, the dotted *u* was apparently ambiguous. In the West Norse area it could be used for /y/, /o/, /ǫ/, perhaps /ø/; /v/ and even /ph/ (Seim 1989, 342–3), and even in the Swedish material (where it is always transliterated *y*) there are examples where it could not possibly denote /y/ (Strid 1989, 16–17 with references). The sound value of dotted *u* in the other West Norse examples now known (Trondheim, Bergen, Isle of Man, Dublin) has been discussed (Hagland 1988, 149–50; 1989, 94; Page 1983, 137–8, 146 n. 29). It seems questionable to ascribe the use of dotted *u* for /o/ to an Icelandic-Greenlandic tradition, based only on the three cross-inscriptions from Herjolfsnes/Ikigaat and the inscription on the Valþjófsstaðir door (which could possibly be Norwegian, Bæksted 1942, 210–11, but probably not Greenlandic, Johnsen 1981, 123). According to the principle of dotting (Seim 1989, 343), dotted *u* could no doubt correspond to different sound or letter values within the wide spectrum which had been covered by the *u*-rune. But in the notation of /o/, /ǫ/ and /y/ the dotted *u* would have to compete with the *óss*- and *ýr*-runes, which would probably be preferred because of their names and position in the futhark. (They all appear in Herjolfsnes III.)

The shape of the Greenland dotted *u*-runes might indicate an early Anglo-Saxon connection without regard to sound value. Perhaps it is also noteworthy that the use of *b* for *f* in the same cross-inscriptions (II and III) has many parallels in the British Isles and in very early inscriptions in Norway, Denmark and Sweden (Johnsen 1968, 34–5 for instance). Magnus Olsen considers this use of *b* in Greenland astonishing, dating back to the time around the millennium, but still surviving into the fourteenth century (1932=1949, 59).

DATING

From much of what has been said above it appears that the crucial point is the dating of the finds from Herjolfsnes/Ikigaat to *c.* 1300. This is obviously generally accepted while apparently based on the result from the excavations published by Poul Nørlund in 1924. However, it is evident that Nørlund is inclined to a rather early dating of the runic crosses: they belong to the older part, the famous garments to the younger part of the find. The type of cross which has semicircular hollows at the intersection (III and VII, Fig. 34.4) 'must undoubtedly be traced to the British Isles where, from the numerous stone crosses preserved, it is seen to have been in extensive use during the centuries previous to and immediately after the year 1000. Thence it spread to Norway and – with or without the intermediary link of this country – to Greenland. Here this type of cross may have survived long after it had been abandoned elsewhere, but it must have been adopted early, at the latest in the 12th century' (Nørlund 1924, 66, 216–19). The final dating, however, depends on Finnur Jónsson's evaluation: 'Thus, on one of these [Celtic] crosses [i.e. no III] there are runic inscriptions which, according to Professor Jónsson, cannot be of earlier date than *c.* 1300' (Nørlund 1924, 219, 67). However, Jónsson's dating seems rather loose, mainly based on a comparison with Icelandic poetry (*Lilja*) and probably affected by the late dating of the Herjolfsnes garments. According to him the cross-inscriptions 'all date from *c.* 1300, a little before or a little after. There can be no doubt that not one of them dates for instance from the 11th or the 12th century' (1924, 289). This is odd, since Nørlund believes 'that the custom [of burial crosses] was known and observed throughout the entire period' of the Norse settlement (1924, 66). Especially if some of the crosses – as already mentioned – were devotional crosses, or processional crosses (Nørlund 1924, 219), it seems very likely that they were made at different times. It is tempting to

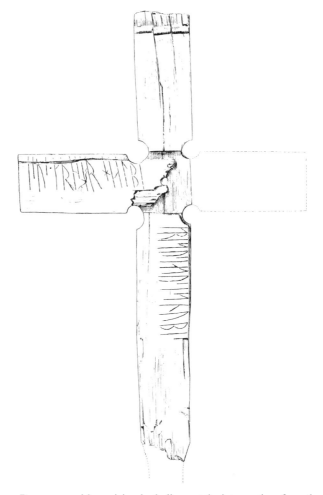

Figure 34.4: Rune cross with semicircular hollows at the intersection, from the cemetery of Herjolfsnes/Ikigaat (VII) with inscription in Norse and Latin. Size *c.* 26 × 38 cm. (Drawing by Peter Linde (Jónsson 1924)).

find associations with the British Isles not only in the 'Celtic cross' shape, but also in the 'Anglo-Saxon' dotted *u*-runes, perhaps also in language-forms like *i s u, i s u s* (for *Jesus*) and *k r o s*. All this might indicate (early) connections with the English church and religious world, which seems very likely, if a priest or member of the clergy composed the inscriptions (Jónsson 1924, 289). However it seems impossible to fix an exact *terminus post quem* for these crosses. Cross VII might originate in the early time of Christianity in Greenland, or it could be conservative in shape and orthography (Fig 34.4). Runological dating based only on the lack of innovations is very risky, but according to the corresponding material from the urban excavations in Norway, my general impression is that these cross inscriptions, except perhaps V, have been dated too late. Also Gudveg's stick could be earlier, from about 1200, when most of the changes in medieval Norwegian rune-writing had taken place (Olsen 1960, 244; Seim 1988, 22).

Though the majority of the Greenland inscriptions were found in connection with archaeological excavations, the dating is rather loose because of the structural complexity of the sites and a certain lack of stratigraphy. According to the report of Ívar Bárðarson, the Western settlement seems to have been abandoned about the middle of the 14th century, but we are not able to point out inscriptions which must be later than that from the Eastern settlement, which, judging from the Herjolfsnes garments, seems to have existed at least until about 1500.

The more recent extensive urban archaeological excavations have created far better possibilities for dating corresponding Norwegian material. The majority of the Trondheim inscriptions is from the later part of the 12th till the beginning of the 14th century (Hagland 1986, 20–1; 1988, 147), while most of the Bergen inscriptions are from the 13th and 14th centuries (Seim 1988, 21–3). This means that corresponding material here comes to an end at the same time as the contacts between Norway and Greenland begin to fail (the Greenland carrier (*knǫrr*) sank in 1369 and was apparently not replaced). But it should not be forgotten that the Iceland tradition of grave slabs from the local basalt with runic inscriptions had started by then (from *c.* 1350 and culminating 1400–1500, Bæksted 1942, 58). From the diplomas concerning the wedding in Hvalsey/Qaqortukulooq 1408, we know of Icelanders staying in Greenland 1406–10 (see Olsen 1932 = 1949, 57–8). The late Icelandic material has some characteristic and dominant rune forms, **ϸ**, (as well as **ↄ,ↄ**), *e* (never denoting a diphthong), **δ**, *s* (full size), and **ϸ**, *d* and *ð* (Bæksted 1942, 38–40, 44), which seem to be local developments (Bæksted 1942, 49–52), though *e* and short *s* with ring are found sporadically in Norway before 1200 (Olsen 1960, 237). In some of the Greenland inscriptions we find the same tendencies: Sandnes/Kilaarsarfik 2 and Kingittorsuaq have *e* with ring (and dots in one case), a rather long dotted *s* is found together with *e* with ring on Vesterbygd 53 d. The *d*-rune with dot on the main stave is found on the Garðar/Igaliku spindle whorl, Sandnes/Ikigaat 3 and Kingittorsuaq. Another (earlier) type with the point under the twig (Vigdis' stone) is found in many Norwegian inscriptions (Liestøl 1979, 233; Stoklund 1987, 197–8).

It is difficult to distinguish between regional variations and chronological differences. To throw light on these questions further investigations are necessary, for example into the Greenland representation of /e/ : /æ/ (and original diphthong), or the *d*-rune for /d/ and /ð/ (Olsen 1960, 237; Bæksted 1942 38–9); Sandnes/Kilaarsarfik 10 *lipuadr*, *Lipvandr* (Moltke 1936, 228) or *Liðvarðr* (Olsen 1949, 79–81). It is noteworthy that, though bind-runes are frequent in the Icelandic inscriptions, they lack the $\widehat{ll}$, $\widehat{nn}$ types (Bæksted 1942, 48).

CONCLUSION

The Greenland runic inscriptions from Narsaq 1 to Kingittorsuaq represent a continuous development from Viking-Age to late Medieval times in accordance with the general changes in runic writing around the North Atlantic. Innovations bear witness to close contact and widespread cultural relations and make it problematic to speak of isolation and to characterise certain features as 'Greenland' peculiarities (except perhaps the so-called 'Greenland' -*r*). It seems questionable on this basis to point out rune-writing Greenlanders' inscriptions elsewhere.

Seen in the light of the datings of the corresponding Norwegian material, now known, the Greenland inscriptions have probably been dated too late, and they have to some extent been taken to form a more uniform group than they are; there is no doubt that they originate from a longer period. The crucial dating of the finds from Herjolfsnes/Ikigaat is apparently not based on archaeological facts, but mainly on Finnur Jónsson's philological arguments from the 1920s. These crosses could be considerably older than from about 1300, and they need not all have been made at the same time.

Appendix

SELECTED INSCRIPTIONS, TRANSLITERATED

Anavik/Ujarassuit V 7 soapstone weight-stone.   mra?|kliăr

Brattahlid II/Qassiarsuk stone.   laiþiiňkibiarkar

Garðar/Igaliku

   grave slab.   uigdis:m̄:d:h|uilir:her:gl|eðe:guþ:sal:he|nar:

   soapstone mould.   . . .l.dur:a:mik·.·

Herjolfsnes/Ikigaat

   ashlar.   +þurfinna+

   cross (wood) II.   kⱮþalmatikrkækⱮþlibāruæl

   III.   þurlibr:kor|þikrⱮstana|m tilůfsokẗy̆rkům̄ar|kⱮþiólmokku

   Va.   mâria:mikai amikbrakil torir

   Vb.   iklatefrakramaesussoaiaônlotePaierksratôn

   (outer panels) Pmaat filiiso

   VI.   maria:ilⱮ ihim|iⱮanisfáþiir isutiusmiusilⱮi|Ɱksunr Ɱkanti

   VII. .isus.kristrhialbi|kristusnatusistnubis

   stick.   +þæsi:kona:uar:lagþ:firi:borþ:i:grønalaz:hafi:ær:guþuih:hit

Kingittorsuaq stone.

   ellikr.sikuaþs:sôn:r.ok.baañne:tortârson:ok:enriþi:osson:lâukardak.in:

   fyrir.gakndag hloþu.uâr date.okrydu: [six cryptic runes]

Napassut fragment of slab.   . . . røssur:asbiærnârsôn+

Narsarsuaq, Uunartoq wooden spoon.   sbon sbon

Narsaq stick 1.

   ×a:sa:sa:sa:is:asa:sat× bibrau:haitir:mar:su:is:sitr:a:blan?. . .

   fuþarkhniastbmly/R

   [cryptic runes]

   ????

Nipaitsoq V 54 meat fork (reindeer bone).   liofrmk

Sandnes/Kilaarsarfik 2 wood.   auemaria:grasiablna

   10 tally-stick.   liþuadr

   11 stick.   ·.·ilon:âPrikum:nonem ·.· elon

   aliy:þ:elon:r:abrsabaot:sion

   ilon:giun:áþ:onay:lux:iairi

   gramaton:saba:ag:misial:gabrel|rafael

Umiviiarsuk V 52 wooden fish.   mariam◀mor◀?tuu◀bittisuoauo

   ikônmikismoiaii

Vatnahverfi

   o 71 whale-bone handle.   +gunnarâ+

   o 71 soapstone plate.   magne

Vatnahverfi

Ø 167 bone.   bæn

Vesterbygd

53 d stick.   ·:· fledin:fûdo:unedeus.meus:omnis:Patris.
eþselô̂þþinieram. numimumnafûr [one line]

REFERENCES

Andreassen, Leon 1980. 'Runakelvi', *Mondul* 6.1, 28.

Bæksted, Anders 1942. *Islands runeindskrifter*, Bibliotheca Arnamagnæana 2, Copenhagen.

Hagland, Jan Ragnar 1986. *Runefunna*, Fortiden i Trondheims bygrunn: Folkebibliotekstomten, Meddelelser nr. 8, Trondheim.

Hagland, Jan Ragnar 1988. 'Runematerialet frå gravingane i Trondheim og Bergen som kjelder til islandshandelens historie i mellomalderen', *Historisk tidsskrift* 67, Oslo, 145–56.

Hagland, Jan Ragnar 1989. 'Islands eldste runetradisjon i lys av nye funn fra Trondheim og Bergen', *Arkiv för nordisk filologi* 104, 89–102.

Hagland, Jan Ragnar 1990. 'Runemateriale som kjelder til islandshandel – ein formasteleg tanke?' *Historisk tidsskrift* 69, Oslo, 106–9.

Jansson, Sven B. F. 1981. *Gästriklands runinskrifter*, Sveriges runinskrifter 15.1.

Johnsen, Ingrid Sanness 1968. *Stuttruner i vikingetidens innskrifter*, Oslo.

Johnsen, Ingrid Sanness 1981. 'Personal Names in Inscriptions in Towns of Medieval Norway', *Michigan Germanic Studies* 7, 119–36.

Johnsen, Ingrid Sanness 1987. 'Die Runeninschriften über Handel und Verkehr aus Bergen (Norwegen)', in *Untersuchungen zu Handel und Verkehr der vor- und frühgeschichtlichen Zeit in Mittel- und Nordeuropa*. Teil 4. Der Handel der Karolinger- und Wikingerzeit. Abhandlungen der Akademie der Wissenschaften in Göttingen, Philologisch-Historische Klasse, Dritte Folge, Nr 156, Göttingen, 716–44.

Jónsson, Finnur 1914. 'Runestenen fra Kingigtórsoak', *Det Grønlandske Selskabs Aarsskrift*, 3–11.

Jónsson, Finnur 1916. 'Grønlandske runestene', *Det Grønlandske Selskabs Aarsskrift*, 63–6.

Jónsson, Finnur 1924. 'Interpretation of the Runic Inscriptions from Herjolfsnes', in *Meddelelser om Grønland* 67, Copenhagen, 273–90.

Jónsson, Finnur 1929. 'Rune Inscriptions from Gardar', in *Meddelelser om Grønland* 76, Copenhagen, 173–9.

Liestøl, Aslak 1979. 'Andres gjorde meg', *Universitetets Oldsaksamling 150 år. Jubileumsårbok* 1979, Oslo, 228–34.

Liestøl, Aslak 1980. *Norges innskrifter med de yngre runer* 6.1.

Liestøl, Aslak 1984. 'Runes', in *The Northern and Western Isles in the Viking World*. Edinburgh, 224–38.

McKinnell, John 1989. 'A New Find from Orkney', *Nytt om runer* 4, 15.

Moltke, Erik 1936. 'Greenland Runic Inscriptions IV', in *Meddelelser om Grønland* 88, Copenhagen, 223–32.

Moltke, Erik 1941. 'In Roussell, Aage'. *Farms and Churches in the Medieval Norse Settlements of Greenland. Meddelelser om Grønland* 89, Copenhagen, 249–50.

Moltke, Erik 1961. 'En grønlandsk runeindskrift fra Erik den Rødes tid', *Tidsskriftet Grønland*, 401–10.

Nedkvitne, Arnved 1989. 'Runepinner og handelshistorie', *Historisk tidsskrift* (Oslo) 68, 348–50.

Nørlund, Poul 1924. *Buried Norsemen at Herjolfsnes*, *Meddelelser om Grønland* 67, Copenhagen.

Nørlund, Poul 1929. *Norse Ruins at Gardar*, *Meddelelser om Grønland* 76, Copenhagen.

Nørlund, Poul 1936. *Viking Settlers in Greenland*, London-Copenhagen.

Olsen, Magnus 1932. 'Kingigtórsoak-stenen og sproget i de grønlandske runeinnskrifter', *Norsk tidsskrift for sprogvidenskap* 5, 189–267 = 1949 revised.

Olsen, Magnus 1933. 'De norröne runeinnskrifter', in *Nordisk kultur* 6, *Runorna*, 83–111.

Olsen, Magnus 1949. 'Sproget i de grønlandske runeinnskrifter', in *Fra norrøn filologi*, Oslo, 52–71.

Olsen, Magnus 1949. 'Runeinnskrifter fra Grønlands Vesterbygd', in *Fra norrøn filologi*, Oslo, 72–84.

Olsen, Magnus 1951. *Norges innskrifter med de yngre runer* 2, Oslo.

Olsen, Magnus 1954. 'Runic Inscriptions in Great Britain, Ireland and The Isle of Man', in *Viking Antiquities* 4, Bergen, 153–233.

Olsen, Magnus 1960. *Norges innskrifter med de yngre runer* 5, under medvirkning av Aslak Liestøl, Oslo.

Page, Raymond I 1983. 'The Manx rune-stones', in *The Viking Age in the Isle of Man*, London, 133–46.

Rask, Rasmus 1827. 'Efterretninger om en i Grønland funden Runesten', *Antiquariske Annaler* 4, 311–14.

Ritchie, P. Roy 1984. 'Soapstone Quarrying in Viking Lands', in *The Northern and Western Isles in the Viking World*, Edinburgh, 59–84.

Seim, Karin Fjellhammer 1988. 'A review of the runic material', in *The Bryggen papers, supplementary series* 2. Bergen, 10–23.

Seim, Karin Fjellhammer 1989. 'Runeinnskrifter fra Trondheim og Bergen som kilder til Islandshandelens historie? Et innfløkt proveniens-spørsmal', *Historisk tidsskrift* (Oslo) 68, 333–47.

Stoklund, Marie 1981. 'Greenland Runic Inscriptions', *Michigan Germanic Studies* 7, 138–49.

Stoklund, Marie 1982. 'Nordboruner', *Tidsskriftet Grønland* 30, 197–206.

Stoklund, Marie 1984. 'Nordbokorsene fra Grønland', *Nationalmuseets Arbejdsmark* 1984, 101–13.

Stoklund, Marie 1987. 'Runefund', *Aarbøger for Nordisk Oldkyndighed og Historie* 1986, 189–211.

Stoklund, Marie 1989. 'Nyfund 1987', *Nytt om runer* 3, 1988, 4–7.

Strid, Jan Paul 1989. '*Ludvig*, *Auðun* och *Oþbiorn*', *Studia anthroponymica Scandinavica* 7, 5–24.

Vebæk, Christen Leif 1952. 'Vatnahverfi. En Middelalders Bondebygd i Grønland', *Fra Nationalmuseets Arbejdsmark* 1952, 101–14.

Vebæk, Mâliâraq 1964. 'En ny runesten fra Herjolfsnes', *Grønlandsposten* 4. juni 1964, 18–19.

35

SETTLEMENT MOUNDS
IN THE NORTH ATLANTIC

REIDAR BERTELSEN   RAYMOND G. LAMB

This chapter is meant as a contribution to the process of formulating new perspectives concerning northern coastal settlement. It is remarkable how archaeological research has been going on in different regions of the North Atlantic area, on similar types of cultural monuments, but with different perspectives and different methods. The discussion, based on these different standpoints is in itself a stimulating experience. The hope is therefore that the perspectives that arise from this rethinking might lead to new research.

'GÅRDSHAUGER' IN NORTH NORWAY

Medieval archaeology in North Norway has focused on 'gårdshauger' (farm mounds) since the mid 1960s. The word 'gårdshaug' was chosen by archaeologists among a series of different terms that are in use among the local population. 'Gårdsgrunn', 'Tofta' or 'Toftan' (pl), 'Gammelgården' or simply 'der heime' are other alternatives used to denote the site where earlier generations had their farm houses. These accumulated mounds of settlement debris have been seen as characteristic of North Norwegian rural settlement. Since discussion has for a long time related mainly to problems of a historical character, the suggested explanations for this phenomenon on the whole considered only internal North Norwegian factors. For a brief account of the farm mound archaeology, see Bertelsen 1992.

State of Research

Of the estimated 1,500–2,000 North Norwegian farm mounds, no single one has yet been excavated totally. The recent excavation of the Haug mound in Hadsel, Nordland (Sandmo 1988) is the most extensive in area, other partial excavations are Trondenes (Ramstad 1964), Grunnfarnes (Stamsø Munch 1966), Saurbekken (Bertelsen 1973), Helgøy (Holm-Olsen 1981), Sandnes (Wik 1985) and Soløy (Bertelsen & Urbanczyk 1985). Around 30 less extensive excavations have been carried out all along the coast from Helgeland the northernmost Finnmark, a total stretch of over 1200 km. Field observations have also involved test pits or cuts of various kinds in a number of mounds. Even if we have data on the character of the deposits from more than 50 mounds, it is far from being a satisfactory situation from an empirical point of view. The investigation methods and the standard of documentation have varied to a large extent. The most serious drawback is, as mentioned above, the lack of large scale excavations.

Apart from excavation, the archaeological surveys of the regional museums in Tromsø and Trondheim have mapped several hundred farm mounds. In addition, the museum collections have thousands of stray finds from these mounds. The estimation of 1,500–2,000 as the total count of North Norwegian farm mounds is based on this information.

Summary of Observations and Results

In spite of the lack of a database that permits detailed comparison, we feel confident that the following observations can be agreed upon. The farm mounds are constituted by a variety of different factors:

- ruins of farm buildings with wooden constructions, turf roofs and turf walls
- middens with household debris such as osteological material, ashes and production offcuts of various kinds
- dung, twigs, peat dust and anthropogenic microbiological material from the barns
- eroded material from standing turf-walled houses.

In some cases, the various kinds of cultural deposits are concentrated in specific parts of the mound at all levels of the deposits, and other mounds show a considerable degree of mixing. Except for floors, very few distinctive levels can be observed in the sections. The accumulations seems to have been a continuous process where only the change in location has created spatial discontinuity (or cuts).

The building up of farm mounds goes back to the latest centuries BC. This means that some of the farm mounds go as far back as farm settlement itself; although this is perhaps an oversimplified statement, it raises the question of the definition of farm. We shall not try to enter this discussion here, the theme is developed somewhat by Bertelsen (1991). We will only suggest that the term *farm* is a difficult concept, it has to be considered as a dynamic through time with the potential for considerable regional variation. For example, a permanent coastal settlement where the main economic activities are livestock breeding, fishing and seal hunting should be included.

In a substantial number of the cases, the present farm buildings still stand on the mounds. This gives us a long time perspective of about 2,000 years. There are, however, indications that a majority of the mounds started to accumulate in the later part of the 1st millennium AD or early in the 2nd. (Bertelsen 1979, 50–3 and 1985, 144–61; Holm-Olsen 1981, 89–91; Jørgensen 1984, 177–84).

It is generally observed that there are good conditions for preservation of organic material in such mounds for artefacts as well as ecofacts. It is however striking that the frequency of artefacts increases dramatically from the 15th century AD. This is clearly demonstrated in the find statistics of the farm mounds of the Helgøy region (Holm-Olsen 1981) and from the Soløy excavation (Bertelsen & Urbanczyk 1985).

Very few of the farm mounds are found off the coast, they are all on the *strandflat*, and just a handful are found more than 1 km from the shore. The settlement pattern is typically dispersed and linear. The linearity is of course mainly a result of the landscape, but the dispersion is a more complex case. It is likely that both cultural and natural factors need to be considered in attempts to explain the settlement pattern.

We have understood farm mounds to be expressions of single holdings ('bruk'), or at the most double farms with a common yard ('tun'). The relation between the mixed farm economy, the size of the population and the carrying capacity of the natural resources are poorly understood, but the carrying capacity cannot be the sole explanation of the dispersed settlement pattern. It is hard to believe that any branch of the economy except the growing of barley has ever been close to the optimal carrying capacity. Barley seems to have been of minor importance when quantity is considered, although it may have had a specific importance.

In the social models based on settlement pattern which have been discussed, there are factors one should believe worked for a clustered settlement pattern, and others that could have favoured dispersion. This theme will be developed further in the section below on social structure. Anyhow, we will consider the settlement pattern as a reflection of a complex cultural system and its relation to nature as well as the cultural system reflects the settlement pattern.

Farm Mounds and Deserted Farms

Differing opinions have been presented concerning the relationship between sites with deserted buildings lacking deep stratified deposits and the farm mounds. Some authors have presented the view that the deserted farms are likely to originate from the later phase of the Early Iron Age (6th century) and that the farm mounds did not start to accumulate until, at the earliest, the High Middle Ages (13th–14th centuries). These two classes of monuments should then be considered as chronologically separate phenomena. The explanation of the relationship between these two classes might then be sought in historical factors.

Other authors have relied upon the indications that both farm mounds and deserted farms are found throughout the whole history of farm settlement in North Norway. The quantitative relationship between these two site types varies through time. For instance, one could suspect that a period of retraction following a rapid expansion would give many deserted farms, and that a period of stability or slow expansion will give us mostly farm mounds and just occasional deserted farms. This view is based on the assumption that it is mostly a question of time and stability of location whether a farm settlement ends up as a deserted farm, or several deserted farms within a certain area or a farm mound.

The possibility of the contrast between farm mounds and deserted farms being a reflection of different cultural behaviour should not be overlooked even if they do represent contemporary settlements. The choice between settling on top of your ancestors' yard or settling beside it, may be an important cultural statement. It may relate to beliefs, to the need for demonstrating legitimate use of the land, to ethnic differences or to other aspects of life.

Ethnic Relations

North Norway was an ethnically complex society during the Iron Age and Medieval Period. Recent investigations (Holm-Olsen 1981; Søbstad 1980; Schanche 1986) have established that farm mounds are much more frequent in Norse districts than in Sami. It is not clear, however, if farm mounds can be looked upon as ethnic criteria. Farm mounds are found in Sami districts and from a theoretical point of view, it is necessary to explain why farm mounds should or should not carry meaning with respect to ethnicity. For the time being, we must rely on the observation that farm mounds are mostly found outside Sami districts and therefore should be considered reflections of Norse settlement.

FARM MOUNDS IN ORKNEY

The great settlement-mounds crowned by still-active farms which dominate the islands of Sanday and North Ronaldsay, have been systematically recorded only since the inception of the Orkney Sites and Monuments Record in 1979 (RCAHMS 1980). Previous Ordnance Survey records relating to three of these sites – Hooking in North Ronaldsay and How and Tofts in Sanday – had noted archaeological features in the immediate vicinity of the farms, without observing the mounds within which these features were contained. The reason for this oversight was the sheer size of the farm mounds, prominent features in the sea level landscape, and their liability to be mistaken for natural hills. The largest mound, at Tofts, rises steeply to a height of 2.5 m, with a surface area in excess of one hectare.

Locally, however, there is a traditional awareness that farms ought to be on top of mounds. A list of placenames in the north end of Sanday, compiled by a farmer, William Skea of Hillhead, who died in 1948, makes several references to mounds under active farms, and to mounds which were formerly the sites of farms (Skea, ms). In general, the largest mounds in Sanday are occupied by farms which have always been important and are still inhabited. Occupied farm mounds appear to be confined to Sanday and North Ronaldsay. On a third island, Papa Westray, farm mounds occur, but mostly as long-abandoned sites. With one exception, they do not compare in size with the Sanday and North Ronaldsay mounds (RCAHMS 1983).

The excavation of the settlement mound at Pool Bay, Sanday (Hunter 1983 and this volume) is very interesting in connection with the problems focused on here and needs to be discussed in more detail elsewhere.

Geoarchaeological investigations have been made into three mounds in Sanday: Westbrough, Langskaill and Skelbrae (Davidson *et al.* 1986). Phosphate, loss on ignition, particle size distribution of the mineral part of the soils, colour and $\delta^{13}C$ values were measured in addition to several radiocarbon datings of stratificational units in the sections. Several of the conclusions are very interesting in relation to the problems discussed above:

> The radiocarbon dates for the three mounds tie in well with the placename evidence, which suggests that the mounds as a class existed at the time of the Norse colonization, or at least when the primary Norse place names were applied in the 9th and 10th centuries AD.
>
> In essence the mounds grew as middens with the major inputs derived from the byres (cut and dried turves, ash); subsidiary inputs would have been derived from domestic reuse as well as from turves used for roofing or windproofing flagstone roofs.
>
> The implication is that farmers did not have to be very concerned with improving the fertility status of their fields, hence the abandonment on sites of dung. This lack of need to fertilise the soils can be explained by the nature of the Fraserburgh Series, which is extensive on Sanday. This soil is derived from wind blown calcareous sands and thus possessed an inherent fertility status. The presence of sand derived soils may explain why there is such a concentration of mounds on Sanday and possibly also on North Ronaldsay.
>
> (Davidson *et al.* 1986, 56–8)

If the date-ranges obtained from the three Sanday sites sampled (which are comparable with the majority of the North Norwegian dates) prove to be typical for the island, it must be asked why agricultural settlement in Sanday dates back to the fourth millennium BC yet farm mounds appear not to form until the first millennium AD. The processes which created farm mounds operated strongly in Sanday and North Ronaldsay, where the mounds attain much larger size than is usual in North Norway. In Papa Westray however mounds are smaller and are usually not associated with farms which are still active, suggesting that the accretion process may have begun at the same time as in Sanday, but did not continue as long.

The sites and monuments survey has covered enough of Orkney, with the same quality of attention as in North Ronaldsay, Sanday and Papa Westray, to indicate that farm mounds do not occur outside these three islands. The special factors which operate to produce the mounds, here as in North Norway, still await definition and we cannot say whether they are cultural or environmental.

FARM MOUNDS IN OTHER REGIONS OF THE NORTH ATLANTIC

The excavation of Stóraborg on southern Iceland (Snæsdóttir 1991) has directed attention to Iceland. The Stóraborg excavation is remarkable due to the fact that it is the only total excavation of a farm mound. The publication of this excavation will be of considerable importance to the understanding of the phenomena discussed here. Although Stóraborg is the first case in Iceland where the farm mound concept is used, the occurrence of settlement mounds do seem to be a common feature in the Icelandic cultural landscape.

Based on very preliminary observations, farm mounds of similar character as the North Norwegian ones occur all around the coast, but they seem to be rare in the valleys. If this impression is valid, the farm mound distribution compares to what is found in North Norway. Another observation made on Iceland is that the farm mound formation is still active in many cases. Ruins of turf walled houses are often seen alongside modern houses. The ruins are still in use as sheds, fences, even gardens, but the construction material is gradually eroding and thus forming a layer of cultural deposits. Many of these buildings are now standing on the top of mounds of deeply stratified deposits.

Neither of the authors of this chapter have been to Greenland, we must therefore rely on publications of investigated farms from the Norse period. It goes without saying that these are all deserted farms and that the time period of continuous settlement in no case can be more than *c.* 400 years. This will probably be too short to form a farm mound that stands out as a feature in the cultural landscape in the same way as those discussed above.

Sven Erik Albrethsen has reviewed the research of Norse sites on Greenland (1982), and his conclusion is that possible stratification on the sites may have been overlooked and that the later farm houses tended to be built at the same spot where the settlers put up their first buildings.

McGovern's excavations of middens indicate a continuous use of the same middens for long periods. Both Albrethsen's and McGovern's observations suggest a farm mound-like accumulation, but maybe without the shifting of location of middens, dung deposits and houses that is observed in most of the North Norwegian cases. But, as mentioned earlier, farm mounds of this possible Greenland type are also known in North Norway.[1]

FARM MOUNDS AS PART OF NORTHERN OR COASTAL MATERIAL CULTURE

If we can agree that farm mounds are particularly frequent in the North Atlantic region, from North Norway in the east to Greenland in the west and south to Scotland, is there then a need for a general explanation of this peculiar distribution? Even if formal criteria indicate that accumulated site formations are similar all over the region, can we then conclude that cultural patterns were equally similar? These questions are at the bottom of the subject framed by this paper, but at this stage of research, we are only able to develop some ideas along the lines of possible general explanations.

Marginal Conditions

Are marginal conditions for farming one factor to consider? The cultivation of cereals and stock breeding do not have the same northern climatic limits. There was probably a zone where cultivated fields were only small patches in favourable locations. The need for fertilising would be far less than further south.

In a situation like the one sketched above, one possible hypothesis is that the highly organic soil that through time accumulated into a farm mound, was just the surplus that was not needed for fertilizing the small fields. There are several historical accounts from outsiders who have observed such an accumulation process and reacted with unsympathetic astonishment. From Trondenes (1879):

> . . . møgen opdyngedes sålænge på alle husets fire sider, indtil det ei blev mueligt at bringe quæget derind, og da måtte de bygge et nyt.

That this has been going on for a while was observed on Senja in 1865:

> . . . tusener av lass gjødsel hvori fæhus på fæhus er nedråtnet, så man finder spor efter dem i 4 á 5 alens dybde. . .

As mentioned earlier, the archaeological information both from Orkney and from North Norway tells us that there are a lot more material accumulating, not only dung. This strictly functional explanation assumes that the inhabitants on the farm unresistingly accepted the conditions made by this surplus of organic refuse. We do not find it easy to believe that human behaviour, even in marginal regions, can be explained as simply as that.

A Specific Coastal Social Structure?

Can there be other differences between northern coastal farming and the situation further south, than just the balance between stock breeding and cereals and the possible restricted distribution to special kinds of soils?

It has been argued elsewhere (Bertelsen 1985, 105–6; Bratrein 1976, 22–4) that North Norwegian farming through the Iron Age up to modern times must have been a branch of the household economy mainly run by women while the men engaged in fishing and seal hunting as they had been doing ever since the Mesolithic. It is of course difficult to find empirical support for this hypothesis in the archaeological record. However, written sources from more recent periods help, even if bureaucratic registers stick to the southern, dominant model of the husband as the farmer. One example is given by Lysaker (1958, 233) referring to a court case in 1738 concerning a quarrel between neighbours on a farm in the Trondenes parish. Among other interesting details is the information that the ploughing and sowing was performed by women.

If the important acts of agriculture were dominated by women as late as this, there is no reason why it should be otherwise earlier. Our hypothesis for the Iron Age society is that the coastal farms were run by a housewife, living together with a fisherman/hunter. However, it is not likely that this holds good for the entire 'farm mound region'.

Fishing/hunting and farming appear to require different social structures. The boat, the crew, the gear, the unpredictable weather, the knowledge of the fishing grounds and the ways of the prey are something very different from buildings on the farm, the plants and the livestock that need protection and controlled reproduction, the cycles of yearly routines and the need for the legitimising of your right to use the land. A farming economy with only half of the household as an active workforce, would perhaps seek extensive forms of production, that could minimise the need for indoor feeding of the animals and keep the need for laborious fertilising to a minimum. Large grazing areas would be sought, also beaches where the animals could find fodder during as much of the winter as possible. Dispersed settlement is the natural solution to such requirements.

Fishing and hunting, on the other hand, are economic activities that tend to go for a more clustered settlement pattern. The fishing villages (*fiskevær*) along the North Norwegian coast are good examples of multiple household settlements. Both the scattered distribution of the best fishing grounds and the need for larger crews than one or two households could support are possible explanations for this tendency. When combined with extensive farming, it is possible that the need for dispersal is more imperative.

A site for the farm had to be selected, and all the various considerations concerning farming had to be met: optimal location of the barley precious fields, good and safe grazing, fresh water, etc.; just as the fisherman had a need for a good harbour and a good view of the nearest fishing grounds so that he would know when to go out even when he gave a hand to of the numerous tasks of farming activity. This list of considerations could be made much longer, but we believe that we have demonstrated already that a many-sided economy like the one we have described, may not give many alternatives when searching for an optimal site of habitation. If the same considerations were made generation after generation, a farm mound would grow under their feet! The indications that support these suggestions are all from the Norwegian coast. It remains to see if similar ideas apply to the rest of the region.

It is also tempting to suggest that a dispersed settlement pattern does not create a need for institutions to regulate the use of land in the same way as a clustered settlement pattern does. Maybe it was good enough proof of legitimate land-use that a person was able to point at the farm mound and claim that it was the manifestation of her ancestors, because everyone understood what a farm mound was? Even if such a possible meaning of a farm mound could have been made unnecessary by later regulations introduced by the state we found it likely that it survived as tradition for a long time afterwards.

The Coastal Farmer as Soil Manipulator

It is suggested above that the typical northern Norwegian coastal farmer of the Iron Age and the Medieval Period was female. A rigid gender based labour division need not be the case for the whole region in question. What seems to be a fairly general feature for the period under discussion is the architecture. The Black Houses of Scotland and the turf houses of Iceland have their similarities in North Norway. Mixed turf and stone walls seem to be a fairly general for most of the North Atlantic up to at least the late 18th century, and in some areas even into more recent periods.

Depending on the climate, the relation of stones to turf and the quality of the wood used in the construction, the life of such houses could vary from a few decades to a few centuries. Highly organic matter accumulates around the houses through erosion and repairs. Cattle that graze or eat seaweed give their daily contributions and it is likely that the standing buildings would function as traps for wind transported material. Even an active farmer may not be able to transport everything out onto the fields. It is also possible that the cooler climate of the north brings about a slower rate of decomposition of organic matter than further south. In such a system, the farm mound will act as a reservoir of cultural deposits. If this bank has a high rate of accumulation, it will tend to build up well stratified deposits. When this rate is low and both the input and output is high, the stratification will be poor. There are endless possibilities for variation.

PERSPECTIVES

Our aim has been to suggest some future lines of research rather than final conclusions. For the time being, we have found that the concept 'farm mound' is useful in our efforts to understand northern coastal settlements through long periods of time. However, one should be careful not to overemphasise the generality of this concept. Integrated documentation of the similarities of farm mounds across the North Atlantic is yet to be achieved.

We have also suggested that the formation of these mounds has possible cultural meaning in addition to their obvious functional aspects. Much energy is needed to investigate this further. In addition to more extensive archaeological excavations, material such as placenames is likely to be of central importance. One obvious perspective that has been mentioned by several earlier authors is the immense information potential embedded in these mounds. The sheer quantity of information is practically endless. More interesting perhaps, is the diversity of data and the challenge this gives to different disciplines when facing the task of integrated analysis.

One such interdisciplinary perspective that can be of general importance to modern archaeology, even on a theoretical level, is the evaluation of man's relation to nature *versus* cultural factors with respect to the shaping of material culture. Let us just ask one simple question for illustration: Is the turf-walled house a solution that the North Norse man took to only because he lacked good timber and needed a warm house? Dissatisfaction with answering 'yes' to this question is a good enough motivation to go deep into the farm mounds and find out.

Acknowledgements

This paper originated in a day of discussion with the geoarchaeologist Dr Donald Davidson of the University of Stirling, Department of Environmental Science (March 1987). The main part of it is written by Bertelsen, except for the section on Orkney, which is written by Lamb. David Griffiths (University of Durham) read the paper out at the Viking Congress and the final version of the paper has benefitted substantially from his advice.

Note

1. Recent excavations and observation also now demonstrate the existence of farm mounds in Faroe with close parallels to North Norway.

REFERENCES

Albrethsen, Sven E. 1982. 'Træk af den norrøne gårds udvikling på Grønland', in *Vestnordisk byggeskikk gjennom to tusen år*, eds Myhre, B., Stoklund, B. & Gjærder, P., AmS-Skrifter, vol. 7, Stavanger, pp. 269–87.

Bertelsen, Reidar 1973. 'Gårdshaugene i Harstad kommune. Et bidrag til områdets økonomiske historie i middelalderen', Unpub. mag.art. thesis, University of Bergen.

Bertelsen, Reidar 1979. 'Farm mounds in North Norway, a review of recent research', *Norwegian Archaeological Review*, vol. 12, no. 1, 48–56.

Bertelsen, Reidar 1985. *Lofoten og Vesterålens historie*, vol. 1, Svolvær.

Bertelsen, Reidar 1991. 'A north-east Atlantic perspective', in *The Norse of the North Atlantic* ed. Bigelow, Gerald F., = *Acta Archaeologica* 61, pp. 22–8.

Bertelsen, Reidar & Przemyslaw Urbanczyk 1985. *The Soløy farm mound. Tromura, Kulturhistorie*, vol. 4.

Bratrein, Håvard D. 1976. 'Det tradisjonelle kjønnsrollemønsteri Nord-Norge', in *Drivandes kvinnfolk. Om kvinner, lønn og arbeid*, eds Bratrein *et al.*, Tromsø-Oslo-Bergen, pp. 21–38.

Davidson, Donald, Douglas D. Harkness & Ian A. Simpson 1986. 'The formation of Farm Mounds on the Island of Sanday, Orkney', *Geoarchaeology*, vol. 1, 45–60.

Holm-Olsen, Inger Marie 1981. 'Economy and settlement pattern, AD 1350–1600, based on evidence from farm mounds', *Norwegian Archaeological Review*, vol 14, 86–101.

Holm-Olsen, Inger Marie 1985. 'Farm mounds and land registers in Helgøy, North Norway: An investigation of trends in site location by correspondence analysis', *American Archaeology*, vol. 5, no. 1, 27–34.

Hunter, John [R] 1983. 'Excavations at Pool Bay, Sanday 1983: An interim report', Unpub. report, School of Physics and Archaeological Sciences, University of Bradford.

Jørgensen, Roger 1984. 'Bleik, en økonomisk/økologisk studie av grunnlaget for jernaldergården på Andøya i Nordland', Unpublished mag.art. thesis, University of Tromsø.

Lysaker, Trygve 1958. *Trondenes bygdebok*, vol. 4, Harstad.

McGovern, Tom 1980. 'Cows, harp seals and churchbells: Adaptations and extinction in Norse Greenland', *Human Ecology*, vol. 8/3. 245–75.

RCAHMS 1980. *The Archaeological Sites and Monuments of Sanday and North Ronaldsay*, The Royal Commission on the Ancient and Historical Monuments of Scotland, Edinburgh.

RCAHMS 1983. *The Archaeological Sites and Monuments of Papa Westray and Westray*, The Royal Comission on the Ancient and Historical Monuments of Scotland, Edinburgh.

Ramstad, Yngvar 1964. 'Utgravingene på Trondenes', *Ottar* no. 41, 3–5.

Sandmo, Anne-Karine 1988. 'Haug på Hadseløya – tradisjoner og forandringer i forhistorisk tid', *Hoðasegl*, vol. 32.

Skea, William. Copy of manuscript in Orkney Archaeological Records.

Schanche, Audhild 1986. 'Nordnorsk jernalderarkeologi, et sosial geografisk perspektiv', Unpub. mag.art. thesis, University of Tromsø.

Snæsdóttir, Mjöll 1991. 'Stóraborg – an Icelandic Farm Mound', *The Norse of the North Atlantic* ed. Bigelow, Gerald F., = *Acta Archaeologica* 61, pp. 116–19.

Stamsø Munch, Gerd 1966. 'Gårdshauger i Nord-Norge', *Viking*, vol. XXX, 25–59.

Søbstad, Tom 1980. *Den sjøsamiske bosetning i Helgøy fram til ca 1700. Publikasjoner fra Helgøyprosjektet*, vol. 5. (mag.art. thesis), Tromsø.

Wik, Birgitta 1985. 'Jernalderen', in *Helgelands Historie*, ed. Wik, B., vol. 1, Mosjøen. pp. 172–264.